THE PLUMPTON CORRESPONDENCE

THE PLUMPTON CORRESPONDENCE

EDITED BY THOMAS STAPLETON
WITH A NEW INTRODUCTION BY KEITH DOCKRAY

Written in the Reigns of Edward IV, Richard III, Henry VII and Henry VIII

ALAN SUTTON

This edition first published in the United Kingdom in 1990 by
Alan Sutton Publishing Limited, Brunswick Road, Gloucester.

This edition first published in the United States in 1990 by
Alan Sutton Publishing Inc., Wolfeboro Falls, NH 03896–0848.

Copyright © in this edition Alan Sutton Publishing Ltd 1990.
Copyright © in Introduction, Keith Dockray 1990.

All rights reserved. No part of this publication may be reproduced, stored in a retrieval system, or transmitted, in any form or by any means, electronic, mechanical, photocopying, recording or otherwise, without the prior permission of the publishers and copyright holders.

British Library Cataloguing in Publication Data

The Plumpton correspondence.
   1. North Yorkshire. (Family) Plumpton, history
   I. Stapleton, Thomas
   929.2′09428′4

ISBN 0–86299–656–2

Library of Congress Cataloging in Publication Data

The Plumpton correspondence: written in the reigns of Edward IV, Richard III, Henry VII, and Henry VIII / edited by Thomas Stapleton; with a new introduction by Keith Dockray.
   p.   cm.
   Reprint. Originally published: London : Printed for the Camden Society by J.B. Nichols, 1839.
   ISBN 0–86299–656–2 : $30.00
   1. England – Social life and customs – Medieval period, 1066–1485 – Sources. 2. England – Social life and customs – 16th century – Sources. 3. Great Britain – History – House of York, 1461–1485 – Sources. 4. Great Britain – History – Henry VII, 1485–1509 – Sources. 5. Great Britain – History – Henry VIII, 1509–1547 – Sources. 6. Plumpton family – Correspondence. I. Stapleton, Thomas, 1805–1849.
DA185.P5 1990   89–36292
942.05–dc20   CIP

Typesetting and origination by
Alan Sutton Publishing Limited.
Printed in Great Britain by
Dotesios Printers Ltd, Trowbridge, Wiltshire.

INTRODUCTION

Keith Dockray
Huddersfield Polytechnic
(Page references in this Introduction are to pages of the original Camden edition.)

Fifteenth-century England has transmitted to posterity four major collections of private letters and papers. Most famous, and rightly so, are those of the Pastons, a gentry family of increasing wealth, status and influence in East Anglia; much used also are the Stonor letters and papers, written or received by members of a prominent and old-established Oxfordshire gentry family; and historians of English commerce in general, and the wool trade in particular, have long drawn enthusiastically on the Cely correspondence, preserved by an industrious family of Merchants of the Staple. Least well known of the four collections, perhaps, are the letters and papers of the Plumpton family: yet these, no less than the other three, are of considerable interest and value.

The Plumpton correspondence, consisting of about 250 letters ranging in date from 1461 to 1552 is, in fact, a source of unique importance for northern society and its preoccupations at the close of the Middle Ages, particularly during the reign of Henry VII when some two-thirds of the collection was penned. Both the letters themselves and a miscellaneous assortment of family papers probably owe their survival, in the first place, to prolonged and acrimonious wrangles between the heirs of Sir William Plumpton (1404–80) for possession of his inheritance and, thereafter, to their transcription on behalf of Sir Edward Plumpton in the early seventeenth century. As a result the Plumptons, a West Riding family with estates particularly concentrated in the Knaresborough area, are the best documented of all fifteenth-century Yorkshire gentry families. Whereas most gentlemen of the time can only be glimpsed imperfectly in sparse remaining records, much fuller portrayals are possible of Sir William Plumpton and his son Sir Robert (*c*. 1453–1523): Sir William, malign head of the family for almost sixty years, became embroiled in the Wars of the Roses as a retainer of the powerful Percy Earls of Northumberland, while his grasping, litigious and even immoral behaviour over many years ensured that his son (another Percy man whose chequered career dominates the correspondence) was destined to spend much of his life fighting to preserve his inheritance. As for the turbulent society in which these men lived, there is much of value here on the law and its manifold shortcomings, marriage, property and family relationships, and the West Riding community of gentry, as well as interesting insight into politics (including several informative newsletters sent back to Yorkshire by family agents in London), economic problems and religious practices in an age of change.[1]

Although copies of earlier letters very occasionally survive, the series proper begins in March 1461 and ends in March 1552.[2] Not surprisingly, most of the letters were addressed to senior members of the family (notably Sir William Plumpton and his son Sir Robert) and sometimes there is evidence that the originals were in the correspondents' own handwriting: Hugh Pagnam, writing to Sir William in about 1465, remarks that his letter has been 'scribled in hast with mine owne hand', although, interestingly, he adds that this was 'in default of other helpe att London' (p. 14). Apart from a sprinkling of letters from kings and rather more from Earls of Northumberland, most of them were written by junior members of the family such as the lawyer Edward Plumpton, fellow gentry with whom the Plumptons had connections of one kind or another (such as the Gascoignes and the Hamertons), or, most frequently, servants and agents of the family like Godfrey Grene and John Pullan.

Regrettably, the letters cannot be recommended for light reading: their literary value is distinctly limited (although they do, perhaps, evoke on occasion the spoken language of fifteenth- and early sixteenth-century Yorkshire); most of them display a no doubt conventional formality in both tone and composition; and an interest in landed property and the laws governing it is a virtual prerequisite for anyone who would seriously venture into them. Even more irritating for the historian is the fact that the originals have disappeared, especially since they were clearly still in existence in the early seventeenth century when they were transcribed for Sir Edward Plumpton (1581–1654) into a small folio paper volume (*Sir Edward Plumpton's Book of Letters* or, as it is more commonly dubbed, the *Plumpton Letterbook*). No less significantly, Sir Edward Plumpton encouraged the compilation of the so-called *Coucher Book* (or *Plumpton Cartulary*): a collection of almost a thousand items relating to the history of the family (commencing in the twelfth century) and including charters, deeds and a number of 'official' letters. Following Sir Edward's death, both the *Letterbook* and the *Coucher Book* (as well as a selection of related transcripts) passed into the hands of the antiquary Christopher Towneley (1606–74) and consequently became part of the Towneley archive. By the time Thomas Stapleton began to work on the Plumpton letters and papers in the early nineteenth century, the originals had vanished and have never been seen or heard of since. Nevertheless, Stapleton, using the seventeenth-century transcripts, was able to publish a remarkably scholarly edition of the *Letterbook* for the Camden Society in 1839 and, in a long introduction, include many items from the *Coucher Book* as well. Thereafter the seventeenth-century *Letterbook*, *Coucher Book* and allied Towneley manuscripts, in turn, disappeared from view until – in 1972 – they suddenly surfaced again and were lodged in the Leeds Archives Department. John Taylor of Leeds University promptly examined them and published his conclusions in 1975: most interestingly, he noted that the first twenty-six pages of the *Letterbook* are missing and rightly bemoaned their loss since they almost certainly included letters to the

Plumptons from kings and Earls of Northumberland (which, had they survived, would clearly have enhanced the collection's value for the historian of both national events and local politics).[3]

The Plumptons, a long-established West Riding family, could trace their history back to at least the twelfth century and every head of the family from the late thirteenth to the early sixteenth century received a knighthood. Several of their principal estates, including the manor of Plumpton itself, were held of the Percy lordship of Spofforth; successive heads of the family in the fifteenth century served as retainers of the Earls of Northumberland; and their own fluctuating fortunes clearly reflected the political ups-and-downs of their patrons. Prudent marriages, too, had greatly benefitted the family since the early fourteenth century, enabling them to extend both their property and influence well beyond their native West Riding. Sir William Plumpton (died 1361), who represented Yorkshire in the parliament of 1331 had married the no doubt wealthy widow of a former Mayor of Newcastle-upon-Tyne. His son Sir Robert (1341–1407), who campaigned in both France and Scotland in the later fourteenth century, secured as his first wife in 1367 Isabella, sister of the Richard Scrope who became Archbishop of York in 1398 and was eventually executed in 1405 for his leading role in a rebellion against Henry IV. This insurrection was also, in part, a Percy-inspired affair, and Sir Robert Plumpton's son (another Sir William) was himself so heavily involved – as both the archbishop's nephew and a Percy retainer – that he too was beheaded as a traitor at York and his head fixed on Micklegate as a gruesome warning to future would-be rebels (p. xxiii). Fortunately for the family, Sir William was not attainted and his father was able to obtain a general pardon for all treasons and felonies on 21 June 1405 (p. xxvi). The succession, too, was well provided for: Sir William had earlier married Alice Gisburn, daughter of a citizen, merchant and three times Mayor of York, John Gisburn, by whom he had no fewer than nine children. Thus when Sir Robert Plumpton died in 1407, his grandson (another Sir Robert, 1383–1421) was able to assume the headship of the family and control of its lands without difficulty. He certainly added greatly to Plumpton wealth and influence by his marriage to Alice, daughter and heiress of Sir Godfrey Foljambe of Hassop in Derbyshire, whose inheritance included substantial estates in Nottinghamshire, Derbyshire and Staffordshire (p. xxvi). Sir Robert also seems to have maintained the family tradition of service to the Earls of Northumberland: Percy patronage probably helps to explain his appointment as steward of the honour of Knaresborough in 1414 (and of the forest as well in 1416) and his appearance on several government commissions; while his own eminence in local society is no doubt reflected in his representation of Yorkshire in the parliaments of 1411 and 1416 and Nottinghamshire in 1414 (pp. xliii–iv). Moreover, as a retainer of Henry V's brother John, Duke of Bedford, he seemingly served in France in 1418–19 and may even have met his death while campaigning there in 1421 (pp. xliii, xlvi, xlix).[4]

At the time of his father's death Sir William Plumpton (1404–80) was still a minor: as a result he became a ward of the Earl of Northumberland and, even after he attained his majority in 1425, his prime loyalty to the Percys never seriously wavered (p. l). Like many young gentlemen of the day, he saw service as a soldier in the war against France: in 1427–8 (when he probably received his knighthood) and, again, in 1435 as a captain in the Duke of Bedford's retinue.[5] From the late 1430s, however, his main interests centred on Yorkshire. In 1439 he became steward and master forester of the royal honour of Knaresborough and, soon afterwards, constable of Knaresborough castle (p. liii): in the years that followed he was to remain closely concerned with the honour's administration.[6] Then, in 1442, the Earl of Northumberland appointed him steward of all his manors and lordships in Yorkshire for life, with an annual fee of £10; and to this was added, in 1447, for his good service, a further £10 (p. lxvi). From November 1439, Sir William's name also appeared on the commission of the peace for the West Riding; while, in 1447–8, he served as sheriff of Yorkshire, and, in 1452–3, of Nottinghamshire and Derbyshire.[7]

During the 1450s, as a retainer of the Earl of Northumberland, Sir William Plumpton became increasingly identified with the Lancastrian regime.[8] Shortly before the first battle of St Albans in 1455, he was summoned to attend a Lancastrian Great Council as a representative of the West Riding, and he may have fought in the battle (where his patron was killed): at all events, he saw the wisdom of obtaining a pardon later in the year.[9] In 1456 he probably took part in a raid over the Scottish border led by the new Earl of Northumberland (p. lxvi), and it was no doubt as Northumberland's man that he appeared on royal commissions in December 1457 and August 1459.[10] Perhaps present in the Lancastrian force at Ludford Bridge on 12 October 1459, he was certainly included, as a commissioner for the West Riding, on the great Lancastrian commission of array of 21 December 1459 'to resist the rebellion of Richard, Duke of York, Edward, Earl of March, Richard, Earl of Warwick, Richard, Earl of Salisbury and Edmund, Earl of Rutland, attainted.'[11] In all probability, he actively supported the Earl of Northumberland and the Lancastrians in the north in the autumn of 1460, culminating in his presence on the battlefield of Wakefield on 30 December.[12] On 12 March 1461, a few days after the Yorkist Edward IV had been proclaimed king in London, orders were issued by the Lancastrian leadership requiring Plumpton and two other knights (Sir Richard Tunstall and Sir Thomas Tresham) 'to summon all liegemen of the forest or demesne of Knaresburgh to set out with them to meet the enemy' (p. lxvii); the following day, 13 March, a letter purporting to come from Henry VI himself at York was directed to Sir William, calling on him 'with all such people as ye may make defensible arraied' to present himself 'in all hast possible' to 'resist the malicious entent and purpose' of Edward IV (p. l). Plumpton almost certainly answered the call and fought for the Lancastrians at Towton on 29 March 1461 (p. lxvii).[13] His son and heir, another William, probably lost his life in the fighting.[14] The Earl of Northumberland certainly perished in what was soon, and rightly, hailed as a great Yorkist victory; as for Sir William Plumpton, the next few years were clearly the most difficult and dangerous of his life.[15]

Like many Lancastrian supporters after Towton, Sir William may well have fled northwards towards Scotland, only to be captured at Cockermouth (in Cumberland) and brought across country to Newcastle.[16] However, he managed to avoid the imprisonment or attainder that might easily have been his fate. On 13 May 1461 he appeared before Chief Justice Robert Danby in the city of York: binding himself in the very large sum of £2,000, he thereby secured the protection of Edward IV against his enemies, but, when the bond expired on 12 July 1461, he surrendered himself to the Tower of London as a prisoner (pp. lxvii–lxviii). How long he remained in the Tower is not known: perhaps his imprisonment lasted until he obtained a general pardon on 5 February 1462.[17] Later that year, on 10 September, he was released from 'all actions of the Crown against him by reason of' his bond of May 1461. Even now his troubles were by no means over, for it was not only the new king and his government that he had to fear. Soon after Edward IV's accession, the widow of Richard Neville, Earl of Salisbury (whose husband had been beheaded the day after the battle of Wakefield) made a formal appeal of murder against Sir William Plumpton, Sir George Darell and a number of others: in connection with this, on 31 May 1462, Plumpton and Darell bound themselves in the sum of £1,000.[18] Sir William's prospects seemed gloomier still when, in late 1463, he was denounced as a traitor by David Routh: Routh's accusations included the receiving of 'false, damnable, diffamatory and slaunderous writing' against the king and secretly aiding 'divers persons coming out of Scotland fro the Kings adversaries' (p. lxix). These were very serious charges and, in view of Plumpton's earlier career, they cannot easily be dismissed. Luckily for him, however, he was acquitted on all counts, and a royal writ dubbed him henceforth 'our true and faithfull liegeman' (pp. lxix–lxx). From early 1464, in fact, Sir William appears to have enjoyed complete liberty – but it was not until the 1470s (with the lifting of the cloud of treason hanging over Henry Percy, fourth Earl of Northumberland) that he finally found security and royal favour once more.[19]

After an absence of almost twelve years Sir William Plumpton was reappointed to the commission of the peace for the West Riding in February 1472 and, apart from a gap of about a year between November 1475 and December 1476, he remained a JP there until his death in 1480.[20] During the 1470s, too, he served as a commissioner of array in the West Riding (in March 1472), while in August 1475 he was included on a commission to treat with the Scots and, in June 1477, to arrest and imprison Scottish marauders in Yorkshire.[21] Presumably, he was now regarded as politically reliable since his patron the Earl of Northumberland was firmly back in favour: certainly he was sufficiently trusted, in February 1472, to be given licence to fortify his manor house at Plumpton.[22] Before the end of 1472 he had become steward of the Percy manor of Spofforth (p. 26) and there are several letters suggesting a fair degree of intimacy between himself and the earl (pp. 26–8). Not that the relationship was always smooth. When Northumberland deprived him of his posts as deputy constable, steward and forester of Knaresborough he was clearly annoyed, especially when the earl granted these offices to his near-neighbour William Gascoigne. Yet, try as he might, he was unable to muster any significant support (whether from

Richard, Duke of Gloucester or the notably well-connected Sir John Pilkington) for his efforts to persuade Percy to change his mind. Similarly, when he was removed from the commission of the peace for the West Riding in November 1475 and appealed to the influential William, Lord Hastings on the matter, he got nowhere. Indeed, his London agent Godfrey Grene firmly warned him of the dangers of 'medling betwixt Lords' (pp. 31–3). Clearly, even in the 1470s, Sir William could obtain no backing whatsoever when he sought to challenge established criteria of royal or aristocratic patronage in northern England.

Sir William Plumpton's son Robert (c. 1453–1523), like his father, soon developed a close connection with the Earl of Northumberland both as a retainer and a member of his baronial council (p. 45).[23] During the last years of Edward IV's reign, this ensured for him a role in resisting what was perceived as a mounting Scottish threat. In September 1480, following a Scottish invasion of the far north, he was summoned 'with all such personnes as ye may make in there most defensible array' to attend on the earl at Topcliffe (p. 40); the threat was still very much there in 1481 (p. 42); and, in 1482, Plumpton did indeed campaign north of the border, in a massive force commanded by Gloucester and Northumberland, and while there probably received his knighthood (p. xcvi).[24] His sympathies during Richard III's reign can only be guessed at: in all probability, he followed the line of his patron Henry Percy, Earl of Northumberland and may even have been in the earl's non-participating force at Bosworth, but there is no solid evidence available.[25]

During the early years of Henry VII's reign, perhaps the most interesting and productive period of his career, Sir Robert Plumpton seems to have enjoyed the Earl of Northumberland's patronage to the full. Initially, the new Tudor king was wary of trusting Northumberland and the earl spent a few months in the Tower of London.[26] Eventually, in January 1486, he was released from captivity and not only permitted to return to the north but once more given wide powers and responsibilities there.[27] As is abundantly clear from a whole series of letters, mostly undated, Plumpton soon obtained his father's former offices in the Duchy of Lancaster honour of Knaresborough, as well as the stewardship of the Percy lordship of Spofforth (pp. 54–5, 74–5, 75–6, 76, 78, 81, 86, 86–7).[28] Soon, too, his political colours were tested. On 15 February 1486 Thomas Betanson informed him, from London, that 'the Kyng proposyth northward hastyly after the Parliament and it is sayd he purposes to doe execution quickly ther on such as have offended agaynst him' (pp. 49–50).[29] No doubt it was in connection with this royal visit that Sir Robert Plumpton, and other Percy retainers, were 'comaunded to be redy upon an ower warning' by their patron (p. 53): certainly, when the king arrived in Yorkshire in April 1486, Plumpton was in the 'great and noble company' of Percy men who rode with the earl to greet him.[30] In 1487 came the first major rebellion of Henry VII's reign. Whether or not Sir Robert Plumpton fought for the king at the battle of Stoke on 16 June, his involvement in the 'mopping-up' operations following Lambert Simnel's defeat is clear (pp. 54–5).[31] Later in the year he was present at the coronation of Queen Elizabeth (p. xcvii). The spring of 1489 saw the outbreak of what was seemingly a serious rebellion in Yorkshire. On 24 April the Earl of Northumberland sent an urgent letter to Plumpton from his manor of Seamer commanding him and Sir William Gascoigne to hasten to Thirsk 'with such a company (as) ye may bring with your ease, such as ye trust, having bowes and arrowes, and pryvy harnest' (p. 61). Sir Robert responded to the summons but, on 28 April, the earl and many of his household servants were set upon at Cocklodge and among those killed was Northumberland himself. Thomas Howard, Earl of Surrey was now sent to Yorkshire to suppress the rebels; he did so with alacrity, and was duly rewarded with the lieutenantship of the north. Sir Robert Plumpton played a sufficiently prominent part in the operation to merit a personal letter of thanks from the king, commending him for his 'true minde and faithful liegance towards us' and praising his 'diligent acquitall for the reducing of our people there to our subjection and obedience' (pp. xcvii–xcviii).[32] Even so, Yorkshire remained in a state of considerable unrest and, in 1492, a further rebellion broke out there. Although rather a shadowy affair and confined to the western part of the county, its suppression by the Earl of Surrey at Ackworth near Pontefract once more entailed a role for Sir Robert Plumpton and, as in 1489, he again received personal commendation from Henry VII (pp. 96–7n).[33] Thereafter he ceased to play any significant political or military role in the north, partly because Northumberland's murder removed his prime benefactor there and the new earl was only a child, and partly because much of the rest of his life was dominated by a gargantuan struggle to defend his inheritance.[34]

As well as providing much insight into political life in general and the political affiliations of the Plumptons in particular at the close of the Middle Ages, the *Plumpton Cartulary* and correspondence must also be regarded as a source of major importance for northern society in the fifteenth and early sixteenth centuries. Most notably, there is a wealth of information here regarding marriage, property and the West Riding community of gentry.[35] A.J. Pollard, in a study of the gentry of Richmondshire, has convincingly argued that:

> Through marriage, through the network of mutual cooperation with which they handled property, and through their other mutual interests, the landowning class of Richmondshire formed a community of their own.

Constant inter-marriage drew them together as a closely-knit kinship group sharing common interests, as did their concern with the possession, protection and extension of their landed estates: in particular, they frequently acted for each other as feoffees to use, witnesses of deeds, executors of wills and arbitrators in property disputes.[36] Much the same is true of the West Riding community of gentry or, even more narrowly, the gentry community of the honour of Knaresborough (who were, perhaps, as clearly within the Percy sphere of influence during the Wars of the Roses as Richmondshire gentry were within the Neville). Certainly, trustees and witnesses of Plumpton deeds tended to be members of local families such as the Babthorpes,

Beckwiths, Gascoignes, Goldsboroughs, Hamertons, Stapletons and Vavasours; many Plumpton correspondents belonged to the same gentry group; and Plumpton marriages, too, were most frequently contracted with neighbouring landowners. As John Taylor has emphasized, the Plumpton letters demonstrate over and over again:

> ... the network of clientage that existed between a family, its friends, and retainers during the later Middle Ages. Thus we have members of the family soliciting each other for favours, communicating information, and preserving some sort of relationship down to the remotest degree of kinship. There are requests from clients 'for good lordshipp and mastershipp' and suggestions are made to the family to 'make your frynds to take your part as frynds shold doe'. Nowhere is the attempt to extend the influence of the family more clearly shown than in plans for marriage alliances, some successful, others abortive, which are found throughout the letters . . . An heir or an heiress was a valuable commodity, and the fortunes of the Plumptons in the fifteenth century centred on the success or otherwise of the various marriage settlements.[37]

The first marriage of Sir William Plumpton (1404–80) set the tone for many that were to follow. Arranged by his parents in 1416 when he was just twelve years old and his prospective wife Elizabeth a mere infant, it was clearly designed to promote (or further) an alliance between the Plumptons and their near-neighbours the Stapletons of Carlton: Elizabeth, daughter of Sir Brian Stapleton, brought with her a dowry of some 360 marks; the couple were provided with a jointure valued at 20 marks per annum from Plumpton estates in Kenalton, Nottinghamshire; and the marriage can certainly be regarded as a success insofar as it produced two sons and a string of eligible daughters (pp. xliii–xliv). Sir William, in turn, seems to have regarded the marriages of his daughters entirely in terms of the advancement and consolidation of family interests: Joan, for instance, was contracted in childhood, in 1454, to marry Thomas, infant son and heir of Robert Roos of Ingmanthorpe, with a dowry of 200 marks and a jointure of 20 marks per annum, and, when this came to nothing, she was matched in 1468 with Thomas Middleton of Kirkby Overblow near Wetherby (bringing with her a marriage portion of £100); Elizabeth was contracted in marriage in 1455 to William Beckwith of Clint near Ripley, with a dowry of £123 6s 8d and a jointure of £10 13s 4d; in 1463 Agnes married Richard Aldburgh (another West Riding man), a match nicely backed by a dowry of 230 marks and a jointure of 20 marks; Catherine became wife, successively, to William Lord Zouch and Sir Gilbert Debenham; Alice was despatched to nearby Goldsborough to become the wife of Richard Goldsborough; Isabel married Sir Stephen Hamerton of Hamerton in Craven; and Margaret was matched, first, with Sir George Darell of Sessay near Thirsk and, after his death in 1466, with John Neville of Womersley near Pontefract (pp. lxxxi–lxxxv).

Clearly, it was particularly necessary that Sir William Plumpton should find suitable brides for his two sons by Elizabeth Stapleton; again, family aggrandizement provided the main spur to his efforts. In August 1446 he managed to arrange a most prestigious marriage for his elder son Robert to Elizabeth, six-year-old daughter of Thomas, Lord Clifford of Skipton-in-Craven. Unfortunately, Robert died in 1450 without consummating the relationship (hardly surprisingly, since his wife was still only about ten years old). Sir William had left nothing to chance, however, for, at the time of Robert's marriage, he had agreed with the Cliffords that, should Robert die without issue, Elizabeth would then marry his younger son William: this she duly did in 1453 and, by the time of William Plumpton's death in 1461, she had given birth to two daughters, Margaret and Elizabeth. Since Sir William had agreed, at the time of his daughter-in-law's marriage to his younger son, that 'they shuld not ligg togedder till she came to the age of xvi yeres', his granddaughters were still well under age at the time of their father's death (pp. lxii–lxiv).[38] Nevertheless, he wasted no time in arranging advantageous marriages for both of them on the understanding that they were his heirs apparent. In November 1463 the keeping and marriage of Margaret, then about four years old, was given to Brian Rocliffe of Cowthorp, near Wetherby, with the intention that she should become the wife of his son John; similarly, in 1464, the governance and marriage of Elizabeth was contracted with Henry Suthill of Suthill Esquire, on the understanding that Henry's son and heir apparent, another John, should marry her. Interestingly enough, Henry Suthill insisted that, if Sir William should take a second wife and have male issue by her, he (Henry Suthill) should have the wardship and marriage of any such male issue on behalf of another of his daughters (pp. lxx–lxxii).[39] This suggests, perhaps, that Henry Suthill already had suspicions regarding Sir William's secret marriage to Joan Wintringham and he must surely have been aware of the existence of Plumpton's (apparently illegitimate) son by her: certainly, neither he nor Rocliffe took kindly to Sir William's manoeuvrings in the 1470s to disinherit his granddaughters in favour of this son.

Sir William Plumpton, it is clear, was nothing if not cavalier in the treatment of his children and grandchildren: yet, when it came to his own private life and personal liaisons, he seems to have been both an individualist and a hedonist. As well as acknowledging two bastard sons by unknown mothers, he chose for many years to maintain an ostensible mistress in his household.[40] Although he almost certainly married Joan Wintringham of Knaresborough in the early 1450s, *before* she gave birth to a son Robert, it was a clandestine match which Sir William did not *publicly* acknowledge. Why he kept its existence under wraps for so long and allowed his son Robert to be thought a bastard has never been fully explained. Once his only surviving son by his first wife, William, died in 1461, the question of Robert's legitimacy or otherwise obviously became crucial: if Robert was legitimate, he must now be the heir to his father's property; if he was not, the bulk, if not the whole, of the inheritance must eventually pass to Sir William's two granddaughters, Margaret and Elizabeth. Probably it was with a view to securing good marriages for them that Sir William continued to suppress evidence of Robert's legitimacy, only intending to reveal it when convenient to himself. Before long, however, he was left with little choice in the matter once the ecclesiastical authorities at York began to take him to task for his apparent immorality in living with Joan Wintringham. In January 1468 he at last acknowledged Joan as his wife, managed to produce several witnesses willing to swear to the validity of the match (including his own domestic chaplain and the parish clerk of Knaresborough), and, as a result, the marriage was duly pronounced valid in July 1472 (pp. lxxiii–lxxvii). Soon afterwards Sir William began actively to promote his son Robert's claims to the family estates and the stage was now firmly set for the years of legal wrangling that were ultimately to prove so disastrous for the Plumptons.

Meanwhile, marriages continued to be mooted and, sometimes, brought to fruition. In 1478 Sir William Plumpton's son by Joan Wintringham, Robert, became the husband of Agnes Gascoigne in the domestic chapel of the Gascoigne family house at Gawthorpe near Harewood (pp. lxxix–lxxx).[41] Agnes died in 1504 and, before the end of September 1505, Robert took as his second wife Isabel (or Elizabeth), daughter of Ralph, Lord Neville. Although he had no issue by Isabel, Agnes gave him no fewer than five sons and eight daughters. The eldest son William (1485–1547) was contracted to marry Isabel, niece of William Babthorpe, in 1496, and several of his daughters also made decent matches.[42] Amid this plethora of conventional business marriages, however, it is nice to find at least one that seems clearly to have involved personal as well as material considerations: the marriage of Edward Plumpton and Agnes Drayate towards the end of the 1490s.[43]

Most Plumpton sons and daughters in the later Middle Ages followed the normal path of marriage: only rarely did they remain single and, if they did, there is little evidence that they were drawn to the religious life. As far as is known, none entered monasteries or nunneries (as young men and women) or joined the ranks of the friars.[44] Indeed, only two members of the family in the fifteenth century seem to have become clerics: Richard Plumpton, nephew of Sir William Plumpton (1404–80), who occasionally surfaces in the role of chaplain (pp. cxxiii, 130); and George Plumpton, brother of Sir Robert (1383–1421), who enjoyed an apparently successful if undistinguished career in the Lancastrian church. Ordained a priest in 1418, he became rector of Grasmere in Westmorland in 1439 as a nominee of the Abbot and Convent of St Mary's York. Several years later, in 1447, he was presented to the rectory of Bingham in Nottinghamshire: within a few months, however, he obtained leave of absence on account of his age and increasing infirmities, resigned the living soon afterwards, and spent his last years as a pensioner in the seclusion of Bolton Abbey in Craven (pp. xxxv–xxxvii).[45]

Although religious observance was an important facet of the later medieval gentry household, neither the *Plumpton Cartulary* nor correspondence contain significant evidence of it. The foundation of chantries was popular in gentry circles, and there is a little on this: in 1345, for instance, Sir William Plumpton (died 1361) founded a chantry at Ripon; while, in 1450, the cleric George Plumpton made provision for the establishment of 'a perpetuall chauntre of a priest' in the parish church of Spofforth (pp. xxi, xxxviii). Several members of the family are known to have become members of the York Guild of Corpus Christi.[46] There is also intermittent evidence of religious bequests: the will of Richard Plumpton, drawn up in 1443, included arrangements for 'a priest to say mass daily and for ever' in Knaresborough and reference to several religious artefacts he wished to bequeath such as 'a psalter covered with red velvet', 'a primer covered with red satin' and a gold crucifix; while Sir Robert Plumpton's will, dated 10 April 1523, provided £10 'to be distributed on the day of his sepulture unto priests, clerks and poor persons' and 6s 8d to the church of Spofforth (pp xxxiii–xxxiv, cxxv).[47]

Clearly, the financial potential of their estates (whether in terms of income generated by the sale of agricultural produce or the rents paid by tenants) must have been a major concern of the Plumptons throughout the fifteenth and early sixteenth centuries: yet, again, there is less direct evidence on such matters here than might reasonably be expected. Nor do agricultural practices or crop yields figure very much, although there is some indication of the increasingly common phenomenon of enclosure in the records: in February 1473, for instance, Sir William Plumpton was licensed 'to enclose and impark all the lands, meadows, feedings, pastures, woods and other tenements in Plumpton'.[48] Another feature of the times was the continuing decline of serfdom, for so long the traditional prop of medieval agriculture; while, as always, there was the unpredictable impact of inclement weather.[49] Only in a single letter, however, is the lid significantly lifted for a moment and the no doubt perennial problems facing fifteenth-century estate-managers briefly exposed. On 21 August 1469 Thomas Billop wrote to Sir William Plumpton from the Nottinghamshire manor of Kenalton:

> . . . I am nott in store att this time of money for to gett your harvest with, withoutyn I might gett it of your tenaunts, or ells for to take of your shepe silver, and that I ware right lothe for to do – letting you witt alsoe that I have bene in the Peake and there I cannott gett no money of Harry Fulgiam, nor of John of Tor, nor no other that owes you, but if I shold take of your cattell, and soe I think for to do; for I have no oxen to gett your corne with, nor none I cannott gett carryed, for every man is so busie with theire owne: for whether is so latesum in this cuntrey, that no man can neither well gett corne or hay – letting you witt that your tenant Nichole Bristow hath not gotten but xii foder of hay, and it is nought good, and the corneland is overfloting with water . . . I was on St Lawrence day att Melton with iiij^x of your shepe to sell, and could sell none of them, but if I wold have selled xx of the best of them for xiij^d a peece, and therefore I seld none (pp. 20–22).[50]

No subject figures more often in the Plumpton letters than litigation and the correspondence constitutes a major source for both the operation of the law and its manifest deficiencies in the fifteenth century.[51] Sir William Plumpton (1404–80) certainly had an insatiable taste for litigation and, judging by the bewildering variety of writs and legal terms (often in Latin) mentioned in the relatively few letters to him, he must have had a considerable personal knowledge of the law. A single letter despatched from London by Brian Rocliffe in the early 1460s mentions three law suits; while, in December 1469, Godfrey Grene reported cases involving 'fishing your ponds att Plompton' and 'your milne att Plompton': indeed, according to

Grene, Sir John Mauleverer had recently accused Sir William of having 'sued all the trew men' in the forest of Knaresborough (pp. 5, 22–3).[52] Sir Robert Plumpton (*c.* 1453–1523) also frequently resorted to the law courts as plaintiff or was, perforce, there as defendant: on 10 February 1490, for instance, Edward Plumpton reported not only that his 'matter in the Excheker is grevous (since) there is iij wryttes agaynst you' but also that, in another suit, 'we must have a *non molestando* out of the Chauncery'; ten days later he drew attention to the recent transmission to his master of 'a box sealed and ther in ij wrytts, one *dedimus potestatem* out of the Chauncere, and another out of the Excheker' (pp. 90–1, 92).

Clearly, all this litigation required the employment of legal advisers, and several of them feature prominently in the correspondence. During the early 1460s Brian Rocliffe, Baron of the Exchequer, certainly performed this function on behalf of Sir William Plumpton, as did Godfrey Grene (who was notably active both in conducting suits and reporting on their progress); Edward Plumpton, a trained lawyer, John Pullan and George Emerson frequently acted in a similar capacity for Sir Robert later on (pp. 5, 7–8, 9–10, 10–12, 90–1, 92–3, 132–3, 141–3, 145–6, 150). Indeed, letters were occasionally sent to Yorkshire from the London Inns of Court: Edward Plumpton wrote from 'Furnywalls Inn' on 13 February 1496, for instance, while John Pullan did likewise from 'Lyncolns Inn' on 29 January 1499 (pp. 117, 133). There is also evidence of fees being paid to such men: on 30 June 1483, for example, Edward Plumpton acknowledged the receipt from Sir Robert of 'my fee xxvi^s viii^d for Pentycost last past' (p. 43).

There is certainly no shortage of information on the cost of litigation, the complexities of legal processes and the prevalence of delay. There is evidence, too, of the manipulation of the law and its officers by the wealthy and well-connected and, on occasion, of downright bribery and corruption. In the mid-1470s, for instance, Godfrey Grene informed Sir William Plumpton of a suit:

> . . . delaid for this terme, but the next terme it cannot be delaid . . . As for all your oder suits, they have the speed the law will give them . . . As for the *supena*, the writt is not retorned in; it seems it will take a delay (p. 30).

In January 1499 John Pullan reported to Sir Robert Plumpton that the 'accion of wast agaynst Sir John Hastings goeth forward as fast as the law wyll serve' and he used precisely the same phrase – 'as fast as the law wyll serve' – in another letter penned later the same year (pp. 133, 141). References to the costliness of the law are suggestive. On 10 February 1490 Edward Plumpton complained that the 'serch and the copy of the wrytts, out of one cort to another, costeth much money, and the fees of them, and great soliciting' (p. 91); in November 1500 George Emerson declared that he had 'retained in the Exchequer, by the advice of Mr Blakewall, Mr Denny, in the Chauncry Porter, and given unto them their fees' (p. 145); and, in a letter to Sir Robert Plumpton in November 1502, John Pullan warned his master that 'the costs and expencs about thes busines wilbe great, therfor I wold ye prepared money to send, uppon all goodly hast' (p. 165). As for the manipulation of the law, it might take several forms. On 23 September 1490 Edward Plumpton reported to Sir Robert:

> This day I have spoken with Master Schereffe, and ther I send Master Blakwall, Master of the Chancery, as the berer can shew to you more by mouth, and they both comend them to you. Master Schereff hath and wyll doe as much in your matter as I can of reason desire him (pp. 99–100).

Similarly, in May 1501, John Pullan advised his master 'to labor as well the Schereffes, as all your frynds, and every country where your land lyeth' (p. 151). More directly, there was always the possibility of influencing the composition of juries or even bribing jurors themselves. In January 1499 Sir Robert Plumpton was urged to 'make specially frynds to the Jurrours, that they may be labored specially, to such as ye trust wylbe made fryndly in the cause' (p. 132); on 12 Feburary of the same year, and in connection with the same case, he was informed that 'it is necessary for you to get a copy of the panel, and then to enquire if any of them or of their wyfes be sybb or allied to Wil. Babthorp, and yf any cause in them beg wherby they may be chalenged' (p. 134); and, in similar vein, on 21 November 1499, he was advised to make 'specyall labor to have one indefferent pannell of the Coroners; they must be labored by sum frynd of yours' (p. 141).

Many legal cases receive only passing mention in the correspondence but, occasionally, they can be followed through. In 1490, for instance, a series of letters demonstrate Sir Robert Plumpton's endeavours to retain possession of Haverah Park in the honour of Knaresborough (pp. 93–99). Even more detail is forthcoming of a dispute in the late 1490s between Sir Robert and William Babthorpe arising, as did an associated legal tussle with Sir John Hastings, out of the marriage of Plumpton's eldest son William to Babthorpe's niece Isabel (pp. 128–35, 141–3, 145–6).[53] Ironically enough, in this long drawn out confrontation, Plumpton was pressing the inheritance rights of a female while – at the same time – vigorously resisting claims to his own estates posed by the daughters of his half-brother William.

During the 1470s the overwhelming ambition of Sir William Plumpton (1404–80) was the promotion of his son Robert's claims to the family estates: yet his two granddaughters, Margaret and Elizabeth, had married into the Rocliffe and Suthill families in the early 1460s on the clear understanding that *they*, not Robert, were his heirs apparent. Since the rules of inheritance in the fifteenth century were nothing if not complex and few titles to property were legally impregnable, it is hardly surprising that a protracted struggle for possession of the Plumpton lands ensued: indeed, it forms the central theme of much of the correspondence.[54] In 1475 Sir William conveyed most of his estates to trustees, for his own use while he lived and that of Robert after his death (pp. lxxviii–lxxix). On the strength of this he succeeded in marrying Robert to Agnes, daughter of Sir William Gascoigne of

Gawthorpe, in 1478, guaranteeing that lands settled on the couple would be unaffected by earlier agreements with the Rocliffes and Suthills, and he also made it clear that he wished all his personal effects to go to Robert (pp. lxxix, lxxxvi). Inevitably, the Rocliffes and Suthills were determined to resist these manoeuvrings, and arbitration machinery had already been set in motion by the time of Sir William's death in October 1480 (pp. lxxx–lxxxi). Battle was now joined with a vengeance until, in May 1482, the various parties agreed to accept the arbitration of a high-powered commission headed by Richard, Duke of Gloucester and Henry Percy, Earl of Northumberland, and made up of members of their respective councils (p. lxxxix). Then, in February 1483, the disputants decided to put their case before the king (p. lxxxix). Edward IV's premature death in April 1483 was followed by Gloucester's seizure of the throne in June: thus it fell to the new king, Richard III, to pronounce on the matter in September 1483. His settlement was a compromise: the heirs-general (Margaret and Elizabeth) were awarded the manors of Grassington and Steeton in Yorkshire, and a series of lands in Derbyshire, while Sir Robert Plumpton was to have the rest of the estates (pp. xc–xcv).[55] Although neither side was fully satisfied, this settlement stood relatively unchallenged for over a decade.

The murder of Henry Percy, Earl of Northumberland in 1489 meant the removal of Sir Robert Plumpton's patron in the north and the new earl was still a child. Plumpton's enemies, no doubt, appreciated his changed circumstances, not least those anxious to overthrow the land settlement of 1483. Moreover, even when the young earl came of age in 1499, it made little difference: he never exercised the power his father had enjoyed in the north, nor did he show much interest in the problems confronting Sir Robert Plumpton. Consequently, Sir Robert could look to no one for the sort of influential support the heirs-general got from Sir Richard Empson. Notorious as Henry VII's agent for investigating the Crown's financial rights and putting the screws on royal debtors, Empson was also concerned to further his own *personal* ends: hence his interest in the Plumpton inheritance.

Early in 1497 Sir Robert received the first clear intimation of Empson's interest in a new challenge by the heirs-general (pp. 120–2). In November 1500 he was informed that 'Master Empson will in hand with you this yere' (p. 147), while in May 1501 he heard that 'they purpose suerly to have an assise this somer' (p. 150). John Pullan reported from Lincoln's Inn on 18 May 1501 that 'the great man E., as far undoubted as I can know, intendeth to have assyses agaynst you'; moreover, since Empson was actively taking steps to ensure the appointment of jurors favourable to himself, Pullan urged his master 'to labor as well the Schereffes, as all your frynds, and every country where your land lyeth' (p. 151). In Nottinghamshire the tactics of Plumpton's opponents were, allegedly, 'to tary and abyde to such tyme as they thinke tyme convenient for to enter into your liflods in this country'; and, although his tenants there were reputedly well disposed towards him, he was urged to make a personal visit (p. 156).[56] For his own part, Sir Robert seems to have sought the support of the Earl of Shrewsbury (p. 158), but his worst fears were soon confirmed when it was discovered that the chosen panel of jurors for Nottinghamshire was likely to uphold the claims of the heirs-general: only 'the great mercy of God, and great labor and cost', he was warned, could prevent 'great hurt to your worship' (pp. 158–60). By the autumn of 1501 it had certainly become clear who was for, and who was against, Sir Robert Plumpton; and, although efforts to influence the jurors on his behalf continued, Empson's reputation seems to have cut far more ice (pp. 160–62).[57] Consequently, at the Lammas Assizes, Plumpton was deprived of his lands in Nottinghamshire, Derbyshire and Staffordshire, while Sir Richard Empson soon received *his* reward in the form of the manor of Kenalton for himself and the hand of Henry Suthill (son of Elizabeth Suthill née Plumpton) for his daughter Joan (p. cvi).

Sir Robert Plumpton did not lack sympathizers for the predicament in which he found himself. Elizabeth de la Pole, for instance, wrote to him on 26 November 1501 deploring:

> . . . the utter and malicious enmity, and false craft of Mr Empson, and such others your adversaries; which, as all the great parte of England knoweth, hath done to you and yours the most injury and wrong, that ever was done, or wrought, to any man of worship in this land of peace. And non more sory therfore, then I myselfe is (p. 162).

The main fear now, of course, was for the Yorkshire estates and Empson, fresh from his success in the Midlands, had every intention of pressing home the other claims of the heirs-general. At the York Assizes early in September 1502, Sir Robert seems to have argued his case with vigour: yet, once more, the verdict went against him and he found himself deprived of the legal right to lands he had occupied for over twenty years (pp. cvi–cvix).[58]

No doubt encouraged by his friends, who were as convinced as he was of the bias of the jurors, Sir Robert Plumpton determined not to surrender possession of his family estates without resistance. Accordingly, a few days after the trial at York, he ordered his wife to 'see that the manor and the place of Plompton bee surely and stedfastly kept' (p. cx), and for months thereafter attempts by the victors to occupy the Plumpton lands were parried, with both Sir Robert's wife Agnes and his son William playing prominent roles (pp. 163–4).[59] Sir Robert himself journeyed to London in order to press his claims personally and, as a series of letters makes clear, he did indeed make strenuous efforts to get the verdict reversed (pp. 165–6, 177–8, 180–1, 181–2, 185, 195–6). He even appealed to Henry VII for protection and the king, in February 1502, created him a knight of the Body and ordered the sheriff of Yorkshire to 'serve noe writs, precepts or other writings' on either Sir Robert or his servants (pp. cxi–cxii, 174).

Meanwhile, resistance at Plumpton continued. Sir John Rocliffe complained that the manor house there was thoroughly fortified against the heirs-general (pp. cxi–cxii) and he and his supporters even petitioned the King's Council in Star Chamber.[60] There is certainly no doubt that Sir Robert ordered strong measures against tenants who refused to pay their rents (pp. 167–9): indeed, some of them were sufficiently harassed to appeal to Thomas Savage, Archbishop of York and acting King's Lieutenant in the north.[61] Savage's interventions, including his indictment of William Plumpton and sixteen of his servants, are chronicled in the letters (pp. 169–74).

Eventually, on 16 July 1503, Sir Robert Plumpton's efforts were rewarded when the king issued an injunction that 'William Plompton, son and heir of Sir Robert Plompton, peacably enjoy the Lordships of Plumpton and Idle' (pp. cxii–cxiii). This at least prevented the heirs-general getting control there, although it did little to clarify the legal situation.[62] The strong support not only of his son William but also his wife Agnes was clearly vital to Sir Robert in these difficult years.[63] Unfortunately, Agnes died in the middle of it all (probably in late 1504 or early 1505) and, although he soon remarried, his second marriage, too, was clearly dominated by the on-going family troubles.[64] The one surviving letter from Isabel Plumpton to her new husband certainly paints a graphic picture of misery:

> Sir, I have sent to Wright of Idell for the money that he promyst you, and he saith he hath it not to len, and makes choses and so I can get none nowhere. And as for wood, ther is none that will bey, for they know ye want money, and without they might have it halfe for nought, they will bey none . . . And your Lenten stoufe is to bey, and I wote not what to do, God wote, for I am ever left of thes fachion . . . Sir, for God sake take an end, for we are brought to begger staffe (p. 198–9).

Sir Robert Plumpton was probably still in possession of at least the Yorkshire manors of Plumpton and Little Studley in 1507.[65] Yet, it is clear, the last years of Henry VII's reign were, for him, dominated by financial worries (pp. cxiii–cxiv, 184–5, 186–7, 196–7, 197–8, 198–9, 204, 204–5): indeed, he and his son William may even have served a period of imprisonment in the Fleet.[66]

The death of Henry VII in April 1509 was soon followed by the downfall of Sir Richard Empson: arrested on fictitious charges of treason, he was found guilty and executed in August 1510. Ultimately, this helped clear the way for a new settlement of the great family conflict for possession of Sir William Plumpton's inheritance, but not immediately. On the contrary, early in Henry VIII's reign, Sir Robert, deprived of whatever protection had been his as a knight of the Body, was arrested for debt and both he and his wife spent some time in the Counter: Sir Robert himself was certainly in the prison from April to August 1510 (pp. cxvii–cxviii). This was the rock bottom of his fortunes. By the end of 1514, however, moves were afoot to arrange a fresh arbitration in the property dispute (pp. 207–10) and, in March 1515, a commission headed by Richard Fox, Bishop of Winchester made a final judgement and award: although hardly a triumph for Sir Robert Plumpton, it did at least give him and his heirs firm possession of the manor of Plumpton (pp. cxix–cxxi). Soon afterwards, in May 1515, William Plumpton (1485–1547) formally took charge of the household and estates at Plumpton: Sir Robert, now over sixty years old, and his wife, agreed henceforth 'to take their ease and reast, and to be at board, [at] the proper costs and charges'; William undertook to pay his father £10 per annum and, ominously, to 'pay yearly xx^{li} of such debts as the said Sir Robert standeth bound for' (p. cxxiv).

William Plumpton Esquire certainly took over control of a much depleted inheritance. At the time of his death in 1480 his grandfather had possessed estates in Nottinghamshire and Derbyshire alone probably worth in excess of £100, while his Yorkshire lands must have been worth a good deal more.[67] On his own death in 1547 William Plumpton held lands in the West Riding, and only there, worth £74: even without allowing for inflation, the change in the family's circumstances is clear.[68] Nevertheless, the Plumptons remained landowners of substance. They were still able to marry well: William Plumpton's eldest son Robert (1516–46) married Anne, daughter of John Norton of Norton Conyers Esquire, in 1538; his second son Denis (1519–96) married Ursula, daughter of Richard Aldburgh of Aldborough Esquire, in 1547; and his grandson William (1543–1602) married Mary, daughter of William Vavasour of Hazlewood Esquire. William Plumpton's will, made shortly before his death in 1547, which included a bequest of £40 to his sister Clare as well as other monetary gifts, certainly does not point to even gentle poverty (p. cxxvii). A significant proportion of West Riding gentry in Henry VIII's reign, in fact, had estates with lower valuations than those of the Plumptons.[69]

By and large, Plumpton letters dating from the reigns of Henry VIII and Edward VI prove an anticlimax for the historian after those of earlier years.[70] The only two exceptions, both probably written about 1536, were from Robert Plumpton (1516–46) to his mother Isabel and they clearly demonstrate the early impact of the Protestant Reformation in London. The young Robert, in residence at the Inner Temple in the mid-1530s, seems not only to have been a convert to the new Protestant doctrines himself but was also anxious to convince his mother of their validity: the fervour permeating the letters is remarkable, not least his exhortations to Isabel Plumpton to 'take heede to the teachinge of the Gospelle' and his despatching of 'a godly New Testament' to Yorkshire for that purpose (pp. 231–4).[71] The supreme irony of all this, however, is that during the reign of Elizabeth I the Plumpton family was to become renowned in the north of England for its unswerving loyalty to Roman Catholicism, a loyalty which finally put paid to any possible recovery of its former political, economic and social status.

NOTES

1. Apart from Thomas Stapleton's comprehensive 'Historical and Biographical Notices of the family of Plumpton of Plumpton' (reprinted here, pp. ix–cxxxviii), there are recent discussions in J. Taylor, 'The Plumpton Letters 1416–1552', *Northern History*, X (1975), pp. 72–87, and K.R. Dockray, 'The Troubles of the Yorkshire Plumptons', *History Today*, XXVII (1977), pp. 459–66.

2. A letter addressed by a group of York citizens to Sir Robert Plumpton in 1416 has been, rather doubtfully, cited as the earliest letter in the English language: Taylor, *loc.cit.*, p. 79. The first letter in the printed edition sequence, dated 13 March 1461 at York and in Henry VI's name, is addressed to Sir William Plumpton (p. 1); the last, dated 6 March 1552, is from Anne Pole to Mrs Isabel Plumpton (p. 258).
3. Taylor, *loc.cit.*, especially pp. 72–81.
4. Ibid., pp. 72–3, 84; *The Parliamentary Representation of the County of York 1258–1832*, ed. A. Gooder (Yorkshire Archaeological Society, Record Series, XCI, 1935), 1, pp. 72–3, 174–6.
5. *Letters and Papers illustrative of the Wars of the English in France during the reign of Henry VI*, ed. J. Stevenson (1861–4), II, ii, p. 436.
6. R. Somerville, *History of the Duchy of Lancaster* (1953), p. 524. Plumpton's early years in office in the lordship of Knaresborough were marked by considerable conflicts regarding demands by John Kemp, Archbishop of York that tenants of the forest should pay tolls at his fairs at Otley and Ripon. Kemp, apparently, fortified Ripon 'like a towne of war' and, in 1441, enlisted large numbers of men to protect his interests; the Knaresborough tenants objected strongly and, on 5 May 1441, a 'great and notable fellowship' led by Sir William Plumpton ambushed the archbishop's men on the road between Ripon and Boroughbridge; during the ensuing skirmish, seemingly, many arrows were fired and some lives lost, and it was certainly several years before peace was restored (pp. liv–lxii). On this affair, see also R.A. Griffiths, *The Reign of Henry VI* (1981), p. 578.
7. C(alendar of) F(ine) R(olls), *1445–52*, pp. 82, 103, *1452–61*, p. 16.
8. Although in receipt of a life annuity from the Earl of Northumberland in February 1453, Plumpton's name seems curiously absent from lists of Percy tenants and supporters indicted for their participation in gatherings at Heworth in 1453 and Spofforth in 1454; however he, along with others described as husbandmen, was reported as engaging in unlawful violence in 1453 in the Craven area of the West Riding: J.M.W. Bean, *The Estates of the Percy Family 1416–1537* (1958), p. 92n; PRO, KB9/149/16.
9. *Proceedings and Ordinances of the Privy Council of England*, ed. N.H. Nicolas (1834–7), VI, p. 340; PRO, C67/41/24 (general pardon, dated 24 October 1455).
10. C(alendar of) P(atent) R(olls), *1452–61*, pp. 408, 518. He was again pardoned on 20 January 1458: PRO, C67/42/16.
11. *CPR, 1452–61*, p. 560. He appeared on a further Lancastrian commission, dated 1 May 1460, concerning lands of attainted Yorkists in the West Riding (p. lxvi); while, following the Yorkist victory at Northampton in July 1460, he was dropped from the West Riding commission of the peace: *CPR, 1452–61*, p. 683.
12. PRO, C1/31/485; KB27/804/67.
13. *Three Fifteenth Century Chronicles*, ed. J. Gairdner (1880), p. 161.
14. Little is known of this William Plumpton (1436–61), beyond the fact that on 13 August 1457 a commission was issued to the sheriff and keepers of the peace in Nottinghamshire to 'arrest and commit to prison William Plumpton Esquire, son and heir of Sir William Plumpton, and George Plumpton, brother of Sir William the father, until they give security for good behaviour, and to repress the societies and gatherings made by them and others at Kenalton (a Nottinghamshire manor belonging to Sir William), and to bring William and George before the King and Council': *CPR, 1452–61*, p. 370. There is no direct evidence as to the exact nature and date of William Plumpton's death: he was alive on 19 February 1461 but dead by 21 September (p. lxvii[n]).
15. At least part of Sir William Plumpton's problems in the early 1460s may have resulted from his own outrageous behaviour following the Yorkist defeats at Ludford in 1459 and Wakefield in 1460. Certainly, Robert Percy, perhaps a former retainer of the Yorkist Earl of Salisbury, soon petitioned the chancellor, complaining that, following the rout at Ludford, Sir William sent armed servants to his house who 'brake the house and closure

of your said besecher' and made off with horses, sheep and other of his possessions. Worse still were Percy's allegations about Plumpton's behaviour at the time of the battle of Wakefield and after: '. . . at the field of Wakefield in the time that your said besecher was taken there the said William laboured to have had his head stryken off. And after that the same William sent divers of his menial servants with force of arms to your said besecher's place, which servants, by the commandment of the said William, riotously broke and entered in the same place and there wrongfully took and drove away horses and sheep, as well as household goods, [to] the value of 100 marks and more. And also from that tyme unto the time the field on Palm Sunday was done, the said William with other rioters and misdoers of his affinity and by his procuring with force and arms kept your said besecher from his said place. So that he for fear to be slain durst not by all that time come thereto to his right': PRO, C1/31/485. Many such complaints were made during the Wars of the Roses and more often than not, as in this case, we have only one side of the story: nevertheless, since Plumpton's career as a whole shows he was often prepared to use violence and force to secure his ends if he thought he could get away with it, the allegations may well contain some truth.

16. C.L. Scofield, *The Life and Reign of Edward the Fourth* (1923), I, p. 175. One source suggests that, after the battle, Plumpton was among those 'adducti erant ad Comitem de Warwyk': *Three Fifteenth Century Chronicles*, p. 161.
17. PRO, C67/45/33.
18. PRO, KB27/804/67; *C(alendar of) C(lose) R(olls), 1461–8*, p. 135. Perhaps it was as a result of this case, and the Percy petition (see above, note 15), that Plumpton secured fresh letters of general pardon on 30 August 1463: *CPR, 1461–7*, p. 285.
19. Only once in the late 1460s does Sir William Plumpton appear on a government commission (*CPR, 1467–77*, p. 55, 10 October 1467) and the records are silent on his behaviour during the crisis of 1469–71. He did, however, obtain letters of general pardon on three occasions: 8 November 1468 (PRO, C67/46/17), 2/3 June 1470 (C67/47/2) and, following Edward IV's restoration to the throne, 2 December 1471 (C67/48/34). Surviving letters do suggest he maintained an interest in political events: for instance, Thomas Middleton sent him news from London on 6 November 1466 concerning events in the capital and possible government appointments in Yorkshire and Lincolnshire (p. 17); while, on 9 December 1468, Godfrey Grene graphically highlighted the increasingly tense political situation with news of the arrest and imprisonment of prominent men of known anti-Yorkist views such as the Earl of Oxford and Sir Thomas Tresham (p. 19).
20. *CPR, 1467–77*, p. 638, *1476–85*, p. 580.
21. *CPR, 1467–77*, p. 349; *Rotuli Scotiae*, ed. D. Macpherson et al. (1814–19), II, p. 452a; *CPR, 1476–85*, p. 50. He appeared on various other government commissions as well: *CPR, 1467–77*, pp. 353, 355, 408, 572.
22. Ibid., p. 421.
23. John Leland, *Collectanea* (1774), IV, pp. 185–7.
24. W.A. Shaw, *The Knights of England* (1906), II, p. 18.
25. Sir Robert Plumpton did obtain a pardon for himself on 24 May 1484 (PRO, C67/51/34) and there is an interesting newsletter sent to him by Edward Plumpton during Buckingham's rebellion on 18 October 1483 (pp. 44–5). Presumably a member of a cadet branch of the family, Edward Plumpton became a lawyer and figures regularly in the letters as a correspondent and adviser on business and legal matters. In October 1483 he was secretary to George Stanley Lord Strange and in this letter he is clearly critical of the rebels, expressing the hope that Buckingham 'shalbe right withstanded and all his malice: and els were great pytty'.
26. News of events in London must have been anxiously awaited in the north during the early months of Henry VII's reign, and there survives a valuable newsletter despatched

from the capital by Thomas Betanson to Sir Robert Plumpton on 13 December 1485 (pp. 48–9). It cannot have provided much reassurance. Reporting news of the king's impending marriage to Elizabeth of York and the doings of his first parliament, it particularly dwelt on the bill of attainder condemning Richard III and many of his more prominent supporters, and it included this chilling comment: 'Howbeit, there was many gentlemen agaynst it, but it wold not be, for yt was the Kings pleasure. Sir, here is much spech that we shall have aschip agayne, and no man can say of whom; but they dem of Northernmen and Walchmen. And much spech is in the Kyngs house and of his householdmen. Sir, other tydings is none here as yett. Ther is much runyng amongst the lords, but no man wott what it is; it is sayd yt is not well amongst them'.

27. As warden of the East and Middle Marches and, perhaps, King's Lieutenant in the North Parts: R.R. Reid, *The King's Council in the North* (1921), p. 73.
28. These letters certainly give interesting indications, too, of the range of duties holding such offices might entail, ranging from taking measures against crimes like cattle stealing and illegal hunting to settling disputes between tenants. On one occasion, for instance, the Earl of Northumberland wrote to Plumpton as steward of his lordship of Spofforth, declaring that 'for asmuch as ye have the rule there under me, I pray you to shew you of semblable disposicion, if any matter of varience hereafter happen within your sayd rule; so that the parties sue not to me, if ye by your discret wisdome can reforme it' (p. 76). Similarly, after expressing concern at certain lawless acts within the lordship of Knaresborough 'where at ye have rule', the earl instructed Plumpton to commit the wrong-doers 'to ward within the castell of Knarsbrough, therin still to remayne unto that ye have further knowledg of my pleasure in this behalfe' (p. 81).
29. Betanson further reported that 'the King will come with great company; as it is sayd, with x hundred men in harnesse, and with him mo than v or six schore lords and knights'. The same newsletter included details of a recent act of resumption put through parliament by the King, Betanson remarking that 'ther be many of his houshold in yt plesyde with yt'. News of the King's progress northwards was supplied to Sir Robert by Edward Plumpton, at Lincoln, in a further letter of 3 April 1486 (pp. 50–1).
30. Leland, op.cit., IV, pp. 185–7. Later in the year, a newsletter written from London by Thomas Betanson on 29 November contained the intriguing remark that 'here is but little spech of the erle of Warwyk now, but after christenmas they say there wylbe more spech of' (pp. 53–4).
31. On 23 June 1487 the Earl of Northumberland wrote to him from Richmond specifically enlisting his support: 'wher it is so that diverse gentlemen and other commoners, being within your office at this tyme, hath rebelled against the King, as well in ther being at this last felde, as in releving of them that were against the Kings highnes, I therfore on the Kings behalfe strictly charg you, and on myne hartely pray you, that ye incontinently after the sight hereof, take all such persones as be within your office, which this tyme hath offended agaynst the King.'
32. Henry VII also made it clear that, in recognition of Plumpton's services, he would remember him 'in time to come in anything that may be to your preferment and advancement'.
33. The king's letter, dated at Sheen 28 May 1492, expressed his 'full speciall thanks' for Plumpton's 'good and agreeable service (in) this last commotion of our subjects in our county of Yorke'.
34. Only very occasionally does he figure on government commissions after 1492: his appearance as a commissioner of array for the West Riding in November 1495 is a rare exception (*CPR, 1494–1509*, p. 52). Nor do most of the later letters contain political news: the report of Perkin Warbeck's fate by John Pullan on 21 November 1499 is very much a rarity (pp. 141–3).
35. For a recent discussion of the nature and importance of fifteenth-century Plumpton

marriages, see K.R. Dockray, 'Why did fifteenth-century English gentry marry?: the Pastons, Plumptons and Stonors reconsidered', *Gentry and Lesser Nobility in Late Medieval Europe*, ed. M. Jones (1986), especially pp. 64–8.

36. A.J. Pollard, 'The Richmondshire Community of Gentry during the Wars of the Roses', *Patronage, Pedigree and Power in Later Medieval England*, ed. C. Ross (1979), pp. 37–59.
37. Taylor, *loc.cit.*, pp. 85–6.
38. Following William Plumpton's death in 1461, his widow Elizabeth took as her second husband John Hamerton; Sir William, seemingly, took the opportunity to renege on an earlier agreement respecting jointure for young William and Elizabeth: PRO, C1/21/330.
39. Careful financial arrangements were made, including Rocliffe's offering a sum of some 400 marks for Margaret, Suthill £100 down plus £233 by instalments for Elizabeth, and Plumpton covenanting estates on behalf of both girls and their husbands.
40. Little is known of Sir William's illegitimate issue. William Plumpton, the elder of the two bastards, became involved in a dispute with his half-brother Sir Robert in the early years of Henry VII's reign concerning Haverah Park in the liberty of Knaresborough (pp. 50–1, 93–5, 97–8); later, however, he supported Sir Robert in his struggle to retain his inheritance (pp. 172–3, 182–3). The younger bastard, Robert, made his home in the city of York and, in December 1490, was elected common clerk of the city, retaining the office until his death in 1507: *York Civic Records*, II, ed. A. Raine (Yorkshire Archaeological Society, Record Series, CIII, 1941), pp. 63, 80, 160. He, too, supported Sir Robert against those seeking to disinherit him (pp. 172–3). In his will, dated 2 March 1507 and proved 14 April of the same year, he made bequests to his brother William and careful provision for his son Richard: *Testamenta Eboracensia*, IV (Surtees Society, 1869), pp. 258–60. This son became a merchant, goldsmith and haberdasher of the city of York, eventually dying at Antwerp in 1544/5: Ibid., pp. 258–60^n.
41. The contract for the marriage of Robert and Agnes, dated July 1477, was between Sir William Plumpton and William Gascoigne Esquire, Agnes's brother, whereby Plumpton agreed to establish a jointure of £20 per annum and Gascoigne to pay £100 as dowry; interestingly, Sir William guaranteed that the estates settled on the couple would be unaffected by earlier agreements with the Rocliffes and Suthills, and bound himself in the very considerable sum of 400 marks for the performance of his obligations.
42. The agreement between Sir Robert Plumpton and William Babthorpe, dated May 1496, included a carefully guaranteed property settlement, although this did not prevent a legal dispute over estates between the two families before very long: pp. xcix–ci, 130–3, 134–5, 141–3. Of Sir Robert's daughters, Joan married Sir Richard Mauleverer of nearby Allerton Mauleverer, Margaret married Arthur Eyre of Padley in Derbyshire and Anne married Germain Pole of Radbourne in Derbyshire.
43. Edward Plumpton's anxious wooing of Agnes, a widow in her forties who was not only 'of good substance' but also 'goodly and beautyfull, womanly and wyse [and] of a good stocke and worshipful', is nicely recorded in three letters to Sir Robert Plumpton, all written in March 1497 (pp. 123–8).
44. Following her husband's death in 1480, Sir William Plumpton's widow Joan did take the veil, perhaps to atone for all the years she had spent as his ostensible mistress in the 1450s and 1460s: *Testamenta Eboracensia*, III (Surtees Society, 1864), p. 344.
45. In 1459 George Plumpton obtained permission from the Archbishop of York to have service celebrated for himself and his servants within the monastery but, by May 1460, he was dead: *Testamenta Eboracensia*, II (Surtees Society, 1855), p. 68n; A.H. Thompson, 'Register of the Archdeacons of Richmond 1442–1477', *Yorkshire Archaeological Journal*, XXX (1930), pp. 65, 127.
46. *Register of the Guild of Corpus Christi* (Surtees Society, 1871), pp. 51, 68, 117, 125, 154, 170.
47. Interestingly enough, the Plumpton letters themselves only tend to refer to ecclesiastical

lands or rights of patronage, not spiritual matters. Sir Robert Plumpton (*c.* 1453–1523), for instance, was employed for a time as steward of ecclesiastical estates at Arkendale near Knaresborough. These lands belonged to the Abbey of Lilleshall, Shropshire, and for a small fee Sir Robert undertook such duties as supervising the tenants, sending reports on events connected with the estates and acting for the abbot in any disputes that arose (pp. 63–66). He probably had a similar connection with the priory of Newbrough (pp. 66–69). On the above, and Plumpton relations with the Church generally, see S.M. Walker, 'The Plumpton Correspondence: An Historical and Social Survey' (unpublished MA thesis, Leeds, 1962), pp. 189–203.

48. *CPR, 1467–77*, p. 421. Yet two years later, in 1475, he was prohibited by the Chancellor of the Duchy of Lancaster from imparking and enclosing within the manor of Plumpton on the grounds that not only did it interfere with the free run of the deer but also checked the free grazing of his tenants: *Victoria County History, A History of Yorkshire* (1907–13), I, p. 509. In May 1488 Sir Robert Plumpton was leasing corn mills at Knaresborough and a water mill at Killinghall from the Duchy of Lancaster: *Materials for a History of the Reign of Henry VII*, ed. W. Campbell, II (1877), p. 300.

49. On serfdom there is an interesting letter from Richard Tunstall to Sir Robert Plumpton, perhaps written in 1487, referring to Sir Robert's apparently claiming a man as his bondman: Tunstall reports the existence of 'evydence of his manumission given by one of your ancestors' which appears to establish the man's right to liberty (pp. 55–6). On the weather, the early months of 1490 certainly seem to have been dire: on 3 January 1490 Edward Plumpton wrote from Latham Hall in Lancashire to Sir Robert Plumpton asking to be excused 'in that I send no wyld fole to you aforne this tyme, for in all Lancashire cold none be had for none money. The snaw and frost was so great, none was in the country, but fled away to see' (p. 89). He was still complaining of the 'great snaw' on 10 February (p. 90).

50. There is also an undated letter from 'tenants and servants of your lordshipp of Idell' to Sir William Plumpton, complaining of their condition and treatment (in particular that 'as for geese, grise, hennys, and copons, your said tenants may none keepe, but they are bribed and stolen away by night to great hurt to your tenants'), and seeking redress (pp. 38–9). Interestingly, too, in the reign of Henry VIII George Johnson wrote to 'Mr Robart Plompton the yonger': 'As for barly, is now much redy and in chambers; for wheat, that such that now ready, the substance is gon. Your men also kiln dry. Beanes is at Gainsborough vi^{li} score, and barley at 4^{li} and xiii nobles a score, and wheat is at Hull ij^{li} a skore' (pp. 236–7).

51. There is a useful discussion of this in Walker, op.cit., pp. 98–113. See also J.G. Bellamy, *Criminal Law and Society in Late Medieval and Tudor England* (1984).

52. Letters written in the 1460s certainly have much to say regarding Sir William Plumpton's involvement in legal actions, generally showing him in an unfavourable light: for instance, they provide evidence of a dispute with Thomas Beckwith of Clint concerning payments Plumpton should have made in connection with the marriage of his daughter Elizabeth to Beckwith's son William (pp. 6–8), including an interesting comment by Brian Rocliffe in December 1465 that 'it is necessary that T. Beckwith be content at this time of x^{li}, for losse of money by suites makes more payments'; also of a legal wrangle with Chapman of Stamford in 1464 (pp. 9–14).

53. These cases are considered in Walker, op.cit., pp. 90–96, where it is noted that a final settlement does not seem to have been reached until 1561.

54. For recent discussions of this, see Taylor, *loc.cit.*, pp. 82–3, and Walker, op.cit., pp. 71–89.

55. *British Library Harleian Manuscript 433*, ed. R. Horrox and P.W. Hammond, III (1982), pp. 133–6.

56. Although Sir Robert was told that a personal visit would be 'a singler pleasure and

comforth' to his tenants and friends and 'a great strength' to himself, he was also urged to 'bryng with you money convenient for your expenses' since no rent was forthcoming from his tenants (p. 156). Moreover, at about the same time, his bailiff reported how servants of his opponents 'beated me one after another' when they discovered he had collected rent for Sir Robert and not for them (p. 157).

57. Robert Eyre, indeed, wrote to Sir Robert in September 1501 expressing surprise that he 'sent nobody to Darby for to take you lodging, for Emson hath taken much lodging for him, as I am enfirmed' (p. 161).
58. Sir Robert later complained to the King that 'Sir Richard Empson by currupt and unlawfull meanes obteyned the favers and goodwills of the sheriffe of the said County of Yorke by givinge of fees and rewards unto him and soe caused the pannels to be made after his owne mynde, and the mynde of Sir John Rocliffe and Dame Elizabeth Sotehill': Walker, op.cit., p. 79, quoting a document in the Dodsworth MSS.
59. There certainly seems to have been violence soon after the trial, during which a servant of Sir Robert's was 'myschevously made away with' (p. 164).
60. In this regrettably undated petition, Sir John Rocliffe, Margaret his wife and Elizabeth Suthill, widow, alleged that Sir Robert Plumpton had 'pute diverse fenyde billes of compleynte unto your Highness' asserting that the judgement against him respecting the manor of Plumpton was a product of 'unlawfull mayntenaunce, corupcion of jurors, and oder synyster and unlaufull meanes'. While judgement was pending, moreover, 'the seid Sir Robert Plompton and William Plompton, his sone, have fellyde and disroyed muche parte of the wode growyng on the seid maner, to the value of £100 and above' and, indeed, still 'daielie felle and distroye the seid wodes': *Yorkshire Star Chamber Proceedings*, IV (Yorkshire Archaeological Society Record Series, LXX, 1927), pp. 26–7.
61. Reid, op.cit., pp. 85–6.
62. A year later, on 17 July 1504, Sir Robert bound himself to the King in a sum of £200, the condition being the 'observance of the judgement or decree given by the King's Council on 6 December last in the matter late depending between Sir John Rouclyf and dame Margaret his wife on the one part and Robert and his son William on the other: *CCR, 1500–1509*, pp. 104–5.
63. Not that they helped sustain any false hopes. On 12 April 1504, for instance, Agnes wrote to her husband that the family income was now suffering badly as a result of the long drawn out dispute: 'I wott not how your house shalbe kept, for I know not wherof to levy one peryworth' (pp. 186–7).
64. Sir Robert's second wife, whom he married about 18 September 1505, was Isabel, daughter of Ralph Lord Neville, eldest son and heir apparent of Ralph Neville Earl of Westmorland (pp. cxiv–cxv).
65. C(alendar of) I(nquisitions) P(ost) M(ortem), Henry VII, III, No. 282.
66. Walker, op.cit., pp. 84–5, quoting a document in the Dodsworth MSS.
67. PRO, C140/78/88. In 1507 the manor of Plumpton was valued at 100 marks, Grassington at £13 12s 4d, Steeton at £29 3s 4d and Little Studley at £4 13s 4d: *CIPM*, Henry VII, III, No. 282 (Yorkshire).
68. R.B. Smith, *Land and Politics in the England of Henry VIII: The West Riding of Yorkshire 1530–1546* (1970), p. 292.
69. Ibid., pp. 290–93.
70. Many of these letters are, regrettably, undated, and most contain little of substance. They do include a couple from Henry Percy, Earl of Northumberland to William Plumpton (pp. 225–7), and several from the wealthy West Riding knight Sir Henry Saville of Thornhill (pp. 246–51), suggesting that the Plumptons maintained good social connections.
71. For a recent discussion of these letters and their significance, see A.G. Dickens, *Lollards and Protestants in the Diocese of York 1509–1558* (1959), pp. 131–6.

THE PLUMPTON CORRESPONDENCE

INTRODUCTION.

AMONG the Collections of Dodsworth, deposited in the Bodleian Library, is a volume (CXLVIII.) containing *Transcripts from writings of the family of Plumpton of Plumpton in Yorkshire.* " This volume consists of two parts :— 1. Copies of Evidences, many of which are very curious and important, being illustrative of ancient usages or connected with public affairs.—2. Copies of the Correspondence of the family, from the reign of King Henry VII. Some of these are on public affairs, others relating to the private concerns of the family."* The originals from which Dodsworth made these copies are referred to by him as Sir Edward Plumpton's Coucher-book, and his Book of Letters; both which manuscripts have been of late discovered to be remaining in the library of Peregrine Edward Towneley, esq., the representative of a family, whose

* Three Catalogues, &c. by the Rev. Joseph Hunter, F.S.A. Lond. Pickering, 1838, p. 237.

CAMD. SOC. 4.

members in former days were distinguished by their labours for the preservation of our gentilitious antiquities, and a gentleman, whose constant urbanity has on more than one occasion allowed a liberal use to be made of the manuscripts in his possession, in order to their being made a source of general gratification through the medium of the press. Availing themselves of this courtesy, for which they beg to express their thanks, the Council of the Camden Society have selected Sir Edward Plumpton's Book of Letters for their fourth publication, with the view to preserve and make known such remains as may be conceived to throw light upon the domestic habits and social manners of our forefathers. The tenor of their occupations in everyday life is a subject, upon which our information has been at all times scant and deficient.

The Manuscript is a small folio volume on paper, and has suffered considerably in the lapse of two centuries from neglect or ill-usage, several pages, besides the cover of thin leather at the back, being at the present time torn away at the beginning of the volume, and at the end. When entire it contained three distinct series of Letters, formed of the several Correspondence of Sir William Plumpton, who died 20 Edw. IV. 1480; of his son Sir Robert, who died 15 Hen. VIII. 1523; and of other members

of the family down to the reign of King Edward VI. The Letters of the time of Sir William Plumpton have been first transcribed into the volume, though not at the beginning; the copy of this portion was made continuously between 8 Dec. 1612, and 1 Feb. following, as appears from the marginal notes: it extends from page 151 to page 179 of the manuscript. Of the Correspondence of Sir Robert Plumpton, with which the volume had commenced, the first remaining letter now stands at page 27, and was originally the thirty-eighth of the series; this letter was copied 22 Feb. 1612-3, and those which follow were transcribed in succession down to 12 May following. This last date is at page 149 of the MS., but the blank space between the two series has been filled up with a letter to " Sir Richard Plompton, chapleyn, at Idell," copied 25 Dec. 1613. The later Correspondence, at the end of the volume, was begun to be copied 2 Jan. 1626, and extended over forty-six or forty-eight pages, as may be collected from the fragments of leaves yet remaining; the last date of transcript now left is of the 19th of the same month. Below may be read part of a letter, having the name " William Hungate" written opposite in the margin; this had been next transcribed, and stood as the thirty-eighth of the series.*

* William Hungate of Saxton, com. Ebor. esq. ancestor to the

The order observed by the copyist was to transcribe, first, the letters of the personage whose correspondence formed the series, next the letters from Sovereigns, then those from Earls, &c. the rank of the writers being the sole classification adopted. Owing to this arrangement, the letters from the King, the Correspondence with the Bishop of Carlisle* relating to Perkin Warbeck *(printed by Sir Henry Ellis, Orig. Lett. vol. I. 1st ser. p. 34),* the letters of the Earls of Surrey and Shrewsbury to Sir Robert Plumpton, together with two letters from himself, of which we find transcripts in Dodsworth and elsewhere, would necessarily have to be sought for in that portion of the Correspondence with which the volume commenced, and is now consequently missing in its present mutilated condition. Dodsworth was at Plumpton in 1633; it is, therefore, probable that he saw the original letters: but he does not appear to have made his transcripts directly from them in

Baronets of that name. The letter has the direction *To his worshipfull Master William Plompton this be delivered,* and what remains reads as follows:

" Right worshipfull Sir, In my most lowly manner I recommend me unto you for all kindness shewed to me and all myne, and for the good chear that you, and my Mistres your wife, maid me at my last being with you. And the cause of my wryting to you at this time . . . . yt will please you to call to your remembrance . . . ."

* William Sever, or Siveyèr, Abbot of St. Mary, York. These four Letters are transcribed in vol. L. of Dodsworth's Collections.

any one instance, as he heads his copy, "In Sir Edward Plumpton's Booke of Letters," and cites the letters as they stood numbered in Sir Edward Plumpton's Book,* nor does he notice any seals. The letters in Dodsworth (vol. CXLVIII.) are twenty-four in number and are all yet contained in the Towneley manuscript, save three; one from the Earl of Shrewsbury (on the same subject as Letter XXXI. p. 65) printed in the *Addenda*, and two others from Sir Robert Plumpton to his wife on matters relating to his suit and household affairs, which will be found introduced into the Historical Notices of the Family of Plumpton prefixed to the Correspondence. In many instances, the copyist of the Letters notes on the page that "this letter hath a seal," but he unfortunately gives no description of the impress. On a blank space at page 192 this *memorandum* has been inserted: " Mrs. Ann Scrope, daughter to Sir Edw. Plompton, did die in December the 16, 1650. Lord Jesus rest her sowle in Heaven. EDWARD CHOLMLEY;" and on the margin of another page is scribbled, "Thomas Cholmley desiers Mister William Fairfax to sufer all he can posible for the good of the comonwelth, and long lookt for will come at

* The Letter from the Earl of Shrewsbury to Sir Robert Plompton, kt. is quoted by Dodsworth as Letter 31. The mistake in writing Knaresborough, 25th Sept. for Woodstock, 23rd (*see Hunter's Catal. p.* 103), is another proof that Dodsworth copied at second-hand; the error was not his own.

last." The Cholmley family resided at Braham, Breame, or Braim Hall, in the immediate vicinity of Plumpton; the year 1650 was the second of the Commonwealth, and the last writing contains an evident allusion to the hoped for restoration of Charles II. At this period the Towneley family were connected by marriage with the Plumptons, and the Manuscript would seem to have been confided to the care of Mr. Christopher Towneley of Carr, the indefatigable transcriber; for in the year 1662 he made copious extracts from the Plumpton Coucher Book, and other books and papers belonging to Sir Edward Plumpton: it has probably ever since continued in the possession of his representatives.

The Cartulary or Coucher Book of Sir Edward Plumpton, which has likewise remained in the same custody, is a very broad folio volume on vellum, containing the deeds and evidences of the family, arranged in chronological order, down to the time of Henry VII. and which were begun to be copied from the originals 15 Mar. 1614, and so continuously to 26 July 1616, 148 pages. At p. 149 *et seq.* are inserted copies of deeds relating to the Plumptons from an old Coucher-book of Fountains Abbey and from another of the Priory of Helagh, as also of such originals as were in the hands of a Mr. Bankes and other individuals: these were transcribed in the years 1616 and 1620. Next follow other evidences of the family, to the reign of King Henry VIII., copied between 15 Jan. 1626-7 and 2 Feb. 1627-8, and written in part upon paper interleaved. At p. 259 are two deeds relating to property at Kirkby-*super*-Wharfe, "copied 29 Sept. 1628, by me, Edward Arthington," who likewise states himself to be the copyist in other places; and at the bottom of the next page is, "*Memorandum*. Notes for Sir Edward Plompton, delivered by Mr. Dodsworth, 18 of March 1633." Pages 285 *et seq.* contained an Index, now deficient in the latter portion; and the volume has been bound up with some ancient Court-rolls of the manor of Plumpton, with which it terminates.

From this Manuscript, and other sources, have been compiled the Historical and Biographical Notices of the family of Plumpton which precede the Correspondence; where such of the evidences as served to illustrate the social position of the successive generations, and to lay bare the economy of their private life, will be found abstracted at length, and in the words of the original. The Letters themselves have also been arranged, as far as possible, in chronological order, so that the preliminary Biographical Notice may serve the reader as a running commentary upon the text. Notes are, moreover, subjoined in more immediate explanation of the matters alluded to, and in identification of the persons named in each Letter; without which, it was felt by the Editor that this domestic Correspondence of a family, however interesting from its antiquity, would be in great measure unintelligible, and of value only to illustrate local history. But with these aids, it is hoped that the Plumpton Letters will be found to contain much that is of interest to the general reader, as leading him to an exact knowledge of the social condition of the English gentry during the half century which preceded the dissolution of monasteries, and the eventful era of the Reformation.

To the Rev. Joseph Hunter, one of the Council of the Camden Society, and the compiler of a late Catalogue of the Dodsworth MSS., I am indebted for information respecting the transcripts made from the Plumpton Papers by that judicious Antiquary, as also for the continuation of the Pedigree of the family from Sir Edward Plumpton to the time of its final extinction in the last century, and for a few valuable remarks introduced among the *Addenda*. To him, as also to Dr. Philip Bliss, and C. G. Young, esq. York Herald, I beg leave to express my thanks for their friendly communications.

T. S.

13, *Wilton Place, Feb.* 6, 1839.

PEDIGREE of PLUMPTON, of PLUMPTON, com. EBOR.

Arms. Azure, five fusils in fess Or, each charged with an escallop Gules.

This is a complex genealogical pedigree chart that cannot be faithfully represented as a simple table due to its branching tree structure spanning multiple generations. The chart traces the Plumpton family of Plumpton, Yorkshire, beginning with:

Sir Robert Plumpton, of Plumpton, com. Ebor., kt.; bo. 7 Oct. 6 Hen. IV. 1404, son and heir of Sir William Plumpton, heir in ward to Henry Earl of Northumberland; died 15 Oct. 20 Edw. IV. 1480 (*Esc.* 20 *Edw. IV. n. 88*), aged 70.

married **Alice**, daughter and heir of Sir Godfrey Foljambe, of Hassop, com. Derb. kt.; one year old 2 Dec. 1388 8 Dec. 9 Hen. V. 1421 (*Esc.* 11 *Hen. VI. n. 5.*); marr. cov. 14 Jan. 16 Ric. II. 1392-3; died before in Spofforth Church.

(Bastard issue: 1. William Plumpton, 2. Robert Plumpton.)

Descending generations include figures such as:
- Sir Robert Plumpton (bo. 8 Mar. 9 Hen. VI. 1430-1; died 20 July 28 Hen. VI. 1450) = Elizabeth, dau. of Thomas Lord Clifford
- Godfrey Plumpton, died before 1 Hen. VII. 1466 = Alice, dau. and coh. of Thomas Wintringham, sister of Joan
- William Plumpton (bo. 28 Feb. 14 Hen. VI. 1435-6; eldest surviving son and heir apparent; died in his father's lifetime, 1461) = Joan, wife of Thomas Middleton
- Robert Plumpton, esq. son and heir (ma. 2 Sep. 30 Hen. VIII. 1538)
- William Plumpton, esq. son and heir, bo. at Waterton, 17 Jan. 7 Hen. VIII. 1515-6 = Anne, dau. of John Norton of Norton Conyers
- Robert Plumpton, son and heir app., bo. at Waterton, 7 Jan. 35 Hen. VIII. 1543 = Anne, dau. of Edward Griffin, of Dingley
- Sir Edward Plumpton, kt. = Frances, d. of Richard Townley of Towneley
- John Plumpton, esq. = Anne, dau. of William Middleton, of Stockeld
- Robert Plumpton, esq. = Anne and heir
- William Plumpton (bo. 1 Oct. 1600) = Catharine, b. 20 Feb. 1602-3, dau. of Sir John Gascoigne
- Robert Plumpton (bo. 21 Feb. 1603-4) = Ellen, betrothed to Griffin Markham
- John Plumpton (bo. 19 Nov. 20 Car. II. 1668; died 2 Dec. 22 Car. II. 1676, s. p.)
- John Plumpton (bo. 27 Apr. 1683) = Elizabeth, 2nd dau. of Sir John Gascoigne of Parlington, Bart. N.S.

Robert Plumpton, son and heir, bo. 23 Apr. 1721; died at Cambray 8 Aug. 1749, s. p.

[Due to the highly complex multi-generational tree structure of this pedigree chart, with numerous horizontal marriage connections and vertical descent lines, a complete faithful representation requires viewing the original image. The above extracts key individuals and relationships visible in the chart.]

HISTORICAL AND BIOGRAPHICAL

NOTICES

OF THE

FAMILY OF PLUMPTON OF PLUMPTON,

COM. EBOR.

The family whose domestic history, during portions of the fifteenth and sixteenth centuries, is brought into such prominent notice through the preservation of the present correspondence, derived its surname from the vill of Plumpton, situate within the parish of Spofforth, in the upper division of Claro wapentake, west riding of the county of York, three miles distant from the town of Knaresborough.

At the time of the Great Survey of England in 1086, of which Domesday Book is the record, the vill of *Plontone*[a] *in Borgescire*,[b] which had belonged entire to Gamelbar under the Anglo

---

[a] *Plumbe* is a woody place, and to this day a clump of trees is called a plump in the north. (See Glossary to *Reginaldi Monachi Dunelm. libellus de admirandis beati Cuthberti virtutibus*, published by the Surtees Society, 1835.)

[b] The wapentake of Borge-scire was so called from Ald-burgh (Burc in Domesday), the capital of this shire or district from the time of the Romans. It is also in one place in Domesday, *f.* 379, *a.* 1, called the wapentake of Gereburg, this prefix being evi-

CAMD. SOC. 4.   *b*

Saxon dynasty, was, in as much as regarded the *suzerainté* of the fief, divided between two Norman followers of the Conqueror, *viz.* William, from Percy in the Département de la Manche, a *seigneurie* owned by the great Norman family of Paynell, of whom he was probably the feudatory; and Gislebert, apparently a member of the no less powerful house of Tesson, who ruled the tract of country in the Département du Calvados, known as *Le Cinglais*, of which Thury-Harcourt is the capital. In this manner the territory of Plumpton came to be divided into two manors respectively held of the honours of Perci and Vesci, the latter being the local surname of another Norman family, on one of whose members, named Ivo, the escheated fief of Gislebert was eventually bestowed.[c] We learn further, from the same in-

---

dently a remnant of the British name Caer, by which all walled burghs were designated. The place of assembly was in a Berewick belonging to it, named Clare-tun, about four miles distant from the burgh, where, as usual, an artificial mound or hoh was raised, called from the tun, Clare-hoh: by a pleonasm, this spot has now the name of Claro-hill. Claro grew eventually to be the name in common use, when the burgh was no longer the capital of the shire.

[c] Vassy *(Vaacie* in Wace*)* is a commune of the Département du Calvados. In Domesday the orthograghy is Veci, and there also in place of Tesson we read Tison. *Taisson,* among the Normans, signified a badger; and that this was the sobriquet given to the lords of Cinglais is proved by their deeds, in which the name is often latinized *Taxo.* Much wider variations than these were, however, common in writing the same proper name, the scribe having to trust solely to his ear for catching rightly the sound of the name as pronounced to him, the subscription of the personage himself to the document being simply a cross mark. It is absurd to suppose, as later genealogists have done, that the Great Standard Bearer of England under King William, by which title of office Gislebert names himself in his charters, was of Anglo-Saxon parentage. The pretended marriage of Ivo de Vescy with the heiress of Tyson, which has hitherto passed current with our Baronagians, is merely the traditional history resorted to in the time of Edw. II. to explain the descent of the baronies of Malton and Alnwick; such late genealogies, unless confirmed by contemporary evidence, must ever be received with extreme caution. It is certain, moreover, that Gislebert Tison left a son and heir named Adam, who in 31 Hen. I. rendered account to the Exchequer of the debts of his father, and of a fine not to plead for his lands until the

---

OF THE FAMILY OF PLUMPTON.

valuable record, that the manor in the Percy fee alone retained its value undiminished from the time of Edward the Confessor, the fee of Gislebert Tison in these parts having been laid waste, for the purpose, no doubt, of forming the royal chace, which acquired the name of "Knaresborough Forest."[d] A portion of the land

---

son of Nigel de Albini (*i. e. Roger de Mowbray*) was a knight. The grand-daughters and heirs of Adam married into the families of Constable of Flamborough and Beauvoir; and from the heads of these families, as well as from Mowbray and Vescy, the monks of Selby deemed it requisite to obtain charters of confirmation to secure to them the possession of the tithes and advowson of the church of Elveley (Kirk-ella), which they had of the gift of Gislebert Tison. Malton was crown land at the time of the survey; but it is not improbable that the defence of the castle of Alnwick, in the turbulent district north of the Tyne, was undertaken by this great military officer, and that he made it the *caput* of his barony. The influence of Robert de Mowbray, the first Norman Earl of Northumberland, may have in that case drawn him in to share in his rebellion, which ended in the expulsion from their seigniories of many Norman barons, whom the Chroniclers omit to name. Under Henry I. he was restored to grace, and re-instated in the possession of Holme-upon-Spaldingmore and of some portion of his lands in Yorkshire, which he transmitted to his heirs; but the *suzerainté* of the escheated honour was retained by Nigel de Albini and Ivo de Vescy, between whom it had been already divided by William Rufus. Even this result appears not to have been obtained without contracting heavy debts in the maintenance of a protracted suit.

[d] Sir Henry Ellis observes, in his notes to the Index of Tenants *in capite* in Domesday, that the lands of Gislebert Tison, consisting of twenty-nine manors, were evidently forfeited upon the ravaging of Yorkshire: ten had belonged to Gamelbar, and one to Gamel. Of six which had belonged to Gamelbar, it is said, "Has terras habet Gislebertus Tison, sed wastæ sunt omnes: tantummodo Biletone redd. iii. sol. redd." Of several manors in Craven no estimated value is given. These six manors are, however, all parcel of the forest of Knaresborough, and in a mountainous and barren tract of country. If they were ravaged by the Conqueror's army in vengeance to a rebellious people, then his forbearance seems most extraordinary, sparing the fertile country nearer to his line of march, and turning aside to spend his fury on these wilds. The love of the Norman princes for the chace need not be dwelt upon; and Domesday furnishes ample proof that entire wapentakes or hundreds were converted from arable into wood and pasture, in order to give "scope and verge enough." The ancient sectional division of the north riding of Yorkshire, called wapentake of Girlestre, gave name to the forest of Galtres, which included within its vast circumference great part of that wapentake, and of the adjoining ones of Bolesford and

---

HISTORICAL NOTICES

was, however, permitted to be afterwards cultivated, upon payment of a rent of five shillings; but before the devastation, this manor, equally with the other, had been worth twenty shillings. The mesne-tenant in the vill of Plumpton in 1086, is named Eldred in Domesday; but this Anglo-Saxon occupant cannot, from existing evidence, be presumed to have been the ancestor of the family who had afterwards the local surname.

Before the first Sunday in Lent, in the year 1168, William de Percy made a return of the knights enfeoffed of his honour, both of ancient feoffment of the time of Henry I. that is, up to the year of his death, and of new feoffment since his death, with their nomenclature, in order that those who had not yet done liege homage, and whose names were not written in the roll of the King, might come in and do it before that Sunday. Of the knights newly enfeoffed, he names, "Nigellus de Pluntona de I. milite."[e] The earliest deed, among the ancient evidences of the family existing in 1612, was, it may be presumed, the one enrolled in the pedigree of Plumpton, as entered in the book of Richard St. George, Norroy, in his Visitation of Yorkshire; it contained a grant of a tenement and two acres of land in Plumpton from Nigellus de Plumton to Gamel, son of Elewin, his *marshal,* and had a seal attached to it with the impression of a knight on horseback holding a drawn sword, the name being circumscribed.[f] Of another deed of this first progenitor, containing

---

Annesti, till its outskirts in later times gradually lessened by successive disafforestments. At the time of its formation, the places of assembly for the men of the wapentakes were necessarily removed without its limits, Girlestre to Birdforth, and Bolesford, where was a ford across the river Fosse, to Bulmer; from these latter places the wapentakes now take their names.

[e] Liber Niger Scaccarii. Hearne, 1774, edit. altera, vol. i. p. 317.

[f] The copy of this deed was numbered 20 in the Plumpton Cartulary, but the page containing it has been almost entirely eaten away by mice. A marginal note, however, remains, indicating its context: "Nigellus de Plumton Gamelo filio Elewini— i domum, i acram in Lafrinwic, i acram in Sabberchdale in Plumton." The names

a much more extensive grant to his *seneschal*, and to which a seal with the same impression was remaining in 1620, I insert a copy from the transcript in Sir Edward Plumpton's Cartulary.

Omnibus sanctæ ecclesiæ filiis præsentibus et futuris, Nigellus de Plumpton, salutem. Sciatis me dedisse et concessisse et hac mea carta confirmasse Roberto filio Huckemani pro homagio et servitio suo quinque bovatas terræ cum omnibus libertatibus et liberis pertinentibus suis infra villas et extra, scilicet, in introitibus et exitibus, in viis et semitis, in bosco et plano, in aquis et ripis, in moris et mariscis, in pratis et pasturis, in turbariis et in omnibus liberis aismentis, scilicet, duas bovatas terræ in Plumton quas pater suis tenuit, cum tofto et crofto et sartis et cum omnibus liberis pertinentibus suis, et præterea duas acras terræ in incrementum versus aquilonem ad Barthestortes, et duas bovatas terræ in Scotton quæ fuerunt Willielmi Coci, et unam bovatam terræ in Ribstain, quam Ricardus le Butiller tenuit cum duobus toftis, quorum ipse Ricardus tenuit unum et Ailine tenuit alterum toftum. Et præterea concessi et confirmavi præfato Roberto in incrementum suæ bovatæ in Ribstain unum toftum cum pomario in Ribstain, scilicet, toftum quod Robertus filius Hulkilli tenuit, et sex acras terræ et dimidiam in campis de Ribstain cum liberis pertinentiis suis et omnibus aismentis suis in omnibus locis et rebus sine retinemento mei vel hæredum meorum infra villas et extra ad ea pertinentibus, excepta bovata terræ ad quam prædictum toftum et una prædictarum acrarum pertinebant; scilicet, unam acram quam Willielmus Straungald tenuit, quæ est

" Nigellus de Plomptona" and " Gamelo filio Elewini" are also legible on the fragments. The Towneley MSS. contain abbreviated copies of the same deed, from which the names of the witnesses may be set down with tolerable accuracy, viz. Robert Vavasor, Hugh de Lelay, Gilbert de Plompton, Richard de Chagge, Richard de Goldesburgh, Matthew de Braham, Robert de Linton, Robert son of Huckman de Plompton, Robert son of Henry de Sicklinghall, Robert son of Jordan de Staneton, William son of Ralph, Richard de Stokeld, Baldwin his brother, Thomas de Dicton his brother, and many others.

inter viam quæ jacet de Ribstain ad Spofford et aquam quæ vocatur Crempel, et unam acram quam Robertus filius Hulkil tenuit, quæ est ultra viam quæ se extendit de Ribstan ad Spofford propinquior viæ de Bram apud austrum, et duas acras et dimidiam quam Ricardus filius Bencelini tenuit, quæ jacent juxta Frodisberi apud orientem, et duas acras in Godwinnesridding, quæ se extendunt super prædictas acras. Quæ scilicet toftum cum pomario et sex acras et dimidiam præfatus Robertus filius Huckeman ante tenuit de dono Walteri filii Nigelli de Stockeld. Omnes autem prædictas terras, tam quinque bovatas quam alias, cum omnibus liberis pertinentiis suis prædictis, concessi et hac carta confirmavi præfato Roberto, habendas et tenendas illi et hæredibus ejus de me et hæredibus meis sine impedimento et retinemento mei et heredum meorum in perpetuum, in feodo et hereditate libere et pacifice et quiete ab omni servitio et omni terrena exactione, faciendo forinsecum servitium, scilicet, pro duabus bovatis terræ et duabus acris in Plumton quantum ad illas pertinet, ubi duodecim carucatæ et dimidia faciunt servitium unius militis; pro duabus bovatis terræ in Scotton, quantum ad illas pertinet, ubi viginti carucatæ terræ faciunt servitium unius militis; pro una bovata terræ in Ribstain et pro sex acris et dimidia cum tofto et pomario quantum ad illa pertinet, ubi decem carucatæ terræ faciunt servitium unius militis. Insuper relaxavi et quietum clamavi de me et hæredibus meis in perpetuum præfato Roberto et hæredibus suis quatuor solidos firmæ et duo calcaria deaurata et duas sagittas barbatas, quæ pertinebant ad me per annum de redditu de prædictis terris, ita quod prænominatus Robertus vel heredes ejus nullum cmnino aliud servitium facient mihi vel hæredibus meis de præfatis . . . . . nisi solum forinsecum servitium, sicut in ista carta sepius dictum est. Ego vero Nigellus et hæredes mei warantizabimus quinque bovatas prædictas et omnia alia prædicta cum omnibus liberis pertinentiis suis infra villam et extra præfato Roberto et hæredibus suis contra omnes homines per prædictum forinsecum servitium sine retine-

mento vel impedimento. Hiis testibus, Roberto le Vavasur, Hugone de Lelaia, Willielmo de Corneburg, Willielmo de Witheton, Alexandro fratre ejus, Roberto de Wiuelstrop, Waltero de Ribstan, Ricardo de Riplea, Thoma de Walkingham, Matheo de Bram, Alexandro de Scotton, Nicolao de Carton, Roberto de Dicthenbi, Waltero de Folifait, Henrico de Brakentwait, Adam de eadem villa, Henrico filio Bauldiwini, Willielmo filio Serlonis, Gilberto le Larden, Thoma de Langewat, Willelmo Mansel, Simone dispensatore et aliis.[g]

To the time of the accession of Henry II. the ancient laws and fiscal system of the Anglo-Saxons had been allowed to remain by the conquerors, and the Norman occupants of the manors and vills of their expulsed predecessors were at first subject to the same burdens. Thus in the venerable roll of the Exchequer Receipts in 1130, we find payments for ferms and Danegeld, but no mention of knights' fees or scutage. The Normans had, however, introduced the continental mode of making grants of land by subinfeudation, of which an early instance is the grant made to Robert de Bruis out of the *Terra Regis*, immediately subsequent to the General Survey of the country in 1086, and which is appended to the record under the title " Hic est Feudum Rotberti de Bruis quod fuit datum postquam Liber de Wintonia scriptus fuit."[h] The universality of this practice naturally paved the way to the abrogation of the Anglo-Saxon constitutions, and the establishment of a system of feudal tenure similar to what was the law on the continent of Europe. As a necessary consequence of this change, Danegeld and the former system of local taxation fell to the ground, and in lieu thereof scutage, or the payment of a certain composition in money for the personal service of the feudatory was introduced. Yet here again the old usage was so far adhered to, that a return was required to be made of the number of carucates in each vill; whereupon the composition for each knight's fee was

[g] Cartul. No. 640.   [h] Lib. Domesd. 332 b.

variously apportioned to a fixed number of carucates according to the capacity of each vill, and according to the greater or less number of feofments made by the tenant *in capite*, and the quantity of service he himself owed to the crown. In proof of this being the mode adopted, I may cite the return made of the carucates in the honour of Richmond and of the tenmantales or tythings in Gillingshire in the thirtieth year of the reign of Henry II., and of the knights' fees of the same honour of old and new feofment, *secundum quod Scutagium debet solvi*;[i] the above charter gives twelve carucates and a half to a knight's fee in Plumpton.

In this reign, in the year 1184, the name of Plumpton acquired a melancholy notoriety from an event, which I relate in the words of the earliest contemporary authority. " While the king was sojourning at Worcester with his army, with intent to make war upon Rhys-ap-Griffin, as is mentioned above, a certain youth was brought there in fetters, sprung of noble lineage, and whose name was Gilbert de Plumton, whom Ranulf de Glanvil, the king's justiciary, had in odium, and sought to put to death; laying to his charge that he had ravished a certain maiden in the king's gift, the daughter of Roger de Guilevast, and kept her to him as his wife; and that in the night-time he broke through six doors in the abode of the girl's father, and took from him a hunting horn and a head-stall, &c. along with the said maiden. He added, moreover, that all these things he carried off by theft and robbery; but the said youth in every point denied what was alleged concerning any violence, theft, and robbery; and upon the issue, he offered to abide the law. But Ranulf de Glanvile wishing to make away with him, because he designed to give the same maiden (whom the said Gilbert had already known after their espousals) in marriage to Reiner, sheriff of Yorkshire, with her father's inheritance, further exhorted those who were to try Gilbert to adjudge him to death; and so it was done, for they sen-

[i] Registrum Honoris de Richmond, p. 24 et seq.

tenced him to be hung; and whilst he was being led to the gibbet, intelligence was brought of the proceedings in his case to Baldwin, bishop of the same city of Worcester. The which bishop, though in great grief for the condemnation of the youth, was, however, exhorted by his attendants to rescue him from death. They said, that he could legally do this, because it was a Sunday that same day, and upon it the Feast of Blessed Mary Magdalen. The bishop (who was a meek and good man) acquiesced in their arguments, and having mounted on horseback, quickly rode after the executioners, who were leading the youth to the gibbet, and had now arrived at the place. Already was the youth with his hands bound behind his back, and with a green band covering his eyes, and an iron-chain round his neck; the executioners being on the point of hoisting the youth up, as the bishop arrived with a multitude of people. Having alighted from his horse, and running up, he stationed himself by the side of the prisoner, thus exclaiming and saying, " I forbid you, on the part of God and Blessed Mary Magdalen, and under sentence of excommunication, to hang this man on this day, because to-day is the day of our Lord and the feast of Blessed Mary Magdalen; wherefore, it is not lawful for you to contaminate the day." The executioners replied, " Who are you?" and " what madness prompts you, that you have the audacity to impede the execution of the King's justice?" But the bishop with no less firmness of heart than of speech, rejoins, " Not madness, but the clemency of heavenly pity urges me; nor do I desire to impede the King's justice, but to warn you against an unwary act, lest by the contamination of a solemn day, you and the King incur the wrath of the eternal God." After some altercation, divine authority at length prevailed; and at the entreaty of the bishop he who was bound is unloosed; nevertheless, he was delivered over to the keeper of the King's castle to safe custody, and in the morning to be led again to execution. But the Lord Almighty, who never deserts those who hope in him, through the merits of the said bishop, granted a longer span of life to the said Gilbert. For when all these matters were reported to King Henry, who, before judgment was pronounced, had withdrawn from the city, from that time forward he cherished the said bishop with a greater love and reverence. Whereupon, immediately, on the same day, in the greatest haste, he sent his messengers to the keeper of his castle, with orders that the youth should not be hung, but kept in prison until he should learn his further will in his respect. Be God blessed in every thing, who saves those who cry unto him, and delivered Gilbert out of the hands of those who bore him malice, and rescued him from the snare of the wicked." [k]

Roger de Hoveden has abridged this narrative, and at the same time somewhat exaggerated the circumstances, making the prisoner to have been already hauled up by the rope when the bishop interposed; in dread of whose anathema the executioners slackened it, and again let him down to the ground. He also remarks that the knight was kept in prison by Ranulph de Glanvill till after the death of the king. Of the reality of this scene which casts such a stigma upon a great name, for to the instigator of this outrage we are indebted for the first treatise upon the forms of Anglo-Norman jurisprudence, those irrefragable documents, the *Annales* of the Exchequer, furnish corroborative proofs. There, in the return made by Ranulph de Glanvill, as Sheriff, for the ferm of the county of York in this same year, the sum of xiiis. is entered in abatement for the expence of conveying Gilbert de Plumpton and his accomplices from York to Worcester; [l] and in the next year he renders an account as Sheriff *de xxixs. iiii*d. *de exitu terræ Gilberti de Plumton de dimidio anno*.[m] The same county was administered by Ranulph de Glanvill down to the second year of Richard I. when John the Marshal replaced him; in the roll of

[k] Benedictus abbas de vita Hen. II. p. 408. Hearne.
[l] Rot. Pip. 30 Hen. II. Extracts *penes me*.   [m] Rot. Pip. 31 Hen. II.

that year, under the heading *De Oblatis Curiæ*, " Nigellus de Plumton reddit compotum de c. marcis pro liberatione Gilberti fratris sui et pro rehabenda uxore sua cum terra. In thesauro liii^{li} et vi^s. et viii^d. Et debet xx marcas." At the same time *Reinerus, Dapifer Ranulfi de Glanvilla*, improperly called Sheriff of Yorkshire by the biographer of Henry II. *reddit compotum de M. marcis pro fine suo et benevolentia Regis habenda et terris suis habendis*.[n] Justice had, therefore, reassumed her sway, and the person in whose favour she had been tampered with was compelled to purchase forgiveness by a heavy fine. In the seventh of Richard I. the same Gilbert de Plumpton was a debtor in ten marks for novel disseisin and recognition of title at Doncaster.[o]

In the 16th Hen. II. for some transgression in his afforested lands, Nigel de Plumpton was amerced at the assize, and the Sheriff of Yorkshire for that year, in his account at the Exchequer, " pro wastis et assartis et forisfactis forestæ de Evervicscira," had acquittance for 6*li*. 13*s*. 4*d*. paid to Henry de Lacy, by precept from the King, *de misericordia Nigelli de Plunton*.[p] The formation of Knaresborough Forest, and its extension over part of the vill of Plumpton, has been already adverted to, and it may be as well shortly to trace the early history of the Honour to which the forest was appurtenant, especially as the heads of the family of Plumpton at a later period exercised the offices of Master Forester and Constable of the Castle of Knaresborough for successive generations. Under Edward the Confessor, Burc, with three berewicks and an extensive soke, constituted a royal manor worth ten pounds: in 1086 the whole of the soke had been afforested, and the value of the manor thereby reduced to fifty-five shillings. King Edward had, also, Chenaresburg in demesne with eleven berewicks, when it was worth six pounds. At the time of the Survey the whole had been afforested, and subjected to an assised rent, as was usual in regard to forest lands, of twenty shillings. In the reign of Henry I. twenty-two pounds (by tale) was the quota of these royal manors to the ferm of the county, which sum was abated to the Sheriff, as they had been given in ferm by that monarch to Eustace Fitz-John, who accounts for them separately in the Exchequer Roll of the 31st Hen. I. which alone has come down to us. *Eustachius filius Johannis reddit compotum de xxii*^{li} *numero de firma de Burg et de Chenardesburg. In thesauro xi*^{li}. *Et in operibus Regis de Chenardesburg, xi*^{li} *per breve Regis. Et quietus est.* It is thus certain that the Honour of Knaresborough did not descend to Eustace Fitz-John, as nephew and next heir of Serlo de Burg, the pretended founder of the castle; but that he occupied it simply as *custos*, and that the works were carried on for the King. This story, which has hitherto past current, rests solely npon the traditional " Stemma Fundatorum," inserted in the Cartulary of their house by the monks of Malton, which, like all genealogical legends of that date, will not bear the test of criticism. During the early part of the reign of Henry II. the ferm of " Burc et Cnardesburc" continued in like manner to be annually accounted for by the Sheriff of York. In the 2d Hen. II. the assised value was lx^{li}; [q] in the 6th Hen. II. it had risen to lxiiii^{li}: but xix^{li} of this sum was abated at the Exchequer by reason of the King's grant of lands and soke to Hugh de Morvill,[q] who doubtless had at this date the custody of Knaresborough, for he fled hither with his associates in crime after the murder of St. Thomas à Becket. In 1177, according to Roger de Hoveden, Henry II. gave the wardship of the castle of *Naresburc* to William de Stutevill, who had served with his father, the Sheriff of Yorkshire, as one of the principal leaders of the royal forces, at the time of the civil war enkindled by the partisans of the young King with the assistance of the Scots; and it is certain, that either

[n] Rot. Pip. 2 Ric. I.   [o] Rot. Pip. 7 Ric. I.
[p] Rot. Pip. 16 Hen. II.
[q] Rot. Pip. de eisdem annis. Extracts *penes me*.

in this year, or soon after, his services were rewarded with a grant of Knaresborough and Burgh, with the appurtenances, to him and his heirs, to be held of the king for the slender service of three knights' fees. The more favourable site of Knaresborough for defence, and the building of a castle there by Henry I., had, it seems, given a supremacy to Knaresborough over the old capital of the shire, so as to cause it to be named first in the grant to Stutevill; at the same time the diversion from the line of the Watling-street, owing to the construction of a bridge over the Ure higher up the river than the Burgh, where the passage had anciently been, probably helped forward its decay. Before the close of the reign of Henry II. another town had sprung up in the vicinity of the new place of traverse, as appears from that monarch having granted franchises, which the *Homines de Pont-de-Burc* fined in ten marks to Richard I. in the sixth year of his reign to confirm.[r] By Richard a fine of two thousand pounds was exacted of William de Stutevill, for permission to retain unmolested possession of " Cnarreburc cum pertinentiis."[s] From King John William de Stutevill also sought a confirmation of his title, and he readily obtained from that pliant monarch a ratification of his father's charter.[t] From this great baron Nigel de Plumpton obtained the charter, which will be found alluded to as " the graunt of Stutvell" in Letter XXVII.

[r] Rot. Pip. 6 Ric. I.
[r] Rot. Pip. 2 Ric. I.
[t] Johannes, Dei gratia, &c. Sciatis nos concessisse et carta nostra confirmasse Willelmo de Stutevill pro servicio suo Knaresbur' et Burgum cum omnibus pertinentibus suis tenenda sibi et heredibus suis de nobis et heredibus nostris per servicium trium militum. Quare volumus et firmiter præcipimus quod prædictus Willelmus de Stutevill et heredes sui post eum, habeant et teneant predictas villas, &c. sicut carta Regis Henrici patris nostri rationabiliter testatur. Testibus. W. Marescallo, comite de Penbroc; G. filio Petri, comite Essex; Roberto de Turneham, &c. Datum per manus S. Wellensis Archidiaconi, et J. de Gray, Archidiaconi Glocestriæ, apud Gildeford, xxii die Aprilis, anno regni nostri primo. *(Rot. Cartarum, vol. I. pars. 1, fol. 1637, p. 54 b.)*

of the Correspondence of Sir William Plumpton, and which I here insert from a copy in the Cartulary.

" Sciant omnes presentes et futuri quod ego Willelmus de Stutevill dedi, concessi, quietum clamavi et hac presenti carta mea confirmavi Nigello de Plumton et heredibus suis pro servicio suo et pro uno equo precio centum solidorum totum vastum forestæ meæ infra divisas suas de Plumton et Roudferlington, scilicet, de Crempell versus occidentem usque ad Osberne-stahe-bec, et de Osberne-stahe-bec usque ad Pudding-stain-cros, et de Pudding-stain-cros usque ad Harelaw, et de Harelaw per magnam viam usque ad Biltonam, et de Biltona per eandem viam usque ad Stokke-brigge, et de Stokke-brigge usque ad Holebec, et de Hole-bec usque in Nidd, et iterum usque ad Crempell. Et si prefatus Nigellus vel heredes sui infra prenominatas divisas sartare vel colere voluerint, libere poterunt non requisita voluntate vel licencia mea vel heredum meorum. Preterea dedi etiam et concessi et hac eadem carta mea confirmavi eidem Nigello et heredibus suis latum cursum per totam forestam meam de Cnaresburgh ad vulpem et leporem, salva venatione mea, scilicet, cervo, bissa, et capreolo. Et si contigerit quod averia sua extra divisas prenominatas exeant, sine visu facti non causabuntur. Hæc omnia supradicta warrantizabimus ego W. et heredes mei prefato Nigello et heredibus suis imperpetuum contra omnes homines libere et quiete et solute ab omni servicio seculari et exaccione. Hiis testibus, Willelmo le Vavasur, Roberto de Mels, Roberto le Vavasur et Malgero fratre ejus, Ricardo de Tanghe, Thoma Lardenario, Adam filio Normanni, Nigello de Stockeld, Ricardo de Brertona, Ricardo de Alneio, Rogero de Creswell, Hugone Lardenario, Ricardo filio Widonis, Ernaldo Bridy, Hugone Pollard."[u]

[u] This deed is numbered 72 in the Cartulary, and has this note appended by the copyist:—" This deed is truly copied the 30 of March 1615, and has . . . . having a grene silk string through it, whereby it is fixed to the deed, and is a man upon horseback . . . . circumference the name of William Stutevill, as may

William de Stutevill died before the feast of the Nativity of St. John the Baptist, 5 John, 1203, and his body was interred in the abbey of Fountains, his gift to that monastery of his fief in the vill of Kirkby Ouseburn having attached to it the condition of sepulture.[v] Robert de Stutevill, his son and heir, had not, at the time of his father's death, quite attained his majority; therefore, on the 11th of July, Hubert Archbishop of Canterbury fined in the sum of four thousand marks to have the wardship and marriage, when Robert assented to his keeping the inheritance in his hands for four years, until he had got back his money, or until he was indemnified for his reasonable expenses.[x] Neither the Archbishop nor his ward, however, lived over the term; and in the 7th of King John, 5 Aug. 1205, Nicholas de Stutevill fined in the enormous sum of ten thousand marks to have livery of his inheritance, viz. of the land his brother William had died seised as of his inheritance, *exceptis castello de Knareburg et Ponte Burgi,* which were to be retained in the King's hands till the whole sum was paid; and of all the lands in pledge that the Archbishop of Canterbury had had in his custody on the day he died.[y] In this interval of time the King had issued a precept (21 Dec. 6 Joh. 1204), to the Sheriff of York to cause the forest of " Cnarreburgh " to be restored to the state it was in when King Henry granted it to William de Stutevill, and to deliver it thus entire to the Archbishop.[z] Among the sufferers by this royal command was Nigel de Plumpton, who, in February 1205-6, had to give a palfrey for leave to hold his land of Rothferlinton and Ribbeston and the appurtenances, with the chattels in the same vill, until the King should come to York, they having been seized into

partely be descerned. but there is a piece . . . ." This page, and several others at the commencement of the volume, have been partially eaten by mice; but the Towneley MSS. contain a transcript of most of the early deeds.
[v] Rot. Chartarum, p. 163.
[x] Ibid. p. 102.
[y] Ibid. p. 166.
[z] Rot. Litt. Claus. p. 16.

the King's hands *pro wasto forestæ*.[a] There the matter was investigated, and the result was a fine of twenty marks for restitution of the land, which was paid into the King's privy purse at Nottingham, 9 March 1205-6, by Brian de l'Isle, the constable of the castle of Knaresborough, and the other officers in charge of the Honour.[b] In the 13th Hen. III. 1229, Hubert de Burgh, Earl of Kent, and Margaret his wife, had a grant to them and their heirs of the " maneria Veteris Burgi et Ponteburg. et Knaresburg," with the castle and honour, knights' fees, soke, and forest, and all appurtenances, as also an assignment of the debt of ten thousand marks which the heirs of Stutevill owed to redeem the same; but in 1233 this great favourite fell into disgrace, and was stripped of his vast possessions. In the next year the Honour of Knaresborough was conferred upon Richard, Earl of Poitou and Cornwall, brother of Henry III. elected King of the Romans;[c] after whose death, in 1272, it descended to his son, Edmund Earl of Cornwall.[d]

The Nigel de Plumpton spoken of above had died in the reign of King John, leaving Juliana de Warewick, h s wife, surviving, between whom and Peter de Plumpton, son and heir of Nigel by his first wife, Maria, a fine was passed (14 *et 15 Johannis)* of the third parts of the vills of Plumpton, Gersington, Idell, and Ribstaine, which she claimed as her dower.[e] Peter de Plumpton was of the party of the barons against King John, and had his lands seized; but, after the death of that monarch, he did fealty and homage to his son, and was restored.[f] To him succeeded Robert,

[a] Rot. de Oblat. et Finibus, p. 317. Hardy, 1835.
[b] Rot. Litt. Claus. p. 66.
[c] Rot. Chart. 13 Hen. III. m. 3.
[d] Ibid. 19 Hen. III. m. 17.
[e] Fin. de eod. anno. *Dodsw. notes from G. f. 25, inserted in the Plumpton Cartulary.* Juliana appears to have been a daughter of Richard de Warewic, and mother of Robert Luvet, who had lands at Gretham, com. Rutland. Her sister, Sarra, married Gilbert de Beningworth. *(Vide Rot. Oblat. et Fin.)*
[f] Rot. Litt. Claus. p. 245 b. and 338 b.

his brother, whose son Nigel de Plumton died in the reign of Henry III. A jury sworn to take the inquisition concerning his lands and heirship, found that he held in *Plumton*, of the fee of William de Vescy, in demesnes, rents, villenages, and other issues from land, without the three dowers of three *Dominæ*, the value of ten marks two shillings and three pence; of the fee of William de Percy, ten marks three shillings; and in the vill of *Nessefeild*, of Peter de Percy, cviii[d] viii[d], rendering for his land there xlii[s] *per annum*. They also found him to have held *Gersington* of William de Percy, rendering one mark of silver *per annum*, and that it was worth ten marks four shillings and one penny, without the dowers above-mentioned; and they say, that Robert is his son and next heir, and of the age of four years and a half, and that the custody of the heir and his marriage of right belongs to *Dominus* William de Percy. Further they say, that he held Idell of the Earl of Lincoln, worth five marks by the year, without the three dowers of three *Dominæ*. The custody of the land in Idle, as not being of the Percy fee, was given by the King to Richard Earl of Cornwall, his brother, to hold till the heir was of age; the writ to notify which matter to the *custos* of the Honour of Pontefract bears *teste* at Westminster, 10 Nov. 29 H. III. 1244. Of the other lands William de Ireby was *custos*, and as such fined in twenty shillings 40 Hen. III. 1256,[g] for an assize to be taken before John de Lessintone, touching the church of Cowthorpe, of which the advowson had been given by Peter de Plumpton, in the reign of King John, to the priory of St. John the Evangelist in

[g] Vide Excerpta e rotulis Finium, Hen. III. rege, vol. I. p. 426; and vol. II. p. 240. The inquisition, of which the substance is given above, is taken from the bundle of escheats de anno LV. r. r. Hen. III.; but there is no date specified in the instrument itself, which must obviously be carried much further back, probably to the time of the minority of the heir of John de Lacy, created Earl of Lincoln 23 Nov. 1232, deceased in 1240: in any case, it is of a date anterior to the grant to Earl Richard of Cornwall of the custody of the land of the heir.

the park of Helagh. It resulted from their title being now questioned by his heir, that all right and claim *in ecclesia de Colthorp* were released to Sir Robert de Plompton by brother Henry the prior, and the convent of the same, under a charter dated at the Park in the month of February, 1274-5.[h] The same Sir Robert de Plumpton, by the style of *Robertus de Plomton, filius et heres Nigelli de Plomton*, confirmed to the noble and religious men, the abbot and convent of Fountains, a right of way through his land at Grassington *(Garsington)*, pursuant to the tenor of the grant of one of his predecessors, the first Nigel de Plomton. This charter bears date at Fountains, A. D. 1275.[i]

In the fourteenth year of the reign of King Edward, son of King Henry, on Saturday next after the Annunciation of Blessed Mary, it was agreed at Knaresburgh, between Edmond Earl of Cornwall and Sir Robert de Plumpton, that the latter and his heirs should have by way of fee *(de certo)* half the amercements from attachments for transgressions committed *de viridi et sicco* in the demesne woods of the said Sir Robert and his heirs within the forest of Knaresburgh, whether the acts of strangers or their own tenants, leviable in the court of the said Earl and his heirs at Knaresburgh, to be received at the hands of the seneschal or bailiff for the time being; but not those from attachments for transgressions in cutting down timber or for waste. Sir Robert and his heirs were also to have the pannage of the swine agisted in their own woods, and to be allowed to assart the demesne woods of Bircom, Loxley, and Halaugh, near Grimbald-brigg, and the hays growing in the cultures of Plompton on the east side of the ditch and hedge extending from Plompton to the bankside

[h] Cartul. No. 90.—" H. T. Joh'e le Vavasur, Stephano Walense, militibus, Willelmo de Katherton, Roberto de Ribbestain, Nigello Pincerna de Dighton et aliis. Dat. apud Parcum mense Februarii anno gratiæ M°CC°LXXIIII°."

[i] Cartul. No. 91.—" H. T. D'no Will'o de Ros, Henrico de Perpoint, tunc senescallo de Knaresburgh," &c.

of Nidd, opposite the gateway of the house of St. Robert of Knaresburgh, called Braistergarth, with the exception of the woods and covers of Grimbald-staines and Hybank; so, nevertheless, that the assarts and cultures remained within the bounds of the chace and forest of Knaresburgh. *Hayboot* and *housboot* were to be allowed of all other woods; and they and their tenants were to be quit of *Castell-boone* and drink-money for the foresters, upon payment of a rent of four shillings a year. The agreement concludes with a saving of the right of common in all places without the inclosures of the parks of the said Earl in their then state, and is attested by Sir Richard de Cornwall, Richard de Goldesburgh, Peter Becard, William de Hertlington, and Richard de Stokyld, knights, and other witnesses of less note.[k]

This Sir Robert de Plumpton closed his career about the 23rd Edw. I. 1295, and was the first of his family to lay aside the quaint device figured on the seals of his immediate predecessors, *viz.* a man riding on a lion crowned, for the armorial *insignia* of his lord paramount, "the Sire de Percy," *d'azur a la fesse engrele d'or;* which he differenced by having each fusil of the engrailed fess charged with an escalop gules.[l] The eldest son of Sir Robert

[k] Cartul. No. 94.
[l] In the roll of arms printed by Nicolas from a MS. of a date intermediate between 2nd and 7th Edw. II. (1308-1314), those of "Sire Robert de Plomtone" are emblazoned, *de azure, a une fesse endente de or, en la fesse v molez de goules*, but in the roll of arms of the time of Edw. III. which belonged to Hugh Fitzwilliams of Sprotborough in 1562, and which has been identified with the roll of arms anciently preserved at Croxton abbey, " Monsire de Plompton " is rightly said to bear, *d'asur sur fes engrele d'or de v points, v cokils gules*. Another later roll of the reign of Richard II. in the possession of the late Rev. J. Newling, B. D. Canon of Litchfield, gives for Plompton this emblazonment, " azure, five fusils in fess or, each charged with an escalop gules." To the transcript of a deed without date (*Cartul. No.* 129), containing a lease of a toft and two oxgangs of land in Garsington to one William Spay from *Robertus de Plompton miles*, the following marginal note is appended by the copyist: "This deed hath the 20 April 1615 a fair seale of grene wax, being the five fusalls and the scallops in the mids of them, and having written in the circumference S. Rob'tus

Plumpton bore the same name as his father: to Robert "filio meo primogenito," and to Lucy, daughter of Sir William de Ros, and to the heirs of their bodies, he gave in frank marriage land to the value of c[s]. rent in Midleton and Langber, with common of turbary and right of stray in the pasture and wood of Nessfield, under a quit-rent of a root of ginger to Sir Patrick de Westwick, in lieu of all suit and secular service, save that the tenants were to grind at mill of Nessfield " ad vicesimum vas."[m] Of the marriage with Ros there was issue Robert de Plumpton, who married Joan, daughter of Sir John Mauleverer, kt. but died before consummation in his father's lifetime; and Sir William de Plumpton, who had succeeded to the property before Monday next after the feast of St. Martin in Winter, 18 Edw. II. 1324.[n] He had to wife Alice, daughter and heiress of Sir Henry Byaufiz, to whom he was married before 14 April, 15 Edw. II. 1322, at which date the manor of Nesfield was settled by Sir Robert Plumpton, his father, upon him and Alice his wife, and the heirs of their bodies.[o] This Sir Henry Byaufiz died in 1325;[p] whereupon the manor of Brakenthwaite, together with lands in Plumpton, Follyfoot, Braham, Kirby, and Little Ribston, which he had held by the curtesy of England, of the inheritance of his wife Cecilia, daughter of William de Plumpton, (descended from Robert, son of Huckman, seneschal of the manor of Plumpton,) was settled by fine, levied

de Plompton—the fusalls and scallops are upon a tryangle whose bottome is uppermost."

[m] Cartul. No. 1002. " Robertus de Plumpton—Roberto filio suo et Luciæ Ros. H. T. d'no Rob'to de Ros, d'no Petro de Ros, d'no Alexandro de Ros, d'no Patricio de Westwick, d'no Patricio de Uluesby, Will'o Graindorge, Nicholao de Melton, Will'o de Hartlington et aliis."
[n] Cartul. No. 170. " Robertus de Flasby, capellanus, &c. recepi de Willelmo de Plompton filio et herede quondam d'ni Roberti de Plompton militis defuncti quatuor libras argenti—Apud Ebor."
[o] Cartul. No. 166. " Robertus de Plompton miles.—Apud Plompton."
[p] Esch. 19 Edw. II. n. 64.

in Hilary term, 19 Edw. II. 1325-3, upon Sir William de Plumpton and Alice his wife, and the heirs of their bodies, remainder to Thomas son of Peter de Midleton, and the heirs of his body, remainder to Marmaduke de Plumpton, and the heirs of his body, remainder to Adam son of Peter de Midleton, and his heirs for ever.[q] Sir William de Plumpton had to his second wife Christiana,[r] widow of Richard de Emildon, mayor of Newcastle in the reigns of Edw. I. Edw. II. and Edw. III. in the seventh year of which last reign he died.[s] She had re-married before 18 May, 12 Edw. III. 1338, being the Monday next before the feast of the Ascension of our Lord, for a settlement was then made of the manor of Grassington in Craven to hold to Sir William de Plumpton and Christiana his wife, and the heirs of Sir William, by Henry de Spofford, chaplain, as feoffee in trust.[t] The same Sir William de Plumpton was the founder of a chantry, at the altar of the Holy Trinity, behind the high altar of the collegiate church of Ripon. The act of endowment is dated at Ripon, on Wednesday the feast of the Conversion of St. Paul, 20 Edw. III. 1345, and was sealed with the seals of Henry de Plumpton, the chaplain first appointed thereto, and of Sir William de Plumpton; which latter bore the impression of a shield, and on it five fusils, with the name written in the circumference.[u] He died 36 Edw. III. 1362, towards the close of the year, as appears by the account of the feodary of the honour of Pontefract of that date, wherein is set down xxv[s]. as the relief of Robert de Plumpton, knight, for the fourth part of one knight's fee in Idell, after the decease of William de Plumpton, knight, his father.[x]

Sir Robert de Plumpton was a deponent in the Scrope and Grosvenor controversy on the 17th day of September 1385, being

[q] Cartul. No. 173. "Finalis concordia, apud Westm. in octabis sc'i Hillarii.
[r] Called de Mowbray in pedigree in Harl. MSS. 1487.
[s] Esch. 7 Edw. III. No. 38.   [t] Cartul. No. 182.
[u] Cartul. Nos. 215 and 216.
[x] Brooke MSS. Collections for Yorkshire in Coll. Armorum.

then of the age of forty-five years, which places his birth in the year 1341, and consequently posterior to his father's second marriage.[y] He appears from this deposition to have repeatedly served in the wars of his time. In 1372 he had gone on board the King's fleet, but falling suddenly and dangerously ill, and being unable to continue this sea voyage, he was compelled to go ashore at the town of Rye; whereupon, the circumstances of his case having first been returned into the Chancery under the seal of

[y] See Controversy between Sir Richard Scrope and Sir Robert Grosvenor in the Court of Chivalry, royal 8vo, 1832. By Sir N. Harris Nicolas, K. H. vol. I. p. 270.—In the biographical notice, it is said that Sir Robert Plumpton was appointed lieutenant of the forest of Knaresborough in May 1387; the original authority for which assertion was doubtless the following charter, numbered 363 in the Cartulary:
Johan de la Pole, cheif senescall de mon tres redoute Sire, le Roy de Castell et de Leon, duc de Lancastre, de North Trent, a Mons[r] Robert de Plumpton, lieutenant del Meistre Forestier de la forest de Knaresburgh, salutz. Vous mande et charge de par mon dit Sire que vous faciez delivrer a Johan Brown de Knaresburgh un Stubb pur merasme, apprendre deinz la foreste illoeqez, pur edifier une meeson sur la terre de mon dit Sire, quil tient par terme des ans a volunte, en la ville de Knaresburgh. Et auxint facez delivrer a William Clerc de Knaresbrough un Stubb pur merisme, apprendre deinz la forest suisdite, pur reparacion des mesons affaire sur la terre de mon dit Sire en la dite ville. Et ceste ma lettre vous ent sera garrart. Escrit a Knaresburgh, le viij jour de Maij, lan du Regne le roy Richard second puis la conqueste, disme. (8 May, 10 Ric. II. 1387.) Number 291 in the same Cartulary is a copy of a bailbond from John son of Robert de Knaresburgh, and John de Makelay of Scotton, to Sir Robert de Plumpton, Constable of the castle of Knaresburgh, dated at Knaresburgh, 26th of October, 11th Ric. II. (1387); but the exact date of his appointment to these lieutenancies is not apparent from either document. In the same memoir he is likewise stated to have had a large family by his wife, Isabella Scrope, whereas Sir William Plumpton was the only son, and there is no evidence as to female issue. Again, the writer of the same notice thinks it most probable that Sir Robert was the issue of his father's first marriage with Alice Byaufiz; but, letting alone the proof to be derived from his age at the time of the controversy, it is also certain that the manor of Brakenthwaite, with the lands which were of the inheritance of Alice, reverted, agreeably to the limitation in the fine noticed in the text, to the posterity of Thomas, son of Peter de Midleton, which could only be in case of failure of issue of Alice. (Plumpton Evidences.) It was in right of this descent that the Midletons of Stockeld quartered the coat of Plumpton, that is, of the seneschals of Plumpton.

Simon Burgh, Constable of Rochester Castle, a writ was sent to the mayor and bailiffs of the town to exonerate him from blame, and instructing them to allow him, with John Heton, his esquire, and his two valets, to return home with all his equipage unmolested.[z]

In the reign of Henry the Fourth, Sir William Plumpton, the eldest son of Sir Robert Plumpton, suffered death upon a scaffold for the part he took in the insurrection stirred up by his uncle Richard, Archbishop of York, whose sister, Isabella Scrope, his father had married. In the history of this commotion in Polydore Vergil, he is represented as the chief actor, a statement which subsequent historians have not thought deserving of credit; I, however, venture to introduce his account into these Memoirs, because that writer's value as an historian appears to me to be somewhat underrated, many of his details being evidently founded upon authentic documents, which have not survived the lapse of time, or which he may have wilfully destroyed, a practice imputed to this foreigner.

[z] Rex Majori et Ballivis villæ de Rye, ac universis et singulis vicecomitibus, majoribus, ballivis, ministris, et aliis fidelibus suis ad quos presentes litteræ pervenerint, salutem. Sciatis quod cum dilectus et fidelis noster Robertus de Plumpton Chivaler, postquam in obsequium nostrum cum flota nostra mare fuisset ingressus, in gravem infirmitatem subito inciderit, sic quod ulterius in viagium nostrum supra mare laborare minime sufficiebat, per quod idem Robertus ad dictam villam de la Rye occasione sanitatis recuperandæ applicuit, prout ipsum ex necessario oportebat, sicut per litteras Simonis Burgh constabularii Castri Roffensis eorum tobis in cancellaria nostra ostensas plenius poterit apparere: Nos volentes pro securitate ipsius Roberti, cum culpa in ipsa occasione recessûs sui ab obsequio nostro reputetur, providere, vobis mandamus quod ipse Robertus, cum Johanne Heton, armigero suo, et duobus valectis suis, a dicta villa de la Rye ad partes suas proprias infra regnum nostrum Angliæ redire et armaturas, harnesia et res sua secum ducere libere permittatis, non inferentes eis seu eorum alicui in personis, armaturis, harnesiis, seu rebus suis ex causa predicta injurium, molestiam, dampnum, violentiam, impedimentum aliquod seu gravemen. Et si quid eis forisfactum fuerit, id eis sine dilatione debite corrigi et emendari faciatis. In cujus, &c. Teste Custode Angliæ, xxii die Septembris anno 46 Edw. III. [1372]. (Plumpton Cartul. No. 270, from an ancient copy in paper.)

"While Henry is thus attentive to his domestic concerns, William Plumpton, a brave and daring knight, formerly of the household of King Richard, along with some of the family of Thomas Mowbray, marshal, whom we have shown above to have died in exile at Venice, first excites the commons of Yorkshire and Durham to revolt, and then collects together a great number of armed men; and he conducts his proceedings with less circumspection than the nature of such an enterprise required, because his soul is mainly bent upon revenge. With him the Northumbrians also take part; and, last of all, the Scots; but these, as will be mentioned below, were not present at the outbreak. The King, meanwhile, informed of the design of the conspirators, for the sake of avoiding instant peril, took up arms, and, without a moment's delay, marched directly to York; and such was his dispatch, that he had arrived there before the movers of the revolt had any certain intelligence of his coming. William Plumpton is instantly taken, and with him some of his associates; among whom was Richard Scrupp, Archbishop of York, who, although his name was in the highest repute for sanctity and virtue, nevertheless, accusers were not wanting to make it suspected that treason attached to him likewise, inasmuch as he sought thus to avenge the death of William, his brother, treasurer of Richard, whom Henry had put to death at Bristol, as I have shown in a former book. Whereupon Henry, having summoned a council of his nobles at York, he ordained an inquiry to be had concerning the conspiracy. At this meeting all unanimously pronounce sentence of death against Plumpton; but as to the others, their judgment was more lenient. However, he having undergone capital punishment in the manner customary of old, the rest likewise are put to death, either by the axe or the gibbet."[a]

The historian here falls into the common error of making Arch-

[a] Polydori Vergilii Anglica Historia. Lugd. Batavorum 1649, 8vo, liber xxi. p. 554.

bishop Scrope brother of the Earl of Wiltshire and thus betrays the aim of his narrative, as meant to extenuate the rebellion of the Archbishop as much as possible. This he does by imputing to him a motive of natural affection which could not exist, and by supposing him to play quite a secondary part, while he shifts the chief blame upon Sir William Plumpton; whom also, as far as existing evidence goes, he falsely represents to have been of the household of King Richard. The verses formerly on the tomb of this unfortunate knight in Spofforth church tell a simpler tale:

> Miles eram dudum, Plompton Will'mus vocitatus,
> Præsulis atque nepos le Scropplis, hic tumulatus.
> Mortis causa sui, michi causa fuit moriendi,
> Mors capitis quippe nostrum male pressit utrumque.
> Anno milleno quater et C. sic quoque quinto,
> Penticostes me lux crastina sumpsit ab orbe.[b]

In the year 1405 the morrow of Pentecost fell on the eighth of June, the feast of St. William of York, which is the day mentioned by Hall as that of their decollation, "on the Monday in Whitson weke." This chronicler erroneously puts "Sir Robart" for Sir William Plumpton, and is exceeding angry with the writers and story-tellers who spread abroad that miracles were wrought at the time of the execution of Archbishop Scrope, as to the King's being striken with leprosy, and the like. He doubtless here alludes to the History of the Martyrdom of Richard Scrope, Archbishop of York, by Clement Maidstone, where it is related, upon the authority of George Plumpton, an ecclesiastic of whom we shall speak largely in the sequel, who was an eye-witness, that on the day of the said decollation, 8th of June, great leprous pustules broke out over the said King's face and hands, and were as prominent as the nipples of the breasts.[c] The vision of the son may,

[b] Cartul. No. 364.   [c] Anglia Sacra, vol. II. p. 369.

CAMD. SOC. 4.   e

however, be believed to have been distorted by the recollection of his father's execution, and by the wish, so natural to mortals, of seeing Heaven avenge our wrongs: the legendary should, at all events, have taken the precaution to look out for a more disinterested witness, before he gave publicity to the tale.

No act of attainder followed upon the execution of the rebels, and Sir Robert Plumpton, the father, obtained for himself a general pardon for all treasons and felonies; to which effect I find letters patent from the King, bearing date at Newcastle-upon-Tyne, 21 June, 6 Hen. IV. 1405.[d] He died 19 April, 8 Hen. IV. 1407,[e] having by his will, dated 26th of February preceding, directed his feoffees, Sir William Gascoigne and Sir Nicholas de Middelton, knights, Richard de Kendale and William de Authorp, parsons of the churches of Ripley and Dighton, to grant the manor of Plompton to Isabel "*ma trescher compaigne*" for her life, with remainder to Robert son of William de Plompton, *son neveue*, in fee, so as to secure to his relict a yearly jointure of fifty marks.[f] This lady was his second wife, and was of Kirkoswald in Westmoreland,[g] she being styled in the deed securing to her a future settlement, bearing date 12 July, 23 Ric. II. 1399, "Isabella quondam vocata de Kirkoswald." Of Isabella Scrope, daughter of Henry first Lord Scrope of Masham, the first wife of Sir Robert Plumpton, mention has been made.

Robert de Plumpton, nephew and heir, was twenty-four years old at the time of his grandfather's death, and yet an esquire. By intermarrying with the heiress of Sir Godfrey Foljambe, knight, whose marriage had been contracted for in his father's lifetime, he added greatly to the wealth and importance of his family, by the acquisition of large estates in the counties of Nottingham and

[d] Cartul. No. 319.   [e] Esch. 8 Hen. IV. No. 15.   [f] Cartul. 331.
[g] Cartul. No. 308 and 309. She remarried before 12 Jan. 1 Hen. V. 1413-4, Sir Nicholas Middleton of Stockeld, and was living his wife 24 May, 4 Hen. V. 1416. (*Ibid. No.* 367 *et* 377.) She is again named 24 Sept. 8 Hen. V. 1420. Vide *postea*.

Derby.[h] His mother was Alice, daughter of John Gisburn,[i] citizen and merchant of York, and coheiress with Isabel, wife of Sir William Frost, kt. to their father. After the death of her unfortunate husband, she made the following agreement with her son Robert.

"Ceste endenture faicte par entre dame Alice de Plumpton dune part, et Robert de Plompton, son filtz, dautre part, tesmoigne, que le dit Robert ad graunte et fraunkement donee au dite dame Alice son miere, sa table sufficaunt et convenable a son degre, et pur Elizabeth et Isabele, feiles au dite dame Alice, & pur Richard son filtz, et pur une noryse, durant une ane pleynement, le primer jour du dit ane commensant en la feste de St. Martyn en yvere

[h] Sir Godfrey Foljambe died on Wednesday next after the Nativity of our Lady 12 Ric. II. (Sept. 9, 1388); and on the 18th November following dower was assigned to his widow Margaret (afterwards the wife of Sir Thomas Rempston, K. G.) in the presence of Sir John Leeke, kt. whose sister she was, and to whom the king had committed the lands of the said Sir Godfrey to farm, Alice his daughter and heir being at the time of his decease little more than a year old. By a subsequent writ, tested at Westminster 16 Feb. 13th of his reign, King Richard granted to the said Sir John Leek the marriage of the heiress for fifty marks, which wardship and marriage he by indenture, dated at Downham-upon-Trent, on the morrow of St. Hilary, 16 Ric. II. 1392-3, transferred to Sir William Plompton, kt. to the intent that she should be matched with his son and heir-apparent, whomsoever he might be, in consideration of c marks, and upon condition of payment of other annual sums till she reached the age of fifteen years. The marriage took place, and after the completion of her fourteenth year Robert Wycard, the king's escheator for the county of Derby, delivered seisin to William de Hardalsey, attorney of Robert de Plompton and Alice his wife, daughter and heir of Godfrey Foliamb, Ch'r, of all lands of which the said Godfrey was seised in demesne as of fee on the day he died, and attested the fact by his deed dated in Collectanea Chaddesden, on Sunday next before the feast of St. Nicholas bishop, 3d of Hen. IV. (4 Dec. 1401). *Vide* inq. post mortem 12 Ric. II. (No. 21.) pro terris quas Avena relicta Godfredi Foliamb, militis, et nuper uxor Ricardi Grene, militis, tenuit in dotem, et Assignationem dotis Margarete que fuit uxor Godfredi Foljambe, Ch'r, fil. Godfredi, fil. Godfredi Foljambe, militis, in Wolley's Collect. MS. Addit. 6675, f. 381, printed in Collectanea Topograph. et Geneal. vol. I. p. 337, Lond. 1834, and *vide* Cartul. No. 292, 294, et 313.
[i] John Gisburn was mayor of York in 1371, 1372, and 1380. (*Drake's Eboracum*, p. 361.)

prochein avenere aupres la date du cestes. Et auxi le dit Robert ad fraunkement graunte a dite dame Alice une chambre, appelle le closetts, ou une petit chambre faite enhaut deines le dit closett, au son propre use, et sufficaunts luminere et fououk.[k] Et si ense seit que la dite dame Alice desire ou voet au fyne du dit ane plus longe-

[k] This lodging must have been in the manor-house of Kinalton in Nottinghamshire, which Robert de Plumpton had in right of his wife, and which he made his principal residence. It had come into the possession of the family of Foljambe either by descent or purchase, before Trinity term 40 Edw. III. 1366, when it was settled by fine upon Godfrey, son of Sir Godfrey Foljamb, kt. and Margaret his wife, and the heirs of their bodies; remainder on the right heirs of Godfrey. (*Thoroton's Notts, vol. I. p.* 155.) This Margaret was the grandmother of Lady Plumpton, and of the blood of the Vilers, lords of Kinalton, Cotgrave, Owthorp, and Newbold, in the county of Nottingham, and owners of lands in the parishes of Eccleston and Croston, in the county of Lancaster, as mesne tenants under the Butlers of Warrington. In the early Visitation of Yorkshire by Tong in 1534, the coat of Vilers, *six lyonceis*, 3, 2, 1, is borne on an escutcheon of pretence in the middle of a shield, *quarterly Plumpton and Foljambe*; but on the tombs of the Drurys in Hawsted church the quartering used for Vilers was *a fess between six lions rampant*. (See *History of Suffolk, Thingoe Hundred, p.* 456, Bentley, Lond.)

PEDIGREE OF FOLJAMBE, of Hassop, com. Derby.

Arms: Sable, a bend between six escallops Or.

Sir Godfrey Foljambe, kt. Second Baron of the Exchequer 18 Edw. III. Seneschal of the lands of the Duchy of Lancaster; died 29 May, 50 Edw. III. 1376; bur. at Bakewell, com. Derby.	=	Avena, dau. of Adam de Ireland by Avena de Holand, lord of Hale, in com. Lanc.; ob. 13 Dec. 6 Ric. II. 1382.	=	Sir Richard Green, knt. 2d husb.
Godfrey Foljambe, son and heir apparent, of Kinalton, com. Notts; died after 45 Edw. III. 1371, in his father's lifetime.	= Margaret de Vilers, mar. 40 Edw. III. 1366.	Thomas Foljambe, of Walton, in com. Derby.	Alvered, ob. 20 June, 5 Ric. II. 1382.	Richard Foljambe. Robert Foljambe.
Sir Godfrey Foljambe, kt. æt. 9 ann. 29 May, 1376, grandson and heir; died 2 Dec. 12 Ric. II. 1388, æt. 21 annorum.	= Margaret, dau. of Sir Simon Leeke, kt.; ob. 21 April, 32 Hen. VI. 1454.	= Sir Thomas Rempston, K.G. drowned 31 Oct. 8 Hen. IV. 1406.		Margaret, wife of Sir Nicholas Montgomery, kt.
Alicia, dau. and heir, æt. 1 ann. 2 Dec. 1388, wife of Sir Robert Plumpton, kt.		Sir Thomas Rempston, kt.; ob. 15 Oct. 37 Hen. VI. 1458.		

ment demurer ou le dit Robert, qu'adoures la dite dame Alice doneray pur son table en la semaygne xii^d; et pur Elizabeth sa feile viii^d; & pur Richard son filz vi^d; & pur Ysabele sa feile vi^d; & pur une gentile feme viii^d; et per une chambrerere, vi^d. Et la dite dame Alice eyaunte tute le eesemente & toutz chosez devaunt nomez durantz le temps que la dite dame Alice fait sa demaunce ou le dit Robert. Et au toutz cez & chescuz condicions tener et pleinement performer ambedeux parties au presentez endenturez eyount myse loure seals. Cestez tesmoignez, John de Mureton, Henri de Mureton, Robert de Skelton, chaplayne, Roger de Spofforth & Nicholas Thornby, chaplaines. Done au Everwyk la neefisme iour du moyse de Octobre, lan du Roy Henri enpres le Conquest sept."[1]

Alice Plumpton was the mother of a numerous progeny, having had, besides her eldest son already named, four other sons, and as many daughters. Some of these are named in the will of their grandmother Ellen de Gisburn, who, after the death of her husband, founded a chantry for the repose of his soul at the altar of St. Nicholas, in the church of St. Martin in Micklegate, in York, and endowed it with a messuage lying between the street of Nether-Ousegate and the cemetery of the church of St. Michael near the bridge of Ouse in York, near Cayllomhall and the river Ouse on either side, the advowson of which she entailed on her daughters Isabel and Alice in turn.[m]

"Ceste endenture tesmoigne que Alice de Plumpton aid resceu de William Frost, John de Moreton, Robert Skelton, chappleyn, executours du testament de Elyn de Gisburn, du legat de testament du dit Elyn, cest assavoir, as iiij fitz du dit Alice, viij^{li}. Item, a Johan sa file, i pece covere et iiij^{li} vi^s viij^d. Item, a Richard, fitz le dit Alice, i pece covere et vi^{li} xiij^s iiij^d. Item, a dite Johan sa file une burse de perell. Item, a Isabele, la file du dit Alice, l bedes argent et iij^{li} vi^s viij^d. Item, a George, le fitz du dit Alice, i pare getebedes bien gaudez dargent. En tesmoignance de quel choyse les parties devauntditz a les partiez de ceste endenture changeablement ount mys lour seals. Done a Everwyke, la xxvime iour dapril, lan du regne notre tres redoute Sire, le Roy Henry quart puise le conquest dengleterre, ixme."[n]

In the partition of her parents' property, Alice Plumpton had allotted to her share a messuage in Skeldergate in York, another upon Byshophill, "et toutz les martisounz, apelles en Knyles *deles of the Kuyes*, que furount Johan de Gysburne en les preetz de Bushopthorp, pres de Everwyk," and a rent of five marks out of lands and tenements in the town of Ripon, together with all the tenements belonging to her said father in North-street, in the city of York.[o] Of this property she made a settlement, 25 Oct. 4 Hen V. 1416, whereby she directed Richard Kendale, parson of the church of Ripley, and other co-feoffees, to make an estate of the lands and tenements in Ripon to her son Thomas and the heirs of his body; remainder, in like form, to her sons Brian and Richard; and the tenements in North-street were similarly settled on her son Richard in the first instance, with like remainders to Brian and Thomas. The premises in Skeldergate were directed to be sold to raise marriage portions for her daughters Isabelle and Katharine, reserving a rent of iii^s vi^d, parcel thereof lately recovered, to augment the chantry in the church of St. Martin, and for prayers for the souls of Sir William de Plompton, Ch'r, and of her her said Alice, of Dame Isabell the mother of the said Sir William, and for the soul of Joan de Chauncefeild.[p]

---

[1] Cartul. No. 325.

[m] Ibid. No. 300. Willelmus Sparrow, capellanus—d'no Thomæ Pynchebek, capellano. Dat. apud Ebor. xxviii° die Maii, A° D'ni millio ccc° nonagesimo sexto, Ric. II. vicesimo.

[n] Cartul. No. 341.

[o] Ibid. No. 293. Done a Everwyke, xiii jours de Januare, lan du reigne le Roy Richard Secound apres la conquest denglelterre quindesyme.

[p] Ibid. No. 381.

Brian Plompton, one of the sons above named, had a legacy of x^{li} and a silver dish with cover, having upon it the arms of Ivo le Zouche, under the will of Stephen le Scrope, archdeacon of Richmond, his cousin, dated 24 Aug. 1418, and proved the 7th of September following, being at the same time one of the executors, in which capacity he had a further legacy of ten marks.[q] Brian was party to a bond dated 31 Dec. 1418,[r] but he, as well as his brother Thomas, who died 18 July 1420, was deceased without issue, in the lifetime of his mother; for by a fresh settlement, bearing date 12 Sept. 2 Hen. VI. 1423, she gave all her lands and tenements, both in North-street York, and at Ripon, to her son Richard de Plumpton and the heirs of his body, paying thereout for the space of four years, to her daughters Isabella and Katharine, xx^s a-piece, unless they died or were married within the term; remainder to George de Plompton her son for life, to dispose of hereafter for the good of her soul and the soul of Sir William de Plompton her husband, and for those of parents, benefactors, and all the faithful departed.[s] This disposition was carried into effect by the feoffees, Richard de Kendale, rector of the church of Ripley, Adam de Wygan, rector of the church of St. Saviour in York, George de Plompton, and Nicholas de Thornby, chaplain, on the 5th of December following, she being then lately deceased.[t] By her will, of which her sons George and Richard were executors, she bequeathed, among other legacies, to her daughter Isabella, "unum par precalium auri cum una fibula de perill, unum tabiletum auri cum imagine Sc'æ Trinitatis et aliorum sanctorum, unam crucem de petris et perillis, unum cofir pruc'æ, unum cofir ornatum cum auriculo, coopertum cum velvet, unum lectum et tapetum cum bollis et liliis, unam matras, duas codices, dua paria linthiaminum de optimis, unum de minoribus, quatuor ulnas panni lanei nigri, tres curtinas de albo et nigro paled, unam zonam optinam deauratam, unam par optimum de trussing cofrise, unum primarium coopertum cum panno rubeo-aureo, et omnes perillos, unum tissehew nigri serici, unum annulum auri cum uno pecudode, sex cocliaria argenti, unam nappam mensalem cum uno tuallo, unam furruram de Bice et medietatem flamineolorum;"[u] to her daughter Katharine, "unum primarum coopertum cum panno de worsted velvet, unum minorem cofer pruciæ, unum coopertorium cum tapeto cum chapellets texto, unum lectum plumale, duo blanketts, duo paria lintheaminum de optimis, unum de minoribus, unum par precalium auri more follium formosorum, unum tabuletam auri cum Salutacione Beatæ Mariæ cum tribus perlis circumpositis, et unam crucem cum xii perlis, et unam togam furruratam cum croppes, & medietatem flameolorum;[x] and to her granddaughter Alice, daughter of Sir Robert de Plompton, knight, "sexaginta precalia de corrall cum sex ganeriis auri."[y] The place of burial of Dame Alice Plumpton was in Spofforth church, where she was laid by the side of her husband, as is told us by the Latin verses, which were formerly inscribed upon the tomb.

> Longo langore dirisque doloribus arte,
> Hic Plumpton Domina clauditur Alicia.
> Mille, quater centum, bis et x, tria jungeque sexto,
> Ad proprium sponsum traditur in tumulum.[z]

---

[q] Testamenta Eboracensia, Part I. p. 385, printed for the Surtees' Society, 1836.

[r] Cartul. No. 400.

[s] Ibid. No. 408; and see Monumental Inscription of Thomas Plumpton in Spofforth church, copied in Dugdale's Yorkshire Arms in *Coll. Armorum*.

[t] Ibid. No. 420.

[u] Cartul. No. 409.   [x] Ibid. No. 422.   [y] Ibid. No. 411.

[z] Ibid. No. 396. The line expressive of the date in this inscription may require explanation. The six first words denote plainly enough the sum mccccxx; and to the sixth word, which is x, you are to add three, making 1423 the total, which was the year of the death of Dame Alice Plumpton, as appears from other evidence. On the same tomb were two other inscriptions in similar style; one of which, in memory of Sir William Plumpton, knight, her husband, in hexameter verse has been introduced

Richard de Plumpton had a pair of orisons of gold left him in the will of the Archdeacon of Richmond, Stephen le Scrope; and was an esquire in the service of Maud, widow of Peter de Mauley the eighth, daughter of Ralph Earl of Westmorland, who, after the decease of her husband in 1415, held the extensive barony which had belonged to him for her life. In her will, made 1st Oct. 1438, and proved on the 4th of that month, Richard Plumpton has a legacy of x^{li}.[a] His own will bears date in 1443, and proves him to have had a grateful recollection of his mistress. Its tenour is as follows:—" My soul I commend to Almighty God, my body to be buried in the church of the house of St. Robert. All my lands and tenements in North-street, York, and in Ripon, I give and bequeath to George Plompton, my brother, brother John Craven, minister of the house of St. Robert, Sir William Normanvill, knight, Ranulph Pygott and Robert Crosse, esquires, in order that they may arrange with the minister and house of St. Robert for a priest to say mass daily and for ever for the souls of my father and mother, my grandfather John Gisburgh, and my grandmother Elen Gisburne, for my own soul, and for the soul of my brother George, and the souls of all the faithful departed; but if this cannot be done, then to dispose of them, as they best may, for the good of the souls above mentioned. I give and bequeath to Master George Plompton my brother, '*unam pixidem argenteam et deauratam, unum psalterium meum parvum, unum par cultellorum vocat*' karving knyves, *et unum par forpicum argenteorum*.' I also will and ordain, that my black cloak furred with with martyrs, and a coverlet of red saten, and a canopy of white silk, be sold, and the price distributed *pro salute venerabilis d'nœ, d'nœ Matildis de Malolacu*. I give to Elen Crosse my best gold ring with a sapphire, and a primer covered with red satin, and ten beads, five of gold in the form of baskets, and five of agate. To Robert Crosse a silvered girdle. To dame Elizabeth Plompton, my niece, (*nepotissœ meœ,*) a gold crucifix. To Elizabeth Hothom a gold ring with an emerald. To Dame Isabella de Bukton a capital gold ring with two images. To Katherine, my sister, a gold cross. To the minister of the house of St. Robert a psalter covered with red velvet, and vi^s viii^d. To brother Richard Fawkes, iij^s iiij^d and 10 beads of amber. To John Smith, chaplain, vi^s viii^d and ten beads of maser. To Thomas Whyttall, chaplain, vi^s viii^d and a pair of long knives. To dame Elizabeth Hothom, recluse, xij^d. The residue to be distributed for the behoof of my soul, of the soul of my mother, and of the soul of Dame Maud de Maulay. Executors, Master George Plompton my brother, Elen Crosse, and Thomas Whittall, chaplain." [b]

George de Plumpton was, as I have already had occasion to mention, in the service of the church. To give him a title, Thomas, prior, and the convent of Landa, of the order of St. Augustin, in the county of Leicester and diocese of Lincoln, assigned him an annual pension of x^{li} for term of life, 4 Jan. 2 Hen. IV. 1400-1; [c] and 3 Oct. 4 Hen. V. 1416, being then a Bachelor at Law, he had a licence from Henry, Archbishop of York and Legate of the Holy See, to receive holy orders.[d] Whereupon, George Plumpton, acolyte, was ordained subdeacon by John bishop of Ely, in the chapel of his manor of Dounham, in the diocese of Ely, 27 Mar. 1417; [e] deacon by the same prelate in the chapel of his manor of Somersham, in the diocese of Lincoln, by licence of Philip the diocesan, 18 Sept. 1417; [f] and priest 19 Feb. 1417-8, in the same chapel of Dounham, by the same Bishop of Ely.[g] In 1438-9 he became rector of the parish church or free chapel of Grismere, otherwise Grassmire, in Cumberland, vacant by the resignation of Master Peter Icford, to which benefice he had been presented by the King as nominee of the abbot and convent of St. Mary's, York, the right patrons.[l] On the 13th Feb. in that year, he was inducted thereto by Walter Capros, chaplain, commissary of Henry Bowett, archdeacon of Richmond, in whose jurisdiction the living was situate.[j] In the next year (10 Feb. 1439-40), he had a faculty from Richard Arnall, sub-dean of the cathedral church of York, and vicar-general of John, Archbishop of York and Legate, to hear reserved cases in confession, and to give absolution to all penitents, save violators of the privileges of the cathedral church of York, and of the collegiates of Beverley, Ripon, and Suthwell, and breakers open of the parks belonging to the Archiepiscopal see for the taking of game therein.[k] In 1447 (12 Nov. 26 Hen. VI.), Master George Plompton, chaplain, had letters of institution to the rectory of the church of Bingham, in the county of Nottingham, upon the presentation of Sir Thomas Chaworth, knight, from John, Cardinal priest of the holy Roman Church, titular of St. Balbina, Archbishop of York, and Legate of the Holy See,[l] and was inducted by proxy 2nd December following, by the official of the Archdeacon of Nottingham.[m] This benefice he probably owed to the good offices of his kinsman, John Lord Scrope of Masham, Treasurer of England (26 Feb. 10 Hen. VI. 1431-2), who had intermarried with a daughter of Sir Thomas Chaworth, and whom the following letter shows to have been the patron of George de Plompton:

To my right trusty and welbeloved Cousin, Sir William Plompton.

Trusty and welbeloued, I greet you wel; praying you that you wil have in tendernesse and favor my welbeloued cousin George of Plompton, your nephew *(recte)* uncle), as towching his annuity, in such wise as he may know this my writing may turn into avail; certifiing mee wherin that I may shew you as much kindnes or ease, the which I wold do with all my hart, as God knowes, who

---

into the text. The other recorded the interment of Dame Isabella Plumpton, his mother, and the day and year of her birth (24 Aug. 1337), in these lines:

Hic cineres Dominæ Plumpton remanent Isabellae,
Quae fuit Henrici filia Scroop Domini.
Mille semel, ter c, ter x, semel v, duo junge,
Bartholomee, tua lux dedit astra sua.

This and the foregoing inscription are transcribed into Sir Edward Plumpton's Cartulary, Nos. 364 and 365, along with this note:—"These are two severall inscriptions both upon one tombe in Plompton quiere in Spofforth church, seene and examined the xviith day of October, 1613, per Fra. Burgoin, rector' ibidem. Milo Nicolson, curat' ib'm, Joh'es Parke, clericus." In the History of the Family of Scrope of Masham, accompanying the publication of the Scrope and Grosvenor Roll, these two inscriptions are correctly given from Vincent's Yorkshire, No. III. fo. 30, save that in the second line of the hexameter inscription *Scropp licet* is put for *Scropplis*, the true reading, an augmentative syllable being added to the name for the sake of the metre.

[a] Testamenta Vetusta, 8vo. 1826. Nichols, vol. I. p. 234; from Dugdale's Abstract, vol. I. p. 736.

[b] Cartul. No. 527.   [c] Ibid. No. 312. Dat. apud Landa in domo nostro capitulari.

[d] Cartul. No. 380. Dat. apud Cawood.   [e] Ibid. No. 386.
[f] Ibid. No. 392.   [g] Ibid. No. 395.
[h] Cartul. No. 442. "Carta testificatoria Hen. Bowett, Archidiaconi Richm. Dat. apud Markingfeild, 2 Mar. 1438."
[i] Ibid. *ubi supra*.
[k] "Ricardus Arnall ecclesiæ Cathedralis Ebor. subdecanus, Reveren^{mi} in Christo patris et d'ni,d'ni Joh'is Dei gratia Ebor. Archiep'i Angliæ primatis et Apostolicæ sedis legati, vicarius in spiritualibus auctoritate, dilecto nobis in Christo Mag'ro Georgio Plompton in utroque jure Baccalario, salutem in omnium Salvatore. Ad audiendas confessiones quorumcunque subditorum dicti Reveren^{mi} patris tibi in foro X'iano confiteri volencium, et eos a peccatis quæ tibi confessi fuerint absolvendos, ac eisdem pro modo culparum suarum injungendas penitencias salutares, nec vota minus solempnia commutanda et cum eisdem dispensanda, etiam in casibus prefato Reveren^{mo} patri seu nobis a jure specialiter reservatis (libertatum et immunitatum ecclesiæ Cath: Ebor: predictæ ac Ecclesiarum collegiatarum Beverlaci, Riponiæ et Suthwelliæ violatoribus, ac parcorum ad Archiep'atum Ebor: pertinentium fractoribus et in eis feram seu feras capientibus duntaxat exceptis, quorum omnium absolucionem prefato Reveren^{mo} patri seu nobis specialiter reservamus) vobis, de cuius conscientiæ puritate et industria circumspecta plenarie confidimus, tenore presencium committimus vices nostras et plenariam in Domino potestatem, ad prefati Reveren^{mi} patris beneplacitum duraturam. Dat. Ebor: decimo die mensis Febr: Anno d'ni Mill'mo cccc^{mo} xxxix^{mo}. (*Cartul. No.* 449.)

[l] Chartul. No. 514. "Dat. in hospicio nostro prope Westm."
[m] Ibid. No. 515.

have you in his keeping. Written at London the nineteenth day of Feveryear.

              The Lord Scroop, tresorer of England.[n]

Within a year after his taking possession of the rectory of Bingham (8 Jun. 1448), Master George Plompton had leave of absence from the diocesan for three years from that date, by reason of his increasing years and great infirmities,[o] during which term the rectory was let by him to farm to Sir Thomas Rempston, knight, for forty marks;[p] but before 11 Feb. 1450-1 he had resigned the living to Sir James Swaledale, retaining, however, a pension of x[li] annually for his life.[q] About the same time (6 Nov. 29 Hen. VI. 1450), he conveyed to feoffees, *viz.* the worshipfull fader and lord, Tho: Spofford, late byshop of Hereford, John Kexby, and William Middelton, clerks, and John Snaith, preist, all the lands and tenements in York and Ripon which devolved upon him after the death of his brother Richard Plumpton, to hold to the uses of his last will,[r] which is dated 14th November following; he thereby declared his intent to be, that they should grant the same premises "to the priest that by the grace of God shalbe made chauntry prest att the alter of Mary Magdalen in the parish kirk of Spofford in the county of York and to his successors, chauntery preists of the same; Trusting in God that I, mine executors, or some of my said welle dispozed feoffez, shall purchase and gett a licence of our soveraigne lord the King to stablish, found, create, and make a perpetuall chauntre of a preist att the aforesaid alter to serve God, and especially to pray to God for the soules of William Plompton knight and Alice his wife, my father and moder, for the soules of John Gisburgh and Ellen his wife, for my prosperity whilles I live in this world, and for my saule after I have taken the universall way, and for the saules of all them of whom said fader and mother, John Gisburgh and Ellen his wife, or I the said George, has had any goods of, and for the saules of all my fader and moder childer, and of all christen saules. Also, I will and grant, that after my decease and from the tyme that the mortsment be made of my forsaid lands and tenements to the Chauntry aforesaid, my nephew William Plompton, knight, and his heirs be the very patrons and giffers therof. Also, I will that for evermore, induring the said Chantry, my worshipfull fader and lord Tho: Spofford, late byshop of Hereford, be specially recommended in all the masses and suffrages to be done by the preste thereof, through whose good lordship and gracious favor, with great costs, I trust in God it shall come to good purpose after myne intent aforesaid."[s]

This venerable ecclesiastic passed the remainder of his life in the seclusion of Bolton Abbey in Craven; and the last memorial of him that has been preserved is a licence from John Sendale, Canon of York Cathedral, Vicar-general of William, Archbishop of York and Legate of the Holy See, for Master George Plompton to have masses celebrated in his presence in any fitting oratory within the monastery or priory of Bolton, for a year from the date thereof, *viz.* 4th Dec. 1459, 38 Hen. VI. with leave for his servants to hear the same.[t] To him at this place the following letter was addressed:

---

[n] This letter is transcribed into the Book of Letters among the Correspondence of Sir William Plumpton, but has been omitted in the series by reason of its diversity of date from the rest.
[o] Cartul. No. 516. "Dat. apud Fulham."
[p] Ibid. No. 517. "Dat. 24 Jun. 26 Hen. VI. 1448." In this charter the rectorial manse is described as a building with thatched roof and mud walls, *rectoria cum tectura straminia et muris luteis.*
[q] Ibid. No. 521. "Dat. Ebor:"
[r] Ibid. No. 518. "H. T. Henrico Percie comite Northumbr: Henrico Percie d'no de Ponyngs, Rogero Ward milite, Rogero Warde armigero, Ric. Lematon cive et mercatore Ebor: Johanne Clark de Spofford parcario, et multis aliis."
[s] Cartul. No. 520.
[t] Ibid. No. 523. "Dat. Riponiæ."

To Master George Plompton at Bolton abbey.

My best brother, I am sory by my troth that I shall nott see you, and cum thus far as to York. God knoweth my intent was not for no great gud that I thoght to desire, but I wott well now ye trusted the contrary. But, brother, it is not unknowne that I am right sickly, and my hart wold have bene gretly comforted to have spoken with you; but I trow, and so doth my daughter, that ye be displeased, denyeing that my writing afore, because she desired a booke of you. And as ever I be saved, she praied me write for either salter or primmer; and my hosband said, halfe apley, prey my brother to gett somwhat to my new chappell. God wot he ment neither gold nor silver, but some other thing for said awter. But I had knowne ye wold have bene displeased, I wold not have writt, for as much as I have speuled my best brother. My sister Dame Isabell liveth as heavy a life as any gentlewoman borne, the which cause me I faired never well since I saw her last month. Hous such, hath nether woman nor maide with her, but herselfe alone. And her hosband cometh all day to my hosband, and seyeth the feyrest langwage that ever ye hard. But all is rong, he is ever in trouble, and all the ioy on earth hath she whan my husband cometh to her; she sweareth there is noe creature she loveth better. Also, brother, I beseech you intirely, if there be any goodly yong woman, that is a good woman of her body and pay, iiij and xx or more, (and I would have one of my owne kin an theare were any), for my selfe and deare brother, and ye or any for you can espie, I beseech you to gitt her for me, as hastely as you may, soune upon Easter, and it may be. I can no more for great hast of my jorny, I beseech the blessed Trinitie with all the saints in heaven give me grace to se you, or I die, to Gods pleasure and your bodyly heale. And, brother, I yede to the lord Scroope[u] to have sene my lady;[x] and be my trothe, I stood thear a large houre, and yet I might neither se lord nor ladye, ad the strangest cheare, that ever I had, of my Mistres Darse,[y] and yet I had 5 men in a suit: there is no such 5 men in his house, I dare say.

              Be your sister.
              KA: CHADYRTON.[z]

The writer of this letter, Katharine Chadyrton, was the younger of the two daughters of Sir William Plumpton, kt. by Alice Gisburne, who yet remained unmarried at the time of their mother's death in 1423. Her husband, it may be presumed, was of the family of Chadderton of Chadderton Hall, in the chapelry of Oldham in Lancashire; but their pedigree is unknown to me, and the Plumpton evidences are unfortunately here of no assistance. Dame Isabel, her sister, whose domestic misery is so feelingly pourtrayed, was the wife of Sir Stephen Thorp of Gowsell or Goxhill, in the county of Lincoln, knight. Her marriage contract bears date 10 March, 3 Hen. VI. 1424-5, and was between Sir Robert de Hilton, kt. and Robert Constable, esq. feoffees of Stephen de Thorp, father of the said Stephen, on the one part, and George de

---

[u] Sir John Scrope, fourth Baron Scrope of Masham, summoned to Parliament from 7 Jan. 4 Hen. VI. 1426, to 26 May, 33 Hen. VI. 1455. Died 15 Nov. following.
[x] Elizabeth, daughter of Sir Thomas Chaworth of Wiverton, co. Notts. kt. Died 6 Edw. IV. 1466.
[y] Eleanor Scrope, daughter of Lord Scrope, married Richard Darcy, son and heir apparent of Sir John Darcy, of Hyrst, com. Ebor. knight, who was dead in his father's lifetime, before 1 Jun. 32 Hen. VI. 1454, when his heir, William, was four years old. John le Scrope, who died 12 Sept. 1452, in his will of the preceding day makes a bequest to "Mistres" his sister, *Magistrici sorori meæ.* There can be little doubt that Mrs. Darcy is here meant, and that it is an error on the part of the compiler of the pedigree of Scrope of Masham, illustrative of the Scrope and Grosvenor Controversy, to give *Magistrix* a distinct place among the children of Lord Scrope. Her husband had died young; and it appears from this letter that she passed her widowhood in the paternal mansion till the period of her second marriage with William Claxton, esq. circa 29 April, 38 Hen. VI. 1460.
[z] This letter is also taken from the Book of Letters, where it is transcribed at the end of the Correspondence of Sir William Plumpton.

Plompton, clerk, and Richard de Plompton, esq. brothers of the said Isabella, on the other part; by it the marriage portion was fixed at 80li, and she was to be jointured to the amount of 10li per annum out of premises in the counties of York and Lincoln.[a] Seisin was subsequently granted to Stephen Thorp, esq. and Isabella his wife, of lands and tenements in the vills of Frismersk and Attenwyk, in the county of York, in the vill of Lednam, and in the vills and territories of Gowsell and Barowe, by Ralph Smith, chaplain, constituted (10 Oct. 4 Hen. VI. 1425) attorney for the above feoffees, and for John Dysney and John Aseyn.[b] He was yet an esquire, 19 Hen. VI. 1410-1;[c] but we have a proof that he was knighted afterward in the title of Dame given to his wife in the above letter, which presents a somewhat curious picture of the social habits of the time. We learn from it that an old infirm priest had with characteristic selfishness, at a time when founding chantries for the good of souls absorbed the wealth of the dying, refused to give even a psalter or primmer to his niece, or to make any present to his brother-in-law's chapel, and had even quarrelled with his sister for making such request. We hear also of a knight's lady left without a single female attendant, and of an inquiry for a poor kinswoman to be hired, *if she be strong and can work for her pay*. And lastly, we have a Dame with five servants in her train made to dance attendance for an hour in the ante-chamber of a greater lady, and then

[a] Cartul. No. 424.
[b] Ibid. No. 412. Frishmarsh, now lost by the Humber, lay between Newsome (also lost) and Patrington, to which last Thorp was a berewick at the General Survey. Lib. Domesd. f. 302 a2.
[c] Ibid. No. 453. "Jacobus Hoton et Will's Ryson ar: concedunt terras, &c. in Thorp juxta Weldik, Wythornwyke, et Bilton in com. Ebor: quæ tenet Rob'tus de Thorpe. jun. ad terminum vitæ suæ—post decessum dicti Roberti, Stephano de Thorpe et Isabellæ uxori ejus et heredibus inter ipsos, &c. H. T. Joh'e Melton de Swyne, Thoma Grimston, Rob'to Hakfeld, Rob'ti Hylierd, armigeris, et Joh'e Aseyn et aliis. Dat. apud Thorpe juxta Weldyke, 12 Mar. 19 Hen. VI." This place is now called Welwickthorpe, from the Wel-wic instead of the Wel-dic, and is a hamlet in the township and parish of Welwick, *Tor-uelestorp* in Domesday.

dismissed, after receiving but strange cheer from the daughter of the house, though the parties were closely connected by ties of kindred, in fact, cousins in the second degree.

To return to Sir Robert Plumpton. He was a knight before the 15th Jan. 1410-1, 12 Hen. IV. when he made a feoffment of his estates in Yorkshire to Henry Lord Fitzhugh, Sir Richard Norton, William Ferman, rector of the church of Kirkby Oreblawer, and Richard Sudberi, rector of the church of Croston;[d] and as such was chosen to represent the shire of York in the Parliament which met on the 3d November, 13 Hen. IV. 1411. In the same reign (1 July, 13 Hen. IV.) I find a grant by Henry Beaufort, Bishop of Winchester, of an annual rent of xxli sterling out of his manor of Whitteny, in the county of Oxford, *pour le bon et greable service que notre trescher et tres bien amé Monsire Robert Plumpton chevaler ad fait et ferra en temps avenir*.[e] In 2nd Henry V. (14 Oct. 1414) Sir Robert Plumpton was Seneschal of the Honour of Knaresborough, as also one of the Council of the King of his Duchy of Lancaster, together with Sir Roger Leche, knight, Chief Seneschal of the lands of the King of his Duchy of Lancaster towards the north part and elsewhere.[f] In 3d Hen. V. (15 Oct. 1415), he was retained to serve the Duke of Bedford for life, in peace and in war, having xx marks as his fee in time of peace, and the usual wages suitable to his degree in time of war, together with *bouche du courte* for himself, an esquire, and his two valets, when at the hostelry of the Prince, or in his company.[g]

[d] Cartul. No. 354.   [e] Ibid. No. 359 and 360.   [f] Ibid. No. 368.
[g] "Ceste endenture fait dentre le haut et puissant prince, Johan fitz et frere des Roys, duc de Bedford, Count de Richmond et Kendale, et Conble d'engleterre, dun part, et Robert de Plompton, Chevaler, dautre part, tesmoigne que le dit Robert est retenuez et demorrez pardevers le dit tres noble et puissant prince a terme de sa vie pour lui servir, sibien en temps de pees come de guerre, au mielz qui resonablement il pourra estre en son pouoir, preignant annuelment du dit haut et puissant prince pour son fe a cause de sa dite demoere vingt marcs en temps de pees de les cofres de mesme le haut et puissant prince. Et sera le dit Robert montéz, armés, et arraiés, come a son degre et estat appartient, et prest de chivalcher oves le susdit tres noble et puissant prince en sa compaignie, a quel temps que a ce fair il sera deper mesme le puissant prince garniz ou requiz, preignant en temps de guerre du dit tres noble et puissant prince, quant travelliera ovec luy, pour luy mesmez, et ses gentz, lesquex il amesnera oves luy par comaundement de le dit haut et puissant prince, tieulx gagez come autres gentilx de lour degree prendront pour le temps, rebatant toutesvoies lafferant de son fe en temps de pees pour lafferant de ses gagez en temps de guerre, en cas qil travaille ove le dit tresnoble et puissant prince a aucuns journes que se tiendra pur un quarter del an ou plus, et nemye pour nulle autre petit journes que se namontera al quarter dan. Et aura le dit Robert quant il travelliera oves le dit tresnoble prince en sa compaigne en temps de pees, ou veigne a son houstell per son comaundement, bouche du courte pour luy mesmes, un escuier, et deux ses valetts, en tiele regarde come au dit tres noble prince il plerra. Et de toutez maners de prisoners et autres profittz et gaignes de guerre quelconques en aucune manere per le dit Robert prisez ou gaignes, le dit tres noble et puissant prince aura la tierce ; et de tous autres ses ditz gentz lesqueulx il aura as gages, de mesme le tres noble prince la tierce de la tierce. Et si aucun chevitaigne ou autre grand sera soit pris per le dit Robert ou aucun de ses ditz gentz, le dit tres noble et puissant prince aura le chevitaigne ou seigneur avant dit, fesant a celly que luy prist resonable regarde. En tesmoignance du quele chose sibien le dit prince come le dit Robert a cestes endentures entrechangeablement ount mys lour sealx. Donne a le manor de Bisshopthorp le xv jour d'octobre, lan du duigne notre soverain sire le Roy Henri quint puis le conquest tierce." (*Cartul*. No. 373.)

[h] Cartul. No. 361.

On the seventh of October, the feast of St. Marcus, Pope, 6 Hen. IV. 1404, Sir Robert Plumpton had born to him a son and heir,[h] afterward Sir William Plumpton, knt. and the same with whose correspondence the series of letters commence. Of this son, when in his twelfth year, the marriage was contracted for on the part of Sir Bryan de Stapilton, of Carlton, com. Ebor. knight, in behalf of his daughter Elizabeth, an infant of the same tender years. The agreement bears date 20 Jan. 3 Hen. V. 1415-16; thereby Sir Bryan accords, that a sum of CCCLX marks be paid to Sir Robert Plumpton for the marriage, he agreeing to settle an estate of xx marks yearly in the vill of Kinalton on his son William and Elizabeth, and their issue. He was further to engage to make a feoffment to Sir Richard Redmayn, knight, John de Moute, esq. Robert Brame and Roger Spofford, chaplains, of the manor of Steton, to secure a rent-charge of XL marks yearly, in case that if the said William and Elizabeth were legally ousted of the estate in Kynalton by Sir Robert or his heirs, or the heirs of Dame Alice his late wife, then the feoffees to convey the same to William and Elizabeth. Within a month after the death of his mother, Dame Alice de Plumpton, Sir Robert was to add x marks to the yearly rent out of Kynalton, except in case Dame Margaret Rempston or Thomas Foljambe[i] pre-deceased his mother, or that she herself happened to die during the minority of her grandson William. There were beside covenants for re-payment of the principal, in case of either of the parties dying without issue, or of divorce before consummation, as well as of a further sum of L marks for the costs of their maintenance. It was also stipulated that Sir Robert de Plompton should not make any feoffment or estate to the disinherison of the said William, his son, of the land which he held, either by descent, or curtesy after the death of Dame Alice his late wife; save only he might give rent-charges of xx marks each to his two younger sons Godfrey and Robert, with right of mutual accretion in case of either of them being promoted to a benefice, or advantaged by marriage, and of survivoship in case of death. Also, he might jointure any future wife he might take to himself, so as the jointure did not exceed c marks. Sir Bryan de Stapilton and Dame Agnes his wife were to have the governance of the said William and Elizabeth during their minority, receiving for their sustenance the rent of xx marks out of Kynalton; but in case Sir Bryan should happen to die, and his widow take a second husband, then Sir Robert was to have the governance of the betrothed parties.[k]

In 1416, 4 Hen. V. Sir Robert de Plompton was Steward of the Forest of Knaresborough, as well as Seneschal of the Honour.

[i] Thomas Foljambe was great-uncle of Dame Alice, the relict of Sir Robert de Plompton, and at the time of her birth was, with his brother Robert, her nearest heir and next of kin. From him descended the knightly family settled at Walton in com. Derb.
[k] Cartul. No. 374. Sir Bryan Stapleton died abroad in 1417, leaving Agnes, daughter of Sir John Godard, kt. his widow, who survived him many years and never remarried.

" Unto the worshipfull and reverent Sir, Monsire Robert de Plompton, steward of the forest of Knaresburgh, or to his deputies, William Bedale, mercer, Richard Bellingham, mercer, John Unthank, spicer, William Garnet, bower, Tho: Constable, fletcher, and Tho: Lincolne, Citizens of York, send honor and reverence; for als mekill als an John of Lawe, chapman, sold unto Richard Clerk of Burebrig a pak with divers mercery therein and a horse for xx^{ie} nobles of the Kings coyn, on thursday next after St. Elen day last past, in the towne of Burebrig, als wee are fully by true men enformed : and for als mekill als it is needfull and necessary thing to all christen men to record and beare witness o' the soth, we do ye to witt that the gude quilk the foresaid John sold att Burebrig was his awen proper gude, and lelely and truly bought and sold, and a gude man of name and fame evere zhit was and is halden amang us, and for na nother nevere zhit was halden ne reccond. And this witnesse we by this our present letter, written and seald att Yorke, the xxiiij day of May in the yeare of King Henry fift after the conquest of England, fourth." [l]

Sir Robert de Plompton made a further feoffment of all his manors and reversions in Yorkshire to Henry Fitzhugh, lord of Ravenswath and Treasurer of England, Dame Margaret de Rempston, Dame Alice de Plumpton his mother, John Grene de Nuby, William Ferman, parson of the church of Kirkby Orblawers, and John Brennand of Knaresburgh, on the 6th November 1416;[m] the purport of which feoffment, by an instrument dated at Plumpton, 1 April, 6 Hen. V. 1418, was declared to be for securing to Godfrey and Robert de Plumpton their annuities of xx marks each ; and if it should so fall out that he the said Sir Robert de Plump-

[l] Cartul. No. 372. St. Elen day was the feast of the Invention of the Holy Cross, 3 May.

[m] Ibid. 384. " Dat. apud Plumpton in festo S^{ci} Leonardi Abbatis, anno r. r. Henr. filii Regis Henr. quarto."

ton, knight, should die before his coming into England, the residue was to be applied according to the directions in his last will. The said feoffees were also to marry his daughters Joan and Alice suitably, and to give xl marks to his sisters Isabella and Katharine for their marriage, and xl^s yearly to his brother Richard of the manor of Nesfield near Addingham.[n] On the 11th day of the same month of April, I find Sir Robert de Plumpton was to be at the muster at Southampton *pour le viage notre Sire le Roy devers son Roialme de France*, in the retinue of the Lord Fitzhugh ; [o]

[n] Cartul. No. 399.

[o] " Ceste endenture fait par entre Monsr Robert de Plompton Ch'r dun part, et John de Pancesbery deverwyke dautre part, tesmoigne que le dit Johr est demoures une home darmes devers le dit Monsr Robert ovec deux archers pur luy servir pur un an entier en un viage notre Sire le Roy devers son Roialme de France, ou autrement en autre lieu, ou luy plerra, lan comenceant le jour del an que le dit John et sex deux archers seront a la mear, prestz pur y fair lour monstres selounque lordenaunce ent fait, et le dit John prendra pur luymesme douuze deniers le jour et chescun le ses archers syse deniers le iour, ovet eskippesson et reskippesson pur cink chevaulx pur luy dit John et sa retenue. Et lavaunt dit John serra tenuz destre bien armes et arraies de novell manere, et il et ses deux archers seront ensy bien et cuvenablement montes et arraiez solounque lours estatz, et tout pretz au port de Southampton le unszisme iour daprill prochein venaunt a y fair touts monstres devaunt les comissioners notre Sire le Roy a ces assignes, a taunt des foitchez, de la mear ou autrement, come ils seront resonablement garniz depart le dit Monsr Robert. Et le dit John prendra gages pur luy et ses deux archers es mayns pur un quart entier del an avauntdit. Preignaunt suertees pur luy et ses deux archers pur ses autres trois quartres del an avaun$t$dit per mesme la forme ou semblable come le dit Monsr Robert prendera de le Sire Fitzhughe. Cest assavoir, le dit John prendera douze deniers le jour, & cescun de les deux archers prendera sise deniers le jour. Et avera le dit Monsr Robert la tierce de toutz prisez & gaignez de guerre, des presoners come des autres choises, per le dit John prises ou gaignez, et le tierce de la tierce de ses deux archers en ascune manere gaignez, en semblable condicion al effect & purport des endentures a mon dit Sr Robert de Plompton faitz de sa retenu devers le Sire Fitzheugh, des queux gaignez, prises, & tierces partes le dit John & ses deux archers ferront a mon dit Sr Robert pleyne conusaunce & notice, si bien prisoners & autres gaignez de guerre, come de lour value, saunce concelement en ascune partie, deinz septz iours apres tielx prises ou gaignez faitz, sur payne de forfair au dit Monsr Robert la value de ycelle concelement. En tesmoignaunce de quele choses les parties suisditz a ycestes indentures extrechangeablement ount mys lour seals. Done a Knaresburgh, la douszisme iour de Marce, lan de reigne notre S^r le Roy Henri Quint puis le Conquest quint." *(Cartul. N° 397.)*

and as about to go abroad, he had the usual letters of protection from the Duke of Bedford, Guardian of England, *tested* at Southampton 29th of the same month.[p] On the 21st of June, 7 Hen. V. 1419, while yet abroad, he contracted for the marriage of Joan his daughter to William Slingsby of Scriven, in com. Ebor. esq., Sir Thomas Rempston, kt. his brother-in-law (son of Dame Margaret Foljambe, mother of Alice, Sir Robert's deceased wife, by her second husband, Sir Thomas Rempston, K. G.) being also a covenanting party on her behalf.[q]

Sir Robert Plumpton was again in England before 27th Aug. following;[r] and on the 24th Sept. 8 Hen. V. 1420, he enfeoffed Dame Alice de Plompton his mother, Richard de Norton, Chief Justice of the Common Bench, Thomas de Rempston, ch'r, John Butler, esq. and John Grene, in his manors of Plompton, Idill, Steton in Aierdale, and Nesfeld, with the advowson of his chantry of the

[p] Carte, Catalogue des Rolles Gascons. fol. Lond. 1743, vol. 2. p. 235.

[q] Cartul. N°. 402. By the contract William Slengsby, esquier, undertook, within six weeks after his coming into the realms of England, to enfeoffe, or cause to be enfeoffed, Sir Thomas Rempston and Sir Robert Plumpton, knights, in lands of his heritage in the townes of Scriven, Knaresburgh Farnham, and Wiclif, to the value of xl marks; to hold to the use and profit of Jenett, one of the daughters of the said Sir Robert, getten of the body of Alison, sometyme his wife, and sister of the said Sir Thomas, during her life, unless the marriage betwixt the said William and hir as here by theis foresaid parties it is spoken and accorded, be not maked. Witnesses, Robert Swillingdon, Giles Dawbeny, Tho. Saint Quintyn, William Hudelston, kts. and William Wakefield, Nicholas Ward, and John Thorp, esquires.

[r] Cartul. No. 403. The deed of this date contains a covenant between Sir R. Plumpton, kt. and Dame Alice Chelray, prioress of Esshold and the convent of the same, whereby the latter, in exchange for a licence to hold in severalty and inclose two assarts, called Over-holme, Nether-holme, Stragilforc, Lang-holme, and Alridrode, which they held of the gift of Neil de Plompton, and other ancestors of the said Sir Robert, in the vill of Idill, agreed to quitclaim to the former all their rights of pasture and pannage in the wood of Idill; provided always, that a chaplain should continue to sing perpetually for the soul of *Dominus Robertus filius Roberti de Plompton*, according to the tenor of a charter made by the same to God and St. Leonard of Eshold. The charters containing these endowments will be found in the Monasticon, new edit. vol. V. p. 472; but the name of Alice Chelray is omitted in the list of Prioresses of Esholt.

Holy Trinity in the church of Ripon, in com. Ebor., and in the reversions of a rent-charge of four marks, issuing out of the manor of Plompton, which Dame Isabell, late wife of Sir Robert Plumpton, kt. his grandfather, had of his grant for term of life in lieu of dower, and of the manors of Gersington in Craven, and Little Studley, after the decease of Alice his mother. [s] But the following indenture shows him to have been at Portsmouth, with archers in his retinue, on the 12th Oct. next ensuing, on his route to cross the sea on an expedition into France.

" This indenture, made the yeare of our soveraigne Lord King Henry the Vth after the Conquest the viiith, betwixt Robert of Plompton, knight, of the to party ; John Fleetham, Tho. Clerke, William Chamberlaine, Robert Barden, Henry of Ripley, Robert Morton, William Cowper, Hugh Coke, of the tother party ; beares witness that the foresaid John, Tho. Will'm Chamberlaine, Rob't Barden, Henry, Rob't of Morton, be left with the foresaid Robert as archers for to serve the foresaid Robert for a twelve moneth, and to take for their service for the foresaid twelvemoneth for their fee, ilkane of them, xl^s, and bouch of Court, clothing, & horsing ; that is for to say, the foresaid Rob't shall deliver unto ilkane of them a horse, and the foresaid John, Thomas, Will'm Chamberlain, Rob't Barden, Henry & Rob't of Morton grants truly to keepe watch and ward as langes to souldiers for to do ; and they that are att horsing of the foresaid Robert truly to pay unto him halfe the gude that they win by war ; and they that are at their own horsing, truly to pay him the third parte at they win be were. And the foresaid Will'm Cowper to take for his fee ii marcs, clothing, bouch of court, and a horse, and for to fulfill and pay truly, and kepe watch and ward as it is said before. And the

[s] Cartul. No. 405. *Dat. apud Plumpton, xxiiii^{to} die mensis Septembris, anno r. r. Hen. V. post conq. Angliæ octavo.* The witnesses were, Sir Thomas de Markinfeld, Sir Roger Ward, Sir Richard de Goldsbrough, Sir Halnath Malleverer, knights, William de Beckwith, William Pensax, William de Hopton, Henry de Chambre, John Pulane and others.

foresaid Hugh to take of the foresaid Robert xx^s, and to serve him for the twelvemoneth like as Will'm beforesaid is boun, and truly to pay and to do all manner of covenants as it is said before. And also the foresaid John, Thomas, Will'm Chamberlaine, Rob't Barden, Henry, Rob't of Morton, Will'am Cowper, and Hugh Coke sall serve him, as it is beforesaid, in what were he goes, to the twelvemoneth fully be ended. In to the witnes of this, the parties beforesaid have setto their sealls. Written att Porchmouth, the xiiith day of October, the yeare of our soveraigne Lord the King beforesaid."^{t}

In the following year, as we learn from an *Inquisitio post mortem*^{u} and from the epitaph on his monument in the church of Spofforth, Sir Robert Plumpton died. It was a tradition in the family that he was slain in France, his death occurring abroad at the time of the siege of Meaux; but the epitaph reads simply,

"*Hic jacet Robertus Plompton, mil. nuper Senescallus de Knaresborough, et Alicia uxor ejus, filia & heres Godfridi Foljambe, mil. qui Robertus obiit* 8 *Decembris* 1421, *quorum animabus propitietur Deus.*"^{x}

The issue of Sir Robert Plumpton and Alice Foljambe were three sons: 1. William, in his eighteenth year at the time of his father's death; 2. Godfrey, married to Alice, daughter and coheir of Thomas Wintringham of Knaresborough, by Alice daughter of John Dobson, before 37 Hen. VI. 1459;^{y} 3. Robert, known only by his father's deeds of settlement; and two daughters, 1. Joan, contracted, as is abovesaid, to marry William Slingsby, of Scriven,

^{t} Cartul. No. 407. ^{u} Esc. 11 Hen. VI. No. 5.
^{x} This inscription, which wants literal exactness, is taken from a copy in the notices of the family of Foljambe, by N. Johnston, M. D. 1701. printed in the Coll. Top. et Gen. vol. I. p. 91. (*Vide No.* 107. *p.* 341.)
^{y} Curia tenta apud Knaresburgh die mercurii p'x' ante festu' Sc'i Laurenci, a^o r. r. Hen. Sexti xxxvii. Alicia nuper ux. Tho. Wintringham—ad opus Johannæ et Aliciæ ux. Godfrid' Plompton, filiarum dictoruin Thomæ et Aliciæ. (*Cartul.* No. 494 & 495.)

21 June, 1419; 2. Alice, whose alliance is doubtful: but either she or her sister became the wife of John Grene of Newby, com. Ebor. esq. previous to the 1st Jan. 5 Hen. VI. 1426-7.^{z}

The wardship of William de Plumpton, till he attained his age, devolved of right upon the Earl of Northumberland as lord of the Percy fee, of which the chief manor in Plumpton was held.

" To all men that heares and sees thes present letteres, Henry Percy, Earle of Northumberland, sends greeting. Knaw ye us have ordayned and assigned our welbeloved William Whitehill, bailif of our best beloved sister of Clifford, as well for to distreyne as to receive the farme of our tenants of Steton in Ayerdale, quilk to us perteyns because of nonage of the heire of Sir Robert Plompton, and the money thereof receyved to deliver to Richard Fairfax, squier, att our costage. And witt ye, that we have charged our Steward Sir John Langton, John Aske, and our officers of Spofforth, to be furthering and helping to you in this matter, if need be, for to distreyne; and this lettere sall be your warrant. Written att our mannor of Toplif, xiii day of September, in the yeare of King Henry sext, after the conquest second." ^{a}

Having now attained his majority, " Willelmus Plumpton, de comitatu Ebor. armiger," procured letters of general attorney, tested at Westminster 27 Jan. 5 Hen. VI. 1426-7, and shortly after set out

^{z} A toutz yceux, &c. Will'm de Plompton, saluz en dieu. Sachez moy avoir done & graunte a mon chier & bien amie frere John Grene un anuel rent de quatre marcz dez issuz et p'fitz de mon manoir de Garsington en Craven, &c. et vesture de son lyverey a son degre, &c. Et le dit John serra seneschall au dit Will'm de toutz ses terres et ten'tz en le counte d'Everwyke au vollour du dit Will'm. En tesmoignaunce, &c. Done apud Plompton le primer jour de Janyver, lan du reigne le Roy Henri sisime puis le conquest quint. (*Chartul.* No. 418.) Alice is put down as the wife of Richard Marley in a pedigree of Plumpton, in Harl. MSS. 1487. A John Marley was a feoffee for the family 12 Jan. 17 Edw. IV. 1478, and William and Isabel Marley are named in Sir William Plumpton's Correspondence; but no proof of consanguinity is to be obtained from existing evidences, and the match is too early for a Herald's Visitation to be relied upon as an authority.
^{a} Cartul. No. 419.

for the wars in France;^{b} from which service he had returned but just before 28 Sept. 9 Hen. VI. 1430, being then a knight.^{c} I next find him involved in a dispute concerning land with Ralph, Earl of Westmorland, which was agreed to be referred to arbitrators, viz. William Lumley and William Garth, esquires, and William Hoton, chosen on the part of the Earl, and John Leek, Thomas Foliambe, esquires, and Richard Byngham, on his part, with Henry Earl of Northumberland for umpire. The bond, conditional upon the performance of this award, is dated 14 Mar. 10 Hen. VI. 1431-2;^{d} but no final decision appears to have been come to at that time, and recourse was had to a second agreement of similar import.

"This bill indented bears witness that the right worshipfull Lord the Earl of Westmerland, Sir John Nevill, knight, and William Nicholson, balife of Ashford, by the advise of Sir Richard Vernon, knight, and other of the counsell of the said Earle and Sir John Nevill, upon that one party, and William Plompton, knight, upon that other party, have compromitted them either party, to stand to the award and arbitrament of a squier and a man of counsell learned in the law chosen upon that one party, and a squier and a man of counsell learned in the law chosen upon that other party, of all manner accions real and personall, quarrells and demaunds had betwixt them, or any of them, before the makeing of this indenture, so that that award and arbitrament be made before the feast of Allhalowes next comeing. And if so be that the said arbitrators may not accord before the said feast of Allhalowes, then the said parties be the advise abovesaid are agreed to abide the award and ordinance in the matter abovesaid of an Noumper to be chosen be the said arbitrators, so that the said award and ordinance of the

^{b} Carte. Catalogue des Rolles Gascons, Normans et François. Londres, fol. 1743, vol. II. p. 257.
^{c} Cartul. No. 425. Will's Repington, ar.—Will'mo Plompton, militi. Dat. apud Amynton in vigilia S'ti Mich'is, anno r. r. Hen. VI. nono.
^{d} Ibid. No. 427.

said Nowmper be made be the feast of the Nativity of our Lord then next comeing. And sufficient suerty in a c^{li} for to be bounden for either of the said parties for to abide the said award and arbitrament of the said arbitrators, and the said award and ordinance of the said noumper. And the day (of) treaty of the said arbitrators to be holden upon the ground that is in debate betwixt the said parties, if (it) like the said Earle, before the utas of St. Michaell next comeing after the makeinge of this indenture. And furthermore the said parties are agreed that eiticon of them shall have a man att York, in the feast of the exaltacion of the Holy Crosse next comeing, in the Chapiter-house of the Cathedrall kirk of Yorke, betwixt the sonrysing and the son setting, for to appointe the said arbitrators, the day of the treaty abovesaid, and persons that shall be bounden in the c^{li} abovesaid; and either of the said parties shall give their man sufficient power thereto. Written att Derby, the xxiiith day of July, in the yeare of the reigne of King Henri the Sext efter the Conquest of Ynglond, xiiith. ^{e} "

In 14 Hen. VI. 1435-6, Sir William Plompton, knt. was a Commissioner with Sir William Gascoigne, Sir Robert Waterton, knts. William Ingelby, Thomas Clarell, Guy Fairfax, John Thwaites, John Gascoigne, and Robert Malleverer, to array men-at-arms, hoblers, and archers, in the Westrithing of Yorkshire, and to send them to the sea coast to repel the threatened invasion; also to make muster of the said troops, and to place signals called *Bekyns* in accustomed and convenient places, to warn the people of the approach of the enemy.^{f} To a deed of this Sir William Plompton, dated at Kenalton, 10 April, 17 Hen. VI. 1439, conveying to feoffees, viz. Sir Thomas Rempston, kt. Dame Agnes Stapilton, Sir Brian Stapilton, kt. Ranulph Pygot, esq. William Rempston, rector of the church of Byngham, Robert Rempston, Richard Redman, senior, esq. Richard Askham, and William Wood, chaplain, his estates in the

^{e} Cartul. No. 434.
^{f} Cartul. No. 436. Teste me ipso apud Westm', 18 Jan. anno regni n'ri 14.

counties of Nottingham, Derby, and Stafford, together with the reversion of what Dame Margaret Rempston held for term of life, a very fair seal remained attached, 27 Apr. 1616, of which the copyist makes note " that it hath the Plompton armes quartered with the Foliamb's arms, and the Roebuck, and was supported by a woman, and hath *Will'm's Plompton de Plompton* written in the circumference, and it is the first deed that is found to be sealled with the same seale."[g]

Sir William Plumpton was Seneschal and Master Forester of the Honour and Forest,[h] and Constable of the Castle,[i] of Knaresborough from about the 17th year of Henry VI. 1439, to the close of that reign, Piers Ardern being deputy the while of William de la Poole, Earl of Suffolk, the Chief Seneschal of the King of his Duchy of Lancaster in the North parts;[k] in which jurisdiction the Honour of Knaresborough had been included from the time of its being granted in 1371 by Edward III. to John of Gaunt, Duke of Lancaster. During his tenure of office, a dispute as to the right of the tenants of the forest of Knaresborough to pay toll at fairs, was made the preliminary to a serious affray with the officers, tenants, and servants of John Kemp, Cardinal and Archbishop of York, on the 5th of May, 19 Hen. VI. 1441, in which lives were lost. The particulars of this affair may be collected from the following declaration, which, as it serves to illustrate the manners of the times, I set forth entire.

" Please the King of his grace to be remembred how that his tenants of the forest of Knaresborough have sewed continually unto his highnes since Michaelmas terme was thre years, and all for his right, desyring by all the bills given to his highnes, that the matter of the right of toll might take such end as his law would; the whilk unto this day could not be had, but ever hath bene adiourned and delayed from tearme to tearme. And the said Archbishop hath, all the said tyme of suite of the said Kings tenants, hath kept his towne of Ripon at fair tymes by night, like a towne of warr, with souldiers hired for their wages like as it had bene in the land of warr, so that none of the Kings said tenants might, ne durst, come att the towne of Ripon, all the said tearme of thre yeares, to utter their caffer, wherewith to pay his farme att tearmes accustomed, for dread of death. Now late this last fair tyme, the Archbishop' officers by his commaundement kept the said towne of Ripon like a towne of warr, with souldiers waged thither out of Tindale and Hexhamshire and of other partes nigh unto Scotland, into the number of cc men of armes, rideing and comeing fro the said parts unto Ripon like men of were, with brest plate, vambraes and rerebrace, greves and quischers, gorgett and salett, long spears and lancegayes ; and the simplest arrayed of all the said persons had either a gestiment, or a hawburgon, or a thick jack, upon him, and either a pricknighate or a sallett upon their heads ; and there

---

[g] Cartul. No. 443. These estates, which had been the property of the Foljambes, comprised the manors of Kenalton, Hassop, Wormehill, Pillesley, Stantonhall, Chelmerton and Combrigge, together with land and tenements in Bakewell, Tiddeswall, Queston, Flagfeld, Martinside, Cumbes, Wardlow, Hurdlow, Spoundon, Lokhaw, Twyford, Turndike, Broughton, Crakemarsh, Monyashe, Chesterfield, and Chaddesden, with the advowsons of chantries in the churches of Bakewell and Mansfeld Woodhous.

[h] Cartul. No. 469. 17 Hen. VI. M[d] q'd Tho. de Thorp & Tho. Brig parcarii parci de Hawray iiij[to] Octob. ult. p'terito deliberaverunt Will'o Plompton, militi, Senescallo ac Magistro Forestario Honoris de Knaresburgh, infra parcum predictum viij[xx]. ferarum, per visum Tho. Beckwith, Rad'i Beckwith, Joh'is Beckwith, ac aliorum, &c. Haverah park (extra-parochial), containing upwards of 2,000 acres, is now divided into farms, the property of Sir William A. Ingilby, bart. in 1439 we learn from this document that it contained 160 head of game. In the Cartulary are copies of the returns of the game, and of the distribution of the same during several years of Sir William Plumpton's occupancy of the office of chief forester in the reign of Henry VI.

[i] Cartul. No. 452. Littera attorn. ad deliberandam seisinam D'no Will'o Plompton, militi, Constabulario castri de Knaresb: Dat. apud Knaresburgh, 3 Jun. 18 Hen. VI.

[k] Cartul. No. 448. Indentura inter Petrum ardern, deputatum Will'mi de la Poole, Comitis Suff: capitalis senescalli d'ni Regis Ducatus sui Lancastriæ in partibus boreal: ex parte una & Johannam nuper uxorem Will'mi Ingilby, militis, defuncti ex parte altera, de firma herbagii & agistamenti parei de Bilton infra dominium de Knaresb: in com. Ebor. Dat. 16 Dec. 18 Hen. VI.

---

came out of Beverley, Cawood, and Yorke into the number of an c persons in likewise arraied, save only speares, lancegaies and breast plate. And the said people, with many other persons of Ripon and Otlay, kept the said towne of Ripon like a towne of warr, takeing some vi[d] a day, and xii[d] a day, and bouch of court, thus waged by Hugh Pakham.[l] And they went robling up the said towne and downe ; they said openly (it was the most continuall language that they had during the said faire), ' *Would God there knaves and lads of the forest would come hider that we might have a faire day upon them,*' and other words of great scorne, rebuke, and provokeing. And this said fellowship, when the faire was done, saw that none of the said forest came thither, so that they might have nothing a doe with them, abode all a day after the faire in the said towne of Ripon, that is to say, on thursday the iiij[th] day of Maie, to take purpose what they would do, or they went out of the country ; for the marchmen were ashamed to come so farr, and not to be noysed with none affray, or they went out of the Country. And so that day the marchmen, by the advice of their persons, took to purpose that they would ride to Yorke with the other persons of York, Cawood, and Beverley, that was xxx miles and more out of their way, and that they would ride throughout Burghbrigg, a towne of the Lordship of Knaresburgh. And certaine persons of Ripon that were well willing unto the aforesaid tenants of Knaresburgh send word unto the said towne of Burghbrigg of their purpose, and the aforesaid tenants of Burghbrigg send word unto Sir William Plompton, that is Justice of and Steward of the said Lordship, of their purpose ; and he sent word againe to Burghbrigg, on the said thursday at even, that the balif with the tenants of the said towne should keep the said towne all that night unto the morne after, that was Friday the vth day of Maie, unto he came himself to se the peace kept, and the good rule and the demeyning of the said towne. And that said nighte certaine persons, into the number of forty persons, went out of the said Lordsh p by nightertale that none of the officers wiste of, over the water of Yure, and went unto Thornton brigg, the whilk is two miles and more fro Burghbrigg, to the intent to have arreasted certaine persons that had spoyled and fairen foule with one of the aforesaid tenants wife of the said forest, att the said towne of Ripon, on a market day late afore this last faire. And on the friday the said v[th] of Maie, Sir William Plompton with other officers came to Burghbrig or the sun rose, and with him into xxiiij persons, for the keping of the peace ; and spirred of the said tenants of the aforesaid towne of the governance and rule that night, and they lett him witt of their persons that were gone out on the said night; and he sent a man to them in all that he might ride, and charged them on the Kings behalf to come againe to the said towne of Burghbrig. And, or the messenger was ridden half a mile without the said towne of Burghbrig, he was perceived of all the said souldiers of the marchmen, and of Yorke, Beverley, Cawood, Otlay, and all of Ripon that they might gett, how they went riding to the said Thorntonbrig, where the said forty persons lay ; for the souldiers were warned by a spie of the said small fellowship that were so gone out att night, and so changed their purpose fro Burghbrig, and thought to have overridden and slayne this said forty persons that lay at Thorntonbrig. And this said messenger seing this great sight of arrayed people, and how they rode the high way unto Thorntonbrigge, rode againe in all that he might into the said Sir W[m] Plompton and told him all the case. And he, with officers of the said forest, rode to themward in all that they might pricke, to thintent to have mett and treate with them of Ripon in saving and keeping of the peace, or they had met with these forty persons, that lay at the said brigg, that knew not of them, nor of their great strengthe, till they sodainly mett and affrayed togeather. And so the said Sir William Plompton, with the aforesaid other

---

[l] Hugh Pakenham or Pagnam was brother of the Treasurer of York Cathedral. A letter from him to Sir William Plumpton will be found among the Correspondence.

officers, rode to them, and peaced all that they might, so that wer ne he had bene there, had mickle mischief fallen; and the said Sir William, with other officers, saved and kept all that were overcomen like to have bene mischeived, and brought them into such ward as they desired: and this shalbe soothed in all that truthe requires."

The Cardinal Archbishop of York had some time previous to this affray made complaint to the King in writing at his manor of Kenington, of the riotous behaviour of those dwelling within the verge of the forest, and had obtained letters under the royal signet addressed to Sir William Plompton and others his officers in the lordship of Knaresborough; by which the King straitly charged him, and by him as well all his tenants and the inhabitants of the said lordship, to keep the peace toward the said Cardinal and Archbishop and his officers and tenants, mainly, of his lordship of Ripon. He now exhibited a fresh bill of complaint, headed, "Thes bene the artikles of the Cardinall of Yorke of the offences and occasion done by Sir William of Plompton, Thomas Beckwith, and other misdoers and rioters of the forest of Knaresbroughe."

By the first of these articles it is set forth, "That Thomas of Beckwith, John Fawks, William Wakefeild, John Beckwith of Killinghall, and many others of the said forest of Knaresborough, and with as they had assocyed to the number of DCC persons or thereabouts, be the covyne and assent of Sir William Plompton, knight, arrayed in manner of war, and in ryotous wise assembled and gadred the xxii[th] day of July, the xviii yeare of the reigne of our Lord the King, against his peace and laws, went the same day to Ottlay, the faire the said towne that tyme being, (the which towne and faire are the said Cardinall and Archbishop as in right of his church of Yorke,) not to buy nor make frut of marchandize their, but rather disposed to bete, as it is semed, wholen and be manassys pretying; and their said forcible comeing put Robert Malleverer, steward, John Thoresby, balif, and other of the said Cardinall and Archbishop officers their, which were few in number and had not supposing of any such assembly, namely, considering the Kings said letters, in great feare and doubt of their persons, saying to them that they should not take, aske, nor receive their any toll of any men of the said forest. And so letted the said steward, balif, and other officers beforesaid, that they might not frely nor surely occupy, nor use the rule and governaile of the said faire, nor gader in the name and right of the said Cardinall and Archbishop the toll due and accustomed. And caused much people, that coming to the said faire to have bought, and sold to departe fro the said faire without their buying and selling; and also letted other to come thither, to the great prejudice, hurt, and harme of the said Cardinall and Archbishop, and great affray of the Kings people."

The second and following articles count divers outrages committed on the person and property of John Walworth, balye of the Cardinal of his lordship of Ripon, dwelling in Thornton wood within the franchise of the said Ripon, in the month of August following, by Thomas Beckwith, John Fawks, Raphe Pullaine and others, by the assent and covine of the said Sir William, and set forth the refusal of Sir William Plompton, Tho: Beckwith and others to treat with Master John Marshall, an officer of the said Cardinal, and Richard Redmayne, esq. for the recognition of the King's peace.

The seventh article contains as follows: "*Item.* The said Raphe Pulleyn, with other of the said misdoers and rioters, in great and notable numbers, by permision, ordinance, and assent of the said Sir William Plompton, Tho. Beckwith, John Fawks, and of the remnant of the said misdoers, arrayed in manner of war and in riotouswise, the Thursday the iiijth day of May last past, att Skitbrigg, lay in waite to beat and to sley the officers, servants, and tenants of the said Cardinall, that had bene att his fair of Ripon, entending upon the good rule and governance thereof, if they had come that way. And semblably the same day was laid att Burghbrig another great and notable fellowship, by thas-

sent as before, to the intent to have beaten and slaine the said officers, servants, and tenants next before rehearsed, if they had come that way. And to thintent that they would not be letted of their said malicious purpose, by any warninge that might have bene given of their said lying there in wait to the said officers, servants, and tenants, wher so was that one William, servant of the said Cardinall of his Citty of York, was past the said towne of Burghbrig toward Ripon nere hand the space of halfe a myle, they doubting least that any warning should have bene given to the said officers, servants, and tenants by the said William, sent fower of their company after him to take him; and so took him, and, magre him, brought him againe to their said fellowship att Burghbrig, and there held him in prison att the house of one John Fery unto the morne about ix of the bell. And when so was that the said misdoers were learned by their especialls, or such as were favorable of their said malicious purpose, that the said officers, servants, and tenants of the said Cardinall, had knowledge of their said lying in waite for them, and were disposed therefore to eschew that way, and to take the way to York-ward by Thornton brig, they dressed them to the said Thornton brig, part of them the said night, and parte on Friday on the morne, by the spring of the day; of the which, parte went into the towne of Helperby, a letle fro the said Thornton brig, on the way toward York, by the which Helperby the said officers, servants, and tenants must passe, and their festned a lidyate in the highway at the towne end of Helperby toward Yorke, with stoks, thorns, and otherwise, to thintent that when the said officers, tenants and servants came thither, they should be stopped their and incumbred. And when so was that the said officers, servants, and tenants of the said Cardinall, the Friday in the morning, the fift day of May, full early in the morning, were neighing the said Thornton brig, comeing fro Ripon, the said Sir Wm. Plompton with a great and notable fellowship of the said forest and other of their said affinity, the which assembled and gadered the same Friday in the morning att the said Burgh brig, came pricking in a route togader with all the diligence that they could, makeing a great and horrible shoute upon the said officers, servants, and tenants, to thintent to take the said Thornton before them, as they so did; the which the said officers, servants, and tenants of the said Cardinall seing, they, in eschewing of bloodshedding and bruses of the Kings peace, left their passage by the said brigg and took them to a feth, half a mile thence, called Braferton forth, to thintent to pass over their, as they so did; the which the said Sir William Plompton seing, sewed with his said fellowship upon them and followed them unto the said towne of Helperby, where the said Tho. Beckwith, Rauf, and others of their affinity, in great and notable number, assembled, also with the said Sir William and his fellowship following, upon the said officers, servants, and tenants of the said Cardinall. And when so was that the said officers, servants, and tenants came to the said yate, finding their passage stopped there, they were compelled by the pursuite and the shote of the said misdoers upon them to seek other waies to passe, as they so did; and passed, some by a long straite lane, and some by breaking of an hedge into a feild, upon whom the said misdoers followed, and drove them into a mire more, neere-hand the space of half a mile fro the said Helperby, noising and crying, "*Sley the Archbishop' Carles,*" and "*Would God that we had the Archbishop here.*" In the which pursuite, assaute, and shote, there was slaine by the said misdoers one Tho. Hunter, gentleman, and Tho. Rooper, yeoman, servants to the said Cardinall, after the tyme that they were yelden to such as called upon them, and bad them yolde them.

"*Item*, in this same great and riotous assault one Xp̄ofer Bee, servant of the said Cardinall, was maymed, that is to say, smitten in the mouth and so through the mouth into the throat, by the which he hath lost his cheeke bone and three of his fore teeth, and his speech blemished and hurt, that it is not easy to understand what he speaks or saies, and may not use therefore the remnant of his teeth and jawes to th'use of eating, as he might before.

Item, in the said assaute and pursuit there was taken by the said misdoers one William Humberstone, also servant to the said Cardinall, whom after that he was yolden, they smote and wounded in such wise that the calf of his legg was neer hand departed from his shin bone, and other many great strokes and wounds gave him, so that he was long tyme afterward in dispare of his life, and shall now never resort to the bodyly strength and heale of his person that he was in before.

Item, in the said assaute and pursuite, one John Creven, servant to the said Cardinall, was greivously beaten and wounded on divers parts of his body by the said misdoers, in especiall in his right legg, the which was neerhand hewen in two, with many other wounds, so that the said John Creven was left as for dead; and so left, lay there after tyme that all other folkes was departed, till was about iiij after noone the same day, at the which tyme happened of the dwellers of the said town of Helperby to come to the place where as he lay; the which finding not fully dead, of compassion and pittie brought him to the said towne of Helperby, and there refreshed him and releived him in such wise that he was turned to life. How it be, that he is perpetually letted of occupying of his crafte of Tayler that he used before, in so much that he may not indure to lay his legg under him in such wise as his crafte would aske.

"*Item*, in the said assault and pursuit were greivously bett, wounded, and hurte by the said misdoers John Burton, Henrie Fox, and William Playne, and other, of the number of xvi persons, servants of the said Cardinall, and the remnant of his said servants greatly affraied and doubted of their lives; and no marvaile that they so were, considering that by the said misdoers were shott to the said servants and tenants of the said Cardinall a m. arrowes and moe, by the which also many of the said Cardinalls officers', servants', and tenants' horses were slayne and greivously wounded.

Item, on the said assaute and pursuite were taken, yolden, and holden as prisoners by the said misdoers Peres of Cawood, and Tho. Mayne, squires, Henry Fox, yeoman, and of the said Cardinalls servants; and some of them labored and treated by them to make them fynance, as they had bene the Kings enemies, and many and divers of them dispoyled of their horses, harnesse, and also gold and silver.[z]

To these several counts Sir William Plumpton made answer in denial or explanation; but, as no further proceedings appear to have been taken in the matter, it may be presumed that a compromise was effected, and that the right of the Archbishop to the "denier of toll" was sealed with the blood of his tenants and servants.

Dame Elizabeth, wife of Sir William Plumpton, is named with her husband in a certificate of admission to the fraternity of the guild of St. Christopher at York, signed by John Skinner, master and guardian, and dated 31 Aug. 17 Hen. VI. 1439;[a] but she was dead before the marriage of her eldest son Robert, (born Thursday, 8 Mar. 9 Hen. VI. 1430-1,[b]) to a daughter of Thomas, Lord de Clifford and Westmorland, was contracted for; on which occasion, on the part of Sir William Plumpton, a feoffment was made, 10 Aug. 24 Hen. VI. 1446, to John Harrington, William Gargrave, Thomas Garth, John Garth, and John Elys, clerk, of his manors of Derley, Stanton, Pillesley, Wormhill, Chaddesden, and Sponden, with their appurtenances, in the county of Derby, together with all lands and hereditaments in the same vills, and in Edinsor, Wardlow, Baukewell, Martinside, Queston, Tiddeswall, Hurdlow, Chelmerton, Flagfeild and Castelton, in the same county, save the nomination of a chantry in

[z] Cartul. No. 455, et seq.   [a] Ibid. No. 446.   [b] Ibid. No. 437.

the church of Baukewell, and two closes called Bussenhay, otherwise Coombes and Betfeld, upon condition that they should enfeoff within five years Robert Plumpton, son and heir apparent of the said Sir William, and Elizabeth daughter of Thomas Lord de Clifford and Westmorland, knight, in the same, to hold to them and to the heirs of their bodies, remainder to the right heirs of Sir William in default of issue being had between them.[c] Within the term, 31 Aug. 27 Hen. VII. 1449, Sir William Plumpton made a second feoffment to John Harrington, son and heir of Sir Thomas Harrington, knight, Sir John Tempest, knight, Thomas Thwaites, Richard Banks of Neuton, Thomas Garth, William Gargrave, Sir Brian Stapilton, knight, Sir John Conyers, knight, Geoffry Pygot, John Vavasor of Neuton, Guy Fairfax and John Fawks, of all his manors and estates in the counties of York, Derby, Nottingham and Stafford, under the same limitations; but with a proviso for re-entry, if either Robert or Elizabeth died without issue had between them in his (Sir William Plumpton's) lifetime.[d] The event thereby contemplated occurred: Robert Plumpton, esq. died on Monday, the feast of St. Margaret the Virgin, 20 July 1450,[e] in the nineteenth year of his age, without having consummated his marriage with Elizabeth Clifford, who three years later was married to William, brother of Robert, and only surviving son of Sir William Plumpton by his wife Elizabeth Stapilton. All evidence relating to this marriage having been subsequently suppressed for reasons which will appear in the sequel, the Plumpton coucher-book here presents a blank; wherefore, for the better understanding of the history of the great suit which forms the leading topic of much of the Correspondence in this volume, I transcribe the following testimony of its solemnization from the Clifford papers at Skipton castle, as printed by Whitaker in his History of Craven.

"Be it knowne to all men, thatt for as much as itt is meretorie and medeful for every true Cryten men to testify and bare true wytnes in every true matter or cause; therefore we William Ratcliffe, being the age of v^{xx} yeres, Nicholas Whitfeild iiii^{xx} xviii yeres, and John Thorn of iiii^{xx} yeres, will record and testify for verrey trawthe, That the lord, Sir Thomas Clifford, marryed Elizabeth, his doghter, unto Roberte Plumpton, the eldest son and heyre of Sir William Plumpton, when she was bot of six yeres of age, and they were wedded at the chappell within the castell at Skypton, and the same day one John Garthe bare her in his armes to the said chappell. And also itt was agreed at the same tyme, that if the forseide Roberte dyed within age, that then the said Lord Clifford should have the second son of the said Sir William Plumpton unto his seid doghter. And they were bot iii yeres marryed, when the said Roberte dyed; and when she came to the age of xii yeres, she was marryed to William Flumpton, second son to the foreseid Sir William, and the seid Sir William promised the seid Lord Clifford that they shuld not ligg togedder till she came to the age of xvi yeres. And when she came to xviii yeres, she had Margarete, now lady Roucliffe. And how as evydenc' hath bene imbeseled, or what as hath bene doon syns, we cannot tell, butt all that ys afore rehersed in thys bill we wyll make yt gode, and, yf nede be, depely depose afore the Kynge and hys counsell, that yt is matter of trawth, in anye place wher we shal be comanded, as farr as is posible for any such olde creatures to be carryed to. In witness whereof we the said William, Nicholas and Jhon hath sett our seales, the xxv^{ith} of October, in the xix yere of the reane of Kynge Henrie the viiith.[f]"

At the time of the marriage of his son, Sir William Plumpton was himself clandestinely married to Joan Wintringham, sister to

[c] Cartul. No. 531. Dat. apud Derley. Witnesses, Sir Richard Vernon, Sir Henry Parpoint, knights, John Curson, Tho: Foliamb, Robert Ayre, and others.
[d] Cartul. No. 535. The witnesses were Sir Robert Roos, Sir Roger Ward, Sir Richard Vernon, Sir Henry Parpoint, Sir Thomas Chaworth, Sir Gervase Clifton, knights, Richard Hamerton, John Curson, William Babington, and others.
[e] Cartul. No. 437.

[f] History of Craven, page 247, 2nd edition.

the wife of his brother Godfrey, and who had given birth to a son; from which cause he was now seeking to effect a settlement of his lands on his heirs male, so as to give a preference to this son by the second venter over any female issue of his eldest son, should he die leaving only such surviving. To try his right to do this, an attempt to alienate parcel of the estate previously settled was made, which his brother by affinity, Lord Clifford, laboured of course to prevent.

" For so much as I, Thomas Lord Clifford and of Westmerland, am enformed at a *nisi prius* is like to pas betwixt my brother Sir William Plompton, knight, and one Thomas Kempe and Alice his wife, for a rent out of certaine lands and tenements in Spondon and Chaddesden, I make knowledge to those trew men att sall pas thereupon, and all other Christen men att this writing sall here or see, att all the lands and tenements att were my said brother Sir William in the said Spondon and Chaddesden, are parcell of the feoffement of the said Sir William' son and heire and my daughter. In witnesse hereof to this my present writing I sett my seale. Written att Hert, tenthe day of July."g

Sir William Plumpton was not however to be diverted from his purpose: for upon his demand, by two several deeds of the same date, viz. 23 Aug. 31 Hen. VI. 1453, Sir Thomas Rempston, knight, (his uncle in half-blood, and sole surviving feoffee under the deed made by his father 24 Sept. 8 Hen. V. 1420, and under his own feoffment of the 18th April 17 Hen. VI. 1439,) entailed all the estate of which he stood enfeoffed in the counties of York, Derby, Nottingham, and Stafford, together with the reversion of what was held by Dame Margaret Rempston for her life, upon Sir William Plumpton and his heirs male, with remainder to Godfrey Plumpton, his brother, and his heirs male.h

But to return to Sir William Plumpton's public career. By

g Cartul. No. 526. Lord Clifford died in 1454.   h Ibid. No. 537 et 538.

deed of the 20th Feb. 19 Hen. VI. 1441-2, Henry Earl of Northumberland and Lord of the Honour of Cockermouth, appointed Sir William Plompton, knight, to be Seneschall of all his manors and lordships in the county of York for the term of his life, with an annual fee of 10^{li}; i to which, 1 Nov. 26 Hen. VI. 1447, was added for his good services a second 10^{li} per annum, issuing out of the manor of Lethelay in com. Ebor.k In 1448 he was Sheriff of the county of York, and in 1452 of the counties of Nottingham and Derby. In 1456 Sir William Plumpton rode northward with the forces mustered by the Earl of Northumberland, for the purpose of making an incursion upon the Scottish borders;l and upon the breaking out of the wars of the Roses, he, as a matter of course, sided with his suzerain and master, the said Earl of Northumberland, and with him fought in support of the House of Lancaster. He is named among the commissioners, the others being John Lord de Clifford, kt. Sir John Melton, ch'r, Sir John Tempest, ch'r, John Hastings, esq. William Gascoigne, esq. Henry Vavasor, esq. John Thwaites, Guy Fairfax, and William Bradford, who, 1 May, 38 Hen. VI. 1460, were, with the Sheriff and Escheator, appointed to inquire concerning the lands, &c. of Richard Duke of York, and others attainted in the preceding Parliament, within the West Riding of Yorkshire.m About the same time, 2 Jan. 39 Hen. VI. 1460-1, Katharine Duchess of Norfolk granted to Sir William Plompton, kt. the office of the chief wardship and mastership of her chace and warren within her honour and demesne of Kirkby Malserd and Niderdale, in com. Ebor. for life, with a fee of v^{li} per annum.n

After Edward had assumed the title of King, and during the time he was on his march into the North, to enter into conflict with the partisans of the dethroned monarch, these two mandates addressed by Henry VI. to Sir William Plompton, kt. followed in

i Cartul. No. 524.   k Ibid. No. 533.
l Vide *postea*, p. xxiv.   m Cartul. No. 545.   n Ibid. No. 546. Dat. apud Epworth.

rapid succession. The first, " tested at York, 12 March, 39th of our reign," contains an order for Sir Richard Tunstall, kt. Sir Thomas Tresham, kt. and Sir William Plompton, kt. to summon all liege men of the forest or demesne of Knaresburgh, to set out with them to meet the enemy; o the second, " geven under our signet, at our cyty of York, the thirteenth day of March," straitly charges " our trusty and welbeloved knight, Sir William Plompton," to repair to the royal presence with his array in all haste possible.p On the 29th of the same month, being Palm Sunday, Sir William Plumpton was present at the decisive battle of Towton, otherwise Saxton field; where William, his son and heir apparent, it seems, was slain,q and he himself either made prisoner by the enemy on that day, or driven by the adverse fortune of his party shortly afterwards to throw himself on the mercy of Edward. On the 13th of May he came before Robert Danby, Chief Justice, in the city of York, and gave bond for the payment of £2000 before the feast of Pentecost next ensuing, whereupon the following writ was issued in his behalf.

" Edward, by the grace of God, King of England and of France

o Cartul. No. 548.
p See Correspondence of Sir William Plumpton, kt. *Letter* 1.
q " *Will'o Plompton ar. filio meo*," is underwritten as witness to a grant of Sir William Plumpton, of the chantry of blessed Nicholas, in the church of St. Martin in Mikelgate, in the city of York, vacant by the death of Henry Cattall, chaplain, *the Custos*, made to Sir William Shorthwait, chaplain, which bears date 19 Feb. 39 Hen. VI. 1460-1. This is the last memorial of his being alive; and he is expressly stated in a contemporary memorandum, containing the births and obits of himself and his elder brother Robert, to have died in the first year of the reign of Edw. IV. 1460-1. (*Chartul. No.* 547.) Thus at a court held at Knaresborough, Wednesday the feast of St. Mathias the Apostle, 1 Edw. IV. Margaret and Elizabeth, daughters and heirs of William Plompton, esq. son of Sir William Plompton, kt. were admitted as copyhold tenants of lands lying in the hamlets of Fellesclif, Bresteyth, and Hamesthwaite, within the vill of Clint, in Harrigat and elsewhere within the vill of Killinghall, and in Knaresburgh, Screven, Ferensby, and Erkendell Lofthouse, saving the right of Elizabeth, late wife of the said William Plompton, for the term of her life. (*Ibid. Nos.* 500 *and* 501.)

and Lord of Ireland, we will and straitly charge all our true liegemen and subgitts, that none of them upon paine of death, under any colour or occasion whatsoever it be, robbe nor spoile William Plompton of Plompton, in our County of York, knight, nor none of his servants, ne tenants, nor none of them; nor contrary to our lawes hurt, trouble, or vex them, or any of them, in anywise, in body or goods. Geven under our privy seale at our Citty of York, the xiiith day of Maie, the first yeare of our reigne." r

The term for redeeming of this bond having elapsed, on the 12th of July, 1461, Sir William Plumpton surrendered himself a prisoner at the Tower of London; and, having been sworn according to custom, was admitted by Sir William Bowischer [Bourchier,] kt. lieutenant of the Tower, to all the liberties and privileges of the place.s He obtained letters of general pardon, 5 Feb. 1 Edw. IV. 1461-2,t and was subsequently, 10 Sept. 2 Edw. IV. 1462, released from all claim by reason of his bond.u But not-

r Cartul. No. 549.
s Will'm's Plompton miles admissus est ad et in omnia libertates et privilegia Turris London p' Will'mu' Bowischer militem locum tenentem Turris p'd'cæ et juratus est secundum consuetudinem eiusdem Turris. In cuius rei testimonium p'sentibus ego p'dc'us Will'm's locumtenens sigillum meum apposui. Dat xii^o de mensis Julii anno regni Regis Edw: quarti post conquestum primo. (*Cartul. No.* 550.)
t Edwardus, &c. Omnibus ballivis et fidelibus suis, &c. Sciatis quod de gratia nostro speciali et ex certa scientia et mero motu nostris perdonavimus, remisimus, et relaxavimus Will'o Plompton militi, alias dicto Will'o Plompton militi, alias d'co Will'o Plumton militi, alias d'co Will'o Plompton de Plompton in Com. Ebor. militi, alias d'co Will'o Plumpton de Plompton in com. Ebor. militi, alias d'co Will'o Plompton nuper de Kenalton in com. Nottingham, alias d'co Will'o Plompton nuper de Knaresburgh in com Ebor. militi, alias d'co Will'o Plompton nuper Vicecomiti Com. Ebor. militi, alias d'co Will'o Plompton nuper Vicecomiti Com. Nottingham et Derb. Chivaler, seu quocu'que alio nomine censeatur, omnimodas transgressiones, offensas, &c. (*Cartul. No.* 551.)
u Edwardus, &c. Omnibus &c. salutem. Sciatis q'd cum tercio decimo die Maii, Anno regni n'ri primi, Will's Plumpton de Plumpton in com. Ebor. miles venerit coram dilecto et fideli n'ro Roberti Danby Capitali Justiciario n'ro de banco apud Civitatem Ebor. et recognoverit se debere nobis duo millia librarum sterlingorum, solvend' nobis

withstanding Sir William Plumpton had afresh letters of pardon dated 30 Aug. 3 Edw. IV. 1463,[x] he was, it seems, restricted from returning home into the North; and was at one time in jeopardy of his life, by reason of the denunciation of one David Routh, son of late Thomas Routh, of Westminster, who laid these overt acts of treason to his charge:

"First, Sir William Plompton, with other persons, within the place of Honslough, the second and third years of the reigne of our soveraigne and liege lord, had receyved, red, and published false, damnable, diffamatory, and slaunderous writing, traiterously by pen and other forged and ymagined against the honor and welfare of our said soveraigne, and the same sent to other suspicious persons to corage and comfort them by the same.

"Also he hath received in the said place divers persons coming out of Scotland fro the Kings adversaries, and secretly cherished them, succored, forbored, and their secrets concealed.

"Also he hath sent messengers into his countrey, which there receyved tidings of his brother men there out of Scotland, fro the Kings adversaries, by his brother assent and his.

"*Item.* When any turble or enterprise was leke to fall hurt or scaythe to the Kings people, the said Sir William Plumpton, with oder suspected, rejoyced, and were glad in chere and countenance."

Upon these charges Sir William Plumpton was tried before the Earl of Worcester, Lord Tiptoft and of Powis, Great Constable of England, and a jury of twenty-four, at Hounslow, shortly before Christmas. Having been acquitted, he obtained a warrant from

in festo Pentecost' ex tunc proximo futuro, sub certa condico'e super eadem recognico'e tunc et ibidem specificat', prout &c. Quibusdam tamen certis consideraco'ibus nos moventibus, &c. remisimus &c. p'fato Will'o omnes et omnimodas acc'ones &c. r'one sive occ'one recognico'is vel condicc'is supradictarum &c. In cuius rei &c. Testo meipso apud Westm' x⁰ die Septembr' anno regni n'ri secundo. Bagott. Per breve de privato sigillo et de data predicto, auctoritate parliamenti. (L.S.) (Cartul. No. 552.)

[x] Cartul. No. 557.

the Constable to be rid of all further molestation on that behalf, dated 20 Jan. 3 Edw. IV. 1463-4,[y] as also the following brief from the King.

"Edward, by the grace of God, King of England and of France and lord of Ireland, To all maiors, sherifs, eschetcrs, baliffs, constables, and other our ministers whatsoever they be, and to all other our true liege people, greeting. We lett you witt, that our welbeloved William Plompton Kt. hath truly, sufficiently, and clearly declared himself of all manner matters that have been said and surmised against him, and so we hold him thereof for fully excused and declared by these our present letters. And we take him, hold, and repute him as our true and faithfull leigman. Wherefore we will and charge you, all and every one of you as much as to him belongeth, that from henceforth ye, nor any of you, neither vex, moleste, greive, trouble, nor him nor any of his, in body nor in goods, otherwise then our lawes will; nor that ye give or shew unto him, or any of his, any ungodly language or countenance, but that ye take him and suffer him to abide and go att his pleasure and ease, there as him shall best like, as other our true leiges do; not breaking this our comaundement, as ye will eschew our great displeasure, and upon payne of punishment by our laws. Yeven under our signett att, &c."[z]

Being now reputed loyal, Sir William Plumpton was restored to his offices of Constable of the Castle, and Master Forester of the Forest of Knaresborough, and to the Stewardship of the Lordship of Spofford, of which he had had grants for life in the previous reign. He also about this time directed his attention to a lucrative disposal of the infant daughters of his deceased son, his own heirs apparent, in marriage; for I find that by virtue of an indenture dated 26th Nov. 3 Edw. IV. 1463, the governance and marriage of Margaret, then about four years old, "cousin and one of the heirs apparent of the said Sir William Plompton, that is to

[y] Cartul. No. 560.   [z] Cartul. No. 561.

say, one of the daughters of William Plompton, esq. son of the said Sir William," was granted to Brian Roucliffe of Colthorp, com. Ebor. gent. third baron of the King's Exchequer, to the intent "that John, son and heire apparant of the said Brian, shall by the grace of God take into wife the said Margret, the marriage of them to be done att convenient and most spedy time att the costs of the said Brian." On the part of Sir William Plumpton, it was covenanted to make to them, and the lawful heirs of their two bodies, an estate out of the manor of Nesfield before the ensuing feast of Pasche; neverthe ess, so as he might retain the whole profits for the first five years, and a rent of x marks by year for the five years next following. For this marriage Brian Roucliffe agreed to give, over what was already paid, cccc marks; under a proviso, however, for the repayment of l^{li}, in case the said John deceased within the next ten years.[a]

The governance and marriage of Elizabeth, the younger coheir, was in like manner granted to Henry Sotehill, esq. by indenture of the 11th of February, 3 Edw. IV. 1463-4, to the intent "that John theldest son and heire apparant of the said Henry, shall with the grace of God take to wife the said Elizabeth, which Elizabeth the said Sir William hath delivered to the said Henry." For the marriage Mr. Sotehill paid a c^{li} down, and gave bond to Sir William Plumpton, Brian Roucliffe, and Sir Richard Hamerton, kt. to pay other ccxxxiii^{li} by instalments. On the part of Sir William Plumpton it was covenanted to make an estate to feoffees, viz. Brian Roucliffe, third baron of the King's Exchequer, Richard Hamerton, kt. George Darell, kt. Richard Aldburgh, kt. John Gresley, kt. Walter Wortesley, kt. Richard Fitzwilliams, kt. John Sotehill of Sotehill, esq. and Guy Fairfax, of manors and lands to the yearly value of xl marks, in order to secure the repayment of the money advanced by Mr. Sotehill, in case the said Elizabeth should happen to die under xiv years of age. It was likewise agreed

[a] Cartul. No. 558.

that if hereafter the said Sir William Plumpton should take a wife and have issue male by her, which ought to be his heir male apparent, that the said Henry should have the wardship and marriage of the same issue male, to be married to one of his daughters, upon payment of cc marks, the day of the delivery of the said issue male. Other covenants were added, securing to John and Elizabeth, as her jointure, a yearly estate of c^{li} value, after the decease of the said Henry Sotehill and of Anne his wife, and of John Boyvile and of Alianor his wife, out of lands of which the said Henry was then and there seised, and binding Sir William Plumpton not to alien nor charge any lands or tenements, whereof he, or any to his use, stood seised, save in favour of any son by his said future wife, that shall be unto him, the said Sir William Plumpton, heir male apparent; and so as he might jointure any wife he should happen to wed in time to come to the amount of c^{li} for life, and also continue the charge upon the estates of xl^{li} a year to Elizabeth, relict of William Plumpton, esq. his son, during the term of her natural life.[b] This last-mentioned lady, the daughter of Thomas Lord de Clifford and Westmorland, and sister of John, the bloody Lord Clifford, slain at Towtonfield, appears to have re-

[b] Cartul. No. 562. The feoffment to Brian Rouclif, third Baron of the King's Exchequer, Sir Richard Hamerton, kt. Sir George Darell, kt. Guy Fairfax, serjeant-at-law, Richard Pygot, serjeant-at-law, Henry Sotehill, esq. Tho. Beckwith, esq. Stephen Hamerton, esq. Lawrence Kighley, and Godfrey Grene, of the manors of Plumpton, Garsington, Steton, Idill, and Stodelay Roger, with the appurtenances, &c. in the county of York, trustees for the purposes of this settlement, bears date 1 June, 4 Edw. IV. 1464. Witnesses, Peter Ardern, one of the King's Justices of the Bench, Brian Stapilton, Richard Aldburghe, kts. Robert Roos of Ingmanthorp, and Ranulph Pigott, esq. (Ibid. No. 565.) For the manors, &c. in the counties of Nottingham, Derby, and Stafford, the feoffees in a deed of the same date are Sir Walter Blount, kt. Brian Roucliffe, third Baron of the Exchequer, Sir Richard Hamerton, kt. Sir George Darell, kt. Guy Fairfax, and Richard Pygott, serjeants-at-law, Henry Sotehill, esq. Thomas Beckwith, esq. Stephen Hamerton, esq. Lawrence Kyghley, and Godfrey Grene, and Edward Goldsburgh, John Byrd, John Askham, Richard Fawbergh, and Thomas Allestre. (Add. MSS. in Brit. Mus. No. 6698.)

married, the same year her husband died, Sir Richard Hamerton of Hamerton in Craven, kt. then a widower;[c] she was yet living his wife 1 Feb. 19 Edw. IV. 1479-80.[d]

The private life of Sir William Plumpton from the time of his wife's death appears to have caused no small scandal in his neighbourhood. Besides being avowedly the parent of two bastard sons, named William and Robert, his offspring by his second wife, Joan Wintringham, by reason of the concealment of their marriage, was long looked upon by the publick in the same light. His intentions in favour of this son by the second venter have been already adverted to; and the covenants cited from the contract made with Mr. Sotehill, show him to have been then preparing the way for his production, at some future period, as the legitimate heir and acknowledged successor to his fortunes. This last act was apparently precipitated by the censures of the Church; for it having reached the ears of the Official of the Civil Court at York, by clamorous report of both sexes, that Sir William Plumpton kept one Joan Wintringham in his house at Plumpton, and had begot on her divers offspring *in amplexibus fornicariis*, to the great peril of his soul and grievous scandal of all the faithful, that officer issued a summons for his appearance before him. Whereupon

[c] Eleonora (*lege* Elizabetha) relicta W. Plumpton fil. et her. D'ni W. Plumpton voluntarie recognovit in capella Sc'i Laurentii infra precinctum manerii honorifici viri D'ni Ric. Hamerton, quod nunquam remisit juncturam suam vel dotem d'no W°. Plompton, 1ᵐᵉ Oct. 1461. (*Dodsworth MSS. in Bib. Bodl. vol. lxxxiii. fol. 79. containing transcripts of deeds remaining in Skipton Castle, Com. Ebor.* 1646. See Whitaker's Craven.)

[d] Omnibus, &c. Elizabeth Hamerton, nuper uxor Willielmi Plompton armigeri, salutem. Noveritis me præfatam Elizabetham remisisse, &c. Willielmo Plompton militi et Roberto filio et heredi ejusdem Willielmi omnimodas actiones, &c. Dat 1° die Feb. a° r. r. Edw. IVᵗⁱ post. conq. Angliæ decimo nono. (*Cartul. No.* 696.) Sir Richard Hamerton, kt. made his will, 3 Oct. 1480, and died the same year. (*Descent in Whitaker's Craven.*)

Sir William Plumpton attended in the chapel or oratory of St. Thomas the Martyr, in the Cathedral Church of York, on Tuesday the 26th day of January 1467-8; and the question being then and there put to him, he publickly declared that he had kept the said Joan in his house, not as his concubine, but as his true and lawful wife, for many years past; and that they had issue between them an only child, begotten of her body after marriage had and solemnized in the parish church of Knaresburgh; but in as much as no banns had been published, and the marriage was a clandestine one, he expressed himself ready on that acconnt now to submit himself to the censure of the Church, and to make satisfaction. Being required to produce witnesses of the truth of what he alleged, evidence was given as below, on Saturday the 13th of February following.

"Sir Robert Littester, chaplain, of the age of forty years, domestic servant to Sir William Plumpton, kt. deposed, that about eleven years ago there was a great muster of Englishmen to oppose the Scots, to which muster the said deponent happened to ride, together with the said Sir William Plumpton, his master, as far as Skipton-upon-Swale; and between the vills of Balderby-in-les-Broome and Skipton, the said Sir William called the said deponent to him, saying, *Robert, do you now return home: and I beg of you to listen well to all I am going to say, and, above all, to what concerns my weal and honour in my household. And because the event of war is dubious, and the solempnization of marriage between me and Joan Wintringham, my wife, has not yet been openly and publickly notified, I hereby make known to you that the said Joan is my true married wife and I her true married husband. And thus I wish and desire you, as you love me, if I happen to die in battle, to testify for the future, wherever it may be necessary.*"[e]

[e] Cartul. N°. 631. In 1456, Henry Percy, earl of Northumberland, warden of the East

During the years following the date of this confession, England was the scene of fierce commotion; rebellion, fomented by the Earl of Warwick, spread on every side, till it drove the Yorkist monarch from his throne, and once more fixed the crown on the brows of Henry. The change was, however, transient; on the fourteenth day of March 1471 Edward landed at Ravenspurn, the fields of Barnet and Tewkesbury were fought in succession, and in May Henry VI. died, leaving his rival in undisputed possession of the Kingdom. During this interval of time, the conduct of the Earl of Northumberland must be our index to that of Sir William Plumpton; "for grete partye of the noble men and comons in thos (North) parties were towards th'Erle of Northumbarland, and would not stir with any lorde or noble man other than with the sayd Earle, or at leaste by his commandement."[f] But, after intelligence had arrived of the landing of Queen Margaret, the gentry of the north parts began to make commotions, which were, however, speedily put down by the tidings of Edward's victory at Tewkesbury; "and dyvors of them made menes to th'erle of Northumberland, beseching hym to be good meane to the Kyng for his grace and pardon."[g] Among others, Sir William Plumpton had letters of general pardon for all offences committed before the last day of September, 11 Edw. IV. 1471;[h] but the King having rewarded the services of the Earl by a grant of the offices of Constable,

[f] "Restoration of King Edward IV." Printed for the Camden Society, 1838, p. 7.
[g] Ibid. p. 32.
[h] Edwardus, &c. O'ibus, &c. salutem. Sciatis de gratia, &c. perdonavimus, &c. Will'o Plompton de Plompton, in com. Ebor. militi, alias dicto Will'o Plompton nuper de Kenalton in com. Nott: militi, &c. omnimodas transgressiones &c. per ipsum Willielmum

Steward, and Master Forester of the castle, lordship, and forest of Knaresborough, and the latter having appointed his brother-in-law, William Gascoigne, of Gokethorp, esq. his deputy, he was compelled to submit to an encroachment upon the rights of his patent office. Of a violent quarrel with the last-named party on this score, some particulars will be found in the Correspondence.

In the meanwhile, the proceedings of the Ecclesiastical Courts for the canonical recognition of Sir William Plumpton's second marriage were continued, and this further evidence adduced in that behalf on the sixth of July, 1472.

"Richard Clerk, parish clerk of Knaresburgh, Yorkshire, of the age of fifty years and more, deposed, that he had known Sir William Plompton for fifty years and more, and Joan Wintringham from the time of her birth—that on a certain friday, which exactly he does not remember, between the feasts of Easter and Pentecost, about twenty-one years ago, in the parish church of Knaresburgh, was solempnized a marriage between the said Sir William and Joan—that at that time he was, as now, parish clerk of Knaresburgh, and was present on this occasion—that the preceding night John Brown, then perpetual vicar of Knaresburgh, sent word to the deponent that Sir William Plumpton intended to marry Joan Wintringham on the morrow, she then sojourning with Alice Wintringham her mother in Knaresburgh, and therefore he bade him wait on him very early the next morning and open the doors of the church for him, and so he did—and very early in the morning of the said Friday came the said Sir William and Joan to the parish church of Knaresburgh—and, they standing at the door of the chancel of the said church within the said church, the aforesaid John Brown came from the high altar

ante ultim' diem Septembris, anno regni n'ri undecimo, contra formam statutorum &c. *Irrot.* Blakwall. Per ipsum Regem.
(*Cartul. No.* 578. *Date in margin,* 2 Dec. 11 *Edw.* IV. 1471.)

in his vestments and solempnized marriage between them in the presence of the deponent, the said Sir William taking the said Joan with his right hand and repeating after the vicar, *Here I take the Jhennett to my wedded wife to hold and to have, att bed and att bord, for farer or lather, for better for warse, in sickness and in hele, to dede us depart, and thereto I plight the my trouth,* and the said Joan making like response incessantly to the said Sir William—that the vicar, having concluded the ceremony in the usual form, said the mass of the Holy Trinity in a low voice in the hearing of the deponent—that there were present at the marriage the said vicar, the contracting parties, Alice Wintringham mother of the bride, Thomas Knaresburgh of Knaresburgh, Richard Askham of Kirkdighton, Richard Exelby of Knaresburgh, and John Croft, his fellow witness, and no more—and immediately after the marriage the said Sir William earnestly entreated those present to keep the matter secret, untill he chose to have it made known—and further, that Sir William was clad in a garment of green checkery, and Joan in one of a red colour."

"John Croft of the age of forty years, domestic servant of Sir William Plumpton in his chamber, deposed to the same effect as his fellow-witness, adding that Jean Wintringham had on a grey hood—that the marriage was celebrated before sun-rise—and that he had kept silence untill within the last five or six years." [i]

Upon the hearing of this evidence, Doctor William Poteman, the official of the court of York, on the 13th of the same month, certified that Sir William Plumpton, kt. and Joan Wintringham, were legally married; [j] and from that time Robert Plumpton, the son by this marriage, was taught to consider himself as the heir apparent of his father's house, and the future owner of his property. Legal obstacles were, however, likely to interpose to prevent the intended eviction of the heirs general, and it became advisable to take fresh steps to effectuate the now avowed purpose of the interested parties. Conveyances were accordingly executed of the several estates of Sir William Plumpton to feoffees, viz. Richard Andrewes, dean of York, William Eure, clerk, Sir John Norton, kt., Ranulph Pygot, John Arthington of Arthington, Godfrey Grene, and Richard Knaresburgh; of the manor of Plumpton, together with the advowson of the chantry of the Holy Trinity in the cathedral church of Ripon, 12 Oct.; [k] of Garsington in Craven 13 Oct.; [l] of Idill, with the advowson of a chantry at the altar of St. Nicholas in the church of St. Martin in Mekilgate, 14 Oct.; [m] of Steton, same day; [n] of Kynalton 30 Oct.; [o] of the manors of Chaddesden, Derley, Stainton, Edinsor, Pillesley, Hassop, Wormehill, Chelmerton, with the advowson of a chantry at the altar of St. Cross in the church of Baukewell, and of another in the chapel of St. Margaret of Elton, and of all hereditaments in the same places, and in Hurdlow, Flagfeld, Queston, Cumbes, Martinside Betfeld, Tidswall, Castleton, Wardlow, Rowland, Baukewell, Calton Lees, Beley, Broughton, Twyford, Spounden, Newbold, and Lokhaw in the county of Derby, Crakemarsh and Combrig in the county of Stafford, Mansfield Woodhouse, Hykling, Owthrop, and Colston in the county of Nottingham, with the advowson of a chantry at the altar of St. Mary in the church of Mansfeld Woodhous, 2nd Nov. and of Okbrook, with the hereditaments there and in Burrosasshe, 6th Nov. 15 Edw. IV. 1475. [p] The said feoffees resettled the same upon Sir William Plumpton for term of his life, with remainder in tail to Robert Plumpton, junior, son of Sir William and Joan his wife, and the heirs of his body, remainder over to Sir William's right heirs; save that as to the manor of Plumpton, of a close with

[i] Cartul. Nos. 582 and 631.   [j] Ibid. No. 583.

[k] In Cartul. No. 586.   [l] Ibid. No. 589.   [m] Ibid. No. 591.
[n] Ibid. No. 593.   [o] Ibid. No. 596.   [p] Ibid. No. 598.

buildings on it called Roughferlington, and of the manors of Garsington and Steton, Com. Ebor., and of Kynalton, Com. Notts., the first limitation was to Sir William Plumpton and Joan his wife for their lives, and in the manor of Okbrook, after the life estate of Sir William Plumpton, certain parcels were to be enjoyed by his bastard sons, William Plumpton, junior, and Robert Plumpton, senior, for the term of their natural lives. [q] Not long after these settlements, Robert Plumpton, junior, was married in the domestic chapel of the manor house of Gokethorp, in the parish of Harwood, to Agnes, sister of William Gascoigne, esq. of that place, daughter of Sir William Gascoigne, kt. late deceased. The contract of marriage bears date 13 July, 17 Edw. IV. 1477, [r] but the licence to the vicar of Harwood for its celebration was delayed till the 13th Jan. 1477-8. [s] In the mean time, the suspicions of those who were interested for the heirs general were roused, and proceedings at law were taken; which resulted in Brian Rouclif, third baron of the King's Exchequer, John Rouclif,

[q] The deeds of settlement bear date as follow: of Plumpton and Roughferlington 23 Oct., of Idell 24 Oct., of Steton 25 Oct , of Garsington 26 Oct., of Kynalton 1 Nov., of Chaddesden, &c. 4 Nov., and of Okbrook 7 Nov. 15 Edw. IV. 1475. (*Cartul. No.* 587, 588, 590, 592, 594, 597, 600 et 603.)

[r] This indenture made the xiiith day of July, the xviith yeare of the reigne of King Edward the iiijth, betwixt Will'm Plompton knight, in that one partye, and Will'm Gascoigne, squier, on that other partye, witnesseth that the said Will'm Plompton, knight, grants unto the said Will'm Gascoigne that Rob't Plompton, son and heire apparaunt to the said Will'm Plompton, knight, shall by the grace of God, take and wed unto his wife Agnes, the sister of the said Will'm Gascoigne, betwixt this day and the feast of St. Andrew thappostle next comyng. And the said Will'm Plompton, knight, shall make or cause to be made unto the said Rob't and Agnes a sufficient and lawfull estate of lands and tenements, to the yearly value of xxli over all manner of charges and reprises, within the lordshipp of Kenalton in the county of Nottingham, within a moneth next after the said marriage had, To have and to hold unto the said Robert and Agnes, and to theires of their two bodyes lawfully begotten, the remainder theirof to the right heires of the said Will'm Plompton, knight. And also the said Wm. Plompton, kt., grants unto the said Will'm Gascoigne that he, nor any other feoffee to his use, shall not make any feoffent or lease of any maners, lands, or tenement that he hath, or that any other person or persons hath, for the agreement betwixt him and Henry Sothill and Brian Roclif, or either of them, but of such maners, lands, and tent as the said Will'm Gascoigne shall be privy to. And also if such evydence and estats as the said Will'm Plompton, knight, hath made of all his maners, lands, and tenta be not thought sufficient to the behoof of the said Rob't and his heirs by the councell of the said Will'm Gascoigne, that then the said Will'm Plompton, knight, shall make or cause to be made all such sufficient estates as the councell of the said Wm. Gascoigne will then avise to be made, fynes and recoveryes onely except; for the which mariage and covenants to be had and performed the said Wil.'m Gascoigne shall pay or make to be paid unto the said Will'm Plompton, knight, a cli of lawful money of England in the manner and forme that followeth, that is to say, xxli att the day of the said marriage, or within a moneth then next after, and xl marke at that day twelmoneth at the marriage is att: and so yearly at that day xl marks to the hole some of the cli be trewly paid and satisfied. And for the payment of the said cli, the said Wm. Gascoigne, with two sufficient persons with him, shalbe bounden unto the said Wm. Plompton, knight, by their several obligacions, according to the dayes of paym't aforesaid. And the said Wm. Gascoigne graunts that he shall of his owne costs and expence pay for the cost of the dynner of the said mariage, and also for the arayment of the said Agnes his sister; for the which covenants well and truly to be performed of the party of the said Wm. Plompton, knight, the said Wm. Plompton, knight, grants that he shall be bounden unto the said Will'm Gascoigne by his obligacions in the some of viijc mark. In witness wherof the parties abovesaid to this indenture interchangeabull have put to their seale the yeare and day abovesaid. (*Cartul. No.* 604.)

[s] Henricus Gillow in decretis baccalarius ac canonicus residenciarius ecclesiæ metropolitic' Ebor. et reverendissimi in Xp'o patris & d'ni, domini Laurentii p'missione divina Ebor. Archiepiscopi, Angliæ primat' et Apostolicæ sedis legati, vicarius in spiritualibus gen'alis, dilecto nobis in Xp'o vicario ecclesiæ p'ochial' de Harwood, sal't'm. Quia Rob'tus Plompton p'ochiæ de Spofford et Agnes Gascoigne p'ochiæ de Harwood matrimonium, ut dicitur, contraxerunt, illudq' in facie ecclesiæ solempnizat' habere intendunt: quodque matrimonium sic, ut prefertur, contract' bannis in utriusq' p'tis p'dict' ecclesiis p'ochialibus per tres dies solempnes inter se distantes, ut moris est, publice editis, licite et libere in capella infra manerium Will'mi Gascoigne p'och' de Harwood p'd' situat' solempnizare seu solempnizari facere valeas, dum tamen alicui ecclesiæ nullum ex hoc p'judicium generetur, et aliquod canonicum non obsistat. licentiam tibi concedimus specialem per p'sentes. Dat. Ebor. xiiio de mensis Januarii, anno D'ni Mill'imo ccccmo lxxviimo.

his son, Thomas Rouclif, and Piers Ardern, esq. becoming bound in a thousand marks to Sir William Plumpton, kt. and Robert Plumpton, junior, his son, that they, the said Brian and John, and Margaret the wife of the said John Rouclif, should abide the award of Thomas Burgh, William Gascoigne, Robert Constable, and Hugh Hastings, knights, Robert Sheffeld, William Eland, Thomas Fitzwilliams, Thomas Middleton, Edward Saltmarsh, Miles Metcalf, John Everingham and John Dawney, concerning all matters in dispute between them. The recognizance bears date 29 May, 20 Edw. IV. 1480;[s] and it was conditioned that judgment should be given before the feast of the Purification of the Blessed Virgin Mary next following. But before that day came, viz. on Sunday the 15th Oct. 1480, Sir William Plumpton died,[t] leaving issue by his second wife, Joan Wintringham, Robert, their only child. The sons by the first marriage have been already mentioned; the daughters were,—1. Joan, contracted in childhood to marry Thomas, the infant son and heir of Robert Rosse, of Ingmanthorp, com. Ebor. esq. before the

Joh'es Gisburn, Canonicus residenciarius eccl'iæ Cath. Ebor. ac Rector eccli'æ p'och' de Spofford, discreto viro vicario p'petuæ eccl'iæ p'ochial' de Harwood vestrove locum tenenti aut vicem gerenti meumque, salutem in D'no. Noveritis me p'fatu' Joh'em Gisburgh, dc'æ ecclesiæ de Spofforde rectorem, publice in facie ecclesie meæ p'ochialis de Spofford anted'cæ banna per tres dies solemnes inter se distantes per capellanum p'ochialem ejusdem ecclesiæ, meum deputatum, intra missarum solemnia cum maior affuerat populi multitudo in eadem. inter honorabilem virum Robertum Plompton, armigerum, filiu' d'ni Will'mi Plompton, militis, dc'æ ecclesiæ meæ de Spofford p'ochianum ex parte una, et honorabilem mulierem, Agnetem Gascoigne, p'ochianam vestram, nuper filiam d'ni Will'mi Gascoigne, militis, nuper defuncti, ex altera parte, legittime edi fecisse, et nullum impedimentu' ex parte dc'i Rob'ti invenisse, quin idem Rob'tus cum eadem Agnete matrimonialiter valeat copulari. In cujus rei testimonium sigillu' meum p'sentibus apposui. Dat. Ebor. xii⁰ die mensis Januarii Anno d'ni Mill'imo ccccmo LXXVIImo. (Cartul. No. 607 and 608.)

s Cartul. No. 610.
t Esch. 20 Edw. IV. No. 22.

CAMD. SOC. 4.

feast of Allhallows in the year 1454:[u] but these espousals were not consummated, and, 24 Aug. 8 Edw. IV. 1468, it was agreed between William Middleton of Stokeld in the parish of Spofforth, esq. and Sir William Plompton, kt., that Thomas Middleton, gent. son of the said William, should take to wife Jane Plompton, daughter of the said Sir William, before the feast of St. Michael; and that the said William Middleton should settle an estate in jointure of lands and tenements in Brakenthwaite and Little Ribstan in com. Ebor. at the costs of the said Thomas, Sir William Plumpton defraying the charges of the marriage and array of the said Jane conveniently, and giving with her a portion of c[li. x].—2. Elizabeth, wife of Sir William Beckwith, of Clint, in the parish of Ripley and liberty of Knaresborough, Com. Ebor. kt. Her contract of marriage is dated 12 Oct. 34 Hen. VI. 1455, Sir William Plumpton and Thomas Beckwith, esq. being the parties thereto. Their agreement was, that William, the eldest son of the said Thomas, should take to wife Elizabeth, the daughter of the said Sir William; the said Thomas to give jointure to the yearly value of x[li]. xiii[s]. iiii[d]. and to bind himself that all lands, tenements, &c. of which he stood sole seized betwixt the water

u "It is accorded between Sir William Plompton, kt. and Robert Rosse, esq. that Thomas Rosse, son and heir apparent to the s[d] Rob't, shall wed and take to wife Johan, daughter of the s[d] Sir Will'm Plompton, kt. before the feast of Allhallowes in the yeare 1454. And that the s[d] Robert shall give jointure to the s[d] Thomas and Johan of lands and tent[t]s to the yearly value of xx marks in Thirleby. It'm that the s[d] Robert shall suffer after his decease to descend to the s[d] Thomas and his heirs, all the manors and lands that he hath by his father, except landes to the yearly value of xx marks for the tearme of the life of Margaret, wife of the s[d] Robert. Item. Sir William Plompton, kt. to pay for the s[d] marriage and jointure cc marks."—(Towneley MSS. G. 24. and see Dodsworth's MSS. vol. L. f. 98 b.) Robert Roos inherited Thirleby, com. Ebor. from Thomas Roos his father, who had it by virtue of a feoffment made by William de Cantilupe, to him and to the heirs of his body.—(Rot. Parl. v. III. p. 79, 80.)

x Cartul. No. 570. Thomas Middelton was of the profession of the Law.

of Nid and Thornton-bek, and in the towns of Muston, Fyley, Halneby, Litle Aton, and South Ethrington, within the county of York, should descend to his son William and his heirs: and also all other lands, &c. of which Elizabeth, the wife of the said Thomas, was jointly enfeoffed with the said Thomas, in like manner: and the lands held by feoffees to his use to go to William and his next heirs male. The marriage portion was fixed at cxxiii[li]. vi[s]. viii[d]. to be paid by instalments; and if the said Elizabeth should die without issue male had of the said William Beckwith, then Sir William Plumpton to be discharged of the surplus, if any, remaining unpaid.[y]—3. Katharine, wife first of William le Zouche, Lord Zouche of Haryngworth and Baron St. Maur *jure matris*, summoned to Parliament 28 Feb. 6 Edw. IV. 1466. He died 14 Jan. 1467-8, his son and heir John being then of the age of eight years, when his widow had Weston com. Warwick and Canworth com. Herts. assigned in dower, and of which she died seized in October, 10 Edw. IV. 1470, being then the wife of Sir Gilbert Debenham, knight.[z]—4. Agnes, wife of Sir Richard Aldburgh, knight, who 20 Apr. 3 Edw. IV. 1463, contracted with Sir William Plumpton to take to wife the said Agnes, his daughter, the father agreeing to give ccxxx marks for a marriage portion by instalments, and to find clothing and array according to her honesty, and the husband to jointure to the yearly value of xx marks afore the feast of St. John next ensuing; the day of "espousayles" to be upon Thursday next after St. Mark day (28 April, 1463.)[a]—5. Alice, wife of Richard Goldsburgh of Goldsborough, com. Ebor. esq. She had jointure of a messuage in

y Cartul. No. 541. Dat. in festo s'c'i Wilfridi Archiep'i anno r. r. Hen. VI[ti]. post conq. Angl. tricesimo quarto.
z Esc. 8 Edw. IV. No. 53, et 11 Edw. No. 40.
a Cartul. No. 555. Sir Richard Aldburgh died 16 Edw. IV.—*Esc. de eod. anno.*

Goldsborough in the tenure of Robert Picard, and of lands and tenements in Newton near Flaxbie, and in Creskeld and Poule, 15 Dec. 1471, by feoffment of Edward Goldsburgh;[b] the contract for her marriage was then of some years standing, the bond being of the date 1 Oct. 5 Edw. IV. 1465, but the espousals were delayed.[c]—6. Isabel, wife of Sir Stephen Hamerton of Hamerton, com. Ebor. kt. whose father had covenanted that he should marry a daughter of Sir William Plumpton, 24 Mar. 25 Hen. VI. 1446-7.[d]

b Cartul. No. 579. Carta feoffamenti Edwardi Goldsburgh facti Ric'o Goldesburgh et Aliciæ uxori suæ. H. T. Will'o Plompton, Ric'o Aldburgh, Joh'e Malliverere, et Will'mo Stapulton, militibus, Rob'to Roos de Ingmanthorp et Will'o Middelton de Stokeld, armigeris, et Thoma Middelton, generos'.—Dat apud Goldsburgh xv[mo] die Dec. a⁰ r. r. Edw. IV. post conq. Angliæ undecimo.
c Cartul. No. 586. Carta obligatoria Thomæ Goldsburgh de Goldsburgh, com. Ebor. et Johannis Norton de Norton, com. Ebor. militis, Willelmo Plumpton militi in ccc marcis solvendis in festo Natalis D'ni prox. futur. Dat. 1mo. die Oct. a⁰ r. r. Edw. IV. post conq. quinto.—(*See Correspondence of Sir William Plumpton, Letter VI.*)
d This indenture made the xxiiii[th] day of March, in the yeare of the reign of King Henry the sixt xxv[th], betwene Sir Will'm Plompton, knight, on thone party, and Richard Hamerton, squier, on thother party, witnes, that where the said Richard is bounden to the said Sir Will'm in an obligation of a c marcs made the first day of March in the yeare aforesaid, payable at the feast of St. Michael tharchangell next sewing, the said Sir Will'm wills and grants to the said Richard by these presents, that if all the lands and tenements, rents, revercions and services, with thappurtenances, whereof Laurence Hamerton, fader to the said Richard, and the said Richard, are ioyntly or severally seazed, and whereof they, or either of them, or any other to their use, to the use of either of them, att this tyme takes the proffitt, discend, revert, remayne, or fall in fee simple or in fee taile, discharged of every rent fra hence forward by the said Laurence and Richard, or either of them, to be granted, to theires male of the said Richard solely, immediately after the decease of the said Laurence and Richard, dower of the said lands and tenements to the wives of the said Laurence and Richard and either of them except, (And except that it be lawfull to the same Richard to make or do make a state of the said lands to Elizabeth, his wife, to the yearly value of xxiiij marcs over all charges and reprises for tearme of her lyfe withoutyn impechment of wast, and also except that it be lawfull to the same Richard to make or do make estate for terme of lives of ii or thre persons att most, ioyntly or severally, of and in the said lands and tenements to the yearly valluee of xl[li] over all charges and reprises and no more,)

OF THE FAMILY OF PLUMPTON.

—7. Margaret, wife of Sir George Darell of Sessay, com. Ebor. kt. He died in April, 6 Edw. IV. 1466, when his widow re-married John Nevill of Womersley, com. Ebor. esq. to whom she was second wife. She died in May, 1487, having survived her last husband five years.[e]

The Correspondence of Sir William Plumpton, any more than the facts elicited in the preceding memoir, presents his character in no very favourable light; fond of litigation, we find him ever letting matters proceed to extremities before taking up his obligations, and to gain time, availing himself of practices "not worshipful"—an adept in deceit, paying court to one mistress, though secretly married to another—fraudulent in his dealings, obtaining money for the marriage of his grand-daughters, when it must have been his fixed resolve to strip them of their inheritance—abusive of his authority, "suing every true man in the Forest," and fearing not to shed blood in the assertion of pretended rights—immoral in his conduct, suffering an innocent wife to labour under slanderous report during years of silence—and time-serving in his loyalty, amassing wealth and coveting offices of trust under Princes of either House. Of the degree of eminence he raised himself to by these unworthy means, a strong proof may be found in the licence which he obtained from King Edward IV. to embattle his manor-place at Plumpton, and to enclose a park there, with liberty of warren and chase.[f] The edifice thus built is noticed by the antiquary Leland in his Itinerary, in these words: "From Grarresborow over Nid river almost al by wood a mile to Pluntone, wher is a park and a fair house of stone with 2 toures longging to the same."[g] At the visitation of St. George Norroy, in 1612, there was remaining in the Hall at Sir Edward Plumpton's this shield, " quarterly, Plumpton and Foljambe, impaling Stapleton with the mullet," the armorial bearings of this Sir William Plumpton and his first wife Elizabeth Stapleton. In the chapel were the coats, Plumpton impaling Clifford—Darell impaling Plumpton—Hamerton impaling Plumpton—and " Argent, a fess between three wolves' heads erased Gules;" perhaps, the arms of office of the Master Forester of Knaresborough Forest.[h]

Some time before his death, 1 May, 18 Edw. IV. 1478, Sir William Plumpton had made an absolute disposition of all his personal effects, moveable and immoveable, in favour of his son,[i] so as to preclude the necessity for any will; consequently, the only memorial respecting him remaining in the ecclesiastical court at York is a commission from the official, dated 10 Jan. 20 Edw. IV. 1480-1, for John Quixley, chaplain, and Richard Plumpton, to collect the debts and make the inventory of the effects of the intestate, which they were to retain in their custody.[k] In regard to the landed estate, it was matter of urgent necessity that the title of Robert Plumpton, the son, should be admitted before the Escheator, and that the office found upon the *inquisitio post mortem* of his father should be returned in that sense to the Court of Chancery. The mode of ensuring this result we learn from the following document :

"This indenture, made the last day of November, the yeare of the reigne of King Edward iiii[th] the xx[th], Betwene William Gascoigne, knight, on that one party, and Edmund Parpoint Excheter for our Lord King in the shyres of Nottingham and Derby on that other party, Witnesseth, that the said William Gascoigne, knight, and the said Exchetor be agreed in manner and forme that followeth; that is to say, that the said Exchetor shall indevor him to do that belongeth him in his said office, as well in the shire of Nottingham as in the shire of Darby aforesaid, to find an office after the decease of William Plompton, knight, now dead, and to make his precept to the Sherife of the said shires, and to write to the saide Sherife to have such men impannelled as abovesaid William Gascoigne shall name. And that the said Exchetor shall cause to his power both the offices, as well in the one shire as in the other, to be found betwixt this and the feast of Nativity of our lord God next comeinge, according to such evidence as shal be shewed there by the counsell of the said William Gascoigne, knight, of all such manners, lands, tenementes, rents, revercions, and services, with other appurtenances, of which the said William Plompton, knight, now dead, was seised of in fe, or otherwise, in the said shires, in his life, or any other to his use. For which the said William Gascoigne, knight, shall pay or cause to be paid to the said Edmund Parpoint iiii[li] for his office so found, retorned and put into the Chauncery of our said sovereigne Lord the King, according to the right and title of evidence above rehersed, and xx[s] for his reward; which putting in shalbe att the charge & cost of the said William Gascoigne, knight. And also the said William Gascoigne, knt. shall save the saide Edmund Parpoint, Exchetor, harmles for the said office so found and retorned. In witnes whereof either party interchangeably to this Indenture hath setto their sealls. Written the yeare and day abovesaid."[l]

Inquisitions were taken according to this agreement before the said Escheator at Derby on the 18th of December, and at Lenton in Nottinghamshire on the 20th of the same month; and in both the feoffment to Master Richard Andrews, Dean of the cathedral church of York and his co-trustees, with the subsequent limitation to Sir William Plumpton for life, remainder to Robert Plumpton, jun. his son, and the heirs of his body, and then to his right heirs, is set forth. In the one, the finding is that *de tali statu inde obiit seisitus, remanere inde in forma predicta*;[m] but the estate in Nottinghamshire having been reconveyed to Sir William Plumpton and Joan his wife conjointly, the finding is that she survived him *et se tenuit intus per jus accrescendi*.[n] The jury upon the inquest in Yorkshire made a like return according to the tenor of the feoffment produced before them, the same I have adverted to above. This office was taken by William Nelilton, Escheator, at *Wedirby*, on Friday before the feast of St. Martin in winter, 10th Nov. 20 Edw. IV. 1480;[o] and in it, as also in the others, are the usual findings of the day of the death of the deceased, and the names and ages of the heirs-at-law, the daughters of William Plompton, esq. son and heir of the said Sir William Plompton, knight, viz. Margret, wife of John Roucliffe, of the age of twenty years and more, and, Elizabeth, wife of John Sothill, of the age of nineteen years and more: save that in the later inquisitions, Margret is returned of the age of twenty-one years and more.

---

[c] MSS. Add. 5530. f. clx. apud Coll. Top. et Gen. vol. i. p. 707. *inter addenda*.

that then the said obligacion be voyd and of none vallue. And also alway forseene, that if it happen no son and heire of the same Richard to have issue with none of the daughters of the said Sir William that then the said obligacion to be voyd and of no value. In witnes of which things the said parties to thes indentures interchangeably have sett their seales, the day and yeare abovesaid."—(*Cartul. No.* 534.) The arms of Hamerton impaling Plumpton were in painted glass in the chapel at Plumpton Hall, at the time of the Visitation of Richard St. George Norroy.—(*MSS. Coll. Arm. c.* 13); and in Long Preston Church under an arch opening the Hamerton quire to the chancel, on the founder's stone, is carved a shield, quarterly, Plumpton and Foljamb. This chantry was founded in 1445, but this carving is of later date than the above indenture, for in the inscription Richard Hamerton, then a *squier*, is called *Miles*. The above contract will therefore have been the reason for giving this unimpaled shield a place here, though no actual marriage had yet taken place between the children.

[f] Cartul. No. 585. Teste meipso apud Westm: decimo-septimo die Febr. anno regni nostri tertio decimo. (7 Feb. 13 Edw. IV. 1467-8).
[g] Leland's Itinerary, vol. i. f. 104. p. 99.
[h] Vis. Ric. St. George Norroy, in Coll. Arm. C. 13.
[i] Cartul. No. 685.   [k] Ibid. No. 628.

[l] Cartul. No. 625.   [m] Ibid. No. 620.   [n] Ibid. No. 710.
[o] Ibid. No. 624. The jurors were Percivall Lyndley, esq. John Arthington, esq. Thomas Hawkesworth, esq. William Exilby, gent. Henry Arthington, gent. John Chambre, gent. William Lyndley, gent. Richard Saxton, John Baildon, William Angrow, William Stead, George Swaile, John Herryson.

The first act of Robert Plumpton, upon succeeding to the property, was to increase the life-estate of his mother, Joan, giving her in Yorkshire the manor of Idle, in addition to Grassington and Steeton which she had by the settlements made in the lifetime of her father;[j] and to her he appears to have borne at all times a singular affection. This is strongly evidenced by the draft of a will, made 13 July, 1482; in it he gives his whole estate to Joan his mother, and Agnes his wife, for their joint lives, before leaving it to Jane, then his only child, and who in the meanwhile was merely to have 400 marks towards her proper disposal in marriage.[k] The claims of the heirs-general continued, however, to be pressed notwithstanding the finding upon the inquest; and 21 May, 22 Edw. IV. 1482, John Roclif, esq. and John Sothill, esq. became bound in a penal sum of £2000 to Joan Plumpton, widow, and Robert Plumpton jun., the condition of which bond was, that they, and all others having right or title through the said Margret and Elizabeth their wives, should abide the award of the prepotent Prince and Lord, the Lord Richard, Duke of Gloucester, the Lord Henry, Earl of Northumberland, Sir William Parr, kt. Sir James Harrington, kt. Sir Hugh Hastings, kt. John Vavasor, serjeant-at-law, Robert Sheffeld, William Eland, Miles Metcalf, and John Dawney, arbitrators chosen by both parties.[l] Subsequently, 14 Feb. 1482-3, the condition of the bond was altered, and the agreement was to abide the award of the King's Majesty, to be given in writing before the feast of the Translation of St. Thomas (7 July) next ensuing;[m] but King Edward IV. dying during the term, 9 April 1483, the bond had to be renewed, 12 Sept. 1 Ric.

[j] Cartul. n. 701, et seq. The trustees for the purposes of this settlement were Sir Christopher Ward, kt. John Gascoign, esq. Richard Knasburg, gent. John Quixley, chaplain, and Henry Fox, valet, and the dates respectively 25, 26, and 27 Oct. 20 Edw. IV. 1480.

[k] Cartul. 714. The feoffees to the uses of this will were Dame Joan Plompton, widow, John Wyntringham, chaplain, and Robert Sykerwham. (Ibid. No. 716.)

[l] Cartul. No. 629. [m] Ibid. 720.

III. 1483,[n] and on the sixteenth of that month this judgment was given:

"Richard, by the grace of God, King of England, and of Fraunce, and Lord of Irland, To all christen people, to whome this our present writing of awarde shall come, greating. Whereas divers variences and discords have beene movid betwyxt dame Johanne late wife of William Plompton knight, and Robert Plompton knight, on that one party, and John Roucliff esquire, and Margaret his wife, John Sotehill esquire, and Elizabeth his wife, cossines and heires of the same Sir William Plompton, that is to say, doghters of William Plompton esquire, sone to the same Sir William on that other partie, for, in, and upon the right, title, clame and intresst of all the lordships, mannors, lands, tenements, and heredaments, with thappertenances, that sumtime were the same Sir William Plompton knight, or any other to his use were or be seasid of, or whearof any of the said parties, or anie other to their use, or any of them, ar or weare seased, and of all other causes, quarels, matters, debates, accions, and demands moved amongst the said parties, wheareuppon the said parties by their escripts obligatories, bering date the xii day of September, the first yeare of our reigne, be baunden either partie to other severally in tow thousand pownde to obey, performe, and kepe our award, ordinance, and doume in and of the premises; and we intending reast, pease, and quiet amongst all our leige people and subiects, have taken uppon us the buisenes and laboure in that behalfe, and repely by goode delibracion have herd and examined the intresst and title of the said parties in the primeses, by the advise of our Lords of our Councill, and of our Judges thearunto called. Thearupon by the assent, consent, and agrement of all the said parties we awarde, ordeine, and deme in the premises in forme following; that is to say, that the same Margret wife to the same

[n] Cartul. No. 721.

John Roucliffe, and Elizabeth wife to the same John Sotehill, shall have a suficient, and lawfull estate of all lordships, mannors, lands, and tennements following; that is to say, the mannors of Garsington and Steeton, in our shire of Yorke, with all other lands, tennements, rents, services, and reversions within the townes of Garsington and Steeton, and alsoe all other lands, tennements, rents, services, reversions, and heredaments, with the appurtenances, within the mannors and townes of Chaddesden, Sponden, Okebroke, Broughton, Wormhill, Whestone, Tidswall, Martineside, Combes, Betfeild, Hurdlowe, Chelmerton, Werdlow, Castleton, Burgh, Neubold, Pillsley, Edinsore, Calton, and Leghes, in our shire of Derby; all which mannors, lands, &c. we exstend to be the yearly rent of ccxxiiij markes over all charges and reprises. And ower that, we awarde the same Sir Robert Plompton, and dame Johne Plompton his mother, and all others having title, &c. to the use of the same Sir Robert and Dame Johanne, or either of them, afore the feast of St. John Baptist next coming, shall make or cause to be made a suficent and lawfull estate of and in all the same mannors, &c. to the same John Roucliffe and Margret, John Sotehill and Elizabeth, and to the heires of the bodies of the same Margret and Elizabeth lawfully gotten; and for defaut of such issue, the remeynder thereof to the right heires of the said Sir William Plompton; in full satisfaction of ccxxiiii marke by yeare over all charges and reprises, be recover, fine, or feoffement, or otherwise, as the councill of the same Margret and Elizabeth shall advise, and be thought reasonable by Sir William Husse, knight, our Cheife Justice, and Sir Guy Fairfax, one of our Justisers of our bench, at proper costs of J.R. and M., J.S. and E. discharged of all grants and statuts maide by the same Robert or dame Johanna, feffe or feffies to the use of them or either of them, or by anie feffments maide by the same Sir William Plompton, whereunto the saide Sir Robert or Dame Johanna were privy. Also we award that if the said Sir William, or any feofie to his use

or the use of his heires, have maide any grant of rent or statute, wherby any of the same grownds, lands, tennements, now assigned by this our awarde to the same Margret and Elizabeth, be charged, that then the same Sir Robert and his heires shall make or cause to be maide a suficient and lawfull estate to the same M. and E. and to the heirs of their bodies lawfully gotten, the remainder hereof in forme aforesaid, of lands and tennements to the yearly value of such charge, as hade, extendeth unto, within halfe a yeare after the same grant of rent or statute truly knowne and understoode. And likewise we award that the said Sir Robert Plompton afore the said feast of St. John Babtist shall have a suficient and lawfull estate of the resedew of all the lordships, mannors, lands, &c. which weare the same Sir William Plompton, or any other to his use, or to the use of his heires. And over that we award that the same J. R. and M., J. S. and E. and all other having title, &c. shall make, or cause to be maide, a suficient and lawfull estate in and of all the aforesaide resedew of the foresaid mannors, &c. to the same Sir Robert, and to the heirs of his body lawfully gotten, and for defaute of such issue, the remainder therof to the right heirs of the same Sir William Plompton, by recorde, fine, feofment, release, or otherwise, as the counsill of the same Sir Robert shall advise, and be thought reasonable by the same Sir William Huse and Guy, at proper costs and expences of the same Sir Robert Plompton, discharged of all grants or statutes maide by the same J. R. and M., J. S. and E. or any of them, feffe or feofes to the use of them or any of them, whereunto the same J. R. and M., J. S. and E. wear prive or of knowledge. The mannor of Nesfelde with thappurtinances, which the same John Rouclife and Margret have of the gift and feofment of the same Sir William Plompton, to be to the same John Roclife and Margret and the heires of their bodyes lawfully gotten, according to the same gift thereof to the same J. R. and M. made by the same Sir W. Plompton, knight; and if thear be ony lands of Nesfeild or

Langbergh, that be no parcill of the mannor of Nesfeild, and that evidently shewed and understoode by the fest of Purification of our Lady next coming affore our said Cheife Judge and Sir Guy, then all such lands and tenements so shewed and understoode as noe parcill of the same mannor of Nesfeild, be to the same Robert and to the heires of his body lawfu ly gotten, and for defaut of such issue, the remainder thereof to the right heires of the same Sir W. Plompton, and to have a sufficient and lawfull estatte made thereof, as is rehearsed afore, att costs and expenses of the same Sir Robert. And over this, we award that the same J. R. and M., J. S. and E. shall make or cause to be maide by ther deede sufficient in law, a sufficient and lawfull grant unto the same Sir Robert Plompton of 40li of rent-charge, with a clause of distresse, yearly goeing out of certain lands and tenements, persil of of the same manners, lands, and tenements, yearly to be paid att feasts of Martinmas and Whittsunday by even portions, for tearme of the life of Elizabeth late wife of the same William Plompton, son of the said Sir W. Plompton, kt. and the grant to be had and maide afore the feast of St. Martin in Winter by the advice of the said Mistresse, att proper costs and expences of the said Sir Robert Plumpton. And moreover, we awarde that if the said Rob., J. R. and M., J. S. and E. his wife, or anie of them or theire heires, by lawfull entre or recovere haud, have and attaine the possession of the mannor of Elton and Stainton, with the appurtenance, in our countie of Derby, or the 5th part of the mannor of Newton besides Blithfield in our countie of Stafford with thappurtenances, that then he or those that so shall happen to have or recover the same manners, lands, and tennements or ani percill thereof, shall have occopy and enjoy the same manners, &c. with the issues and proffits of the same, unto such time as the partie which so recovereth be fuly satisfied of the moyte of such costs, as he or thaye have done abowte the recovery or attaining of the same, the said costs to be assessed by the othe of him or them that so maketh or beareth the same. And if thear be any agreement maid, whearuppon any recoveres shall be had for the right and title of every of the said lands and tennemens by the said parties or any of them, that then the same recompence shalbe equalie devided betwene the same parties, that is to say, the one moyte therof to the same Sir Rob. Plompton, and that other to the same J. R. and M., J. S. and E. their wifes.° And moreover, if the same Johanne Plompton, or Sir Robert Plompton, or either of them, or any other in their name or for them, any time s th the feast of Pentecost, xxi yeare of the reigne of King Edward the iiii, our Brother, have received, taken, or levied any rents, services, issues, profits or revenewes of anie of the forsaid mannors, lands and tennements above awarded to the same J. R. and M., J. S. and E., which weare dewe or paable at any tearme or day after the said feast of Whitsonday, we award that the same Dame Johanne and Robert shall content and pay unto the said J. and M., J. and E. all such rents and revenues affore the said feast of Pasch next coming after making of this our award; and in likewise if the same J. R. and M., J. S. and E. or any of them &c. And as for all such evidences, escripts, and munyments as concerneth all the said

° The manor of Elton had been the property of Sir Edward Foljambe of Tideswall, com. Derby, kt. whose issue having failed before 4 Edw. IV. 1464, the inheritance was claimed by Sir William Plumpton as heir-general, and by Thomas Foljambe of Walton, com. Derby, esq. under a special entail. In that year the latter gave to Richard, Earl of Warwick, and William, Lord Hastings, Chamberlain of the King, the manor of Tideswell com. Derby, and lands in Tideswell, Hucklow, Wormhill, Abney, Longsden and Button (*Coll. Top. et Gen. vol. i. p.* 347); and 8 Apr. 19 Edw. IV. 1479, Dame Cecilia Fuljambe, relict of Sir Edward Fuljambe, knight, in her widowhood, granted to Sir William Plompton, kt. her manor of Elton, com. Derby, with the appurtenances in Elton and Stainton, and a fifth part of the manor of Newton, near Blithfeild in the county of Stafford, and released absolutely to him all right and title therein. (*Cartul. No.* 593.) What was the result of this suit does not appear; save that no proceedings were taken by Sir Robert Plumpton after this adverse award in favour of the heirs-general, which necessarily cast a slur upon his title *virtute doni*, and rendered it of little avail in any claim as against them.

mannors, &c. or any parcell of them, we awarde that the same Sir Robert Plompton shall deliver all such evidences, &c. which the same Sir Robert haith, or any other to his use, &c. which by this our award be assigned to the same Margret and Elizabeth, as is above speccfied, to the same M. and E. by the feast of Pasch next coming. Also we award that the same J., M., J. S. and E. shall deliver all such evidences &c. which by this our award be assigned to the same Sir Robert; and therein we award that all such evidences, escripts, or muniments be delivered by the advice and discretion of the said Cheife Juge and Sir Guy afore the feast of St. John Babtist next coming. Over this we award that if the aforesaid manner of Elton and Stainton or the 5th part of the same mannor of Newton be recovered, or the possession therof attained, as is rehearsed above, that within the space of half a year after the same paiment, he or those that shall happen to recover or ateine the lawfull possession in and of the same, shall make or cause to be made unto him soe paying the same halsendale, a suficient and lawfull estate of the moyte of the same mannors, lands, and tennements so recovered and attained, to have to him and the heires of his body gotten in manner and forme as is above rehearsed. And if ther be any article, clause, or matter comprehended in this our award, which by reason of consions of right oweth or should be reformed, it so to be interpritted and reformed afore the true interpirtion, effect, and intent of this our award by us and our Juggies, or counsill for reformation of the same. In witnesse whereof we have sined this our present award with our owne hand, and the same with our privie signit, the 16 day of the month of September, the first yeare of our reine." P

Substantial justice appears to have been done by this award, and its conditions were peaceably acquiesced in by both parties for a lengthened series of years. But it was the misfortune of Sir Robert Plumpton to have lived in the days of a monarch who, under the pretence of a rigid enforcement of the law, sought only the means to gratify his avarice. By the greedy and rapacious lawyers, his tools, every defect of title or breach of statute, which might furnish the pretext for a suit or fine, was eagerly caught at in order to swell the revenue, while they themselves reaped the reward of their bare-faced maintenance, whichever side they advocated. In this manner was the claim of the heirs-general revived by the notorious Empson; but before I detail the proceedings consequent thereupon, which ended in reducing Sir Robert Plumpton to beggary, it will be proper to give some account of his public career.

Within two years after his father's death, Sir Robert Plumpton, when serving with the Earl of Northumberland, was knighted by the Duke of Gloucester in Hoton-feild beside Berwick, 22 Aug. 22 Edw. IV. 1482; and, in company of the same Earl, he rode to meet King Henry VII. in his progress towards York, in the first year of his reign.

" By the way in Barnesdale a litill beyonde Robyn Haddeston (*lege* Robyn Hudde ston) thErle of Northumberland with right a great and noble Company mete and gave his attendaunce upon the King; that is for to say, with 38 Knyghts of his feedmen, beside Esquiers and Yeomen. Part of those Knyghts names are ensuen. Sir .... Multon, Sir Tyme, Lorde of Seint Johns (*lege* Sir Robert Multon, sometyme Lord of Seint Johr's), Sir William Geiston (*lege* Gascon), Sir Robert Counstable, Sir Hugh Hastings, Sir William Evers, Sir John Pikering, Sir Robert Plompton, Sir Pers of Medilton, Sir Christofer Warde, Sir William Malary, Sir Thomas Malyver (*lege* Malyvera), Sir William Englishby (*lege* Engleby), Sir James Strangways, Sir Rauf Rabthorp, Sir Thomas Normanvile, Sir Martyn of the See, Sir Robert Eilliart, Sir Rauf Crathorn, Sir William Bekwith, Sir Robert Utreyte, Sir Thomas Metham, Sir Richard Counyers, Sir William Darcy, Sir Stephen

P *Cartul. No.* 722.

Hamton (*lege* Hamerton), and Sir William A. Stapleston (*lege* Stapleton); and so proceded that same Mondaye to Pomfret, wher his Grace remaynede unto the Thursday next following.^q"

Sir Robert Plumpton likewise attended, in the retinue probably of the Earl of Northumberland, at the coronation of Queen Elizabeth, wife of Henry VII., in the third year of that reign, 25 Nov. 1487; on which occasion his youthful nephew, William Gascoigne, was created a Knight of the Bath.[r] Among his Correspondence will be found a pressing letter from the same Earl, dated 24 April, 4 Hen. VII. 1489, charging him to come, with his nephew, Sir William Gascoigne, and with such armed followers as he could trust, to the town of Thirsk, on the Monday following the date thereof. That Sir Robert obeyed this summons, and was thenceforth actively engaged in suppressing the insurrection of the Commons of Yorkshire, which commenced with the massacre of the Earl of Northumberland " besides Thurske, near Blackmor Egge, on Saint Vitalis day, the 28th day of April" (Tuesday), and was followed by a successful assault upon the city of York, this letter of thanks sent from the Court is a sufficient token:

"Trusty and wellbeloved wee greet you well. And whereas wee understand by our squire Nicholas Kinston (*lege* Knifton),[s]

one of the Ushers of our Chamber, your true mind and faithful liegiance towards us, with your diligent acquitall for the reduceing of our people there to our subjection and obedience, to our singuler pleasure and your great deserts; wee hartily thanke you for the same, praying for your persevering continuance therein. Assureing you, that by this your demeaneing you have ministered unto us cause, as gaged to remember you in time to come in any thing that may bee to your preferment and advancement, as ever did any our progenitors to our nobles in those parties. And as any office of our gift there falls voyd, wee shall reserve them unto such time as wee may bee informed of such men, as in the said parties may bee meet and able for the same, praying you that if there shall happen anie indisposition of our said people, ye will, as ye have begun, endeavour you from time to time for the speedy repressing thereof. And, furthermore, to give credence to oure Squire aforesaid on such things as wee have commanded him at this time to shew unto you on our behalfe. Given under our signet at our mannor of Sheene, the thirteenth day of October."[t]

The lord Percy, at the time of his father's death, was only in his twelfth year, having been born 12 Jan. 17 Edw. IV. 1477-8, and consequently unable to take upon him the rule of the North, now grown hereditary in his family; the King, therefore, established in the government the Earl of Surrey, Sir Richard Tunstall, and Sir Henry Wentworth. In the second year of the Earl of Surrey's being there, the men of Yorkshire once more rose in

---

^q Lel. Coll. vol. iv. p. 185, from a MS. in the Cotton library. Sir Robert Multon was Prior of St. John's, Clerkenwell, in 1474; in which year (14 June) he was made Warden of the East and Middle-Marches jointly with the Earl of Northumberland. (*Claus.* 15 *Edw. IV.* m. 26.) In 1477 he resigned his office of Prior and was succeeded by Sir John Weston.

^r Lel. Coll. vol. iv. p. 219, where the name is misprinted Gasixyne, and afterwards in the list subjoined of knights present at the ceremony, Gaston. Dame Gascoigne, his mother, sister of the Earl of Northumberland, likewise heads the list of " Ladyes " of the court given by the Herald on this occasion, as " Dame Gaston ; " but in reading printed copies of ancient manuscripts, the t and c should be always made mutually convertible, as from its being impossible to distinguish these letters from one another as written, their right appropriation can only be determined by extraneous knowledge.

^s The name of this Esquire of the Body to King Henry VIII. is printed Kinston in

CAMD. SOC. 4.   O

Rot. Parl. VI. 345. a. but in Leland's Collectanea, where his name twice occurs in the Herald's Ceremonial which has been quoted from above, the reading is Kuyston and Ruyston, with an interlineation over it Kyffton. I apprehend, therefore, that the real orthography was Knyfton, and that he was identical with Nicholas Kniveton of Mercaston, com. Derby, esq. living at this period.—(*Wolley's MSS.*)

^t From a copy in the Towneley MSS. Whitaker has printed this letter in an abbreviated form, probably from Dodsworth's transcript, in his History of Craven, with the date of the thirtieth of October instead of the thirteenth; and this same date is also in the Towneley MS. G. 24.

rebellion in the West part of the country, and in May 1492, the rebels were defeated by the forces under his leading at Ackworth besides Pomfrett. At this field, Sir Robert Plumpton was present,[u] and demeaned himself so well, as again to merit the special thanks of the Sovereign " for his good and agreeable service in this last commotion." The royal letter bears date 28 May, 7 Hen. VII. 1492, and the precautions recommended by it for the time to come, in order to secure the service of " assured men," show strongly the feelings of disaffection towards Henry, which at that time pervaded the North.[w]

Sir Robert Plumpton had probably been confirmed in the offices of Constable of the Castle of Knaresborough and of Master Forester under the Earl of Northumberland, as well as in the Stewardship of the Lordship of Spofford, immediately after the death of his father; for it will be seen from the Correspondence that he exercised the powers they conferred for a lengthened period during this reign. Such being his credit and authority, he was enabled to contract for an advantageous alliance on behalf of his eldest son, William, when he had reached his twelfth year. By an indenture, dated 11 May, 11 Hen. VII. 1496, between Sir Robert Plompton, knt. and William Babthorp, gentleman, it was covenanted and agreed, " that William Plompton, son and heire apparant to the said Sir Robert, shall with the grace of God marry

and take to wife Isabell Babthorp, cossin and heire to Dame Isabell Hastings late deceased, late wife to Sir John Hastings, kt. and neace to the said Will. Bapthorpe, before the feast of St. Michell tharcangill next coming . . . . . Also it is agreed that the said Sir Robert shall beare the costs of tharray of the said William his son . . . . and the costs of the meate and drink to be expended at the marriage . . . . and that the said Will. shall beare the cost and charges of tharray of the said Isabell the day of her first marrage. Also it is covenanted and agreed between the said parties that the said Isabell shall have to hir heire the maner of Sacompt in the county of Hertford, and Watterton in the county of Lincolne, and all other lands &c. in the said countie of Hertford, and in Hotoft, Amcotes, and Watterton, in the countie of Lincoln, and in Estoft, Selby, and Kerkby-upon-Wharfe, in the county of York, except certain closes in Selby called the Flates, whereof Sir Robert Babthorp, kt. or Dame Elizabeth his wife, grauntseder and grauntmoder to the said Elizabeth,[x] or Sir Raufe Babthorp, kt. unkell to the said Isabell, or any of them, were seased of ani estaite of enhirretance, without let of the said Will. Babthorp or his heirs for ever . . . . . And over this it is agread that the said Will. Babthorp shall have, him and his heire, all those lands, tennements, and hereditments with their apurtenances in the parish of Hemyngburgh, Midleton-upon-the-Would, Northcave, Hundsley, Lofthouse, and Wistow, in the county of York, and in Colby in the county of Lincolne, whereof the said Sir Robert Babthorpe, Sir Raufe Babthorpe, knights, or Mr. Thomas Babthorp, clark, or any of them, weare seased of any estaite of any enhiritance, and also the said closes in Selby before except, in satisfaction of all those lands &c. that wear or be entailed to any of the name of Bapthorpe, his anchestors, or to the heir male of any of their

---

^u See the letter of the Earl of Surrey to Sir Robert Plumpton in a note at page 96 of the Correspondence, where mention is made of Robert Beck (*see Letter XX*), a servant of the latter, having found a gelding belonging to the Earl, which had been lost upon the field of battle.

^w See this letter also at page 96, note a. Through erroneous calculation of the regnal year, the battle of Ackworth is there represented to have been fought in the spring of the year 1491, instead of 1492, which the date, 28 May, 7 Hen. VII., refers us to. That this last was the right year, also appears from the inscription on the tomb of the Earl of Surrey at Thetford; in which the suppression of the insurrection, and the execution of the chief leaders, are referred to the same year as the King's expedition to the Continent and the siege of Boulogne.

^x Elizabeth and Isabell were used indiscriminately at this period in England, as well as abroad, to denote the same proper name.

OF THE FAMILY OF PLUMPTON.

bodies, without let &c. And shall have all the evidence &c. tuching the said lands &c. and t'ofice of the Steward and Master Forester of the Forest of Galtres. . . . . . And that the said Sir Robert Plompton, kt. shall have all the evidence &c. conserning the residew of the mannors &c. that any time weare the said Sir Robert Babthorpe, Rauffe Babthorpe, or anie ancestors of the said Isabell . . . . Also the said Sir Robert Plompton granteth by theas presents that he shall make, cause, asure, suffice a lawful estate, to be maid before the said feast of S^t. Michell to Nicholas Mydleton, Richard Grene, Robert Haldynby, esquires, and Richard Plompton, clerk, of lands and tenements to the clearly value of xx mark over all charges, to the use and intent that the said feofes shall make estate of the said lands and tenements with their appertinances to the said Will: Plompton and Isabell, &c. within six weakes next after the said Isabell cometh to the age of xvii yeare. . . . . In witnes &c." ^y The feoffment required by the last covenant was made on the 14 Sept. 12 Een. VII. 1496, and comprised the manor of Hassop, with the appurtenances in Hassop and Rouland, in the county of Derby; from which date it may be presumed that the marriage was solemnized on the appointed day. ^z

^y Cartul. 781.   ^z Ibid. 783.

PEDIGREE OF BABTHORPE, OF BABTHORPE COM. EBOR.

Arms: Sable, a chevron Or between three crescents Ermine.

Sir Robert Babthorpe, kt. of Babthorpe, com. Ebor. and Sacomb, com. Herts. Executor to King Henry V. Died 22 Aug. 14 Hen. VI. 1436. Bur. at Hemingbrough. = Elianora, dau. and heir of John de Waterton, of Waterton, com. Linc. esq. Feoffment before marriage dated 12 Sept. 11 Hen. IV. 1410. (Impalement in ch. of Hemingbrough.) = Bridget, dau. of . . . . Pilkyngton, of . . com. Lanc. (Impalement in ch. of Hemingbrough.)

Ralph Babthorpe, son and heir, of Babthorpe, com. Ebor. and Waterton, com. Linc. esq. Slain at the battle of St. Alban's, 22 May, 33 Hen. VI. 1455. Esquire of the King's Body. = Katharine, dau. of . . . . Ashley of . . . . Had Sacomb, settled in jointure 11 Sept. 8 Hen. V. 1420. Died 27 Aug. 1 Edw. IV. 1461. Buried at Hemingbrough.

HISTORICAL NOTICES

It was shortly after the marriage of his son, that Sir Robert Plumpton received intimation, in a letter from Edward Plumpton, that the lawyer Empson intended " to attempt matters against

Ralph Babthorpe, esq. eldest son. Sewer to King Hen. VI. Slain 22 May, 33 Hen. VI.; buried with his father at St. Alban's. s. p.	= Margaret, dau. of Thomas Mitford and Isabella his wife. Feoffmt. on marriage 20 July, 19 Hen. VI. 1441.	Sir Robert Babthorpe, kt. son and heir, æt. 32 ad mort. patris. Died. . . . 6 Edw. IV. 1466.	= Elizabeth, dau. of Sir William Ryther, of Ryther, com. Ebor. kt. Hac. lands in Hotoft com. Linc. and Kirkly-super-Wharfe, com. Ebor. ex done patris in matrim. 23 June, 19 Hen. VI. 1441. Died. . . .	Thomas Babthorpe, Clerk, Prebend of Howden. Died 13 Oct. 18 Edw. IV. 1478; bur. at Howden.

Sir Ralph Babthorpe, kt. son & heir, æt. 22 ad mort. patris. Died 7 March, 6 Hen. VII. 1490.	= Margaret, d. of William Middelton, of Stockeld, com. Ebor. esq. Living 12 Nov. 21 Hen. VII. 1505; had in dower.	Robert Babthorpe, next brother. Died 11 May 11 Hen. VII. 1496.	= Katharine, dau. of Thomas Hagthorpe, of Brackenholm, com. Ebor. esq. & wid. of . . Eleson, of Selby, com. Ebor.)	William Babthorpe, of Osgodby, com. Ebor. esq.; in the entail of Babthorpe, by covenant 11 May, 11 Hen. VII. 1496. Died 20 Hen. VII. 1504.	= Christiana, dau. of Henry Sotehill of Stokfaston, com. Leic. Hen. esq. 2 Apr. 1540, buried in Grey Friars, London.	= William Babthorpe, esq. Living 29 Apr. 2 Hen. VIII. 1510. 2d husband.	Thomas Babthorpe, clerk. Provost of the Collegiate Church of Hemingbrough. Died 8 Hen. VIII. 1517.

Isabella, dau. and heir, æt. 15 ad mort. patris. Marriage covenant before 20 June, 1 Ric. III. 1484; enfeoffed of lands in Babthorpe, Bramyngburgh, Hemynghurgh, Beokenholme, Selby, Thorpe & Estoft, com. Ebor. 20 July, 8 Hen. VII. 1493. Died . . 11 Hen. VII. 1496.	= Sir John Hastings, of Fenwick, com. Ebor. kt. æt. 22 ad mort. patris. 7 Jun. 4 Hen. VII. 1489. Tenant of Babthorpe, & Sacombe, per legem Angliæ. 2d wife, Katharine, dau. of . . . Aske of Aughton, com. Ebor. Died . 20 Hen. VII. 1504. Buried at Norton-Priory, s. p.	Isabella, dau. of Robert Babthorpe, & cousin & heir of Dame Isabella Hastings. Marriage covenant 11 May, 11 Hen. VII. 1496, being then a minor and in ward to William Babthorpe, her uncle; solemnized 29 Sept. in the same year. WIFE OF WILLIAM PLUMPTON, ESQ.	(William Eleson; dau. w. of . . . . Girlington, a quo Robert and a dau. w. of Ralph Aldborough; a dau. w. of . . . Compton, a quo Thomas.)	Sir William Babthorpe, kt. son and heir, inf. æt. ad mort. patris, æt 29 Apr. 2 Hen. VII. 1510; in ward to his mother and uncle. One of the Council of the North. Died 1 and 2 Ph. and M. 1555.	= Agnes, dau. of Brian Palmes, of Naburn, com. Ebor. esq.

Issue died young.

SIR WILLIAM BABTHORPE, to whom the manor of Babthorpe was awarded 20 Oct. 7 Eliz. 1565.

---

him in the title of the heire of John Suttell." ^a Accordingly, in the course of the three years next following, this too celebrated personage procured the legal estate of the surviving feoffees under the deeds of settlement on the marriages of the heirs-general, though not without exposing them to be persecuted by Sir Robert Plumpton and his servants,^b to be conveyed to certain clerks, Robert Bubwith and Richard Burgh, in whose name a suit was commenced, as feoffees to the use of Sir John Rocliff and Margaret his wife, and of Elizabeth Sotehill, widow. In May, 1501, Mr. Pullan writes word, " that the great man Empson," as far as he could know for certain, intended to have assises against Sir Robert Plumpton; and warns the latter, that, availing himself of the favour it was in his power to show, as one of the King's Council sitting for assessing fines upon such as had not taken up their knighthood, he was secretly labouring to ensure a verdict, by having the persons thus made friendly placed upon the panel for the trial of the assize, in the counties where the lands lay.^c The ground of action alleged will be best understood by transcribing a memorandum of the original declaration in the cause:

" Sir William Plompton, ch'er, seisi de divers maners in les Contes de Everwick, Nott. Derb. et Stafford, avoit issue per un feme, Robert et William; et puis le dit Sir William fyt covenaunt ove Thomas, Signieur de Clifford, que le dit Robert espouse Elizabeth, file de dit Sig^r de Clifford. Et le dit Sir William graunta quil ferra feoffment a les dits Robert et Elizabeth des maners, terres ove tenements, a la valure de xl^{livs}, a aver a eux et les heires le dit Robert et le dit Elizabeth ingenderount, le remainder al droit heires le dit Sir William. Et que touts auters maners et hereditaments que li dit Sir William ou autre a son use adonques avoit, devoit apres le mort le dit Sir William remainer descender et reverter a le dit Robert et a ses heires sauns disinheritance ou incumbrance de ceo ent a fair per le dit Sir William et ses feoffees. Et puis le dit Sir William de touts ses maners, terres et tenements in les Contes de Everwike, Nottingham, Derb. et Stafford enfeffet Jehan Tempest Ch'er et autres in fee, sur condition que les dits Feoffes, quant ils serount per le dit Sir William requises, enfeofferount le dit Sir William et un tiel en fee quil espousa, de certein de dits maners a la valure c. marcs, a aver a eux pur terme de lour vies, le remainder al dit Robert et a ses heires, et quil ferroit autre estate des tenements a la valure xx marcs a un fitz le dit Sir William qui le nomera pur terme de vie, le remaynder a le dit Robert et a ses heires in fee. Et de touts les residieu des tenements avant dits, que les dits feoffes apres le mort le dit Sir William enfeffe le dit Robert et ses heires en fee, pourveu touts foits, que si le dit Robert morust, vivant le dit Sir William, que ben lirra a le dit Sir William in touts les tenements avant dits, ultre les tenements a le dit Sir William, ses femes et ses fits en le furme avant dit &c. donés et lessés, a rentrer. Puis le dit Robert deins xiiii aunz &c. Et puis le dit Sir William relzeroit (resserroit) les premers covenaunts de marriage covenantés ove Seigneur de Clifford, que le dit William, adonque son fitz et heire apparaunt, espouseroit le dit Elizabeth; et le dit Sir William graunta quil ferra feoffment a les dits William et Elizabeth des certens maners et tenements a le valure de xl^{li}, a aver a eux et a les heyres de le dit William del corps le dit Elizabeth engendrés, le remaynder pur default tiel issue al heyres de le dit Sir William. Et outre graunta quil ferra anuel estate de auters terres et tenementes a les ditz William et Elizabeth a le valure x^{li}, a aver a eux et apprendre les profitz apres la mort Margaret de . . . . . . aylesse (ayeule)^d a le dit Sir William. Et auxi le dit Sir William graunta quil ferra escripts indentés de les premises in

^a Vide Letter XCIV. p. 120.   ^b Letter XCV. p. 122.
^c Letter XCIX. p. 150.

^d Margaret de Rempston, who died very aged on the 21st April, 1454.

due et loiall maner, accordant a les dits escripts endentés faits sur le dit premer . . . . . marriage ; per force de quele le dit William espousa le dit Elizabeth, et avoit issue inter eux deux files, silz, Margaret et Elizabeth. Et le dit William devia. Puis le dit Sir William fit covenant ove Briane Rocliffe pur certen summes dergent a lui paiés, que le dit Margaret, un de ses heyres apparaunts, espousera Johan fitz et heyre apparaunt a le dit Brian, et outre graunta quil ne autre de ses feffes ferroit alyenacion ne discontinuance dacun de ces manors et hereditaments, mes quils entierment apres son mort descenderont et returneront a les heyres le dit William, per force dequel le dit John espousa le dit Margaret, heyre le dit Sir William. Et apres le dit Sir William graunta a un Henry Sotell pur certens summes dergent a lui payés, que Elizabeth, son cosin et auter de ses heyres, espousera un John fitz et heyre apparaunt a le dit Henry. Et outre graunta quil ne nul de ses feffes ferrount acun feoffment ne discontinuance, sil ne soit a seluy qui serra son fitz et heyre male apparaunt, excepts terres et tenements a le valure de c^{li} quil poit doner a terme de vie ou des vies. Come appeart en un Indenture fait lan le tierce le Roy Edward le iiij^{te},^{e} le dit Sir William inffeffa un Richard Fawbergh et autres persons de touts ses terres et tenementes en les Countés de Notingham, Derby, et Stafford, per force de quel ils fueront ent seisis tanque per le dit Sir William disseisés. Et le dit Sir William issint eut seisie et enfeffa le dean de Everwik et auters en fee, qui prist estates a luy pur terme de vie, le remaynder a un Robert Plumpton Ch'er et a ses heyres de son corps engendrés. Et apres le dit Sir William murroit. Apres que mort le dit Sir Robert entra, sur que le dit Richard Fawbergh et les feffees entraient, devant le statute de Richard le tierce. Et

^{e} This deed of feoffment is suppressed in the Cartulary, but a copy has been preserved in the same MS. from which this declaration has been taken, and from which it appears that the true date was 1 Jan. 4 Edw. IV. (see p. lxxii.)

CAMD. SOC. 4. *p*

un Richard Fawbergh, un des enfeffés qui surveyquist son confeffes, reentra et enfeffa ^{f} ceux qui port le . . . .

Item le dit Syr William Plumpton enfeffa un Richard Redman et autres de touts ses terres et tenements en le Counte de Everwyk en fee per force de quel ils fueront seises tanque per le dit William disseiez ; et le dit Syr William re-eyaunt seisin enfeoffa auters persons en fee ; sur que bien le dit Richard, qui fuit en le graunte, entra et enfeffe auters persons al use Margaret et Elizabeth." ^{g}

For the lands lying in the counties of Nottingham, Derby, and Stafford, of which Sir Robert Plumpton had retained possession by force of the award of Richard III. viz. the manor and vills of Kinalton and Mansfield-Woodhouse, the manors of Derley, Stanton, Hassop with Rouland, Combridge, and Crakemersh, trials were had at the Lammas Assizes in the autumn of the year 1501, when, owing, perhaps, to Empson having taken " much lodging " and the way " he undermyneth," ^{h} verdicts were recorded in favour of the above-named feoffees. This result obtained for the prime mover in the cause a grant of the manor of Kinalton, *habendum et tenendum eidem Ricardo Empson et assignatis suis pro termino vitæ ejusdem Ricardi ;*^{i} and about the same time, by his procurement, the son and heir of Dame Elizabeth Sotehill, Henry Sotehill, then a minor, was married to his daughter Joan, or Jane Empson.

The proceedings on the trial, by which it was sought to eject Sir Robert Plumpton from the patrimonial inheritance in Yorkshire, are made known to us in the following memorial.

" For as much as it is meritorius to every Christian man to

^{f} This feoffment was made before 2 July,15 Hen. VII. 1500. *Vide* Letter CXXIV. n. a.
^{g} Add. MSS. in Brit. Mus. 6698. Wolley's Collections. *Ex MS. Joh'is Sudbury, olim de Alfreton, com. Derb. Attornat.*
^{h} Letter CXXVII. and Letter CXIX.
^{i} Cited in *Inq. post mortem Elizabethæ Sotehill*. At the date of this grant Sir Richard Empson had not been knighted.

certyfie the trewth in such cawses as they shalbe required for the declaration of trewth to be had in the said causes, and that Sir Robert Plompton, knight, hath required us to certifie the demesner of Sir Richard Emson, knight, at the assise that Robert Bubwith and Richard Burgh, prestes,^{k} arained against the said Sir Robert at York of the maners of Plompton and Idell to the use of Sir John Roucliffe and Margret his wife, and Dame Elizabeth Sotehill and the sircumstance thereof. Therfore it is that we whose names hearafter ensueth upon our trewth testyfie that the foresaid Sir Richard Empson, acompened with Edward Stanhopp,^{l} Gervis Clifton,^{m} Robert Dimmoke^n and William Perpoynt,^{o} knights, and other gentlemen and yeomen to the number of 200 persons and moe, and divers of the garde of our Soveraigne Lord the King arayed in the most honnorable liverie of his said garde, came to Yorke to maintaine the foresaid Robert and Richard in the said assise, and theare abode with the said companie at their costs and charges to the time that the said assise passed against the foresaid Sir Robert. Also we testifie that John Vavasor Justice then associat to Umfray Conysby Justice to the said assise then shewed in open courte a fine exemplified under the greate seale of England saing that therin wear comprised the foresaid manors taled to the heires generall of Sir William Plompton, and the Counsell of the foresaid Sir Robert desired hearing therof and might not have it by no meanes. And then the frinds of the said Sir Robert trusting it to be trew upon the credence that they gave to the foresaid Sir John Vavasor labored for a

^{k} The declaration above transcribed gives Richard Redman as the name of the feoffee who conveyed to Bubwith and Burgh, but in the Cartulary is a copy of a grant to the same parties from John Ingilby, esq. of the manors of Plompton, Idell, Steveton, Garsington in Craven, and Little Studley near Rippon, in com. Ebor. dated 7 May, 17 Hen. VII. 1501. *(Cartul. n.* 818.)
^{l} Sir Edward Stanhope, of Rampton, com. Nott. kt.
^{m} Sir Gervase Clifton, of Clifton, com. Nott. kt.
^{n} Sir Robert Dymoke, of Scrivelsby, com. Linc. kt.
^{o} Sir William Pierpoint, of Holme, com. Nott. kt.

treaty ; whearupon Sir Marmaduke Constable knight ^{p} and Brian Palmes ^{q} wear chossen arbitrators for the foresaid Robert Bubwith and Richard Burgh, and Sir William Gascoigne knight and William Eleson ^{r} for the foresaid Sir Robert. Which iiij arbitrators met at the chapel of Yorke Brige for the said matter, and then and theare the said Sir William Gascoigne and William Eleson desired to have hearing of the foresaid fine and might not have it. And then the said Sir William Gascoigne and William Eleson went to Sir Robert Plompton and shewed him the ofer of the said Sir Marmaduke and Bryan which he refuse and said that he would not departe with noo party of his land, for he said that he had very knowledge that the fine that was sheweth belonged to Wylliam Mydleton, and that the foresaid manors wear not comprised therin. Whearupon the said Sir William Gascoigne and William Eleson went to the foresaid Chappell, and thear shewed to the foresaid Sir Marmaduke and Brian that they had knowledge that the foresaid manors wear not tailed to the heires generall of Sir William Plompton, and said that they weare tayled to the heires male of Sir William Plompton, and the said Sir William Gascoigne opened a box and said to the foresaid Sir Marmaduke and Bryan, " hear ar the dedes whearby the foresaid mannors ar tayled to the heires male of Sir William Plompton," and saide he would no further treate in the matter and so brake the treaty. In witnes and trew testimonie of which premises We William Gascoygne, Christofer Warde knights,^{s} Henry Vavosor, Thomas Pigot, Henry Ughtred, Thomas Fairfax, Richard Maulevery, Richard Kyghley, Nicholas Gascoigne, Robert Chylton, Thomas Ratcliffe, Walter Baylton, Thomas Nawdon, Walter Woode, Esquires, William Lindley, Richard Wod, Lancelot Wod,

^{p} Sir Marmaduke Constable, of Flamborough, com. Ebor. kt.
^{q} Brian Palmes, of Leathley, com. Ebor. called Serjeant 18 Nov. 1511.
^{r} William Eleson, of Selby, gent. ; half-brother to Mrs. Isabel Plumpton, wife of William Plumpton, esq. eldest son of Sir Robert.
^{s} Sir Christopher Ward, of Givendale, com. Ebor. kt.

Percivell Lindley, George Oglestrope, Edmund Richworth, Robert Oglestrop, Thomas Knarsbrough, William Aldbrough, Robert Knarsbrough, William Scargill, Raufe Moure, John Douning, William Scargill yonger, gentlemen, William Dickinson, Thomas Saxton, Thomas Wood, John Graver, Tho: Dickinson, John Hardistie, Will. Paver, Will: Beshe, Rob't Dickinson, Nickolas Atherton, Tho: Dickinson, Roger Dickinson, John Beckwith, Rob't Gelsthorpe, Will: Beaston, John Graver yonger, Stephen Hardistie, Raufe Stanfeild, Stephen Gyll, Rob't Richardson, Myles Gill, Myles Wood, Rob't Dickinson, John Gefray, John Pullaine, Thomas Kendell, Stephen Beaston, John Fairborne, James Wod, Percivill Whytehead, Tho: Brædebelt, Will: Robinson, John Bradbelt, John Scaife, Tho: Bayldon, Edmond Mydlebroke, Tho: Exelby, Rob't Wayde, James Holynaghe, James Helme, Richard Barker, Henry Readshaw, Will: Shutley, John Swayle, Rob't Folyfote, Thomas Kyghly and Richard Coundall, yeomen, with others, we have put our seales. Given the 18 day of January the yeare of the reigne of our most dread liege King Henry the VII after the conquest of England the xx[th]." [t]

Among the transcripts of evidence in the Towneley MSS. relating to the family of Plumpton, is also this *Memorandum* of the challenges made by the defendant: " Upon a pannell for the Assizes 18 Hen. VII. there are exceptions against the Jury by reason the persons were either relations or had dependance on the parties interested, by which it may appeare who wer the principall sticklers in that great Contraversy for the Complenant—Sr William Conyers [u] . . . . Rad'us Ryther ch'r, Nicholas Skyres Esq. serviens Viccomitis,[w] Joh'es Dodsworth ar. serviens Will'i Conyers, Jacobus Cure (Eure?) serviens d'ni Henrici Clifford, Will's Nesfield ar. consang. querent. D'nus Ric'us Aldburgh miles consang: Henry Wakefeild gen: serviens Ric'i Aldburgh, Joh'nes Chamber serviens Ric'i Aldburgh, S[r] Rich: Hamerton, Ralph Nevill, John Nevill, Brian Stapleton, John Tempest, ... Pudsey."

Notwithstanding the verdict thus given against him, Sir Robert Plumpton was determined not to surrender possession to the claimants without a forcible resistance. The following letter was dispatched by him with this view to his wife from York on Friday after the trial, 9 Sept. 18 Hen. VII. 1502.

To my entyrely and right hartily beloved wife, Dame Agnes Plumpton, be this Letter delivered.

My deare hart, in my most hartily wyse, I recommend mee unto you, hartily prayinge you, all things laid apart, that you see that the manor and the place of Plumpton bee surely and stedfastly kept; and alsoe that I have this Tuesday at even 6 muttons slene, to bee ordained for the supper the said Tuesday at nighte: and alsoe that yee cause this said Tuesday a beast to be killed, that if neede bee, that I may have it right shortly. As for my nephew Gascoigne, my couzen Pygot,[x] my brother Ward,[y] Ralph Nevill,[z] Ninne Markinfeld,[a] Thomas Fairfax,[b] Nicholas Girlington,[c] with many other frends and lovers were with mee at supper this night. And thus I betake you to the keepinge of the Holy Trinity, who preserve you evermore to his pleasure. From Yorke

[t] Cartul. No. 824. "Copied the 12th of November (1627), having 69 seals besides them that is broken off."
[u] Sir William Conyers, of Hornby, com. Ebor. kt. first Baron Conyers.
[w] Sir Thomas Wortley, of Wortley, com. Ebor. kt. was Sheriff of Yorkshire in 1502.

[x] Sir Randolph Pygot, of Clotherholme, com. Ebor. kt. Cb[t] 1503, buried in Ripon minster.
[y] Sir Christopher Ward, brother-in-law to Sir Robert Plumpton.
[z] Ralph Nevill, of Thornton, com. Ebor. esq. son-in-law of Sir Christopher Ward.
[a] Sir Ninian Markenfield, of Markenfield, com. Ebor. kt. Will dated 1 Oct. 1527, proved 5 July 1528. Buried before the high altar of St. Andrew, in the collegiate church of Ripon.
[b] Sir Thomas Fairfax, of Walton, com. Ebor. kt. married Anne Gascoigne, niece of Dame Agnes Plumpton.
[c] Nicholas Girlington, of Hackforth, com. Ebor. esq. *jure uxoris*, who was Margaret dau. and coh. of Thomas Montfort.

this Tuesday (*lege* Friday), the morrowe next after the nativity of our Lady.

By your owne lover Robert Plompton Kt.[d]

In the reasonable hope that the King would have a grateful recollection of his former services, Sir Robert Plumpton had also in this emergency direct recourse to the Crown for protection.

" In most lamentable and piteous wise sheweth and complaineth unto your most gratious highnes your daylye Orator and . . . . . Robert Plumpton Kn[t], how that Sir John Rocliffe, dame Margaret his wife, and Elizabeth Sothill, through the great . . . . . maintenance and supportation of Richard Empson, &c. have recovered by assize lands of the value of 500[li], whereof your orator and ancestors have beene seased above 300 yeares &c. And the said Sir John and Richard, not regarding the displeasure of God nor of your Grace, intend to attach and cast in prison the body of your beseecher &c. Wherefore the said Orator hath and ever shall bee best content to put his said whole lands to the judgement and award of your most noble Grace and councell, or upon any two Judges. And wherefore, most gracious Soveraigne Lord, your said poore Orator, at the reverence of Almighty God, humbly beseecheth your grace that hee may have protection . . . . for a whole yeare &c. and shew the same how craftily and by maintenance hee is disherited of all his said lands, which without onely the helpe of your Grace he can never recover."

To this Sir John Rowcliffe answered, " that all was done by processe of the Kings Laws, and that Judgment cannot bee examined but by writ of . . . . or attainder, yet they submit to make good the said Judgment &c. recovered by the said Assize. And

[d] Dodsworth MSS. in Bib. Bodl. Oxon. vol. CXLVIII. f. 62. In 18 Hen. VII. 1502, the feast of the Nativity of our Lady, 8 Sept. fell upon a Thursday, and this letter being written on the morrow of the feast, the date would be Friday. That Tuesday is a mistake of the writer through inadvertence is also obvious from the contents of the letter, which refer to that day as remote. There is a transcript of this letter in the Towneley MSS.

. . . . hath fortifyed the same &c. with guns, bowes, crossebowes, bills, speares and other weapons &c. as if it were in . . . . . of warr, soe that ne the Sheriffe ne other officers of the Kings &c. cannot and may not serve the Kings processe without jeopardy, and perill of mans lives, manslaughter, and murder, to the worst and most perillous example that in this land hath been seene sith the Kings reigne &c." [e]

The appeal of Sir Robert Plumpton was, however, favourably listened to by King Henry VII., who forthwith made him a Knight of his Body, thus screening his person from arrest; and sent " To our trusty and welbeloved Sir William Conyers, Sheriffe of our County of Yorke, &c. that hee serve noe writs, precepts, or other writings, upon Sir Robert Plumpton, Knight of our Body, or his servants," &c.

This was followed by another precept, to Sir Christofer Ward and Sir William Calverley, kn[ts]. " that William Plompton, son and

[e] During Sir Robert Plumpton's visit to the Court, the manor-place of Plumpton had been left in charge of his wife and his eldest son William, with directions to distrain upon all tenants who, by reason of the warning on the part of Sir John Rocliffe and Dame Elizabeth Sotehill, should refuse to pay the rents due at Martinmas. This was done; and they, not being able to recover their cattle and household stuff, thus seized, by replevy in the usual manner, made complaint to the Archbishop of York, who in vain interfered on their behalf. Whereupon he caused William Plumpton and sixteen of his servants to be indicted, and when the jury would not return a true bill, he made them to do so by a threat of punishing him who made refusal. William Plumpton, however, still set the Archbishop at defiance, and under a promise of assistance in case of need from Sir William Gascoigne, determined to resist all attempts on the part of Sir John Rocliff to plough the land, by force of arms, and to treat the tenants who did not acknowledge him as their landlord, as trespassers. (See *Correspondence of Sir Robert Plumpton, Letter CXXXIV. et seq.*) Into the Cartulary is copied a writ of *capias*, directed from William Conyers, kt. Sheriff of Yorkshire, to Thomas Spinke, bailiff of the wapentake of Clarro, against Richard Coates, and divers other husbands, laborors, yeomen, shermen, a webster, and a smith, at the suit of William Plumpton, esq. of a plea of trespass, returnable on Thursday next after *quindena Pasch.* to bring their bodies to the castle at York. " Dat. in castro Ebor'. sub sigillo officii mei xx die Apr. anno r. r. Hen. 7. XVIII." *(Cartul No. 820.)*

heir of Sir Robert Plompton, peacably enjoy the Lordships of Plumpton, and Idle, and the rents, &c. Dated Collyweston 16 July."[f]

The further steps taken by Sir Robert Plumpton in his matters, will best appear from the following letter, written by him to his Lady, upon occasion of her second journey to London, and dated Tuesday 13 Feb. 19 Hen. VII. 1503-4.

To my right hartily and mine entyrely beloved wife, Dame Agnes Plompton, bee this delivered.

Best beloved, in my most harty wyse I recommend mee unto you. Soe it is, I mervaile greatly, that yee send mee not the money that yee promised mee to send with John Waukar within 8 dayes after you and I departed, for I am put to a great lacke for it. Therefore, I hartily pray you, as my especiall trust is in you, to send me the said money in all hast possible, and alsoe to send me money, for my cost,is very sore and chargeable at this tyme: for I have spent of the money that I brought from you more then v[li]. For very certaine, Sir Roger Hastings[g] is at the point of undoinge, because hee hath not money to pay where he ought to pay. Therefore, deare hart, I pray you to remember mee. And as for my matter, there is noe mooveinge of it as yet, but the Kings grace is the same man hee was at my last departinge from his grace; and my lord of Winchester,[h] and Mr. Lovell,[i] Mr. Gylforth,[k] Mr. Weston,[l] with all our good friends, are to mee as they were at my last departinge. And as shortly as I can have any way certaine of my matters, I shall send you word. Nevertheles, my adversaries had laboured to have had a privy seale against mee; but my lord of Winchester and Mr. Deane of the Kings Chappell would let them have none to tyme were that they understood . . . . . whether I was in sicknes or nay. And for diverse consideracions and greate hurts might falle to you and mee and our children hereafter, I heartily pray you to remember to hast the money unto mee, as my especiall trust and love is in you, as knowes the holy Trinity, who preserve you evermore to his pleasure. From London in hast, the Tuesday next afore St. Valentines day, by your lovinge husband, Robert Plompton, kt.

Postscript by Richard Plompton, Priest. Madam, your bedeman servant, Sir Richard Plompton, hartely prayes you to remember all the matters above written, for my Masters adversaries and yours purveys them to bee still with the Kings grace, and entends to impoverish my Master, and all those that will take his part and doe for him.[m]

The reply of Dame Agnes Plumpton to this letter will be found in the Correspondence of Sir Robert Plumpton, Letter CXLIX. and in the Letters which there follow may be seen the course of conduct pursued by "the adversaries." In this same year, and probably in the month of August, Dame Agnes Plumpton died; after whose death her husband, Sir Robert, remained a widower for about a year, when he was again united to Isabella, daughter of Ralph Lord Nevill, eldest son and heir apparent of Ralph Earl of Westmorland, by his second[n] wife, Edith, daughter of Sir William Sands, of the Vine, com. Hants. kt. and sister of the accom-

[f] Towneley MSS. The King was at Collyweston in July 1503. (*Lel. Coll. IV. p.* 265.)
[g] Sir Roger Hastings of Roxby, com. Ebor. kt.
[h] Richard Fox, Bishop of Winchester, Lord Privy Seal, ob. 14 Sept. 1528.
[i] Sir Thomas Lovell, K. G. Treasurer of the Household and President of the Council.
[k] Sir Richard Guildford, K. G.   [l] Sir Richard Weston, kt.

[m] Dodsworth MSS. in Bib. Bodl. Oxon. vol. cxlviii. f. 62. " In Sir Edward Plumpton's Booke of Letters." *See Introduction.*
[n] Lord Nevill married first, in presence of King Henry VII. and his Queen, the daughter of William Paston, esq. Of the death of this Lady, the Herald, whose valuable memorials have been printed by Hearne, in the *Collectanea Lelandi*, has this notice: "The King, the Quen, and my Ladie the Kings moder, beganne Crysmas at Westmynster, and at that season ther wer the Meazelles soo strong, and in especiall amongis Ladies and Gentilwemen, that sum died of that sikeness, as the Ladie Nevill, daughter of William Paston." This was in the fifth year of Henry VII. 1489, and she must have died issueless, as her sisters, the wives of Sir Gilbert Talbot and Sir John Savill, knts. were the heirs of William Paston. Lord Nevill's second marriage

plished courtier Sir William Sands, K. G. advanced to the degree of a Baron of the Realm, by the title of Lord Sands, 27 April, 15 Hen. VIII. 1523, and introduced by Shakespeare under that title in his historic play of Henry the Eighth. The covenants for the settlement of her jointure bear date 18 and 20 Sept. 21 Hen. VII. 1505; and the same was charged upon such lands as Sir Robert Plumpton had purchased in the vills and fields of Knaresborough, Mathe or Matge Lofthouse near Knaresborough, Huby, Helthwait-hill near Harwood, Aketon, Spofforth, and Arkendale, under a feoffment to Sir William Sands, kt. Sir John Rainsford, kt. Sir John Norton, kt. Edward Rainesford, esq. and others. Her father, the Lord Nevill, had been dead[o] since 13 Hen. VII. 1498, and the Lady Nevill, her mother, was probably at this time the wife of Sir Thomas Darcy, K.G. created a Baron before the close of the reign of Henry VII.; and whom King Henry VIII. in the first year of his reign, made steward and surveyor of all the lands beyond Trent then in the Crown, during the minority of his step-son, Ralph Earl of Westmorland, brother of Dame Isabell, otherwise Elizabeth, Plumpton.[p] By her, who survived him, and remarried Lawrence Kighley of New-Hall near Otley, com. Ebor. esq.[q] Sir Robert Plumpton left no issue.

In the following year Dame Elizabeth Sotehill died, upon whose death an inquisition was taken, 16 Jan. 22 Hen. VII. 1506-7, of the lands of her inheritance which she had recovered by assize in the county of Nottingham against Sir Robert Plumpton; and some time after, another writ, *ad melius inquirendum post mortem Elizabeth Sotehill viduæ*, was sent to William Crouche, the Escheator of the county of York. In pursuance thereof, an inquest was taken at

was likewise solemnized in the royal presence, as appears by an authentic list of *Marriages in the King and the Quenes presence, where summe officers of arms have ben present.* Among these entries we have, " Item. The Lord Nevill furst to the doughter of William Paston; after to the suster of Sir William Sands." (*Coll. Top. et Gen. vol. i. p.* 22, *from a MS. of the time of Hen. VIII. penès D'n'm Tho. Phillipps, Baronettum.*)

[o] Edward Strangwyshe and William Pollard were presented to the living of Brancepeth and the Mastership of Steindrop College, by Richard Fox, Bishop of Durham, respectively on the 12th and 20th July, 13 Hen. VII. 1498, *ratione custodiæ terrarum et tenementorum quæ nuper fuerunt Radulfi nuper comitis Westmorland et minoris ætatis Radulfi heredis ejusdem et nunc comitis Westmorland in manibus dicti Episcopi existentis.* Both the Earl of Westmorland and his son, Lord Nevill, were with the army under the Earl of Surrey, which entered Scotland in July 1497; and the latter was one of the conservators on the English side of the truce concluded at Aytoun, 30 Sept. 13 Hen. VII. 1497. When this truce was renewed, 12 July, 1499, the name of Lord Nevill, as being then dead, was omitted, but all the other conservators are the same on both sides. The precise date of his father's death is unascertained; but we know from the report of Leland, an excellent authority, as almost contemporary, that the Earl died for grief at the loss of his son, at Hornby Castle in Richmondshire, and lay buried in the parish church there. (*Lel. Itin. vol. i. f.* 60.) The infant heir was brought up at Court; and among the privy purse expences of Henry VII. are payments in 1499, " for a horse, bridell, and sadell for young Nevill, 11s. 8d. For a Kendall cote for litell Nevil, 3s. 4d." *Excerpta Historica. Bentley,* 1831, *p.* 122.

[p] In 1503, the Lady Nevill was one of the Ladies who accompanied the princess Margaret, the affianced Queen of Scotland, to the Court of that Realm; at which date the first wife of Sir Thomas Darcy, Dowsabella, daughter of Sir Richard Tempest, of Giggleswick in Ribblesdale, com. Ebor. kt. was yet living; for after her husband had met the royal train at the entrance of the town of Berwick, of which he was captain, and received the Queen into the place, "she was conveyed and brought to the Castell, wher she was receyved by the Lady D'Arcy honestly accompanyed." (*Vide De rebus Anglicanis opuscula varia, apud Lel. Coll. vol. iv. p.* 279.) Lady Nevill, for she retained that more ancient distinction of title after her union with Lord D'Arcy, died at Stepney, 22 Aug. 1529, and was buried at the Friars Minors in Greenwich, in Kent, leaving issue by her second husband an only daughter, Elizabeth, married to Sir Marmaduke Constable of Flamborough, in com. Ebor. kt.

[q] By indenture made 10 March, 10 Hen. VIII. 1528-9, betwixt William Plompton, of Plompton, esq. of the one partie, and Lawrence Kighley, of Newaly neare Otley, esq. of the other partie, the lands, &c. lying in Roughfarlington, in the countie of York, except the new house and the orchard, together with other premises in Plumpton and Knaresborough assigned to Dame Isabell Plompton, late wife of Sir Robert Plompton, knight, and now wife to the said Lawrence, in the name of her feofment, were exchanged for a rent-charge of xx marks annually during the joint lives of the said Lawrence and Isabel; and if the said Lawrence fortune to die living the said Isabell, she to enter upon and have the same during her natural life. (*Cartul. No.* 856.) Dame Isabel Plumpton was second wife to Lawrence Kighley, esq.; his first wife was Ann, daughter of Thomas Lyndley, of Scutterskelf, com. Ebor. esq. to whom her issue by him were coheirs. (*Vide Pedigree of Lyndley, in Graves' History of Cleveland.*)

Pontefret, 20 Nov. 23 Hen. VII. 1507, by the oath of Thomas Ellis, esq. George Moore, gent. and others, of which the finding was, that Robert Bubwith and Richard Burghs, clerks, by virtue of a recovery specified in the same writ, were seised *(inter alia)* in their demesne as of fee of the manor of Plumpton with its appurtenances to the use of Margaret, wife of Sir John Rowcliffe, kt. and of Elizabeth Sotehill, and of their heirs,—that they had been so seised until they were disseised by Sir Robert Plumpton, kt.—that the said Robert Bubwith had died, and that the said Richard Burgh was yet surviving,—that on the day the said Elizabeth Sotehill died, viz. 21 Sept. 22 Hen. VII. the fee and right of the said manor with its appurtenances belonged to the said Richard Burgh and his heirs, by right of survivorship, to the use abovesaid. This and the previous Inquisition were returned into the Chancery *per manus Ricardi Emson militis*, who still continued intent on asserting the legal claims of the heirs-general, now doubly dear to him, as centering in part in his own blood ; for Henry Sotehill had died in his mother's lifetime in 1505, leaving by Joan Empson twin daughters, Joan and Elizabeth, who had only completed the first year of their age on the feast of the Ascension of our Lord next before the death of their grandmother, i. e. on the 21st May, 1506.r

Meanwhile, the continuance of the dispute brought along with it a heavy expence, and the straits to which it gradually reduced the family of the subject of these Memoirs, will be found strongly depicted in a letter from Dame Isabel Plumpton to her husband, inserted in the Correspondence. After the accession of Henry VIII. these difficulties so increased upon Sir Robert Plumpton, now no longer protected as an Officer of the Court, that he was arrested for debt, and committed prisoner to the Counter. Of his sojourn there I find this memorial in the Cartulary :

r Henry Sotehill, of Stockfaston, com. Leic. esq. who died thus young, was buried in the Grey Friars, London. *(Coll. Top. et. Gen. vol. v. p. 269.)* Both Inquisitions are copied at length among Plumpton Evidences in the Towneley MSS.

Item, that I Sir Robert Plompton, knight, and Oliver Dickinson, my servant, hath paid unto Hew Reding, the Keaper of the Counter in the Pailtre, and his wife, al manner of duties for meat, drinke, and fire, since the 12th day of May, the second yeare of our soveraigne Lord King Henry the eight, unto Mydsomer eve, the same yeare—44s. 10d. And the foresaid Sir Robert Plomton cam untill the foresaid counter first the xxiiij day of Aprill, and paid for every maile of meate unto the foresaid xii day of May, iiij^d for himselfe, and ii^d for his servant. *Item*. the foresaid Sir Robert Plompton paid by the hands of Oliver Dickinson to the wife of the said Hew Reding, the Thursday next after Mydsomer day, the same yeare, for his bed and his chamber—xx^s.

Item. The foresaid Sir Robert Plompton was discharged by Hew Reding for meat and drinke, the xiiii day of July, the yeare abovesaid.

Item. The foresaid Sir Robert Plompton come into comens with Oliver Dickinson his servant the 25 July unto super againe

Item. Edward Soole paid unto Hewgh Reding, the xxx day July, for the board of Sir Robert Plompton and his servant—xx^s.

Memor. That Sir Robert Plompton and dame Ezabell, his wife, hath paid unto Mrs. Reding, the 5 day of August, the yeare abovesaid, for al manner of meate, drink, and bedding, and al other things for himselfe, his wife, and servant—iiij^{li}, and is even for every thing to this present day of August.s

But if beggary and imprisonment were the lot of Sir Robert Plumpton, a more dreadful doom awaited his arch-enemy, Sir Richard Empson, whose maintenance and barratry in the preceding reign now brought down upon his devoted head the vengeful clamours of the victims of his oppressions. On the seventeenth day of August, in this same second year of King Henry VIII. he was led forth to execution, and, with his accomplice Dudley, beheaded on Tower Hill, upon a false pretext of treason to the

s Cartul. No. 836.

State. His death appears to have opened the doors to a compromise of this protracted suit ; although that course, perhaps, was now become a matter of necessity on the part of Sir Robert Plumpton. In the first year of Henry VIII. (22 Aug. 1509,) the custody of Joan and Elizabeth Sotehill above-mentioned, with their marriage, had been granted by the King to Sir William Perpoint of Holme, com. Notts, kt. who had married their mother, the daughter of Sir Richard Empson, and widow of Henry Sotehill, esq. Of him the marriage of the eldest of these coheirs had been purchased by Sir Marmaduke Constable of Flamborough, com. Ebor. kt. as a match for his fourth son, John Constable, esq. who from that time had her wardship. With the last-named knight, who was nearly allied to all parties, a meeting was appointed to be held at York, for the Tuesday after the feast of the Translation of St. William, 10 Jan. 6 Hen. VIII. 1514-5, by Sir William Gascoigne, on the behalf of his uncle and cousin, Sir Robert and William Plumpton, to treat of the matter in traverse between them, and Sir John Rocliffe and his coparceners ; whereat it was agreed that the said parties should abide the award of the Bishop of Winchester, the Lord Treasurer, the Earl of Surrey, and other arbitrators indifferently chosen.t A bond, under penalty of a thousand marks, was entered into by Sir Marmaduke and John Constable, Sir John Rccliffe, and Sir William Perpoynte, to Sir Robert Plompton and William Plompton, 20 March following, to have effect, " so that the same awarde, ordinance, and jugement be maid and given afore the feast of Easter next ensuing ;"u and on the 27th of the same month the following judgement was pronounced in pursuance thereof :

"To all christian people, to whome this present writing indented shall come, heare, or se, we Richard, by the sufrance of God Bishop of Winchester, Sir Thomas Lovill, knight, Tresurrer of The most honorable houshold of our Soveraigne Lord the King,

t See Letter CLXX. et. seq. p. 207. u Cartul. No. 840.

Robert Brudnell, one of the Justices of our Soveraigne Lord, and John Earnley, generall attorney of the said Kinge, send greting in our Lord. Wheeras thear hath bene divers variances and debaites late moved and had betwene Sir John Rouclife, knight, and dame Margret his wife, one of the cossines and heires of Sir William Plompton, sometime of Plompton in the county of Yorke, knight, Sir William Perpoynte, knight, gardien of Elizabeth Sotehill, another of the cossines and heires of Sir William Plompton, Sir Marmaduke Constable thelder, knight, and John Constable, esquire, gardine of Jane Sotehill, another of the cossines and heires of Sir William Plompton, on thone partie, and Sir Robert Plompton of Plompton aforesaid, knight, and William Plompton, son and heire aparent of the said Sir Robert, on thother partie, of and upon the right, &c. we the foresaid arbytrators, calling afore us the Councils of the foresaid parties, hearing and seing their titles, &c. at the special request and by the consent of the foresaid parties, award, ordeyne, and deame of and upon the same, manner and forme following.

"First, we award, ordeyne, and deame that the foresaid Sir Robert Plompton and Will. Plompton his son, shall have and injoy from henceforth the foresaid mannor of Plompton, and all the messuages, lands, &c. within Plompton, or within the parish of Spofford aforesaid, within the said county of York, to have and to hold all the same mannors, &c. to the same Sir Robert and Will: his son during their lives, and after their disease to the heir male of the body of the said Sir Robert Plompton lawfully begotten, and to the heirs males of their bodyes lawfully begotten, and for defaut of such heires males, the said mannors, &c. to remaine and come to the foresaid Dame Margret Rouclife, Elizabeth Sottehill, and Jane Sottehill, and to their heires, as cossines and heires to the foresaid Sir William Plompton, knight.

"Also we award, ordeine, and deame that the foresaid Sir John Rouclife, and Dame Margret his wife, the foresaid Sir Will: Perpoynte, and Dame Jane his wife, mother of the foresaid Elizabeth and Jane, when they shall be therto required, and the foresaid Sir Marmaduke and John Constable, and the foresaid Elizabeth and Jane, at the full age of the said Elizabeth and Jane, by fine, deade with warranty against thabbut of Westminster and his successors, and otherwise, shall do, sufer, and cause to be done all such things reasonable, as the foresaid Sir Robert, &c. shall devise for the making sure the foresaid mannor of Plompton, &c.

"Also we award, ordeine, and deame, that the foresaid Sir John Rouclife, &c. shall have and enjoy the resedeu of all the foresaid mannors, &c. to them and their heires, according to their inheretance to them from the aforesaid Sir Will: Plompton, knight, descended, &c.

"Also we award, ordeine, and deame that Sir Anthonie Seale, clarke, shall have and enjoy his Chauntre in Ripon, which he now hath, according to the statutes and ordinaries of the same Chauntre; *the Chantry to be hereafter in the gift of such as be lords of the manor of Plumpton, if it may be so proved of right to belong; all other benefices to remain to the heirs general.*

"Also we award, ordeine, and deame, if it can be proved afore us the said arbytrators, or any of us, within a yeare next after the date of theise presents, that the foresaid Sir Robert Plompton hath purchased any lands, tenements, and hereditaments within the foresaid mannors, &c. or at his cost and charges hath redeemed or brought home by reason of any title auncestrell any lands, &c. and the same lands, &c. be of like yearly value over all charges, as the foresaid lands, &c. in Studley Rogers aforesaide be yearly worth over all charges or debittes, that then the foresaid Sir John Rouclife, &c. shall have to them and their heires of the forsaid Dame Margret, Elizabeth and Jane Sotehill, according to their forsaid olde inheritance, all the foresaid lands, &c. and the foresaid Sir Robert Plompton shall then have to him and his heires all the foresaid lands, &c. in Studley Rogers aforesaid, *any over-*

plus to be made good in money, after the rate of xvi years purchase."ᵛ

By way of collateral security for the performance of the award by Elizabeth and Jane Sotehill when they came of full age, or by their husbands, if married, an estate of 40ˡⁱ per annum out of lands of the proper inheritance of Sir William Perpoynt and Sir Marmaduke Constable was, by covenants of the same date as the award, agreed to be limited to feoffees, to be conveyed to Sir Robert Plumpton and William his son, in case of any refusal on their part; the legal cost of which feoffment was either to be borne by Sir Robert and his son, or they to pay 53s. 4d. to Sir William Perpoynt and to Sir Marmaduke and John Constable.ʷ And as a further assurance, in Hillary Term, 7 Hen. VIII. 1515-6, Sir John Norton, kt. Sir Richard Maulevery, kt. Sir Thomas Fairfax, kt. and Sir William Maulevery, kt. recovered against Sir Robert Plumpton, kt. and William, his son and heir apparent, the manor of Plumpton with all appurtenances in the parish of Spofford, they having called to warranty Sir John Rouclife, kt. and Margaret his wife; and to the same four knights Richard Burgh, clerk, the survivor of the party in whose name the assize had been brought, made a release in full, 10 July, 8 Hen. VIII. 1516. Subsequently, at the special request of Sir Robert Plumpton and his son, and in pursuance of articles of agreement dated 6 March, 10 Hen. VIII. 1518-9, the four knights named in the recovery conveyed to William Ingleby and Guy Wilstrop, esqrs. Robert Plumpton, junior, esq. son of the said Sir Robert Plumpton, and Thomas Angrom, clerk, a messuage called Rough Farlington, and all other the lands in Rough Farlington, (save two closes held by

ᵛ Cartul. No. 841.
ʷ Cartul. No. 840. In Michaelmas Term, 7 Hen. VIII. Sir Bryan Stapleton, kt. Sir Richard Sacheverell, kt. Sir Thomas Fairfax, kt. and Sir William Mauleverer, kt. recovered against Sir William Perpoynt, kt. the manor of Woodhouse, with appurtenances in Cukney, com. Nott. of the inheritance of Sir William, in fulfilment of this covenant. (*Ibid. No. 863.*)

Richard Plumpton, chaplain,ˣ for term of his life, and of those the reversion,) another messuage called Morhouse, also lying within the demesne and manor of Plumpton, and three burgages in Knaresborough, to the use of Sir Robert Plumpton, and Isabell, or Elizabeth, his wife, and to the longer liver of them, to secure thereout a jointure of 20 marks; and a further estate of the yearly value of ten pounds was to be made to the same feoffees, for raising annuities for the three younger sons of Sir Robert Plumpton, to commence after his decease, viz. the said Robert Plumpton the younger, Marmaduke Plumpton, and Nele Plumpton, the remainders being to the heirs male as specified by the award. At the same time the manor of Plumpton, and all the other lands and tenements so recovered, were conveyed to Thomas Linley, Robert Lampton, John Birnand, esquires, to hold to the use of Sir Robert Plumpton for term of his life without impeachment of waste, and after his decease to the use of William Plumpton and of the heires male of his body coming, and for default to the heirs male of Sir Robert Plumpton.ʸ

The domestic economy of the family, after they had obtained this final confirmation of their title to the ancient residence of their knightly race, is somewhat curiously exhibited in the following document, which I transcribe entire from the Cartulary.

"This indenture made the 2 of May, in the 7 yeare of King Henry the 8, betwixt Sir Robert Plompton of Plompton, knight,

ˣ Richard Plumpton, chaplain, was son and heir of Godfrey Plumpton, next brother of Sir William Plumpton, named in the entail to the heirs male made by his brother in his lifetime. After the settlement in performance of the award, Sir Richard released all right and title in the estates of Sir William Plumpton, to William son and heir apparent of Sir Robert Plumpton, kt. by deed dated 20 Aug. 11 Hen. VIII. 1519, and witnessed by Sir William Gascoigne, senior, kt. Sir Richard Mawlevery, kt. Sir Thomas Farfax, kt. Robert Teske, Minister of the house of St. Robert near Knaresbrough, Richard Chirdin and others (*Cartul. No. 851.*); which release he renewed 20 Dec. 15 Hen. VIII. 1523. (*Ibid. No.* 854.)
ʸ Cartul. No. 867, 869, et 870.

on the one partie, and William Plompton, son and heire to Sir Robert, esquire, on the other partie, witnesseth that it is agreade betwixt the said parties, in manner and forme following. First, it is agreed that the said Will: Plompton shal have ordering and charge of all the houshold and goods therto longing, and his said father, and my Lady his wife, to take their ease and reast, and to be at board with the said William at the proper costs and charges of the said Will: Also the said Sir Robert hath granted to the said Will: al the revenewes and profitts of all the lands and tenements with the Lordship of Plompton, to the intent that the said Will: shall stand and be charged with all manner costage belonging to the said house and houshold, that is to say, meate, drinke, and wages. Also it is agreed that the said Will: shall stand to and be charged with his brothers and sisters in all things neccessary, except Clare, his sister, which his said mother hath promised to beare the charge of hir close. Also it is agreed that the said Will: shal have delivered al such quick goods and deade, as is belonging unto the said house, be bill indented, and to deliver as many agayne in like forme, except reasonable cause to the contrarie. Also it is agred that the said Will: shall at his owne libertie take al such servants as he thinks neccessary and profitable for the wele of the said house, except that the said Sir Robert his fader shal have thre at his owne pleasure, such as he will apointe. Also it is agreed that the said Will: shall pay or cause to pay to the said Sir Robert his father 10ˡⁱ yearly, to be paid at 2 several times, that is to say, at Whitsonday 5ˡⁱ, and Martinmas 5ˡⁱ, or within xii dayes next folowing. Also it is agreed that the said Will: shall pay yearly xxˡⁱ of such debts as the said Sir Robert standeth bound for, after making and deliveri of this indenture, so that he may peasobly occupie the said rents, revenewes. and profits from the day abovesaid to the said debts be fuly content and paide; and every yeare to accounte to his said father of all his receite and exspences, that his said father may know suerly what overplus may be saved towards the contencion of the said debts. Also it is agreed that the said Will: shal be the letting of al such farmes as shal be voyd by the advice and councill of his said father; also woodseling by the advise of his father, unto the said debts be paide. Provided always, that if theare be any break or varience of cr in the premises, that then both parties to call for the Minister of St. Roberts, and Sir John Alan, parson of Burghwalles, and then he order the cause. In witnes of all the premises either partie to theise indentures hath set their seales, the day and yeare abovesaid."[z]

Sir Robert Plumpton, being now upwards of seventy years of age, and feeling his end approach, made the following testamentary disposition, 10 April, 14 Hen. VIII. 1523. He gives 10[li] to be distributed on the day of his sepulture unto priests, clerks, and poor persons. To the House of St. Robert 8d. per annum for ever out of Blaky farme in Knaresburgh. To the church of Spofforth 6s. 8d. To the House of St. Robert all the right he had in Thorp-Garths in Scotton. To Robert Plumpton his son, for term of his life, six marks in money, to Marmaduke his son 5 marks, to Nigell his son 5 marks, which sums William Plompton his son and heir was to pay at twe terms of the year. To Clare Plompton his daughter 20[li]. To Magdalene his daughter 20 marks, to be paid by the said William out of his lands and tenements. To Isabella Plompton, his wife, all the goods in his chamber after his death, and the half of all his other goods. He makes Marmaduke Plompton his executor, and William Plompton his son and heir, and Isabella his wife, supervisors.[a] How soon after signing this instrument he expired, or on what day his remains were interred in the family vault in the church of Spofforth, have not been recorded; but the first act in which his son's

[z] Cartul. No. 843.
[a] Copy of the will in Towneley MS. G. 24. Witnesses, Sir Richard Plompton, chaplain, William Garthing, chaplain, Oliver Diconson, Ralph Knowle, and others.

name appears, as being then in possession of the estates, bears date 20 Dec. 15 Hen. VIII. 1523, and contains a release in full made to him by Richard Plompton of Plompton, clerk, son and heir of Godfrey Plompton, esq. of all right and interest in the manors of Grassington, Steton, Plompton, Westhall, Langbar, and Idle, in the county of York, and in the former property of the family in the counties of Nottingham and Derby.[b]

Some account of the dispute between William Plumpton, son and heir of Sir Robert Plumpton, and William Babthorpe and the male branch of that family, founded upon his claim to the entire inheritance in right of his wife, the heir general, will be found in the notes to the Correspondence; and I shall here only add the following extract from the Itinerary of Leland the Antiquary, who visited Yorkshire in the reign of Henry VIII. "Plomton of Plomton, a mile from Gnaresburghe. This Plomton hath by the heire generall a good parte of the Babthorps lands: but Babthorp the Lawyer kepith Babthorpe self, that is, as I remember, in Holdernesse."[c] And in another place: "From Gnarresborow over Nid ryver, almost al by wood, mile to Plunton, wher is a parke, and a fair house of stone, with 2 toures longging to the same. Plunton is now owner of it; a man of fair lands, and lately augmented by wedding the daughter and heir general of Babthorpes."[d] It would seem also that the old quarrel was partially revived between William Plumpton and Sir John Roclife of Colthorp, kt. by reason that the latter, upon the chantry of the Holy Trinity in the collegiate church of Ripon becoming vacant, had deputed William Cooke of Ripon, chaplain, and Henry Bell, to present Stephen Clarkson, chaplain, to the same; who was admitted on their pre-

[b] Cartul. No. 854.
[c] Lel. Itin. vol. VIII. pt. 2nd. f. 68 b. Sir William Babthorpe, kt. son of William Babthorpe of Osgodby, gent. possessor of Babthorpe at the date of this journey, was a lawyer and one of the King's council in the north. (See State Papers, part iv.) Babthorpe is not, however, in Holderness, but in the liberty of Howdenshire.
[d] Lel. Itin. vol. I. f. 104, p. 99.

sentation. Whereupon, William Plumpton brought his action against Christopher Cragley, clerk, and the abovenamed persons; and a jury was summoned 30 May, 22 Hen. VIII. 1530, in fine recognition in the octaves of Pentecost, whether Sir Robert Plumpton, kt. was legitimate or a bastard, and as to the right of the said William Plumpton to present a fit person to the said chantry.[e]

William Plumpton, esq. made his will 1 July, 1 Edw. VI. 1547: among the bequests were 40[li] to his sister Clare Plompton, and to Denis Plompton his son two parts of all his lands, until he have received the sum of £200; out of which sum he was to give 20[li] to Anne Plompton, one of the daughters of Robert Plumpton, his son and heire, late departed, when of the age of 21 years, and 20[li] a-piece to each of her sisters, Mary and Isabell, in like manner, with right of survivorship, as also 10[li] to William Plompton, son of Robert Plompton, deceased, when of age, and 40[s] to Robert Plumpton his (the testator's) nephew and servant. By it he confirms an annual rent-charge of 40[li] to Dennis Plompton, and small annuities to John Poule, Marmaduke Bellingham, Thos. Garden, and Richard Darcy, out of the manor of Plumpton; as also certain other annuities to Anne Plompton, widow, late wife of Robert Plumpton, deceased, and to Robert and Neyle Plompton, his (the testator's) brothers; "and if any of them dye within 17 yeares next, that then the said Dennys to have the proffits of two parts devided into three parts, towards the helping of my poor kinsfolks. And I give to Robert Sethill my servant, for writing of this my last will, 6s. 8d. To the poor folks 40s. Isabell Plompton, my wife, and Dennis my son, to be my executors, and my nephew Richard Arthington, and my brother Richard Yorke, supervisors of this my last will, and to either of them 20s."[f] Wil-

[e] Cartul. No. 857.
[f] Towneley MS. G. 24, p. 302, taken of an old manuscript. Witnesses, Tho. Gascoigne, esq. Thomas Plompton, Richard Ampleforth, Tho. Hawks, Chr'ofer Mauson, Wm. Stevenson, Rob. Settill, Roger Hall, Rob. Haukes, and others.

liam Plumpton died on the 11th of the same month, being then aged 62, and was buried at Spofforth.

Robert Plumpton, his eldest son, born at Waterton, 17 Jan. 7 Hen. VIII. 1515-6, married 2 Sept. 30 Hen. VIII. 1538, Anne daughter of John Norton, of Norton Conyers, com. Ebor. esq. but died in his father's lifetime, aged thirty-one, and lies buried at Luddington, in the isle of Axholme, the parish church to Waterton, where he resided. His widow subsequently remarried Robert Moreton of Bawtry, com. Ebor. esq. to whom she was second wife.

William Plumpton, son of Robert, and heir to his grandfather, was born on the feast of St. Anthony, 17 Jan. 35 Hen. VIII. 1543-4, and being a minor when the succession devolved upon him, fell in ward to the King. By indenture, 16 Nov. 1 Edw. VI. 1547, made between King Edward VI. of the one partie, and Thomas Bill, esq. one of his Highness' physicians, of the other partie, by the advice of the Councill of his Grace's Court of Wards, the manor of Plumpton and tenements in Ripon, late the property of William Plumpton, esq. were demised to the said party, he paying to the feodary of the Westriding of the county of York, 8l. 15s. 8½d. over and above the annuities to the uncles of the ward, Robert and Neyle, and 13[li]. 13s. for the dower of Isabell, late wife of the said William Plumpton; provided always, that all things granted to Anne, mother of the ward, and to Dennys Plompton and Ursula his wife, were excepted and reserved. And 9 Feb. 2 Edw. VI. 1547-8, the same Thomas Bill, esq. granted to Isabel Plompton, widow, the custody and marriage of William Plumpton, cosin and heire of William Plompton, esq. deceased, and all other the premises made from the King's grace unto the said Thomas.[g] Dame Isabel Plumpton died 30 June, 6 Edw. VI. 1552, leaving

[g] Towneley MS. G. 24, containing transcripts from a book of Plumpton Evidences called the Red Book, is the authority for the statements in this latter portion of the Historical Notices of the family.

her grandson yet a minor; and who, by an inquisition taken 8 Nov. 6 Eliz. 1564, was found to be of the age of 20 years and 9 months. Having completed his full age 18 Jan. 7 Eliz. 1564-5, William Plumpton had a writ of *Ouster-le-mayn*, first of February following, from Sir William Cecil, kt. Master of his Majesty's Court of Wards, and Robert Keilway, Surveyor of the same. He had also livery, 31 May, 7 Eliz. 1565, of all the lands which descended to him as cousin and heir of Dame Isabel Plumpton above-named, his grandmother; and in this same year he revived the claim to the manors of Babthorpe and Osgodby, and such parcel of the ancient inheritance of the Babthorpes as had been retained by the male branch of the family. The latter were, however, confirmed in possession by the award of Richard Weston and John Walshe, two of the Queens Majesties Justices of the Common Pleas, made 20 Oct. 7 Eliz. 1565; and William Plumpton had, moreover, to give 160li. that a fine might pass between him and Sir William Babthorpe, kt. in the ensuing Hilary Term, (29 Jan. 8 Eliz. 1565-6,[h]) of the manor of Watterton, with the appurtenances in Watterton, Amcotes, Colby, Hotoft, and Luddington, and of the free piscary in the water of Trent, called Maredykegarth, in order to assure these premises against all subsequent claim.

William Plumpton married to his first wife Mary, daughter of Sir William Vavasour of Hazelwood, kt. and by her had issue a son, Robert, and two daughters. By indenture, 27 Nov. 10 Eliz. 1567, between Sir Ingram Clifford of Colthorpe, com. Ebor. kt. and Dame Anne his wife, and William Plumpton of Plumpton, com. Ebor. esq. it was agreed, that "in consideration of a marriage to bee had and solemnised betwixt Ellen Clifford, daughter and sole heire of the said Sir Ingram and dame Anne, and Robert Plumpton, son and heir of William Plumpton, before Easter next," that Sir Ingram and dame Anne should settle all their lands upon feoffees, viz. Robert Morton of Bawtry, esq. and William Wydmerpoole of Wydmerpoole, esq. that is to say, the manour of Cowlthorp, and Brerton, Steton, Idle, Nesfeld, Studley, Eastburne, Glusburne, Thorpe, Wray and Longbargh, com. Ebor. Kinalton, Mansfeild and Woodhouse, com. Nott. Edinsor, Hassup, Darley, Pillisley, Wormehill and Chelmerdon, Cowmes, Martinside, Baukewell, Rollesley, Tydswall, Weston, Worderplow, and Hurdlow, Flagg, Twyford, Moxdale, Betfield, Stanston, Harberch meddow, Turnedikes, Spondon, Bargshosham and Lowh, com. Derby, to hold the said lands to the use of Sir Ingram and dame Anne, and the longer liver of them, and after to their sons in order of primogeniture to be begotten on the bodies of Sir Ingram and Dame Anne, and then to Robert Plumpton and Ellenor, now their daughter and sole heir, and the heirs of their two bodies. Dame Anne Clifford had inherited the estates of the family of Roucliff; and it is deserving remark, that if this marriage had taken place, the long disputed lands that went away with Dame Margaret Roucliff, would have returned and again been united with the ownership of Plumpton. Providence ruled otherwise; both infants died, and 3 December following, Sir Ingram Clifford released William Plumpton from his bond obligatory in 2000li for the fulfilment of the articles contained in this covenant.[i]

The death of Robert left Ellen and Mary, his sisters, the heirs apparent of William Plumpton, during his first wife's lifetime; and between Thomas Markham of Ollerton, com. Notts. esq. on the first part, the said William Plompton of Plompton, their

[h] Fin. Term. Hill. 8 Eliz. coram Jacobo Dyer, Anthonio Browne, Rich. Weston, et Joh. Walshe.

[i] In the Towneley MSS. this note accompanies the transcript of the covenant: "Robertus Plumpton filius et heres Will'i Plumpton ar. obiit sine prole."

father, on the second part, and Edmund Thurland, esq.[k] and Anthony Lathom, gent. on the third part, it was covenanted, 8th Jan. 19 Eliz. 1576-7, that Griffin Markham, son and heir apparent of the said Thomas, before he accomplished the age of fifteen years, and if he die before that time, then Robert Markham, gent. second son of the said Thomas, shall marry Ellen Plumpton, eldest daughter of the said William, before she be of the age of fifteen years, or if she die before that time, then Mary, his second daughter, before she be of the like age. In consideration of which marriage the said William Plumpton agreed to suffer a recovery of his manors of Plumpton and Rudfarlington, and all others the messuages, &c. in the hamlets of Plumpton and Rudfarlington, Spofford, Knaresborow, Aketon, Folyfet, Kirkeby-Wharfe, and Adlingfleet, in the county of York, of the manor of Sacomb, and all messuages &c. in the hamlets of Sacomb, Stonden, Wadsmill, Watton, and Stapleford, in the county of Hertford, and of the manor of Watterton, and all lands, tenements, &c. in the county of Lincoln, so as the feoffees, Frances Waferer and William Mason, gent. should stand seised thereof to his use for life, remainder in tail male to his sons, and in default to the heirs of the bodies of his said daughters as should marry the said Griffin or Robert, with other remainders over, and provided that the marriage so limited for such daughter do not break by her default; the said William to have a power of jointuring such wife or wives as he shall marry to the amount of 50li a year, and if he fortune to have any issue male by any other wife than by Mary, now his wife living, after the time of any such marriage, that then, within three years after such issue had, he shall pay unto the said Griffin or Robert, as shall marry the said Ellen or Mary, the sum of 1000 marks: and the said Thomas Markham was to suffer lands of the yearly value of 200li to descend to his son and heir, and to give dower in 100 marks yearly. The daughters here named never reached maturity; and, their mother having died, William Plumpton covenanted, 29 March, 22 Eliz. 1580, to take to wife Anne Griffin, sister of Edward Griffin of Dingley, com. North[n]. esq. on whom the jointure of 50li per annum was settled, and for whose portion her brother was to pay, the day after marriage, 500li, the gift and legacy of Edward Griffin her father, and 300li at Pentecost, 1581: but the uses of the previous settlement were not to be disturbed, save only as far as the admission of the daughters of the second marriage to take in coparcenary with those of the first, in default of male issue.[l]

William Plumpton had been educated in the doctrines of the ancient faith, and the alliances of the family were made with such only as shared in the same conviction of its truth. In Yorkshire, and the other Northern counties, the Catholics in the reign of Elizabeth continued for a while to be formidable both by their numbers and property; but their power was broken by the ill-success of the attempted rebellion of their chiefs, the Earls of Northumberland and Westmorland. Few escaped exile, imprisonment, or forfeiture; and one after another their estates passed into the hands of strangers, or were extended by the crown for the payment of the fines for recusancy. Among the Burghley Papers in the Lansdowne collection is one indorsed "A trybe of wicked people," and containing a genealogy of the Catholic families of Norton, Moreton, Thurland, and Plumpton; where, after shewing that "Plumton of Plumton, esq. had issue by his wife, the daughter of Norton, Plumtone now of Plumton," this note follows: "he was

[k] Edmund Thurland of Gamston on Idle, com. Notts. esq. brother-in-law of William Plumpton.

[l] Towneley MSS. *ubi supra*.

in the lait rebellion and asewered his lands and now gone over" (seas), *i. e.* to Flanders.[m]

William Plumpton made his will 7 Jan. 44 Eliz. 1601-2, by which he enjoined his body to be buried in Plumpton Quire in Spofforth church, and gave to Ann his wife 100^{li} and a third of all his goods—to Peter his son for life, and to his wife, his executors and assigns, for twenty-one years after his decease, all the lands he bought of John Acclome, esq. in Kirkby-*super*-Wharfe, and the Ings there, called Horrington Ings, he paying no rent during life, and they 8^{li} during the term—to Thomas his son, such part of the said manor of Kirkeby-*super*-Wharfe as he bought of William Fairfax, esq. and Francis his brother, in like form—to John, his son, all that part of the said Lordship which did descend unto him, in like form, save that the rent for the term was to be but 6^{li}, and if this were controlled, then to have all those lands which he (the testator) bought of Robert Morton, esq. and Robert his son, in Watterton in the county of Lincoln—to Richard his son one burgage in Knarisburgh called Wintringham Hall, and an annuity of 12^{li} out of Waterton, after the death of his wife—"to my son William one annual rent of 20^{li} out of Waterton after the death of Anne Plumpton, my wife." To his daughter Clare he bequeathed 200 marks; and if she depart not from his son and heir, then to have meat, drink, &c. and 5^{li} for apparell. To his daughters, Elizabeth, Frances, and Luce, 8^{li} yearly till they married or accomplished the age of twenty-four years, and then portions of 400^{li} each, or 200^{li} if their marriage was without the consent of their mother. The real estate (except the manor of Sacomb in the county of Hertford, afterwards sold to Sir Philip Boteler of Woodhall, kt. and the lands in Kirkeby-*super*-Wharfe abovenamed,) to remain settled to the uses declared by the deed of 8

[m] Lands. MSS. 27. Plut. 73 f. *(Burghley Papers.)* Surtees has printed this paper in the Appendix to his Lives of the Bishops of Durham, prefixed to his first volume of the History of Durham, p. clx. but with some misreadings, as of *Antony* for *Plumtone*.

Jan. 1576-7, viz. first to his issue males, and in default to his issue females, "so as the said issues females pay to Clare Plompton my daughter 200^{li}," with remainders as to the manors of Plumpton and Rudfarlington to Richard Plumpton, son of Dynnis Plumpton, to William Plumpton, late of Adlethorpe,[n] to Robert Plumpton brother of William, to John Plumpton son of Nigell Plumpton, and to Robert Plumpton brother of John, successively, in strict tail male, and, in default, to the right heirs of Edward Plumpton his son for ever. To Anne his wife, he gave his manor of Usflet[o] for her life; and after her decease, and after the death of Frances wife of his son Edward Plumpton, [whose jointure of the capital messuage of Rudfarlington and 40^{li} per annum was to surcease at the death of Anne,] the same manor, together with the reversion of the lands in Kirkeby-*super*-Wharfe, was to remain to his son Edward and his heirs male, &c. His armour, his best horse, and all his goods and chattels at Plumpton, he gave to his eldest son, and appointed his brother Edward Griffin supravisor, with a legacy of 10^{li}, and a gelding of 10^{li} price. Lastly, he made Anne Plumpton his wife sole executrix, and if she intermarried or refused probate, then Francis Smith of Ashby Folvile and Francis Smith his grandchild, William Midleton of Stockeld, esq. Thomas Ingleby, and William Metcalfe of the Inner Temple, to be executors, and to every of them he gave 5 marks. "*Item.* 20 nobles to bee dealt to the poore on the day of my funerall." Six days after executing this testament, viz. on the 13th of January, William Plumpton died, being the Wednesday next before the feast of St. Anthony, his birth-day, when he would have completed his fifty-eighth year, and was buried at Spofforth.[p]

[n] Addlethorpe is a farm-house in the township and parish of Spofforth.
[o] Ousefleet, in the parish of Whitgift, com. Ebor.
[p] In the church of Spofforth is yet remaining in a niche an uninscribed monument, having on it the recumbent effigy of a knight in armour cross-legged, on his shield the coat of Plumpton. *(See Archæolog. vol. VI. pl. xlvii. p. 338.)*

Sir Edward Plumpton, kt. the transcriber of the family Evidences out of which these Notices have been compiled, the eldest son of his father's second marriage, was born at Dingley, in the county of Northampton, at the house of Edward Griffin, Attorney-general to Queen Mary, father to Anne Griffin his mother, 22 Sept. 23 Eliz. 1581.[q] He married Frances, daughter of William Arthington of Arthington in the county of Yorke, 13 Sept. 41 Eliz. 1599, when in his eighteenth year. The covenant for the marriage is dated 18 July preceding, and is an indenture tripartite between William Plompton of Plompton, com. Ebor. esq. and Anne his wife of the first partie, and William Arthington of Ripley in com. Ebor. esq. and Sampson Ingleby of Spofforth in the foresaid county of York, gentleman, of the second partie, and Edward Plompton, son and heire apparent of the said William Plompton and Anne, and Frances Arthington, one of the daughters of William Arthington of Arthington, com. Ebor. esq. deceased, of the third partie. It witnesseth that "whereas a marriage is agreed upon between the said Edward Plompton and the said Frances Arthington, neice to the said William Ingleby and Sampson Ingleby,[r] on this side and before Christmas, now for the making of a jointure to the said Franceis, the said William Plompton and Anne agree to suffer a fine of the manor or lordship of Urslit *alias* Uslet, known by the name of Willough Parke *alias* Wilfe Parke, sometime parcell of the possession and inheritance of Sir Richard Bozome, knight, with all appurtenances, as also of all that sometime the land of Robert Haldenby of Haldenby in the county of York, esq. and of Francis Haldenby his son, lying in

[q] *Ex libro per manum propriam Edwardi Plompton. (Towneley MSS.)*
[r] William Arthington married Catharine daughter of Sir William Ingleby of Ripley, kt. Treasurer of Berwick, and High Sheriff of Yorkshire 7 Eliz. 1574.

the parish of Whitgife, in the county of York, to the said William and Sampson, and to their heirs, to hold to the use of the said Anne for life, and after her death then to the use of the said Edward and Frances, and the longer liver of them, remainder to the said William Plompton and his heirs; and till the estate so appointed came into possession, they to have the manor, farm, or capital messuage called Roughfarlington or Rudfarlington, in the township of Plompton, and an annual rent-charge of 40^{li} a year out of the manor of Plompton, during the life of the said Anne." By her Sir Edward Plumpton had a numerous offspring, of whom John, the eldest surviving son who came to years of manhood, married Anne, daughter of Richard Towneley of Towneley in the county of Lancaster, esq. The covenants for this marriage were made 20 Dec. 3 Car. I. 1627, between Sir Edward Plompton of Plompton kt. Dame Frances his wife, and Ann Plompton, widdow, his mother, upon the first part, Richard Towneley of Towneley in the county of Lancaster esq. upon the second partie, and Sir Raphe Ashton of Great Leaver, in the said county, Bart. Sir Peter Midleton of Stockhill in the county of Yorke, kt. Savile Radcliffe of Todmerden in the said county of Lancaster, esq. and William Norton, son and heir of William Norton of Sawley, com. Ebor. upon the third partie, the same to take place before Pentecost next ensuing. The portion of the lady was £2,000; in consideration of which large sum, and for the better advancement of the said Dame Frances, Anne Plompton, and Anne Towneley with convenient jointures, it was agreed to make estate to the feoffees last named of all the manor of Plompton and Roughfarlington, all the mannor of Watterton and Amcotts and Barton Stather, and all the manor of Urslett *alias* Willough or Wilfe Parke, with the mansion-house, [formerly reputed as part of the inheritance of Edward King and Mary his wife, or of Sir William Cordall, kt.

and Dame Mary his wife, deceased], who were to resettle the same upon their several issue in strict tail male.

But the Civil Wars, in which with zealous loyalty so many Catholic families embarked life and fortune, greatly impoverished Sir Edward Plumpton and his son, who held the rank of Captain in the Royal army, and to whom 15 Apr. 14 Car. I. 1638, the father had yielded up the complete control of the property, reserving only to himself the building called "Lower Tower in Plompton," in consideration of an annual rent of 200li, he being then indebted in the sum of 1139*l*. 7*s*. 8*d*. as appears by a schedule annexed to the deed. The will of John Plompton of Plompton, in the county of York, esq. is dated 21 July, 20 Car. I. 1644, and contains this recital: " First in regard I am in great debt, I doe give unto Sir William Ingleby of Ripley, kt. and bart. William Midleton of Stockehill, esq. Henry Arthington of Arthington, esq. and Christopher Towneley of the Carr, gent. and to their heirs for ever, all those my two several mannors and mannor houses of Watterton and Uslet *alias* Wilfe *alias* Willough Parke, to sell the same towards the payment of the several sums in the schedule, hereunto annexed:" these sums reach to a total of 6393*l*. 16*s*. 10*d*. The testator at the time of making this will had been hurt in the wars, "at Hessamoore, during the siege of York," i. e. 2 July, 1644, the day that Prince Rupert was defeated by the Parliamentary forces, on the moor between Hessay and Marston: from which last-named village this field has been likewise called the Battle of Marston-moor. After languishing for several days at Knaresborough, whither he had been removed, he died and was interred in the church of that town.

Sir Edward Plumpton married, the same year his son died, a second wife, Frances, daughter of Richard Chamney, esq.; to whom in his will, dated 26 Jan. 1654-5, "as having been partaker with him and a comfortable yokefellow in these times of his sufferings and as having had and received with her a convenient portion," he bequeaths all his estate real and personal, " and all his right in one lease granted by the late Committee at York, and confirmed by the Committee at Haberdashers' Hall, to Mr. Richard Rodes of Knaresburgh:" which lease was no doubt held under a secret trust in behalf of the testator, his property having been sequestrated by the Parliament.

The year in which probate of this will was taken out is not annexed, nor do I find any Plumpton *Memoranda* extending beyond the year 1663 among the transcripts in the Towneley MSS.; but the inserted Pedigree of the family has been supplied with the later descents from one communicated by Richard Wilson, esq. Recorder of Leeds, in 1755, to Thomas Wilson, and entered by him in his Book of West Riding Genealogies, now in the Public Library at Leeds. Robert Plumpton, esq. the last of his line, conformed to Protestantism, but returned again to the faith of his ancestors. He died at Cambray in France, unmarried, 8th Aug. 1749, to which place he had gone to confer with his aunt Anne, a Benedictine Nun, who recovered him to the Catholic Church. After his death, the estate of Plumpton, then reckoned worth about 700*l*. a-year, was sold by Mrs. Anne Plumpton and her coparceners to Daniel Lascelles, esq. who, designing to make it his seat, pulled down Plumpton Hall, (or Plumpton Tower, as it was frequently called,) and formed about its site extensive pleasure-grounds; but, after having begun the erection of a new building, he desisted and went to live at Goldsborough Hall, another of his purchases, on the opposite side of the river Nidd, and which, like Plumpton, had once been the residence of a knightly family. From this gentleman descends Edward Lascelles, Earl of Harewood, Lord Lieutenant of the West Riding of Yorkshire, the present owner of the lordship and domain of Plumpton.

PLUMPTON CORRESPONDENCE

FROM

SIR EDWARD PLUMPTON'S

BOOK OF LETTERS.

LETTERS

WRITTEN TO SIR WILLIAM PLOMPTON,

WHO DIED 20. YEAR OF K. EDWARD THE FOWRTH.

LETTER I.

To our trusty and welbeloved knight, Sir William Plompton.

By the King. R. H.[a] Trusty and welbeloved. we greete you well, and for as much as we have very knowledg that our great trator, the late Earle of March,[b] hath made great assemblies of riotouse and mischeously disposed people, and to stirr and provoke them to draw unto him, he hath cried in his proclamations havok upon all our trew liege people and subjects, thaire wives, children, and goods, and is now coming towards us, we therfore pray you and also straitely charge you that anon upon the sight herof, ye, with all such people as ye may make defensible arraied, come unto us in all hast possible, wheresoever we shall bee within this our Realme, for to resist the malitious entent and purpose of our said trator, and faile not herof as ye love the seurty of our person, the weale of yourselfe, and of all our trew and faithfull subjects. Geven under our signet at our Cyty of York, the thirteenth day of March.[c]

(13 *March* 1460-1.)

[a] Henry VI.
[b] Edward Earl of March took the title of Edward IV. 4 March 1460-1.
[c] The battle of Towton field or Saxton field was fought on the twenty-ninth of March following, being Palm Sunday, whence it was sometimes called Palm Sunday field. Sir William Plumpton's eldest son was among the slain. (*See Memoirs.*)

LETTER II.

Unto my right reverent and worshipfull maister, Maister Sir William Plompton, knight.

My right reverent and honorable maister, All humble recomendation praemised, please you that I receaved of your servant John Smith xl marks, and your letter to the Tresorer and Barons of the exchequer for respitt of your day to xv[na] Hillary,[a] which would not be graunted but soe I have gotten that one shall appeare for you att the day of account and soe to be appeared for in the pipe,[b] and then for to be prepared in the next tearme; and soe I have labored a felaw of mine to be your Atturney in the Court, for I may nought be but of Counsell, and he and I shall shew you such service all that time and afterward that shall be pleasing unto you. And soe shall ye have day or respitt to the xv of hillary next coming, then to be opposed of your greenewax; at which time ye may nott faile to send hider all your bookes and some readie man for to answer unto him, for I nor my said felaw may nott attend thereupon, and also to be here yourselfe than or before to pursue for your pardon,[c] and to gree all your demaundes att once. And I trust to god for to gett you downe your greenewax[d] if that I may, thof it cost you mony; soe ye wrote unto me, beseeching our

[a] 27 Jan.
[b] See Madox's Exchequer for the mode of passing an account at the Exchequer, and as to a Sheriff being apposed by the Barons upon the summonce of the Pipe. Sir William Plumpton had been Sheriff of the county of York in 1448, and of Nottingham and Derby in 1452.
[c] Sir William Plumpton obtained his letters of general pardon and release, 5 Feb. 1461-2; wherein, among other designations, he is styled "nuper vicecom. com. Ebor. mil. *alias* nuper vicecom. com. Nottingham et Derb. chivaler." (*Vide Chartul. continent. evidentias familiæ de Plumpton, No.* 551.)
[d] The estreats out of the Exchequer, sent to the Sheriffs to be levied, were sealed with green wax.

lord to gif you good speed against all your enemies and in all your matters. Written in hast at Westminster the fift day of November.

(5 *Nov.* 1461.)   Your servant, BRYAN ROCLIFF.[c]

[c] Bryan Rocliff of Cowthorpe, com. Ebor. (*See Memoirs.*) He was made third Baron of the Exchequer, 8 May, 1 Edw. IV. and therefore in condition to show service to his client at the time of writing.

LETTER III.

To my right honnorable and reverant Coussin Sir William Plompton, knight.[a]

Right worshipfull and reverent Coussin, after dew and hartyly recommendations,—Be the advise of my master, Sir John Markam,

[a] The nature of the variance spoken of in this letter may be collected from the evidences in the Plumpton coucher book. A writ of appeal had, it seems, been brought by "Thomasyn, late the wife of Henry Perpoint, sometyme of Holme, esquire," (whose son this Henry was) against " Robert Grene, late of Plompton beside Knaresburgh, in the county of York, gent." of the death of the " said Henry Perpoint, sometyme her husband, in the shire of Nottingham ; " and, on the other hand, a counter-writ had been sued by " Richard Grene, of Plompton, neveww and heir of John Grene, late of Plompton," (which John was brother-in-law to Sir William Plumpton, and serving as his steward) against " John Perpoint, late of Rodmathwaite, in the county of Nottingham, gent. and others," of the death of his " said uncle John Grene, in the shire of York." These homicides had been committed in an affray on Papplewick-moor in Nottinghamshire 35 Hen. VI. ; and 10 Feb. 37 Hen. VI. 1458-9, the same parties had agreed to abide by the award of Sir John Melton, knight, John Stanop, esq. and Richard Elingworth, counsellor, arbitrators chosen on the side of Perpoint, and of Sir William Vernon, knight, William Babington, esq. and Richard Neel, counsellor, on the side of Plumpton, with John Viscount Beaumont for umpire. The civil dissensions probably prevented the final settlement of the variance at that time. Then came the proposal contained in this letter of Sir Richard Bingham, but which was not acceded to, as the final award was subsequently made pursuant to a bond dated 24 May, 2 Edw. IV. It is in the sole name of Richard Bingham, " one of the King's Justices of the bench," and bears date " on Friday on the morne after the ascension of our lord," 28 May, 1462. *(Chartul. No. 552.)*

Chiefe Justice,[b] I comonde with Henry Pearpointe Esquire[c] for the variance that is betwixt you and him, and he is agred, if it please you, to put all thing that is in variance betwixt you and him in the said Sir John and me; and if ye will doe the same, we for the ease of you both and the rest of the contry will take the matter upon us, and we will apoynt you both ; and apoynte you to be at Notinggam upon the Mondey next after Law Sunday next coming at even, you to be lodgd theare, upon the long Raw in the satterday market, at your pleasure, and the said Henry against St. Mary kirke; and every of you not to excede xij persons, and ye and every of your persons to be single arrayd, and in noe other forme, and the place of metting for you and us to be at St. Petter kirke; and if this please you, I trust to God the matter in variance betwixt you and him shall take good conclusion: and therfore how ye will agre in this matter I pray you send word in writing to my son Richard Bingham, that he may let my master Sir John Markam, Henry Perpoint, and mee have knowledg of your dispotition in the said matter. The day of your trety shal bee at Notingham upon the tewsday next after Low Sunday betimes, and my said master and I shal so behave us betwix you, that yf you both wil bee reuled by reason, ye shal both bee wel eased, with the grace of God, which keep you ever. Written at Midlton, the eight day of January.

Your poor Cosin,

(8 *Jan.* 1461-2.)   RICH. BINGHAM, knight.[d]

[b] Sir John Markham, made chief justice of the King's Bench, 1 Edw. IV. removed 8 Edw. IV.

[c] Henry Pierpont of Holme Pierrepont, esq. son of Henry Pierpont, esq. and Thomasyn, daughter of Sir John Melton, knight.

[d] Sir Richard Bingham, knight, a justice of the King's Bench and the writer of this letter, was of Middleton, com. Derb. and agreeably to the custom of the time, calls Sir William Plumpton his cousin, inasmuch as his son Richard Bingham, junior, who is named in the letter, had married Margaret, daughter of Sir Thomas Rempston, knight, uncle by the half-blood to Sir William Plumpton.

LETTER IV.

Unto his right reverend and honorable master Sir William Plompton, knight, in hast.

Right reverend and honorable Sir, and mine especiall good maister, after all humble recomandations, with dew regraces and hartly thankings of your kind mastership unto me undeserved, effectualy my trust is desiring continuance. Please you that I have communed with Beford in your mater as ye wrote to me, and I cannot find him disposed that he will eyther grant you any yeares of payment, or els to be content by any soum yearly to be paid, and he will agre to no treate but if he have some money in hand, and so he haith taken his *exigi facias de novo* and is with us called in the hustings ;[a] marveling me that after writing by letter and comunication by mouth, ye tender not hartyly that matter, considering the other obligation which might be executed against Plumtre of Nottinggam,[b] if ye wold doe your devor, beseching you to remember your honestie and wellfare. And Sir, I have tretid with Wigmore and at few words, I find him right hard and strange and soe ye bene iij[c] called in Midlesex; wherfore ye must purvay hastely remmedy, for he will noe more trust faire wordes as he saith ; thus remiting matters to your discrett wisdom, whom the holiest enspire to your profit and pleasure, my advis being allwaies redy. Written in hast at London, the 19th of May.

Your servant, BRIAN ROCLIFE.

(19 *May, anno circiter* 1462.)

[a] Hustings, the court for causes in the City of London.
[b] John Plumtre of Nottingham died April 1471.—See Thoroton for an account of this family.
[c] A defendant was to be called in court five times before judgment of outlawry could be given.

LETTER V.

Unto his reverent maister Sir William Plompton, knight, in hast.

In speciall my verray good maister, after due recomendations; my maister the Chief Baron[a] comuned to my lord Treasorer[b] of certaine matters, and soe my lord opened that Thomas Beckwith[c] was his Awnte son, and he would make him eschetour; saying, that he loved you right well and would fayne an end were taken betwixt you and Beckwith, willing my said maister to take upon him the rewle, and would undertake Beckwith to be ruled by him, if he would take it upon him, who disclosed this unto me, nott certaine that ye would agree. And I answered that I supposed ye would agree to all reason, enforming him of the trewthe of the matter to my cuning after your information; soe that if such writing be had unto you by the advice of your trewe in reason, in reason it is to be agreed with reason, as my simplesse seemeth, saveing your better advise. And Sir, Beford hath spoken with me, sayeing that the matter is broken up in the default of Sir Harry,

[a] Richard Illingworth, made Chief Baron of the Exchequer 10 Sept. 2 Edw. IV. 1462.
[b] John Earl of Worcester, Lord Tiptoft and Powis, was Lord Treasurer at this period. He is stated to have married Elizabeth, daughter of Robert Greyndour, of which name of Greindour, or Graindorge, there was a family of some consequence in Craven, whose heir-general was Nesfield of Flasby, a manor acquired by this match. The intermarriage with the family of Beckwith may therefore have been on the part of the wife's relatives ; any how a near affinity seems to be indicated by this letter.
[c] The Eschetour of the county of York, 2 Edw. IV. was Thomas Beckwith of Clint in com. Ebor. esq. whose eldest son and heir apparent William had married Elizabeth daughter of Sir William Plumpton before 26 Jan. 34 Hen. VI. 1455-6. At that date Elizabeth, the wife of Thomas Beckwith, who is stated in the pedigree of the family to have been a coheir of Heslarton, was living, and lands in Hawnby, Filey and Muston are named in the settlement upon the marriage of their son William Beckwith. By the same deed Sir William Plumpton was bound to pay a certain sum by annual instalments for his daughter's portion, and from a subsequent letter it would seem that x[li], parcel of this sum, had been kept back, probably on the ground of his daughter not having issue male, it being one of the conditions of the bond that all payments should thenceforth cease, upon her dying without having any such alive. (*Chartul. No.* 541.)

that kept no tyme, and soe he purposes to continue and take out his suite, whom with soberness I entreate, affirming that ye will be here this tearme, and as long as I may, but I have noe grant of him. And Colt hath spoken to me for the remainder of the money, which he should send with the Bill of issues and for costes. And Beford hath spoken with Plomptree for the other obligation under sewertee, and soe in manner of a certante of payment, but now it is deatt the lyeing at large. Thus matters remitted to your said discretion whom our lord govern and haf in his keeping. Written in hast in the temple the fourteenth day of October.

(14 *Oct. anno circiter* 1462.)   Your servant, BRYAN ROCLIF.

LETTER VI.

Unto his singuler good maister Sir William Plompton, knight.

Right worshippfull my singuler good mastre, as my dewtie is, with intier regraces I recomend me unto you, whose honor ioy and prosperitie I beseech the blessed trinitie to encrease dayly as I would haf of my simple person. Sir, I thank you among inumerable other, of your comfortable letter that you now take your disport att your libertee.[a] And as touching my lord,[b] I shall ride to M——— to him within these 4 daies and doe my part, and as I shall find him, so shall I certifie you. Sir, as anenst Scatergood I hafe yett taken a longer continuance unto new yeare day, and I would fayne that it were att an end; thof it cost you mony for countermaunding and noysing; that would be had by privy seales, for they go light cheape, and send me your will therein. Sir, it is necessary that T. Beckwith[c] be content at this time of x^{li}, for losse

[a] Sir William Plompton had about this time been confined on a false charge of carrying on a treasonable correspondence with the fugitive Lancastrians. (*See Memoirs.*)

[b] John Nevill, Earl of Northumberland and Lord Mountague, between whom and the Earl of Warwick the estates of the House of Percy were divided, after the accession of Edward IV.

[c] Thomas Beckwith. (*See note to Letter V.*)

of money by suites makes more payments. Sir, if it like you that Richard F——— aftre this yoole might entend upon me toward London, seing your presence now here, and ye might forgo him, I would have of you knowledge, for other have labored me, whome I respite therefore. Butt dissease or displease would nott I you in any wise. As for Gouldesburgh yett mett we nott, but now I trust that ye shall confirme all that first was named, and for Gods sake performe it (*quia mora trahitt periculum*) or his brother Edward[d] goe to London att twentie day of yoole, and ellis will it straunge and delay. And think how ye lost Robart Ros son.[e] Your daughter and myn, with humble recomendations, desireth your blessing, and speaketh prattely and french and hath near hand learned her sawter. Sir, Henry Suthill hath knowledge of her feofment,[f] as a man tould me secretly, but for all that I trust all shalbe well, with the grace of the blessed trinitie, who quyte you and send you all your desires. Writen in hast at Colthrop on fryday.[g]

(*Dec.* 1463.)   Your serviseable brother,[h] BRYAN ROUCLIFFE.

[d] Edward Goldesburgh, third Baron of the Exchequer in 1484. The writer of the letter apparently alludes to the then projected match between Richard, eldest son and heir apparent of Thomas Goldesburgh of Goldesburgh, com. Ebor. esq. brother of Edward Goldesburgh above named, and Alice, one of the daughters of Sir William Plumpton. The father's bond for the marriage bears date in 1465. (*See Memoirs.*)

[e] "Robert Ros' son," with whom and another daughter of Sir William Plumpton a match had previously miscarried, was Thomas, eldest son of Robert Ross, of Ingmanthorp, com. Ebor. esq.

[f] Margaret Rocliffe, the wife of John Rocliffe, eldest son of the writer, was granddaughter of Sir William Plumpton. Her feofment on marriage (dated 26 Nov. 3 Edw. IV. 1463) had, it seems, been kept secret from Henry Suthill, esq. who in Feb. 1463-4 contracted for the marriage of the other co-heir.

[g] The date of this letter was probably the Friday next preceding Christmas (*Yule*) day, which in 1463 fell on a Sunday. The manor seat of the Rouclifes was at Colthrop, otherwise Cowthorpe, a parish-town in the upper division of Claro, com. Ebor. The church there was built by this Brian Roucliffe, and in the choir on a flat stone are the effigies in brass of him and his wife, bearing betwixt them the model. It was consecrated in 1458; and he died 24 March 1494.

[h] From the time of the marriage of his son with the grand-daughter of Sir William Plumpton, Brian Rocliff contracted that degree of affinity with the latter which it was usual to distinguish by the name of brother in social intercourse, and this change in his mode of signature denotes the priority of date which attaches to the preceding letters.

LETTER VII.

To my right worshipfull maistre Sir William Plompton, kt.

Right worshipfull maistre, I recomend me unto you. Please it you to witt the minister of St. Roberts has taken 2 suits, one of trespas for delving his ground att St. Robert, another of debt and detinue both in a writt, debt 12 marks, which as I understand by Horberey should be lent to you. Be the place (*plea*) of the detinue for a chalise shold be lent to you; also the writts were out, but I caused Horberey *per album breve*, so the sheriff shall have none paid for the writts, by the avise of Mr. Rocliff.[a] I pray you send answerre against the next tearme; also had I understood for certain what goods Folbaron and Walker had of yours, I shold have bene answerd this terme by Horberey not guilty, which is the best issue you can have: I pray you send word against the next terme. Also Whele had sent out *exigi facias de novo* against Holden, Hanworth[b] and West, or I came here, and said they were returned *quarto exactus*; he had given them to short a day. Whearfore he said he wold write unto you for an excuse, and pray the *exigi* against West may be withdrawen: I promissed he should take no hurt by the proces. Also Whele sends you a *capias utlegat.* against Harldre by Rauf Annias, but he delivered it to the Sheriff. I shall send you another with the Copie of your

[a] The phrase *per album breve* ought perhaps to be understood of a bribe given to Horberey, acting as attorney on behalf of the minister of the house of St. Robert at Knaresborough (at this date Robert Boulton), for the staying of these writs.

[b] Thomas Holden and William Hanworth were with William Husworth, William Rute, Christopher Craven, Richard Dryver, Richard Warter and John Ripley, freres and brethren of the house of St. Robert, John Cock and William Barker, indicted and outlawed during these suits by Sir William Plumpton. (*Chartul. No.* 573.)

new suites and a *venire facias* against the ministre. Mr. Rocliff hath labored effectually this tearme for your matter of Stamford,[c] and for my lady Inglestrop[d] for your sake, and to Pake[e] also; and also he dined with my lady and thanked her hertely for your sake. I trust by his labour your matter of Stamford shall take a good end with the grace of God, who have you evermore in his keeping. Written att London 14 february.

(14 *Feb.* 1463-4.)   Your servant GODFREY GRENE.

[c] Chapman of Stamford. (*Vide postea, Letters VIII. and IX.*)

[d] Joan Lady Ingaldesthorp. (*Vide postea, Letter X. note b.*)

[e] Pake, *quære* if intended for Hugh Pakenam or Pagnam, whose letter is among the correspondence, No. X.

LETTER VIII.

Unto my reverend and worshipfull master, Sir William Plompton, kt.

Reverend and worshipful master, after all due recomendations had; Sir, as for your suites against the minister[a] and others, they shalbe called upon as effectually as I can, and with the grace of God shall take as good speed as the law will suffer, howbeit that Horbury sais that ye and the minister stand in comprimise to abide the award of Sir John Malivera[b] and others, and that he hath in comaund to continue the suite of the minister by reason of the same; notwithstanding, your suit shall proceed untill the time ye send otherwise in comaund. And as for the byeing of the velvett, the mony upon the obligacion of Mr. Suthill[c] is nott

[a] Robert Boulton, minister of the house of St. Robert near Knaresborough. See Letter VII.

[b] Sir John Mauleverer of Allerton, com. Ebor. kt.

[c] Henry Suthill esq. was bound to pay for the marriage of the grand-daughter and heir apparent of Sir William Plumpton a certain sum by instalments, the first of which became due 24 June, 1464. Suthill was married to the only daughter of John Boyvile of Stockfaston, or Stockerston, com. Leic. which property was inherited by his issue; he was himself a younger son of Gerard Suthill of Ledburne, com. Linc. (a shoot from the ancient stock of Soothill in the parish of Dewsbury, com. Ebor.)

paid; he said Barnby wilbe here with it this tearme. God send grace it be so, for Mr. Byngham,[d] Tho. Eyr, and Chapman of Stamford, everichone of them attends after his part this tearme. And as for the suits I shall borow untill the time the other come. There is a yong man, a mercer in the Chepe, the which a Michaelmas purpose to sett up a shop of his owne, the which mercer makes great labor to my lady and to Jeffrey Dawne for my sister Isabell to marry with her;[e] lyvelode he hase none, a Norfolk man and of birth no gent. as I can understand; what he is worth in goods I cannott wytt. Mercers deals nott all together with their owne proper goods. How be it my lady P. hath proferred him faire, that is to say, xl[li] in mony of my lady and her freinds and my lady to find her thre yeare if he will, and Jeffrey hath proferred to lend him for iiij yeare a hundreth merce, the which mony is ready in a bag if they agre. I moved unto my lady and Jeffrey, as far as I durst for displease, that the mony was muche without she had some twentie of other of lyvelods or of goods, to the which my sister, as fare forth as she durst, abode upon; by the which they brake and nott concluded. And my lady and Jeffrey agreed well to the same, notwithstanding my sister ne I cannot think it is for her to refuse my ladies labour nor agreement, but wholie to put her to my ladies rule and ordinance, and so she did att all times. How be it my lady said to her it shold come of herselfe, and she answerred that of her selfe she could nott ne wold nothing do without the advise of you and her freinds, but whatsoever my lady thought she shold do, she wold do it unwitting you or any of her freinds. Whearfore I

and was at this time following the profession of the law, from which he appears to have derived considerable wealth, so as to enable him to contract for the heiress of Plumpton.

[d] Richard Bingham the younger.—See Letter III.

[e] Geoffrey Dawne was probably of the family of Dawney of Cowick, com. Ebor. but the connexion with the writer and the lady P. in whose service Isabel Grene was at this time, has not been ascertained.

beseech you as hastely as it please you, to send me word of your intent, for she and I wold faine do that at might be most to your pleasure and her profitt. Also Mr. Byngham hath spoken to Mr. Rocliff and me to witt what day ye wold be in Nottinghamshire, and I could not answere thereto; ye may send him word as it please you. Also I am not very certaine of the day and yeare that your milne dam was broken; I pray you send the certaintie this terme and ye may, that it may be amended if it be wrong. And all your other matters shalbe called upon with the grace of God, who have you evermore in proteccion. Written at London the xiiii[th] day of June.

Also as for the mercer, I understand he profers now to find surety that if he die, she is to have a C[li] besides her part of his goods after the custome of the Cittie.

(14 *June* 1464.) Your servant GODFREY GRENE.

LETTER IX.

Unto the reverend and right worshipful Sir William Plompton, knight, my singular good master, be this delivered.

Right reverend worshipful Sir, intirly beloved brother, and singularly my good master, after al faithful and due recommendations præmised and special regraces and thankings, as I have mo causes than I can write, which our Lord acquit, where I by non power am restrained, desiring him dayly for your honor prosperity, ioy, and longanimity, to bee encreased to your pleasur; Sir, like you to remember, the conclusions of the matter taken betwixt you and Chapman of Stamford by Husee[a] and mee, that yee for to have his releas general should pay 100s., wherof I paid 4 marks in hand which you paid mee again; and now this term by

[a] William Husee was at this time a counsel learned in the law; made serjeant 9 June 1479, Chief Justice of the King's Bench 7 May 1482.

the advise of Huzze, thorowh importune clamor of Chapman, and you to bee in quiet delivering your acquittance, I paid 33s. 4d. afore Husze to Chapman, so that now you bee utterly out of his dammage. And, Sir, I conceived, by the remembrance of my cosin Mr. Midleton,[b] that yee willed mee to buy to you, black velvet for a gown. But, Sir, I pray you herin blame my non power but not my will, for in faith I might not doo it, but gif I should run in papers of London, which I did never yet, so I have lived poorly therafter; for and I might els haue doon it, I shold not have spared. But the wis man saith to us, *Impedit omne forum carentia Denariorum.* And that prooves here now: I dare not write al my complaint. Sir, Thomas Eyr[c] clamoreth upon mee importunly for money, so that gif I had any of my own, I wold have stopped him, and so as I might have promised him this next term, which like you for to send hither than: for and hee begin his suit now, he wil not bee so easily entreated. And also, Sir, I pray you specially for to send mee money fro Nesfield,[d] according to your appointment and saing at our last departing, for and ye knew how it stands with mee here, I trust verily yee wold tender mee the more. And, Sir, the rather I pray you, for I purpose to have your son John Roclif to court at beginning of this next terme, where my charge of him in array and other exspences, shal encreas to the double, as God knowes, whom I beseech entirly, for to have you in his keeping, and graunt you all your desires. Written in hast in the midle temple, tertio die

[b] Thomas Middelton, son-in-law of Sir William Plumpton.

[c] Thomas Eyr, citizen and draper of London, and Elizabeth his wife, late wife of Nicholas Yeo, late citizen and alderman of London, acknowledge to have received of Sir William Plumpton, knight, by the hands of Brian Rouclif, ten marks in part payment of a larger sum, 10 May, 5 Edw. IV. 1465. (*Chartul.* No. 567.)

[d] The manor of Nesfield, com. Ebor. had been settled in jointure upon Margaret Plumpton at the time of her marriage with John Roclif, the son of the writer, but Sir William Plumpton bargained to retain the issues for five years from 26 Nov. 1463, the date of the contract.

decembris. Sir, Sir Henry Vavasor[e] was gone hence or I wist, so that I might not speak to him for the wapp: my Thomas may go to him and speed I trow.

(3 *Dec.* 1464.) Your servisable brother, BRIAN ROCLIFF.

[e] Sir Henry Vavasour of Hazelwood, in com. Ebor. knt. high sheriff in 1470.

LETTER X.

To my right especiall and singuler good mastre Sir William Plompton, kt.

Myne owne speciall and singuler master, with all my hole heart and service I recomend me unto your best beloved good mastership, humblie thanking it for all that I am bound to thank itt for. Please it the same to knowne that from my departure out of London after Christenmes into good fryday last was kam, I not to my lodging were ye saw me last, ne never since that time herd I word nor wryting from you; nor over that, I understand not by any wryting that my brother the tresurer[a] hath sent me sith that time, that he receaved the letter which I sent him by your Mastership: whearfore I send John Hawkins bearer hereof now to se your gretliest desired welfare, trusting that by him againward I shall hastely be ascertained thereof, with all your commaundements and desires, which I shall ever be desireous to observe as fer as my simple power may to atteine, with the mercy of our lord, whom I beseech to have your singuler and best be trusted mastership in his most safe gard and goverment, graunting it as much prosperitie, hertes comfort, and welfare as your gentl heart with his pleasure best shall like to desire. Scribled in hast with mine owne hand in default of other helpe att London the 21 of June, which day your dayly Bedewoman my huswif desired that by this rude sedule, she may humblie be recommended to your most loving mastership, and to signifie how God bred her to be delivered of

[a] John Pakengham, treasurer of the cathedral church of York from 1459 to 1477, in which year he died. See his monumental inscription, Drake's *Ebor.* p. 499.

her son Nicholas on Tewsday the 4 of this month, and how that on Saturday last was my daughter Agnes accepted into the habitt of St. Dominike ordre att Dertford, like as the said bearer kan enforme your mastership; which wold also lyke to knowe how that now of late I was with my lady Ingolshorp,[b] whose ladyship is well recovered of the great sicknes that she hath endured many day past, at which time my mistres Isabell Marley was in good hele, thankid be God, and lett me witt how she likes right wele and greatly is bounden to my lady. My master Rauf Haukins and mistresse his wife, now being lodged at the lions, my mistres F. S. now being att Wulwich with her brother and sister kin and others your well willers, servants, and bed folkes in this country were in hele att the makeing hereof, thanked be God. I conceive there is displesure hanging that ye saw not my lord Chamberlaine[c] upon his being in the north, as well for that ye comfort not my said maistresse S. ne none of her frencs in the matter ye know of, for the which I have bene often called upon sith Paske : it were to be done as me seemeth to make writing from you to my maistres S. thanking her of her trew and loving heart, excuseing the non accomplishment of her desire in such wis as yee can well enough, and soe to put her out of dispaire, for as I understand she hath offers great by right worshipfull. In the matter touching the £48 13s. 4d. I have opened the specialties thereof unto John Hawkins, to whom in that behalfe please your maistershipp to give faith and credence.

(21 *June, anno circiter* 1465.)   HUGH PAGNAM.[d]

[b] Joan Lady Ingaldesthorp, relict of Sir Edmund de Ingaldesthorp, who died 2 Sept. 1456, and sister of John Earl of Worcester. Her daughter was married to John Nevill, Earl of Northumberland, and after 1469 Marquis Montague.

[c] William Lord Hastings, Lord Chamberlain to King Edward IV.

[d] Hugh Pagnam was probably an ancestor of the family connected with the county of Kent in the reign of Edw. VI., when a Hugh Pakenham owned *jure ux.* the Moat in Ightham. His correspondence with Sir William Plumpton apparently had for its motive the urging on a declaration of marriage to the lady named

Mistress F. S. on whom Sir William Plumpton had made a favourable impression. This letter will therefore have been written before the secret marriage of Sir William had been divulged in 1468. Mr. Rocliffe's labour to "Lady Inglestrop," spoken of in Letter VII. was, it may be conjectured, simply with a view to the obtaining a place in the household of that great lady for Mrs. Isabel Marley, a niece of Sir William Plumpton, as we find her residing with the "Lady Ingolshorp," and greatly bounden to her at the date of this letter.

LETTER XI.

To my right trustie and welbeloved Sir William Plompton, knight.

Right trustie and welbeloved, I grete you wele, and whereas I am enformed that ye pretend clayme and title to a closse called Spencer close, belonging to my welbeloved Thomas Scarbroughe,[a] whearin with others I stand enfeoffed, I therefore desire and pray you that ye will suffer the said Thomas the said closse in peaceable wise to have and occupie without vexation or trouble, unto time that by such persons as thereupon by your both assent being elect and chosen, the matter be thoroughly determined whether of you the same oweth to have of right. And our Lord have you in his keepeing. Written att Toplife the ninetenth day of September. Therle of Warwick and Salisbury grete chamberlaine of England and Captaine of Calais.

R. WARWICK.[b]

[a] Thomas Scarborough was of Glusburne in Craven.

[b] Richard Nevill, Earl of Warwick and Salisbury, held Topcliffe with the other manors and lordships of the Percies in Yorkshire, from 1461 to 1469, when Henry Percy was restored.

LETTER XII.

To my worshipful Maister Sir William Plompton, knight, bee this bil delivered.

Right worshipfull Sir, I recommend me to your good mastership, letting you wit, as touching the matter betwixt my coussin Golfray Greene[a] and Nyccoll Gotman, that my Lord Chauncler has given in commaundment unto Master Patman to make prossis against my Coussin Godfrey, to bring the issues and profits that he hath received of a Chauntre, for which the varience shold begin, and else to cours him from day to day : and therfore provide by your wisdome such remmede in his behalfe, as you semes best. Also if ye speake with my Lady Stapleton,[b] if it please ye to commend me unto hir gud Ladyship, and let hir understand that I delivered hir letters that she sent me, and that Mr. Borough[c] desired hir in any wise that she shold kepe it secret and let no person have knowledg; but that he shold kepe still the ward of my master hir son, notwithstanding he is and wil be redy to kepe all appoyntements that are made in every article. The King, my Lord Chauncler,[d] and the Earle of Warwick ar at London; he came to the towne with 300 horse and more, as it is said. My Lord of Clarence is riden to Tutbery, and the Earle of Woster to Walles, to Denbe as it is said. I sopose Sir James Harington[e] shall be Sherife of Yorkeshire; Sir John Conyers[f] and Sir Henry Vaveser is in the bill. Sir Robart Constable[g] is Sherif in Lincolnshire. As for tidings I can none wryte, but I have sold both my horse, good morrel and his felow; and as for my bay horse, at your neighborhad fro Harwod park by his commaundment, I purpose to take no such as yet. No more at this tyme, but the holy Trinytee have you in his blessed keeping. Written at London the Thursday after alhalow day.   Your servant

(6 *Nov.* 1466.)   THOMAS MIDLETON.

[a] Godfrey Greene was probably of the family of Grene of Newby, com. Ebor. which was allied to the Middeltons of Stocke d., and of which place was John Grene, who married Joan, sister of Sir William Plumpton.—(*See Memoirs.*)

[b] Lady Stapleton was Isabella, daughter and coheir of Sir Thomas Rempston of Rempston, com. Nott. kt. and relict of Sir Bryan Stapleton of Carlton, com. Ebor. kt. who died 3 Edw. IV. leaving Bryan his son and heir a minor.

[c] Sir Thomas Burgh or Borough of Gainesborough, com. Linc. kt. ancestor of the Lords Borough.

[d] George Nevill, Archbishop of York.

[e] Sir James Harrington of Brierley, com. Ebor. kt. Sheriff of Yorkshire in 1467.

[f] Sir John Conyers of Hornby, com. Ebor. kt.

[g] Sir Robert Constable of Flamborough, com. Ebor. kt. Sheriff of Lincolnshire in 1467.

LETTER XIII.

To my right reverend and most especiall good maistre Sir William Plompton, knight.[a]

Right reverend and my moste speciall gude maistre, I recomend me unto your good mastership, and as touching your *nisi prius*

[a] The news communicated by Godfrey Grene in this letter furnishes some additional historical information to fill up the meagre outline of the events of the time, as given in the chronicles. To begin with the "remarkable fragment" printed by Hearne in the same volume with "Sprotti chronica," p. 295; it is there narrated, "this vii[th] (*lege* viii[th]) yere Margarete sustir unto King E. bifore saide departid frome the King, and rode thurgh oute London behynde the Erle of Warwicke, and rode that nigt to Stratforde Abbay, and from thens to the se syde, and went into Flaundres to Brugis, where she was maryid with grete solempnite. And within short space aftir, thois astates, as the duchess of Northfolke with othir, retournid in to England, in whois Company were ii. yong gentilmen, that one namid John Poyntz, and that othir William Alsford, the which were arestid bicause in the tyme of the forsaide mariage they hadde familiar communication with the duke of Somersett and his complicis there, in the which they were bothe detectid of treason : whereupon one Richard Steris skinnar of London with thois ii. were behedid att the toure-hill the xxi. day of Novembre." This extract is from a contemporary and well-informed writer, and accords with the news in the letter, save that the day of execution is spoken of in the latter as being Monday before St. Andrew day, i. e. 28 November (instead of Monday se'nnight, 21 November) and the name Steris (or Starres. *Rot. Parl.* vi. 292 5) is written "S[t] peirs," an error no doubt of our copyist in 1612. In Fabyan is this notice of the events of the year 1468, 8th Edward IV. "This yere, and xxi. day of Novembre, a servaunte of the Duks of Exceter, named Richard Sterys, after his jugement, was drawen thorughe the cytie unto the Tower Hylle, and there parted in ii. pesys, that is, the hede frome the body. And upon the daye followynge, two personee beyng named (the one) Poynys and that other Alforde, were drawen westwarde to Tyborne, and there whan they shulde have been hanged, there chartours were shewyd, and so preservyd.

"And about this season or soon after, was the Erle of Oxenforde, which before tyme was taken by a surmyse in ielosy of treason, awaytyd for and arrestid, and after delyvered." (*Fab. Chron. London,* 1811, 4to. p. 657.)

against Fulbaron, it were well doon that ye appointed with Mr. Danby[b] at what place and what day in his comeing home after the next tearme ye would have it served; soe that I might have word the begining of the next tearme, to take out the writt, according to your appointment. Also as for the writt against Geffray Malivera, John Cockle, Rich. Croft, Hanson and other, I stand in doubt whether Mr. Midleton and Mr. Ros greed you and Sir John Maliveras[c] thereof, or no, because they are his men; notwithstanding if they agreed you nott, and ye send me word, I trust to have an exigent the next tearme. My Lord of Oxford is comitt to the tower, and it is said kept in irons, and that he has confessed myche thinge; and on Munday afore St. Andrew day one Alford and Poiner, gentlemen to my Lord of Northfolk, and one S[r] peirs, Skinner of London, were beheaded; and on the morne after was Sir Thomas Tresham[d] arest and is comitt to the tower: and it is said he was arested upon the confession of my Lo. of Oxford, and they say his livelyhood, and Sir John Marneys[e] livelihood, and divers other livelihuds is given away by the king. Also there is arest Mr. Hungerford, the heir unto the Lord Hungerford, and one Courtney, heir unto the Earle of Devonshire, and many other, whose names I know nott; and it is said that Sir Edmund Hungerford[f] is send for. And also the yeomen of the Crowne bene riden into diverse countries to arrest men that be apeched. Also it was told me that Sir Robt. Ughtred[g] was send for, but I trust to God it is not so, who have you evermore in his blessed proteccion. Written at London, 9 of December.

Your servant GODFREY GREENE.

(9 *Dec.* 8 *Edw. IV.* 1468.)

[d] Sir Thomas Tresham, of Rushton, com. North[n]. kt. a zealous Lancastrian, beheaded at Tewkesbury in 1471.

[e] Sir John Marney, of Layer Marney, com. Essex, kt. ancestor of the Lords Marney.

[f] Sir Edmund Hungerford, kt. was great-uncle to Sir Thomas Hungerford, Knight.

[g] Sir Robert Ughtred of Kexby, com. Ebor. kt.

The surmise of treason against the Earl of Oxford was not without cause; for, on the 18th July, nine days after the marriage of Margaret to the Duke of Burgundy, we find him writing to Sir John Paston, Knight, from Canterbury, to order him three horse harness, as though it were for himself, together with two standard-staves, and concluding his letter in these words, "I trust to God we shalle do right well." But the Earl's fortitude appears to have failed him upon being committed to the Tower; "it is said he has confessed myche thinge," writes Sir William Plumpton's correspondent. Of his accomplices, Hungerford and Courtenay were executed; " and this yere," to use the words of a contemporary writer,* " was Syr Thomas Hungreford, Knight, sunne to the Lorde Hungreforde, and Henry Curteney of right Erle of Devenshere, behedid at Salisbyre;" the others here named were, with the Earl, restored to grace.

[b] Robert Danby, Chief Justice C. P. in 8 Edward IV. 1468, a Knight in 1471.

[c] Sir John Mauleverer of Allerton-Mauleverer, com. Ebor. kt.

* Chron. ap. Lel. Coll. vol. i. part 2, p. 500. It is stated by Dugdale that Sir Thomas Hungerford was seized and tried for his life at Salisbury on Monday preceding the feast of St. Hilary, 8 Edward IV. when he had judgment as a traitor, and suffered next day. But according to the record he was arraigned with Courtenay on Monday next after the feast of St. Hilary, i. e. 16 January 1468-9, for treason charged to have been committed on the 21 May, 8 Edw. IV.; and it was on the next day that, after a trial and conviction by jury, both were sentenced to execution. (*Vide Rot. Parl. vi.* 306 b.) Henry Sotehill was attorney for the King on the occasion.

LETTER XIV.

Unto my worshipfull master Sir William Plompton, knight.

Right worshipfull maister, I recommend me unto you, praying you that you will cause the clothe that the wooll was packed in for to come againe with the shipp, for I borrow it wheare that ye saw that I borrow it; of that of your servants aforetime have borrowed two packcholthes and other geare, which they had never againe: letting you understand that I have given the shipman of his hier x[s], and he for to have his whole payment, when he deliver the goods which he receaved, which is xxxiij[s] iiij[d]. Whearfore I pray you that ye see that he be content of the said some, for I am nott in store att this time of money for to gett your harvest with, withoutyn I might gett it of your tenaunts, or ells for to take of your shepe silver, and that I ware right lothe for to do—letting you witt alsoe that I have bene in the Peake and there I cannott gett no money of Harry Fulgiam, nor of John of Tor, nor no other that owes you, but if I shold take of your cattell, and soe I think for to do; for I have no oxen to gett your corne with, nor none I cannott gett carryed, for every man is soe busie with their owne: for whether is so latesum in this cuntrey, that men can neither well gett corne nor hay—letting you witt that your tenant Nichole Bristow hath not gotten but xii foder of hay, and it is nought good, and the corneland is overflotin with water—letting you witt that I have gotten the hay in Heththornemeen that was left after lammas day, as ye comaunded me for to do—letting you witt that I have a counterpais wheith of the wheight stone that the wooll was weyed with, and that ye se that the stone be kept that the shipman brings. Also letting you witt that I delivered the shipman viij paire of blanketts, that is not in the bill indented, and a hanging of old linen cloth that the coverletts are trussed in—letting you witt that I was on St. Lawrence day att Melton with iiij[x] of your shepe to sell, and could sell none of them, but if I wold have selled xx of the best of them for xiij[d] a peece, and therefore I seld none—letting you witt that I sent unto you with William Plompton[a] and with William Marley[b] v[li], and also xxv[s] which was borrowed of Bryan Smith, which I must pay againe, and therefore I am not perveyed of money for to gett your harvest with—also that you gar the malt be windowd, or it be laid in any garners, for ells there will brede wyvolls in it, for I could nott gett it windowd before it went to the ship, because that I could not gett no helpe, and therefore I upheaped with a quarter, xxi quarters for xx quarters; and also six of your cheeses hase two markes that I know be the best of them. Noe more I write to you at this time but that the holy Trinity have you ever in his keeping. Written in hast by your servant THOMAS BILLOP att Kinalton,[c] the munday afore St. Bartholomew day, 9º Edw. 4.

(21*st Aug.* 1469.)

[c] Kinalton in com. Nott. a seat of Sir William Plumpton, kt. which came to him from the Foljambes.

LETTER XV.

To my right worshipfull maistre Sir William Plompton, knight, this letter be delivered.

Right worshipfull master, I recomend me unto your good mastership; Sir, I have sent to you by the bringer of this letter, a *venire facias* against the minister of St. Robert's, for he hath pleaded not guiltie for fishing your ponds att Plompton; if so be your writt be well served and the issue tried for you, the punishment will be grevieous to them, for it is gyffin by a statute.[a] Also I have sent you a *venire facias* against Dromonby, parson of Kynalton; he hath pleaded—he withholds you nothing, in accion of detynu of the goods, delivered him by Heynes. Also the copie of the pleadings betwixt you and the minister for your

[a] William Plumpton, bastard son of Sir William Plumpton, Kt. (*See Memoirs.*)

[b] William Marley, it is presumed, was nephew to Sir William Plumpton, son of Richard Marley and Alice Plumpton. Isabel Marley was their daughter. (*See Letter X.*)

[a] The writ of *venire facias* against Robert Bolton, the minister of the house of St. Robert near Knaresborough, and his fellow canons Richard Dryver, William Rute, John Malle, and William Usworth, for fishing in the ponds of Sir William Plompton, Knight, at Plompton, on the 20th day of February, 3 Edward IV. 1463-4, and taking breams, pike (*dentrices*), tench, and roches, sent by Godfrey Grene with this letter, was returned unexecuted by the sheriff in the following Hilary Term, by reason of the time being too short; and another was issued, returnable in Easter Term.— Teste R. Danby apud Westm. 12 Feb. 9 Edw. IV. 1469-70. The parties ultimately bound themselves (10 May 1471) to refer all matters in dispute to arbitration; for which purpose Robert Roos, of Ingmanthorp, and Lawrence Kighley were chosen on the part of Sir William Plumpton, and Robert Gascoigne and Thomas Clapeham on the part of the minister, who made their award on Saturday after the Ascension day, 11th Edward IV. 23 May, 1471. (*Chartul.* No. 571 *and* 573.)

milne att Plompton; it were well done that ye had a speech with Mr. Midleton of the forme of the pleadings, and of the matter both of the title of his milne, and your milne, and of the freholdes of both sides the water, for that your counsell may have instruccion thereof: it hath cost you money this terme, and yett no conclusion but to change the pleadings the next terme at the pleasure of the parties. Mr. Midleton had great labour therewith, I profferd him no rewards because ye may reward him yourselfe as it please you. Maister Fairfax[b] had x[s] for that matter all on. Mr. Suttill labored effectually; I tould him he shold be rewarded of the mony in his hands, and said lightly he would have none; so I wot whether he will take or no: he hath nott all paid yett. I pray you, against the next terme, send me word how I shall be demened in rewards giveing, for and it go to matter in law, it will cost mony largely. Also I have sent you a *Capias utlegat.* against Hargreve of Fuston: Sir John Malevera gave me a chalenge for him, and said he was outlawd under my trety: I told him I treted never; I bare your message to him, and that was a continuance for the matter against Fulburn, but nott for Hargreve. And he said ye had sued all the trew men to the king, to my lord, and to him in the forest, sith that ye come home; and that he shold complaine to the king and to the lords thereof; and I said, I trust to God ye shold come to your answere. And he said that shold not lyg in my power to bring you to do, for he wold deele with you and yours, both be the law and besides the law; and said he wold cutt the clothes notwithstanding. He was full angrie and hastie what time he said soe, and I was with Mr. Roclif the same time he gave me this chalenge, and Myles Willesthorp[c] was with him, and said no word. And Maister Roclif asked him what the matter was, if he might any ease; and he answered him, that ye desseyved him and all that ye dellyd withall: and Mr. Rocliff said he trust to God,—who have you evermore in his proteccion. Written at London, the vth day of December.

          Your servant
(5 Dec. 1469.)   GODFREY GRENE.

[b] Serjeant Guy Fairfax, called in 1464, was made King's Serjeant 28 April 1468.
[c] Miles Willesthorp, of Wilsthorp, com. Ebor. esq.

LETTER XVI.

To the right worshipfull and right reverend Sir William Plompton, knight, Custos of the Castle of Knaresburgh.[a]

Worshipfull and reverend Sir and our right good mastre, we recomend us unto you; and please you to have krowlech that our trustie freind, Thomas of the Logge, hath of late tame bene greveously vexed and troubled for certain matters that ye have knowlich of; so that yett, without that he trusteth specially above all things unto you, he dare not come at his owne house, unto his right great hurt and hindring: and as we have knowledge, the matters are in your will and throughe your good lordshipp . . . . Wheafore we beseech you in the lowliest wise we can or may, that ye vouchsafe to shew unto him your good lordshipp and mastershipp; for, if the matter shold be tryed by his neighbours, we deem the countrey should be found of his appeale; soe, that because of this our simple writing and request, he may under your protection have his goods unto his proper use under sufficient baile, and that he be not put into the wrongs that may cause his undoing, wherein ye shall deserve thanks of God, and your good lords at your coming to the kings house, with our dayly service att all times. Written att Windsor, the 14 of September. And it please to deliver unto

[a] The suits against the dwellers in the forest, spoken of in Letter XV. denote that Sir William Plompton held at this time the appointment of Chief Forester of the forest with that of Custos of the castle of Knaresborough, which same ofices he had also held in the reign of Hen. VI. and from whom he had had a grant of the latter for the term of his life.

Robert of Tymble[b] a Stub[c], the which Mr. Controller granted unto his ward for him and his wife.

    By your servants JOHN FELTON groom of the Chamber,
      and JOHN WARD[d] groom of the Eurey.

(14 *Sept.* 146..)

[b] Great Timble, in the parish of Fewston and liberty of Knaresborough, was one of the vills of the forest.
[c] Stub, a timber-tree.
[d] John Warde is named with others in Letters Patent bearing date at Westminster, 29 Apr. 6 Edw. IV. (*Rot. Parl.* v. 596 b.).

LETTER XVII.

To my right trusty and hartely welbeloved Sir John Mauliverer, knight.

Right trusty and hartily welbeloved, I greet you oft tymes wel. Letting you wete that Sir William Plompton, knight, hath sent unto me, and complayneth him that Thomas Wade[a] and Richard Croft dayly threats to beat or slay his servants, and seeketh them about his place; wheafore I desire and pray you to cause the said Thomas and Richard to surcease and leave theire said threatnings; and if they have any matters against his said servants, lett them complaine unto me therof, and I shall see that they shall have such a remedy, as shall accord with reason; and that ye faile nott hereof, as my speciall trust is in you. And God keepe you. Written att my Castle att Warkworth, the seaventh day of December. The Earle of Northumberland and Lord Mountague, wardin.[b]

(7 *Dec.* 1464-9.)   NORTHUMBERLAND.

[a] Thomas Wade of Knarysburgh, yeoman, a zealous Yorkist, convicted of treason, as an adherent of the Earl of Lincoln on the fourth of June, 2 Hen. VII. 1487, and attainted 19 Hen. VII. 1503. (*Rot. Parl.* vi. 545.)
[b] John Nevill, Earl of Northumberland (from 27 May 1464 to 25 Mar. 1470), Lord Montagu, and Warden of the East Marches. He was likewise President of Yorkshire.

LETTER XVIII.

To our right trustie and welbeloved Sir William Plompton, knight, Stuard of the lordshipp of Spofford, and to the balife of the same, and to ether of them, The duc of Glocestr, Constabl and Admirall of England.

R. GLOCESTRE.[a] Right trustie and welbeloved, we grete you well. And wheras att the freshe pursuit of our welbeloved Christopher Stansfield, one Richard of the Burgh, that had take and led away feloniously certaine ky and other cattell belonging to him, was take and arested with [in] the said manor att Spofford, wheareat they yett remaine; wheareore we desire and pray you that upon sufficient suerty to be found by the said Caristopher to sue against the said felon, as the law will, for that offence, ye will make delivery unto him of the said cattell, as is according with right: shewing him your good aide, favour, and benevolence, the rather att the instance of this our letters. And our Lord preserve you. From Pontfrett, under our signett, the thirteenth of October.

(13 *Oct.* anno circiter 1472.)

[a] Richard Duke of Gloucester, made High Constable of England 29 Feb. 1472, resided at Pontefract as chief Seneschal of the King's Duchy of Lancaster in the North Parts, and by virtue of his office leased to his beloved Sir William Plompton, knight, the ferm of the corn mills of Knaresborough and the new mill of Bilton, together with the office of bailiff of the burgh of Knaresborough, for the space of twelve years, rendering for the first xx marks, for the second xlvi s. viii d., for the said office of bailiff xlvi s. viii d.; which deed bears date 29th September, 12 Edw. IV. 1472 (*Chartul.* No. 584). The lordship of Spofford, in which parish Plumpton lay, belonged to the Earl of Northumberland, who had there a manor-place with a park.

LETTER XIX.

To my right trusty and welbeloved Coussin, Sir William Plompton, knight.

Right trusty and with all myn hart my welbeloved Cossine, I grete you hartily wealle, and desire and pray you that my welbeloved servant Edmund Cape may have and occopie the office of the baliship of Sesey,[a] as his father did tofore in time past. My trust is in you, that the rather for this mine instance and contemplation, ye will fulfill this my desire, and I will be as wellwilled to doe things for your pleasure. That knoweth our Lord, who have you in his blessed keping. Written in my manner of Topclife, the seventeenth day of August.

Your Cossin, H. Northumberland.[b]

[a] Sessay, a parish town in the wapentake of Allertonshire, was the residence of the family of Darell, of whom Sir George Darell, knight, died 8 Edw. IV. 1466, having married Margaret, daughter of Sir William Plumpton. The application of the Earl of Northumberland, on behalf of his servant, for the office of bailiff, makes it probable that Sir William Plumpton had then the wardship of the heir of Sir George Darell.

[b] Henry Percy, restored to the earldom of Northumberland in 1470, and to the estates of the family in Yorkshire, was the fourth Earl of the name.

LETTER XX.

To my trusty and welbeloved Cossin, Sir William Plompton, knight.

Right trusty and withal my hart my right welbeloved cosin, I gret you wel, and desire and pray you to labor Sir Richard Aldborough,[a] to caus him to deliver unto my cosin, dame Isabel Ilderton,[b] such beasts and cattel as he retayneth and withholdeth from her: for she hath no other mean to help herself with, unto that a determination be had betwixt Thomas Ilderton and her, of the livelyhed that standeth in travers betwixt them. Cosin, as ye love mee, that ye wil endevor yourselfe for the performance of the præmisses, wherin you shal deserve great thank of God, and to mee right great pleasure. That knoweth our Lord, who have you, cousin, in his blessed keeping. Written in my manor of Lekingfield, the twenty-five day of September.

(25 *Sept.* 1471-6.)   Your Cousin, H. Northumberland.

[a] Sir Richard Aldborough, kt. married Agnes, daughter of Sir William Plumpton, and was dead 16 Edw. IV. 1476. (*Esc. de eod. ann.*)

[b] The family of Ilderton were " of that ilk " in Northumberland, near Wooller.

LETTER XXI.

To my right trusty and welbeloved Coussin, Sir William Plompton, knight.

Right trusty and welbeloved Cossine, I grete you wele; and wheras varience dependeth betwixt you and my right welbeloved servant, Robart Birnand,[a] I therfore right hartyly desire and pray you therin nothing to doe, unto that I come into the contry. As my trust is in you, conforme you to the performing of this my desire, as ye intend to doe me pleasure: and our blessed Lord have you, kussin, in his blessed kepping. Wryten in my maner of Lekingfeild, the sixt day of June.

(6 June 1471-9.)   Your Cossine, H. Northumberland.

[a] Robert Birnand, of Nidd near Knaresborough, esq.

LETTER XXII.

To my right worshipfull and reverent maister, Sir William Plompton, kt.

Right worshippfull and reverent Sir and maister, I recomende me unto you. And please your good maistershipp to witte, there is a Clerke att York, the whilke purposes to say his first mes the sunday next after the feast of the nativitie of our Lady the Virgin[a]; and if ye wold vouchsafe that he might have a morsel of venison agenst the said sunday for Robart Manfeld sake, and trewly I shall lett him wytte both how ye did to his kinswoman against her wedding, and now for this said priest; for he is full brother to the said woman, and they are both right neare of his kin. I am siker he will thank you full hartely, fro I lett him witt, and that shalbe in all the gudly hast at I may, with the grace of

[a] 8 Sept.

God, who encrease your good estate to his pleasure. Written in hast att York, the friday next before the said feast.

Your owne servant and Bedeman, John Johnson of Yorke.

LETTER XXIII.

To my reverent and worshipfull maister, Sir William Plompton, knight.

Right reverent and my full worshipfull maister, I recommend me unto you in the hertelyest wise I kan. And for as much as a poore widdow, called Ellen Helme, is my son-in-law Will. Nesfields[a] tenant, is greeveously vexed in her sons; whearfore I pray you hartely to be their tender and especiall maister, as I and my said son may have cause to doe you service, the which we shalbe ready to doe, with Gods grace, who have you in his blessed keeping. Written at Newton on St. Cudberts day

(20 *March* 14 . .)   By your awne, Rich. Banks.[b]

[a] William Nesfield, esq. was of Flasby in the parish of Gargrave in Craven.

[b] Richard Banks, of Cold Newton or Bank Newton, in the same parish, esq. This match with Nesfield is omitted in the pedigree of the family of Banks inserted in Whitaker's History of Craven.

LETTER XXIV.

To my right reverend and worshipfull Maistre, Sir William Plompton, knight.

Right worshippfull Sir, I recomend me unto you good mastershipp; Sir, as for a *supersedias*[a] for yourselfe, there will not be gotten, without I shold put in sufficient men to be suerties; for there is a new rule made in the Chancery now late, that no sureties shalbe accepted, but such as be sufficient, and twenty of the old common sureties dischardged: so it is hard to gett suerties for a yoman. And as for the supliants, I have dayly labored, sith your man come, to gett a man to aske the suertie; and so I fand one which hath bene of old a *supersedias* mounger, and was agreed with him that he shold gett me a man to aske it, and he and the man shold have had v[s]. for their labor; and so he said unto me and Thom. on Saturday last that it was done, and desired mony for the mans labor and for the sealing, and we shold have them forth withall: and so he hath driven us from morne to even, and in conclusion deceyved us, and hath receved vii[s]. vi[d]. And I may nott arreast him nor strive with him for the mony, nor for the decept, because the matter is not worshipfull; and so there is none odere meane, but dayly to labor him to gett the writts, and so I shall, and send them to you asoune as they may be gotten: the labor is great and perillous, and the anger is more, because of the decept. As for the suit of Tulis executor, it is delaid for this terme, but the next terme it cannot be delaid; therefore it were well done ye sought up your writtings, and all the circumstances of making the obligacion, and whear it was made; for there is none will make a plea, without he have some matter to make it of: and also the court will nott admitt a forreine plea, without the matter be somewhat likely to be true. As for all your oder suits, they have the speed the law will give them, as Horbury will enforme you, when he comes home. As for the *supena*, the writt is nott retorned in; it seemes it will take a delay. I have sent you a copie of the letter, and a *supersedias* for Ward of Breeton; and as for your awne, if so be ye will that I put in sufficient suerties for you, ye may have one; but saveing your better advise, me think it nott necessary so to do, without oder cause shold require: for as strong in the law is a *supersedias* of a Justice of the peace, as in

[a] There were two kinds of appearances before the *quinto exactus* to avoid an outlawry, viz. an appearance in deed, that is, to render oneself, &c. and an appearance in law, that is, by purchasing a *supersedeas* out of the court where the record was.

the Chancery. And as for your bottles, there came no samon men here of all this sumor, but I understood they will come now hastely; by the next at comes they shalbe sent, with Gods grace, who have you evermore in his blessed proteccion. Written att London, the xth day of July. Thomas can enforme you of novelties in this countrie better then I can write.

(10 *July, anno circiter* 1475.)   Your servant GODFREY GREENE.

LETTER XXV.

To his right worshipfull maistre, Sir William Plompton, kt.

Right worshipfull Sir, I recomend me unto your good maistership; Sir, as for the suit against you by the executors of parson Tuly, had not it fortuned that there was a default founden in the writt, it had bene so that ye had bene condemned, or els an *exigi* awarded against you; for as for the matter of your plea, there would noe man plead it, ne it would not have bene except, if it had bene pleaded. Sir, there is an indenture upon the same *oblige*, the which wold serve much of your intents, and it might be found. Also, Sir, now of late I have receaved from you diverse letters, of the which the tenure and effect is this; one, that I shold labour to Sir John Pilkinton,[a] to labor to my lord of Glocester or to the king; they to move my lord of Northumberland[b] that ye might occupie still at Knaresborou.[c] Sir, as to that, it is thought here by such as loves you, 'at that labour should rather

[a] Sir John Pilkington, one of the knights of the king's body. (*2da pars Pat.* 13 Edw. IV.)
[b] Henry Percy, Earl of Northumberland, had obtained Letters Patent from the King, granting him the offices of Constable, Steward, and Master Forester of the castle, lordship, and forest of Knaresborough, within the County of York. (*Rot. Parl.* vi. 344 b.)
[c] Sir William Plumpton had had a grant of the keeping of the castle of Knaresborough for the term of his life in the reign of Hen. VI. (*Rot. Parl. vol.* v. 347 a.)

hurt in that behalve then availe; for certaine it is, as long as my lord of Northumberlands patent thereof stands good, as long will he have no deputie but such as shall please him, and kan him thank for the gift thereof, and no man els, and also doe him servise next the king: so the labour shalbe fair answered, and turne to none effect, but hurt. And as to another point comprised in your writing, that is, to enforme the lords and their counsell of the misgovernances of Gascoin[d] and his affinitie. Sir, ye understand that in every law the saying of a mans enemies is chalengeable, and rather taken a saying of malice then of treuthe, where, by the correction of the same defaulte, the complainer hath no availe; and so certainly by your counsell is thought here, that it wold be soe taken, and in no other wise, how be it that it be trew: and also a disworship to my lord of Northumberland, that hath the cheif rule there under the king. And as for the matter, to informe my lord of Northum: counsell how ye were entreated at Knasboro—Sir, we enformed my lords counsell according to your comaundement, and they enformed my lord, and my lord said he wold speak with us himselfe, and so did, and this was the answerr: that the cause why he wrote that no court of Sheriff turne shold be holden, was for to shew debate betwixt you and Gascoins affinitie, unto time he might come into the country and se a derection betwixt you—and that he wold 'at the 3 weeks court were holden for discontinuance of mens actions—and that he entended not to dischardge you of your office,[e] ne will not as long as ye be towards him—and that as soune as he comes into cuntry, he shall see such

[d] The quarrel between Plumpton and Gascoigne probably had its origin in the latter having been appointed to have the custody of the castle of Knaresborough by the Earl of Northumberland, to the exclusion of the former, and regardless of his right in virtue of the grant of King Henry the sixth. In the Chartulary is a bond from William Gascoigne of Gokethorpe, esq. to keep the peace towards Sir William Plumpton and to refer all matters to the arbitration of the Earl of Northumberland. The instrument is dated 27 Oct. 11 Edw. IV. 1471. (*Chartul. No.* 576.)
[e] Office of Bailiff of the Burgh of Knaresborough. (*See note* to Letter XVIII.)

a derection betwixt his brother Gascoin[e] and you, as shalbe to your harts ease and worship. And that I understand by his counsell, that it shalbe assigned unto you by my lo: and his counsell, what as longes to your office, and Gascoin nott meddle therewithall; and in like wise to Gascoyne. And as for the labour for the bailiships and farmes, Sir, your worship understands what labour is to sue therefore; first, to have a bill enclosed of the King, then to certein lords of the Counsell, (for there is an act made that nothing shall passe fro the King unto time they have sene it,) and so to the privie seale and Chauncellor: so the labour is so importune, that I cannot attend it without I shold do nothing ells, and scarcely in a month speed one matter. Your maistership may remember how long it was, or we might speed your bill of Justice of the peace; and had not my Lo. of Northumberland been, had not been sped for all the fair promisses of my Lo. Chamberlaine.[f] And as for the message to my Lo. Chamberlain, what time I labored to him that ye might be Justice of the peace, he answered thus; that it seemed by your labor and mine, that we wold make a jelosie betwixt my Lo. of Northumberland and him, in that he shold labor for any of his men, he being present. Sir, I took that for a watche word for medling betwixt Lords. As for any matter ye have to do in the law, how be it that it be to me losse of time and costly to labor or medl, as yett I am and alwayes shalbe readie to doe you service and pleasure therein, with the grace of God, who have you evermore in his blessed protection. Written att London, the eight day of November.

Your servant,
(8 *Nov. anno circiter* 1475.)   GODFREY GREENE.

[e] William Gascoigne, esq. was brother-in-law to the Earl of Northumberland, having married Margaret the Earl's sister.
[f] William Lord Hastings, Lord Chamberlain.

LETTER XXVI.

To my right trusty and hartely beloved brother, William Gascoygne.

Right trusty and right hartily beloved brother, I greet you well. And forasmuch as I understand that ye have put under arrest in the Castell of Knarsbrough one Thomas Ward, for suerty of peace; he finding sufficient suertie to answere to the King our soveraigne Lord, I will that ye suffer him to be at his larg without longer enpresonment. Not failling hereof, as my trust is in you, and our Lord have you in his kepping. Written in my mannor of Lekinfeild, the xix day of June.[a]

Your Broder,
(*Ante* 19 *June* 1479.)   HEN. NORTHUMBERLAND.

[a] The date of this letter is prior to 20 Edw. IV. 1480; at which time William Gascoygne of Gawkthorpe, com. Ebor. esq. the brother-in-law of the writer, Henry fourth Earl of Northumberland, was already a knight. Sir William Gascoigne died 4 Mar. 2 Hen. VII. 1486 (*Inq. virtut. officii*, 11 *Jun.* 4 *Hen. VII. Ebor.*), leaving his son William under age. To Dame Joan Grastock, the executrix of his will, William Ryther acknowledges to have received (8 April, 9 Hen. VII.) ten marks, six from Sir William Ryther his father, and four from herself. Sir William Gascoigne, the son, was in his twentieth year, 4 Hen. VII. 1489, and then a knight. (*Chartel. No.* 750.) One of the daughters is named in the will of her maternal uncle, the Earl of Northumberland, dated 17 July, 1485: "Also I will that my neice Elizabeth Gascoigne have to her marriage c markes." (*See abstract of the will, Coll. Top. et Gen. vol.* ii. *p.* 65.) She married (in 1494) George Talboys, son and heir of Sir Robert Talboys, Lord of Kyme and Redisdale; the same who is spoken of as Mr. Talbose in a subsequent letter. John Gascoigne and Ralph Gascoigne, esqrs. were brothers to the Sir William Gascoigne who died in 1486; Dame Agnes Plumpton, and Dame Margaret Ward, his sisters. Of these we find mention in the present correspondence; a pedigree (*MS. Add.* 5530, *f.* CLX.) adds Elizabeth and John, said to have died unmarried, and Humphrey who died young.

LETTER XXVII.

To the right reverend and worshipfull Sir William Plompton, knight, this to be delivered.

Right reverent and worshipfull Sir, I recomend me unto your good mastership. Please you to witt that I labored to Mr. Pilkinton and to the Chaunceler[a] diverse times for your letter fro the King, and promissed me to move my lord to speak to the King therefore; neverthelesse it was not doon, but when the King comes to London, I shall labour therefore againe. Your writts and *certiorare* are labored for, and shalbe had, how be the judges will graunt no *certiorare* but for a cause. Ailmer wife was like to have bene non suit in her appeale, for her day was *octabis martini*;[b] but Whele and I certified the judges that she wold come if she were in hele, and out of prison. The judges gifnes her no favour, for they say they understand by credible informations, that these men be not guiltie, and is but onely your maintenance; and so one of them said to me out of the Court. And Guy Fairfax[c] said openly att the barre, that he knew so, verily they were not guilty,—that he wold labor their deliverance for almes, not taking a penny; and I seing this, took Mr. Pygott[d] and Mr. Collow.[e]

(*Anno circiter* 1476-7.)   GODFREY GRENE.

[a] Thomas Rotheram, Bishop of Lincoln, made Lord Chancellor, 1475.
[b] 18 November.
[c] Guy Fairfax, King's Serjeant. (*See note to Letter XV.*)
[d] Richard Pigot, called serjeant 7 Nov. 1464.
[e] William Colow, called serjeant 9 June 1479.

LETTER XXVIII.

To my most reverent and worshippfull maister Sir William Plompton, knight, be this delivered.

After all lowly and dew recomendations, I lowly recommend me unto your good maistershipp; certifieing your maistership I sent you by one Wil. Atkinson a letter and the copie of the answerre of the privie seale, and a box with 6 peeces, 5 sealed and one unsealed; and, Sir, the box sealed for your maistershipp took me no more. First, they tooke me 7, and 2 filed together that were of one, the graunt of Stutvell[a] and the peticion thereon; and they tooke away the petition, and soe I had but 6, whilk I send your maistershipp by the said William in the said box sealed; and if it were so, and the letter delivered to you with the copie, I desire you send word. As for your say, I have sent you a peice of 2 yards and a halfe broad by Grethum of York, the first of Lent. As for the other peice, there is none of lesse bredth then 2 yards; for if I could have any, I should have sent it with the other. And as for the cloth of my ladies, Hen. Cloughe putt it to a shereman to dight, and he sold the cloth and ran away; and Hen: mett with him, and gart him be sett in the Countre, till he founde sewerte to answer at the Gildehall for the cloth. And soe he hath sewed him till he had judgment to recover, which cost him large money; and when he shold deliver it, he delivered another peice, butt that Henry hapned to understand after the recovery wheare he had sould it; and soe it is had againe and it is put to dyeing, and as soune as it is readie, I shall send it by the carrier, for it was fryday in the second week of Lent or it was gettin againe. And as for suites in the Kings bench again them in Brereton, and in the Common place again Will. Pulleyne and his suertes, are in proces; and fro they be in exigent, ye shall have the exigent sent you, as soun as it will be sped. And for the day of appearaunce of Ailmer wyfe, is *mense Paske*;[b] so that she be here the morrow after *mense Paske*. I shold have sent you word or that, but that I had nott the *habeas Corpus* against John Esomock, and Robart Galaway, and for to see that we were not beguiled by the day of returne and day of appearance; be it my day. And soe I send you now the *habeas corpora* and a coppie thereof, and you must desier the sheriffe to serve it, yf so be that ye agre not. And also, Sir, that ye will send word as soon as ye can, if the principalls were delivered not att York, and what way is had betwixt you and them, and if there be any towne or hamlett in Craven that is called Medilton, and that ye send word. And as for your cope, I have cheaped diverse, and under a hundred shillings I can by non, that is ether of damaske or sattin, with flowers of gold; and I send you a peice of baudkin, and another of impereal, to se whether ye will hafe of, and the price. And the bredth of it is elme broade; 3 yards, besides the orffrey, will make a cope: to have of whilk it please you, ether to be made ... or there. And if ye will have it to be made here, it will stand ye to 6 marks or more, with the orfrey and makeing, and that is the least that I can drive it to. The orffrey 32s., the lining and making 8s., and as for a broderer, I can find none that will come soe farre, but any work that ye would have, to send hither and they will do it; and in no other wise they will as yett grant me, but I shall that I may to gett one. Alsoe, Sir, I send your mastership the bill of the expences and costs that I have made since I came hither, and please you to see it and send money the next terme. All other thinges, whilk ye will I do, and I shall doe therein that I ether may or can. I beseech your mastership to recomend me lowly to my lady; and if I durst, Sir, the matter betwixt my brother Robart and Mr. Gascoines sister,[c] me think, is to long in makeing up, for in long tarriing comes mekell letting. And I beseech the blessed Trinitie have you in his continual keeping. From London, the first day of Aprill.

Your servant in all,

(1 *April* 1476.)   ROBENETT P.[d]

[a] For the grant of Stuteville, see *Memoirs*.
[b] *Mensa Paschæ*, the month or quinzaine of Easter, i. e. the eight days preceding and the eight days following Easter day. It commenced 7 April in 1476, the year this letter was written.
[c] The contract for the marriage of Robert Plumpton, only surviving legitimate son of Sir William Plumpton, with Agnes, sister of William Gascoign of Gokethorp, esq. was signed 13 July 17 Edw. IV. 1477, and serves to fix the date of this letter to the month of April in the preceding year.
[d] Robenett or Robert Plumpton was a bastard son of Sir William Plumpton, and was usually distinguished from his legitimate younger brother by the epithet of senior.

LETTER XXIX.

Complaynts of your servants of Hidell,[a] John Rycroft and Wil. Rycroft.

To our maister and lord, Sir William Plompton, knight.

Beseketh your good maistershipp all your tenants and servants of your lordshipp of Idell, Wil. Rycroft yelder, Wil. Rycroft yonger, John Rycroft, Henry Bycroft, and John Chalner except. And at it please your good mastershipp to heare and consider the great rumor, slaunder, and full noyse of your tenants of your said lordshipp, att they shold be untrew peopell of their hands, taking goods by mean of untrewth; and for as much as the said Wil. Rycroft yelder, Wil. Rycroft yonger, John Rycroft, Henry Bycroft, and John Chalner are dwelling within your said lordship, they all not having any kow or kalves, or any other guds whearby they might live, nor any other occupise, and fair they are beseen,

[a] Idle in the parish of Calverley, liberty of Pontefract, a lordship belonging to Sir William Plumpton.

and wel they fair, and att all sports and gamies they are in our country for the most part, and silver to spend and to gameing, which they have more readie then any other within your said lordship; and to the welfare of our soveraigne lord the King and you, nothing they will pay, without your said tenants will fray with them, whearfore they are in regage to divers of your graves; and by what meanes they in this wise, with 5 persons being in houshold, are found, God or some evill angel hase notice hereof. And as for geese, grise, hennys, and copons, your said tenants may none keepe, but they are bribed and stolen away by night to great hurt to your tenants. And for as much as these persons afore rehersed are not laboring in due time, as all other of your tenants are, but as vagabonds live, your said tenants suppose more strangely by them. Whearfore att reverence of God and in way of charitie, your said tenants beseketh you to call all them before you, and to sett such remedy in these premisses as may be to your worshipp, and great proffitt to your tenants, and in shewing of mikle unthriftiness, which without you is likely to grow hearafter, and your said tenants shall pray to Almighty God for your welfare and estate.

LETTERS

WRITTEN TO SIR ROBERT PLUMPTON, KT.

WHO DIED THE 15TH YEAR OF K. HENRY THE EIGHTH.

LETTER I.

To my Right welbeloved Robart Plompton, esquier.[a]

Right welbeloved frinde, I greet you well. And wheras the Scotts in great number are entred into Northumberland, whose malice with Gods helpe I entend to resist; therfore on the King, our soveraigne Lords behalfe, I charg you, and also on myne as wardeyn,[b] that ye with all such personnes as ye may make in there most defensible arrey, be with me at Topliffe uppon Munday by viij a clocke, as my trust is in you. Written in Wresill,[c] the vij day of September.

Your Cousin,

(7 *Sept.* 1480.)   HEN. NORTHUMBERLAND.

[a] Robert Plumpton, esq. eldest surviving son of Sir William Plumpton, kt. was knighted in Hoton-field beside Berwick, 22 Aug. 1482.

[b] Henry Percy, Earl of Northumberland, was Wardens of the East and Middle Marches in 1480; in which year, upon its being signified that, notwithstanding the cessation of arms, the King of Scots had invaded the English Marches, he was commissioned by the King to muster all able-bodied men, &c. (See *Collins's Peerage, tit. Percy Earl of Northumberland.*)

[c] Wressle-castle, near Howden in the east riding of Yorkshire, was built by Thomas Earl of Worcester, and was a favourite residence of the Percies.

LETTER II.

To my old Lady Plompton[a] *be this bil delivered.*

Right worshipful and my especial good Lady, I recommend me unto your good Ladiship, evermore desiring to wit of your welfare. And, madam, I pray you to call to your Ladiship how gude precher I have been to my master, at gon is,[b] and to you. And, madam, there is one duty awing unto me, part wherof was taken or my master deceased, whose soul God have mercy, and most part taken to your selfe since he died: taken by Henry Fox and by Henry of Selay, your servants, of whilk I send you one bill with Henry Fox. The sum is 19^{li}. 2^s. 9^d. wherof I have received by Henry Fox in money 3^{li}. and in 2 fat oxen, price 36^s. Sum at I have received is 4^{li}. 16^s. so remaines there behind 14^{li}. 6^s. 9^d. Madam, if case be that ye will have sende word for Sir John Wixley,[c] that drawes 6^{li}. 6^s. viij^d.; so is ther owyng to me 9^{li}. 1^d. And I besech you, madam, that I myght have my money; I have forborne it long. Ye know well, madam, the great troble that I was in, and the great cost and charggs that I had this last yere past; and, madam, ye know well I have no lyfing, but my bying and selling: and, madam, I pray you sende me my money, as ye will I doe you service, or els to send me word when I shall have it, for it cost me much money sending for. And Henry Fox bad me send my rakning at Ripon, and I should be answered to my money, for Herry received most part of stufe of me; and if ye will not answere me therfore, Henry must answer therfore. Ma-

[a] Joan, daughter of Thomas Wintringham, of Knaresborough, gent. second wife of Sir William Plumpton, kt. survived her husband, and was living 19 Oct. 12 Hen. VII. 1496. (*Chartul. No.* 785).

[b] Sir William Plumpton, kt. died 15 Oct. 20 Edw. IV. 1480.

[c] Sir John Quixlay, chaplain, was with Richard Plumpton appointed by the official of York, 10 Jan. 1480-1, to take the inventory of the effects of Sir William Plumpton, kt. who had died intestate. (*Chartul. No.* 622.)

dam, thar is one Casson in taking, of that towne to; considring of gud service (*a line omitted*) at Sir John Dedyser, my master, and you in your great troble. For sute, madam, I lost all that I payd for him, and that was long of your Ladyship; for when I wold have followed him, ye dyside me nay, for ye sayd ye had rather lose the towne. And therfore I besech you to loke if ther be any thing I may dow for your Ladiship, or for my master your son;[d] I shall be redy with grace of God, who preserve your Ladyship. Written at York, on friday after St. Peter day.

Be your owne,

(*July, anno circiter* 1481.)   WILLIAM JODDOPKAN.

[d] Robert Plumpton, esq.

LETTER III.

To my welbeloved Robart Plompton.

Right welbeloved, I gret you well, willing and charging you to be with me in all hast possible after the sight of this my writting; not failing herof, as ye will answere to the Kings highnes and to me at your perill. Written at Lekinfeild,[a] the last day of December.

(31 *Dec.* 1481.)   HENRY NORTHUMBERLAND.

[a] Leckonfield, near Beverley, where the Earls of Northumberland had a manor-place.

LETTER IV.

To my right trusty and welbeloved freind, Sir Robart Plompton, Kt.

Right trusty and welbeloved, I greet you well, and will and charg you on the King our soveraigne Lords behalfe, and also on myne, that ye, with all such persones as ye may make defensibly arrayed, be redy to attend upon the Kings highnes and me, upon our warnyng, as ye love me and will answere to the King at your perill. Written at Lekingfeld, the ixth day of October.

Your Cousin,

HENRY NORTHUMBERLAND.

LETTER V.

To the right honorable my especyall good master, Sir Robart Plompton, knyght.

After all due recomendations premysed, pleaseth your mastership to wyt that I have received my fee xxvis. viiijd. for Pentycost last past, sent to me by my fader servant, William Coltman, in my most humbly wyse thanking your mastership therfore ; nevertheless I marvell greatly that your mastership wrote not to me, comaunding me to doe you some service at London. Sir, you know my mynd and service, and I am right sory and any synister wayes of my adversaryes be shewed unto you, and not of my deservyng; if yt be so, your wryting had bene to me more comfortable then much goods, considryng althings done aforetyme. Such as be your adversaryes in your old matters [a] hath bene with me at London, Master Bryan Roclife, Palmes and Topclyffe, comyning and desyring further to proced in our matters ; and saying, ye clame suyt, service and seute, of ther maner of Colthorpe, and for the same merce him in your court at Plompton : if yt be so, in my mynd yt is necessary to aske, distreyne, and levie the sayd amerciments. Pleaseth it your mastership in my most humble wyse to recomend me unto my good ladyes, and to my power service, as I have bene and ever wylbe to my lyfes end, as more at the larg the brynger of this shall shew unto you by mouth, to whom I pray you give credence. In short space ye shall know more for the best, with the grace of *Jesu*, who your mastership preserve. At London, the last day of June.

Your humble servant,

(30 *June* 1483.)   EDWARD PLOMPTON.[b]

---

[a] From the time of the death of Sir William Plumpton, the succession of Sir Robert Plumpton to the estates of his father had been disputed on behalf of the heirs general, one of whom was married to the son of Master Bryan Roclife. A reference to the crown for arbitration had been agreed upon in the reign of Edw. IV., which was rendered ineffectual by the death of that monarch. There was now a desire to proceed further, and the matter was for the present settled by an award of Richard III. dated 16 Sept. in the first year of his reign. (*See Memoirs.*)

[b] Edward Plumpton, gentilman, had letters to act as general attorney for Sir Robert Plumpton, kt. dated 4 Jan. 1 Ric. III. 1483-4. (*Chartul. No.* 729.) Prior to which date he had a rent out of Nether Studley, given to him and Agnes his wife by Sir Robert Plumpton, which he entered into a bond to release, 10 Dec. 1483. (*Ibid. No.* 728.) He was a younger son of Godfrey Plumpton, (brother of Sir William Plumpton, kt. Sir Robert's father) who was living 26 Sept. 1483. (*Ibid. No.* 723). His father married Alice Wintringham, sister of Dame Joan Plumpton, by whom he had Sir Richard Plumpton, chaplain, his heir, also a correspondent of Sir Robert Plumpton. Alice, the wife of Godfrey Plumpton, had become a widow before 20 July, 1 Hen. VII. 1486. (*Ibid. No.* 737.)

LETTER VI.

To the right honorable and worshipfull my singuler good master, Sir Robart Plompton, knyght, these be delivered.[a]

The most humble and due recomendations premysed, pleaseth your mastership to recomend me unto my singuler good lady your moder, and my lady your wyfe ; humble praying your good mastership to take no displeasure with me that I sent not to you afore this, as my duety was. People in this country be so trobled, in such comandment as they have in the Kyngs name and otherwyse, marvellously, that they know not what to doe. My lord Strayng[b] goeth forth from Lathum upon munday next with x ml. men, whether we cannot say. The Duke of Buck: has so many men, as yt is sayd here, that he is able to goe where he wyll; but I trust he shalbe right withstanded and all his mallice : and els were great pytty. Messengers commyth dayly, both from the Kings grace and the Duke, into this country. In short space I trust to se your mastership ; such men as I have to do with, be as yet occupied with my sayd lord. Sir, I find my kinsmen all well dysposed to me ; if your mastership wyll comand me any service, I am redy and ever wylbe to my lifes end, with the grace of *Jesu*, who ever preserve you. Wrytten at Aldclife, uppon St. Luke day.

Your most humble servant,

(18 *Oct.* 1483.)   ED. PLOMPTON.

---

[a] This letter was written on the very day on which the Duke of Buckingham first openly appeared in arms at Brecknock against King Richard III., and gives us some interesting information respecting his proceedings, as to his seeking to make partisans in the county of Lancaster, in aid of his attempt. But the King at this time was secure in the allegiance of the powerful Earl of Derby, and of his son George Stanley, Lord Strange, to whom the writer was secretary ; the approach of the latter, with ten thousand men, doubtless mainly contributed to the dispersion of the Duke's forces, and the crushing of his rebellion.

[b] George Stanley, Baron Strange of Knockyn, died 15 Dec. 13 Hen. VII. 1497.

LETTER VII.

To my right hartely beloved cousin, Sir Robart Plompton, kt.

Right hartely beloved cousin, I commend me unto you. And wheras I conceive, that wheras award was ordred in the matter of variance depending betwixt John Polleyn[a] on the one partie, and Georg Tankard[b] with other taking his parte on the other party, I am enformed that the said parties bene now at traverse in that behalfe, contrary to such derections as were taken. I, willing the pacefying and reformation herof by the advyse of you and other of my counsell, desire and pray you, Cousin, at your comyng to me at Yorke uppon thursday next comyng, to cause the sayd Georg and the other persones to com with you ; and that ye shew your good will for the performance herof, as my very trust is in you, whom God kepe. Written in my Castell of Wresell, the xiiij day of Februarie.

Your Cosin,

HEN. NORTHUMBERLAND.

---

[a] John Polleyn of Knaresborough, esq. son of John Polleyn the elder, gentleman.

[b] George Tankard, gentleman, was brother of William Tankard, ancestor of the Tancreds, Baronets, of Boroughbridge, com. Ebor. He was a witness to a deed, 15 Dec. 20 Edw. IV. 1480. (*Chartul. No.* 702.)

LETTER VIII.

To the right worshipfull Sirs, Sir Robart Plompton, Myles Wylstrop, and to John Pullan, Robart Barnand, be this letter delivered.

Worshipfull Sires, I recomend me to you. My nephew Halnath[a] hath bene with me, and shewed to me a wyll made upon a feftment, at my brother Sir John goyng over see, on whose soule *Jesu* have mercy ; by the which I understood that my nephew Halnath and Robart shold have, ether of them, iiijli. by the yere, terme of ther lyfes. If they can shew the wyll under seale according to the copie, the must neds have ther iiijli. Also they shew that Myles Wylstropp, John Pullan, Robart Barnand, and Nycholas Ward[b] was with my brother at his death ; to whom my sayd brother sayd, that he wold that this will were fulfilled and performed. If this be the trew, it is a great evydence. As for my sister entrest, I

---

[a] The writer of this letter was, it appears, a brother of the House of St. John of Jerusalem at Clerkenwell, and of the family settled at Allerton Mauleverer, in the county of York. Sir John Mauleverer, his brother, is said in the pedigrees of the family to have married a daughter of Banks of Newton in Craven, by whom he had a son named Thomas, whose wife was a De la River of Brandsby, com. Ebor. ; and a daughter Grace, married to John Pullan, of Knaresborough, esq. ; but this and the following letter add considerably to the genealogies of the family, hitherto in print, in furnishing us with the names of the writer himself, and those of his nephews Halnath and Robert, sons of his brother William. Sir Thomas Mauleverer, knt. was a feed-man of the Earl of Northumberland in 1486, and contracted for the marriage of his son Richard to Joan, daughter of Sir Robert Plumpton, knt. 20 May, 7 Hen. VII. 1492. He died before 2 Sept. 11 Hen. VII. 1495, leaving Elizabeth his wife surviving. (*Chartul. No.* 763 *and* 779.)

[b] Nicholas Ward was a younger brother of Sir Christopher Ward, of Gevendale, com. Ebor. knt.

shall comyn with wyse lerned men, and shew to them how the matter stands betwene my sayd sister and my nese, as nere as I can. I shall shew them of the exchang, and of the closser bysyde Sober Hell,[c] and also what the law will, if my sayd sister was agreed afore wytnesse that my nephew shold have my sister joynter and dower for terme of hir lyfe, if yt be by endenter. I remitt yt to your wysdomes, besechyng you all to se that ther be no troble among them, to I send the certayne of all the premisses. Gylbard shalbe with you by Trenete Sunday, or sone after, and bryng you the certaynte of every thing, by the grace of *Jesu*, who preserve you. Wrytten at Clerkinwell, the xiii of May.

HALNATH MALIVEREY.

[c] Sober Hill is the name of two farm-houses in the township of Newby-Wiske, near Northallerton.

LETTER IX.

To the right worshipfull Sir Robert Plompton, John Pullan, and to Robert Byrnand, and to every of you be thes delivered.

Right worshipfull Sirs, I recomend me unto you, letting you wytte that I have comond with lerned men to understand wher my syster in law may enter into her joynter and dower, or no. They say, for as much as the erytance and right of the same was in my nevew after the death of his father, on whose soule *Jesu* have mercy; at whose death my sayd sister let to ferme her joynter and dower to my sayd nephew, hir son, afore wittnese, terme of hir lyfe, the which is thought by them that be learned, is a surrender in the law: wherfore she must byd by such comonds as was betwyxt hir son and hir. As for my brother William, if it may be shewed under his seale or synmanuell, or if the sayd wyll be lost, if ther be iiij worshipfull men that will swere upon a booke, that they saw the wyll, and that my sayd brother at his death desired them that the same wyll myght be performed, my nephewes must needs have their porcion, and every person to have after thayr porcion. Also yt is thought by the forsayd lernedmen, that if my sayd nevew had a c[li]. of his father goods, yf it were spended afore his death, his father seckturs may have no accion agaynst his seckturs. Ye have right wyse and descret learned men in Yorkshire; ye may enquere of them, if it please you. *Jesu* preserve you. Written at Clerkynwell, the xx day of May.

Yo[r] owne, HALNATH MALLYVERER.

LETTER X.

To his especiall gud master, Sir Robart Plompton, Kt. deliver these letter.

Sir, if it please your mastership, on the satterday after our Lady day,[a] the Parlament was prolonged unto the xxvii day of January, and then it begineth againe. Sir, my lord Schanchler publyshed in the Parlament house the same day, that the Kings gud grace shall weede my lady Elizabeth (and so she is taken as quene); and that at the marage ther shalbe great justyng.[b] Also, Sir, ther be divers lords and gentlemen attended by the Parlament, which be these; and first, Richard late Duke of Gloucetter, John Duke of Norfolk, Thomas Erle of Surrey, Francis Lord Lovell, Walter Lord Ferres, John Lord Such; knyghts, Sir James Heryngton, Sir Robert Heryngton, Sir Richard Charleton, Sir Richard Ritliff, Sir William Barkley, Sir Robart Brakenbery, Sir Thomas Filkynton, Sir Robart Mydleton; esquires, Walter Hopton, William Catisby,

[a] 10 Dec. 1 Hen. VII. 1485.
[b] The roll of parliament for 1 Hen. VII. it is presumed, is defective, as no memorandum of the prorogation, spoken of in this letter, is to be found in the printed copy; but a petition of Margaret Agard, daughter and heir of Geffrey St. Germayn, refers incidentally to its reassembling on the xxiii of January, which numerals we should perhaps here read instead of xxvii. The Chancellor's notification of the King's marriage is therefore unrecorded, and the date obtained from this letter becomes a valuable acquisition to the historian.

Roger Wake, William Sapcott, Homfray Stafford, Wylliam Clarke, Galfryd Seyngermen, Watter Watkyn, herold of hermes, Richard Revell of Darbyshire, Thomas Pulter of Surrey, John Walste, John Kendall secretory, John Buke, John Ratte, William Brampton: the are attended for certayne. Howbeit, ther was many gentlemen agaynst it, but it wold not be, for yt was the Kings pleasure. Sir, here is much spech that we shall have aschip agayne, and no man can say of whom: but they dem of Northernmen and Walchmen. And much speca is in the Kyngs house and of his householdmen. Sir, other tydings is none here as yett. Ther is much runyng amongst the lords, but no man wott what it is; it is sayd yt is not well amongst them. Sir, I send your mastership a letter by Roger, Mr. Mydleton' man. Sir, if ther be any newer things, your mastership shall have word, if I can gett it caryed from London. *In die* Sent Lucie Virgin.

Your bedman, Sir THO. BETANSON.

(13 *Dec.* 1485.)

LETTER XI.

To his singuler gud master, Sir Robart Plompton, Kt. deliver these.

Sir, if it please your mastership, I have made a letter unto you afore Christenmas of such tydings as I know; but I was deceyved, for I went your mastership had had it to within this ij dayes: and so ye shall have one other with it both. Sir, if yt please you, these bet the tydings that I know. The Kyng hat resumyde by the Parlamentt into his hands all maner patayns, jeftys, offyzs, that he dyd jiffe from the ij day of August unto the iij day of January, and that be many of his houshold in yt plesyde with yt. Also he hath resumyde all maner gyfts, patayns, offezs, that was geven from the xxiij (*lege* xxxiii) yere of King Herre the vj[th], by King Edward the iiij[th], or by King Edward his son the vth, or by King Richard the iij[th], into his hands.[a] Also it is in actte in the Parliament, that all maner huntyng in parkes, chases, forest belonging to the Kyng, is made felony.[b] Also, Sir, the Kyng proposyth northward hastyly after the Parlament, and it is sayd he purposes to doe execution quickly ther on such as have offended agaynst him. Sir, other tydings I know none as yet. Sir, I besech you recomend me unto both my gud Ladis, and I send them a pauper of the Rosery of our Lady of Coleyn, and I have regestered your name with both my Ladis names, as the pauper expresses, and ye be acopled as brether and sisters. Also, Sir, these lords and gentlemen that was attaynted, they gytt no grace, as yt is sayd. No more, but I besech your mastership to be gud master unto my father, and I shalbe your bedman, with Gods grace, who hope you evermore in great joy and felycyte. From London, *in crastino* St. Valentin. Also, Sir, the King will come with great company; as it is sayd, with x hundred men in harnesse, and with him mo then v or six schore lords and knights. Also the Duke of Bedford[c] goes into Wales to se that country. Also it is in actt, that all maner of profycyes is mayd felony.[d] Sir, oder tydings I know none as yet, that be certayne.

Your servant and bedman, Sir THO. BETANSON.

(15 *Feb.* 1485-6.)

[a] The act of resumption of all patents, &c. from the xxxiii[rd] year of Hen. VI. to the ii[d] of August 1 Hen. VII. is on the printed copy of the Rolls of Parliament; but its extension to the iii[d] of January is not recorded.
[b] This act is on the Statute Roll.
[c] Jasper Tudor, created Duke of Bedford, 27 Oct. 1485.
[d] In its present defective state this act is not found on the Parliamentary Roll.

LETTER XII.

To my singuler good master, Sir Robart Plompton, kt.

After most due recomendacions had, pleaseth your mastership in my most lowly wyse to recommend me unto my singuler good lady. Sir, this day com Wylliam Plompton[a] to labor for Haveray Parke,[b] and brought to me nether byll, wrytteng, nor commandement by words, nor token, fro your mastership; and therof I marvell, considering that at your instaunce I suffered him to occupie the same parke and office for this tyme: and for that cause I am not in certente, whether ye be his good master or noo. Wherfore he hath not spedd as he myght have done if your wrytting had com; notwithstanding, yt is well. Sir, my lord [c] kept his Easter with my lord of Oxford at Laveham,[d] and come to the King uppon fryday last,[e] and comes with the King to Yorke; and my lord of Darby departeth from Notingham into Lancashire. Sir, therle of Oxford, my lord Chamberleyn,[f] with diverse other estates, cometh to the King to Notingham, and so forth to Yorke, as more at large the brynger shall shew to you by mouth. Sir, the first gift that my lady of Syon gave to me, was a par of Jeneper beads *pardonet*, the which I have sent to you by the bringer; and if I had a better thinge, I wold have sent it with as good a will and harte: and any service that ye wyll comand me, I am redy, as knoweth our Lord, who preserve you. At Lyncolne, the iij day of Apryll.

(3 *April* 1486.)   Your servant, EDWARD PLOMPTON.

[a] William Plompton, bastard son of Sir William Plumpton, kt.
[b] Haverah Park was a royal chase in the liberty of Knaresborough, and parcel of the duchy of Lancaster, of which the Earl of Derby was at this time seneschal in the North parts.
[c] The Lord Strange. (*See Letter* LXII.)
[d] John, Earl of Oxford, had a capital manor at Lavenham, com. Suff.
[e] In the year 1486, Easter day fell on the 26th of March, at which time the King was sojourning at Lincoln, being then on a progress towards the north parts of the kingdom; but he had reached Nottingham before the end of the week, and was yet there when this letter was written. (See an account of this progress in *Lelandi Collectanea, vol. IV. editio altera. p.* 185.)
[f] Sir William Stanley, Lord Chamberlain.

LETTER XIII.

To my right worshipfull master, Sir Robart Plompton, Kt.

Reverend and my right trusty good master, due reverence done, know ye I am at your comaundment, with prayer for you, my gode lady your wyfe, and mother, and your children. My lord [a] faryth well, and recomends him unto you, with harty thanks of your good and fast love, which he entendeth to content your mynd for. Sir, yt is so that Sir Alexander [b] hath a *dedimus potestatem* dyrect to thabot of St. Mary in York, Sir Richard Tunstall [c] and Sir John Hart; [d] for the which matter my lord hath wrytten to thabot and Sir John Hart in recomendation of Sir Alexander. Wherfore, when expedient tyme shalbe apoynted, my lord wilbe glad and well content that ye se the deling, and as ye understand that yt will lest you, certyfie me by your wryting derected to me; and thus almighty God preserve you. From Greenwich, the xviii day of November.

By your loving and due beadman,
(18 *Nov. anno circiter* 1486.)   Master HENRY HUDSON.

[a] The Earl of Northumberland is doubtless the lord to whom the writer alludes, he being then with Court at Greenwich.
[b] Sir Alexander Lee, rector of Spofforth, is the person here spoken of. (*See Letter* LXXVII.) Plumpton was in this parish.
[c] Sir Richard Tunstall, kt. Steward of the honour of Pontefract.
[d] Sir John Hart, rector of the church of St. Martin in Micklegate, York, from 1476 to 1519.—(*Drake's Eboracum, p.* 472.)

LETTER XIV.

To my right hartely beloved Cousins and frinds,[a] *Sir William Inglebie,*[b] *Sir Robart Plompton, Sir William Beckwith,*[c] *Kts. and John Gascougne, Esquier.*[d]

Sir Randall Pygot,[e] Sir William Stapleton,[f] Sir Piers Middleton,[g] Sir Christofer Ward,[h] Sir Thomas Malliverer,[i] John Hastings, [k] John Rocliffe [l] were comaunded to be redy upon an ower warning.

Your Cousin, HEN: NORTHUMBERLAND.

[a] The knights to whom this brief notification was made by the Earl of Northumberland were his feed-men, receiving his wages. When King Henry VII. made his progress into the north parts in the first year of his reign, the Earl met him by the way in Barnsdale, a little beyond Robin Hood's stone, with thirty-three knights of his feed-men, besides esquires and yeomen.—(*Lel. Coll. vol. IV. p.* 185.)
[b] Sir William Ingleby, of Ripley, com. Ebor. kt.
[c] Sir William Beckwith, of Clint, com. Ebor. kt.
[d] John Gascoigne, esq. uncle to Sir William Gascoigne, of Gawkthorp, com. Ebor. kt.
[e] Sir Randall Pigot, of Clotherholm, com. Ebor. kt.
[f] Sir William Stapleton, of Wighill, com. Ebor. kt. He died 16 Dec. 1503.
[g] Sir Piers Middleton, of Middelton, com. Ebor. kt.
[h] Sir Christopher Ward, of Givendale, com. Ebor. kt.
[i] Sir Thomas Malliverer, of Allerton, com. Ebor. kt.
[k] John Hastings, of Fenwick, com. Ebor. esq. afterwards Sir John Hastings, kt.
[l] John Rocliffe, of Cowthorpe, com. Ebor. esq. afterwards Sir John Rocliffe, kt.

LETTER XV.

To his worshipfull master, Sir Robart Plompton, Kt. this delyver.

Right worshipfull and my singuler gud master, I recomend me unto your mastershipe, and unto both my gud Ladys, and unto all gud masters and fryndes, your servants. If it please your mastership to here of me, and where I abyde, I serve in the Sepulcre church without Newgaytt. Ther is a woman was borne in Selby. I have x marke and no charg, and the terme tymes I have meat and drynke of my lord Bryan, cheife judg of the common place; [a] and this christenmas I goe with him into the country to his place, and comes agayn the next terme. Wherfore, if it wold please your mastership to send me a letter how ye, and my Ladys, with all your houshold, doth, for yt were to me great comforth; and if ther be any thing here that I can or may do, send me word, and I shall indever me to do, yt, as is my dewty. Sir, as for tydings, here is but few. The King and the Quene lyes at Grenwych; the Lord Perce [b] is at Wynchester: the earle of Oxford is in Essex: the erle of Darby and his son be with the King. Also here is but litle spech of the erle of Warwyk [c] now, but after christenmas, they say ther wylbe more spech of. Also ther be many enimies on the see and dyvers schippes take, and ther be many take of the kyngs house for theves. Other tydings I know non. Also they begyn to dye in London; there is but few pariches fre: at summer they die faster. Then I purpose to come into Yorkshire, with Gods grace, who kepe you and your lovers evermore. At London *in vigil*. St. Andrew apostle.

(29 *Nov.* 1486.)   Your dayly bedman, THO. BETANSON.

[a] Sir Thomas Brian, kt. Chief Justice C. P. Writ tested at Westminster, 20 Sept. 1486.
[b] Lord Percy, eldest son of the Earl of Northumberland, to which title he succeeded 28 Apr. 1489.
[c] Edward Plantagenet, Earl of Warwick, then a prisoner in the Tower.

LETTER XVI.

To my right trusty and welbeloved cousin Sir Robart Plompton, kt.

Cousin Sir Robart, I commend me unto you; and wher it is so that diverse gentlemen and other commoners, being within your office at this tyme, hath rebelled against the king, as well in ther being at this last felde, as in releving of them that were against the Kings highnes, I therfore on the kings behalfe strictly charg you, and on myne hartely pray you, for your owne discharg and myne, that ye incontinently after the sight hereof, take all such persones as be within your office, which this tyme hath offended agaynst the king, and in especiall John Pullen and Richard Knaresborough: and that ye keepe them in the castell of Knaresbrough,[a] in suer keepeing, to the tyme be ye know the kings pleasure in that behalfe. And that this be not failed, as ye love me; and to give credence unto this bearer, and God keep you. Written at Richmound, the xxiii day of Juyn.[b] Se that ye faile not, as ye love me, within the time, and as ever ye thinke to have me your good lord, and as ever I may trust you.

Your Cousin,
(23 *June* 1487.)   HEN: NORTHUMBERLAND.

[a] This letter shews Sir Robert Plumpton to have succeeded his father in the offices of bailiff of the burgh, and *Custos*, of the castle, of Knaresborough under the Earl of Northumberland.

[b] The field of Stoke had been fought upon the 16th of June immediately preceding the date of this letter.

LETTER XVII.

To my right worshipfull cousin, Sir Robart Plompton, knyght.

Right Worshipfull Cousin, I recomend me unto you; and forasmuch as it is shewed to me, that ye doe make a pretence and clame to a man, called William Wroes, dwelling within thoner of Pomfret, wher I am officer, premyssing that he should be your bondman; wherin I have sent his evydence of his manumission, given by one of your ancestors, called Sir Robart Plompton, with dyverse other wryttings, that bynds the said Sir Robart and his heires under a certain payne, which is expressed in ther sayd wrytings, that ther shall never no pretence, nor clame, be made by them, nor none of ther heires, for the said bonde, but evermore perpetually to be at lyberty. Wherfore, Cousin, insomuch as the sayd William is dwelling within the honour, wher I am officer, I nether can, nor may, see that he be wronged, if it may lye in me to amend it; therfor I will and pray you. that if ye intend to make

any such pretence and clame, then that ye wold send to me some of your counsell, so that I may understand wherby ye pretend your tytle, and if your tytle be good, ye shall have such answere, as of reason ye shalbe content with. I pray that I may have an answere in wrytting from you of these premysses.

Your Cousin,   RICHARD TUNSTALL.

LETTER XVIII.

To my right worshipfull cousin Sir Robert Plumpton.

Right worshipfull Cousin, after due recomendations, I comend me unto you, letting you wytt I am enformed ye are good master unto my cousin John Baylton, praying you of your good contynuance therin for my sake. Sir, I understand my cousin Sir Christofer Ward hath put him ther to an occupation of the Kyngs. Sir, if ther be any man that wold wrong him therin, I desire you therin that you will be his good master for my sake, as I may doe you any pleasure hereafter, which I shalbe redy, with grace of God, at altymes, who have you in his keeping.

Be your owne   WILLIAM CALLVERLEY the older.[a]

[a] William Calverley, esq. of Calverley and Esholt, com. Ebor. Agnes, daughter of Sir John Tempest, knt. was living his widow in 1489; their eldest son was of the same name as his father. It appears from the pedigree in Thoresby, that Amice, sister of William Calverley, esq. was the wife of a Mr. Robert Baildon, 24 Hen. VI. The John Baylton here mentioned was doubtless their descendant.

LETTER XIX.

To my right hartely beloved Cousin, Sir Robart Plampton, knight.

Right trusty and welbeloved Cousin, I gret you hartyly well. And wheras I conceive that ye prepared yourselfe to have ridden with me to this day of trewe,[a] and now remembring, that

[a] The days of truce for the meetings of the great commissioners of the East and Middle Marches were fixed, by the treaty of 1483, to be held on the first of December

it were not only to your great labor, but also to your cost and great charg, therfore I take me oorly to your good wyll and thankfull disposition, for the which I hartely thanke you, and am right well content and pleased that ye remaine still at home. Written at Derham, the xix day of November.

Your Cousin,
(19 *Nov.* 1486-7.)   HEN. NORTHUMBERLAND.

at Reading-burn; and as warden of the West and Middle Marches, Henry, Earl of Northumberland, was the first of the Conservators of the truce agreed to at London, to commence from 3 July 1486, and to continue for three years.

LETTER XX.

To the right worshipfull Sir Robart Plompton, Kt. be thes delivered.

Right worshipfull Sir, I recommend me unto you, and wher ye have shewed by your curtace letter, of late to me derect by one Robart Becke your servant, beryng date at Plompton, the vi day of September, that your servants and lovers, John Person and his brother, should be greatly vexed and trobled by Wylliam Whit[a] and his servants; Sir, as touching the same William, in the beginyng of the troble and variance betwyxt the servants of his and John Persons, his bretheren, and other, he was innocent, as fare as I, my brethren aldermen, and other the common counsell of the Cyttie of York, by any wayes and meanes can understand; and the same Wylliam hath shewed unto us, that he at no tyme have given cause to the said Person so to deale with his servants, as they tofore have doun. And further, Sir, the sayd John Person and his brother bene fraunchesid and sworne to the Kyng and maior of the citie of Yorke for tyme being, to be and deale according to the effect of there othes. And if any variance or troble, tofore this, have bene betwixt my cocitisins, that they, according to ther duties, have shewed them in the same to the maior for tyme being, and to none other; and he to se an end betwyxt them

[a] William White was mayor of York in 1491.

and right wold, so that no more inconvenient should fall by reason of the same. Sir, I am the man, and take God to record, without favor or parcialite, to adoon the same in the premyses to the sayd John Person, and other in the premyses, and they had shewed them in the same varience unto me, as ther dutyes had bene. Wherfore, Sir, if it like you, and by your advice, the sayd John Person and his brother to come home, both my brethren and I shall endevor us, in the sayd varyance and troble, to make a good and a loving end, and the better for your pleasure. And further, Sir, of my brethren behalfe and myne, we pray you to give credence to this bearer, and Jesu preserve you. In hast from Yorke, the ix day of September.

By your aune ROBERT HAVOCK[b]
Maior of Yorke and his brethren Aldermen.
(9 *Sept.* 1488.)

[b] *Sic, sed lege* Robert Hancock. He was mayor of York in 1488.

LETTER XXI.

To my right worshipfull master, Sir Robart Plompton, kt. be these delivered.

Reverent and worshipfull Sir and master, I recomend me unto your mastership, beseching Allmyghty *Jesu* to preserve your worship and welfare to his pleasure and your harts comforth. Sir, plese yt you to understand, my servant Thomas Coke, now late being with your mastership, hath shewed unto me parte of your mynde and entent, by the which I conceyve ye wold I dyd your mastership a pleasure, and if I so myght or may, it wold be to me comforth. Howbeyt my sayd servant shewed unto me none of your mynd, how or what tyme I shold be content therof againe, if I might so do. Wherfore, Sir, if yt wold either be pleasure or ease to you that I should doe you such a pleasure, as I wylbe right glad to doe, if I shold therfore screane myself, and my frynds also, and not put me therfore to hurt; so that yt will like your mastership to send me wrytting, by the bringer herof, what tyme yt will please you to have yt, and how and what tyme I shalbe content therof againe, and I shall put me in dever to fullfill your intent, and doe your pleasure in that behalfe, or any other thing to your comandment, be the grace of *Jesu*, who ever preserve your worship. At Hassopp, the tuesday next afore St. Thomas day the apostle.

(December 1482—8.)   Be your tenant and servant,
STEPHEN EYRE of Hassopp.[a]

[a] The manor of Hassopp, com. Derb. had been let by Sir William Plompton kt. and Robert Plumpton, esq. his son, to Stephen Eyre, esq. for the term of twelve years from Michaelmas 1479, and indentures were sealed between the parties 1 Feb. 19 Edw. IV.—(*Chartul.* No. 695.) The date of the letter is prior to 9 Jan. 4 Hen. VII. 1488-9, when the lease was renewed by Dame Joan Plumpton, and Sir Robert Plumpton kt. to Katharine Eyre, late the wife of the said Stephen Eyre.—(*Ibid.* No. 751.)

LETTER XXII.

To my master, Sir Robart Plompton, kt.

In my most humble and fayhtfull wyse I recommend me unto your mastership, and to my singuler good lady. This day in the mornyng I spake with my master Gascoyne at Poymfrett, and he comended him to you and to my lady; and then I spake with Sir Rich. Tunstall, and had great commyning with him of *per et contra*. Sir, I wold advise your mastership cause William Scargell to take good regard to himselfe and not to use his old walkes; for and he doe, he wylbe taken, and brought to fynd such surety for peace and otherwise, as shalbe to him inconvenient: notwithstanding, the said Master Tunstall gave to me right curteouse words at my departing; but therto is no great trust. For the tyme it is good to dreed the worst, insomuch as the land lyeth in his rule, in the honor of Poymfret. Sir, as for such matters I had with Robert Lenthorpe,[a] he will give me no perfitt answere unto the begining of the terme; in the meantyme he will speak with a doctor, and send to me a letter to London by one Watkinson of Poymfrett, attorney of the common place, and then your mastership shaibe answered of the premises, with Gods grace, who ever the same preserve in prosperouse felicitie long tyme to endure. From Poymfrett, the xi day of January.

  Your humble servant,
(9 Jan. 1488-9.)   EDWARD PLOMPTON.

[a] Robert Leventhorpe, of Leventhorpe, in the parish of Swillington, com. Ebor. esq.

LETTER XXIII.

To my right worshipfull Cousin, Sir Robart Plompton, kt.

Right Worshipfull Cousin, I recomend me unto you, and whereas I late wrote to you for one Skaggell[a] to have come to me, for a matter of causes betwixt him and certayn other, with myne officer, Thomas of Pomfret; wherin I understand by such an answer as I had from you since, that he will not be advertysed by you therin. Cousin, I eftesones will desire and pray to advise him to come, for and he will not, I intend to shew his obstynance to the King and his counsell, which if I so doe, I thinke it will not be for his ease. And also I intend, when I can finde a convenient tyme and place, to attach him, if he thus contynew in his sayd obstynance.

  Your Cousin,
RICH. TUNSTALL.

[a] William Scargill, of Thorpe-Stapleton, com. Ebor. esq. (*See preceding letter and postea.*)

LETTER XXIV.

To the right worshipfull knyght, Sir Robart Plompton.

Right worshipfull sir, I commend me to you, and am full sory that ye should be displeased agaynst the writting, which came last to you in my name. I comaunded the officer to writ to you in my name, but I saw not the same after. Sir, ye have alway bene good master to our house and I pray you so to contynew. and in any thing which ye are myscontent with, it shall be amended by the sight of yourselfe. And I besech you be good master to this bearer, for he is giltles in this matter. And as for our land, we pay our dymes therfore, and trust in you that ye will not ses none thereof, wherby we should have cause to make further labor; for it is not the Kyngs mynd to ses no dymeable land, and we have no suit land, but it is dymable, as God knoweth, who preserve you ever.

  Your lovyng freind,
the PRIOR OF NEWBROUGH.[a]

[a] Newbrough, or Newburgh, a township in the parish of Coxwold, com. Ebor. was the site of a priory for Canons regular of the order of St. Augustin, which was endowed with lands in the parish of Spofforth, of the fee of Mowbray, their founder.

LETTER XXV.

To my right hartely beloved Cousin, Sir Robart Plompton, Kt.

Right hartely beloved Cosin, I comannd me unto you, and for right weighty consideration me moving concerning the pleasure of the Kings highnes, on the behalve of his grace, charg you, and on my desire pray you, that ye with such a company, and as many as ye may bring with your ease, such as ye trust, having bowes and arrowes, and pryvy harnest, com with my nepvew, Sir William Gascougne, so that ye be with me upon munday next comeing at nyght, in the towne of Thirske; not failing herof, as my speciall trust is in you, and as ye love me. Written in my mannor of Semar, the xxiiii day of Aprill.

  Your Cousin,
(24 *April* 1489.)   HEN. NORTHUMBERLAND.[a]

[a] This summons was sent on the Saturday immediately preceding the day of the riot at Cocklodge, in which the Earl of Northumberland was slain, being Wednesday, the feast of St. Vitalis, 28th of April, 1489. For his services in suppressing this commotion, Sir Robert Plumpton was in this same year (30 Oct.) thanked by King Henry. (*See the letter of Hen. VII. in the Memoirs.*)

LETTER XXVI.

To right worshipfull Sir in God, Sir Robert Plompton, kt. be this byll delivered in hast.

Right worshipfull Sir, after dew recomendations, pleaseth you to know, that after as I am enformed, one John Bailton of Knarsbrough, of layt bought and received of my kinsman, the brynger, a ton of wyne, for the which he hath nought content; and now for his offence all his goods standeth under arrest and in your will. I wold and hartely pray you, that my sayd kynsman myght for my sake, either have his wyne againe, or els contentation therefore, after there comaunds; and ye therfore shall have my good hart in any thing I may doe for you. So knoweth our Lord, who have you in his protection. From Fountayne, this same tewsday.

  Your owne, JOHN ABBUT OF FOUNTAYNE.[a]

[a] John Darneton, abbot of Fountains from 1478 to 1494. (*And see note to Letter XVIII.*)

LETTER XXVII.

To my right worshipfull and enterly beloved gossep, Sir Robart Plompton, knyght.

Right worshipfull and my full trusty enterly beloved gossep, after all harty recomendations as I can thinke, I pray you hartely to be good and tender master and lord to Thomas Hirst, my full speciall freind, in such matter as he hath to labor unto you; and the more tender at this my poore prayer and instaunce, and for the love of my godson, to whom I besech Almyghty God to give good grace to encrease in vertue, and you, with my lades, your mother and your wyfe, my comered, to preserve in worship and favour, unto his pleasure and harts ease. From Kyrkestall in hast, upon munday next before St. Luke Evangelist.

Your poore gossep and true lover,

THO: ABBOT OF KIRKESTALL.[a]

[a] Thomas Wymbersley, Abbot of Kirkstal from 6 April 1468 to 1498.—William was the name of the eldest son of Sir Robert Plumpton, and it was to him that the abbot had probably stood godfather.

LETTER XXVIII.

To my right worshipfull brother, Sir Robart of Plompton, deliver these.

Right worshipfull Brother and Sister, I hartely recommend me unto you. Where ye have made a search, they for me thanke you hartely therfore, and I shall do service to you, and I may, therfore. I beseech to make a thorow search for my matter, as my trust is to you, and I will be ruled according to right, as my frynds, and ye in specyall, thinke that I should be. No more at this tyme, but the holy Trenetie have you in keeping. I pray you give credence to the bringer of this byll.

Your loving brother, SIR STEPHEN HAMERTON.[a]

[a] Sir Stephen Hamerton, of Hamerton and Wigglesworth, com. Ebor. kt. succeeded his father Sir Richard in 1480, and married Isabel, half-sister of Sir Robert Plumpton. (*See Memoirs.*) He died 16 Hen. VII. 1500-1.

LETTER XXIX.

To the worshipfull in God Master Plompton, knight, these letters be delivered in hast.

Right worshipfull Sir, I comand me to you, beyng glad to here of your welfaire. Sir, I hartely thank you for my tennaunts of Arkenden,[a] praying you of good contynuance, and also for your wryting, the which ye send unto me towching to the lands of myne in Arkenden. Sir, I have sent to you by my servant, Thomas Morton, the copie of my evydents of the ix acres of land, the which they clame intrest for the King. And I trust that I have sent to you such wrytting as shall discharg that matter. Sir, I pray you that ye will shew my matters according to right; and after your good mynd, for I remytt all unto your good wysdome. Sir, yt is so that I am a yong beginner of the world in my office; and Sir, for your good will and counsell I will that my officer reward to you yerly vi^s. viii^d. as was rewarded to other men afor tyme, praying you of your good contynuance, and any thing as I can, I will, as knoweth God, who have you in his blessed keeping. Amen. Written at Lilleshull, the xxvi day of May.

Your loving frind, THE ABBOT OF LILLISHULL.

[a] Arkendale, in the parish of Knaresborough, had been given to the abbey of Lilleshull, com. Salop, by Hilaria Trusbut in the reign of Hen. II. with housebote and haybote in the woods of Kirkdighton and Ingmanthorp. (*Mon. Ang.* vol. I. p. 146^b.) She was the wife of Everard de Ros. Sir Robert Plumpton, as was usual with men of worship at the time of writing, acted as steward for the abbey.

LETTER XXX.

To the right worshipfull Sir Robart Plompton, kt. be this letter delivered.

Right worshipfull Sir, I recomend me unto you, thanking you, as hartely as I can, for your great kyndnes and gentlenes shewed to me, and to my poore tennaunts in Arkenden. And wheras ye have written to me that one Robart Walkinham[a] is injuried and wronged of his tennor in Arkenden, contrarie to right and concience; wherfore I purposse, sonne after Whitsontide next comyng, to send a brother of myne and other officers to Arkenden, and ther to have a court to be houlden, and right to be had according to reason and good concience, with the grace of God, who have you in his governance. Written in hast on Tewsday in the ii^d weeke of lent.

Your good lover, THE ABBOT OF LILLESHULL.

[a] Robert Walkingham, of Plumpton, was living 1 Dec. 1483. (*Chartul.* No. 724.)

LETTER XXXI.

To Sir Robart Plompton, kt. in Yorkshire, be this letter delivered in good speede.

Right worshipfull Sir, we recomennd us unto you. And so it is that dame Joyes Percy hath shewed unto the Earle of Schrewesburie,[a] which is our very good lord, and tender lord in all our rightfull causes, how ye enwrong her of certayne lands lying within our lordship of Erkenden, were ye be our steward; wherein the said lord hath made labor unto us for the sayd Dame Joyes, and desired us that we wold she be not wronged in hir right: and considering how good lord he hath bene, and yet alwayes unto us ys, and remembryng allso, that we, being men of the holy church, owe not to suffer any wrong to be done to any maner of persones within our Lordship, may no lesse doe but effectually tender the sayd lords desire in that behalfe. Wherfore we desire you, that ye will see the sayd Dame Joyes to have all that which she of right ought to have within our Lordship of Erkenden foresayd, so as she find hir not greved, nor have cause to make any more labor to the sayd lord for hir remedy therin. For and she doe, we must sett some other person in your rome, that will not wrong hir; for we may in no wyse abyd the displeasur of the sayd lord. Tendering therfore this our desire, as we trust you; and our Lord have you in his governance. From Lillishull, the xxviii day of May.

Your good loving ABBOT OF LILLESHULL.

[a] The Earl of Shrewsbury (George) wrote himself to Sir Robert Plumpton from Ashby on the 8th of July, in behalf of Dame Joyce Percy, who was then attending on his wife, in respect to certain lands purchased by S r Robert Percy, her late husband, to which Sir Robert Plumpton laid claim.—This letter was one of the twenty-six, of which the transcripts formed that portion of the Towneley MS. which has been torn off (*see Introduction*); but it is one of the few letters of this correspondence which were copied by Dodsworth from the MS. in 1633. (Vol. CXLVIII. Bibl. Bodl.) Sir Robert Percy was probably of Scotton, near Knaresborough, where a family of the name was at this time settled.

LETTER XXXII.

To my most trusty good master, Sir Robart Plompton, knight.

Right honorable and my most trusty good master, in as humble wyse as I can thinke or say, I comennd me to your sayd mastershipp. And, Sir, according to my dutie I thank you of all gentle mastership unto me shewed, and to my frinds, beseching you of contynuance. Morover, Sir, pleaseth you to understand the affect of my desire at this tyme. It is so here by us at Cukeswald,[a] the clarkship therof standeth avoyd, saffe it is observed be the meanes of 2 children, sones to the clarke lait deseased; wherin, good master, I beseech you tenderly, that it wold please you to writ to Sir Robart Owtreth,[b] that he wold at request of your mastership send wrytting to his tennants of the sayd towne, first to his keper Georg Dayvell, Robert Cropwell, and John Barton, then all other in generall, that my brother, your trew servant, myght have that service of the clarkship, trustyng to God he should please the parishioners according to his dutie, and I evermore your trew and faythfull prest and bedman. That knoweth Almyghty *Jesu*, who you, my most trusty good master, preserve to his pleasure. At Newburgh in hast, *in festo S^{cti} Georgii Martiris.*[c]

Your owne prest and bedman,

SIR WILLIAM CATTON, Chanon of Newburgh.

[a] Coxwold, a parish-town in the immediate vicinity of the priory of Newburgh or Newburough.
[b] Sir Robert Oughtred, of Kexby, com. Ebor. kt.
[c] 23 April.

LETTER XXXIII.

To the right worshipfull and my specyall good master, Sir Robart Plompton, knyght, deliver these in hast.

Right worshipfull master, I recomend me unto you, thanking you of your benyngne mastership shewed unto me, for the which, Sir, without feyning I am, and shalbe, your trew and faythfull beadman. Beseching your mastership after the contemplation of this byll, that it wyll please you to stand good master unto the brynger herof in such matters as he shall shew unto you. Sir, he hath bene with us, and spoken with Sir Thomas Morwyn, and with Sir William his brother, and with other dyvers of our brethren, the which recomend tham unto your mastership; and he hath shewed unto them his intent and desire, the which we intend, with Gods grace, to endevor us to fullfill, if our power may so extend, in the which we besech you to take no dysplesaure; wherin ye shall bynd me, with all afore rehersed, to impend unto your sayd mastership our prayer and service, according unto our duety, by the grace of *Jesu*, who preserve you ever more to his pleasure. At Newburght in great hast.

Your chaplayn and bedman,
Sir Thomas Thorp, Chanan.

LETTER XXXIV.

To Sir Robart Plompton, knight, be these delivered.

Right worshipfull Sir, and my especiall good master, I comend me to you, thanking you much for my veneson, for it did me great stead. I beseach God to encrease your veneson. Sir, ther is certaine money owing to me in Follifait,[a] the which I beseech you that it wold please you to comannd them to pay it to the bringer of this

[a] Follyfoot, in the parish of Spofforth, was in the lordship of Plumpton.

byll, my servant; he shall shew you which they be that owe the money. As touching the tenement in Pannall,[b] I let it to John Wilson to the behalfe of another man, and the sayd John was his suretie the farm should be content; and I caused my servant to aske farme of this Wylson, and he sayd that they had discharged him, that he should not occupie, for they wold put in a tennant at your pleasure. Sir, if it so be that they discharged him, suppose it will please you that I be content the farm, or els remyt it to the sayd Wylson; it is run two yeares, to the sume of 2iiij^s. As touching the matters he hard at the syse, I caused some to be thyn at this tyme, as God knowes, who preserve you evermore to his pleasure.

Your owne beadman,   Cellerer of Newburgh.

[b] Pannall, now a parish-town, was in the forest of Knaresbrough.

LETTER XXXV.

To Sir Robart Plompton, knyght, be thes delivered.

Right worshipfull Sir, I recommend me to you. I thank you, Sir, of your labor and good will. Sir, it is so that I have no more of the ferm content of that at is owing, but xiiij^s. Also Robart Goles brought with him a byll of alowaince for Aykton Kilne, and I have answered him, that he shall have as much as is our charge to do; therfore it was sene by our tenants, and set to a valow what should be our charge to do, and that shall he have: I understand it was either 25^s or 27^s. Also, Sir, as for as touching William Paver ferme, I am not content; I put it in respate till I come over, for he sayth that he hath payd for suyt of court at Spofforth ij yeare, and also fee ferme for one yeare, and he thinks to have the farmhould for 2vij^s. viii^d. in one yeare; but he shall not, and so I send him. The brynger herof shall shew you more credence herein. Sir, if it please you, upon tewsday come a sennyt, I would have your court at Follyfait, that I might make levy of our fermes that

are behind. Sir, I say no more, but *Jesu* have you in his keping. Written at Newbrough, this day, by your owne beadman,
Cellerer of Newburgh.

LETTER XXXVI.

To my right worshipfull master, Sir Robart Plompton, kt. this bill be delivered.

Right worshipfull Sir, I recomend me unto your mastership; please it you witt, that I understand that my cousin, Ralfe Hawgh,[a] sendeth to your mastership for such dues as was granted to his mother and to him, by my master your father, and you, under your seales; the which writting and your seales, to come before men of worship and discretion, I am certayne, when ye se him, will not be denyed: for your seals be well knowne, and to show in money other matters in this contry, the which are of great charge. Wherwith, it please your mastership, that after my poore advice, take a direction with him at this tyme; for it will els be proces turne to more cost, and that wold I be right sory fore. From Padley, on Sunday next before St. Mary day in Lent.

From yours,   Robart Eire.[b]
(*anno circiter* 1488.)

[a] Ralph Haugh, of Derley, com. Derb. gent.
[b] Robert Eyre, of Padley, com. Derb. esq.

LETTER XXXVII.

To the right honorable and my especiall good master, Sir Robart Plompton, knight, be this letter delivered.

After all due recomendations had, please it youre mastership to witt that Ralfe Haugh, according to the agrement and award[a] betwixt you and him made, hath delivered into my hands all such

[a] The award bears date 1 June, 4 Hen. VII. 1489. (*Chartul*. No. 756.)

evydence as he hath concernyng your mastership, endefferently to be kept unto such tyme as a sufficyent and lawfull estate be made unto the sayd Ralfe of a yerly rent of v mark, for terme of life of the sayd Ralfe;[b] that is to say, a feoffament of trust indented made by your mastership unto me and other of the maner of Darley with the appurtenances, and a letter of atturney according to the same; also ii obligations, one of ccc marke and another of x^{li}. Wherfore I besech you to be good master, and to make him a lawfull estate acording to the award, at which tyme all the sayd evydence shalbe delivered unto your hands, or to your assigne, and if ther be any service or pleasure that I may doe, it shalbe done at my power, by Gods grace, who ever preserve you body and soule. Written at Padley, the iiijth day of August last past.

Your owne,
(4 *Aug*. 1489.)   Robart Eyre, squire.

[b] In the Plumpton coucher book (No. 757) is a copy of a grant from Sir Robert Plumpton, Kt. to Ralph Hauh, gent. of an annuity of five marks out of the manor of Hassop, dated 12 July, 5 Hen. VII. 1490, witnesses, Robert Eyre, John Roklay, and Thomas Meverell, esqs.

LETTER XXXVIII.

To my lady, Dame Jane Plompton, at Plompton.

Madame, in my most humble wyse I recomend me unto your good Ladyship, and let you wyte that I have spoken with Master Receyvor;[a] iiij houres space he tarryed me, and he is right lovingly disposed in every thing toward my master and all his, if he have, or may have cause therto: and thus I have left with him to be at

[a] In the Plumpton coucher book (No. 755) is a copy of a receipt from Richard Harpur, receiver-general of the King's rents of his Duchy of Lancaster, for £9. 3s. 2d. had of Sir Robert Plumpton, kt. for the farm of the mills of Knarsbrough, parcel of the said Duchy, by the hands of Edward Plumpton, dated 8 March, 5 Hen. VII. 1489-90.

Knarsbrough, the wednesday next after saynt Eline day.[b] And ther, or afore that tyme, if they mete, to do his dutie to my master curtesly, and after that, to be as favorable, and to shew his good wyll to my sayd master in every thing he may doe, as we wyll desire; and then I purpose with Gods grace to be there. And afore the langage that Alan shold say, it is not so; he sayd none such langage. The mylner told Alan that his farme was redy, and if yt so be, I pray you cause the mylner to deliver it to Benson, and if not, to make yt redy agaynst the Receyver come thither; for this I have promysed, and unto that tyme we mete, I besech you speake to my master, that no uncurtes dealing be had with none of his servants. Also ther is a ax[c] that my master clameth the keeping of; I pray you let them have and occupie the same unto the same tyme, and then we shall take a dereccion in every thing, as well in the premyses, as otherwyse, to my masters pleasure and entent, with Gods grace, who preserve you and him both, and all yours.

Fro Habberforth, this present Thursday.

Your most humble servant,

(anno circiter 1489-90.)   Ed. Plompton.

[b] 3 May, the feast of the Invention of the Holy Cross, called St. Elline day. (*Vide postea, Letter CXXI. note* [d]). This name for the feast has escaped the observation of Sir Harris Nicolas, in his admirable Chronology of History. (*Lardner's Cabinet Cyclopedia. New Edit.* 1838.)

[c] Ax, *quære* if the mill-dam. See *Blount's Law Dictionary, sub voce Hatches or Hacches*.

LETTER XXXIX.

To Sir Robart Plompton of Plompton Kt. be these delivered.

Sir, after my dowte of comendations remembering, in my most harty maner I recomend me unto you. Sir, I desire you to beare in remembrance mony the which you caused to be borowed upon my husband and me; the which money I dyverse tymes sent for, and ye have dyverse tymes appoynted me to send for it;

and when I send for it at your poyntment, you brak day ever with me, whereby I canot get my money. Therfore I desire you to send me word how I shalbe answered of yt, by this bearer, for if I may have it, I were loth to troble you. If you will not send me word how I shall have yt, I wyll take my next remedy; that you shall well know, yt shalbe to your paine and they that borowed yt. No more at this tyme, but *Jesu* preserve you to his pleasure. Written at Killinghall, by your loving and frind,

Mawd Rose.

LETTER XL.

To my worshipfull Lady Plompton thelder.

Right reverend lady, with due recomendacions. I have wounder that ye doe so unkindly to me, but of great nede I wold not have sent. I lent to my kynsman c. marke, I have yt not; they have forfit cc. marke. And for the lake of yt, I send more besily to you, praying you to send me iij[li] by this messinger without delay, and than it is but xl[s] owing, of the which I shall suffer to Pasch; and *Jesu* preserve you. Wrytten at Cristall[a] in hast,

by your B. Roos.

[a] Kirkstall.

LETTER XLI.

To my right hartely beloved Cousin Sir Robart Plompton, kt.

Right hartely beloved Cousin, I commennd me unto you; and wheras I conceive that ther is a grudge depending betwixt you and Sir William Beckwith, knight,[a] I, entending the peacifyng thereof, desire and pray you to forbere and contynue to do any

[a] Sir William Beckwith, kt. one of the feed-men of the Earl of Northumberland, (see *Letter XIV.*) was dead before 19 Aug. 11 Hen. VII. 1496, when Elizabeth, his relict, released to Sir Robert Plumpton, kt. and his heirs, all right and title in the lands of which their father, Sir William Plumpton, kt. died seised. (*Chartul No.* 782.) See also *Letter V, note* [c] *at page* 6.

thing in that behalfe against the sayd Sir William unto my next commyng into Yorkshire. And then, I shall shew me in such wyse for the reformacion therof, as I trust shall agre with right law and conscience. Wherefore I pray you to conforme you to the accomplishment herof, as my very trust is in you. I have wrytten in like wise unto the sayd Sir William. That now God conserve you. Wrytten in my castell of Warkworth, the xvi day of July. Over this, Cousin, ye shall understand, that the sayd Sir William Beckwith will committ him unto my rule in all behalves, and therfore I pray you to se the premysses performed.

Your Cousin,
Hen. Northumberland.[b]

[b] As it is impossible to distinguish with certainty between the undated letters of Henry the fourth Earl, and those of his son the fifth Earl of Northumberland, in every instance, I have inserted several consecutively in this place, though there can be no doubt that this letter is to be attributed to the father. The son was born 13 Jan. 1477-8, and had a special livery of his lands in the thirteenth year of Hen. VII. before he had fully attained his majority; his letters will therefore date from after the year 1497-8.

LETTER XLII.

To my Right hartely beloved Cousin, Sir Robart Plompton, Kt.

Right hartely beloved freind, I commend me unto you, and pray you to apply your comyng unto me, according unto such order as was taken of late tofore your departure from me; and that ye faile not hereof, as my very trust is in you. Written in my Castell of Wresull, the xx day of Januarie.

Yore Cousin,
Hen. Northumberland.

LETTER XLIII.

To my Right hartely beloved Cousin, Sir Robart Plompton, Kt.

Right hartely beloved Cosin, I commend me unto you, and

for certaine considerations me movyng, I will and desire you that ye incontynent after the sight hereof, cum hether unto me, all excuses and delayes laid a part, that it be in nowise failed, as ye intend the pleasure of the Kings highnes, and as ye love me. Written in my mannor of Lekingfield, the vi day of Aprill.

Your Cousin,
Hen. Northumberland.

LETTER XLIV.

To my Right hartely beloved Cousin, Sir Robart Plompton, Kt.

Right trusty and welbeloved cousin, I commennd me unto you, and desire and pray you that in such things as my right intierly beloved Cosin, Mary Gascougne, [a] hath to doe with you, as touching hir right of herytaunce, that ye will give unto hir ayde and supportance, as right law and conscience will, as my speciall trust is in you, whom God keep. Written in my mannor of Semar, the first day of Aprill.

Your loving Cousin,
Hen. Northumberland.

[a] This Mary Gascoigne may have been the daughter of Ralph Gascoigne, esq. who had, it seems, been possessed of a house in Plumpton, the fine of which was parcel of the evidence of William Middelton in 1502. (*Vide Letter of Sir William Gascoigne, kt. postea.*)

LETTER XLV.

To my Right hartely beloved Cousin, Sir Robart Plompton, knight.

Right hartely beloved Cousin, I commennd me unto you, and desire and pray you to cause suer search to be made, what horse and cattaille ther be, that goes in my spring within my parke at

Spofford;[a] and such as can be found their, I pray you to se them dryven and voyded out therof: and also henceforth, that ye will se neither horse nor cattell goe within my said spring, as my speciall trust is in you, whom God preserve. Written in my mannor of Semar, the ij day of Aprill. Over this, Cousin, I hartely pray you to se my said parke vewed, and that the dere within the same may be easily delt withall, and what remaines within the same I pray you to certefie me, after the said vew be taken.

Yor loving Cousin,
HEN. NORTHUMBERLAND.

[a] It appears from this and the following letters, that Sir Robert Plumpton was steward of the manor of Spofford under the Earls of Northumberland, as his father had been before him.

LETTER XLVI.

To my Right hartely beloved Cousin, Sir Robart Plompton, Kt.

Right hartely beloved Cousin, I commennd me unto you. And wheras I of late hath had in ward two servaunts of Thomas Myddleton,[a] for hunting within my parke of Spofford, which I send unto you by my servant, Richard Saxston, praying you therfore,

[a] Thomas Middleton, married to a sister of Sir Robert Plumpton, has a brass to his memory in the church of Spofforth, with this quaint epitaph:

> With humble prayer I beseech thee
> That this scripture shall here or see
> To say *De profundis* if you letterd be
> For the soules of Jone my wife and me
> Thomas Middleton sometyme man of law
> Under this stone am laid full lawe;
> If thou be unlearned and cannot reed
> For our soules and all christen soules med
> Say a *Pater Noster* and *Ave* and a Creed.

Above was the shield of Middleton of Stokeld impaling Plumpton. (*Dugdale's Yorkshire Arms, MS. in Coll. Arm. And see Letter XII.*)

to take an obligation of them, and two sufficient men bounden with them in the sume of xx^{li}, to be of good bearing and in law themselfes upon viii dayes warning, whensoever I send for them; not failing herof as my singuler trust is in you, whom God keepe. Written in my mannor of Semar, the xxvii day of March. Over this, Cosin, I hartely thanke you in executing my commaundement.

Your Cousin,
HEN. NORTHUMBERLAND.

LETTER XLVII.

To my Right hartely beloved Cousin, Sir Robart Plompton, knight.

Right hartely beloved Cousin, I commennd me unto you. And wheras variance and discord is dependyng betwixt my servant, Thomas Saxston, and Richard Ampleford, of my Lordshipe of Spofford, the cause wherof, as I am enformed, hath bene, or this, shewed unto you; and if it hath not, I desire and pray you reply to exammæn it, and therupon to shew your lovyng diligence, not onely to se the peace kept in this behalfe, but also to sett the sayd parties at agrement, so that this matter may be pacefied. And for asmuch as ye have the rule ther under me, I pray you to shew you of semblable disposicion, if any matter of varience hereafter happen within your sayd rule; so that the parties sue not to me, if ye by your discret wysdome can reforme it, as my very trust is in you: and in your thus doyng, ye shall shew unto me thankfull pleasure. That knoweth God, who preserve you. Written in my castell of Warkworth, the xv day of June. Cousin, I pray you to se this matter pacefied, that there be no more calling upon me therfore, as my very trust is in you.

Yore Cousin,
HEN. NORTHUMBERLAND.

LETTER XLVIII.

To my most speciall good master, Sir Robart Plompton, knyght, be this delivered in hast.

Right worshipfull and my especiall good master, I recomend me unto your mastership, thanking your mastership hartyly of your kindly and hartely mastership shewed unto me, undeserved of my partie as yet. I besech Almyghty *Jesu* that I myght doe that thing, that myght be pleasure to your mastership; ye shall have my service. I have many things to thank your mastership for, and especially for Richard Ampleforth, the which I besech your mastership to be his good master, to helpe, ayd, and assist him in his necessitie; and wher he thinks that he offendeth to your mastership in any behalfe, he shall amend it at your pleasure. Your mastership shall understand his wyffs confescion, as she hath shewed it unto me. She besecheth your mastership to be hir good master, and to helpe hir and sucker hir in hir great necessity, and to set hir in rest and peace anente Thomas Saxton; for without your mastership wilbe good master to hir husband and to hir, she shall never be in rest and peace. And if she wilbe a good woman, it is a good and gracious dede to your mastership to help hir; and if I knew that she wold be a myskidyd woman, I shold never speake word to your mastership for hir, nor to no other. Also I besech your mastership to be good master to John Myming, your owne servant; I trust veryly that you have a trew servant of him to his power, to whome I pray your mastership to give credence. I besech God thank your mastership of the great reward that you gave the sayd John Myming, whom you sent into Bishopprike[a] to me. No more at this tyme, but I am your servant, as God knowes, who your mastership preserve to his pleasure. At Knaresbrough in hast.

Your servant,
JOHN MORRE.

[a] The County of Durham was in common parlance called the Bishoprick.

LETTER XLIX.

Unto my master, Sir Robart Plompton, knight.

Right worshipfull master, I recomend me unto you evermore, desiring to here of your prosperity and welfare, the which I besech almyghty *Jesu* to mercy to his pleasure, and to your most hartiest ease; and also praying you to comend me unto my lady your moder, and to my lady your wyfe. And also praying you to be my good master, (for I understand a man of Spofforth, which I had his wyfe in cure, will arest me,) for I can not goe fourth of place of master John Fous,[a] nor without his lordship, but your baylaies will arest me, as I understand by them that loves me. Wherfore I pray you take this matter into your hands, Sir; and also praying your mastership that I may have a letter, by this man, of you, that I may goe where I shall. Ye understand that I have receved x*s*. and xx*d*., and of that silver I have spent x*s*. of medcins; and also, Sir, as you and this man agres of this silver, what he shold have againe, he shall content him. Whatsoever of his concience he will have againe, he shalbe contented. As fast as I have silver, I will come to you and pay you, with grace of God, who have you in his keping. Wrytten at the place of master St[eward.] Aleffant day of moneth of March.

By your well loved servant,
Maister ANTHONY.

[a] John Fawkes of Farnley, com. Ebor. esq. Steward of the Forest of Knaresborough, living 10 Hen. VII. 1494-5. (*See Pedigree of Fawkes in Thoresby.*) In a north window of Knaresbrough Church was the coat, Ar. a [mascle] sa. and a woman kneeling by it. Underneath, Dame Mary Faukes. (*Dods. MSS. vol. CLX. fol.* 186.)

LETTER L.

Unto his right worshipful master, Sir Robert Plompton, Kt. in hast.

My ful especial maister, I recomende me to you. Pleas it you to wyte, that this same day I have delivered mee a letter from my lord of Northumberlond, wherby his lordship hath streitly charged Mr. Nevil[a] and al his servants, and me, as tomorow, to be at Toplif, both there to see his woods, parke, and game, and furthwith by his servant to be ascertayned in every behalfe, according to his said writing. For so it is, Sir, that ther are complaynts mad of the keepers of the game, wherein my lord is sore displeased withall, as I shall shew to you hereafter. Wherfore, Sir, I pray you to take noe displeasure for that I am not with them at Knarsbrough, as tomorow. Sir, I pray you to send me word by this bearer, how my sayd lord and Mr. Gascoygne departed in all matters;[b] and also what day Mr. Gascoygne ridds up towards London from his place at Gaukthorp. And, Sir, I trust that my servant, this bearer, shal find you his good master, as wel in the reports made to you of him, as in other matters for which he is bounde to you. And thus, Sir, it is not for you to forgeet the matter that I wrote to you in, concernyng Sir John Wixeley;[c] so you her many

[a] Ralph Nevill, of Thornton-bridge, in the parish of Brafferton, near Topcliffe, esq.
[b] Sir William Gascoigne, kt. father of Master Gascoigne here named, and to whom Letter XXVI. p. 34, is addressed, had had in his life time the custody of the castle of Knaresborough under the Earl of Northumberland. At his death, the son was under age, when his wardship may have devolved upon the Earl, his uncle ; but from this time, 4 Mar. 2 Hen. VII. 1486, Sir Robert Plumpton acted as deputy for the Earl, and had the custody of the castle of Knaresborough: at least, the contents of the letters next following imply that such was the fact.
[c] Sir John Whixley, chaplain. (*See note to Letter II.*)

askers of guds, and thus *Jesu* keepe you. Written in hast at Rippon, the thursday next after Candlemas.

Your servant, RICH. GREENE.[d]

[d] Richard Greene, esq. was with Nicholas Middilton and Robert Haldynby, esqrs. and Richard Plumpton, clerk, a co-feoffee of the manor of Sir Robert Plumpton, kt. lying in Hassop and Rouland, com. Derb. 15 Sept. 12 Hen. VII. 1496.

LETTER LI.

Unto the right worshipful Sir Robart Plumpton, Kt. deliver these.

Right worshipfull Sir, I commend me to your mastership, certifying you that I have shewed William Tankard[a] your comandment, that he shold have warned the tenaunts to pay no farme to William Aldburgh ; and he letting them pay farme to his mother, and wold not warne the tenaunts to pay none. And as for taking of William Aldburgh, he sayd he wold not take him, for ye let him alone and ye myght have taken him, and ye wold; and may take him when ye wyll. I besech you be so good master unto me, and sett me and my husband tenaunts in rest of him. To God send my husband home, so that I compleane no further for noe remedy, as my trust is in your mastership, as God knowes, who preserve you to his pleasure. From Newby,[b] on Munday after Salmesday.[c]

Your Beadwoman ELIZABETH GREENE.[d]

[a] William Tankard, otherwise Tancred, was, it seems, at the date of this letter, bailiff of Boroughbridge, parcel of the liberty of Knaresborough, in which Sir Robert Plumpton had jurisdiction, and where the disputed lands lay.
[b] Newby, in the parish of Topcliffe.
[c] Soul-mass-day, Nov. 2.
[d] She was, it seems, the wife of Richard Greene above named and from the contents of the letter, appears to have claimed as of her inheritance the land of William Aldborough, by reason of the son's illegitimacy.

LETTER LII.

To my right hartely beloved Cousin, Sir Robart Plompton, Kt.

Right hartely beloved Cousin, I commennd me unto you, thanking you for my servant Rich. Greene ; and desire and pray you, that if Bastard Aldborgh, Richard Leds, or such other as of late, as I am enformed, have made revery and withdrawen goods, contrayrie to the Kings lawes, within the lordship of Knarsbrough, where at ye have rule, can be come by, ye committ them to ward within the castell of Knarsbrough, therin still to remayne unto that ye have further knowledg of my pleasure in this behalfe. Over this, Cousin, where as I have assigreed my servant William Bullocke to levy and receive such rents and fermes, and also arrerages, as are due and growen of the lands that late were William Aldburgh', wherin ye and I, with other, stand infeoffed, and to be reserved to that my pleasure therin be understanden. I therfore desire and pray you, if any person would interupt him in the execution herof, ye will shew your good will in the lawfull defending therof, and also in the geting of all such hay as is upon the sayd ground ; not fayling herof as my speciall trust is in you, whom God kepe. Written in my Castell of Werkworth, the xxxi day of July.

Your Cousin,
HEN. NORTHUMBERLAND.

LETTER LIII.

To my right worshipfull master, Sir Robart Plompton, knight, be thes delivered.

Right reverent and worshipfull master, I recomend me to your mastership, certyfiing you that John Pullan and I meett this day at Castley, which John brought with him Herry Dickinson and John Tomlinson to support him, and to testyfie his talke. Sir,

the dayes men cannot agre us, so Mr. Mydleton[a] to make the end. Wherfore I wold besech your sayd mastership, that yt wold please you to cause some of your servants to goe to the sayd Mr. Midleton, and the bringer herof to goe with him [to whome I besech you give credence] that ye and the sayd Master Midleton wold assigne a day and a place, that I may know the same and attend upon him. Beseching your sayd mastership, that yt wold please you, if ye so may, to be at the end-making, or els I fere me we shall have no end for myn avantage, and all by the meanes of the sayd John Tomlinson ; for he seketh all the meanes that he can to put me from yt, as I am enformed, both to the said Nicholas Midleton, and also to my lord of Fountance. Sir, I shold have comen to your mastership, but I must ned ride to Conresburgh for matters of my moders in law ; wherfore I besech your mastership to pardon me. No more at this tyme, but the blessed Trinetie preserve you in worship to his pleasure. Writtin at Arthington hall, the iiijth day of Apryll.

By your owne servant,
WILLIAM ARTHINGTON.[b]

[a] Nicholas Middelton, of Stokeld, com. Ebor. esq. living 12 Hen. VII. 1496. (*See Letter L. note d.*)
[b] William Arthington, of Arthington, in the parish of Addle, com. Ebor. esq.

LETTER LIV.

To the right reverent and worshipfull and my especiall good singuler master, Sir Robart Plompton, knight.

Right reverent and worshipfull and my specyall good master, I hartely comend me unto you, thanking your mastership of your tender and loving favour shewed to my poore kynsman, John Wynpenne, now late brynging a letter from my lord to your mastership, and me, and other moe. Beseching you to be his good master touching his right according to conscyence, this holy tyme, upon Wedensday at your court. And wher your mastership wold that I shold wayt upon you ther that tyme, I wold have bene right glad so to doe, but because that I understand that Richard Danby, to whom my lord hath wrytten, lyke as to other, cannot be ther as than. Wherfore I besech your mastership, at the reverence of God, and be way of almes and charytie, to assigne a tyme and place, wher the sayd Mr. Danby, Richard Grene, and I myght awayte upon you for the sayd matter, and I shalbe redy both for that, and to your service, by the grace of God, who evermore preserve and kepe your worship and good health. Wrytten the iiij day of Aprill, at Qatton.[a]

By your loving servaunt,
WILLIAM ROWKSHAW, preist.

[a] Watton, in the east riding of Yorkshire, where was a priory of Gilbertines.

LETTER LV.

To his right worshipfull master, Sir Robart Plompton, kt. deliver these.

Right worshipfull Sir, in the most hartyest wyse I recommend me to you, thanking you of your tender mastership shewed me in all causes. Please yt your mastership to wyt that I am somewhat in hevynes, for such sicknes my wyfe hath, once or twice at the least every day, puts her in joperty of hir life with a swonnyng; that the morow next after the assise I passe not from hir. Wherfore, Sir, I besech you to take no displeasure, that I se not you and my lady at Plompton no rather. And wherfor . . . . that your mastership hath Robart Ward, clarke, in your ward at Knarsbrough; Sir, I purpasse to persew the law against him in ther names, whomes cattell he heretofore helped to stele, now eftsones: entending the same to have done forth of the lordship, if

so be that the awenners of the same cattell will mayntayne ther sute in ther name at my cost. And in the meane tyme I pray your mastership that this pure woman, the bearer hereof, beadwoman to your mastership, may have suerty of peace of the same Robart, which I trust she will desire of your mastership of him. Written at Newby, the Wedensday next after our lady day in Lenten. And as for William Bulloke, I shall shortly send him to your mastership to know your gud advice and counsell, and all causes concernyng me.

Your servant, ROBART GREENE.[a]

[a] Robert Grene, groom of the pantry to King Edw. IV. had a grant of the office of Bailiff of Burghbrigge, in the county of York, for terme of his life, 8 Sep. 2 Edw. IV. 1462 (*Rot. Parl. V.* 593 b.); and was probably the same person as was concerned in the affray upon Papplewick Moor 35 Hen. VI. and described of Plumpton, near Knaresborough. (*See note to Letter III. p.* 3.)—Robert Greene, who married Isabel, sister of William Tankard, of Boroughbridge, and was of Newby, I presume to have been his grandson, son of Richard and Elizabeth Green, and the writer of this letter.

LETTER LVI.

To my uncle, Sir Robart Plompton, kt. deliver these in hast.

Worshipfull uncle, I recomend me to you as hartely as I can thinke; and wher yt is that my servant, John Tomlynson, hath taken a farmehold of the abut of Fountayns, after the desseyse of the tenant that dwelleth theron, which the abott wyll record the taking: and it is so that the sone of him, the forsayd tenaunt, clameth the farmehold after his father dysseys, and he never toylke the sayd farmehold of the abott, nor of none other man, but my sayd servant, John Tomlinson. Wher it is so, uncle, at the matter betwyxt my servant and John Forest is put to iiij men, and the owmpreght of you; yt is so, uncle, that I shold have bene with you the same day, butt that I had letting and busynes. But I besech you be gud master to my servant, as my speciall trust is in

you; and at such a way may be taken to right, and well to my servant. And I beseech you give credence to the berer.

Your cousin and servant, RICHARD ALDBURGH.[a]

[a] Son of Sir Richard Aldburgh, of Aldburgh, com. Ebor. kt. and Agnes Plumpton, his wife.

LETTER LVII.

To his hartly beloved good master, Sir Robart Plompton, kt. be these delivered.

Right worshipfull and my especyall good master, I recommend me unto you, e. c. shewyng you, that at the last end of this terme, Sir Richard Aldburgh sold take of me awort, as it is made me to know; praying your mastership to speake to your attorney, and poynt yt, if yt so be, and what charge or cost ye be at, I shall content. No more at this tyme, but *Jesu* preserve you in all causes.

Your bedman and servant, JOHN TOMLYNSON.

LETTER LVIII.

To the right worshipfull Sir Robart Plompton, knyght.

Master Plompton, I recomennd me unto you, and thanke you for your letter; and it happyn(ed Miles went with me[a]) that day, with whom I have broken the matter. I felt him well disposed, and even forthwith I have sent my mynd to Sir Thomas Maleverer,[b] that he wilbe appliable to reason and doe wel. I shall in hast have word againe from him. I pray you labor herin, and soe

[a] The words between brackets are in paler ink, their place having been at first left blank. We should probably read, *Miles Willesthorp was with me*, for the words attempted to be decyphered which had puzzled the copyist.

[b] Sir Thomas Mauleverer, of Allerton, knight bannaret, died before 2 Sept. 11 Hen. VII. 1495, leaving Elizabeth his wife executrix, and a son and heir Richard, married to Joan, daughter of Sir Robert Plumpton. (*Chartul. No.* 799.)

will I doe; and in conclusion, if other of them be obstynat, and will not be counselled by frinds, the Kings grace will be myscontent with him, whatsover he be, and I, and you. Written in hast at my poore mannor of Overton.[c]

Your owne, WILLIAM, ABBAT OF YORKE.[d]

[c] At Overton the abbots of York had their chief country residence. Over this word is written in the pale ink *Wreton*.

[d] William Sever, alias Seveyr, elected Bishop of Carlisle, 11 Dec. 1495.

LETTER LIX.

To my right trusty and welbeloved Cousin Sir Robart Plompton, kt.

Right trusty and welbeloved Cousin, I grete you hartely well. And if you have suffered any person, that was under your ward, within the Castell of Knarsbrough, to be delivered at the desire of Sir Thomas Wortley, Kt.[a], I lett you witte that I am not therewith contented. Wherfore, Cousin, see that this be reformed, and not to suffer any person within the said Castell to depart thence, unto that ye have knowledg of the pleasure of the Kings highnes, or from me; as my speciall trust is in you, whom God kepe. Written in thabbey of Funtayns, the xxvi day of Juyn.

Your Cousin, HEN. NORTHUMBERLAND.

[a] Sir Thomas Wortley, of Wortley, com. Ebor. was a knight of the King's body to Edw. IV. Rich. III. Hen. VII. and VIII. and traditionally reported to have been a man of principal power and consequence in his neighbourhood. (*See Hunter's Hallamshire and South Yorkshire.*) This letter is a corroborative proof of the influence attached to his requests.

LETTER LX.

To my right hartely beloved Cosin, Sir Robart Plompton, kt.

Right hartely beloved Cousin, I commennd me unto you, and desire and pray you to caus a bucke of season to be taken, within the forest of Knarsbrough under your rule, to be delivered unto this bearer, to the behaufe of the mawer of the Cyte of Yorke and his bredren, and this my writting shalbe your warrant. Wherfore I pray you that this be thankfully served, as my speciall trust is in you, whom God keepe. Written in my manor of Lekinfeild, the xxviii day of Juyn.

Yor Cousin, HEN: NORTHUMBERLAND.

LETTER LXI.

To my master, Sir Robart Plompton, knight.

Pleaseth your mastership, after all due recomandacion, to wyte that this day was hanged at the tower hill iiij servants of the Kings; wherfore, the brynger herof can shew to you by mouth.[a] Other newes, as yet, here is none. Sir, afore your indentures of Mr. Chaunceler, he maketh none unto Candlemesse next, and then he will have a generall awdite, where ye, and all other, shall have your lesses out; and in the meane tyme, every man to ocupie ther owne farmes, notwithstanding the premysses: put ye no doubt therin,

[a] These four were Edward Frank, Henry Davy, John Mayne, and Christopher Swan, who about the first day of December, vth yere of the reigne of King Henry VII. at London, had communication with one Thomas Rothwell, otherwise called Thomas Even, late of London, priest, how they might take out of the King's ward Edward the Earl of Warwick, John abbot of Abyndon supplying money for the purpose; and afterwards, viz. on the xxth day of Decembre, in the said vth yere, conspired to compass their design at Abyngdon, for which acts they were attainted of high treason.—(See Rolls of Parliament, vol. VI. p. 436 b, where the printed text, besides having in one place vith yere for vth yere of the King's reign, is also wrong in the day of the month of December, which should be the xth, calculating by the date of their execution, as ascertained by this letter.) The herald, whose valuable memorial of the ceremonies at Court in the early years of the reign of Hen. VII. has been printed by Hearne in the Collectanea Lelandi (vol. IV.) notes that, "the Abbott of Abyndon and Harry Swan, and oder, wer attaynt of Treson in that Parlement, and Edward Franke, Harry Davy, Tailleur of London, and .... were beheaded at Tourhill."

for ye shalbe sure therof, assone as any man of his.[b] I have spoken with Nicholas Lenthorpe,[c] and fele him well dispossed toward you. Sir, if ye send therfore at Candlemasse, send to Mr. Hemson[d], by the token, I gat him a warrant for a doo of my lord[e] in his parke of Hals yerely. If it please you to assigne me, send me word what increse and approment ye wyll give, and I wyll applie my mynd and service to your pleasure and wele. Sir, I purpose to se your mastership, or to send this Cristinmase, if I may goe home. This day my lord knoweth not whether he goeth home afore this tyme, or noo. If we goe home, I wyll send; if not, I pray you send to me afore Candlemasse. Remember Clement Simpson. Pleaseth your mastership to recomend me to my singuler good lady. And your owne faythfull servant, as knoweth our Lord, who preserve you. Wrytten at London, the xvij day of December.

Your humble servant,
(17 Dec. 1489.) EDWARD PLOMPTON.

[b] This information has doubtless reference to the renewal solicited of the leases granted to Sir Robert Plumpton by the deceased Earl of Northumberland, whose office of Constable, Steward, and Master Forester of the castle, lordship, and forest of Knaresborough, had only been a grant for life, though afterwards reconferred upon his successor, when he was out of ward.

[c] Nicholas Leventhorp, esq. was Receyvour of the Honours of Pountfrett and Knaresburgh, an office held by patent. (Rot. Parl. 1 Hen. VII. vol. VI. p. 341 b.)

[d] Master Hemson, otherwise Empson, afterwards Sir Richard Empson, kt. the well-known tool of Henry VII.'s legal extortions, had it seems, even at this period, attained to considerable emtinence in the practice of the law, a knowledge which he afterwards perverted to such unworthy purpose. Of this celebrated individual much interesting matter will be found in the subsequent letters, and in the Memoirs of the family of Plumpton, prefixed to this volume of correspondence.

[e] George Stanley, Lord Strange. Hale was a manor of the Earl of Derby, in the county of Chester.

LETTER LXII.

To the right honorable my especya'l good master, Sir Robart Plompton, kt.

After the most humble and due recomendation had, please yt your mastership, that in the most humble lowly wyse I may be recomended unto my singuler good ladies; praying you to have me excused in that I send no wyld fole to you afore this tyme, for in all Lancashire cold none be had for none money. The snaw and frost was so great, none was in the country, but fled away to see; and that caused me that I sent not, as I promysed. Sir, Robart, my servant, is a true servant to me, neverthelesse he is large to ryde afore my male, and over weyghty for my horse; wherfore he hartely desireth me to wryte to your mastership for him. He is a true man of tongue and hands, and a kind and a good man. If yt please your mastership to take him to your service, I beseech you to be his good master, and the better at the instaunce of my especyall prayer. Sir, I have given to him the blacke horse that bar him from the feild;[a] and if ther be any service that ye will comand me, I am redy, and wilbe to my lives end at your comandement, all other lordship and mastership layd aparte. My lord kepeth a great Cristinmas, as ever was in this country, and is my especyall good lord, as I trust in a short tyme your mastership shall know. My simple bedfelow, your bede-woman and servant, in the most humble wyse recomendeth hir unto your mastership, and to my ladys good ladyship, and your servants; as knoweth Jesu, who preserve you. Wrytten at Lathum,[b] the iij. day of January.

Your most humble servant, ED. PLOMPTON,
(3 Jan. 1489-90.) sectory to my lord Straung.

[a] "Lord Strange brought with him to the field of Stoke a great Host, enough to have beaten all the King's enemies, only of my lord his father's, the Earle of Derby's folks, and his," writes a contemporary annalist. (Lel. Coll. edit. ult. vol. IV. p. 213.) —Edward Plumpton had, it seems, with his servant, ridden in this company.

[b] Latham Hall in Lancashire, the well-known seat of the Earls of Derby.

LETTER LXIII.

To my master, Sir Robart Plompton, Kt.

In my most humble and faythfull wyse I recomend me to your good mastership, and to my especyall good ladyes. Sir, at my departing I rode according to your comandement by my lady Delphes,[a] a full trobleous way in that great snaw; notwithstanding, I cold not speed of your matters at that tyme. But now she is at London, and promyses me well; the which I trust, as yet, shall speed, afore your atturney come to London, within this vi dayes. He cometh ever at the last Retorne, in the end of the terme; that causeth me to have more busines than nedeth. Your matter in the Excheker is grevous; there is iiij wryttes agaynst you.

[a] Lady Delphes. The family of Delves were owners of the manor of Crakemarsh, com. Stafford, in which place the Plumptons had inherited lands by descent from the Foljambes. Sir John Delves, kt. was slain at the battle of Tewkesbury, 4 May 1471, and lies buried in the church of Wibbenbury, com. Cest. under an alabaster tomb, having effigies of a man and his two wives, with the epitaph, Hic jacet Johannes Delves miles et Elena uxor ejus, necnon Johannes Delves armiger, filius et heres predicti Joh'is, &c. The son here named had been beheaded after the battle of Tewkesbury, and was one of the few attainted in the following Parliament for being present at that field, by the name of John Delves, late of Uttockeshater, in the county of Stafford, esq. By his wife, eventually the heiress of Babington, of Chilwell, com. Nott. he had left only daughters; so that when the attainder was reversed, 22 Edw. IV. 1482, the heirs males, as well as the heirs generals, of the said John Delves, and every person feoffee to the use of them, or any of them, were expressly declared to be restored by the act to their original status, save only that the manor of Apedale, which had been granted by letters patent to James Blounte, esq. (15 Edw. IV. 1475), was to remain to him and to his heirs male. This same gentleman, afterwards Sir James Blount, kt. married one of the daughters of John Delves, esq. in whose right, as coheir with Ellen, wife of Robert Sheffield, of Butterwicke, in com. Linc. esq. he had possession of Crakemarsh, but of which some part was at this time yet held in dower by Lady Delves, the second wife and relict of Sir John Delves, kt. the grandfather. The manor of Doddington in Cheshire passed to the heirs male, and is the seat of the present representative of this branch of the family.

Whereof, I have a *dedimus potestatem* out of the Escheker, and another out of the Chauncere, both derected to Sir Guy Fayrfax, to resayve your hothes and my ladyes. The serch and the copy of the wrytts, out of one cort to another, costeth much money, and the fees of them, and great soliciting. If I had them now redy, I wold have sent them to you; when they be, I pray God send to me a good messinger, or els I must neds send my servant. Afore the iij[th] wrytte, for the entre into Wolfhountlands, all the counsell that I can gett, can shew no way, as yet, necessary for you; save onely I have labored the wrytt proceding agaynst you to be reteyned unto the next terme, and in the meane tyme to purvey our remedy. Fech your pardon and my ladyes, and send them both; for without they will helpe us, I wote not well what to doe in the matter. Incontinent upon the comyng home of master Farfax, ye and my lady ride to his place [b] with your wrytts, for so I am agreed with him; and as hastely as ye can gett down, send up the sayd wrytts with his sertyfycat, for then we must have a *non molestando* out of the Chauncery to discharges. The premysses maketh my purse light; to wryte partyclarly the charges, I have no tyme now. Bylby taketh to me no money; nevertheless when I have, or may make any, your matters shall not slake, nor abate, unto such tyme as your mastership send, as is above sayd. All other matters concerning you to the Kyngs grace and his counsell, I can send to you no word therof as yet. I trust in short space to doe, with Gods grace, who preserve you. Wrytten in great hast, the x day of Feb.

Your most humble servant,

(10 *Feb.* 1489-90.)[c]   Ed. Plompton.

[b] Sir Guy Fairfax, kt. one of the Justices of the King's Bench, had his place at Steeton in the Ainsty, com. Ebor.

[c] This and the following dates are ascertained from a letter of the 6 Nov. 1500, (*vide postea*) in which the suit respecting Wolf-hunt-land in Mansfield Woodhouse, com. Nott. is spoken of as having been pleaded ten years ago, which reference carries us back to 1490;

and the renewed mention of the "great snow" warrants the conjecture, that the severe winter, when the wild fowl fled away from the frozen meres of Lancashire to the sea, was the one which is marked by the date of this letter.

LETTER LXIV.

To my singuler good master, Sir Robart Plompton, kt.

In my most humble and faythfull mynd I recomend me unto your good mastership, and to my especyall good ladyes; certyfiing your mastership, that I delivered to Sir Richard Thornton, prest, upon Sunday last, to bryng to you, a box sealed, and ther in ij wrytts, one *dedimus potestatem* out of the Chauncere, and another out of the Excheker, both derected to Sir Guy Fairfax, and my poore wrytting therwith, the which was right simple, but I besech you have me excused. Though I wryte not at all tymes, as my dutie is to do, Sir, I had never so great busines as I have now for your matters. I know not the causes, but much payne I had to avoyd your appearance in your proper person, as ye shall more at large know by mouth, when I shall speake with you; that shalbe at your comendement. Hall demanded of me grene wax, that I knew not of, and I desired of hym a byll, what he asked of you, and his bokes wanted, he cold give me none; but I trust he wyll not be hasty upon you therfore, and if he be, let Henry Fox speake with him in my name, and pray him to suffer unto my comyng home. I made to him such chere as I cold at London. I have found meanes to convey the wryt, shold goe to the Schereffe of Notinghamshire agaynst you, unto the next terme; then Gode send us good speede therwith. Afore Easter, send upp your pardons, wrytes of *dedimus*, and escapetes of instruccion what plee we shall make for you in the Excheker, of, and how, and wherby ye enter your lands and maketh clame;[a] the matter is litle, and ioyus, with

[a] This relates to the suit concerning Wolf-hunt-land in Mansfield Woodhouse,

Gods grace, I purpose to be ever all this vacacion, and unto the next terme. I send to you a letter by Robert Beckwith, and more of every thing concerning you and your servants your atturney can shew. I wold, if I myght by wyshe, speak with you one hour, and yt pleased *Jesu*, who preserve your mastership in prosperous long to endure. Wrytten at London, the xx day of Febr. My lord Straunge came to the Kings grace uppon Munday last; my lord of Northumberland [b] is in good health, blessed be *Jesu*. Please yt your mastership to commend me to my master Gascoyn, if I cold doe to his mastership any service in thes partes, I wold be glad. Robert Blackwall [c] hath sent to you a pattent to seale, as appereth by the same, shewing to him your pleasure of vi[s] viii[d] by yere; and that he toke to no regard: the world is so covettus, I wott not what to say, nor nought I wyll, *parum sapienti sufficyt*.

Your servant,

(20 *Feb.* 1489-90.)   Ed: Plompton.

adverted to in the preceding letter. It was parcel of the lands of the Foljambes, and so called from its being held by the service of winding a horn, and chasing the wolve in the forest of Shirwood.

[b] The Earl of Northumberland was then in his thirteenth year.

[c] Robert Blackwall was son of Richard Blackwall, of Blackwall, com. Derb. who by a lease dated 28 Aug. 1489, held Flagg House in the same county, for a term of twelve years from 25 Mar. 1490, under Sir Robert Plumpton. This lease was renewed to Robert Blackwall, gent. [to hold for another term of twelve years after the ending of the former in 1502,] by Sir Robert Plumpton, kt. 19 Sept. 1499, with a clause that he should retain ten shillings out of the rent for his fee previously granted. (*Chartul. No.* 798.)

LETTER LXV.

To the right honorable and my especyall good master, Sir Robart Plompton, kt.

In my most humble and faythfull wyse I recomend me unto your good mastership, and to my especyall good ladys. Sir, the iij day of May I received your wrytting, and incontinent I labored to David, and spake with him according to your desire; and ther is great labour made to him for to put you from Haveray parke,[a] and offered to him x[li] by yere, and a reward of c[s]. Notwithstanding, I have made such labor; and caused him to be agreable to let yt to you for vi yeare, viii[li] by yeare, and ye to send vi marke to him at Whytsonday next to London, and then and ther ye to have your indentures sealed and delivered, and ye to enter and begine the vi yeare to you and your assignes. Sir, David wrytteth to you in favor of Wylliam Plompton bastard,[b] and for his excuse; and all is but a collor, for doubtles, and I had not layd yt to David discretely dyverse wayes, yt had bene gone from you, for I mad many meanes, or he wold make to me any grant: and because your mastership wrote that ye wold not for xx[li] but ye had yt, according to my dutye, I diligently applyed it to accomplish your pleasure therin. Sir, afor the arbage, doubt yt not; for sir Henry Wentforth,[c] nor yet none other, can have it, nor nothinge that belongeth to David. Sir, yt is well done ye remember to send this money, and have your indenturs in all hast possible, and if ther be anything that I know not, that ye wold have comprised within the same indenture, send to me word. Sir, I marvell much of William Plompton, that he sayth that I am not true. I never did him harme, but at your comandement I have done

[a] David Griffith, one of the council of Thomas Earl of Derby, and executor of his will (dated 26 July and proved 9 Nov. 1504), held Haveray Park, in the honour of Knaresborough, by virtue of a patent at this date. The Earl of Derby had held the office of chief steward of the duchy of Lancaster, north of Trent, of which the honour of Knaresborough was parcel, from 1 Hen. VII.

[b] Bastard son of Sir William Plumpton, kt.

[c] Sir Henry Wentworth, of Woodhouse, com. Ebor. kt. was at the date of this letter High Sheriff of Yorkshire, and then stationed at Knaresborough to keep the peace of the disturbed districts.—(*See the following Letter.*)

much for him. Yt is no marvell he that is not naturall, that he cannot love and owe his service to you, though he love not me. I trow, he love all ill that is faythfull and true to you. Sir, what soever any man say, I am, and wilbe, to you and yours true and faythfull while I live, with Gods grace, who preserve you. From Furnyswall, *vi die* May.

Your humble servant,
(6 *May* 1490.)   EDWARD PLOMPTON.

LETTER LXVI.

To the right honorable my singuler good master, Sir Robart Plompton, Knight.

In my most humble wyse I recommend me unto your mastership, and to my singuler good ladys. Late ye wrote to me a letter, the which I received upon Whitsonday at nyght, touching the departing of Sir Henry Wentworth and incontinent upon yt, I toke a bote, and went to Grenewich, and shewed the matters to my lord of Derby; and he appoynted me to attend uppon him unto he spake with the King, and so I did; and the Kings grace will in no wyse that Sir Henry Wentworth departe from your country,[a] as more at larg I shall send you word in hast, when I have more sure messinger. Sir, I pray you shew to my ladys

[a] The King, before returning to keep the feast of Whitsuntide, (7 June 1489,) at Nottingham, from the progress on which he had set out to quell the Yorkshire insurgents, "established in the northe parties the Erle of Surrey, Sir Richard Tunstall, and Sir Henry Wentworthe." (*Lel. Coll. vol. IV. p.* 247.)—The absence of the latter from his post at Knaresborough at the date of this letter was, it seems, justly to be feared, notwithstanding a year had passed since the dispersion of the malcontents; and in fact, in the second year of the Earl of Surrey's government, *teer was an insurrexion in the west part of the countrey, with* whom the said Erle *with the helpe of the Kynges true subyetts fought in the feld at Akeworth besides Pomfrett.* (*See monumental inscription of the Earl of Surrey at Thetford,* Weaver's *Funeral Monuments, p.* 386.)—At this field Sir Robert Plompton was present, as we learn from the following letter, another of

that Byrd of Knasbrough spake to me for certaine things to send them; and he cold cary none, for he went to Hales and many other pilgramages. Wryte in a byll such things as they wold have, and send to me. Sir, ye have a faythfull fryend and servant of Davy ap-i-Kriffith, but I marvell that ye sent not the mony at Pentycost. I am douted that he vary from his grant, ther is so great labor made to him for Havarey. Notwithstanding his letter send to you in the favor of W[m]. Plompton, I am through with him affor my lord of Derby, that ye shall occupie, and put and depute under you whosoever ye wyll, at your pleasure; and so shall your indentures be made, ye observing all covenauntes. And ever your owne to my pore power, as knoweth our Lord, who your good mastership, and my good ladys, with all yours, preserve. From London, *crastino Corporis.*

Your most humble servant,
(11 *June* 1490.)   ED. PLOMPTON.

the torn off series, but of which a second copy has been preserved in Dugdale's Yorkshire Arms. (*MS. in Coll. Arm. p.* 105 *b.*)

To my worshipfull Cousin, Sir Robert Plumpton, knight.

Right worshipfull Cousin, right hartelie I comend me unto you; and wheares I am enformed that a servant of yours had a gelding of myne, which I lost on the feild, I desyre and pray you that my servant, this bearer, may have a sighte of him, and yf the said geldyng be myne, that then ye will cause him to be delivered unto my said servant, as my singular trust is in you, whome our Lord have in his blessed safeguard. Written in the castle of Sheriff-hutton, the 6th day of Maye. Cosen, I have some proofe that your servant Robert Beck hath my gelding; one knoweth him well, told it me. I pray you, Cosen, fail not to send me the geldinge with the hand.

Your loving cozen,
THOMAS SURREY.

The date of this letter is 6 May, 7 Hen. VII. 1491, and on the 28th of that month Sir Robert Plumpton was honoured with the following gracious letter from his soveraign.

To our trusty and welbeloved knight, Sir Robert Plumpton.

Trusty, &c. For the good and agreeable service you did unto us in this last commotion of our subiects in our county of Yorke, wee can (*give?*) you our full speciall thanks,

LETTER LXVII.

To my master, Sir Robart Plompton, knight.

In my most humble wyse I recomend me unto your mastership, and to my especyall good lades. Sir, I marvell much that your mastership sendeth not the iiij[li] for David; he made to you a grant conditionally that ye shold content and pay to him at London iiij[li] at Pentycost last past, wheruppon ye sent to me a byll that he shold be payd at Mydsommer, and to content his mynd I shewed to him your letter; what I shall say to him, or what excuse to make, I cannot tell. Sir, remember ye may have his parke, xl[s] yerly under the price, by my labor; and if he change and let yt to another, blame not me: I have done my duty. William Plompton hath bene at London with David, and made much labor agaynst you for his fee; and otherwyse, shewed to me a copy of a state and feftment, mad by my master your father to certaine feofes, to his beofe, of lands and tenementes to the value of x mark yerly, for terme of his lyfe, the remaynderie to the ryght heire of William Plompton knight: wherupon he intended to labor a prive

and shall not forget the disposition you have beene of in that behalfe, &c. Wee therefore, intending to provide for the time to come, desire you that forthwith, and by as wise wages as yee can, yee put yourself in a surety of your meniall servants and tennants, and to know assuredly how many of them will take your part in serving us according to your and their duties foresaid. When yee have demeaned the matter in this wise, which wee would that you did as above with all diligence, then we pray you to certifie our cozen, the Earl of Surrey, of the number of such assured men, &c. Dat. Shene 28 Maii 7 H. 7. (*From a transcript in C. Towneley's MSS. taken from Sir Edward Plumpton's MS. when entire.*)

The well-read historian of Hallamshire has remarked, that the Earl of Surrey's inscription is perhaps the only memorial of the second Yorkshire insurrection; the proof from these letters of its historical exactness may therefore be strongly urged to shew the value of the correspondence now given to the public by the Camden Society. The battle of Ackworth is, moreover, further ascertained to have been fought in the spring of the year 1491.

scale to bring you before my lord Chaunceler and the Kings counsell, the which I have stoped as yet.[a] Sir, I pray you send me word in all hast possible of your mynd in this matter, and in especyall the money for David; and our Lord preserve you. Wrytten in hele in great hast uppon St. Peter even. Sir, they begine to die in London, and then I must departe for the tyme and other men do. I wold make you sure of Awerrey, or I departe, fro David.

Your servant
(28 *June* 1490.)   ED. PLOMPTON.
1495.[b]

[a] William Plumpton, of Kirkby Overblars, com. Ebor. gent. afterwards, by deed obligatory dated 1 Oct. 6 Hen. VII. 1490, submitted himself to the award of Sir Robert Plumpton, kt. with the advice of his council, Thomas Middleton and others, in regard to all matters in dispute between him and Sir Robert. (*Chartul. No.* 759.)
[b] *Sic, sed lege* 1490.

LETTER LXVIII.

To my Cousin Sir Robart Plompton, K[t].

Cousin, after dew recomendations I comend me; certifyng you one my honesty, I payd my palesses of Avarey parke,[a] duryng the tyme I occupied, xxx[s], dischargeng one of the palas to the Kings grace. Wrytten on our Lady Day, Assumption.

Your Cousin,
(15 *Aug.* 1490)   RANDALL PIGGUTT.[b]

[a] Palings, *palicea*. The persons who had the care of them were called Palessers. According to the award of Sir Robert Plumpton, given at Plumpton 22 Nov. 1490, and made in pursuance of the bond of William Plumpton, late of Kerkeby Orblass, bastard, the latter was to pay 30[s] sterling, received for the herbage of Haweray in the yeare 6th Hen. VII. and 20[s] owing to the palessers of Haweray for the same term. (*Chartul. No.* 761.)
[b] Sir Randolph Pigot, of Clotherholme, com. Ebor. kt.

LETTER LXIX.

To the right worshipfull and my good master, Sir Robart Plompton, kt.

Right worshipfull Sir, I comend me to you, and yt is so that I am through with my brother, Edward Plompton,[a] touching Haveray parke, and hath made a pare of indentures betwixt you and me touching the same;[b] and now, at our lady day in lent next comyng, ther is to be payd due to me viij^{li}, which, I trust your mastership, wilbe redy at that day: and any service yt list you, comannd me; I am yours, as knowes God, who keepe you. At Waryngton, the last day of August.

(31 *Aug.* 1490.) Your, Davy Hervy.[c]

[a] David Griffith was, it appears from this letter, brother of Agnes, the first wife of Edward Plompton, and through this connexion the latter probably got placed in his situation of secretary to Lord Strange.—See also Letter VI. as to his reception by his kinsmen in Lancashire.

[b] This lease is transcribed in the Plumpton Coucher-book, No. 758, and purports to be between David app Griffith of the one party and Sir Robert Plompton, knight, of the other, whereby the office of the keeping of Haverey Parke, with the herbage and pannage, &c. was granted for the term of six years to the latter, at a rent of viij^{li} to commence from lady day next coming; Sir Richard Langton and Sir John Langton, clerk, being sureties in 20^{li} for the performance of the covenants on the part of Sir Robert; the date, 26 Aug. 6 Hen. VII. 1490.

[c] *Sic, sed lege* Griffith.

LETTER LXX.

To my master Sir Robart Plompton, knyght.

In my most humble wyse I recomend me unto your good mastership, and to my especyall good Lades. This day I have spoken with master Schereffe, and ther I send Master Blakwall, Master of the Chancery,[a] as the berer can shew to you more by mouth,

[a] In the windows of the choir of the church at Mansfield Woodhouse, com. Nott. was this painting and scroll; "a man with a shaven crowne kneeling, a booke open

and they both comend them to you. Master Schereff hath and wyll doe as much in your matter as I can of reason desire him. At Nothingham, uppon Munday come a senit, must we fynd a office for you. I have bene with Thomas Horton, by the advice of Mr. Schereffe, and pennyt ij inquisicions of dyverse wayes; if one will not serve us, the other shall. Sir, ye have a simple tenant in Maunsfeld Woodhouse. I wold have sent him to Rich: Saxton, for to mete with me at Mr. Schereffs, and he absent him. Any service ye wyll comand me, send me word, and I am yours, as knoweth our Lord, who preserve you. Wrytten at Southwell, the xxiij of September.

(23 *Sept.* 1490.) Your servant, Ed. Plompton.

before him."—*Blakewall unus Magistrorum.* (MS. of Gervase Hollis, Bibl. Harl. N. 6829.)

LETTER LXXI.

To my master Sir Robart Plompton, knyght.

In my most humble and lowly wyse I recomend me unto your mastership, and to my singuler good lady. Sir, I sent to you late wryttings of all matters by Sir Edward Bethom, prest. I thinke long unto I here word from you, whether they come to you in tyme, or noo, and of your welfare. Sir, I had no word seth I parted from Plompton, as many as hath comyn to London. I cannot gyt myne entent of my lady Delphes, wherfore I have comyned with Masters Blunt and Shefeld[a] in this forme; the say they will take yt in ferme, or els make yt exchaunce with you of lands lyeing in Yorkshire, or els pay to you redy money therfore; which of thes iij wayes ye wyll take, I pray you take advise, and send to me word as hastyly as ye can, for they will not tary here; and I will have no further comunycation therin, tyll I know your pleasure and mynd, for they wyll take hold at a letle

[a] See note [a] to Letter LXIII.

thing. All such newes as I here, John Bell can shew ye by mouth, for he made so great hast, I had no leasure to writt more at larg of al things at this tyme. I thinke long till I here from your mastership, the which *Jesu* preserve. At London, the iiij day of November.

Your most humble servant,

(4 *Nov.* 1490.) Ed. Plompton.

LETTER LXXII.

To my master Sir Robart Plompton, knyght.

"The replycacion of Margret Scargill to the answere of William Scargill.[a] The same Margrett sayth, that the byll put by her agaynst the sayd William is good and true in every poynt, and that the same John Scargill, named in the sayd byll, made such wyll of the same maner, landes, tenements and other premyses, and every of them, as is surmytted by the same byll; and over that, sayth althings as in the saydbyll is surmytted: all which matter she is redy to prove, as this cort will award, and prayeth as in hir byll is desired."

Sir, in my right humble and tender wyse I recomend me unto your good mastership, and to my singuler good ladyes. Sir, I sent to you the copie of the replycacion of Margaret Scargill, wherupon my lord Chaunceler hath, at our speciall desire, comand a *Dedimus potestatem* to Sir Guy Fayrfax, to heare and examyn ther proves and ours both, in Yorkshire; wherfore I wold advise your mastership to shew your copies of ther byll, our answere, and ther replicacion to Mr. William Fayrfax, that he may be perfitt by them, and your instruccion in the matter, and to be for William Scargyll afore Master Sir Guy, at that day of

[a] William Scargill, of Thorp Stapleton, esq. was father of Sir Robert Scargill, kt. who lies buried under a splendid tomb in the church of Whitkirk.—(*Whitaker's Loidis et Elmete.*)

his sytting, with all other proves most necessary for him; and in any wyse se that William Scargill agre with Watson, and bryng him up with him to London to release his suerty for the peace, or else he must fynd other suertyes, and that is costly: and if he fayle, he must go to ward, or els loose c marke, and every one of hus iiij l marke, the which God forbyd shold be. Sir, afore your lands in Crakenmarsh, I can not deale with my lady Delfs; I find hir varyable in hir promyse; wherfore I have, according to your comandment, letten them in your name to Mr. Blunt by indenture, as more at larg appereth by the same, the which I sent to you within this box inclosed under my seale; and ye to subscrybe your hand, and to send a servant of yours with the same box and indentures to thabbay of Dale,[b] and ther to se thabbot and convent seale the obligation for suerty of your rent, as in them is specified, and to wryt his name down to deliver one parte to Mr. Blount, and retine another parte for you with the obligation. All such matters as ye wrote for by Georg Croft, dout not for them; I have and shall remember them to thaccomplishment of your mynd, with grace of *Jesu*, who you and yours long preserve in prosperous felicite to endure. From London, the xxvij day of November.

Your humble servant,

(27 *Nov.* 1490.) Ed. Plompton.

[b] Dale Abbey, in the county of Derby.

LETTER LXXIII.

To my worshipfull master, Sir Robart Plompton, kt.

Right worshipfull Sir, I recomend me to your mastership, and yt is so that the Kings grace hath appoynted my lord to wayt upon his grace, now at this his noble vage into France; wherfore I must take homely upon your mastership, and desire you to helpe me with my fee for this yere, for I am distytute of money; and this my wrytting shalbe your discharg and warrant to delyver yt to the berer herof.[a] And if yt may be done now at this tyme, I am bounden to you to doe you any pleasure that lyes in my power, with Gods mercy, who preserve you, my gud master, and I pray you to take credence to Rich: Shaw, this berer, in my behalfe. The iij day of February.

(3 *Feb:* 1491-2.) Your owne servant, DAVID GRIFFITH.

[a] It was not till the month of October in the year 1492, that Henry VII. sat down before Boulogne, and on the 20th of that month, 8 Hen. VII. Geffrey Townley, servant to Sir Robert Plumpton, paid 8[li] to William, abbot of Whalley, to be delivered to Dame Fr. Gryfin. (*Chartul. N°.* 766.)

LETTER LXXIV.

To my right worshipfull master, Sir Robart Plompton, kt. this bill be delyvered.

Right worshipfull Sir, I comend me unto your mastership; it is so I received of your chaplain in the New Castle under Lyne 8 pounds. And also I send to you my brother Midleton,[a] and pray you that ye wold content him of this yeare farme. And Christ keepe you. At Preston, the 8 day of October.

From your servant, DAVID GRIFFITH.

[a] Brother-in-law, *quære* if the Lancashire family of that name.

LETTER LXXV.

To my Cousin, Sir Robart Plompton, be thes delivered.

Right worshipfull Cousin, I commend me unto you, letting you wyt that ther is a neighbour of myne, this bearer, William Medley, naler, which geysted with two of your servants in Haywras[a] x bests, Thomas Ward, and Wylliam Thorp; and when this poore man

[a] Hayrah or Haverah Park, where cattle were agisted.

come at Michellmes for his cattell, ther lacked one of the best, which was worth xii[s] and better: and your servants wold have delyvered him other cattell for his, both that was fare fro the value of his. Wherfore, Cousin, I hartely pray you to be his good master to this man, and that ye wold call your sayd servants afore you, and that he myght be payd for his best that he lacks, as I may doe for you in like cause, which I shalbe glad to doe, as God knows, who ever preserve you to his pleasure.

By your Cousin, WILLIAM MERKINFEILD.[b]

[b] William Markinfield, esq. brother of Sir Thomas Markenfield, of Markenfield-hall, near Ripon, com. Ebor. kt. who died in 1497. He is named in the will of his nephew Sir Ninian Markynfield, kt. dated 1 Oct. 1527, proved 5 July 1528.

LETTER LXXVI.

To my worshipfull unkl, Sir Robart Plompton, kt.

Right worshipful uncle, I recomend mee unto you. Sir, it is so that my lord of Surrey hath written to mee, by the labor of Rich: Cholmley,[a] to be with him on Thursday next folowing in the matter depending betwixt mee and John Thorneton; wherfore, uncle, as my most especial trust is in you, praing you to be with mee at the day appointed, as I may deserve it to you in tyme to come, with grace of *Jesu,* who preserve you. From Sessay, 4 day of January.

Your loving Cosin, THOMAS DARREL.[b]

[a] See note [b] Letter LXXVII.
[b] Thomas Darrel of Sessay, com. Ebor. esq. son of Sir George Darrell, kt. and Margaret Plumpton.

LETTER LXXVII.

To the right worshipfull Sir Robart Plompton, kt. at Plompton.

Right worshipfull Sir, after all due recomendations, please it

you to know, I have latly bene in the bishopryk of Durham, by the Kings comandement, for leveing of such arrerages and other dutyes, as were due to the late byshop decessed, whose soule God pardon; and ther it was shewed unto me by certayn frinds of Mr. Alex. Lees,[a] and also by his old servant, Lawrance Canwike, who ye know, that ye without your duty belonging to the sayd Mr. Lee, wherwith all the Kings comyssioners and I marvelled that ye wold so doe. Wheruppon the sayd Lorance, with other his master frynds, wer in mynd and fully determyned to have made complaynt of you unto the Kings grace in that behalfe; and then, Sir, in avoyding of such inconvenients as myght have ensued to you by reason of the same, and also for such speciall favour as I owe unto you, I caused them to surcease ther purposse unto the tyme I had wrytten to you, and known your mynd in that partie. Wherfore, Sir, I pray you, according to the Kings comandement, which I have sene, and also for your singuler wele, that ye will see the said Larance content of parte of the sayd duty at this tyme, and so to finde him a suffycyent suerty for the residue, as ye and he can agre. And, Sir, if ye endever not yourselfe for the accompleshment of the premysses, I have promysed them to wryte to the Kings grace for the contentation of the same, which I wold be loth to doe. Sir, I doubt not, so ye will deale herin, that it shall not mis-

[a] The fragment in Hearne, to which reference is made in note [c], Letter X., after mention of the warning given to Edward IV. by the serjeant of his minstrels of the project of his enemies to seize upon his person, when he was in the North in the month of September, A.D. 1470, breaks off with this unfinished sentence; "And sodeinly upon that came one Maister Alexander Lee a priest —" This personage was, it seems, rector of Spofford in 1493, in which year, 12 Jan. 1492-3, died John Sherwood, Bishop of Durham. In the Coucher book is copied a receipt from Thomas Taylor, chaplain, one of the factors of Master Alexander Lee, rector of the parish church of Spoford, acknowledging payment by Sir Robert Plumpton, kt. of 26[s]. 8[d]., the whole sum of the tithes of Plumpton, and dated 1 Feb. 1493-4. (*Chartul. No.* 770.) It is therefore probable that he had some preferment in the diocese of Durham, which was the occasion of his non-residence.

care; and, Sir, of your toward mynd herin I pray you that I may be answered by my servant, this bearer, to whom I pray you give credence. And I am yours. At Cotingham, the xvi day of June.

(16 *June* 1493.) Your owne, RICHARD COVERLEY.[b]

[b] I suspect that Coverley should be read Cholmley, and that the name is a mistake of the copyist in 1613. Richard Cholmley was in fact one of the guardians of the bishoprick of Durham after the demise of Bishop Shirwood, his appointment bearing date 11 April, 8 Hen. VII. 1493. (*See* Surtees' *Durham.*)

LETTER LXXVIII.

To my right hartely beloved Cousin, Sir Robart Plompton, kt.

Right hartely beloved Cosin, I comaund me unto you. And for as much as I am distetute of runyng hounds, I desire and pray you to send me a copple with my servant, this bringer. And of thing like I have fore your pleasure, it shalbe redy. Written in my lodging at Spetell of the street,[a] the xxix day of October. Over this, Cousin, I pray you to send me your tame haert, for myne dere ar dead.

Your Cousin, HEN: NORTHUMBERLAND.

[a] Spittle in the Street, com. Lincoln.

LETTER LXXIX.

To my cousin, Sir Robart Plompton, knyght, be these byll.

Right worshipfull Cousin, I recomend me unto you, desiring to here of your wellfare; praying you to give me ij eople of conyes to stocking of a litle ground that I make at Ryther, and I shall doe you as great a pleassure. I pray you that I may be recommend to my lady your wyfe. We have rest; and past this summer, I wyll pray you to come and kill a bucke with me. I pray you, Cousin, that the bringer hereof, my servant, may have the conyes, and *Jesu* keepe you. At Rither,[a] this fryday.

(1490—1520.)

By your Cousin,
RALFE RYTHER.[b]

[a] "We have rest," that is to say, no bucks were to be killed out of the stock in the park at Ryther in that year.
[b] Ralph Ryther of Ryther, com. Ebor. esq. *ætatis* 40, 6 Hen. VII. 1490, when he succeeded to the family estates. He died 2 April 1520, being then a knight.

LETTER LXXX.

To his worshipful Cosin, Sir Robart Plompton, kt.

Right reverend and worshipfull Cosin, I commend me unto you as hertyly as I can, evermore desiring to heare of your welfare, the which I besech *Jesu* to continew to his pleasure, and your herts desire. Cosin, please you witt that I am enformed, that a poor man somtyme belonging to mee, called Umfrey Bell, hath trespased to a servant of youres, which I am sory for. Wherfore, Cosin, I desire and hartily pray you to take upp the matter into your own hands for my sake, and rewle him as it please you; and therin you wil do, as I may do that may be plesur to you, and my contry, the which I shalbe redy too, by the grace of God, who preserve you.

By your own kynsman,
ROBART WARCOPP, of Warcoppe.[a]

[a] Warcop, in the county of Westmerland.

LETTER LXXXI.

Unto my right worshipfull master, Sir Robart Plompton, kt. be this delivered in hast.

Right worshipfull Sir, after my duty I recomend me unto your mastership, beseching you to be good master to Henry Gulles concerning one farmhold in Follifit, which John Gulles now holdeth; that if ye can git John Gullese good wyll, that ye wilbe so good master unto Henry Gullese that he may have yt, and the better master for my sake. No more at this tyme, but *Jesu* preserve you.

Your own to his power,
JOHN SWALE of Staynley.[a]

[a] John Swale of South Stainley, com. Ebor. esq. ancestor to the Baronets of that name. Follyfoot is a hamlet in the parish of Spofforth.

LETTER LXXXII.

To my right worshipfull master, Sir Robart Plompton, kt. delyver these.

Right worshipfull Sir, I oftymes comend me unto your mastership, and for so much as ther is a matter betwixt John Marshall and his mother, I understand, Sir, that his mother hath put hir matter to your mastership. Sir, and it be so, he shall byd your mastership in likewise. Wherfore, Sir, I pray you hartely, and as ever I may do you service, for to be good master to John Marshall, and the better for this my prayer; for, Sir, I have spoken of that matter herbefore, and they sayd at they wold have bydene my rule. Sir, I am well pleased that ye have a rule in that matter, or any other matter in this country; it pleases me well, for, Sir, I will take your part in any matter ye have here, or in any other place. Sir, I pray you hartely that ye wold, for my sake, to let the matter rest to that I may speake with your mastership, for this my prayer. Sir, I am to you as I was to my master, your father, and so shall I be while I live, with grace of God, who kepe you. Morover, Sir, it is letten me wytt that they have enformed your mastership, that John Marshall labors to a gentleman in this country; Sir, it is not so, and that shall ye well know when I speake with you, and *Jesu* keepe you.

By your trew cousin and man,
THOMAS HAKSWORTH.[a]

[a] Thomas Hawkesworth, of Hawkesworth, com. Ebor. esq. *vixit* 8 Hen. VII. (See pedigree in Thoresby's Ducatus Leodiensis, 2nd edit. 1816, *p*. 173.)

LETTER LXXXIII.

To Sir Robart Plompton, or els to Master William his son.

Right worshipfull master Plompton, as hartely as I can I recomend me unto you, desyring you to be good master unto this poore woman, the bearer hereof. Sir, it is so that a servant of yours hath gotten a child with hir, the which is lost for lacke of keeping, as God knowes. She hath kept it as long as she may, whils she hath not a cloth to her backe but which I have given hir, since she came to my service. And if it wold please you to heare this poore woman speake, I trust to God ye wilbe good master to hir, and rather the better for my sake. And if I had not bene, she wold have rune hir way; and all this wile I keep the child of my own proper cost, and will doe, till I here some word from you, as knowes God, who preserve you.

By your owne to his powr,
WILLIAM WITTCARS.

LETTER LXXXIV.

To Sir Robart Plompton, kt. this be delivered.

Right worshipfull master, I recomend me unto your mastership as hartely as I can, in my most lowliest maner. Sir, the cause of my wrytting to you at this tyme, is this; that it may please your sayd good mastership to helpe my moder in hir right, as to get hir by your good meanes such small dutyes, as is owne hir by such a person as she shall shew you the name of: if that your mastership, after that you have sent for him to your sayd mastership, comon the matter ripely with him. And if than that ye can bring him to no reasonable end, then I besech your mastership to send me word by wrytting how he wilbe demeaned, and therafter I shall entreat him according; for if he will take none end with hir at your desire, I shall sharply sue him by the comon law, as shortly after as may conveniently. No more to you at this tyme, but *Jesu* preserve you. At London, the xxvii day of May.

By your servant, JOHN WALKER.

LETTER LXXXV.

To his worshipfull master, Sir Robart Plompton, knight, be thes letter delivered in hast.

Most reverent and worshipfull Sir, I recomend me unto your mastership in the most lowly wyse, ever me glad to here of your prosperytie and welfare, which I besech almyghty God to encrease to his pleasure, and your harts desire; letting your mastership understand, the lowest price of the male, which your mastership spake of, is 2iiij[s] viii[d]. as the maker therof sayeth. And yf yt please you to send for yt shortly, he shall kepe yt; or els, he shall make one other, when yt please your mastership to send him word iij dayes before the tyme that it please you to have it. No more to your mastership at this tyme, but the Holy Trenite have you in his keeping.

By your owne bedman, SIR EDWARD BIRTBY.

LETTER LXXXVI.

To my right worshipfull master, Sir Robart Plompton, kt. be this delivered.

Most honorable and worshipfull master, of whom myne intellygence and service lyes unto, with all due recomendations in the most humylitywise that I can thinke, or may, I recomend me unto your worthy estate, beseching you of this simple wryting and matter to give audience and intelleccyon, under what forme the wrytting is made to you in preve. Please you to understand, the cause of my writing is this; your lordship of Stanton,[a] where that I dwell, is made lesser of rent, and halfe your valow, [and yt may contynew so and be suffered of you and yours,] be the gressing of xx oxen be yere. For ther be such men dwelling in Stanton that thus deale, that will no other way but so ; they will have yt, by ther seying, be yt right or wrong. And yt please yow to send your counsell over to hold a court, he shall have such infomacion be us that be your tenaunts, that your lifflod shall be saved and kept unto you and yours, with the grace of God, who have you in his blessed keeping. And uppon this conclusion, and it please you so to do, that you seek up your evydence of a place is called Renald Riding, under what forme you have yt, for except your evidence specyfie, you be lyke to goe without yt. And if yt please you that these things here wrytten shalbe performed, I besech you that I may have answere, for to make your tenaunts perfect under what forme ye wold have them demeaned, and they, and I, to be redy to do you a pleasure with our body and our goods, with the grace of God, who defend you and yours. Amen.

[a] Stanton Hall, a manor belonging to Sir Robert Plumpton, in the county of Derby, of the lands of the Foljambes.

LETTER LXXXVII.

To my master, Sir Robart Plompton, knight.

In my right humble wyse I recomend me unto your good mastership. I have receyved your wrytting and the credaunce of your servant. And in stopping and letting of your prevy seale, at the instance and especyall labour of my Master Gascoygne,[a] my lord Prevey Seale [b] hath done that he myght with reason, insomuch that he lettyt yt, and comaunded Mr. Bele, clark therof, that none shold passe, unto such tyme as all the lords of the Kings counsell commanded yt to passe, upon his surmyse and complaynt, wherof I sent to you a copye. And when we sought no remedy, we found the meanes that Ch. Kilborne, and sufficient suertyes with him, shold be bonden in a reconusance of x^{li} to content and pay the cost and charg, if his surmyse and byll of complaint be founden insufficyent and not true. My sayd Mr. Gascoygne hath dyligently applyed your matter, as much as is possible for to doe, as your servant Geffray can shew unto you more at large every thing by mouth ; and as yet he can get no surtyes. Wherfore my lord abbot of St. Mary Abbay [c] shewed to me this day, that his servant Kilborne wold have a writ, *subpena*. Sir, for that I have lade good watch. Also my lord abott told me this day, that Edmound Thwaites hath sene his evedence, and sath that your mylne standeth upon his ground and more, and that he is not your ward. Wherby I perceive well, he haught a favor and good lordship to his servant Kilborne. He desired the matter to be put

[a] Sir William Gascoigne, kt. nephew to Dame Agnes, wife of Sir Robert Plumpton, appears to have enjoyed considerable influence at court by reason of his near relationship to the Earl of Northumberland.
[b] Richard Fox, Bishop of Durham, Lord Privy Seal in 1495.
[c] William Siver or Siveyer. See a letter from him *ante No.* LVIII.

upon my lord of Surrey and him. And I answered, that the matter concerned your inheryance, and a matter of land, the which cold in no wyse be rightfully determynted without learned counsell. Sir, I trust we shall so provide for him here, that he shal not have all his intent, with Gods grace, who preserve your good mastership, and my singuler good ladys, and all yours, long tyme to endure with encrease of grace and honor. From Furnywalls Inne, the xxvi of October 1495.

Your humble servant,

(26 *Oct.* 1495.)   Ed. Plompton.

LETTER LXXXVIII.

To my singular good master Sir Robart Plompton, knyght.

In my right humble wyse I recomend me unto your good mastership, and to my singuler good lady. Afore, my lord of Carlel [a] hath passed so by the way, at his lodging at Poumfret and Scroby,[b] that as yet I spake not with his lordship. I spake with his servants, and they shewed to me Ch. Kilborn rideth not up with him. Yt was shewed me that uppon Thursday last [c] ther was a great Justice sat at Wentbrig ; I wold fayne know what was done ther, and afore that, in such matters as concerned you. Master Tailbose [d] was at Colliweston [e] uppon tuesday, wedensday, and thursday last, as the

[a] William Siver or Siveyer, Abbot of St. Mary, York, had been elected bishop of Carlisle, 11 Dec. 1495.
[b] Scrooby in Nottinghamshire.
[c] Thursday, 7 Jan. 1495-6.
[d] Sir George Tailbois of Kyme, com. Linc. kt. married to Elizabeth Gascoigne, niece of Dame Agnes Plumpton.
[e] Collyweston was the residence of Margaret, the King's mother, countess of Richmond and Derby. Edward Plumpton was in the service of Lord Strange, son of the Earl her husband.

bringer can shew; els I wold have written much more. My lord of Darby departith towards London upon munday come a senit. Davy [f] recomend him to your mastership, and when we come to London, ye shall have a strayt restreynt for Haveray. Our lord preserve you and all yours. At Stampforth,[g] *crastino Hallarii*.

Your humble servant,

(14 *Jan.* 1495-6.)   Ed. Plompton.

[f] David Griffith.
[g] Stamford is in the immediate vicinity of Colly-weston.

LETTER LXXXIX.

Unto my singuler good master, Sir Robart Plompton, Kt. be thes letter delivered in goodly hast.

Right reverent and my singuler good master, I recomend me to your good mastership, to my gode lady your mother, and my lady your wyffe. Please yt your mastership to know, that I have received your letter sent to me by Robart Benson, and hath hard his commyng from you. And I have bene and labored to the Clarkes of the previe signit dyvers tymes afore the making herof, and to my lord presedent, after thentent of your wrytting ; and the day of the delyverie of this wrytting by the sayd Robart Benson, Percyvall Lanton and I went to the Tower to speake with my lord Pryvey seale,[a] as the clark of the Kings signit advised us, thynking that to be our next way, if so were that we wold not advise you to com not up by the pryvie seale. For ther was a byll put into the Parliament, a litle before Christynmas, that no privie seal shold goe against no man, but if the suer therof wold find suerty to yeld the parties defendants ther damages, and after that intent yt is sayd, that the lords of the counsell behave themselfe. And the most dylygent labor and way that the sayd Percyvall and I can doe our good master in his behalfe, we shall ende-

[a] Richard Fox, Bishop of Durham, Lord Privy Seal.

vor ourselfs, for to the sayd Percyvall, for both his labour at the last terme and this terme, ye be much beholden unto; and the sayd Lanton is generall atturney to my said Lord Privey seale. And as for Edward Plompton, he is not commyn to London at the making of this simple wrytting. Also, Sir Robert Blawall, your atturney in the Kings Escheker,[b] hath shewed me, that Edward Plompton hath not payed the money for respityng of your homage in the sayd Escheker, as he promysed me and your menyall servant Geffray Tounley the last terme; and by great labour of the sayd Blakwall, he hath saved your issues to this terme, and he will lay down no penny. And it is so that I have promysed payment or I come home, and with the grace of God so shall I make pacement; and at my comyng home, I shall shew to your mastership al things more clerely, praying your sayd mastership be not displeased with my homely wrytting. Written in the even and in great hast. For parte of your matters I have spede, and parte of my ladies matters also, and as touching the remnent of your matters, I shall indevor me for you as farre as I can, with the grace of God, who preserve you and all yours to his pleasure. Wrytten the thursday next after the puryfication of our lady the Virgin last past. Anno xi. h. vii. Yor servant,

(4 Feb. 1495-6.)   EDW: BARLOW.

[b] Sir Robert Blackwall, clerk, Master in Chancery. (See note [a] Letter LXX.)

LETTER XC.

To my good master Sir Robart Plompton, knyght, at Plompton, in hast.

Plese yt your good mastership to understand, your servant and atturney, Mr. Owen Barley, desired mee to labor to my lord of Duresm,[a] that sum meanes might be found to excuse your appearance, if the privy seale were delivered unto you, which one Kilburn labored against you this last term; and according to his desire, I have labored at diverse times. My lord shewed me dyverse things, which was shewed him in that matter, as I shall shew your mastership at laser. And in conclusion this is his mynd; if the privie seale be delivered you afore his comyng home into that country, which, I trust, wilbe about the iiij[th] weeke of lent, thin he wold ye shold set stale yourselfe, and send a servant to me, as shortly as ye can, and he and I shall purvey a remedy, that ye shall take no hurt therby. And if the privie seale be not delivered afore my lords comyng home, than he sayeth, that he will send for the partie, and cause the matter be examyned endefferently; and thus he was content, that I shold wryt unto your mastership. And therfore dowt not in this matter, but take your ease, and in no wyse charg yourself with comyng upp for this matter, thoffe the prive seale be delivered unto you. Herein, I assure you, I shall give as great delygence, as the matter were myne owne. And thus our lord God preserve your mastership to your most comforth. At Lyncolnes Inne, the ix[th] day of February, by the hand of

Your servant

(9 Feb. 1495-6.)   PERCIVALL LAMBTON.

LETTER XCI.

To my master Sir Robart Plompton, knight, at Plompton.

In my right humble and harty wyse I recomend me unto your good mastership, and to my singuler good lady. The ix day of February I received your wrytting, the which was to me great comforth. The contents therof was moved to my lord Prive seal afore that, by Percyvall Lambeton, as he shewed to me, and as he

[a] Richard Fox, Bishop of Durham.

---

hath wrytten to you the scanty in every thing of my lords mynd in that behalfe; the which, me semeth, right good and necessary for you. And yt pleaseth you, when my lord cometh into your country, to se him, and ride a myle or ij with him, and wellcome him to the country; yt will doe good many wayes. Sir, afore credaunce of Ewene Barle, he gave none to me but for these premyses, and that, I thinke, nedeth no more labor nor cost; for when my sayd lord had answered reasonable therin, yt sufficeth for the same. Also I send herin a byll of discharg for your fine, and I wold I myght have content the same fyne at the last terme, [but I spared for the more advauntage,] for ye payd none syth Trenetie terme unto now. And your owne, and ever wylbe, to my power, as knoweth our Lord, who ever preserve you and yours in prosperous long tyme to endure. From Furnywalls Inn, the xiij of February.

Your humble servant,   ED. PLOMPTON.
(13 Feb. 1495-6.)   1495.

LETTER XCII.

To the right worshipfull and my right hartely beloved frind Sir Robart Plompton, knight.

Right worshipful Sir, I comend me unto you, with all my hart thanking you of the great love and favor, that ye have shewed unto my nephew, the comander of Rybston;[a] and not only unto him, but as well unto his servants and tenaunts in these partyes, as well in his absence as in his presence: praying you so to contynew, and ye may be assured, if ther be any thing that I may doe for you or for any of yours, ye shall alway find me redy to my power. John Trongton, the brynger hereof, shall shew unto you in what case the matter standeth in, that is betwixt my nephew and John of Rocliffe;[b] and I pray you give credence to the sayd brynger hereof, and *Jesu* keep you. Wrytten at St. Johns, the iij day of September.

Your owne,

Sir JOHN KENDAL, prior of St. John.[c]

[a] Sir John Tong. (See Letter XCIII.)

[b] John Rocliffe of Cowthorpe, esq. afterwards Sir John Rocliffe, Kt.

[c] Brother John Kendal, Turcopolier of Rhodes, was the commissary and deputy of Pope Sixtus IV. throughout the globe, in aid of the expedition against the Turks A.D. 1480, tenth of his pontificate. To those who should contribute to this object, he had authority from the Holy See to grant faculties to their confessors in reserved cases, together with plenary indulgences; and for that purpose had with him printed forms on parchment, to which he affixed his seal. One of these to Dame Joan Plumpton has been copied into the Cartulary (No. 699), and as attention has been drawn to this personage from his having been the subject of the earliest contemporary English medal in existence, its perusal will probably gratify the curiosity of the reader, and I have given a transcript of it below. See also the remarks of Sir Frederic Madden concerning these forms. (*Archæolog.* vol. XXVII. p. 172, note [g].) The medal is engraved in Pinkerton's Medallic History of England, 4to, 1790. Sir John Kendal succeeded Sir John Weston as Prior of the Hospital of St. John of Jerusalem, Clerkenwell, but the exact date is not ascertained; the earliest discovered is the year 1491. He occurs ten years after, and is stated to have died in November, 1501.

Frater Johannes Kendal Turcipelerius* Rhodi, ac commissarius a sanctissimo in Christo patri et domino nostro, domino Sixto, divina providentia, Papa quarto, et vigore

* The military dignity of Turcopolier, or General of the Forces of the Order, which at first was inseparable from the post of Grand Prior of England, [and the latter might be held by a foreigner,] was subsequently attached absolutely to the English nation, or *Langue d'Angleterre*, in the Order. (Vertot, *Hist. de l' Ordre de Malte*, vol. I. p. 206, 4to. 1726.) In 1480 Brother John Boucq, were Turcopoliers of the Order, in which same years John de Weston and William de Weston were Grand Priors of England. I observe the name of Brother Thomas Ploneton among the brethren of the Order present at the siege of Rhodes in 1480, who I presume was of the Yorkshire family, and probably nephew to Dame Joan Plompton.

literarum suarum, pro expeditione contra perfidos Turcas, Christiani nominis hostes, in defensione Insulæ Rhodi, et fidei Catholicæ, facta et facienda, concessarum, ad infrascripta per universum orbem deputatus. Delectæ nobis in Christo, Dominæ Johannæ Plompton, salutem in domino sempiternam. Provenit ex tuæ devotionis affectu, quo Romanam ecclesiam revereris, ac te huic expeditioni sanctæ et necessariæ gratum reddis et liberalem, ut petitiones tuas, illas præsertim quæ conscientiæ pacem et animæ tuæ salutem respiciunt, ad exauditionis gratiam admittamus. Hinc est quod nos, tuis devotis supplicationibus inclinati, tibi ut aliquem idoneum et discretum præsbiterum secularem, vel cuiusvis ordinis regularem, in tuum possis eligere confessorem : qui confessione tua diligenter audita, pro commissis per te quibusvis criminibus, excessibus et delictis, quantumcunque gravibus et enormibus, etiamsi talia fuerint propter quæ sedes apostolica sit quovismodo merito consulenda, iniectionis manuum in episcopum vel superiorem, ac libertatis ecclesiasticæ offense, seu conspirationis in personam aut statum Romanæ Pontificis, vel cuiusvis offense inobedientiæ aut rebellionis sedis ejusdem, ac præsbitericidii casibus duntaxat exceptis, in reservatis semel tantum, in aliis vero non reservatis totiens quotiens fuerit opportunum, debitam absolutionem impendere, et pœnitentiam salutarem iniungere, ac omnium peccatorum tuorum de quibus corde contritus et ore confessus fueris, semel in vita, et semel in mortis articulo, plenariam remissionem et indulgentiam, auctoritate apostolica tibi concedere possit, dicta auctoritate, qua per ipsius sedis literas, sufficienti facultate muniti, fungimur, in hac parte indulgemus. In quorum fidem has literas nostras, sigilli nostri appensione munitas, fieri iussimus atque mandavimus. Dat visesimo secundo die mensis Aprilis, anno Domini MCCCCLXXX ac pontificatus præfati sanctissimi domini nostri, domini Sixti Papæ quarti, anno decimo.

(699. *Deed. Copied on tuesday the 13 of februarii*, 1626, *having then a seal.*)

LETTER XCIII.

To my right worshipfull, and my right hartely welbeloved neghbor and fadyr, Sir Robart Plompton, knight.

Right worshipfull and my right entirely beloved Sir and father, I recomend me unto you, and thank the same for your loving dealing in my absence shewed to my tenaunts and servants, and especially to my servant Tromton, this bringer, for the good mastership shewed to him at Yorke to your cost and charge. My sayd servant shall shew you my further mynd, to whom it will please you to give credence, and also that I may be recommended to my good lady and mother, your wyfe. *Jesu* preserve you. At London, the xi[th] day of March.

Your owne son, Sir JOHN TONG,
commander of Rybston and Mownt S. Johns.[a]

[a] At Great Ribstone, in the parish of Hunsingore, near Knaresborough, and at Mount St John, in the parish of Feliskirk, north riding of Yorkshire, the Knights Hospitallers of St. John had commanderies. A John Tong was mayor of York in 1477, so that the writer of this letter was probably his son, to whom at his birth Sir Robert and Lady Plumpton had stood sponsors. We learn, from the preceding letter and elsewhere, that he was nephew to Sir John Kendal, prior of St. John's, Clerkenwell, the chief house of the Order in England, and in the list of burials in the Priory Church are the names of William Tong, Margaret Tong, and Isabel Tong, the first being also a brother of the Order. In the volume of the Archæologia referred to in the proceding note, Sir Frederic Madden has printed a curious document, which purports to be the confession of one Bernard de Vignolles, dated at Rouen, 14 Mar. 1495-6, and wherein he accuses "Sire Jehan Quendal, grant prieur de l'ordre de Saint Jehan de Roddes, Sire Jehan Thonge, son nepveu, pareillment chevallier du dit ordre," and others, of treasonable designs to compass the death of the King by necromancy, and of entertaining a correspondence with Perkin Warbeck, and wishing for his establishment on the throne. (Vol. XXVII. p. 205.)

LETTER XCIV.

To my singuler good master, Sir Robart Plompton, kt.[a]

In my right humble wyse I recomend me unto your good mastership, and to my singuler good lady ; acertaynyng you that ther is in thes partes a great talking, of those that belong and medle

[a] We have in this letter the first intimation of the scheme hatching by the too celebrated lawyer, Empson, the infamous tool of Henry's rapacity, to oust Sir Robert Plumpton from the lands, which should have been made secure to him by the award of King Richard III. The progress of the suit will be traced with interest in the series of letters which follow, and which step by step reduced the unfortunate knight to such straits, that at the commencement of the next reign we find him a prisoner in the Counter, and depending on his son's bounty for subsistence. He had, however, the satisfaction to live to witness the tragic end of his once all-powerful adversary.

with Mr. Hemson,[b] that he intendeth to attempt matters agaynst you in the title of the heire of John Suttell.[c] Wherin he moved and brake the same unto Mr. Gascoyne,[d] of whom he had a discret and good answere, as thus. He desired my sayd Mr. Gascoyne to be favorable to him in the premysses ; and he answered to him, and sayd thus : " if your matter were against any man in " England except my uncle, I wold take your parte ; but in this ye " must have me excused," with dyvers words more concerning your honour and wele. Sir, the sayd Mr. Hemson moved this matter greatly, and maketh his frinds ; and divers that he hath broken his hart and mynd too, hath told me the same, and his saying afore,

[b] Richard Empson, esq. was chosen speaker of the House of Commons in the Parliament that met on 17 Oct. 7 Hen. VII. 1491 (*Rot. Parl. VI.* 440) ; and was one of the serjeants-at-law, chosen by act of Parliament to be feoffees for the King of his Duchy of Lancaster, 19 Hen. VII. 1503, in which year he was knighted. (*Ibid.* 522 and 537 b.)

[c] Sir John Suttell, or Sotehill, of Stoke Faston, or Stockerston, com. Leic. kt. who had married Elizabeth, grand-daughter and one of the heirs at law of Sir William Plumpton, kt. was then lately deceased, he having made his will in July 1493, and it having been proved 7 Oct. 1494. His eldest son was named Henry, and at his death a minor, as he was in ward to his mother 11 Hen. VII. 1495-6, (*History of Suffolk, p. 436, note e fol.* 1838,) the same year as the date of this Letter. Dame Elizabeth Sotehill survived to 21 September, 22 Hen. VII. 1506, when she died, leaving her twin granddaughters, her infant heirs. She and her husband were buried at Stockerston, in the south aisle of the church, the chapel of the Lords of Stockerston. " On the floor of the south aisle," says Mr. Smith, writing in the year 1747, " close by the last (monument) towards the south wall, inlaid in brass, were the figures of two persons, the man in armour, and both in a posture of prayer ; at his feet the figures of eight sons, at hers of two daughters ; inscription round the edge quite gone. Over his head, *O pater in celis, me tecum pascere velis. D'ne miserere, &c.* From her mouth a label, *Nos precibus matris salvet sapiencia patris*. Over their heads, their arms ; quarterly, 1 and 4, Sotehill ; 2 and 3, quarterly, Boyvile and Murdac, impaling, quarterly, her coat, 1 and 4, Plompton of Plompton, Ebor. ; 2 and 3, Foljambe of Kenalton, co Nott. This impalement identifies the parties ; and moreover, another manuscript recites an invocation for prayer for the soul of John Sotehill who died in 1493, which was then in glass in the same church. (*See Nichols's Leicestershire, Vol. II. p.* 823.)

[d] Sir William Gascoigne of Gokethorp, kt.

as they knew. If yt plese your mastership, to cause your loving frinds and servants to have knowledg therof. Sir, I shewed to a gentleman, that is of counsell and fee with Master Hemson, and a companyon of myne, how that Kyng Richard, in his most best tyme, and the first yere of his reigne,[e] having you not in the favor of his grace, but utterly against you, caused them to have a parte of your lands by his award and ryall power, contrary to your agrement and all right conscience ; the which I trust to God wylbe called agane. Sir, ye have many good frinds and servants, and moe, with Gods grace, shall have ; this is the matter I thinke no dout yn. Ye have a great treasour of Mr. Gascoyne. If ther be any service your mastership wyll comand me, yt shalbe done to the uttermost of my power, as knoweth our Lord, who preserve you. Written in Furnyvalls Inne, the iij day of Feb. 1496.

Your humble servant,
EI: PLOMPTON.

(3 Feb. 1496-7.)

[e] 16 Sept. 1 Ric. III. 1483. For the particulars of this award, *see Memoirs*.

LETTER XCV.

To the right worshipfull Sir William Gascoygne, Kt. deliver these.

Master Gascoygne, after most harty comenndations, pleaseth you to wyt that Richard Falbarne, late clarke to Bryan Rowclife, according to the trust put in him, hath made estate of dyvers maners, lands, and tenementes, late Sir William Plompton, in the county of Yorke[a] ; wherwith, as it is sayd, Sir Eobart Plompton taketh dyspleasure, and his servants speake such words and so

[a] The feoffment of Sir William Plompton, of Plompton, com. Ebor. kt. of his manors and lands in the counties of Nottingham, Derby, and Stafford, under which Richard Fawberg had the legal estate as surviving feoffee, was dated 1 Jun. 4 Edw. IV. 1464. The conveyance by the latter here spoken of, was made before 2 July, 15 Hen. VII. 1500, of which date is the letter of attorney to William Saucheverell and William Sanderson from Robert Bubwith, clerk, and Richard Burrow, chaplain, who claimed under it, to take seisin in their names. (*MS. Add.* 6698.)

demene them selfes, that the poor man for dread dare not apply his busines. Sir, I heare that you be frend to the sayd Sir Robart, I pray you move him that the pore man may passe his busines in Gods pease and the Kyngs, the rather at this my motion; ore that ye wyll please to send me word of his disposition, to thentent I may further doe and provide, that best may be, fore the poore mans suerty in this partie, and that I may know the sayd Sir Robart is disposition by you herein; wherby ye shall bynd me to do you good pleasures, iffe that be in me. So knoweth our Lord God, who preserve you. Fro Gascoyn,[b] the vii day of September.

     By yours verely,   RICH. EMPSON.
(7 Sept. 149–.)

[b] *Sic, sed lege* Easton, the name of the seat of Sir Richard Empson in the county of Northampton. (See *Baker's Northamptonshire, Easton-Neston.*)

LETTER XCVI.
To my master, Sir Robart Plompton, kt.

In my humble and most hartyest wyse I recomend me unto your good mastership, and to my singuler good lady. Sir, yt is so that certaine lovers and frinds of myne in London hath brought me unto the sight of a gentlewoman, a wedow of the age of xl yeres and more, and of good substance; first, she is goodly and beautyfull, womayne and wyse, as ever I knew any, none other disprie sold: of a good stocke and worshipful. Hir name is Agnes. She hath in charg but one gentlewoman to hir daughter, of xii yer age. She hath xx marc of good land within iij myle of London, and a ryall maner buylded therupon, to give or sell at hir pleasure. She hath in coyne in old nobles, c^{li}—in ryalls, c^{li}—in debts, xl^{li}—in plate, cx^{li}, with other goods of great valour; she is called worth m^{li} beside hir land. Sir, I am bold upon yor good mastership, as I have ever bene; and if yt please God and you that this matter take effect, I shalbe able to deserve althings done and past. She and I are agreed in our mynd and all one; but hir friends that she is ruled by, desireth of me xx marke jointor more then my my lands come too; and thus I answered them, saying, "that your mastership is so good master to me, that ye gave to my other wyfe xii marke for hir joyntor in Stodley Roger, and now, that it wyll please your sayd mastership to indue this woman in some lordship of yours of xx marke duryng hir lyfe, such as they shalbe pleased with: and for this my sayd frinds offer to be bounden in m^{li}." Sir, upon this they intend to know your pleasure and mynd prevely, I not knowing; wherfore, I humbly besech your good mastership, as my especyall trust is and ever hath bene above all earthly creatures, now for my great promotion and harts desire, to answer to your pleasure, and my wele and poore honesty; and I trust, or yt come to pase, to put you suertie to be discharged without any charg: for now, your good and discret answere may be my making. For, and she and I fortune by God and your meanes togyther, our too goods and substance wyll make me able to doe you good service, the which good service and I, now and at all tymes, is and shalbe yours, to joperde my life and them both. Sir, I besech your good mastership to wryte to me an answere in all hast possible, and after that ye shall here more, with Gods grace, who preserve you and yours in prosperous felicyte longtyme to endure. Wrytten in Furnywall Inne in Olborn, the ij day of March 1496.

     Your humble servant,
(2 *March* 1496-7.)   ED. PLOMPTON.

LETTER XCVII.
To my singuler good master, Sir Robart Plompton, Kt.

In my right humble wyse I recomende me unto your good mastership, and to my singuler good lady, your wyfe; and wher it hath pleased Almighty *Jesu* of his grace, by meanes of my lovers and frinds, to bryng me to the sight and acquantance of a gentlewoman in London, whose name is Agnes, late wife of Robert Drayate, gentilman, who is a woman that God hath indued with great grace and vertue. She is wyse and goodly, and of great substance, and able for a better man then I am. Notwithstanding it pleaseth, so that I myght content her frinds mynds for her joyntor of xx marke by yere that they demand of me. My answare is to them, that I have no lands but in revercion; and that yt pleaseth your good mastership to give my last wyfe xii marke by yeare out of your lands, and my especyall trust is, that it will please your mastership, for my promotion, and in especyall for my harts desir and wele, that faythfull is set upon this sayd gentlewoman, to grant and make sure to hir a jointer of xx marke yerely over all reprises, during her life. And I besech you so to do, and that the berer herof may be certayne of your mynd in the premysses, and also answere to them by your wrytting of the same. This don, incontinent after Easter I trust in *Jesu* to fynish this matter; for they demaund of me certayne lands and goods, as more at large appereth within a byll here inclosed, the which I observed in every poynt to thaccomplishment of ther pleasures. Sir, you know I have no lands, nor lyving in substaunce, but onely of you; and this hapen, I shall be more able to do your mastership service. From London, in my sayd master lodging, the x of March, 1496.

John Chasser of Lyncolnes. Your humble servant,
Sir William Chamber, Chaplaine. * ED. PLOMPTON.
Edward Chesseman.[a]
(10 *March* 1496-7.)

* The names endorsed were apparently the friends of the lady, who intended to communicate with Sir Robert Plumpton upon the proposed settlement. A plan for their mystification is curiously developed in the next epistle of Edward Plumpton.

LETTER XCVIII.
To my singuler good master, Sir Robart Plompton, Kt.

In my most humble wise I recomend me unto your good mastership, and to my especyall good lady. Sir, I sent a letter this last weke to you by James Colton, servant to Master Gascoyne, to shew to your mastership my fortune at this tyme. If your mastership be, (as I doubt no other in my mynd, nor with my words to noble men of worship, but that ye be,) my good master, the which hath, and ever shalbe, to your honour and profitt, though I have afore this bene chargable to you, now, I trust in God, as true and profitable to be, as ever I was, and much more, and able to restore and amends make of all cost done to me afore tyme. Sir, I besech you after your most discret mynd and wysdome to answere this messenger, that shall com to you for this joyntor of xx marke, both in words and in your wrytting, so that yt be to your honour, my poor honestie, and truth, and making in this world; for uppon that answere lyeth my great wele, and if yt were otherwyse, my utter undoing for ever, the which God forbyde. Yt shall cost your mastership no peny more, nor charge to you; for if your mastership say to him that ye are content, and will grant and make to him this joyntor incontinent after our marriage, when we two shall come to you, and so shew yt lovingly to the sayd messenger, and in your wrytting to them agayne, then all is done: for when I am maryed to her, thes men that now are counsellers shall bere but litle rome. And therfore, this is a matter of no charg, and to me great promotion all maner of wayes. She is amyable and good, with great wysdome and womanhead, and worth in land yerly xx marke and more, to you at hir wyll, the which, I trust in God, shalbe loving for you and yours in tyme to come for ever. Also in gold and silver, coyned and uncoyned, D^{li}, I thinke veryly, as I perceyve by hir. Beside hir lands, in all she is worth m^{li} marke and more. She hath refused for my sake many worshipfull men and of great lands; some of them hath offered to hir xl^{li} joyntor within London: notwithstanding, she is to me singuler good mystres, as after this your mastership shall know. This same day she gave to me a chayne of gold, with a crosse set with a ruby and pearles, worth xx^{li} and more. And because that ther messinger shall bryng my letter with him that they se, for I closed yt afore, to show your mastership my mynd, I besech your mastership to cause him that shall come with these lettres from my mystres and hir counsellors, to have good chere, [and that I trust to deserve,] and to send to me a bill by the same, as yt shall please you. Sir, I have sent to you ij yerds of whit dameske for a cowrenet, as good as I cold bye any, and I wold have sent much more things, save only my businesse is great. Also I have payd your fyne in the Excheker, but I take not out a discharge unto the next terme, because I purpose to get a grant more. Also I besech your mastership to shew that sayd messinger, that ye had no word from me this vi weke, and no man in your place to know from whence this berer come, lest that ther messinger shold understand of my sending. Please yt your mastership to give credence unto this berer, and let him departe or the other man come with the letters; and all such service as yt pleseth you to comand me, yt shalbe done, with Gods grace, who evermore preserve you and yours in health and honor. Wrytten in Furnywalls Inne, the 19 day of March, 1496. I humbly pray your mastership to cause the messinger to speake with my Lacy, and if hir ladyship wold send by him a token to my master, yt shall avale hir another of xx tymes the valor. Now, and my good lady wold of hir great gentlenes and noble mynd send a token, as is within wrytten, I cold never deserve yt to hir, for yt shold be to me great honesty, and the greatest that ever I had; for by your mastership and hir, I am put to more worship than ever I shold have comyn to. Sir, as I wrote in, I was purposed to have sent a fellow of myne to your mastership, but now I send this my wrytting by Preston, servant with my master Gascoyne. Pleaseth your mastership to kepe this byll, and whatsoever you doe for me in word, cost, and wrytting, yt shalbe mine, when we be maryed, to relesse and unbynd; and so I will. Sir, I besech you, pray my lady to make the messinger that shall come from my mystres good chere. I know not as yet what shall come, but as I am infirmed, a gentilman of Clementts Inne. I besech your mastership, and my good lady both, to take no displeasure with my simple wrytting this tyme, for my mynd is set so much otherwyse, that I cannot perfictly do my duty. Our Lord preserve you.

(19 *March* 1496-7.)
Your servant,
EDW. PLOMPTON.

LETTER XCIX.

To my singuler good master, Sir Robart Plompton, Kt. deliver these.

In my right humble wyse I recomend me unto your good mastership, and to my singuler good lady. Sir, I have bene at Sacombe,^{a} and had theder with me from Ware William Barloe, goodman of Christofer and William Waman, now for the tyme baly; and of thos I have bylls, of the which I sent to your master the copies, of such woods as is sold late. The maner goeth downe and decayeth, and all the houses about yt; the woods are clene destroyed and ligly to be in hast. I have given and done, as fare as I myght, in comandment and charge for further felling, and carying such as are felled and remane ther. Necessary it were, me seames, that ye made a bargan with Master Hastyngs,^{b} and it wold be. It is a fayre lordship, and yt were well gidded; it is ix myle to compasse about. Sir, I have done good ther and avantaged much wood and tymber, both as well felled as not felled, and my doings wyll stand. I have put the byers in great fere. I pray you, master, in all hast possible send to me word of your mynd in the premysses and all other, and a byll of such lands as ye are content to departe with to Kilborne^c in exchange, and if ye wyll have the *surcrortr.* Our Lord *Jesu* preserve you and all yours. From London, the xvi of February.

(16 *Feb.* 1496-7.)
Your humble servant,
EDWARD PLOMPTON.

^{a} Sacomb, com. Herts, had been a manor belonging to the family of Holt. By deed bearing date 11 Sept. 8 Hen. V. 1420, and sealed in red wax, with a seal of arms, comprising in the scochen of the same a chevron and three squereells scehine (*seiant*), Richard Holt, clerk, brother and heir of Hugh Holt, of the county of Northampton, Esq. gave the said manor, with the advowson, to Sir Robert Balthorp, Kt. together with certain lands in Staunton and Epcomp, in the same county;* to hold for life, with remainder in tail to Ralph Babthorpe his son and Katherine his wife, and the heirs of their bodies; and in default, to the right heirs of Sir Robert. Witnesses Thomas Bishop of Durham, Robert Tirwhit, John Leventhorp, John Hotoft, John Fray, and others. (*Chartul. No.* 791.)

^{b} Sir John Hastings, of Roxby, com. Ebor. kt. had married Elizabeth, or Isabel, daughter and heir of Sir Ralph Babthorp, of Babthorp, com. Ebor. kt., and in her right had possession of the manor of Sacombe, com. Hert. She dying without surviving issue, between the years 1489 and 1496, the reversion of this inheritance of the Babthorpes came to Isabel, daughter and heir of the next brother of Sir Ralph Babthorpe, called Robert in the pedigree, after the death of Sir John Hastings, who was tenant by the curtesy of England. This lady was contracted to marry William, eldest son of Sir Robert Plompton, 11 May, 11 Hen. VII. 1496, before the ensuing feast of St. Michael, she being then under seventeen years of age and in ward to her uncle, William Babthorp of Osgodby, com. Ebor. esq. (*Chartul. No.* 781.) The object of the visit of Edward Plumpton was therefore to prevent waste on the part of Sir John Hastings, which would be prejudicial to his young master, the expectant heir in right of his wife.

^{c} Thomas Kylborne, yeoman, sold some property in Plumpton to Sir Robert Plumpton and William Plumpton his son 28 Jan. 17 Hen. VII. 1501-2. (*Chartul. No.* 806.)

* Standon-wood, in the parish of Sacomb, is marked on the Ordnance Map, but Epcomp is a name that nowhere appears; though I find in the nvaluable record of Domesday *Seuechampe, Stuochampa,* and *Thepecampe,* all there noticed. The change of the second name to Staunton or Standon is a curious instance of the corruption of orthography. To the historians of Hertfordshire, Standon, Epcomp, and even the armorial bearings of the family of Holt, appear to have been alike unknown. Holt of Aston, near Birmingham, had the squirrel for a crest.

LETTER C.

To Sir Richard Plompton, Chapleyn, at Idell.

Sir, as hartylie as I can, I commaund me unto you; and within a box to my Lady, to whom I pray you I may be recommended as hir servant, is the fest of *Nomen Jesu* with *Utas,* and also the fest of the Transfiguration,^{a} that ye desired me to send to you. As for the price of them, ye and I shall agree at our next cominge togither. I doubt not ye know that the *venire facias* againe Ellis of York^b com not according to our comunicacion; I wold it com up servid any wyse this terme. Sir, with Bryan Pullen of Gawkthorp I send a letter to my master and yours of all the . . . . . . about the matter here at London agrine Babthorpe,^{c} as that none other way wold be in any wise; but the *venire facias* com in served by one Thomas Rokeby, servant to Mr. Constable

^{a} The feast of the Holy Name of Jesus was kept on the seventh of August, and that of the Transfiguration on the sixth, the former being solemnized with an octave or Utas. Manuscripts containing the office of the Church appointed for each feast were doubtless what were sent to the chaplain by the writer of the Letter.

^{b} John Ellis of York. (*See Letter* CII.)

^{c} Notwithstanding the terms of the agreement made between Sir Robert Plumpton and William Babthorpe of Osgodby, when the marriage of Isabel Babthorpe was the Servant.^d The copie of the retorne and panell I send to you inclosed herin for more surtie, as tother letter is delivered. Sir, to speake of the labor I maide to the contrary, I have written the circumstance therof in my master letter, and surelye it was to the uttermost of all my power. It is so now, I understand, they will have a *habeas corpora* againe the Jurrours *retornable octabis Trinitatis*, so that they may have a distres with a *nisi prius* againe Lammas Assise.^e Therfore, Sir, betwen you and my lady ye must cause speciall labor to be made, so it be downe prevely, to such of the Jurrours, as ye trust wilbe made frindly in the cause. Sir, in the box is a bonet of velvet for . . . . . . Mawlevery^f according to my Ladies infirmacion; the price therof is x^s. viii^d. so that I layd dowen xx^d more then my Lady toke to me for beyng therof. Also, trussed to the same box is a dagger to Mr. Pole,

contracted for, whereby provision was made for assuring to the latter and his heirs, " all those lands, tenements, and hereditaments with their appurtenances in the parish of Hemingburgh, Midleton-upon-the-Would, North Cave, Hundsley, Loftsome, and Wistow in the county of York, and in Colby in the county of Lincoln, with their appurtenances, as also certain closes in Selby called the Flates, in satisfaction of all those lands, tenements, and hereditaments with their appurtenances which wear or be intailed to any of the name of Babthorp, his anchestors, or to the heire male of any of their bodies, without let or interruption of the said William Plompton and Isabell, or any other son of the said Sir Robert, husband to the said Isabell, and theire of the said Isabell, for ever;" it appears that now William Plumpton and his wife sought to dispossess Babthorpe of these lands in right of her claim as heir general. The father and son were thus singularly circumstanced; the right to the estates of the one depending upon his making good his title as heir special, and to his wife's inheritance of the other, upon his proving that there was no bar to the descent to heirs general.

^d Robert Constable, Serjeant-at-law. Joan, his daughter and heir, married Thomas Rokeby, of Mortham, com. Ebor. esq.

^e Lammas Assize was the assize held in the months of August and September.

^f Mrs. Mauleverer was the eldest daughter of Sir Robert and Dame Agnes Plumpton.

according to his mynd; I pray you show to him it cost viii^d more then his money. As for the *subpena*, with all other matters that longeth to my master and yours, they shalbe send with the next trusty messenger that cometh home. And thus *Jesu* be your preserver. From Lyncolns Inne, at London, this munday next afore Candlemas day.^g

(28 *Jan.* 1498-9.)

^g John Pullan was the writer of this letter; the subscription has been accidentally omitted in the MS. (*See next Letter.*)

LETTER CI.

To his especyall good master Sir Robart Plompton, knight, at Idell, in hast.

Sir, please yt your mastership to understand that I sent a letter to you with Bryan Pullan of Gawkthorp of all the cyrcumstance of the matter betwene my master and your son and his wyfe, and William Babthorp; and as that none ther wold be. But the *venyre facias* com in servid. Sir, so yt is now that suerly they intend to have a *habeas corpora* agayn the Jurrours with a *nisi prius* this next assise in Lent, at Yorke. Therfore, Sir, ye must make special frynds to the Jurrours, that they may be labored specially, to such as ye trust wylbe made frindly in the cause. Sir, I have letten Mr. Kyngesmell^a see the dede of gift of the chaunchry of Elton,^b and shewed to him as your mastership presented in after the deith of the last Incumbent, which presentee was

^a Master John Kingsmill, Serjeant, called 10 Sept. 1496.

^b Chantry in the chapel of St. Margaret at Elton, com. Derb.

in by the space of iiii or v dayes at the least, and desired of hym to have his best counsell. And he answered to me thus; that *subpena* lay not properly in the case: but the best remedy for your Incumbent was to have assise at the common law, if any land belonged to the sayd Chaunchre. And if he had no land, then to have a spoliacion in the spirituall court agaynst the preyst that now occupyeth, because he is one disturber, or els to suy a *quare Impedit* at the comon law. And so is to take no *subpena*. And for these causes I rest to know your pleasure . . . . wryting. Sir, as for the *subpena* agaynst Sir John Hastyngs, I shall remember it. The accion of wast agaynst Sir John Hastings goeth forward, as fast as the law wyll serve. And if ther be any other service to doe, it shalbe done to all my power, with Gods grace, who be your preservor. From Lyncolns Inn at London, this tuesday next Candlemas day.

Your servant and bedman,

(29 *Jan.* 1498-9.)   JOHN PULLAN.

LETTER CII.

To my worshipfull master, Sir Robart Plompton, kt.

After due recomendations, please yt your mastership to understand that of late I was at Yorke, wher I understand ye have an accion hanging against myne host, John Ellis of Yorke, wherof I am right sory, for the good hart I bere to him, that he shold myscontent your mastership and give you cause of accion. Neverthelesse, Sir, I have broken my mynd, and he is not that man that wold displease your mastership in no wyse, nor troble you in any matter; and for any fault, whatsoever yt be, abyde your owne judgment and award in every poynt, and be corrected in all causes after your owne mynd, if yt please your mastership so to take him.

And over this, he shall come to your mastership and submyt himself according to his duety, as yt is abovesayd. And, Sir, if your mastership be thus content, I trust ye will se him have fre lyberty in comyng and goyng, and if yt please your mastership to be thus content, and that I come with him to you, I trust to God he shall so deserve at his departure, ye shall have cause to be his good master. And so as I may, I besech you to be, upon this humble submyssion, for I have advysed him so to doe, the which he is right glad and aplyable, and thus our blessed Lord ever preserve you. Wrytten at Harwood, the Sunday after Candlemasse day; and by this bringer I besech your mastership I may know your good mynd.

Your loving servant,

(3 *Feb.* 1498-9.)   THOMAS LYSTER.

LETTER CIII.

To his Right worshipful master, Sir Robert Plompton, kt. be this delivered.

Right worshipful Sir, I recomend me to you. By your letter I understand William Babthorp will have a *nisi prius* at this next assizes. Sir, it is necessary for you to get a copy of the panel, and then to enquire if any of them or of their wyfes be sybb or allied to Wil. Babthorp, and yf any cause in them bee wherby they may be chalenged. And also to make labor to them that they appeare not, or els to be favorable to you according to right, and enform them of the matter as wel as ye can for their consciences. Sir, for Mr. Kingsmel, it were wel doon that he were with you, for his auctority and worship; for he may speke more plainly in the matter than any counsel in this country will, for he knowes the crafty labor that hath been made in this matter, and also he will not let for no maugre. And yf the enquest passe against you, he may shew you summ comfortable remedy, for I suppose with good counsell you may have remedy; but, Sir, his coming wilbe costly to you. Sir, I purpose with the grace of God to be at Knaresburg upon tewsday next coming, and if ye be there or any for you, I shall shew you more of my mind. No more, but God preserve you and further treweth. Written the 12 day of february.

By your servant at litle power,

(12 *Feb.* 1498-9.) WILLIAM ELESON.[a]

[a] William Eleson of Selby, com. Ebor. esq. son of John Elson who died 14 . .-1509, and has a monumental inscription in the abbey.—(*Burton. Mon. Ebor. p.* 410.) He afterwards married a daughter of Sir Robert Plumpton.

LETTER CIV.

To his right worshipfull master, Sir Robart Plompton, kt.

Right worshipfull Sir, I comend me to you. Sir, this day I receyved your letter, by the which ye desyred me to be at Helagh[a] upon Myghellmas even. Sir, that day I may not keepe, for I must then be at Malton for my lord Clifford,[b] for keeping of his court; but if it please you to send to Mr. Babthorppe, which is yet at Dighton,[c] to appoynt fryday or satterday before Myghellmas day, or fryday or satterday next after Myghellmas, I shall then attend of you, with the grace of God. And of the day that ye appoynt, I pray ye send me word by my servant. Sir, I pray you

[a] Healaugh, a parish town in the Ainsty, com. Ebor.
[b] Henry Lord Clifford and Westmoreland, inherited Malton, com. Ebor. from his mother Margaret, daughter and coheir of Henry Bromflete, Baron Vescy.
[c] Kirk-Dighton, near Plumpton.

hold me excused of the breaking of my promyse, for I was vij nyghts from home more then I weut I shold have bene when I rodde forth. And thus God preserve you. Wrytten at Selby the Wedensday.

By your servant,

WILLIAM ELESON.

LETTER CV.

To my right worshipfull Master, Sir Robart Plompton, kt.

Right honorable Sir, I humbly recomend me unto your mastership. Please yt your mastership, I wold be right glad that ye wold have a comynyng with my master in such matters as in parte I have shewed you, Sir. Sir, I have so spoken to my master, if ye please to be at Poumfrett on Munday, ther and then my master will meet you, and ther your mastership to know in those ye wilbe content; and or els your mastership will pardon me the reversion of Kirkbe,[a] and I wyll abyde with my master, Sir John Hastyngs.[b] Sir, I thinke, if ye please your mastership, I have desarved a dobellett in laboring him to showe your mastership pleasure. No more to you at this tyme, but *Jesu* have you in his proteccion. Wrytten at Watterton, on Wedensday after St. Edward day.

By your servant,

(20 *Mar.* 1499.) JOHN TAYLOR.

[a] Kirkby-Wharfe, a parish town in the liberties of St. Peter and of Pontefract. Sir Ralph Babthorp, father of Dame Isabel Hastings, died seised *inter alia* of two messuages and forty acres of land in Kirkby, held of the King as of his duchy of Lancaster. (*Esc.* 5 *Hen. VII.*) With Waterton it was at this date held in dower by Margaret, widow of Sir Ralph Babthorp.
[b] Sir John Hastings, kt. was deceased before 16 Nov. 20 Hen. VII. 1504, when by their deed of that date William Plompton, esq. and Isabel his wife bestowed the office of bailiff of their manor of Savacum, com. Hert. on Edward Oglethorp. (*Chartul. No.* 823.)

LETTER CVI.

To the right worshipfull Sir Robart Plompton, kt. delyver these.

Right worshipfull Sir, in my best maner I lowly recomend me to you, hartely desiring your welfare, thanking you of the patience that ye sufferred at my poore place, I being from home. God give me grace once to see you ther againe, that I may make you better chere and doe you sume pleasure. Moreover, Sir, it pleased you to write to me of a gentlewoman for my son; [a] Sir, God give me grace to deserve it, and I thank you hartely that it pleased you so lovingly to remember both him and me. Sir, her frinds bene worshipfull, and I am a poore gentleman. Well I wotte they will learne, whosoever they medle withall, what landes and substance he is of. I am willing to depart with him in lands and in goods, as he may lyve, so that I may have, according to reason, money; or els lands, and to give money. And, Sir, I am moved in a place of worship and have made promyse to see a gentlewoman. Howbeit, lyke as I doe, ye shall have knowledg, and shalbe glad to be moved and counsell by you, trystyng ye will be good master and lover to me. And thus *Jesu* preserve you. At Gotham in hast, scribbled with the hand of your owne at my litle powre

JOHN SAINT ANDREW.[a]

[a] John Saint Andrew of Gotham, com. Nott. esq. the writer of this letter, was succeeded by a son of the name of William, who married Margaret, daughter of John Aston of Haywood, com. Stafford, esq. by his wife Elizabeth Delves, on or before 16 Hen. VII. 1500-1. (*Thoroton's Notts.* 4to. 1797, vol. i. p. 40, *and Clifford's Tixall, p.* 147.) This letter of the father for his son's disposal in marriage, shows how absolutely a matter of bargain all such contracts were. Here, there is a question between two gentlewomen, and the father has no objection to two strings to his bow; so that the friends of the one are to be made acquainted with the offers of the friends of the other gentlewoman, and then I presume the highest bidder would be sure to speed best.

LETTER CVII.

To my right worshipfull master, Sir Robart Plompton, kt.

After due recomendations to your good mastership and hartely desire of your welfare, for which of duty I am ever bound to pray for, and sithe I hard say that a servant of yours was deceased of the sicknes, which hath bene to your disease, I am right sory therfore.[a] Wherfore I wold advise your mastership, my lady, and all your houshold many,[b] from henceforth to make promyse, and keepe yt, to fast the even of St. Oswald;[c] kyng and marter, yerely; and that promise truly entended to be performed, I trust verely ye shalbe no more vexed with that sicknes. And thus the Most Mighty preserve yow and yours, this fest of Exaltacion of the holy ghost (*sic, sed lege* Cross).

(14 *Sept.* 1499.) Your servant ROBART LEVENTHORPE.[d]

[a] This and the following letter were apparently written in the year of the great plague in England, 15 Hen. VII. 1499.
[b] Many, meny, or meiny, a family. (*See Hallamshire Glossary, by Rev. J. Hunter, App. p.* 155.)
[c] The feast of St. Oswald was kept on the fourth of August.
[d] Robert Leventhorpe of Leventhorpe-Hall, in the parish of Swillington, com. Ebor. esq.

LETTER CVIII.

To his right worshipfull father, Sir Robart Plompton, kt. be these delivered in most godly hast.

Right honorable and worshipfull father and mother,[a] in the most

[a] German Pole, the writer of this letter, married Anne, daughter of Sir Robert Plumpton, in the lifetime of his grandmother Elizabeth Pole, who was a party to a pair of indentures between her and Sir Robert Litton, kt. bearing date 28 Nov. 10 Hen. VII. 1495; for the fulfilment of the articles of which contract, she gave bond to Sir Robert Plumpton, kt. 28 Aug. 15 Hen. VII. 1499. (*Chartul. No.* 797.) A subsequent letter, written by her to Sir Robert Plumpton, indicates that these indentures

lowliest wyse that I can, I mekely recomend me unto you, desiring to here of your welfare and prosperitie, the which I pray almyghty *Jesu* long to continue to his pleasure, and to your most joy, and comfort, and harts ease. Also, father, my brother William [b] hartely and mekely recomendeth him unto you, and unto my lady my mother, desiring you of your dayly blessing. And I allso lowly pray you of your dayly blessing, the which is as glad unto me, as unto any child that you have, for I have no other father [c] but you, nor no other mother but my lady; for my speciall trust is in you. Therefore I pray you take me as your poore son; a beadman for my prayer you shall wyt I life. Sir, if it pleaseth you to know that a munday my brother was at Thornton brygge,[d] and I were; all, blessed be almyghty *Jesu*, be in gud health. And my sister Margaret,[e] and my wife, and my sister Elinor [f] lowly recomend them unto you and unto my lady, praying you of your daly blessing, the which is better unto them then any worldly goods. Veryly, Sir, Master Nevell nor Mrs. Nevell,[g] neither of them was at home; but his brother was at home, and he made us very great chere as myght be. Also, Sir, I am very sory that the death seaseth not at Plompton, but I trust to almyghty *Jesu* that his

had reference to an assignment of lands in jointure to her grandson, German Pole, and his wife, Anne Plumpton. *(Vide postea, Letter CXXVIII.)* The bond was probably signed about the time of the consummation of her son's marriage, and I ascribe this letter to the same year, 1499, from the mention made of the pestilence at Plumpton.

[b] William Plumpton, eldest son of Sir Robert Plumpton.

[c] John Pole of Redburn, com. Derb. was the father of German Pole; he, as well as his wife Jane, daughter of John Fitzherbert of Etwall, com. Derb. esq. died in the lifetime of Ralph Pole, the grandfather of the writer, before 7 Hen. VII. Their marriage covenant bore date 14 Aug. 13 Edw. IV. 1473, and German Pole their son was aged nine years 25 July, 8 Hen. VII. 1492. *(Esc. 8 Hen. VII. n. 23.)*

[d] Thornton-bridge, in the parish of Topcliffe.

[e] Margaret Plumpton, married in the following year to Arthur Eyre, esq.

[f] Eleanor Plumpton. *(See the letters concerning her marriage, postea.)*

[g] Ralph Nevill of Thornton-bridge, esq. and Ann his wife, daughter of Sir Christopher Ward of Givendale, com. Ebor. kt. John Nevill was his brother.

great mercy and grace (*some words are here omitted*) send to my lady hir joy and comforth, and to all your frinds, as my daly prayer shalbe therfore. Sir, the cause of my wryting is but to heare of your gud welfare, the which is to me great joy and comforth. And, Sir, I lowly pray you and my lady, my mother, to take this letter in good parte, for it is wrytten hastyly with my own hand, and without the 'vise of any other body; for I trow you had rather have it of my owne hand, then of another bodyes. Also, Sir, John Tynderley [h] recomendeth him unto you and unto my lady, my mother, gladly willing to heare of your welfare. No more unto you, good father, nor mother, at this tyme, but pray the holy Trenytie to have you in his blessed keepinge.

Your good son and beadchild,

(*anno circiter* 1499.)   GERMAN POLE.

[h] He was probably owner of the house at Ripon, under whose roof the younger branches of the family of Plumpton had sought a shelter from the plague, then raging in the vicinity of their own home.

LETTER CIX.

To my right worshipfull brother, Sir Robart Plompton, kt. this byll be delivered.

Right worshipfull brother, I recomend me unto you, and to my lady, and also to my daughter and yours,[a] with all my other yong cousins, desiring hartely to here of your welfaire and theres both, which I besech *Jesu* preserve unto his pleasure and your harts comforth, ever thanking you, and my lady both, of the great worshipe and gud chere, that I and my frinds had at my last beyng with you. Brother, yt is so that your farward, Christofer Law, is departed of this word and hath left behind him a wyfe and vii

[a] Margaret Plumpton, who was at this date contracted to marry the eldest son of the writer. *(See Letter CXI. postea.)*

smale children, wherfor I hartely pray you to be gud master unto hir, so that she might have hir farme, and the rather for my prayer. And if it please you, when your servants come over in this contry, that they will have my mynd in the letting of the sayd house; and I trust to take such wayes therin, as shalbe for your worship and profit both, as *Jesu* knoweth, who ever preserve you. At Padley the tewsday next afore St. Luke day [b] in hast.

Your loving brother,

(15 *Oct.* 1499.)   ROBART EYRE.

[b] 18 Oct.

LETTER CX.

To his especyall good master, Sir Robart Plompton, knight, be these delivered.

Right worshipfull Sir, I recomend me unto your mastership. Sir, laytly I sent wryting to my father to convey to you, which I trust be comes to your hands afore this tyme; in which wryting is conteyned how the Justices of the Common Place awarded a new *venire facias* betwyxt my master, your son, and Wylliam Babthorpp; and also in a lytle byll therin, is contayned the names of such persones as the sayd Wylliam Babthorpp entended to have had reconnyd in the first *venire facias*. I wold your mastership made specyall labor to have one indefferent pannell of the Coroners; they must be labored by sum frynd of yours. Sir, the proces in thaccion of West goeth forward, as fast as the law wyll serve. Sir, I receved two letters from you with xxvi[s] viij[d], and all such copies, as was conteyned in your wryting. Sir, so yt was that Parkin Warbek and other iij were arreyned, on satterday next before the making herof, in the Whithall at Westmynster for ther offences, afore Sir John Sygly, knight marshall, and Sir John Trobilfeild; and ther they all were attended, and judgment given

that they shold be drawn on hirdills from the Tower, throwout London, to the Tyburne, and ther to be hanged, and cutt down quicke, and ther bowells to be taken out and burned: ther heads to be stricke of, and quartered, ther heads and quarters to be disposed at the Kyngs pleasure.[a] And on munday next after, at the Gildhalle in London wher the Judges, and many other knyghts, commysioners to inquer and determayn all offences and trespasses; and theder from the Tower was brought viij presoners, which were indited, and parte of theme confessed themselfe gyltie, and other parte were arreyned: and as yet they be not juged.[b] I thinke the shall have Judgement this next fryday. Sir, this present day [c] was new barresses made in Westmynster hall, and thether was brought Therle of Warwek, and arrened afore Therle of Oxford, being the Kyngs grace comyssioner, and afore other Lords, (bycause he is a pere of the Realme) whos names followeth ;[d] the Duke of Bokingham, Therle of Northumberland, Therle of Kent, Therle of Surrey, Therle of Essex, the lord Burgenny, lord Or-

[a] "Anno Domini M.iiiicxcix. In thys yere, the xvi day of November, was areyned in the Whyte Hall at Westmynster the forenamed Parkyn and iii other," is the simple advertisement of Fabyan. Hall has, "and so he, beyng repulsed and put backe from all hope and good lucke with all hys complice and confederates, and Jhon Awater, sometyme Mayor of Corffe in Ireland, one of hys founders and hys sonne, were the sixten day of Novembre arreyned and condempned at Westminster." Hall here uses the word founders apparently in the sense of fautors, i. e. partisans, but the names of the father and son conjointly arraigned with Perkyn Warbeck are unrecorded. As the trial was before Sir John Sely, Knight Marshal, and Sir John Turbervile, Marshal of the Marshalsea (*Rot. Parl. vi.* 367), the offences charged must have been the attempt to break out of the King's ward, and treasonable practises committed out of the Realm.

[b] These were Astwood, Bluet, and others, who had assisted Perkyn Warbeck in making his escape. The day of their trial was Monday Nov. 18.

[c] Thursday 21 Nov. 1499.

[d] In the MS. this list of the Peers who sat in judgment upon the Earl of Warwick is very incorrectly copied: thus, in the names Deyngham, Daubeney, and Dacre, the initial letter is changed into a B, and for Zowch we read Rowch.

mond, lord Deyngham, lord Broke, lord of Saynt Johns,[e] lord Latymer, lord De la Warre, lord Mountioy, lord Daubeney, lord Hastings, lord Barns, lord Zowch, lord Sentmound,[f] lord Willughby, lord Grey of Wylton, and lord Dacre. And ther Therle of Warweke confessed thenditments that were layd to his charge, and like Judgment was given of him, as is afore rehersed. When thes persones shalbe put in execution I intend to shew to your mastership right shortly; and give credence unto this berrer. From Lyncolns Inne at London, this xxi day of November. By your servant and bedman,

(21 *Nov.* 1499.)   JOHN PULLAN.

[e] This title of Lord of Saynt Johns must be intended to designate the Prior of St. John's, as there was no other Lord of Parliament bearing the title at this period. As a military order, the knights of St. John were not, it seems, affected by the usual restriction upon ecclesiastics against deciding upon matters of blood.

[f] Richard Beauchamp, Lord St. Amand, corruptly written Sentmound. (*Vide Rot. Parl.* vi. 245 *b*, 273 *b*.)

LETTER CXI.

To my right worshipfull brother, Sir Robart Plompton, kt. these be delivered.

Right worshipfull Brother, I recomend me unto you, and to my lady your wyfe, and to my daughter and to yours, with all my other cousins your childred, desiring to heare of your welfarie and thers both, which I besech *Jesu* preserve unto your most harts comforth; evermore thanking you and my gud lady, your wyfe, of the great and worshipful chere I and my kynsmen had with you. Brother, ye be remembred how the writings of the covnaunte of marage of my son and your daughter, as it be not made upp by the 'vise of learned counsell; wherfore, if it please you to apoynt any day, and please about the beginyng of Lenten, when that I myght wayt uppon you, I wilbe glad to wayt upon you, and

a learned man with me: and all such promyse as I have made on my party shalbe well and trewly performed, with the grace of *Jesu*, for ye shall find me ever one man. Also, brother, I pray you that ye wold send me by my servant, William Bewott, this bringer, the payment which I shold have of you att Candlemas last past, for I have put myselfe unto more charge, since I was with you, then I had before.[a] For I have maryed another of my daughters, and I have begon to make a wall about my parke that I shewed you I was mynded to do, which, I trust, when ye see it, ye will like it well. Praying you not to fale herin, as my trust is in you, and to give credence to this bringer. No more but *Jesu* preserve you. Written at Padley on St. Valentyne day with the hand of your brother,

(14 *Feb.* anno 1499-1500.)   ROBART EYR.

[a] Robert Eyre of Padley, com. Derb. esq. had covenanted to grant the marriage of his eldest son, Arthur Eyre, to Sir Robert Plumpton, kt. for 250 marks; he to be matched with Sir Robert's daughter, Margaret, for whose keep fifty shillings were to be henceforth allowed out of each instalment. A receipt for twenty marks, parcel of this sum, bears date 4 Aug. 15 Hen. VII. 1500. (*Chartul. No.* 800.)

LETTER CXII.

To my right worshipfull Cousin, Sir Robart Plompton, Knyght.

Right worshipfull Cousin, I hartyly recomend me unto you, desiring you to send me my letter John Talloyr delyvered you. Please yt you to do soe much for me in this terme, to leyn me and send unto me by this berrer, James Potsay, v marke. I by this wrytting, faythfully I promise you to content and pay you the sayd v markes by the date of this my bill at Mighellmas the next; and for that deflaut, I clearly dyscharg me, and ye to have all my lands and rents at Kyrby uppon Wharfe for ever. And also I desire you to take credence unto this berer which knowes my mynd;

and also this letter may recomend me unto my lady your wyfe. And evermore fare ye well, the xxx[t] day of August.

Your kinsman,

ROBART HASTINGS.[a]

[a] Robert Hastings, esq. and William Dalyson of Laghton in Lindsay, com. Linc. gent. submitted their differences to the arbitration of Sir Robert Plumpton, Sir John Hastings, knights, and Nicholas Mydleton, esq. 23 Sept. 13 Hen. VII. 1497. (*Chartul. No.* 790.) He was probably a younger brother of Sir John Hastings, who under Dame Margaret Babthorpe had acquired lands and rents at Kirby-Wharf.

LETTER CXIII.

To the right wyrshypful Sir Robert Plompton, kt. in hast.

Right wyrshipful Sir, and my special good mastre, after dew recomendations had, I hartily thank your good mastership that it wold please you to cause mee to bee praied for. I beseeche Almighty God that I may live to do you such service therfore, as may contente your mastership. I received your letter by Mr. Sygskyke, clerk, and 2 ryals closed therin; and according to your commandement I have retained in the Exchequer, by the advice of Mr. Blakewall, Mr. Denny;[a] in the Chauncery, Porter, and given unto them ther fees. I have delivered all your letters, and from Mr. Blakwall, I trust, ye have answer by one of Mr. Gascoygne servants. And also for all things compresed in your first letter that I received by John Wadd, as touching any accion to be taken agenst you, or any *diem clausit extremum* for any office to be founde, I shall doe therin as much as lyeth in my power, that your mastership may have knowledg therof. If ther be any such wryt made, yt must be in Porters office, and he hath promysed me that ther shall none passe, but he shall give me knowledg therof; and if ther come any *Inquizicio virtute officii*, it must come into the office, wherat Mr. Deene is dayly: wherfore, I trust to

[a] Edmund Denny, made fourth Baron of the Exchequer 6 May 1514.

God that your mastership shall have knowledg, if any such things fortune. They have made search in the Escheker for the perdon that was pleded, suppose the title had bene made therin as here to Sir William, and when they saw that it was by feffment, they were not well content. The names that are in the byll for to be schereff; *Not: and Derb:* Sir Ralfe Langford,[b] Ormound,[c] and Such;[d] *Yorkshire*, Sir William Bulmer,[e] Sir William Engelby,[f] and Sir W. Griffith.[g] Sir Humfrey Stanley[h] labors to be Schereffe in Staffordshire: herof I shall acertan you, as sonne as the byll cometh from the King. I have receyved from your mastership xl[s]; at the end of this terme, I shall send you a byll of all the matters of this terme; and as for the accion which procedeth against Sir John Hastyngs, I shall contynue yt to the next terme, by the grace of God, who ever kepe you and yours. From London, with the hand of your servant, the x day of November.

GEORG EMERSON.

Sir, also yt was shewed unto me by one Master Newdigate, that thes names for *Not: and Derb:* were put in the byll by the labor of the sayd Master Newdigate,[i] at the request and desire of Sir William Meryngs heire.[k] And yt please your mastership, me semes that yt were well done to send unto Mr Meryng, to know wheder he wilbe frindly in thes matters or no; and if he may doe any thing with the above named personnes.

(10 *Nov.* 1500.)

[b] Sir Ralph Langford, of Longford, com. Derb. kt.
[c] John Ormond, of Alfreton, com. Derb. esq. obiit 1507.
[d] William Zouche, of Morley, com. Derb. esq.
[e] Sir William Bulmer, of Wilton, com. Ebor. kt.
[f] Sir William Ingilby, of Ripley, com. Ebor. kt.
[g] Sir Walter Griffith, of Burton Agnes, com. Ebor. kt.
[h] Sir Humphrey Stanley, of Pipe, com. Staff. kt.
[i] John Newdigate, called Serjeant, 18 Nov. 1511.
[k] Sir William Mering, of Mering, com. Nott. kt.

LETTER CXIV.

To his right worshipfull and especyall good master, Sir Robart Plompton, knight, be these delivered in hast.

Right worshipfull Sir and my especial good master, with due recomendation, please yt your mastership to understand that Master Gryffith is Schereffe of Yorkshir,[a] Sir Ralfe Longford of Not. and Derby,[b] and John caston[c] (*lege* Aston) of Stauforthshire; and as for the Eshetours, in Staffordshire as yet, as fare as I know, is non. Ralfe Sauchevereth of Hopwell[d] is Eschetour of Notinghamshire and Derby, and as farre as I understand, W[m] Crowch, that was Custymer of Hull, is Eschetor of Yorkshire. My lord of Carlele[e] hath authorytie to make Eschetor ther; and as fare as I know, or can learne, the sayd Crowch occupieth still ther. And as yet, as fare as I can understand, ther is noe office found, nor as yet reconed, nether into the Chaunchry, nor yet into the Eschequer, after the death of my master your father. I shall lye in awayte, as much as I can, therfore. I pled for your mastership x yere agoo a Perdon for Wolfe-hunt lands about Maunsefeild in Shirwood;[f] by which plee ye clamed the land by fefement of my master, yore father. A gentilman, that is of counsell with Master Empson, enquered for the same plee and saw yt; and was sory that ye had not clamed the saide land as son and heire. Other tydings ther be none, but that make you redy; for suerly, as farre as I know, Master Empson will in hand with you this yere, and as farre as I can know, by assise. And I besech you, that I may

[a] Sir Walter Griffith, High Sheriff of Yorkshire in 1501.
[b] Sir Ralph Longford, High Sheriff of Nott. and Derb. in 1501.
[c] John Aston, esq. High Sheriff of Staffordshire in 1501, afterwards Sir John Aston, kt.
[d] Ralph Saucheverell, of Hopwell, com. Derb. esq.
[e] William Sewer, Bishop of Carlisle and Abbot of St. Mary, York.
[f] Perdon, i. e. *per donum*, by which plea the land was claimed under a gift special. (*See Letters LXIII. and LXIV.*)

be recomended to my good lady, my lady your wyfe, with Master Pole[g] and my mystres his wyfe. My master[h] recomendeth him to you and prayeth you to remember his l marc now, for he sath that he hath nede therof. And *Jesu* preserve you. From London, in great hast, as apeareth, the xvi day November.

Your servant, ROBERT BLAKWALL.[i]
(16 *Nov.* 1500.)

[g] German Pole, son-in-law of Sir Robert Plompton.
[h] Robert Lytton, esq. Under Treasurer of England in 1493, afterwards Sir Robert Lytton, kt. is probably here indicated by "my master:" the debt was owing for the marriage of the daughter of Sir Robert Lytton to German Pole in 1495, in which contract Sir Robert Lytton had an interest. (*See Letter CVIII. note* [a].)
[i] The name of Sir Robert Blackwall, clerk, is found among those appointed to be receivers of petitions in the Parliaments 1 Richard III. 7, 11, 12, and 19 Henry VII. (*See Letters LXIV, note* [c], *and LXX, note* [a].)

LETTER CXV.

To my hartyly beloved Brother, Sir Robart Plompton, knyght.

Brother, I recomend me unto you. This Sunday my nephew Sir William Gascoygne is ryden from home towards Colyweston,[a] and whether further or nay I know not; howbeit, I trow better, he had not. Brother, he desired me to wrytt unto you, praying that ye wille content unto this bringer, my Cousin Robart Hastings, iiij mark and xxd. now dew unto him at this Martymasse last, which is right gredy therupon, and gladly my nephew wold he were content. If ye wold any thing to London, send me word; that I can, for I thinke I send one right shortly after my nephew. Thus farewell. At Gaukthorp, this Sunday.

Your owne at his power,
JOHN GASCON.[b]

[a] Coly-Weston, com. Northampton, where the King's mother resided.
[b] John Gascoigne, esq. brother to Dame Agnes Plumpton, wife of Sir Robert Plumpton, kt. and uncle to Sir William Gascoigne, of Gokethorp, com. Ebor. kt. from whom see next Letter.

LETTER CXVI.

To my Uncle Plompton, be thes delivered.

Uncle Plompton, I comennd me unto you. And where I should have bene with you to morow at Selbie, in good fayth it is so that I was yesterday so crased and sicke that I kept my bedd all day, and this day I am not of power to goe, nor ride as yet. And also there is with me my uncle Ward,[a] Thomas Lawrance,[b] Ralfe Nevell,[c] and others; but that notwithstanding, if I had my health, I should be with you. And if ye cannot conclud tomorrow, appoynt a new day, and I shalbe glad to be with you with grace of *Jesus*, who ever keepe you. Scribbled at Gaukthorp, this fryday in hast.

Your nepho,
WILLIAM GASCOYGNE.

[a] Sir Christopher Ward, kt. of Givendale, com. Ebor. He married Margaret daughter of Sir William Gascoigne, kt. sister to Dame Agnes Plumpton, and aunt to the writer of this Letter. He died 14 Hen. VIII. (*Esc.* 14 *H.* 8. *n.* 68.)
[b] Thomas Lawrence, son-in-law of Sir Christopher Ward. By his wife Margaret he had no issue.
[c] Ralph Nevill of Thornton-bridge, com. Ebor. esq. married Anne, another daughter of Sir Christopher Ward, kt.; both were deceased before 14 Hen. VIII. (*Esc. ubi supra.*)

LETTER CXVII.

To his worshipfull Uncle, Sir Robart Plompton, kt. deliver these.

Right worshipful Uncle, I comennd me unto you, praying you to send me all such evidence, as ye have concernyng any lands or tenements in Tokwith;[a] so that I may have them at Tadcaster this nyght, for the matter is in communication there: and the sayd evidence shalbe safly kept for you, as knoweth Almyghtie

[a] Tockwith (Ainsty) parish of Bilton, com. Ebor.

Jesu, who evermore preserve you. Written at Tadcaster this fryday.

Your nepho,
WILLIAM GASCOYGNE.

LETTER CXVIII.

To the worshipfull Sir Robart Plompton, kt. deliver these.

Right worshipfull Sir, and my especiall good master, after due recomendations had, I hartyly thanke your mastership for many great things done for me afore this, beseching Almighty God that I may doe your mastership some service therfore. I receyved your letter by George Crose, and as for all your great matters, as yet nothings sayd; yet yt is shewed me that they purpose suerly to have an assise this somer. Wherfore I trust your mastership doth provide for the best remedy, which after my mynd is to make many frinds and of the best. I send unto your mastership closed in this box the sawar[a] for the Inditement, according to your comandement, which is *retornabile xv Trinitatis*. And thus Almyghty *Jesu* preserve your mastership and all yours to his pleasure. From London, the first day of May, with ond of your servant to his power.
(1 *May* 1500.) GEORG EMERSON.

[a] Sawar, *quære* whether the writ to the sheriff was so called, because of the clause *si feceri te securum?*

LETTER CXIX.

To the right worshipfull and his speciall good master, Sir Robart Plompton, kt. deliver these.

Right worshipfull Sir, I recomend me unto your mastership, letting you understand that laytly I wrott to you a letter of your matters; where was, that the great man E.[a], as far as undoubted as I can know, intendeth to have assyses agaynst you. Wherfore tyme is to labor as well the Schereffes, as all your frynds, and every country where your land lyeth. It is for that the said great man E. with other of the Kyngs coursell, sitting for assessyng of fynes for knyghts,[b] . . . . which may doe hym pleasure, he is intreated sececretly to owe his good will; ye may have trial by lyklyhed what ther answere shalbe: thus he under myneth. But let you for no labour. All such copies of your matters resteth in my keeping. And this was your lawiers conclusion; that your mastership should take a sure frynd to se all your evydence (which I thynke after my mynd must be Mr. Eleson),[c] to this intent: that your sayd counsell may have all the estayts made by your graynser and father,[d] as well uppon marrage lesses, as other wayes, and in lykwyse, how all the sayd estats come home agayne, wrytten *verbatim* in paper: and to have all your new esvedence by your father to John Norton and others, and estats made to have to your father for terme of lyfe: and to send copies of all matters proving matrymony betwyxt my sayd master your father, and my lady your mother: [e] and further prove which of the sayd feffees was

[a] Empson is here meant.
[b] The fines levied upon persons who had not taken up their knighthood, was one of the extortions in which Empson was an active agent for the crown. By partially favouring individuals, he secured their services when empannelled as jurors for the trial of the assise against Sir Robert Plumpton.
[c] William Eleson, esq. (See Letter CIII. note [a].)
[d] Sir Robert Plumpton and Sir William Plumpton, knights.
[e] See *Memoirs* for what relates to the clandestine marriage of Sir William Plumpton and Joan Wintringham, his second wife. This lady was living 19 Oct. 12 Henry VII. 1496, when she passed some copyhold lands in the court at Knaresborough to her son, before Thomas Coghill, the bailiff of the liberty, *(Chartul. No. 785,)* but was dead in the following year, 1497, when by reason that Sir Robert Plumpton had given for the repose of her soul the twentieth part of a ducat to the re-building of the greater hospital at St. Jago de Compostella, her name was to be associated with all those prayed for by that community, with a share in all spiritual indulgences according to the tenor

present at possession. Loke they be at London the begining of this next terme, with xl[li] . . . . . . Sir Richard [f] and ij men, and the sayd copies. If Mr. Eleson can fynd any of your lands talled to the here male, send copies therof; I thinke none be. And thus the holy Trenety send good speed to yours. From Lyncolns Inn, at London, this tuesday in the crose dayes.[g]

                Your servant,   JOHN PULLAN.[h]

I find no sure frends in all cause but George Emerson. Yaxley and Frowick, serieants, and Brook and Edgar are your counselors.[i]

(18 *May* 1501.)

of the bulls of Popes Innocent VIII. and Alexander VI. *(Chartul. No. 788.)* The informalities attending her marriage required atonement, and in the Chartulary are copied numerous certificates of the Indulgences which her husband and herself had obtained in return for alms bestowed on different religious communities both at home and abroad. Dodsworth, among his Church Notes, has the following memorandum: "Knaresborowgh Church, 28 Sept. 1622. There is a quire in the south side called Plumpton's quyer, which belonged to a house in the town called Wintringham Hall." *(Dodsw. MSS. in Bibl. Bodl. CLX. fol. 186.)* The same antiquary has also preserved to us this description of a painted north window then remaining in the same church. "A man in ar. kneeling, on his breast b. 5 fusells in fesse or, *(Plumpton)*; his wiefe behind him, on her breast the former coat paled with ar. a (inescocheon) ent. an orle of martletts, g. *(Wintringham)*; under, *Orate pro a'i'a*. . . . . . . *Plumpton et etiam pro a'i'a d'n'i Will'mi Plumpton qui istam* . . . . *anno* . . . . Qu'rly. b. 5 fusells in fesse or, and sa. a [bend] ent. 6 [escalops] or, *(Foljambe)*; paled with it, an [inescocheon] ent. 9 martletts in orle, g." Dodsworth appears to have either overlooked the escallops on the fusells, the distinguishing charge in the coat of Plumpton, or they had become imperceptible from lapse of time.

[f] Sir Richard Plumpton, chaplain, is probably here intended.
[g] Cross week was Rogation week, and the cross days the three days, Monday, Tuesday and Wednesday before the feast of Ascension, or Holy Thursday
[h] This letter was in a tattered state when copied by Sir Edward Plumpton, 21 April 1613. The two sentences here printed as a postscript are written in the margin of the page of the MS. and at the foot of the letter is added, "much is omitted becaus it is riven."
[i] John Yaxley and Thomas Frowyk, serjeants, called 10 Sept. 1496. Richard Brook, counsellor, called serjeant 10 Nov. 1511. The following is a copy of Serjeant Yaxley's retainer, *(Chartul. No. 802.)* "This bill indented at London the 16 day of July, the 16 yeare of the reigne of King Henry the 7th witnesseth that John Yaxley, Sergent at

the Law, shall be at the next Assises to be holden at York, Nottin. and Derb. if they be holden and kept, and their to be of council with Sir Robert Plompton, knight, such assises and actions as the said Sir Robert shall require the said John Yaxley, for the which premisses, as well for his costs and his labour, John Pulan, Gentlman, bindeth him by thease presents to content and pay to the said John Yaxley 40 marks * sterling at the feast of the Nativetie of our Lady next cuming, or within eight days next folowing, with 5[li] paid aforehand, parcell of paiment o' the said 40 marcks. Provided alway that if the said John Yaxley have knowledg and warning only to cum to Nott. and Derby, then the said John Yaxley is agread by these presents to take onely xv[li] besides the said 5[li] aforesaid. Provided alwaies that if the said John Yaxley have knowledg and warning to take no labor in this matter, then he to reteine and hold the said 5[li] resaived for his good will and labor. In witnesse herof the said John Yaxley, seriant, to the part of this indenture remaining with the said John Pulan have put his seale the day and yeare abovewritten. Provided also that the said Sir Robert Plompton shall beare the charges of the said John Yaxley, as well at York as Nottingbam and Derby, and also to content and pay the said money to the sayd John Yaxley comed to the said Assises att Nott. Derb. and York.

"(*Copied the 5 of October* 1627, *having a seal.*)   JOHN YAXLEY."

            * 26*li*. 13*s*. 4*d*.

LETTER CXX.

To the Right worshipfull, and his especiall good master, Sir Robart Plompton, knight.

Right worshipfull Sir, I recomend me unto your mastership, letting you understand, that latly I sent dyvers letters to you; thaffect of which letters was, that your adversaries intendeth suerly to attempt the law against you. Therfore I can wryt no other thing to your mastership, but oftymes remember my wryting; it toucheth your worship and wele. Therfore make your frynds to take your part, as frynds shold doe, as well in Nott. Derb. as Yorkshire, and God, I trust, shall be steresman in every ryghtwyse cause. Master Robert Constable, servant,[a] shalbe Justice of assise in Cornewall, Devonshir, and other west countryes, with Master Frowike; so that I trust, he shal not be al this

[a] See Letter C. note [d].

assise. Such pronunstications as a speciall freind lent to me, I copied them, as your worship shall see, and receive herewithall closed. As for all other causes, this bringer can shew to you by mouth, as larg as I can wryte, as *Jesu* knoweth, who preserve you. From Lyncolns Inne, at London, this Whitsonemunday.

        Your servant and beadman,

(31 *May*, 1501.)   JOHN PULLAN.

LETTER CXXI.

To my right worshipfull master and brother, Sir Robart Plompton, knyght.

After lowly and all due recomendations, I recomend me unto your good mastership and good brotherhode, praying the same, that yt will please you to send me by this berer the Martynmese farme for such lands and tenements as ye have by lease made betwixt you and me. And, Sir, as I suppose, insomuch as ye pleased not to content me at the uttermost day lymytted in the sayd lease, ye wylbe agreable that I enter to the sayd lands and tenements; wherfore, so I pray you to send me word in a byll by this berer, whether ye will that I enter to the same lands and tenements, or that ye will hold them still, and content according to the same lease. And, Sir, in so much as this is the first day of breach of your payments, I wyll nothing attempt therin, to I have word from you by this bearer, if it may so please you. And Almyghty *Jesu* preserve you in prosperouse lyffe, long to endure. From Yorke the xii[th] day of January.

        Your servant,

               ROBART PLOMPTON, of Yorke.[a]

[a] Robert Plumpton of York, was another of the bastard sons of Sir William Plumpton, kt. and brother of William Plumpton of Kirkby-Overblow, gent. (See Letter XXVIII. note [d].) The land and tenements lay at Ockbrook, com. Derby, and the deed by which they were held has already been brought under notice in Letter LXVII.

LETTER CXXII.

Unto Sir Robart Plompton, knight, be this letter delivered in hast.

Right worshipfull Sir, I recomend me unto you, desiring to here of your welfare; certifiing you I have receyved your letter and hath spoken with Sir Edmond Batmon, and he is right glad of the mocion, and wyll abyde by yt for his dede, and by all things that his attorney doth in his name, and so will shew to all men that spurns[a] him any wher. But he is feard lest they wyll not appeare without a *suppena*, and if ther be any thing, that ether he, or I, can doe you service or plesure, we are yours. No more at this tyme, but *Jesu* preserve you. Wrytten at Darley in the Peke, the VI day of March.

By your lover and servant,
HERRIE CULLUMBELL.[b]

[a] To spur, to ask. *See the Hallamshire Glossary, by the Rev. Joseph Hunter, F.S.A. Lond. Pickering,* 1829.
[b] Henry Collumbell of Derley, com. Derb. esq.

LETTER CXXIII.

To our right woshipful master, Sir Robart Plompton, kt. be this letter delyvered in hast.

After most lowly and all due recomendations, we lowly recomend us unto your good mastership; certyfying you, that as fare as we can understand or know, John Rocliffe and John Sothell[a] ar come to Kynreston place,[b] and ther purpose to tary and abyde, to such tyme as they thinke tyme convenient for to enter into your liflods in this country, and take distor (*distress*). And we have bene at dyverse places of your liflods, and finds your tenants well disposed toward you; and sithen, the most part of gentlemen in this country, and especyally the Eyres, so that ye wold come yourselfe and be sene amongst your tenants and frynds, the which were to them a singler pleasure and comforth, and to yourselfe a great strength. And to bring with you not over the number of xx horse at the most, and such as may have your advise and counsell to take derection, the which may be to the suerty of your lyflod and tenants. And if ye can gett master Mydleton, bryng him with you, or Richard Grene, or some other, and come to Hassop, for we have deseuvered us, and some departed tham. And with the grace of *Jesu*, and ye come betwixt this and tuesday, that all things shalbe to your harts comforth in tyme to come. But, Sir, they have bene here diverse tymes, doing for your wele and pleasure, and thinkes ye will, or dar, not put you in jopartie for your owne; for and ye come, they will put them in dever to do any thing that may be to the wele of your liflod and tenants. And, Sir, bryng with you money convenient for your expenses, for as yet . . . . here be now (*noe*) rent teyned. Now (*noe*) over to you at this tyme, who the holy Trenety have you in his keping.

By your servant,
(*Anno* 1501.) ROBINIT PLOMPTON, with other moe.

[a] Sir John Sotehill, the husband of Dame Elizabeth Sotehill, was at this time deceased, and his name is here improperly introduced through the inadvertence of the writers. Master Anthony Clifford was, it seems, the attorney for Dame Elizabeth Sotehill in these matters, but the legal estate and right of entry had vested in Robert Bubwith, clerk, and Richard Burrow, chaplain, by conveyance from Richard Fawberge or Fulbarne, the surviving feoffee of the original settlement, alleged to have been made by Sir William Plumpton, kt. in the fourth year of the reign of Edward IV. (*See Letter XCV. note* a.)
[b] Kinston Place, anciently *Cheniston*, in the parish of Radcliff-upon-Soar, com. Nott. was at this time a seat of the Babingtons; "and a very fair house they had there," says Thoroton.

LETTER CXXIV.

To my right worshipfull master, Sir Robart Plompton, knight.

After my duety, pleaseth your good mastership to wyt, that Sir John Rocliffe and Master Anthony Clifford send for me to Notingham; and when I came ther, they asked me whether I had brought mony, and I shewed them ye had received it alredy, and then they were very angree with many sore words. I was never so werie and soferd of my life, since I was borne. And they wrote every word I said and more; and I trow, but that they were in troble before, I shold never have escaped them. And all ther servant beated me one after another. I trust I shall hold me at home, if they send for me. And ever they thratte me that I shold goe to London, and if I wold come up unsent for, that shold be the better for me; and if I taryed tyll I were sent for, I shold be undone. Wherfore, Sir, I pray you let yt be loked to, if they wold take out any accion against me. I bere me much of Master Sacheverell, which is your stuard; but they had me in that case, whatever they sayd I durst not say nay, nor I wist not what I sayd, nor what I did.

Your bayley and servant,
(*Anno* 1501.) WILLIAM SANDERSON.[a]

[a] By letters bearing date 2 July, 15 Hen. VII. 1500, Robert Bubwith and Richard Burrow constituted William Saucheverell and William Sanderson their attornies, to take possession of the manors of Edensor, Derley, Stanton, and Pillesley, com. Derb. and of Combridge and Crakemarsh, com. Stafford, which they had by force of the feofment made by Richard Fawberge to them and their heirs. (*See Letter XCV.*)

LETTER CXXV.

To my right worshipfull brother, Sir Robart Plumpton, kt. these be delivered.

Right worshipfull brother, I recomend me unto you. Brother, I have received your letter, be the which I perceived ye be mynded to be with my lord of Schrewsbury on munday next, be noune of the day; and that ye wold have me to meet you by the way. Brother, my lord is at Wynfeld, and my lady both, and I wilbe glad to wayte upon you at Hegham, a myle from Wynfeld,[a] or els at Chesterfield, whether it please you. Brother, I am afrad lese this labour be vayne, for in certayne I caused all the labour to be made possible at this tyme, both to my lord and to my lady, and he wold not be turned; for he myght not, and keepe his truth and promyse made afore. Notwithstanding, sithe ye be comyng on your way, I thinke it is well done, ye to speake with my lord yourselfe, as prevely as ye can; and thus *Jesu* kepe you. At Padley, the sunday next afore the feast of St. John Baptise.[b]

Your loving brother,
(20 *June* 1501.) ROBART EYRE, esquire.

[a] Wingfield, in Derbyshire, a capital manor of the Earl of Shrewsbury.
[b] 24 June.

LETTER CXXVI.

To my worshipfull master, Sir Robart Plompton, knyght, be these delivered.

In my most humble wyse, Sir, I recomend me unto you and to my lady. Also, Sir, it is so, according to your wrytting that ye send me by Robart Smyth, I sent a letter in your name to William Rossell,[a] and he sent me a copie of the Inpanell that Rocliffe and Suttell intends shall passe agaynst you for your maner of Kenalton and the towne also,[b] which Inpanell the sayd William Rossell had of the underschereffe of Nottingham, and he gave him therfore 11[s]; which Inpanell is so favourable mayd, as I understand by dyvers of your frynds now of layt, wylbe great hurt to your worship, except the great mercy of God, and great labor and cost. Also, Sir, I have spoken with the baylay of Byngham Vapentake, and he will owe you as mekell fovour, as is in him to doo, for hes master Beron[c] servant, and his name is Edmund Mylnes; and so I understand by him, his master wold doe also, if he were labored. Sir, I have teryed at Kenalton this satterday, for because I cannot have my money that I should have had of him, and my horse wold bere me no further; and this satterday I have bought another horse of Robart Towyll of Nottyngham, for which I have payd him v nobles, of which sume Thomas Haym of Kenalton hath lent me for your sake and my ladis xx[s], which I have promysed in your name shalbe payd unto him agayne, with the grace of God. Sir, I send unto you a copie of the Inpanell that William Rossell sent unto me, and all these that is at the end of the names ar Hundrythars, as I understand by the baylife of the waypentake of Byngham, and other of your frynds and lovers. And also, Sir, Robart Smyth (xx[s]) ard John Reger (x[s]) hath lent me xxx[s] for your sake and my ladyes. As for John Willemett,[d] hath payd me iiij[li]. As for William Tufell,[e] hath maryed Mr. Beron sister; and as I understand, Mr. Berron may cause him and other of the Inpanell. Therfore I thinke, by my simple advice, that ye caused Mr. Beron to be spoken withall, for if I myght have had space, I shold have labored him in that matter. Sir Thomas Babington,[f] and a lerned man, called William Wyneswold, is greatest labourers agaynst you in this matter, as is shewed me by your lovers. And as for Richard Trumyll, he is houshold servant unto Sir Henry Wyllowby;[g] and thus I betake you to the keping of the holy Trenete. From Kenalton, the sunday next after Natyvytie of St. John Baptest.

By your Beadman and servant,

(27 *June* 1501.)   SIR RICHARD PLOMPTON, Prest.

[a] William Rossell, a younger brother of John Rossell of Ratcliff, com. Nott. esq.

[b] This suit had been brought in the names of Robert Bubwith and Richard Burgh, clerks, against Sir Robert Plumpton, kt. for the recovery of the manor of Kinalton, com. Nott. and was tried before John Vavasor, Justice of Common Pleas, and John Fisher, Serjeant, Justices *pro hoc vice*, at Nottingham, at the Lammas Assizes, in the year 1501, when the verdict passed for the Claimants. Whereupon Sir John Rocliff and Margaret his wife, and Elizabeth Sotehill, widow, demised the said manor to Sir Richard Empson, kt. for the term of his life, who, besides this reward for his maintenance, further procured, about 20 Hen. VII. 1504, his daughter to be married to the heir of Dame Elizabeth Sotehill.

[c] Sir Nicholas Byron of Colwick, com. Nott. kt. obiit 13 Jan. 19 Hen. VII. 1503-4.

[d] By an indenture made 24 July, 10 Hen. VII. 1495. Sir Robert Plumpton leased the manor of Kenalton, "from the feast of the Invencion of Holy cros, called St. Elline day, next coming unto the end of ix yeares," to John Willymot for 22[li] yearly rent. The latter was to furnish to Sir Robert Plumpton meat and drink for his servants, and provender for twenty horses, for the space of four days, twice in the year, and if he abode for a longer space, then to pay three farthings for herse litter and hay for a day and night, and 1½d. for going at grass in the summer time for a week. Sir Robert and his servants were also to occupy the hall, chambers, bakehouse, brewhouse, kitchen, and stable belonging to the said manor, at his coming there, and in his absence the said John to occupy the hall and the chambers at the over-end of the hall, with all other houses of office; the tenant was moreover to find meat and drink for the stewards and receivers of Sir Robert Plumpton coming on business. (*Chartul.* No. 778.)

[e] William Turvile of West Leke, com. Nott. esq.

[f] Sir Thomas Babington of Kinston, com. Nott. kt.

[g] Sir Henry Willoughby of Wollaton, com. Nott. knight banneret.

LETTER CXXVII.

To my right worshipfull brother, Sir Robart Plompton, kt. deliver these.

Right worshipfull brother, I recomend me unto you and to my lady, your wyfe, and to my daughter Margret. Brother, I spake with Frowick on Satterday next after St. Bartelmewday,[a] and I enquired of him whether the assisse held at Nottingham and Darby, or not; and he answered and sayd, that he cold not tell, nor man els, unto munday next after, for that day the Kings grace had comanded all the Judges and Servants to be with him at Richmond, and whether he wold comand them to kepe your Servants, or to tary for other besines at that tyme, he west never. Also, brother, as for your parte of your panell, I am promysed suerly they will appere, whose names ar closed in a byll; but as to the attachment of the proces for your sute,[b] is not yet, as fare as I understand. But I send about it unto the Shereffe as sone as Hare Harlad com from you, for sume remedy ther, if he myspede. I have sent you part the names of the enpannell for Suttell and Rocliffe, which be in the end of the Hye Peyke, of the which divers have promysed me not to appere, and moe I trust for to stoppe. Marveling ye sent nobody to Darby for to take you lodging, for Emson hath taken much lodging for him, as I am enfirmed. Also I shall wate one you at Nottingham one sunday next, except ye comand me contrary, praying you to send me answere shortly.

Your loving brother, ROBART EYRE, esquire.[c]

(*September* 1501.)

[a] In the year 1501 the feast of St. Bartholomew (24 Aug.) fell on a Tuesday, the Saturday next after would therefore be the twenty-eighth, and the Monday following the thirtieth of August.

[b] Sir Robert Plumpton had brought a cross action in the name of his feoffees, Thomas Lindley, John Swale the elder, Richard Kyghley, John Alleyn, clerk, and William Lindley, against Sir John Rocliff, kt. and Margaret his wife, and Elizabeth Sotehill, widow, for lands in Edinsour and Pillesley, which lands had been awarded to the heirs general by King Rich. III.; and by the King's writ, tested at Westminster 4 Aug. 16 Hen. VII. 1501, John Vavasor and John Fissher were appointed Justices for the trial of the same, in the county of Derby. A similar suit was instituted for the recovery of the manors of Garsington and Steeton in Yorkshire, which, by a writ of the same date, Humphrey Conyngesby and James Hobert, serjeants, were appointed to try before them as Justices at York. The attachment has, however, reference probably to proceedings in Chancery on the part of Sir Robert Plumpton, by reason of the parties not appearing under the *subpena*. (See Letter CXXIX.)

[c] Robert Eyre of Padley, died 13 Nov. 19 Hen. VII. 1504, when Arthur his son and heir was of the age of twenty-three years. (*Esc.* 28 *Jan.* H. 7, n. 253, *pars* 1.)

LETTER CXXVIII.

To the right worshipfull, my full singuler good master, Sir Robart Plumpton, knight, this letter be delivered in hast.

Right reverent and worshipfull and my singler gud master, in the most humble and lowly maner that I can, I recomend me unto you, and unto my gud lady your wyfe, desiryng to have knowledg of your prosperous helth, worship, and welfayre, which I besech almyghty Jesus long to contynue to his pleasure, and your most comforth. Hartely beseching the gud Lord that redemed me and all mankind upon the holy crosse, that he will of his benigne mercy vouchsafe to be your helper, and give you power to resist and withstand the utter and malicious enmity, and false craft of Mr. Empson, and such others your adversaries; which, as all the great parte of England knoweth, hath done to you and yours the most iniury and wrong, that ever was done, or wrought, to any man of worship in this land of peace. And non more sory therfore, then I myselfe is. If it were, or myght be in my poore power to remedy the matter, or any parcell of the matter, in any maner, condition, or dede, and whereas I may doe no more, my dayly prayers shalbe, and have bene, ever redy, with the grace of *Jesu*. And wher it is so that I am bounden to pay to your mastership, or to your assignes, certayne money by yere, to the sume of x[li], at ij tymes, for such lands as be assigned in ioynter to my nephew, Germayne Pole, and my cousin, his wyfe and your daughter, I have delivered and payd to his hands for this last past Martynmas rent v^{li}, trustyng that your mastership is contented therwith. What parte, or how much thereof, my sayd neveu, Germayne, hath sent to your mastership, I am ignorant, saving that he shewed me that he sendeth you but x^{li} towards the exibicions of my nese, his wyfe. I required you as my singler trust is in you, to send me acquitaunce for my discharg, for the payment of this sayd v^{li}; and moreover I besech you to send me word in writting by the bringer hereof, how I shall pay my rent from hence forward, and to whom I shall pay it; and as it pleaseth you by yore owne writting to comand me, I shalbe redy to performe it, by the grace of *Jesu*, who ever preserve your gud mastership. Wrytten at Rodburne in hast, the morow next after St. Kathren day.

Your true and faythfull beadwoman
(26 *Nov.* 1501.)   to hir power, ELIZABETH DE POLE.[a]

[a] The writer of this earnest letter was Elizabeth, daughter and coheir of Sir Reginald Moton of Peckleton, com. Leic. kt. who died in 1445, and widow of Ralph Pole of Radburne, co. Derb. esq. who died 31 May, 1492. (*Vide Letter CVIII.* note [c].) German Pole was her grandson, and in the letter mention is made of money paid to "my nephew," which epithet (as in the Latin from which it is derived) equally designated a nephew, the son of a brother or sister, and a grandson. His wife is in like manner "my nese," or "my cousin;" and the remittance for schooling shews her to have been yet of such tender years as not to have left the paternal roof. German Pole was, however, with his wife in Derbyshire in 1502, before he had fully attained his age. (*Vide Letter CXXXII.*)

LETTER CXXIX.

To his worshipfull master, Sir Robart Plompton, kt.

Right worshipfull Sir, in my lowliest wyse I comend me to you. Sir, I purpose with the grace of God to be with you or Martynmas,[a] if I may. This day I must ryde to Yorke, and how long I shall tary ther, I can not shew you. And as for compleanyng to my lord Archbishop of any ryott,[b] the tyme is not now. When I speake with you, I shall shew you more of my mynd, with the grace of *Jesu*, who, I besech, preserve you, &c.

Your servant
(November 1502.)   WILLIAM ELESON.

[a] 11 Nov.
[b] To the attempt on the part of the lessors of the plaintiffs, Rocliffe and Sotehill, to eject Sir Robert Plompton from his manor of Plumpton, a forcible resistance had been made by him and his servants, and a riot had ensued in which his servant, Geffrey Towneley, appears to have lost his life. *(See Memoirs.)*

LETTER CXXX.

To my right worshipfull Cousin, Robart Plompton, Kt. be these delivered.

Right worshipfull Cousin, I recomennd me unto you, desiryng to here of your wellfayre. Cousin, I understand there there was a servant of yours, and a kynsman of myne, was myschevously made away with, which I am sory fore. Cousin, I desire and pray you to be good master to Nycholas Lee, my lyaufe, as touchinge his goods, and the better at the instance of this my wrytting; and if ther be any thinge that I may doe for you, yt shalbe redy to you, as ever was any of my ansitors to yours, which, I enderstand, they wold have bene glad to do any pleasure to. Written at Townley, on Salmes day[a] last past.
(2 *Nov.* 1502.)   JOHN TOWNLEY, kt.[b]

[a] 2 Nov. All Souls-day, otherwise "Soulemas day."
[b] Sir John Towneley of Towneley, com. Lancast. kt. born 1473, died 1539. The kinsman here alluded to was doubtless Geffrey Towneley, whose name has occurred more than once in the correspondence; and of whom the last memorandum in the Cartulary is to the effect, that David Griffith had received of Gefferay Towneley, servant to Sir Robert Plompton, knight, ix^{li} for his fee of Hawwarrey parke, at Leyrpole, 5 Oct. 14 Hen. VII. 1498. (*Chartul. No.* 795.) It is presumed that he lost his life in the riot adverted to in the preceding letter.

LETTER CXXXI.

To the right worshipfull Sir Robart Plompton, kt.

Sir, after my duety remembred unto your mastership, please it you the same to know, that by instant labour I have gott a copie of the wryt of thassisse and playnt agaynst you, to the intent therby to have a wryt of error; which wryt, by the advise of your counsell, which I had togither, is put to making: and for the expedition therof, it shall want no dyligence, nor calling uppon.[a] For the costs and expencs about thes busines wilbe great, therfore I wold ye prepared money to send, uppon all goodly hast. And your learned counsell thinketh veryly, if the law may be indefferently hard, that the proceeding in the sayd assies is error. It is so that master Frowyke is made Cheife Justice of the Common place,[b] and therfore ye must myse his counsell; and that I forthinke. Sir, I have delivered your letters, as well to Mr. Under tresorer,[c] as to Blackwall; and Mr. Tresorer shewed me aparte how your wryting was. I desired him, seeing your great troble and cost, to spare the payment that ye owed him for a season; and that he sayd he myght not doe in no wyse, because he had appoynted such summes of money as ye owe him, to pay it to other persons; and further sayd, that he could not do no other wayes but attempt the law agaynst you and your suerty, if ye pay not according to your wrytting. I intreated him as specially as I could, to spare you for a season, but it wyll not be; therfore make shift to pay him, or els you and your surty wilbe sued. Ever after this, as I may have knowledg in all your matters to your comfort, I shall wryt to your mastership, with the grace of Almyghty God, who send you and all yours ther healths also. From Lyncolns Inne, this sunday next after All Saints day. Sir, for all other matters this berer can shew you at large, for a proteccion, and what your lerned counsell sayd therin.

Yor beadman JOHN PULLAN.
Frynds the Bishop of Rochester[d] and Docter Warghhan.[e]
(6 *Nov.* 1502.)

[a] By deed bearing date 7 May, 17 Hen. VII. 1502, John Ingilby, esq. as the heir of, or surviving feoffee in some settlement made by Sir William Plumpton in the reign of Edw. IV. conveyed his estate in the manors of Plumpton, Idill, Steveton, Garsington in Craven, and Little Studley, near Ripon, to Robert Bubwith, clerk, and Richard Burgh, chaplain, to which Thomas Ros, Richard Goldsbrough, John Acclome, and James Ros, esqs. subscribed as witnesses *(Chartul. No.* 818); and at the assizes held at York in the month of September in that year, the parties thus enfeoffed had recovered the manor of Plumpton against Sir Robert Plumpton. *(See Memoirs.)* It was now sought to discover error in the proceedings, and at the same time application was made for Sir Robert Plumpton to be appointed a Knight of the King's Body, in order that he might have in the meanwhile the privilege of being protected against civil process and arrest.
[b] Thomas Frowyk, Chief Justice C. P. Writ tested 30 Sept. 18 Hen. VII. [1502]. Obiit 17 Oct. 1506, buried at Finchley. Dugdale in his *Origines Judiciales* has made the year of his appointment 1503, by a mistaken calculation of the *Annus Domini* corresponding with the regnal year of Hen. VII.
[c] Sir Robert Lytton, kt. Under Treasurer of England.
[d] Richard Fitz-James, Bishop of Rochester. Appointed 17 May, 1497.
[e] Edward Vaughan, Treasurer and Prebendary of St. Paul's. Appointed Bishop of St. David's 13 June, 1509.

LETTER CXXXII.

To his right worshipfull father, Sir Robart Plompton, kt. deliver thes.

Right worshipfull father, in the most humble and lowly wyse that I can, or may, desiryng to here of your prosperous health, worship, and welfaire, which I hartely besech Almighty Jesus encrease and contynew to his pleasure, and your most comforth.

Father, I am very desirous to here from you, and to know how you do in your matters. I can noe more doe therein, but hartely pray to God to helpe you in your right, and send you gud speede. And I pray you let my wyfe have some word from you by this next carryer, how you doe in your sayd matters; and she and my sister Ellynor humbly recomend them unto you, and pray you for your dayly blessing. And both they, and I, pray you that we may be recommended unto my brother William Plompton and all your folkes. (And we rehersed them by name.) And thus the holy Ghost guid you and all the matters that you labor about. Scribled in hast the viii day of November. Father, I can not yet tell whether I come to London my selfe on this side Christenmas or not; my servant, the bringer hereof, shall shew, as sone as he hath the certenty, whether I shall come or be at home.

Your loving sone to his smale poore,
GERMAYN POLE.

(8 Nov. 1502.)

LETTER CXXXIII.

To the worshipful Sir Robart Plompton, kt. be thes delivered in hast.

Sir, in my most hartiest wyse I recommennd me unto you, desiring to heare of your prosperitie and welfaire, and of your good spede in your matters; certyfiing you that I, and my sone William, with all your children, are in good health (blessed be *Jesu*) with all your servants. Sir, ye, and I, and my sone, was content at your departing, that my sone should take the farmes at Martingmas of his tenants, or els cast them forth and prayse ther goods; and so my sone hath done with some of them. And here are the names of them that hath payd me; Robart Wood, Peter Cott, John Gloster, Robart Taler, William Bentham. Sir, it ys let us to understand that thers other tenaunts, that are cast forth, hath bene at Cothorpe,[a] and made one ragman [b] to compleane on my sone and you, that ye take ther goods from them. And that is not soe, for my sone hath sent for the neighbours of Knaresbrough, and Harrygate, and Spofforth, to set pryse on ther comon and cattell after ther consience; and my sone hath set to streys some in ther layes,[c] for ther is some that will not apply to his mynd. And they purpose to get on discharg for my sone, that they may be set in agayn, and he not to occupie; therfore I pray you to take good heed therupon. And they have set there names in the ragman that hath payd my sone; that they know not of, nor will not be conselled therto. Also, Sir Richard Goldsbrough hath taken an ox of William Bentham, that was dryven over the water [d] with ther cattell of the towne of Plompton, that he caused to be put over, for the sayfgard of ther cattell. And when he came for his ox, he answered him and sayd; Sir John Roclife had wrytten for certayne tenaunts to be so taryed by him, and spirred him, whose tenaunt he was, and he shewed him whos he was. And he will not let him have them without a replevie, and I trow he will dye in the fold; for I sent William Skirgell and William Croft, and they cannot get him without a replevie. And therfore if ye can find any remedie, I pray you for; and also I pray you to send me some word, as sone as ye may, of your good speed. No

---

[a] Cowthorpe, the seat of Sir John Rocliffe.

[b] Ragman, a word derived from Rag, to rate or reproach, Isl. *raega*, to accuse, and here applied to signify the paper to which the accusing or complaining parties had set their names. This word may yet be traced in the cant expression, round-robin, which, I apprehend, is simply a corruption of round-ragman. Bully-reok, in Shakspeare's Merry Wives of Windsor, should be read Bully-rag. (*See Brockett's Glossary of North Country Words, voce Rag. Newcastle-upon-Tyne, 8vo. 1825.*)

[c] That is to say, my son has levied a distress upon some of the cattle in their leas, meaning thereby the pastures which were not common.

[d] Goldsborough lies on the opposite side of the river Nidd, facing Plumpton; of this place, Sir Richard Goldsborough, kt. was at this time owner.

---

more at this tyme, but I betake you to the keping of the Trenetie. From Plompton in hast, the xvi day *Novembris*.

By your wife, Dame
AGNES PLOMPTON.

(16 Nov. 1502.)

LETTER CXXXIV.

To my trustie and well-beloved William Plompton, Esquire, be thes delivered.

Trustie and welbeloved I greate you well, and let you wit that on the behalfe of dame Elizabeth Sutell,[a] and other the inhabatants dwelling in the lordship of Plompton, I am informed, that wheras acording to the Kings lawes theare hath bene exhibite a replevie for such cattell, as ye latle hav taken for a distres within the said Lordship; yet not onely will not obey the same, but continueth in maner contrary to the Kings laws, right, and good consciences, as well in taking their cattell, as other houshold stuf; if it so be, to their utter undowing, if ye that should be sufred; as by their lamentable complaints mad at large, I am informed. Wherfore, the premeses considred, I desire you, and in the Kings name command you, imeadetly and furthwith, upon the delevery of this replevie, that ye obay the precept of the same, according to law; and els, upon the sight of this my writting, that ye, or your councell learned in your name, dres you to appear afore me, thear to shew me som reasonable cause, what so to doe ye make refusall. And of this faill not, as ye will answer at your perrill. At my castell of Cawood, the xxv day of November.

Yors, TH. EBORUM.[b]

(25 Nov. 1502.)

---

[b] Thomas Savage, Archbishop of York. Translated from London 12 April 1501. Ob. 2 Sept. 1507.

LETTER CXXXV.

To the worshipfull Sir Robart Plompton, kt. be thes delivered in hast.

Right worshipful Sir, in my most harty wise I recommend me unto you, desiring to witt your prosperytie and wellfayre; letting you understand that I and all your children is in good health (blessed be *Jesu*) with all your servants. Lettyng you to understand that my Lord Archbishop sent one servant of his unto my son William, chardging him in the Kyngs name to sette in the tenaunts agayne; and if he wold not, he wold send to the schereffe, and cause him to poynt them in agayne. And so I sent one servant to the schereffe, and the schereffe shewed my servant that my Lord had wrytten unto him for to poynt them on agayne. But my sone kepes them forth as yet, and therfor I trow my lord Archbishop will compleane of my son and you; and sath, that he will indyte them that was at castyng out of them. And, Sir, I pray you that you be not myscontent, that I sent not to you, for indeed I make the labor that is possible for me to make, and as yet I cannot speed; but as shortly as I can, I shall spede the matter. No more at this tyme, but the Trenytie have you in his keeping. Scribled in hast, at Plompton, this sunday next after St. Kateryne day.

By your wiffe, dame
AGNES PLOMPTON.

(27 Nov. 1502.)

---

[a] Dame Elizabeth Sotehill or Sutell, widow, died 21 Sept. 22 Hen. VII. 1506, leaving her twin grand-daughters, Joan and Elizabeth, daughters of Henry Sotehill, her son, her cousins and next heirs, and then in infancy, having only completed their first year on the feast of the Ascension of our Lord last past, 21 May, 1506. (*Esc.* 22 Hen. VII. n. 102.)

LETTER CXXXVI.

To the worshipfull Robart Plompton, knight, be thes byll delivered in hast.

Right worshipful Sir, in my most harte wyse I recommend me unto you, desiring to here of your welfare and good speed in your matters. I and all your children is in good health (blessed be *Jesu*). And, Sir, so it is, as God knowes, that I have mayd as great labor as was possible for me to make, to content your mynd in all causes; and now I have mayd the usance of xx^{li}, and sent you with Thomas Bekerdike to content where ye know. And I pray you to send some wrytting to Thomas Meryng [a] for the repayment of the money and your discharg. Sir, it is so that my lord Archbishop hath indytt my sone William and xvi of his servants, on tewsday was a senit. But Anthony Cliforth gave in the bill of dytement against my sone and his servants, but the quest would not endyte them. But my lord Archbishop caused them; or els he bad them tell who wold not, and he should ponishe them, that all oder should take insample. And I cannot get the copie of the indytement, for my Lord hath it in his hands. No more at this tyme. The Lord preserve you. From Plompton in hast, this St. Thomas day.

By your wife, dame

(21 Dec. 1502.)   Agnes Plompton.

[a] Thomas Meryng was one of the Collectors of the tenth granted to Henry VIII. in the fourth year of his reign; his receipt for 21s. from Robert Smith, constable of the vill of Plumpton, bears date 18 Oct. 4 Hen. VIII. 1512. (*Chartul. No. 857.*)

In Dodsworth's MSS. in the Bodleian library is a transcript of a letter from Sir Robert Plompton addressed to his wife about this time, soliciting money, and stating that his suit was not yet gone into. (*Dodsw. vol. cxlviii. f. 62-63.*)

LETTER CXXXVII.

To master Thomas Everingam, be this bill delivered in hast.

Cousin Thomas Everyngham,[a] I recomennd me unto you, thanking you of your good mynd and will at all tymes; praying you, that ye will take the labor and payne upon you to come and speake with me betwyxt this and tewsday next, as my speciall trust is in you; and that ye faylle not therof, as I may dow for you as much in tyme to come. No more at this tyme, but the Trenyte kepe you. From Plompton in hast, this Sant Maury day.

By yours at my power

(15 Jan. 1502-3.)   Dame Agnes Plompton.

[a] Thomas Everingham of Rockley, com. Ebor. esq.

LETTER CXXXVIII.

To Sir Robart Plompton, knight, being lodged at the Angell behind St. Clement Kirk, without the Temple barr, at London, be thes delivered.

After most harty and due recomendations, I recomend me unto your mastership and brotherhode, and to my lady your wyfe, beseching Allmyghty God evermore to preserve and prosper you. Sir, on munday last come a servant of Sir John Roclyfs from Mr. Emson to Brian Palmes, and caused him forthwith to take his waye toward London; and as I am enfirmed, the sayd servant shewed that at the comyng up of Bryan Palmes,[a] thei shold have an end with you, and if ye had any land, that ye shold be charged with my brother William and me. Therfore, Sir, if ye and thei drawd to an end, as I besech allmyghty *Jesu* to send you a good end after your pleasure and mynd, see how ye shall stand charged anenst us, and whether ye shalbe charged with the one, or with

[a] Brian Palmes, junior, son of Guy Palmes, Serjeant-at-law, called 18 Nov. 1511.

both. And, Sir, wher ye sent me word by Georg Barbor to search for the call of the exigent in the castell of Yorke agayn you, my cousin your son, or any other of your name, or servant; Sir, on tewsday last was the court in the Castell, and then was ther none exegent called agaynst you, none of your servants, nor of your name. But ther are ix playnts by *Replegiare* by ix of your tenaunts against you, my cousin your sonn, Sir Richard Plompton, and dyverse of your servants. But how many playntts, and how many defendants, as yet, I can not get any knowledg; for the Schereffs clarck sayth, his master hath all the records and notes, and the playntyffs that day was essoined. And thus almyghty *Jesu*, our Lady, Saint Mary Virgin, Mary Magdalene, with all the Saints in heven, as I shall dayly besech, prosper and spede you in all your great besines. Scrybled in hast, the vith day of February.

Yours at prayer and power,

(6 Feb. 1502-3.)   Robart Plompton of Yorke.

(*Indorsement.* Sir Thomas Granger of Yorke delivered this letter.)

LETTER CXXXIX.

To my right trusty and welbeloved William Plompton.

Right trusty and welbeloved, I commend me unto you, and trust that such derrection, as was of late taken by me, and by your assent, for matter in varrience betwene you and Sir John Roccliffe, be not owt of your remembrance; which was, it to rest unto the first sonday in Cleane Lent.[a] I understand that notwithstanding, ye use your selfe, as it is to me complayned, contrary to that agre-

[a] First Sunday in Clean Lent, or *Quadragesima* Sunday, fell on the fifth of March in 1502-3.

ment, as in felling down ashes and other woods in soundry maners; wherfore I will eftsones dessire you that ye withdraw yourselfe from so doing, unto such time that we heare from your father, which is now at London; and thus far you well. Written at Ribston, the xvi day of February.

(16 Feb. 1502-3.)   Yours,   Tho: Eborum.

LETTER CXL.

To my trusty and welbeloved William Plompton.

Right trusty and welbeloved, I greet you well, and greatly marvill that ye, notwithstanding my oft wryting unto you for reformation of dooing contrary to the apoyntment taken for the matter in varience betwene you and Sir John Rotelif, to be determined by the first Sonday in Lent, use yourselfe in senestor maner. As wher it was agred, in the mean time, ye to have your fewell nesesary of such bowes of trees that best might be spared, not hurtting the bodyes of the same; and as I understand, ye take both bodyes and bowes, and fell them downe by the rowths, and that contrary to your said apoyntment. But, Sir, I wold advise you to doo otherwise. If ye will not be reformed, I acertaine you that the said Sir John shall be for me at liberty to take his most avantage. And wheras it hath pleased the Kings highnes to grant unto your father his letter of protexion, which, used as ye use them, shold be contrary to his lawes, and occation to the breach of his paice; wherin I know his Highnes pleasure, by his letters latley derected unto me, not intending to have his grant derogatorie unto justice, wherunto I will and neds must have respect: and thus far ye well. Written at my castle at Cawod, the xxiiij day of Febuary.

(24 Feb. 1502-3.)   Thomas Eborum.

LETTER CXLI.

To my uncle Sir Robart Plompton, kt. be thes byll delivered in hast.

Uncle Plompton, I recomannd me unto you as hartely as I can, shewing you that my lord Archbishop hath sent a letter to my cousin William your son and a byll closed therin; which byll and letter I wold ye gave good heed to, and understand whether it be Kings comandement, or nay. And also John Vavasour of Newton is departed to mercy of God, sence ye departed from home, and I have inquered of the age of his son and heire, which shalbe at full age within a moneth, and then I am in a suerte to have the release of him.[a] Also there is a marcige moved betwyxt the sone of Sir John Roklife and Jane Ughtred, syster to Henry Ughtred,[b] and great labour have they made to my lord of Northumberland for the same, which I have stoped as yet. And thus the sayd Sir John Rokclife, Henry Ughtred, and Anthony [c] drawth all one way; and I understand they will make more labor to my sayd Lord hastely, for which cause I will goe to Lekinfeld the next weke, where I shall know further herein of my lords pleasure, which I know is your especiall good Lord: and as I can know furthere, I shall send you wrytting shortly. And also, as I understand, your adversaries will lay a fine against you, which fine is parcell of William Midleton's evidence, and is the fine of the house in Plompton that was my uncle Ralfe Gascoygne.[d] I pray you to send me some good tydings, as sone as ye can, of your good speed in your matters, which I besech Gude may be to his pleasure, and your comforth and myne; and thus our Lord kepe you. At Gaukthorpe in hast, the second sunday in Lenten.

Yore nephew,

(19 Mar. 1502-3.)   WILLIAM GASCON.

[a] By deed, bearing date 6 Aug. 18 Hen. VII. 1503, John Vavasour of Newton, esq. released to William Plompton, esq. all the right and title he had by reason of any feoffment made by Sir William Plompton, kt. grandfather of the said William, to his father n Plompton, Folefote, Idill, Girsington, Braem, Stotheley, and Steton. (*Chartul. No.* 421.)

[b] Henry Ughtred of Kexby, com. Ebor. esq. afterwards Sir Henry Ughtred, kt.

[c] Anthony Ughtred, made Knight Banneret at the battle of Spurs.

[d] See an account of the proceedings relating to this fine in the Memoirs.

LETTER CXLII.

To the worshipfull Sir Robart Plompton, knyght, be thes delivered in hast.

Right worshipfull father and mother,[a] I recomend me unto you, praying you of your dayly blessing; and all my brethern and sisters is in good health (blessed be *Jesu*) and prays you of your dayly blessing, and my lady mother also. Sir, I marvell greatly that I have no word from you (and my cousin Gascoyne also) under what condition I shall behave me and my servants. Sir, it is sayd that Sir John Roclife will ploue, but we are not certayne; and if that they come, my cousin Gascoyn saith well therin, for he will se them on that mannor that they will not like: and bytts me and my servants keep house, and he will send us x bowes, and us ned. Sir, your frinds trowes ye beleve fayr words and fayr heightes, and labors not your matters; for they trow that ys not the Kings mynd, nor knowes not of ther dealing, that they indyte you, and me, and your servants, as ye may se by the Judgment herof. Sir, I have sent you ij letters, derected from my lord Archbishop; the which I have answered him, that I will keepe the Kings peace. And also I meane sent him word, whether the tenants should occupy

[a] It appears from this letter of their son, that Sir Robert and Lady Plumpton were both at this time in London, soliciting the King's interference.

or no. And it is my cousin Gascoyns mynd, that they shall occupy for the tyme; and therfor I besech you send me word, how I shold do in every cause, and my servants also. Sir, your frinds thinkes that thes indytements ar for you, and it be shewed to the King or his Counsell. Both my cousin Gascon, and my brother Elson,[b] as your counsell, gives you so to do. And also I besech you send me word, as shortly as ye may possibly. No more at this tyme, but the Trenietie kepe you. From Plompton, on saint Benedic day. By your son,

(21 Mar. 1502-3.)   WILLIAM PLOMPTON, Esquier.

[b] See Letter CIII. note a.

LETTER CXLIII.

To his right worshipfull Sir Robart Plompton, knyght, this byl be delivered.

Right worshipfull Sir, after due recommendations had ecrn, I understand by my lady that your mastership hath spoken with the Kyngs grace, wherof I am very glad. Sir, I wold avise your mastership, that if the King command your mastership to nayme any of his counsell, which ye wold shold have examination of your matters, to refare that unto his grace, and that your mastership name none; for if your mastership shold name any, peradventure the King wold thinke parcialty in them, and also your frinds shold be knowne. If yt like your mastership, yt were best for to shew the Kyngs grace that ye wold refuse none of his counsell, except Mr. Bray,[a] Mr. Mordaunt,[b] and such other as are belonging to Mr. Bray. Sir, at the reverence of God, keepe your frynds secret to your selfe, for fere that ye leese them. I remit all these matters to your wisdom, and thus I beseech Almighty *Jesu* send your mastership good speed. At London, with the hand of your servant,

(*Anno* 1502-3.)   GEORGE EMERSON.

[a] Sir Reginald Bray, Knight Banneret and Knight of the Garter, one of the chief counsellors of King Henry VII. made his will 4 Aug. 1503, whereby he appointed Master Richard Empson, one of his executors; an intimacy which fully justifies the advice here given to Sir Robert Plumpton to make an exception to his being chosen. The will was proved 28 Nov. 1503. (*Testamenta Vetusta, vol. ii. p.* 446.)

[b] Sir John Mordaunt of Turvey, com. Bedf. kt. King's Serjeant. Will dated 5 Sept. and proved 6 Dec. 1504. (*Ibid. p.* 462.)

LETTER CXLIV.

To his right worshipfull and most especiall gud father in law, Sir Robart Plompton, kt. be thes delivered.

Right worshipfull and my most especiall gud father in law, in my most umbele maner I recomend me most hartely unto you, and unto my lady my mother in law, gladly desiringe to have knowledg of your prousperyte, wellfayre, and harts ease, the which I besech almyghty *Jesu* long to contynew and increase unto his pleasure, and unto your most joyfull comforth and gladness. Sir, if it please you to understand, that since my last coming into Darbyshire, it was infirmed me, that ther was in Staforthshire a parcell of land, the which should be ther at Combryge and Cramarsh,[a] that was not recieved the recovery of the size at Nottingham and Derbye. Wherfore, Sir, I toke upon me in your name to send unto the tenants for as much rent as they were behind, since the last payment that was made unto Sir John[b] or Preston;[c] and they desired my servants to com agane, as that day sennyt, and they should either have the rent, or be suffered to streyne on such guds as they fond on the ground. And so they did com

[a] Combridge, in the parish of Rowcester, com. Staff. and Crakemarsh, near Uttoxeter, in the same county.

[b] Sir John Rocliffe.

[c] Preston, servant to Sir William Gascoigne, kt. (*See Letter XCVIII.*)

againe as they had apoynted them, and in the meane season, thorow the meanes of one Berdall of Assope, ther had bene iiij of Suttell and Roclife servants, the which wold have had the rent; and your tenaunts answered, that they knew not wherfore that they should pay them, and so they went ther way. Howbeit, they sayd they wold be ther shortly againe, and for that cause they wold not pay my servant, as for at that tyme. Howbeit, they promysed them upon ther fayth that they shall not pay one penny unto the tyme that they have some word from you.

Furthermore, Sir, if it please you to understand of the great unkindnes that my grandam hath showed unto me now latly, as the bringer herof can more planly shew you by muth, to whom I besech you to take credence on. For be ye sure, Sir, that I was never so unkindly delt with; all is because that she well know it that ye are asunder, therfore she thinketh that she may give and sell all at her owne playsure. I will besech you for the reverence of *Jesu* to be so gud father unto me and my wyfe as to mayntayne it that is my ryght, and to se a remedy for it, as my speciall trust is in you above all other creatures livinge. Furthermore, I wold desire you that I may have knowledge how that you do in your matters, for I here tell that you dyd well. That wold be the most joyfull tydings unto me that ever was, or ever shalbe, as knoweth the blessed Rode of Rodeborne, who save you in his blessed keepinge. Amen. I will besech you, Sir, that this simple letter may recomend me unto my brother William, and my brother Maliverey, with both my sisters, and my sister Eyre, with all your housholld.

By your humble son and beadman,
(*Anno* 1503.)
G. DE LA POLE.

LETTER CXLV.

To his right worshipfull father, Sir Robart Plompton, knyght, thes letter be delivered.

Right worshipfull and my most singuler good father in law, in my most humblest maner I recommend me right hartely unto you, and unto my lady my mother in law, inwardly desiring to have knowledg of your wellfare and harts ease, the which I besech almyghty *Jesu* of his infinyt mercy and grace shortly to send you, unto your most joyful comforth, and to the pleasure of your harte. So it is, Sir, that I understand by the letter that I received from you, that ye have the Kings protection ryall, the which is the most joyfullest tydings that ever I hard, since the tyme that I was borne of my mother. For now, I doubt not but with dew labor mad unto the Kings grace, and with the gud counsell of your lovers and frinds, all the vexation and troble that ye have had now laytly for your matters, by the grace of the blessed Trenity, shall turne unto your joyfull comforth and harts ease, considering how falsly, and how unrighteously, the size is past against you, contrary to the law either of God, or man. Furthermore, Sir, I have bene at Combrige for your rent at your tenaunte, William Smith, and I received of him for one yeares rent xl^s. the which I send you by the brynger hereof. Howbeit, I lay at outside ij dayes or I cold have it, he was so fearfull to pay it because of Sir Robart Shefell [a] and Emson; and he desireth you to be his gud master and beare him out, that a be not vexed nor trobled therfore, for be ye sure he is stedfast unto you. And I wold have had rent in Crakmarsh, but the tenaunts wold pay me none; and I wold have streaned, but ther could no man shew me which was

[a] Sir Robert Sheffield of Butterwicke, com. Linc. kt. (*See Letter LXIII. note* [a].)

your ground. Wherfore, I supposed that it should have hurt your matters to have streyned, not knowing your ground from his. Also, Sir, I desired you in my last letter to be so gud father unto me, as to com speake with my grandam for diverse matters, the which longeth unto my profit. Howbeit, I have no gud answere of you. But now I will desire you, for the reverence of *Jesu*, to doe for me as I will do for you, if my power were unto my will, and make it in your way to com speake with hir for the welfare and profit of your daughter, my wyfe, and me. Many a gentleman in Darbyshire marvelleth, I being so nere my age, that ye will not com and speake with hir for my right; and if ye come, it will save me greatly, more then ye know, in dyvers matters that I shall shew you of, by the grace of *Jesu*, who have you in his gloryous keeping.

Your owne son and beadman,
(*Anno* 1503.)
GERMAN DE LA POLE.

LETTER CXLVI.

To the right worshipfull Sir Robart Plompton, knight, be this delivered.

Right worshipfull Sir, I recomend me unto you. Sir, one John Frobiser, one of the Coroners in the county of York, hath bene with me and shewed me your wrytt of atteynt with a panell,[a] whereupon ye were well agreed at Yorke afore him and all his fellowes, as he seeth; and at they should send the writ to me to returne in ther names, because they were not expart in making ther returne, because it is somewhat diffuse, and because of this your wryttyng: and that ye (*omission*) and the Impanall is not good and indifferent for you, I have not medled, nor will not, at the desire of the Croners, without your assent. And so they have determyned enough themselves to send the sayd John Frobiser, in all ther names, to put in the same writt; and therfore I will advise you, if ye will labour the Kings grace herin, to make all the speed ye can, and tery not for any other cause, for this matter towches you nere. I cannot intreat the sayd Frobiser to keep the wryt in his hands, but to put it in at the day, as he and all his fellows were agred for his and ther honestyes and truth in this matter; for they have warned the panell Jurie, and the other partie, to kepe ther day at London, according to the wrytt. And therefore, without ye be at London afore, and geit some comandement from the Kings grace to the sayd Coroners to kepe the sayd wrytt in ther hands, or els to amend the returne, and this must be done and labored with affect; and therfore, I will advise you to make your ready to ryde on Monday next at the furdest, for els ye will come behind. And thus far ye well, and God give you as gud speed in this matter, as I wold have my selfe. From Doncastre,[b] this Sunday.

By yours,
(*Anno* 1503.)
T. STREY.

[a] This was a writ of attaint to examine the judgment given by the jurors at the Assize, in order to its being reversed; but it was discontinued, and Sir Robert Plumpton had a precept "To Our trusty and welbeloved Sir William Conyers, Sheriffe of our county of Yorke, &c. that hee serve noe writs, precepte or other writeings upon Sir Robert Plumpton Knight of our body or his servants," and another to Sir Christopher Ward and Sir William Calverley, Knt^s. "that William Plompton, son and heir of Sir Robert, peacably inioy the Lordship of Plumpton and Idle and the rents," &c. Dat. Colly Weston, 16 July. (*Towneley MS.*) Sir William Conyers was Sheriffe of Yorkshire in 1503.

[b] John Frobiser resided at Doncaster. See an account of the family in Hunter's South Yorkshire.

LETTER CXLVII.

To my right worshipfull master and brother, Sir Robart Plompton, knyght for the King's body.

After most harty and due recomendations, I recomend me unto your mastership and brotherhode; and wheras my brother William, like as I shewed you a byll, hath in his name and myne put a byll unto the Kings grace agaynst Rocliffe and Suttell, which hath made answere, as appearethe in the byll I sent you by Ball. And the Kings counsell comaunded my brother Wylliam to goe and enter into Ocbroke; and so, in his coming home, he went thether, and wold have entred, and William Sawcheverell wold not suffer him. And he shewed the copie of our deed, and he wold not admyt it; but the tenaunts sayd, if he come againe afor alhallowes, and bryng the deeds under seale, they shold endever them to pay us. And I thinke to send Sir Robart North thither with him, in the weke next afore alhallowmase. Wherfore I pray you that ye will lett Sir Robart have the ij^d deed with him in a box, which is of feoffment, thider, to the intent abousayd; and ye shall have them delivered againe unto you, or my lady, whether ye shal please. And if you wyll my brother Wylliam bring them up to you unto London, I shall bynd me that he shall trewly deliver you them. And of your gud mynd and pleasure in thes premyses, I pray you that ye will vocksafe to send me knowledge in writing. And, Sir, I understand your adversaries reporteth, your matter shalbe determyned by the Kyngs Judges and Sergiants, and ther, I dout me, ye gitt but litle favor. Therfore the sonner ye goe up, I trust yt be the better for you. And almyghty *Jesu* preserve you, and send you gud speede in all your busines, and that shalbe my daly prayer, as God knoweth. At York, this Munday.

(*Anno* 1503.)   Your servant ROBART PLOMPTON.

LETTER CXLVIII.

To his right worshipfull and welbeloved frind, Sir Robart Plompton, knight.

Sir, I recomend me unto you, and pray you take no displeasure that I can not content your mynd, insomuch that I am not certayne what day, or tyme, to be called up for certayne matters concerning the weyll of my house. Many other causes reasonable to be shewed, the which long to writt. I fere me greattly to be overcharged, or I witt. And thus our Lord preserve you. From Kyrkestall, the second day of December. I have good plegges that will serve me of nothinge at my nede; the which I am full like to sell and displese the owners, now at my need.

Your beadman, WILLIAM THE

(2 *Dec.* 15—.)   ABBOT OF KIRKESTALL.[a]

[a] William Stockdale was abbot of Kirkstall from 20 Dec. 1501, but died before 3 Dec. 1509, when William Marshal was elected his successor, the vacancy after whose death was filled up 21 July 1528.

LETTER CXLIX.

To the worshipfull Robart Plompton, knight, be this byll delivered in hast.

Right worshipfull Sir, in my most hartie wyse I recomend me unto you, evermore desiring to here of your prosperytie and wellfaire, and good sped in your matters, shewyng you that I and all your children is in good health (blessed be *Jesu*) and prays for your blessing. Sir, it is so now that I have made you thewsans of the money, that ye sent to me for, and I have sent it you with John Walker at this tyme; the which I shall shew you how I mayd schift of, at your comminge. And I pray you that ye be not miscontent that I sent it no sooner, for I have made the hast that I could that was possible for me to do. And also, Sir, I will not lett Tho: Croft wife plow nor occupie her fermeald, but saith she shall not occupy without yer life. And also I pray you to send me word how you speed in your matters againe, as soon as ye may; and also to send me word where ye will your horses to come to you.

No more at this time, but the Trinity keep you. From Plompton in hast, the xixth day of March.

By your wife,

(19 *March* 1503-4.)   Dame AGNES PLOMPTON.

LETTER CL.

To the right worshipful Lady, my lady Plompton, be this byll delivered.

Madam, in my most harty maner I comend me unto your Ladyship, thanking you of your reward delivered unto me by Edmund, your servant. Madam, here hath bene this day with Master Schereffe,[a] Edmund, your owne servant, and also Edmond Ward, your tenaunt which was arested at Knarsbrught by dew of a warant delyvered to the Balife. Master Shereffe is good master unto him, as he can shew you, for this writt shalbe at none harme, nor never ether named in the wrytt with him, at this terme. Nevertheless, I wold advise you wryte to London to some of your counsell, that the wryte may be answered to, or els, I thinke veryly, ther shall another *capias* com against them the next terme; which if ther doe, I doubt ther wilbe labor made to Master Schereffe for taking of them, which I wold be loth to doe, as knoweth God, who keepe you. Att Ryther, this tewsday in Ester weeke.

By your poore kinsman,

(9 *April* 1504.)   WILLIAM NORVANVILL.

[a] Sir Ralph Ryther of Ryther, com. Ebor. High Sheriff of Yorkshire in 1504, 19-20 Hen. VII. William Norvanvill, or Normanvill, was his Under Sheriff. See the letter of Dame Agnes Plompton, inclosing a copy of the above, to Sir Robert Plumpton in London, which follows.

LETTER CLI.

To the worshipfull Robart Plompton, knight, be these delivered in hast.

Right worshipfull Sir, in my most hartiest wyse I recomend me unto you, desiring to here of your prosperytie and welfare, and good spede in your matters, the which I marvell greatly that I have no word from you. Sir, I marvell greatly that ye let the matter rest so long, and labors no better for your selfe, and ye wold labor it deligently. But it is sayd that ye be lesse forward, and they underworketh falsly; and it is sene and known by them, for they thinke to drive it that they may take the Whitsonday ferme: and so it is sayd all the country about. Sir, I besech you to remember your great cost and charges, and myne, and labor the matter that it myght have an end, for they have taken on *capias* and delivered for certayne of your tenants. And so they have taken Edmund Ward at Knarsbrough and arrest him; the which is a great nossen in the country, that they shall get such prosses, and ye dow none to them, but lett them have there mynd fullfilled in every case. And the other tenaunts cannot pays ther housses, but they shalbe cagid; and also willing none of your servants shall not pas the dowers, but they mon be trobled. And also they have stopped the country, that ther will no man deale with any of your servants, nether to bye wod, no nor nothing els. Therfore, I pray you that ye will get some comandment to the Scherefe that the prosses may be stoped. Also, Sir, I send you the copy of the letter that came from the Undersherefe, and the copy of the causes, and the letter that come from William Elison; the which I had mynd in for loyssing of Edmund Ward, for I have gotten him forth by the wayes of William Ellyson. And also, Sir, I am in good health, and all the children (blessed be *Jesu*), and all your children prayes you for your daly blessing. And all your servants is in good health, and prays delygently for your good speed in your matters. And also it is sayd, that they have cagments for them that hath bought the wood, that they dare not deale therwith. For without ye get some comaundement, I wott not how your house shalbe kept, for I know not wherof to levy one penywroth. No more at this tyme, but the Trenietie keepe you. From Plompton in hast, the xii day of Aprill.

       By your wyfe,
(12 *April* 1504.)   Dame AGNES PLOMPTON.

LETTER CLII.

To Sir Richard Plompton be thes byll delivered in hast.

Sir Richard Plompton, I recomend me unto you, dessiring and prayng you that ye will se some remydy for thes prosses, that they may be stopped; and that ye will goe to my lord Dayrsse,[a] and make on letter for me in my name, and shew him how they delt with my housband tenaunts and servants, and ye thinke it be to dowe. And I pray you that ye will se that nether thes, nor none other prosses, pas, but be stoppyd, as my speciall trust is in you. For I have sent up the copy of the *capias*, with one letter from William Elesson and one other from Under Sherife, that ye may, after the scest of them, labor as ye thinke best by your mynd. Also, Sir Richard, I pray you to remember my other [*order*]; for Thomas Stabill hath taken the west Rod and the est Rod, and hath mayd the fenses, and so she hath no gresse to hir cattell; and also they sow hir land, and will not let hir occupy nothing as yet, and that discomfortheth them much. No more, but the Trinete kepe you. From Plompton in hast, the xiii day of Aprill.

(13 *April* 1504.)   By me Dame AGNES PLOMPTON.

[a] Thomas Darcy de Darcy, Chl'r, was summoned to Parliament, 17 Oct. 1 Hen. VIII. 1509, the same year in which William Lord Conyers had also his first summons upon record. The latter, it is known, bore the title of Lord Conyers in 1506, and now the evidence of this letter, that Sir Thomas Darcy was a Baron in 1504, makes it more than probable that both these noble personages sat in the Parliament which assembled on Thursday, 25 Jan. 19 Hen. VII. 1503-4, and that the writs of summons are lost. Moreover, the Herald whose diary of the ceremony of the interment of King Henry VII. on the 8th, 9th, and 10th days of May 1509, is printed by Hearne, (*Lelandi Collectanea, vol. IV.* p. 303,) likewise calls him "the lord Darcye, beinge Captayn of the Garde;" so that it is certain he had the title before any summons for the new Parliament in that year was issued.

LETTER CLIII.

To the worshipfull Robart Plompton, kt. be thes byll delivered in hast.

Right worshipfull, I in most hartee wyse recomennd me unto you, desiring to heare of your wellfaire and good speed in your matters, letting you understand that I am in good helth, with all your children (blessed be *Jesu*), and pray you of your daly blessinge; and all your servants is in good health and is right glad to here of your welfare. Sir, one the eving after the making of this letter, your servant Edmund Robyson come home, and so I understond by your letter, that you wold understand if Sir John Roclife servants have received any ferme in Yorkshire, but therof I can get no knowledg as yet. But they have sold oke wood at Nesfeld, and lettes them stand to the tyme of the yere, one oke that is worth xl^d for xij^d; and also they have sold aches at the same place: and the okes are sold to William Clapame and Richard Clapame, and the aches to the towards there about. And also at Idell, they have sold holyn to James Formes and to Thomas Quentin and William Aches, and herof I can geet no more certaintie as yet. And also there is no mo of your tenaunts to get as yet, nor your servants nether, at this tyme; but the Trenitie have you in his blessed keepinge Scrybbled in hast, the fryday next after St. Marke day.

       By your wyffe,
(26 *April* 1504.)   Dame AGNES PLOMPTON.

LETTER CLIV.

To his right reverent and worshipfull master, Sir Robart Plompton, knight, or my lady his wyfe, or ayre, William, or my mistres, or Sir Richard, his chaplan, or any of them, deliver this byll.

Most honorable and worshipfull and my especiall good master, after the most hartyest maner I can, or may, I recomend me unto your mastership. Sir, I am a poore beadman of yours, and I am alwayes right glad to here of your welfare, my lady your wyfe, master William, your son, and my mystres his wiffe, and all your childer, and all your good frinnds and lovers. Sir, the cause of my wrytting to your mastership at this tyme; your mastership remembers that John Toyllar left me with the keyes of your schawittry,[a] to keepe for your behalfe in the defalt of a better. Sir, I had the keyes levered me, when John Toyller come to your mastership; and had a fellow lemett to keepe the said schawnter with me, and he fayled me in my most neede. In the defalt of him ther come another poore man, as my selfe, whose name is called Ingland, and we two keeped yt well and trewly to the tyme that your servant came and discharged us, whose name called Broweke, your servant. I levered him the keyes, afore John Tayller in Bondgate, to Sir Thomas Aykryg behalfe, by the comanndement of Broweke, your servant. Touching . . . . . . Akryg promysed to content all maner of dues. I beseech you, Sir, the most enimies that I have within Rypon is Robart Squire and his wyffe, touching the ryght that John Toyller knowes right well. Desiring your mastership to send me word with this pure boy, how I shalbe demeaned and under what forme, and *Jesu* preserve you. Sir, I am yours at all tymes.

   Your servant and a poore beadman of yours,
           JOHN EYRE.

[a] In the Collegiate Church or Minster at Ripon, an ancestor of Sir Robert Plompton had founded at the altar of the Holy Trinity beyond the high altar, a chantry, which it appears from this letter was screened from the rest of the church and under lock and key. At the foot of the page in the MS. is written, *words are omytted bycause they are ryven out.*

LETTER CLV.

(*No address.*)

Right worshipfull and my singuler good master, in the most humble and lowly maner that I can or may, I humbly recomend me unto your good mastership, and unto my good lady your wyfe, desiryng hartely to here of your welfaire, and also of your good speed in your weighty and great matters, which I have prayed for, and shall doe dayly. Sir, I receyved a letter from you, which bare dayt the viii day of June, and in that letter ye wrote to me, that it was my sone Germyne mynd, and yours, with other his frynds, that I should occupie still att Rudburne, as I have done in tymes, as long as we can agre; upon condition that I wold be as kynd to my sayd son Germyne, as he intendeth to be to me. I pray Jesus that I may find him kynd to me, for it is my full entent and purpose to be kynd and lovyng unto him and his, whersoever I come. But thus the matter is now, that I have taken another house within the Freres at Derby, which is but of a smale charge, and ther I entend to dispose myselfe to serve God dilygently, and kepe a narrow house and but few of meany; for I have such discomforth of my son Thomas unfortunate matters, that it is tyme for me to get me into a litle cornner, and so wyll I doe. I will besech you and him to take no displeasure with me for my departing, for it wilbe no otherwyse; my hart is so sett. Moreover, as touching the custodie of all such evidence, as I have now in my keeping, concernyng thenherytance of my sayd son Germyne, a gentleman of your acquantance, Mr. Herry Arden, hath bene in hand with me for them, and I have shewed him, whensoever and to whom it shalbe thought by you most convenyent tyme of the delyverance of them, I wylbe redy to delyver them, for I will be glad to be discharged of them; for I will flitt at this next Mighelmas, as I am full mynded, or sonner, with Gods grace. I pray you contynew my gud master, and owe me never the worse will therfor; for it ryseth on my owne mynd to give over grett tuggs of husbandry which I had, and take me to lesse charge. And with Gods grace I shalbe as kynd to him, and to my daughter, his wyfe, as ever I was in my life, as well from them, as with them. With the grace of *Jesu*, who ever preserve you. Wrytten at Rodburne in hast, the xth day of July.

By your poore sister and trew beadwoman,

(10 *July* 1504.)   ELIZABETH POLE.[a]

[a] Dame Elizabeth Pole had numerous offspring by Ralph Pole or de la Pole, her husband, who died 31 May, 7 Hen. VII. 1492. Her eldest son John married Jane daughter of John Fitzherbert, of Etwall, com. Derb. esq. but both died in the lifetime of Ralph Pole. (*See Letter* CVIII.) Their son German was heir to his grandfather, and the custody of his lands during his minority had been granted to Elizabeth Pole, widow, and Thomas Pole, which latter was a merchant of London. This letter will therefore have been written after he attained his majority in 1504, when it became a question whether his grandmother was to continue still to occupy the family mansion at Radburn. Elizabeth Pole in this letter calls her grandson, son, and his wife, daughter, instead of nephew and niece, or simply, cousin, as in her former letter; but it is evident from her subscribing herself " sister," that she here writes *in loco parentis*, and uses the expressions of affinity suitable in this regard.

LETTER CLVI.

To my right worshipfull father-in-law, Sir Robart Plompton, kt. be this delivered.

Right worshipfull and my most singuler good father-in-law, in my best maner I hartely recomend me unto you, right glad to here of your welfare, the which our Lord contynew long unto his pleasure and your most comfort. Father, the cause of this my wryting unto you of myn own hand, is for a matter that no man knoweth of but onely my wyfe, and I, and the partyes. Father, this is the matter; ther is a gentleman, the which has maryed one of my naunts, whose name is Randolpe Manwring,[a] and he beareth great love and favor unto my sister Ellynor, and she doth likewise unto him the same. And the gentleman hath desired me to wryte unto you, to know if ye can be contented that he have hir in marage to his wyfe; the which if that ye so be, he wilbe glad to meat you in any plase, that it please you to apoynt, and to have a communication in the matter. And I thinke in my mynd that he wilbe contented to take lesse with hir than any man in Inglond wold doe, being of his avyowre, because of the great love and favour that is betwyxt them. And, father, this I will say by myn uncle Manwryng; his land is a c marke, and also he is as godly and as wyse a gentleman, as any is within a m. myle, of his hed. And, Sir, all the whole matter lyeth in you and in noe man els; but if that she were myne owne borne sister, I had lever that she had him, knowing him as I doe, than a man of vi cymes his land. Father, how that ye are disposed in this matter, I besech you that I may have answere, as shortly as ye can; for my sister Ellynor putteth herselfe utterly unto that thing, that is your mynd. And my wyfe and I will doe the same, by the grace of *Jesu*, who send you shortly a good end in your matters. Amen.

Your son,

(*Anno* 1504.)   GERMAYN POLE.

[a] Randal Mainwaring of Carincham, com. Cest. esq. married Margaret, daughter of Ralph Pole of Radburn, com. Derb. esq. (*See pedigree of the family in Ormerod's Cheshire.*)

LETTER CLVII.

To my right worshipfull father-in-law, Sir Robart Plompton, kt. this letter be delivered in hast.

Right worshipfull and my most singuler good father-in-law, in the best manner that I possibly can, I hartely recomend me unto you with effectuall desire to here of your welfare and gud speed in your great matters. And likewise, Sir, doth your poore daughter my wyfe, and my sister Ellynor, desiring to have your dayly blessing. Father, I have word brought me, by one Duckmanton of Moginton, from you, that you had a joyfull end in all your matters, the which were unto me the joyfullest tydings that cold be thought. Howbeit, Sir, I have had great marvell, that I have not, since that tyme, hard some word from you. Father, pleaseth yt you to understand, that I have comuned with my uncle Maywheryng, according to the effect of your letter; and veryly, Sir, I can no other wyse perceive by my sayd uncle, but that he is reasonable in all causes. For first, he wilbe contented to make hir xx marke joynter; and as for such essew as God sendeth them, it is noe doubt but he wyll so provyd for them, that they shall live like gentlemen or gentlewomen, whichsoever God suffereth. And veryly, father, I am right sure that my sister Ellynor had rather have hym, you beyng so content, then a man of far greater lands. And also, father, I know wher that my sayd uncle myght have great marraiges, both with great lands, and guds. Wherfore, Sir, yfe yt is your mynd that the matter goe forward, and the preferment of my syster, your daughter, in this behalfe, I pray you that I may have shortly knowledg in writting, what your mind is in this matter, and what you be worthy to give for his large proffers. And, you being any thing resanable, I am right sure that ye shall like my sayd uncle, as well as ever you liked any man, by the grace of *Jesu*, who preserve you. Written at Rodburne in hast upon Martingmas even.

By your son-in-law,

(10 *Nov*. 1504.)   GERMAYN POLE.

LETTER CLVIII.

Unto the worshipfull knight, Sir Robert Plumpton.

Right worshipfull father, in my most hartyest maner I recomend me unto you, desiryng to here of your prosperous welfayre, the which I besech *Jesu* to contynew and increase unto his pleaser. Father, so yt is that I lent my lady your wyfe, of whose soule God have mercy,[a] viii marke and a ryall, of which summe I have received all save iiij marke, the which remayned still in my lady your wyffe hands; for which matter I sent a letter unto my lady your wyffe, on whose soule *Jesu* have mercy, by Olyver Dickenson, your servant, for the same money. For the which I besech you for to be gud father unto me, that I may have yt at my need; and if it, or I, did you any good, I am right glad, and shalbe glad to be at your comandement after the old maner. Also, father, I pray you that I may be recomended unto my brother, your sone, with all your servants. Father, I pray you remember the suertyshipe that belongs unto, to my brother your sone. No more at this tyme, but I besech you as dayly wellwiller, that I may have knowledg by the bringer herof, how that ye do in your great matters, the which I pray *Jesu* give you good speed, who have you in his gloryous keeping.

(*Anno* 1504-5.)   HENRY ARDARN.[b]

[a] Sir Robert Plumpton, kt. married his second wife, Isabel Neville, about 18 Sept. 21 Hen. VII. 1505, and we know that his first wife, Agnes Gascoigne, whose death is here referred to, was living as late as 10 July, 1504; (*See Letter* CLV.) so that this letter will have been written in the intervening year.

[b] Henry Ardern was probably a younger son of the family of that name settled at Park Hall, near Birmingham, com. Warwick; but I am unable further to identify him, or to state which of the daughters of Sir Robert Plumpton he married. His connection with the Poles would seem to indicate that the match with Randal Mainwaring had been broken off, and that he married Eleanor Plumpton, then residing with her sister Mrs. Pole.

LETTER CLIX.

Hulme, Lynacr, Algrathorp. In teritoriis de Trubervi, Bramenn Lyvacr et Chesterfeld Padenhale.[a]

Sir, wheras it is commoned by your adversaryes that if the Kings grace, through the favor which his counsell beareth you, grant you any lifflod now, they trust herafter to recover it againe by the law, for they have ther recovers exemplified under the Kings great seale to the same intent.

Item. They talke, that wher ye intitle you by reason of a dede intayled by Sir Robert Plompton and dame Alice his wyffe, daughter and heire of Sir Godfrays Foliambe, made unto sir Thomas Rampeston and other; they say, if the sayd sir Robart intaled his owne inherytaunce, the intale of his wiffs inherytaunce was to be avoyded by *Cui in vita*,[b] by many and diverse dyscontynuaunces, which are exemplified. And they have them redy to be shewed herafter, when they see ther tyme for all such causes. Sir, by the advice of your counsell learned, shalbe unto the Kings grace that all former recovers and other tytles, which your adversaryes hath against you and your heires, may be voyded, and adnuled, and revoked; and that ye, by the advice of your learned counsell, by autoryty of Parliament, recover, or otherwise, as your

[a] The heading to this legal opinion in the MS. appears to be wholly irrelevant to the subject matter of it. The places there named I presume to be the hamlets of Holme, Lynacre, Hackingthorp, Troway, and Bramley in Derbyshire; and that under the name of Chesterfield Padenhale is denoted the place of which there is this record in the Domesday survey of the manor of Newbold, to which Chesterfield was only a berewick. "Soke. In Greherst and Padinc four oxgangs of land to be taxed; it is waste." (*Vide Domesd.* 272 b. 1.)

[b] *Cui in vita* is a writ of entry which a widow hath against him to whom her husband alienated her lands or tenements in his lifetime. For the grounds of the title set forth by Sir Robert Plumpton, see *Memoirs.*

counsell thinketh most expedient, herafter may be in suerty for all manner recoverse, dyscontynuances, or any other clame that you adversarys, or their heires, myght have against you and your heires. And this for Gods sake ye se done and perfytly fynished, and *Jesu* evermore preserve you.[c]

(*Anno* 1504-5.)

[c] During the remainder of the reign of Henry VII. the influence of Sir Robert Plumpton, now a Knight of the King's body, and of his friends at Court, was, it seems, sufficient to counteract the measures of Empson, at least so far as to be permitted to retain possession of Plumpton and the Yorkshire estates, notwithstanding the verdict against him at the assize. (*Vide Inq. post mortem Eliz. Suthell liberat. Cur.* 12 *die Februarii anno* 22 *Hen. VII. per manus Richardi Emson militis pro manerio de Kenalton et terris in com. Nott. et* 11 *die Decembris* .... *per manus Ric'i Bunney per* .... *Emson pro manerio de Plumpton, com. Ebor.*) The estates in Derbyshire had been in possession of the feoffees to the use of the heirs general since the eve of the feast of St. Michael 17 Hen. VII. the year of their recovery by assise before the Justices. See a *compotus* of Edward Browne, bailiff and collector of rents there for the use of Richard Burgh and Robert Bubwith, clerks, from the feast of the Exaltation of the Holy Cross, 19 Hen. VII. to the same feast in the following year. (*MS. Add. Brit. Mus.* 6698.)

LETTER CLX.

To my Lady Plompton.

Myn own good Lady Plumpton, I recomende me unto you and to your gud husband, and right sory I am of his and your troubles. If I could remedy it, but God is where he was, and his grace can and will poorvey every thing for the best, and help his servant at their most needes, and so I trust his hynes, he wil do you. My lord, my husband, recommends him unto you both, and sends you yowr obblegasiyn; and has receyved but 4^{li} and a marke of the 20^{li} and 2^{li}: the remnant my lord gives your good husband and you. And I pray Almighty *Jesu* send you both wel to do, as your own herts can desire. Written in hast with the hand of your mother, the 28 day of April. Give credence to this good bearer, for surely he love you full well.

EDITH NEVILL.[a]

[a] Edith, wife of Ralph Lord Nevill, eldest son and heir apparent of Ralph, Earl of Westmoreland, was daughter of Sir William Sands, of the Vine, com. Hants, kt. by Edith, daughter of John Cheney, of Shirland, com. Derb. kt. Her husband died in the lifetime of his father, before 12 July 13 Hen. VII. 1498, at which time his father was likewise dead; for the death of his son, says Leland, so affected the Earl his father, that he quickly followed him to the grave, dying at the seat of his son-in-law William Lord Conyers, at Hornby in Richmondshire, in the church of which parish he lies buried. (*See Lel. Itin. vol. I. f.* 80.) His widow, at the date of this writing, had become the second wife of the ill-fated Lord Darcy of Templehurst, whom Henry VIII. in the first year of his reign, probably by reason of this marriage, made steward and surveyor of all the King's lands beyond Trent, during the minority of her son. (*Orig.* 1 *Hen. VIII. rot.* 62, as cited by *Dugdale.*) That there was other issue of the marriage of Ralph Lord Nevill with Edith Sands, beside Ralph, fourth Earl of Westmoreland, and an elder brother, buried at Brancepeth, who died young, is evinced by this letter, though hitherto unnoticed by genealogists. Dame Isabel Plumpton, their daughter, was married to Sir Robert Plumpton, of Plumpton, com. Ebor. kt. about 18 Sep. 21 Hen. VII. 1505, for by deed of that date, the latter conveyed to Sir William Sands, kt. (afterwards the first Lord Sands), Sir John Rainsford, kt. Sir John Norton, kt. Edward Rainesford, esq. Thomas Ratcliffe, gent. Thomas Pigot, esq. Richard Mauleverey, esq. and William Croft, chaplain, all his lands and tenements lying in the vills and fields of Knarsbrough, Matheloftus near Knarsbrough, Heuby, Elthwatehill near Harwode, Ripon, Acton, Spopherd field, and Arkendon, in the county of York; which feoffees settled the same premises the day but one following upon Sir Robert Plumpton, of Plumpton, kt. and Isabella his wife, and either of them, the longer liver. (*Chartul. No.* 825-6-7.)

LETTER CLXI.

To the right worshipfull Sir Robart Plompton, knyght, be these delivered in hast.

Right worshipfull Sir, I recomend me unto you, being glad to here of your welfare. Sir, according to the promyse that ye made with this bearer, the last tyme that he was with you, I pray you that I may have my money now at this tyme, for I must occupy much money within thes iiij dayes, as this bearer can shew you. And if ye delyver it to this sayd berer, then he shall deliver to you your exigent, and also an acquitance for the sayd money. And if ye will not delyver it at this tyme, I will send no more to you for it, but the berer shall goe to the Shereff with this exigent, and have from him a warrant to have the sayd money, or els to take your body, the which I wold be as sory for, as any man in Yorkshire, if I myght other wayes doe, as knowes our Lord, who keepe you in worship. At Staynley, this St. Martyn even.

Yours to his litle power,

ROBART CHALONER.

LETTER CLXII.

To Sir Robart Plompton, kt. be thes letter delivered.

Sir, in the most hartyest wyse that I can, I recomend me unto you. Sir, I have sent to Wright of Idell for the money that he promyst you, and he saith he hath it not to len, and makes choses (*excuses*) and so I can get none nowhere. And as for wood, ther is none that will bey, for they know ye want money, and without they myght have it halfe for nought, they will bey none; for your son, William Plompton, and Thomas Bickerdyke hath bene every day at wood sence ye went, and they can get no money for nothing,—for tha will bey none without they have tymmer tres, and will give nothingo for them: and so shall your wood be distroyed and get nought for it. Sir, I told you this or ye went, but ye wold not beleve me. Sir, I have taken of your tymmer as much as I can get of, or Whitsonday farme forehand; and that is but litle to do you any good, for ther is but some that will len so long afor the tyme. And your Lenten stoufe is to bey, and I wote not what to do, God wote, for I am ever left of thes fachion. Sir, ther is land in Rybston feild, that Christofer Chambers wold bey, if ye will sel it; but I am not in a suerty what he will give for it. But if ye will sel it send word to your son what ye will doe, for I know nothing els wherwith to help you with. Sir, for God sake take an end, for we are brought to begger staffe, for ye have not to defend them withall. Sir, I send you my mare, and iij[s] iiij[d] by the bearer herof, and I pray you send me word as sone as ye may. No more at this tyme, but the Holy Trenyttie send you good speed in all your matters, and send you sone home. Sir, remember your chillder bookes.

Be your bedfellow,
ISABELL PLOMPTON.[a]

[a] This letter from the grand-daughter of a mighty Earl of Westmoreland feelingly exhibits the straits to which she and her husband were now reduced. No lands of the ancient inheritance of the Plumptons and Foljambes could be sold, where the title of all was impeached, or if a purchaser presented himself, it was only upon obtaining a collateral security fixing lands purchased by Sir Robert Plumpton in his own lifetime, or which had come to him under another title, as through his mother; unless indeed some substantial person could be found to become bound for their peaceable enjoyment. Thus John Slingsby the younger, esq. bought, 10 Oct. 20 Hen. VII. 1504, lands in Studley Roger of Sir Robert Plumpton, kt. and William, his eldest son and heir apparent, but with a condition annexed, that Richard Mauliverey, esq. and Walter Baildon should be at the same time enfeoffed by the vendors in lands in Wetton and Huby near Harwood, to be conveyed to the purchaser, "if the said lands in Studley Roger be recovered from the possession of the said John Slingsby." (Chartul. No. 823.) Of the annoyances to which Germayn Pole, who bought the lands at Combridge in Staffordshire, was subject, his letters which follow bear testimony. To make head against the expenses of this protracted struggle with the more legal claims of the heirs general, the rents of such tenants as did not yet refuse to own Sir Robert Plumpton as their landlord were forestalled, and the wood on the estate was felled. But this last resource failed him: the dealers held back in order to drive an usurious bargain with a necessitous man. The sum of 3s. 4d. was, it seems, all that could be mustered on the present occasion; meanwhile, the store-rooms at Plumpton were empty and the season of Lent was approaching, when the usage of the time made it a sin to taste flesh, and therefore needful to lay in stock-fish and other like provision. Well might Lady Plumpton tell her husband "we are brought to begger-staffe;" ere long she became with him the inmate of a gaol. (See Memoirs.)

LETTER CLXIII.

To the right worshipfull Sir Robart Plompton, knight.

Right worshipfull Sir, in my best maner I comend me unto you; and understood that but layte ye have made clame and pretence unto a certayne land in Rybstone,[a] of long tyme in the tennor of one John Ampleforthe, the which, above the tyme wherof is any memory, hath belonged unto the parson of Spofford for the tyme beying, wher, though all unworthy, at this tyme I occupie the rowme, and the same land without any let or interuption hath had at his disposicion, as is well knovne to all ancient and aged persones within the Lordship of the same, and nygh in the country therunto. Wherfore, Sir, I trust veryly of your wyssdome ye will not in that matter, nor in noe other, anything attempt against the right of me, and my sayd Church, more than ye have heretofore done in the tyme of my predecessors, or of ther deputs and fermors. And if ye nedely will, I must defend me and my sayd right as I may, and so will; nevertheles, if I may have the right of my church with your love and favor, I wold be right glad, for right loth I wold be, not compelled, to be in troble with you, or any worshipfull of my parishe. Therfore, Sir, I requier you to let me have my right peasiably, as my predecessors tofore hath had, and so doing, ye shall have my service, and otherwise not, as this berer, my servant, to whom please yt you to give credence, shall more largly shew you on my behalfe. Wrytten at Pettewoorth, the xxvii of January, with the hand of him that wold, having noo cause to the contrary, owe you his service.

ROBART PICHARD,
parson of Spofforthe.

[a] Could this have been the land in Rybston field, of which Lady Plumpton speaks in the preceding letter? If so, the attempt to sell it appears only to have added to the Knight's misfortunes in drawing down upon him the wrath of the rector of his parish, and the displeasure of the powerful Earl of Northumberland. (See next Letter.)

LETTER CLXIV.

To my right trusty and welbeloved Cousin, Sir Robart Plompton, knight.

Cosin Sir Robart Plompton, I commennd me unto you, and am informed that ye pretend a tytle and clame unto a litle land in Rybstone, the which without tyme of mynde hath belonged unto the parson of Spofford the tyme being, and hath always bene at his disposition to now lait that, as I perceive, ye be aboutward against all right to imbarre and exclud my Chapleyn, now parsonn ther, and . . . . . my service of the same; wherof I greatly marvill, considring his predesessors alway hertofore hath quietly and peasibly had it. And furthermore, well assured I am, Cousen, that my chaplayn wold not covit to have it, but for the . . . . . aforsayd, and in the right of his Church; the which, for that I . . patron thereof, I must and will, in that I can, helpe to defend, as myne owne inheritaince. Wherefore, I desire and pray you noe further to intromete you with the sayd land and right of his church, more then ye have in tyme past, in the dayes of other his predesessours; and in case ye nedely will, wherof I wold be right sory, know ye veryly ye cannot have my good will and favour. And that, morover, it shalbe greatly against my will, that ye or any other shall wrong me in the right of the same, whill I live. Written in my mannor of Petworth, the last day of Januarie.

Your loving Cousin,
HEN: NORTHUMBERLAND.

LETTER CLXV.

To the right worshipfull and my most entyerly beloved, good, kind father, Sir Robart Plompton, knyght, lying at Plompton in Yorkshire, be thes delivered in hast.

Ryght worshipfull father, in the most humble manner that I can I recommend me to you, and to my lady my mother, and to all my brethren and sistren, whom I besech almyghtie God to mayntayne and preserve in prosperus health and encrese of worship, entyerly requiring you of your daly blessing: letting you wyt that I send to you mesuage, be Wryghame of Knarsbrugh, of my mynd, and how that he should desire you in my name to send for me to come home to you, and as yet I had no answere agane, the which desire my lady hath gotten knowledg. Wherfore, she is to me more better lady then ever she was before, insomuch that she hath promysed me hir good ladyship as long as ever she shall lyve; and if she or ye can fynd athing meeter for me in this parties or any other, she will helpe to promoote me to the uttermost of her puyssaunce. Wherfore, I humbly besech you to be so good and kind father unto me as to let me know your pleasure, how that ye will have me ordred, as shortly as it shall like you. And wryt to my lady, thanking hir good ladyship of hir so loving and tender kyndnesse shewed unto me, beseching hir ladyship of good contynewance therof. And therfore, I besech you to send a servant of yours to my lady and to me, and shew now by your fatherly kyndnesse that I am your child; for I have sent you dyverse messuages and wryttings, and I had never answere againe. Wherfore, yt is thought in this parties, by those persones that list better to say ill than good, that ye have litle favor unto me; the which error ye may now quench, yf yt will like you to be so good and kynd father unto me. Also I besech you to send me a fine hatt and some good cloth to make me some kevercheffes.

And thus I besech *Jesu* to have you in his blessed keeping to his pleasure, and your harts desire and comforth. Wryten at the Hirste,[a] the xviii day of Maye.

By your loving daughter,
DORYTHE PLOMPTON.[b]

[a] Temple Hirst in the parish of Birkin, com. Ebor. the seat of Lord Darcy.

[b] Dorothy Plumpton had, it may be presumed from the context of this letter, been placed in some menial situation in the household of Lady Darcy, which the young lady did not think meet for her rank. The Lady Darcy was mother of Sir Robert Plumpton's then wife, and hence perhaps the motive for her step-daughter being so bestowed. (See *Letter LIX. note ª*.) I may here remark that among the usual authorities for the genealogies of the extinct Baronage of the kingdom great discrepancy is apparent respecting this lady and her connexions. Dugdale writes the name Elizabeth, citing as his authority MS. J. 3 in Offic. Arm. fol. 71 b, and affirms she died 22 Aug. 1529, and was buried at the Friars Minors in Greenwich. Collins copies Dugdale, but makes her the first wife, *ex stemmate*. It is, however, certain that both George Darcy and Arthur Darcy, sons of her husband by a former wife, daughter of Sir Richard Tempest, of Giggleswick, in Ribblesdale, com. Ebor. kt. had reached manhood before 6 Hen. VIII. 1514, when they were co-feoffees with others for the uses of the marriage settlement of Sir Marmaduke Constable, the younger, and Elizabeth, the daughter of Thomas Lord Darcy; which marriage had been contracted for in the preceding year by Sir Marmaduke Constable, the elder, of Flamborough, kt. and Sir Robert Constable, his eldest son, father of the younger Sir Marmaduke, in consideration of the sum of 800 marks, given with her by her father. *(Petition of Sir Robert Constable, 5 Eliz. Archer's MS. p. 168, penes W. Constable Maxwell, de Everingham, com. Ebor. Ar.)* Banks and Edmondson recite the wives in their proper order, but, as well as Dugdale, without being aware of or having been first married to the Lord Nevill, and upon his authority adopt the name of Elizabeth. But in a MS. *Baronagium Angliæ* by Wm. Smith, Rouge Dragon, anno 1597, now in the possession of Lord Stourton, under the title of Sandes, she is rightly named Editha, and her two husbands, Ralph Nevill and Thomas Lord Darcy of Templehurst, are both mentioned, the only error being the addition of the title of Earl of Westmoreland to the name of her first husband. It was, moreover, no doubt in compliment to her that one of the daughters of George Lord Darcy was named Edith, afterwards the wife of Sir Thomas Dawney of Cowick, com. Ebor. kt. The proof of this second marriage of Edith Lady Nevill is otherwise interesting, as establishing the near degree of kindred which existed between the last unfortunate Earl of Westmoreland and the infamous Sir Robert Constable, who sought to betray him to Queen Elizabeth. (See *Sadler's State Papers*.) Her daughter, Dame Isabel Plumpton, survived her husband Sir Robert Plumpton, and was 10 Mar. 20 Hen. VIII. 1528-9, the wife of Lawrence Kighley of New Hall, near Otley, esq. *(See Memoirs.)*

LETTER CLXVI.

To the right worshipfull Sir Robart Plompton, kt. in hast thes.

Right worshipfull Sir, my duty remembred, I recomend me to your good mastership, praying you to be good master to me as to send me iiij^{li}, according to your appoyntment afore my master Gascoygne, at Harwode; the which appoyntment was, that I should send for yt within viii day of Martynmas day. I thinke, by the grace of God, to goe to London within thes 2 or iij dayes, and therfore I send to your mastership more hastyly, for because I wold have it with me to pay for the cost of the same suyte. And therfore I besech you to bestowe no more labor in this behalfe, and this my letter, the which this berrer can delyver to your mastership, shalbe a sufficient discharg of all debts and outlares by reason of the sayd oblygacion, as knoweth *Jesu*, who keepe you in worship. At Wakfeld, the xvi day of December.

Your owne to his power,
ROBART CHALONER.

LETTER CLXVII.

To the right worshipfull Sir Robart Plompton, kt.

Right worshipfull Sir, in the best maner that I can I recommend me to you, praying you to send me the money which my father lent you at London, the which is iiij^{li}; for your son Edmund[a] promysed me at London, if I wold suffer the exigend, which I had agaynst you, not to goe out agaynst you, that I should have the money now at my comyng into the countre. And therfore, if so be ye will deliver to this berer the aforesayd money, he shall deliver to you the exigend, and an acquitance sealed with my sygnett for the same; and if not, I will put the exigend into the schereffe hands, and then ye shalbe outlawd shortly. For if I had not kept it in my hands, ye had bene outlayed or now, as knoweth *Jesu*, who preserve your mastership in worship. At Standley, the xvi day of Aprill.

Yours to his power,
ROBART CHALONER.

[a] This is the only notice I have met with of Edmund Plumpton; he probably died unmarried in his father's life-time.

LETTER CLXVIII.

To our right worshipfull Sir Robart Plompton, kt.

Right worshipfull, after all due recomendations pleaseth you to understand, that of late you made great instante labors unto our singuler good lord, my lord Archbyshop of Yorke, for a chauntry of the Trenite, within the church of Rippon, possessed by Sir Anthony Sole; and also ye shewed to our lord Archbishop that the foresayd Sir Anthony was intrused. Wherupon your informacion, our sayd Lord Archbishop comaunded, by a letter to the foresayd chapitor of Rippon derected, to admitte Sir Richard Plompton by your presentacion, for because the foresayd Antony was presented by Richard Emson, and also that he was his chapelaine, and not after the true order of law admytted. Master Plompton, according to our sayd Lord Archbyshop, at his departing out of England,[a] comaunded to me John Carvar, his Vicker generall, and John Wythers, his Surveyor and generall Reasonner, to wryte unto you that the foresayd Sir Anthony hath be possessed this iij quarters of a yeare and more peassably; and also presented by the Kinge, and nothing belonging to Rich. Emson: and no *Quare impedit* of your parte suyd, and as now without remedie by that wryte. Wherfore, we exhort you and hartyly desire you to patiently suffer this poore preist to occupie peassiabely his poore chawntory with all the profitte and commodity to the said chawntory belonging (without any desire and commaundement of your parte to the tenaunts, fermors and occupiers of the same), without any furder besines or trouble, and it nothinge preiudiciall to your tytle of londis. And thus doing, ye shall please almyghty God, and to cause our forsayd lord Archbishop to be more synguler good lord in all your causes, busines, and trobles. And thus our Lorde God have you in his keeping. From Yorke, the xxix day of October, by your faithfull and loving frynds at ther litle powers, as God knoweth.

JOHN CARVER,
Vicar generall.
JOHN WYTHERS.

(29 Oct. 1509.)

[a] Christopher Bainbridge, Archbishop of York, appointed proctor for King Henry VIII. at the Papal See, 24 Sept. 1509. He died in the Holy City. *(See Drake's Eboracum.)*

LETTER CLXIX.

To the right worshipfull Sir Robart Plompton, Kt. be thes byll delivered, or to my lady his wyfe.

Master Plumpton, I comend me unto you; letting you understand that the Scherefe of the shire of Lancaster sent a balife to my house with a wrytt, and hath seysed into the Kings hands al my lands and goods, unto such tyme that the marchant of London be content of a c^{li}. which Sir John Luth,[a] a knyght, and I were surty to for you, and the whole summe is layd to my charge; wherin I marvell greatly that ye shewed that ye had goten longer day to

[a] *Sic, sed lege* Bothe. Sir Robert Plumpton, kt. and William, his son and heir apparent, were bound in a statute merchant to Sir John Bothe, of Barton, in com. Lanc. kt. and Hamelett Harington, of Hayton-bay, com. Lanc. esq. in a £100, to indemnify them against Morgan Williams, citizen of London, who had advanced this sum upon their security, which instrument bears date 1 Jan. 1 Hen. VIII. 1509-10. *(Chartul. No. 833.)* This debt was not acquitted till 9 May, 8 Hen. VIII. 1516, when it was agreed that costs should be awarded according to the judgment of Sir Robert Sheffeild, knight, counseler to our Lord the King, and of Master John Veesy, clerk, Dean of the King's chappell. *(Ibid. No. 847.)*

pay it in at Whitsontide and Candelmas. Wherfore, I pray you to se a way that I may be discharged, as shortly as ye can, so that I may occupy my land and goods. If ye will not so doe, I must sue my statute marchant on you and ayre William, your sone, which I wold be loth, and ye had such dayes granted as ye shewed me. Ye must, at the least, send to London to the marchant, and get him to send downe to the Schereffe, that I may be discharged. And if ye will not do soe, I will up to London, and sue out my statute marchant, as shortly as I can. Take credence to the bearer therof. At Hyton, the eight day of May.

HAMNET HARYNGTON,
Esquire.

LETTER CLXX.

To my right worshipfull Cousin, Sir William Gascon, be these delivered.

Right worshipfull Cousin, I recommend me unto you. And where it was appoynted, for the matter in traverse betwyxt my Cousin Plumpton, my cousin Roclife, and his cooparseners, the meetyng to be at Yorke, upon fryday next afore St. Wyllia day,[a] supposing than it had bene the morning next after the twelt day. Cousin, in that matter we toke the day wrong, for that same fryday is veryly the twelt day. Wherfore, that it will like you to apoint some other day, for that day cannot keepe for causes aforsayd. And if it like you to appoynt the Munday or Tewsday next after St. William day, or any day in that weke, I having knowledg from you, I shall not fale to keepe the same day that ye list to apoynt. And the cause why I am desirus to know the day now, is cheifly because I wold common with Sir Wyllyam Parpoynt, who is now comyng fro beyond the see, and know his mynd thorowly in this matter afor our meting. And thus I besech *Jesu* preserve you. Wrytten at Holme, the xi day of November.

Your loving Cousin,
MARMADUKE CONSTABLE, of Flaunborgh.[b]

(M^d. to appoint the Tewsday next after twelt day.)
(11 *Nov.* 1514.)

[a] The feast of the translation of St. William, Archbishop of York, was kept on the Sunday next after the Epiphany. In the year 1515, 6 Hen. VIII. the Epiphany, or Twelfth Day, fell on a Friday.

[b] King Henry VIII. Aug. 22, in the first year of his reign, granted to Sir William Perpoint, knight, of Holme, com. Nott. the custody of Joane and Elizabeth Southill, and their marriage. (*Rot. Pat. pars* 1ma. 1 *Hen. VIII.*) He had also, July 24, 2 Hen. VIII. the custody of the lands and tenements which were Henry Sothills and Elizabeth Sothills, widow, as long as they remained in the King's hands. (*Ibid. pars* 2da. 2 *Hen. VIII.*) At the same time Sir William Pierpoint married Joan, the widow of Henry Sotehill, and the mother of these twin sisters, his co-heirs; she, it has been mentioned, was the daughter of Sir Richard Empson, kt. who towards the close of the reign of Henry VII. had been made Chancellor of the Duchy of Lancaster. (*See Thoroton's Notts. edit.* 1797, *vol.* i. *p.* 176.) The wardship and marriage of Joan, the eldest co-heir, was subsequently purchased by Sir Marmaduke Constable of Flamborough, com. Ebor. kt. conjointly with his fourth son, John Constable, esq. afterwards a knight, who eventually married the lady, and resided at Kinalton. He died 13 Eliz. 1571, leaving issue by her three daughters: 1. Anne, the wife of George Babington, esq. in her right of Kinalton, by whom she had no issue, and secondly, of Sir Anthony Thorold, of Marston, com. Linc. kt. whose only daughter by her became the wife of George, son and heir of Sir Gervase Clifton, of Clifton, com. Nott. kt. and carried the representation of the ancient house of Plumpton, together with the estate at Kinalton, to the family of that surname; 2. Cecilia, first wife of William Bevercotes, esq. and secondly, of Clement Oglethorp, esq. She had issue by both husbands, and upon the partition of the land which was the Lady Jane Constable's, late of Kinalton, com. Notts. by virtue of an indenture bearing date 28 Mar. 19 Eliz. 1577, between Cuthbert Bevercotes, esq. of the one part, and William Oglethorp, esq. of the other part, the moiety of the lordship of Clifton (*Steton ?*) was assigned to the former, and the moiety of the lordship of Idel to the latter. (*MSS. of J. C. B. in Coll. Arm.*) 3. Catharine, without issue. Elizabeth, the second of the daughters and co-heirs of Henry Sotehill, was married to Sir William Drury, of Hawsted Place, com. Suff. kt. of whose descendants a full and detailed account will be found in the History of Suffolk, "Thingoe Hundred,"

lately published by my esteemed friend, John Gage, esq. Director S. A. who since the demise of his brother, the late Robert Joseph Gage Rookwood, of Coldham Hall, in Stanningfield, com. Suff. esq. without surviving issue, has, upon succeeding to the estate, assumed also the name of Rookwood. (*Hist. and Antiquities of Suffolk, p.* 428, *London,* 4to. Bentley, 1838.)

LETTER CLXXI.

To my right worshipfull Coussin, Sir William Gascoine, be thes dellivered.

Right worshipfull Coussin, I recomend me unto you; and this Saterday, at thre of the clock at after nowne, I received your letter, whearby I perceive that both ye and my coussin Plompton is content to kepe the tewsday next after the twelt day at York. And whether ye think to be theare that tewsday at viij clock, and have communication in that matter upon wednsday by viii or ix of the clock in the morning, or els to be theare the monday at night, and have our comunication upon the tewsday, this I had nede to know, before I send to my cossin Parpoint, because he comes farre, and I wold not disapoint him. And furthermore, Coussin, ye rehearse to me in your said letter that you have spoken with my cossin William Plompton in the matter that ye comond with me of, and that ye trust at our metting to give me such answer in that matter, as I shall be content. Coussin, as towching the matter betwixt Sir Robart Plompton, and Sir John Rouclif and his cooparseners, if my sayd coussin be of any towardnes to take end, and to be ordred by frinds in that matter, I shall well content both in that and other things . . . . frind apoynted to kepe the day at York, such as ye have appoynted. And as for any answer, or other communication with my Cossin William Plompton, in any other matter, but onely this old matter betwixt my coussin Sir Robart Plompton, his father, and Sir John Rouclif and his cooparseners, I trust verrely that ye think, that I of my honestie may neither common, nor take answer in that matter. And so if that be the princepall cause, or any part of any meting, I wold neither ye, nor I, lost no labor, but rather remit all matters to the Common Law. And, Coussin, for the more perfit and suer knowledg of your mind, touching this day of our metting, I shall send a servant of mine, who shall not faill to be with you upon Thursday at viii clock next coming, and to bring me suer writting from you in that behalfe. And thus our Lord preserve you. Written at Holme, the xix[t1] of November.

Your loving coussin,
MARMADUKE COUNSTABLE,
of Flaynbrough, knight.

(19 *Nov.* 1514.)

LETTER CLXXII.

M^d. for the matter of varyance betwyx Sir John Rocliffe, Sir Wiliam Perepoynt, John Constable, on the one party, and Sir Robart Plumpton and William his son on the other party; it is thus ordred by the assent of both the parties, the sayd partys shall abyde thaward of my Lord Wynchester, my lord Tresourer, my lord of Surrey, Robert Brudnell, William Fayrfax, Justices, Bryan Palmes, John Newdgate, Sargaunts at the law, Sir John Norton, knyght, Richard Sawcheverell, or Sir Andrew Wyndysour, betwixt this and the next assise; and nether of the sayd partyes shall vex other, nor ther partakers, servants, tenants for ther sakes, by entre, dystresse, wrytt, prive seale, indytement, nor other wyse betwixt this and the said assise.

WYLLIAM FARFAX.[a]

[a] Sir William Fairfax, Justice of the Common Pleas, eldest son of Sir Guy Fairfax, of Steeton, com. Ebor. kt. Chief Justice of the King's Bench, died 6 Hen. VIII. 1515. Only three of the arbitrators here named signed the final award, John Earnly, the King's Attorney-general, being the fourth. (*See Memoirs.*)

LETTER CLXXIII.

To my right worshipfull father-in-law, Sir Robart Plompton, kt. be these delivered.

Right worshipfull father, in the most loving maner that I can, I hartely recomennd me unto you, and to my lady my mother-in-law, your wyfe; and likwise my poore wyfe, your daughter, recomends hir unto you and my sayd lady, and prayeth you of your daly blessing. And we desire hartely the knowledge of your prosperous health, worship, and welfare, the which I besech Almyghty Jesus long to contynue to encrease to his pleasure, and your comforth. And, father, if you be remembred, I wrote a letter unto you laytly, and sent it unto you by my servant; in the which letter I instaunced and desired you to shew your fatherly kindnes unto my poore wife and me, and to be so gud father unto us, as to make a sure meane that we myght peaseably enjoy and occupie the land that I bought of you in Combryg in Staforthshire, (for I thought, that unles the sayd land in Combryge were specified in this award, now made betwixt you and Roclife and the heires of Suttele, or els of a liklyhod they wold enter upon me and disposses me,)[a] and you send me word, that you thought they wold not have it, nor medle with it. But thus it is, that now within this fortnyth ther were servants of Sir William Parpoints and Sir John Roclifes determined to take away the goods that they could find upon the ground; and so had they donne, but that the tenaunt fortuned to here tell of ther coming, and in all possible hast came to give me warning. And so, by the helpe of gud masters and frinds, at the last, by fayre means, with very great payne, entreated them to spare distreyning, till such tyme as I had sent unto you to know what remedy you wold provide herin. Wherfore, at the reverence of God, and for the love that you owe unto my poore wyfe and me and our children, remember how we stand unto you, and be so gud and kind father unto us to find the meane, that we may peasiably occupie that litle land, which I bought of you and truly payd for; and it shalbe to a discharge of your conscience and, with Gods grace, comforth in lykewyse, for it shall ever succeed in your bloud. Father, I besech you thus to doe, to take the payne upon you to make such labor unto Sir John Roclife, that he will, at your instauncie and by the mediacion of such of your frinds as it shall please you to cause to labor unto him, make a release of that land in Combrig. Father, if it please you to doe your best herin, I doubt not, with Gods grace, but you shall well bring this matter to passe, considring the familiaritie betwixt you and him now, and that is like to be. Thus doing, you bynd me and all myne ever to do you that pleasure, that may be in our smale power; and not doyng thus, all that know you and me myght well speake upon it, that I should, considryng how I stand unto you, pay such a sume of money to you, and not to be made sure of my bargen. And beside, yt wold be to me as great discomforth as lightly cold happen me, which wold greve much more then the losse of my money, or of my land. And, as you know right well, I have Slyngsby bonden as your surty in an obligation of x^{li} for the perfirmance of your bargan, which I have redy in my keping. And the Lord preserve you. From Redburne in hast, upon Trenetie Munday.

By your faythfull loving son,

(*4 June* 1515.)   GERMAYN POLE.

[a] The award had been made 27 Mar. 6 Hen. VIII. 1515, and in it the lands at Combredge in Staffordshire were not specified; bnt an agreement was subsequently come to by the parties, 12 Nov. 17 Hen. VIII. 1515, to refer to arbitrators the proofs concerning the lands called Comrig, in the county of Stafford, and the question whether the advowson of the chantry of Ripon, in the county of York, was appurtenant to the manor of Plumpton, in the county of York. (*Chartul. No.* 845.) The result was in favour of Germayn Pole, and the lands purchased at Combridge continued to be the property of his descendants, as appears by the escheats.

LETTER CLXXIV.

To the right worshipfull and singuler gud father, Sir Robart Plompton, Kt. be these delivered in hast.

Right worshipfull and my full singuler gud father, in the most humble and lowly maner that I can, I hartely recomend me unto you, and to my lady your wyfe, and in lykewise doth your daughter, my poore wyfe, and hartely prayeth you of your dayly blessing, desiring the knowledg of your prosperous health and welfaire. Father, so it is that upon a truth, of thursday last, oon Richard Bardall of Hessope came in the names of Roclife, Parpoynte, and Counstable[a] to my tennant in Combryg, and also to Crake[marsh] and in ther names comaunded my tennant that he should from henceforth pay me no rent, but to make his rent redy for them, shewing eich one of them wold send a servant thither for the rent betwixt this and Martynmas; and told him playnly that they must have the sayd land, because it was nether in ther wryting, nor in yours. Father, you sent me word laytly by my servant, that you had made it sure to me without any daunger. Yt pleaseth you to let him se your wrytings, and, as I understond, both by you and by him, it is nether expressed in the wrytings that towch them, nor you. Yet, notwithstanding, upon mine honestie, they make this sturrying therin, and so yt is to thinke, that if they may find any hole or colur therin, they will troble with me for the same; and yt were great pytie that I shold have ony troble for that thing, that I have bought and truly payd for. Wherfore, at the reverence of God, and for the love that you owe to me and my wyfe, and our children, to make a sure way for me now at this terme at London. And I pray you send me word what tyme you will goe or send to London, and I will send one of my servants to meet you or your deputie ther. And at his comming whom, bringing me word that you have made it sure to me without daunger or jopartie, forthwith you shal have payd you that, that myne uncle Sir Alban[a] promysed you, and at all tymes the best that in me may be to you and all yours, duryng my natural life, by the sufferance of *Jesu*, who have you in his eternall keping. From Rodburne in hast, the iij day of October. Father, I besech you at such tyme as recoveres or assurances shalbe made, that it will please you to let it be expressed by name, that they may be avoyded or expulsed from ther clame therin.

Your loving son,

(3 *Oct.* 1515.)   GERMAYN POLE.

[a] Sir Alban Pole was a younger son of Ralph and Elizabeth Pole, probably in Holy Orders.

LETTER CLXXV.

To my uncle Plumpton this letter be delivered in hast.

Uncle Plompton, I commend me unto you. It is so I am like to have busines for the lordship of Harwood. The Kinge is my good and gracias Lord, and hath granted it to me, with all the revenos and profitts thereof, duryng the nowne age of the heire of Heire Ridman.[a] And as I am enformed, such folkes as be not my lovers, wold bysie them in the cause; how be it, they have no matter of law, nor right therin. Wherfore I desire you, if there be any cause or matter of danger against me in that behalfe, that ye will be with me, with such company as you can make, at such tyme as I send to you; at which your comyng ye shall se a reason-

[a] Joanna, only child of Henry Redman, son and heir apparent of Edward Redman, esq. lord of a moiety of Harewood, com. Ebor. was five years old in 6 Hen. VIII. when her grandfather died. (*See Pedigree in Whitaker's Loidis et Elmete.*)

able suerty to beare me in the cause. And what ye will doe herin, I pray you send me word in writting be this bearer. And thus our Lord keepe you. At Gaukthorpe, the xviii day of December.

Your nephew,

(18 *Dec. anno circiter* 1515.)   WILLIAM GASCOYGNE.

LETTER CLXXVI.

To my Uncle Plompton be these delivered.

Uncle Plompton, I recomend me unto you, desiring you to call to your remembrance the byrth of my nephew William Farfax,[a] which was borne with you at Plompton, and let me have the dayt of his birth. Also I pray you let me have the dayt of the marraige of my cosin Hair and your daughter,[b] which ye have in wrytting, as I am enformed ; and ye thus doyng bynds me to doe you as great a pleasure, which I shalbe glad to doe, with the grace of God, who preserve you to his pleasure, and thus fare ye well. From Gawkthrop, the third day of March.

Your

(3 *March* 15—.)   WILLIAM GASCOYNE.

[a] William Fairfax, twin-brother with Sir Nicholas Fairfax, of Gilling, com. Ebor. kt. sons of Sir Thomas Fairfax, of Walton, com. Ebor. kt. by Anne, daughter of Sir William Gascoigne, of Gawkthorpe, com. Ebor. kt. and the Lady Margaret Percy, and sister to the writer of this letter.

[b] Arthur Eyre, son and heir of Robert Eyre of Padley, com. Derb. esq. was contracted to marry Margaret, daughter of Sir Robert Plumpton, kt. before 4 Aug. 15 Hen. VII. 1500.

LETTER CLXXVII.

To my right worshipfull master, Sir Robart Plompton, kt. deliver these in hast.

Right worshipfull Sir, after my loving maner I hartyly recomend me unto your good mastership, desiryng evermore to here of your good health and wellfare, the which Almyghty Jesu preserve and contynew to his pleasure, and to your singuler comforth. Sir, the speciall cause of my wrytting to your mastership at this tyme, is this ; my lady Ward, your sister,[a] hartely desires your mastership that ye wold be so good brother unto hir, as for to let hir have Mrs Clare, your daughter, to beare her ladyship companie this tyme of Christynmas at Gauthorp : that done, she wer much bound to your gud mastership. Letting your mastership to understand, that she is a hevy gentlewoman ; wherfore, I cannot say. Letting your mastership to know that Mr. Nevell is come home, and master Watter Stryckland in like maner.[b] As for other newes, I here of none. Desiring your mastership to send hir Ladyship your mynd by wrytting, or els by word of mouth be the berer of this letter, after what maner she shalbe ordred touching the premysses of this byll. No more to your mastership at this tyme, but almyghty Jesu have you in his keeping, and all yors. Amen.

Your owne servant to his poer,

JAMES EMYSONN.

[a] Margaret, daughter of Sir William Gascoigne of Gawkthorp. com. Ebor. kt. by his wife Joan, daughter and heiress of Sir John Nevill, of Althorp, com. Linc. kt. wife of Sir Christopher Ward of Givendale, com. Ebor. kt. and sister of Dame Agnes, wife of Sir Robert Plumpton, kt.

[b] Sir Christopher Ward died 14 Hen. VIII. 1522. (*Esc.* 14 *Hen. VIII. n.* 68.) when it was found that Margaret the wife of Lawrence, (then *sine prole,*) Joanna wife of Sir Edward Musgrave, kt. *ætatis* 23 *annorum*, Catharine, wife of Walter Stirkland, esq. æt. 22, Johanna, wife of John Constable, esq. twin with the last, and Anne, wife of Ralph Nevill, (who with her husband were then both dead,) should have been his daughters and heirs.

LETTER CLXXVIII.

To my right worshipfull master Sir Robart Plompton, kt. deliver thes in hast.

Right worshipfull Sir, in my most humble maner that I can, I recomend me to your good mastership, and also to my good lady ; letting your mastership understand that Nicholas, the messenger, hath delivered a byll into the Stare Chamber of all the prevey seles that he delivered in the north country : and as many as apereth not, the Counsell derecteth proses against them. Howbeyt, I made aledgment for your mastership, wherwith they are content, and hath given day to All-hallow day. And they lay to your charge lxxxiij^{li}, that your mastership shold be debtable to the King for the lordship of Plompton, for ij yeres, in King Herre the VIIth dayes. This must be answered at the next terme. And, Sir, ther is a suyt against your mastership in the Excheker for introshon.[a] And, Sir, as for my yong master, that hath none end as yet.[b] Sir, the Kings grace and the queens lyeth at Wodfeld ; and yt is sayd of a certayne that ther comes a lyget from Rome to my lord Cartdenall, and shall bring to my lord Cardenall the paypis with full authoryty and power of all maner of things in the Reame of England.[c] No more to your mastership, but the Holy Ghost have you in his keping. From London in hast, the xxviii of June.

By your servant,

(28 *June* 1516.)   JOHN D.

[a] This suit must relate to the forcible possession retained of Plumpton in the reign of Henry VII. after recovery by assise at the Common Law. Sir Robert Plumpton was now, it seems, made a debtor to the King for the rents and profits received during this intrusion, till he was again in by due course of law.

[b] The dispute with Babthorpe. (*See next Letter.*)

[c] Cardinal Wolsey obtained these powers from Rome by bull dated Dec. 22, 1516. *Rymer's Fœdera, tom. XIII.* p. 573.

LETTER CLXXIX.

To his sister Isbell Plompton[a] *be thes delivered.*

Sister, I hartelie commend me to you. Edmond, your servant, shewed me that ye are aferred that the agrement that my lord of

[a] It has been asserted in a preceding note, but upon insufficient grounds, that William Eleson or Elson, the writer of this letter, whom William Plumpton calls his brother in Letter CXLII. and who here addresses Mrs. Isabel Plumpton as his sister, had eventually married a daughter of Sir Robert Plumpton, the above modes of expression being supposed to indicate that he was the brother-in-law of the parties. That there was no such connection, when the Letters inserted at p. 134-5, and p. 163, were written, is manifest from their address and subscription. Now of these letters, one is ascertained to have been written 12 Feb. 1498-9 ; the next is of later date ; while the third cannot have been sent before the month of October or November in the year 1502 ; subsequently to which date, and to the date of William Plumpton s Letter, viz. on the 12 Apr. 1504, he is named by Lady Plumpton, but not as " my son," a distinction to which if he was entitled no mother-in-law would have omitted in a familiar letter of the time, when affinity and relationship in a much more remote degree were so respectfully cherished. To explain the connection between the parties, we must therefore have recourse to other evidence. In the Visitation of 1584 by Glover, Robert Babthorpe, the father of Mrs. Isabel Plumpton, is represented to have married a wife named Katharine, and from a tricking of a coat of arms, *sa. a chevron engrailed or,* a line is drawn appropriating it to her. Archer, as cited by Burton from Smales, p. 124, corroborates Glover, and adds that she was daughter of ———— who died in 1461. (*See Pedigree of Babthorpe in Burton's Mon. Eboracense,* p. 437, *note* [b].) The above coat Edmondson assigns to the family of Hagthorpe, a local name derived from a vill in the same township as Babthorpe, viz. Brakenholme cum Woodal, in the parish of Hemingbrough ; and I find a Thomas Hagthorpe de Brakenholme, a witness to a deed of release from Alice Keighleston to Ralph Babthorpe, esq. dated 10 Jan. 17 Hen. VI. 1438-9. (*Towneley MSS.* G. 24.) Robert Babthorpe must necessarily have died before 11 May, 1496, when the representation of the Babthorpes had vested in his daughter Isabell or Elizabeth as heir general, then in her seventeenth year ; * (*see Letter XCIX.* note [b].) and upon comparing the date of his

* By the contract of marriage, 11 May, 11 Hen VII. it was covenanted that Sir Robert Plumpton should convey to feoffees, Nicholas Mydletcn, Richard Grene, Robert Haldynby, esq. and Richard Plumpton, clerk, lands to the value of 20 marks

Durram [b] hath made with Bedell [c] shold hurt your title in Bapthorp. Sister, be ye nothing afeard therof, for ye shal have as good remede now as ye might have had before, and as that if your Cossin wear at full age; for his non age shall not hurt you.[d] If

[daughter's birth with the age of Ralph his elder brother, who was found to be 22 years old when his father died, 6 Edw. IV. 1466, (Esc. de eod. anno.) it may be conjectured that he was about thirty when he married. It is also certain from a comparison of dates and circumstances, that William Eleson was many years the senior of Mrs. Isabel Plumpton, for we find him in 1501 esteemed a lawyer of such approved counsel, as to be considered the fittest person to investigate the complicated evidence supporting the title of Sir Robert Plumpton to the estates claimed by the heirs general. (See Letter CXIX.) From these inferences I draw the conclusion, that Katharine, wife of Robert Babthorpe, daughter of ——— Hagthorpe, had had a first husband, and that William Eleson of Selby was the issue of such marriage, and brother in half blood to Mrs. Isabel Plumpton. On a stone in the north aisle of the abbey church of Selby, near the font, was inscribed, *Hic jacet Joh. Elson, qui obiit* 14...1509, who, if the date be correct, was probably another brother, and not father of William Elson, as heretofore assumed in the note to Letter CIII. Of other issue, mention will be made in a subsequent note.

[b] The manor of Babthorpe was held of the Bishop of Durham.

[c] Christiana, the widow of William Babthorpe of Osgodby, remarried William Bedell, esq. and survived to 8 April, 31 Hen. VIII. 1540, as appears from the register of Sepulchral Inscriptions existing temp. Hen. VIII. in the church of the Grey Friars, London. "Christiana Bedell, uxor Willelmi Bedell, armigeri, et filia Henrici Suttell de Stockfaston, de com. Leicestrie, armigeri. Ob. 8 Apr. 1540." (See *Coll. Top. et Geneal. vol. V. p.* 289.)

[d] William Babthorpe, son of William Babthorpe of Osgodby and of Christian Sotehill or Suttell, (erroneously described as a daughter of Mr. John Soothill in the pedigree of Babthorpe in Burton,) was yet a minor, 29 Apr. 2 Hen. VIII. 1510, when Thomas Babthorpe, clerk, provost of the Collegiate Church of Hemingbrough, bound himself in the penal sum of £100 to William Plumpton, the obligation to be void " if the said Thomas Babthorp and William Bedell, during the nonage of William Babthorp, should keep the award of Thomas Darcy, Lord Darcy, and Sir Marmaduke Constable, knight, (late) Sherif of Yorkshire,]

any presept com from the Sherrif to take your cattell, obey ye it not, for no cattell should be taken therby but your husband cattell, and he hath none; and so may ye make the bayly answer. And take good hede of your cattell, and of keping of your place[e] now, whiles your husband is at London. And I pray God send you good spede in your matter. Written this Monday.

By yours,
WILL. ELSON.

[arbitrators indifferently chosen by the parties, of and upon the right and title of the manor of Babthorpe and the lands and tenements in Brackholme and Hemingbrough, which the said William claimeth in the right of Isabel his wife, and of the lands in Watterton, in the county of Lincoln, which the said Thomas claimeth in right of the foresaid William Babthorpe, now being under age, the award to be given before the feast of St. Michael the Archangel next ensuing." (*Chartul. No.* 835.)

[e] William Crouch, the Escheator in the county of York, testifies by deed that on Friday, 3 Apr. 21 Hen. VII. 1506, he had given quiet seisin and possession of the manor called Babthorp, with its appurtenances, in the county of York, and of the manors or vills called Brakenhome, Estofte, Selby, and Hunigsley, in the same, to William Plumpton, esq. in right of Isabella his wife, cousin and heir of Isabella Hastings, late wife of Sir John Hastings, kt. according to the precept in a writ dated 13 Feb. last past to him directed. (*Chartul. No.* 828.) But before the date of this letter the opposite party had, it seems, regained possession, and the manor was now in the occupation of William Bedell in right of his wife as her dower. The place, therefore, here alluded to must have been Waterton, in the Isle of Axholme, to which a counter claim had been set up in the title of the heir male.]

LETTER CLXXX.

To my right worshipfull and my especiall good father Sir Robart Plompton, kt. be thes delivered.

Right worshipfull Sir, after dew recomendations had, I homly recomend me unto you and to my lady and mother-in-law, beseching you for your dayly blessing. Sir, I have bene dyverse tymes before the judges for my matters, but I can have none end

as yet, except my cousin Babthorp myght have all the lands in Hemyngbrough .... and I to have Waton, Northcayffe, Medelton, Wystou, and lands in Beverley to the valow of xl[s], and forest land in Selby to the valow of xx[s], and iij[li] land more, or lx[li] in money; and to give answer the first day of the next tearme.[a] Wherfore, Sir, I beseech you for your best counsell therin by this bearer. And as for your owne matter before Master Dance, Olever hath wrytten to you the scertayntie therof; and as for Mr. Woyd, I had money so much to do as to stope the outlawery this terme. Wherfore, Sir, I besech you to make some search therfore, for yt is a great danger, as the world is at this day, as *Jesu* knowes, who preserve you in health. Wrytten at Sacum, the x day of June. Sir, I besech you give credence to this bearer.

By your owne son to his litle power,
WILLIAM PLOMPTON.

[a] The dispute between " William Plumpton and Isabel his wife " of the one party, and " William Babthorp, gent. and Anas [Agnes] his wife, of the other party," concerning the ancient estates of the family of Babthorpe in Yorkshire, was continued till after the death of Sir Robert Plumpton, kt. his father, for by bond dated 2 May, 16 Hen. VII. 1524, it was agreed to refer all matters to the arbitration of Sir Lewis Polard and Sir Richard Broke, kts. two of the King's Justices of the Common Pleas, and to Sir William Gascoigne, kt. Treasurer of the right reverend father in God, Thomas Lord Cardinal, Legate of the See of Rome, Archbishop of York, Primate and Chancellor of England, and to Ralph Swillington, Attorney to our Sovereign Lord the King. (*Chartul. No.* 855.)

LETTERS

WRITTEN TO MR. WILLIAM PLOMPTON, ESQUIRE.
WHO DYED PRIMO ED. 6.

TO MR. ROBART PLOMPTON, ESQUIRE.
WHO DYED 38: OF HEN: 8.

AND TO MRS. ISABELL PLOMPTON,
WHO DYED 6: ED. 6.

LETTER I.

To the right worshipfull Mr. William Plompton, esquire.

.... your frinds of the sid of .... Bapthorps,[a] that som of your Learned Councill did convay, and besid, clame evidence which neyther yourself, nor any of your frinds, wold have done at any meting; therfore, it is

[a] In the Cartulary is the copy of a bond for a thousand marks from William Babthorpe, esq. to William Plumpton, esq. dated 27 June, 11 Hen. VIII. 1519, to be void upon condition " that the said William Babthorp and Agnes his wife, and all seised to their use, or to the heirs of the said William Babthorp, should perform the award of Robert Brudnell and Humphrey Coningsby, knights, two of the King's Justices, arbitrators indifferently chosen between the above bounden William Babthorp and Agnes his wife, and the said William Plumpton and Isabel his wife, upon the right and title of the lands that were Sir Ralph Babthorpe, knight, or any of his ancestors ;

thought that you meting with such Learned Councill shall take litle efect. But if ye would take one substantiall frind or ij, and he likewise take one or tow, and at my coming home, soe to meate, I shall be glad to meate with you at such time and place as shall be apoynted by you both; and take with me such as is both of good experience and learring, trusting so to set a finall end . . . . you and them. I trust we shall commun . . . . ther of our matters; and of your mind in the premises, I pray you to acertaine me, and thus hertyly fare ye well. From Aknig,[b] the xviii day of July.

Hertyly yours asured,
THOMAS BURGH.[c]

the award to be given before the feast of St. Luke next ensuing, and if no award given, then the parties to abide the umpirage of Thomas Lord Cardinal, Legate of the See of Rome, Archbishop of York, prymate and Chauncler of England, if given before the feast of All Saints." *(Chartul. No.* 850.) This proposed settlement of the difference between the families must, however, have failed, for the bond was again renewed 2 May, 16 Hen. VIII. 1524, when Sir Lewis Polard and Sir Richard Broke were the Justices chosen for arbitrators, with whom were joined Sir William Gascoigne, Treasurer to Cardinal Wolsey, and Raufe Swillington, the King's Attorney. *(See note to Letter CLXXX.)* The award was to be given at the feast of Pentecost; but if ever made, it was set aside. This letter implies a third attempt to adjust matters, which was also of no avail, for the ancient claims were revived in the next generation, and not finally set at rest until 20 Oct. 3 Eliz. 1561, when Richard Weston and John Walsh, two of the Queen's Justices of the Common Pleas, awarded to Sir William Babthorpe, kt. the manors of Babthorpe and Osgodby, and to William Plumpton, esq. the manor of Watterton, and lands in Estoft and Hunesley, in com. Ebor. and in Hotoft and Caldby Ayncotes, in com. Linc. *(Towneley MS. of extracts from the evidences at Plumpton.)*

[b] *Quære* Hackney?

[c] Thomas Burgh of Gainsborough, com. Linc. k:. summoned to Parliament 3 Nov. 21 Hen. VIII. 1529.

LETTER II.

To the right worshipful Mr. Plompton of Plompton this deliver.

Right worshipfull Sir, in my hartyest maner I commend me to your mastership and to my mistres your wife, thanking you of the good chear ye maid me at my being with you. Sir, the cause of my wryting unto you at this time is to beg of your mastership to . . . . to me for God . . . . else ye utterly undo me. Wherfore, I besich your mastership that I may know your mind in wryting, for I trust, seing I am your tennant, ye will not put me owt, except it wear for som great cause, that ye would ocupy it yourselfe, as ye promised me at the begining. Sir, the gentleman that you said should have it, sayes that the first motion came of you and [not] of him. Sir, ye spoke with me that you wold have had som good ling fish; wherfore, I send your mastership part to se how you like them, and if ye do like them, send me word in wryting what substance ye would have, and I shall helpe to provide you therof, or salt fish in likewise, for I supose ye shall have as good a penneworth now as ye shall have afterward. And thus our Lord have your mastership in his keping. At Beverlay, the first day of December.

Your loving frind and tennant at your pleasure,
CHRISTOPHER HUDSON.[a]

[a] Christopher Hudson was at this time tenant of the Babthorpe lands in Beverley, mentioned in Letter CLXXX., near which town is Hunsley, perhaps the most ancient residence of that family; for round the early seal of a Ralph de Babbetorp, engraved in the volume relating to the Priory of Finchale, published by the Surtees Society, 1837, is the inscription, *Sigill. Radulphi de Hundesle.* This vill, n the township and parish of Rowley, five miles from Beverley, gives name to the division of the wapentake of Hart-hill, called Hunsley-Beacon.

LETTER III.

. . . . *worshipfull Mr. Plompton of Plompton theis.*

. . . . in my hartyest wise I recommend me unto you. Sir, whear I was with you upon a time, and did . . . . e you to be good and loving kinsman to me conserning a litle farmehold lying in Kirk Stainely of vis viii[d] by yeare, and belonging to your Chauntre preist in Ripon; even so I hartely require you by this simple letter to be good kinsman to me in the same, as it may do to lie in my lytle power to do you such like pleasure, that I may have it for my farme paying. Cousin, if ye be good to me, I trust your chauntre prist and I shall agre. Sir, I spoke with my Cousin, your son, at York, at Lamas Sise, and desired him to be meadiater to you for me in that behalf; and he told me againe, that he put no dought but that ye would be good and favorrable to me. Sir, ye so being shall bind me, to my litle power, to do you pleasure, as knoweth our Lord who preserve you at his pleasure. From Lytle Burton, the v day of October. By your loving kinsman.

MARMADUKE WAVELL.[a]

[a] Marmaduke Wyvill, of Little Burton, com. Ebcr. esq. ancestor to the Baronets of that surname, resident at Constable Burton, in Richmondshire.

LETTER IV.

To my right trusty and welbeloved Wiliam Plompton, esquire.

Right trusty and welbeloved, I great you hartely well; and whear there is done and traversed betwixt you and the tennants of Folefeit Poole, of my lord and father Lordship of Spofforth, for our Courte in this time within his said township of Folefout, and as I understand, ye are contented to bide the order of me and others of the said Lord and my fathers cowncell of and upon the premises, so that an end wear maid before months day next. And so it is now at this time, that I have had and yet hath such buisenes, as I can not attend it this time; whearfore, I pray you be contented to give sparing to the next head Cort at Spoforth, at which time ye shall have an end, with my Lord and fathers favor and mine. And if ye doe break and make iij or iiij gaps in Folefout feild, as ye clame to doo of coustam yearly, thearwith I am content at this time, so that ye doe make noe more buisenes therin to the time when the said matter be ordered or determined. And herof at this time, I pray you, faile not, as my trust is in you. Written at the castle of Wresill, the xviii day of September.

H. PEARCY.[a]

[a] Henry Percy, eldest son of Henry, fifth Earl of Northumberland, succeeded his father in the 18th Hen. VIII. 1526, but the day his father died appears to be unascertained.

LETTER V.

To my right welbeloved William Plompton, esquire.

Right trusty and welbeloved, I recomend me unto you, signefiing unto you I am informed on the behalfe of my right welbeloved in God, the prior of the Monestry of St. John Evangelist, Helagh Park, of my foundation,[a] of certaine traverses depending betewt him and owne Georg Fulbarne for the right and intrest

[a] Leland in his Itinerary says, "From Helagh pryory, scant a mile to Helagh village, I saw great ruins of an ancient manor of stone, with a fair wooded park thereby, that belonged to the Earl of Northumberland. It was, as far as I can perceive, sumtymes the Hagets' land." Geoffrey Haget was the founder of the monastery in Helagh-park, for Regular Canons, of which Richard Roundale was at this date Prior; but how or at what time the lands and representation of the Hagets were acquired by the Percies, I have not seen any account.

of one spring liing within the tewinship of Litle Ribston, within my Lordship of Spoforth, which, as I perceive, you have bought of the said Georg, and so entendeth to fell it to your los. I desire and also chargeth you that ye sufer the saving of it, unto the time the better we may know to whom the right of the same belongeth. Written at Livingfeild, the xvii day of December in the xix yeare of the reign of our sovraign Lord, King Henry viii.
(17 Dec. 1527.)   H. NORTHUMBERLAND.[b]

[b] Henry Percy, sixth Earl of Northumberland, K. G. ob. 1537, s. p.

LETTER VI.

To my very good Lady Rokesby[a] *deliver this.*

Madam, in my best and hartest maner I recomend me unto you, and I dout not but ye have hard of the uniust and crafty dealing of Gervis Cawwood against me. Your late husband, whose sowle God pardon, was clearely expulsed and put forth of his ofic, which he had under the Chapter seale for tearme of his life, by the said Cawood, and the said Cawod received your

[a] This letter was copied into the manuscript the 2 of June, 1626; and a note by the copyist written in the margin informs us that "this Lady Rokesby lived and died at Plompton." We learn from a subsequent letter that a Newport of Boynton, com. Ebor. was her son, and that her husband Rokeby was buried at *Resby* Church. Risby is in the township and parish of Rowley, and was the seat of the family of Ellerker in the reign of Hen. VIII. There does not, however, appear to have been any chapel erected there, with a right of sepulture; but as the name of Rowley is of modern growth, the place being not named in Domesday, perhaps the parish church commonly went under the name of Risby. We have in that case a clue to her identity; for in the curious Memoir of the family of Rokeby, entitled, *Oeconomia Rokebiorum,* 'printed by Whitaker in his Richmondshire, and of which the date is 1565, mention is made of a Richard Rokeby, third son of Ralph Rokeby, of Mortham, com. Ebor. esq. a soldier and servant to the Lord Scrope of Bolton, whose standard he bore in Flodden-field, who had issue by his wife ——— daughter of ——— Ellerker of Risbye, esq.

husbands fee, and what accounts and reckinings he maid unto your late husband thereof, I know not. And that if I may know from you how many yeares the said Cawod reseived your hosbonds fee, if ye doe acertin me therof, and make me a letter of atturney unto some of your frinds, aboufe to clame your arreareges, I will send him forward for your helpe, the best I can. And I pray you to accertaine me the truth by your writting by this bearner. And thus our Lord send you good life and long to his pleasure. Written att Holme in Spald. this 22th day of Aprill.
By your loving frind,
ROBART CONSTABLE, knight.[b]

[b] Sir Robert Constable of Holme in Spaldingmore, and of Flamborough, com. Ebor. kt. succeeded his aged father, Sir Marmaduke Constable, 29 Dec. 10 Hen. VIII. 1518; and having taken part in the insurrection known as the Pilgrimage of Grace, he was executed for high treason, and his body hanged in chains over Beverley Gate, at Hull, in the month of June, 28 Hen. VIII. 1536. (*Memoirs of the Constable family, penes me.*)

LETTER VII.

To my good Lady Rokesby at Plompton.

Madam, in my harty wise I recommend me to you, and right so doth my wife; and we are very glad that ye be in good health, and that I hear you like so well with Mr. Plompton. And I send you your Indenture by this berrer, which hath stayd your son, Newport; then I trust ye shall hear more of him, but good toward you. And when your prest at Boynton had song out all your ten pound, he kepes him still at his cost, and will kepe a prest sining at Boynton, as long as he lives, which exsample ye began.[a] My coussin Portington,[b] as I doth sopose, hath brought

[a] On a stone in Boynton church was this inscription: Hic jacet Thomas Newport et Elizab't uxor ejus, filia et heres Joh'is Boynton, filii et heredis Do'i Rob'ti Boyn-

your through[c] to Resby Church, to be laid of your husband Rokesby by this time. And our Lord preserve you long in your health. At Everingham, this xvii of December.
Your own asured,
MARMADUKE COUNSTABLE, kt.[d]

ton militis, q'i Tho's obiit xv°. die Novembr. A°. D'i. M°CCCCXXIII. quorum animabus propitietur Deus. Amen. On another, Hic jacet Will's Newport, armiger, qui obiit decimo die mensis Novembris, Anno. Do'. M.CCCCLXXX° cuius aie propitietur Deus. (*Bointon church, 14th Nov. 1620. Dodsw. MSS. in Bib. Bodl. v. CLX.*)

[b] In the 24th of Hen. VIII. 1532, Master Thomas Portington paid to the fabrick of the collegiate church of St. John of Beverley 3d. 6s. for the free rent of three cottages and one oxgang of land in Bentley, then in his tenure. (*Scaum's Beverlac, p.* 24.) Bentley adjoins Risby in the parish of Rowley. Portington, from which this family took their local surname, is at no great distance, in Howdenshire.

[c] Thruff-stone, a tomb-stone. Sax. thruh. (*Brockett's Glossary.*)

[d] Sir Marmaduke Constable, of Everingham, com. Ebor. kt. in right of his wife Barbara, daughter and eventually sole heir of John Suthill of Everingham, esq. She died 4 Oct. 32 Hen. VIII. 1543, and he 12 Sept. 1545.

LETTER VIII.

To my good Lady, Dame Anne Rokesby, be this delivered.

Maddam, after my most louely I recomend me to your ladyship, evermore desiring to wit of your good wellfare, which is my dayly prayer to Jesus to inquete to your harts most comfort. Maddam, I doe wryte to you praying not your ladyship to be wroth with my husband for the money that he received of my M[rs] your daughter, that he send not to you by this bearner. It was my consent; for in good faith, madam, in a maner we weare eether to have lost our farme, for M[r] Trey is so trobled in the law, that he may not forbeare his rent no whyle. Madam, I bad my husband take your money, and I said, I trust your Ladyship will not be discontent for your money for a season; the which shall be befor Lamas, by the grace of God. For in good fayth, madam,

we must have else sold iij of our key, the which had bene a great hindrance to us. For in good faith we buy that we spend in our house, and I am faine to eate browne bread and drink small alle myselfe, and lives as hardly, as God knowes, and must do for this yeare. I trust to God it shall be ammended the next yeare; for, I thank God, we had not a better cropp toward this good whyle. And God reward your Ladyship; we had lived most hardly, if that your Ladyship had not bene. And I pray you, madam, let not my M[rs]. your daughter wit of it, for then she will never trust my husband, nor me. God reward hir, which I am much bownd unto. I can doe nothing for your Ladyship and hir, but for to pray for your prosperete. I pray you, madam, let not my husband know of this letter, and send me word trewly with this bearner in a little bill of your owne hand, ij or iij words, that he know not of your mind. No more, but Jesus kepe your Ladyship in good health.
By your power beadwoman,
ANN ABOTT.

LETTER IX.

To the right worshipful and his welbeloved Cousin William Plompton, esquire.

Right worthy and welbeloved Cousin, in my full hertely maner I recommend me to you. The cause of my writing to you at this time is, that I wad be very glad to speake with you as touching Cousin, Sir Robart Sheifeld,[a] whose soule Jesus have mercy; for my frinds in Linconshire hath letten me have understanding that ye have some knowliging in the thing touching that matter, the

[a] Sir Robert Sheffield of Butterwicke, com. Linc. kt. died 14 Nov. 24 Hen. VIII. 1532.

which I would desire you that I may know. For surely if ye can let me have knowledge of any thing concerning the same, ye do us a great pleasure, and a great deace of charrety to bring to knowledg, for I assure you I would take great paine to come to perfit knowledge. Wherfor, Coussin, if it would please you that I might know your mind secretly in wryting by this my servant, or that it like you that I might speake with you myselfe, I will be at Harrwood of Monday next, with grace of God, and that ye will take a litle paines to come thider, that I might speak with you. I shall take paines to labor twice as far, if ye call of me, with grace of Jesus, who kepe you. From Liversay, this Saterday after Martinmas day.

(16 Nov. 1532.)

By your lover asured,
ROBART NEVILL, knight.[b]

[b] Sir Robert Nevill of Liversedge, com. Ebor. kt. son of Thomas Nevill, esq. and Isabel, daughter of Sir Robert Sheffield, kt. Recorder of the City of London, named in a former Letter. *(See Letter CXIV.)* He died 10 Aug. 1516, and had by Ellen, daughter of John Delves, esq. Sir Robert, his successor, Isabel or Elizabeth above named, and other children.

LETTER X.

To his mother at Plompton be this letter delivered.

Right worshipful mother, I humbly recommend mee unto you, desiring you of your dayly blessing, praing *Jesu* long to continew your helth to his pleasur. Mother, I thanke you for the . . . . . you send mee, for yf you were not, I were not able to live; for this same Christmasse hath cost mee as much as you send mee. Wherfore, I am afraid I shal not have money to serve mee to Easter. Also I wold desire you to send mee word of the letter that I wrote to my father and you, for to moove my Lady Gascoin to write to my lord, her brother,[a] not to bee only his servant, but of his houshold and attending unto him; for els he wold do as other lords do, knowes not half their servants. Wherfor, I desire you that you wil moove my lady Gascoin to write so to my lord, that I may bee his houshold servant. Also, mother, I wold desire you to mark wel my letter, that I sent you by Mr. Oughtred;[b] and here I send you a godly New Testament by this bearer. And yf the prologue bee so small that ye cannot wel reade them, ther is my fathers book, and they are bothe one, and my fathers book hath the prologue printed in bigger letters. Yf it wil please you to read the introducement, ye shal see marvelous things hyd in it. And as for the understanding of it, dout not; for God wil give knowledge to whom he will give knowledg of the Scriptures, as soon to a shepperd as to a priest, yf he ask knowledg of God faithfully. Wherfor, pray to God, and desire Jesus Christ to pray for you and with you. No more to you at this tyme, but God fill you

[a] Margaret, Lady Gascoyne, second wife of Sir William Gascoyne of Gawkthorpe, com. Ebor. kt. was daughter of Richard Nevill, Lord Latimer, who died 22 Hen. VIII. 1530, and sister of John Lord Latimer, among whose houshold servants the writer of this letter, the eldest son of an esquire of no mean degree, seeks to be admitted. This connection with Lord Latimer, who died in 1542, probably brought about the marriage of Robert Plumpton with Ann Norton, 2 Sept. 1538, he having attained his majority on the 17th of January preceding, and whose brother Richard Norton was married to this Lord's sister. At the date of this letter, Robert Plumpton was a student of the Inner Temple, and, it would seem, deeply imbued with the new doctrines, which the study of the Scriptures, now thrown open by the discovery of the art of printing to the interpretation of each one's private judgment, had lately introduced to the world. The zeal he here manifests for the conversion of his father and mother to the novel investigation was, however, fruitless; the family ever adhered to the ancient faith. He died at Waterton in the 38th of Hen. VIII. 1546, about Christmas, at the early age of thirty-one; but it is probable that his sentiments underwent a considerable modification after his connection by marriage with the Nortons, who were among the most zealous sticklers for Papacy in the North Country.

[b] Robert Ughtred, of Kexby, com. Ebor. esq.

with al spiritual knowledge, to the glory of God, the helth of your soule, and the profit of your poor nieghbor. Written at the Temple, the 12 day of ianuary.

(*Anno circa* 1536.)

By your sonn,
ROBERT PLOMPTON.

LETTER XI.

To his right worshipful mother bee this delivered with speed.

Right worshipfull mother, I humbly recomende me unto you, desiringe Jesus longe to continewe your healthe to the pleasure of God. Worshipfull mother, I am bounde to write to you, yea and you were not my mother, because it hathe pleased God of his inestimable goodnes to send me some understanding in the Scriptures; for everie man or woman that it shall please God to sende knowledge in the Scriptures is bounde to instructe theire brethren in the lovinge of the Gospell. Wherefore, it is my dutie to instructe you, most principalle of all other, which hathe shewed to me so muche kindenes, besides all motherly kindenes. Wherefore, I desire you, moste deare mother, that ye will take heede to the teachinge of the Gospell, for it is the thinge that all wee muste live by; for Christe lefte it that we shoulde altogether rule our livinge thereby, or els we cannot be in favour with God. Wherefore, I woulde desire you for the love of God, that you woulde reade the Newe Testament, which is the trewe Gospell of God, spoken by the Holy Ghoste. Wherefore, doubte not of it, dearly beloved mother in the Lorde, I write not this to bringe you into anie heresies, but to teache you the cleare light of Goddes doctrine. Wherefore, I will never write nothinge to you, nor saye nothinge to you, concerninge the Scriptures, but will dye in the quarrell. Mother, you have muche to thanke God that it woulde please him to geve you licence to live untill this time, for the gospell of Christe was never so trewly preached as it is nowe. Wherfore, I praye to God that he will geve you grace to have knowledge of his Scriptures. Ye shall heare perceive what the profession of our Baptisme is, which profession we muste have written in our hartes. Which profession standeth in twoe thinges; the one is the knowledge of the lawe of God, understandinge it spiritually as Christe expoundeth it, Math. v. vi. and vii. chapters; so that the roote and life of all lawes is this, Love thy Lorde God with all thy harte, all thy soule, all thy mighte, and all thy power, and thy neighboure as thy selfe for Christes sake. And love onely is the fullfillinge of the lawe, as saithe S. Paule, and that whatsoever we doe and not of that love, that same fullfilleth not the lawe in the sighte of God. And what the lawe doth meane ye shall finde in the prologue to the Rom: in my fathers booke, called the Newe Testament. I write unto you because that I knowe you have a fervent . . . . and his lawes . . . . .

(*Rest wanting.*)

LETTER XII.

To my welbeloved son Robart Plompton at the Iner Temple in London be this.

Son Robart Plompton, I hertely recommend me to you, and sending you and your brother[a] God blesing and mine. The cause of my writing to you now; that I wold you should helpe this bearrer, yong Letham, in such buisenes as he hath in the Court of Augmentation, for certaine power for yong children of one Berkine, deceased, as conserning one farme hold, late belonging to the hold of St. Robarts, which you know I did speake to the Ansurer[b] for the use of the said children, and he permised not to suit them. That notwithstanding, John Benson would have en-

[a] Denis Plumpton, seond son of the writer.
[b] The person who answered to the Court of Augmentation for the rents and profits. This Court was first erected in the 27th year of the reign of Hen. VIII.

tred; and now made many great riots upon the said children, and therfore he is indited with divers persons with him. And now further, he hath brought a preve seale against old Leathom and yong Leathom, and also the eldest child; and for that divers and many of ther frinds hath moved me to wryte to you to help them in the said matter. And if it be that you can make any frinds, to shew Mr. Chaunceler the planer and through in every thing (and this bearrer can instruct you), and then, I pray you, do the best for them. And also I would have you to speake with Mr. Latham, the goldsmith,[b] Lanlord to Robart Oliver, and shew him how that he will not make his diches and fences belonging to his farme, but that my corne and gras is spoyled at Watterton by that meaner. And if he will not seake remedy therof, let Mr. Fox enter a action of trespas against the said Robart Oliver for dispoyling my gras at Watterton to the valew of five mark. And as far as I fele, Mr. Norton[c] comith not up. I shall make your rents to be gathered, and send it to you as shortly as I can. And thus hartely far you well. From Plompton, this 14th day of November.

By your loving father,
WILLIAM PLOMPTON.

[b] Ralph Latham, of Upminster Hall in Essex, citizen and goldsmith, had, with other issue, a daughter Alice, married to John Twisleton, citizen and goldsmith, alderman of London.—*Vide* letter from their son Christopher, who was afterwards in possession of this property at Waterton, *postea*.

[c] John Norton, of Norton Conyers, esq. whose daughter Robert Plumpton married 2 Sept. 30 Hen. VIII. 1538. This letter is apparently subsequent to that match.

LETTER XIII.

To my loving frind William Plompton of Plompton, esquire.

Mr. Plompton, after my herty comendation, whereas some contreverse hath bene betwen Sir Wiliam Mydleton [a] and Sir Oswold

[a] Sir William Mydleton, of Stockeld, com. Ebor. kt.

Wilesthorpe [b] for a tith, which the said Sir William Mydleton hath certaine yeares had in his own hands; for as much as afore me they be condescended and agred, that the said tith shall be gathred and inned by some man indeferrent, and in place semblable, and of all other hath thought you most convenient and indefrent frind to chouse such men as shall se the ining, and ordering therof as to the place: this is, first on my behalfe, and eftsones theirs, to desire you hertely to take the paines betwene them, to apoynt alwayes such men as place indeferent, so that it may remaine in the said place and custode, to such a day as they have apoynted that further order shall be taken for the same. And thus far you hartyly well. From Cawood the ix day of August, 1539.

Your loving frind,
(9 *Aug.* 1539.) EDW: EBORUM.[c]

[b] Sir Oswald Wilsthorp, of Wilsthorp, com. Ebor. kt.
[c] Edward Lee, Archbishop of York, ob. 10 Sept. 1544, æt. 62.

LETTER XIV.

To Mr. Robart Plompton the yonger be this delivered.

Right worshipfull Sir, my deuty donne unto your mastership, and as letting you know that I have received your indenture and delivered it to Robart Poclington; and he is content with that, sauffing that he wold desire your mastership to set in the indenture whear that he should pay his money at his rent dayes. For the indenture specefies, his money unpaid xxi dayes, you or your heires to recover of him all the hole, which wear a undowing to him, to take that he should make his living on for the place unknowne whear that he shold pay his rents, or what place. And I also letting you know that Mr. Leades flate with him verry fast afar his neighbors, since he cam from you. As I say, he shall not occupy it but has the lase, for he hath no right to it, nor you neither. And he said, he had no lawfull warning that he will tak a discharge for, but that he will occopy alsoe. I bad Poclington plow and put him of over the lands, that he have no intrest; and send me word what his deade is and his words, and I shall send you word. For in your absence, I bad him send me word, and I shold come over to him and se what he sayes and take his answer. And also if it please you to send me money, I will do the best for you I can at all times. As for barly, is now much redy and in chambers; for wheat, that such that now ready, the substance is gon. Yowr men also kiln dry. Beanes is at Gainsbrough [a] vi li score, and barley at 4 li and xiii nobles a skore, and wheat is at Hull at ij li a skore. I pray you send me word in a bill what ye will have don as conserning his writing in all condittions, and thus Jesus preserve you.

By yours to his litle power,
GEORGE JOHNSON, Clerk.

[a] Gainsborough in Lincolnshire, the nearest market-town to Waterton, the residence of Robert Plumpton, called the younger during the life-time of his uncle Robert Plumpton of Knaresborough. The writer of this letter, though in holy orders, appears to have acted as steward for Mr. Plumpton in his absence.

LETTER XV.

Too the right worshipfull and his singuler good master, Mr. William Plompton, esquire, at Plompton Hall, in the countie of York, give theis.

Right worshipfull, my deuty to you premised, in my most hartyest maner I recomend me unto you, and likewise to my good Mistres your wife, trusting in Jesus that you with all your children be in good health, the continuence wherof I pray Jesus increase. It may please you to be advertised I have received your gentle letters, datted at Plompton the ix of January, by the which you required me to helpe Tho: Compton, your nephe,[a] to some honiest ocopation at London, with him to be bownd prentis; which I wad gladly to the uttermost of my power and the helpe of my frinds have don, as I am bownd, in case he had come unto me, as he did not. The bringer of your said letters informed me that your said nephew was determend to kepe in his owne countrie, and not to cum to London. And where your pleasure in your said letter is, that I shold give you notise if theare wear any thing in varience within your maner or lordship of Sacomp, to the intent you might send your pleasure therin by your baly, at his next coming to Sacomp. Sir, thear is one thing in varience for title of copehold land ther, which one Edward Glidall, your late farmer, hath; which land was somtimes one Flegs, unto the which one Flege now maketh title and hath don long times past. And abowt Christmas last past, the same Flegge delivered a *supenea* to Glidall for the same, as I am informed, but what is don therin I know not; of this matter, Settill, your servant, can informe you better then I. Allso, ther is one Slepe dweling abowt St. Albones, who at your last Court thear maid clame to a percill of grownd of your said copehold in the tenner of Marston, of the which the same Marston hath a cope. Soever the le (*nevertheless*), said Slepe aledgeth that his brother, of whom the said Marston bought the same ground, never maid surrender therof, according to the custome of your maner; albeit, it apereth plainely in a bill remaining with the said Merston, that the brother of the said Slepe sold unto Merston all his intreast in the said coppehold. The same Slepe at your last court required your baly ther, with the asent of the said Merston, to make search in your court rowls if any such surrender wer maid, acording as it is mentioned in the said copie remaining with the said Marston, [which cope, as

[a] Thomas Compton was perhaps of the family of that name at Willingham, com. Lincoln, and nephew in half-blood to the wife of William Plumpton. (*See note to Letter CLXXX.*)

I remember, was maide in the fowerth or fifth yeare of the reign of our Soveraigne Lord the king that now is,] where the said rowle could not be found; howbeit, theare was all the rowles of this King reigne but onely that of that yeare. Sir, as me thinks, your rowls thear be not kept as they ought to be; the cofer wherin your said court rowles lieth is nought and the lock therof not worth a pene, and it standeth in the church at Sacomp, wheare every man may come at his pleasure. Wherfore, in my simple mind it should be nesary for you to provide sum other meane for the safe custody of your said rowles. Also, Sir, sith the time I have bene your farmer ther, I have paid, and must pay within tow yeares next to come, vi fiftens for the farme of your maner of Sacomp, the first payment xxiiij^s, the second xxx^s viii^d, and either of the other fower yeares xxiiij^s, which amounteth in the hole viii^{li} x^s viii^d. I marvill greatly that your said manor shold be so highley charged, considering the hole fiftene of your towne of Sacomp is but lix^s. I could never se no writing of the sesment therof, but only by the report maid of your tennants ther by word of mouth. Sir, I wright this unto you, because in case you have any sertinty therof in wryting, I might know it. I wold be sory to charge your said maner with any more then ought of right to be; and yet I have paid the same, bycause I am loth to stand in contentions with my neighbors . . . . the truth therin be known. Further, I have received the letter sent to you by Sir Philip Butler, knight,[b] wherin he wrighteth that you have bene insensed against him by the report of lewd and evill disposed persons; by whome he meaneth the same, I may not judge: howbeit, I think rather by me then any other. His sones ar discontented with me, because I kepe grey hounds and hownds at your said maner, saieng that it becometh not me to kepe grey hownds and hownds so near theyr fathers nose, with many other things

[b] Sir Philip Boteler, of Woodhall, in the parish of Watton-at-Stone, com. Herts. kt.

which I remite for lake of time. And whear your pleasure is in your said letter, that I shold shew Mr. Butler that in case he wold give you such fine for your milne of Sacomp as your baly did demaund for the same, you wear contented that he shold be amited tennant therof; Sir, sith the receit of your said letter I have not spoken with the said Mr. Butler, because I have bene and yet am at London, as this bearrer can informe you. Albeit, at this *Hillarii* tearme I spoke with one Mr. Hide, who maried the said Mr. Butlers daughter [c], and lieth and continueth within the said Mr. Butlers, and is the greatest doer about him; to whome I shewed your pleasure therin, requiring him to informe Mr. Butler therof, and of your said pleasure. Wherupon the said Mr. Hide said, that you demaunded an unreasonable fine for the same, and that his father did ofer you double the fine that ever was paid by any man for the same. And further he said, that in case ye wold not take such fine, as shold stand with reason and good conscience, he trusted that my lord Chauncler of England, upon the matter hard before him, wold ses such fine for the same as shold stand with right and good consience. And whear, also, the said Mr. Butler, amongst other things, wryteth in his said letters that your tennants thear be daly in his danger, and that he might put men daly to trobles, if he wold; Sir, I trust ye have no tennant thear, but that is the Kings trewe subiect, and obedient to Gods law and his graces. And as long as the be so, I dought not but that we, having so noble and gratious a King as we have, power men shal live in rest, doing their deuty to his grace, as they and all other ar most bownd to do. Sir, Mr. Butler of himself is a good and gentle knight, in case he wear not otherwise counciled, as knoweth *Jesu*, who ever preserve you and all

[c] Anne, daughter of Sir Philip Butler, kt. married Leonard Hide, esq. *Pedigree in Clutterbuck's Herts.*

yours in good and prosperus health with long continuance of the same to his pleasure. From London the xxii day of Febuary.

Your fermar and servant,

JOHN DODINGTON.[d]

[d] In Sacombe Church, on the floor in the chancel, was a stone with this inscription, "Here lieth buried the bodie of John Dodington, of Sacombe, gentleman, who deceased a faithfull Christian the viith daie of Januarie, in the yeare of our Lord God 1544, who was husband to Eleanor Dodington, whose grave is joyned here to his on the right side; after whom he survived seven yeares and seaven weeks and left alive at his departure by her his only wife three sons and six daughters.

Cygnea qui terris modulati carmina mortis,
Dulce polo vitâ nunc melos usque canunt."

LETTER XVI.

To the right worshipfull Mrs. Isbell Plompton, this with speede.

Right worshipfull and my singler good Mistres, my duty to you premised, in my most hertyest maner I recomend me unto you. Pleaseth you to understand I have received your letter; by the which I understand that your pleasure is, that I shuld lett Edward Glydal have such parcels of ground of your maner of Sacomburs, as which he think to be nessary for him, and which parcils I think be minded to be let. Mistres, as yet I have let no persill of the same your maner to no person. So ever the les, I have oferd Glidall, that if I let any persill of the sam, that he shold have the perfirment therof before any other person, and as farr as I can prevaile, he hath in mind to have ney percill of the same land. He hath taken a farme of my Lord of Essex, and that he intendeth to inhabit and dwell; and his eldest son, which lately dweld in a coppie hold of his father in Sacomb, hath taken and dwelleth in a farme of Mr. Holts in Lankeshire abowt Wouden.[a] And the same copiehold the said Edward Glidall wold have me to

[a] Woolden Hall in Eccles parish was the seat of Thomas Holcroft, esq. in 1595. He probably purchased from the Holts.

take of him and put in acount therin my self, and that then I shold and might tack land of the sam your said maner to the said coppiehold I shuld think expedient; and I as yet am not minded to take any copehold. Soevertheles, yf Glidall himselfe or his son be minded to occopie any of the said land that I shall be minded to let, he shall hav the preferment therof, and your comaundment in that behalfe, or in any other thing that in me lieth, to be observyd and kept to the best of my power by the same, as Jesus [knoweth], who preserve you in good and prosprus health with long continuance of the same. In hast from London the xxiith of Febuary.

Your servant and to comaund,

JOHN DODINGTON.

LETTER XVII.

To the right worshipfull and his singuler good Master, Mr. William Plompton, Esquire, this.

Right worshipfull, in my most hartyest maner I commend me to you and likewise to my good Mistres your wife, trusting to Jesus that you and all your children and famila be in good health. And wheare I perceive by Robart Settell, your servant, that the perty who oweth the lease you sent unto me to be exemplefied, thinketh long for the same and suposes the same lease to be lost; Sir, truth it is, the same lease is and remaineth in the custody of Mr. Henley of the Court of Augmentation of the King's Majesties Crown, and is assigned with the hands of Mr. Chauncler and Counsell of the Court aforsaid, and upon the iiij day of this present month of June was delivered to Duke, clarke of the said Councill, to ingross in parchment, and then to be sealed with the seale of the same Court, which shall be done ard finished within fower or 6 dayes next coming. And shortley also, I shall send you the same with a bill of such somes of money, as I have and shall disburse for the same ; so that I trust the said party have no cause to mistrust the having therof. He may not have that leases in revertion be sold on Alowed Sent Leasur.[a] And frindship, as knoweth our Lord God, who ever preserve you. Scribbled in hast at London the 6th day of June.

Yours to comaund,
JOHN DODINGTON.

[a] Alured St. Leger, *quære ?*

LETTER XVIII.

To the right worshipfull Mr. William Plompton, esquire.

Right worshipfull Sir, my deuty to you premised, in my hartyest maner I commend me unto you and to my Mistres your wife ; pleaseth yt you to understand my Master hath wryten his letter to Mr. Goldsbrough for a do for your mastership in Bilton park or the park of Heay at your pleasur. I trust it will be signed, and if it be not, my Master desires your mastership to send him word therof. The same letter is herin closed ; and I pray your mastership, if ther be any service that I [may] doe your mastership, it will please you to commaund me as your servant. And thus Almighty God to preserve you. Scribled in hast, the viith day of October.

Your servant to comaund,
JOHN DODINGTON.

LETTER XIX.

To the right worshipfull William Plompton of Plompton, in the county of York, Esquire, deliver with sped.

Right worshipfull, in my most hertyest maner I commend me unto you, and likewise to my good Mistres your wife, and very glad wold be to heare of your good health and all your children. Theas be to certifie you that it hat pleased God Almightie to take into his mercy the late person of Sacomp, Mr. John Petty.[a] He departed this transetory life upon Easterday last at vii of the clock before nowne, whose sowle I pray Jesus perdon ; and let us pray that he that shall succede him, be of no worse sorte than he hath bene. I and all my neighbors hartyly desire your mastership, iv also he that shall have the same be minded to be resident and abid upon the same personage, than that you will move him that cumes [for] Sir Christopher Bird, person, who honestly did kepe the cure under the forsaid late person, and the maintenment of God service ; and may be his depete, as he was to the other late person, wherof I and all your other tennants wold be very glad. Sir, I have sent you the Kings writ of *dedimus potestatem* by Mr. Birnand with a letter, sealed in a box, which I trust is come to your hands ; and what your pleasure shal be to commaund me in the premises, I pray you let me know, and I shall be glad to accomplish the same. And I pray you have me hartyle commended to Mr. Robart Plompton, your son, and to my Mistres his wife, and to Mr. Dinis, your son, and to Mr. Birnand. And I pray you informe Mr. Birnand his son is mery and in good health, thanks be to Jesus, who ever preserve you and all yours. Scribbled in hast at your maner of Sacomp, the Monday next after Easter day.

By your to commaund,
(26 *Mar.* 1543.) JOHN DODINGTON.

[a] Richard Sharp, clerk, was, upon the death of Mr. John Petty, priest, admitted to the living of Sacombe 3 May 1543, upon the presentation of William Plumpton, in right of Isabella his wife. *Clutterbuck's Herts. ex reg. Longland*—where the name Palfreman is manifestly an error for Plumpton.

LETTER XX.

To the right worshipfull Mr. Plompton of Plompton, in Yorkshire, this be delivered.

Also, in my most hartiest manner, as unaquainted, I have me hartile commended unto you. And wheraras I am informed by Oliver, my tennant, that the Kings Majesties oficeres requireth of you and of me and divers other tennants of Watterton to be contributors to the charges and staving of the watters of Ancotes, and that you have suficient writing for your discharg and mine in that behalfe ; therfore, this shall be to desire you, in voidin further trobles and charges that might insue against us both, that you will deliver unto my said tennant a trew coppe of the said writing, if you have any such : whearby I and my frinds and counsill with your frinds and councill at this next tearme may might togeather, and may take som order and derection in that behalfe, as may be for the safte of us and our heires, if your deed will maintaine the same. And further, whear I am informed by my said tennant that you have partley denied him his wey to his mor, which my tennants have alwayes hertofore had ; desiring you, therfore, that he may gentle have the same, as one gentleman and gentlewoman may use one another with favor, and in so doing, you shall receive at my hands such pleasur as I and my frinds can do for you, as knoweth our Lord God, who ever have you in his keping. From Dertford, the xxviii day of December.

By your loving frind,
CHRISTOPHER TWISLETON.[a]

[a] Christopher Twisleton married Anne, daughter of John Beer of Dartford, com. Kent, esq. The family afterwards settled in Yorkshire, and were of Barlow, otherwise Barley, in the parish of Brayton, near Selby.

LETTER XXI.

To my cosen Plompton of Plompton, this deliver with spede.

Cossin Plompton, in as harty manner as I can think I recomend me to you. First, all your frinds ar in good health heare. I have bene very sick since ye went, but I am well now, I thank God. I have vewed Christall ; the rent of it, as it is now letted, xs iiijd score, xvli viiis ; and Arthington is above xxli at the end of xvi yeares : the will be iij score pownd above the rent. And the woods, my man sayes, he dar give a thowsand marke for them, but he thinks without dowt he will make a thowsand li. I have written to my Cossin, Henry Savill of Lapset, to go thorowgh with my Lord of Canterbury for it. Acording to the comunication, and ye and my Cossen, John Gascoyne, shall have a part, if ye will wryte to me that ye will stike to it ; and Robart Savill and Henry Savill of Lapsit will stand to tow parts. I think the woods will give us our money and more ; and the lease cleare to be gotten, for laying out of the money till we can make it againe of the woods. I have sent you a rental of it, what it is, every cloase. I pray you let my Cossen, John Gascoyne, se this letter and the rentall. Kepe it secret from all other. I pray God send us merry meting. All written in my ship, at Timmoth.

Your asured kinsman,
HENRY SAVILL.[a]

Cussin Gascoyne, your children ar mery.
(*Anno circa* 1543.)

[a] Sir Henry Savill of Thornhill, Tankersley, and Elland, com. Ebor. K.B. The monastery of Kirkstall and nunnery of Arthington had been part of the religious plunder acquired by Cranmer, Archbishop of Canterbury, in exchange for other lands, 34 Hen. VIII. 1543, in trust for whose younger son, Thomas Cranmer, it was held by Peter Hammond and others in the 4th of Edw. VI. (*Burton's Mon. Ebor.*) The bargain for the lease spoken of in this letter it may be presumed was adhered to on

the part of the Savills only. Robart Savill of Howley, the illegitimate son of Sir Henry Savill, must have afterwards also acquired the reversion in fee, as this estate has descended with his other property to the Erudenells. Of the other parties who were to be admitted to a share in the speculation, Henry Savill of Lupsett, the surveyor, was ancestor to the legitimate branch of Savill, and William Plumpton and John Gascoigne were related in equal degree to Sir Henry Savill, whose lineal ancestor had married a Gascoigne. The dating of this letter from aboard ship at Tynemouth furnishes a new biographical feature in the life of Sir Henry, whose letters show him to have had all the heartiness of the sailor, unbounded in his hospitality, and devoted to sporting.

LETTER XXII.

To my Cossin Plompton of Plompton, this be delivered.

Cossen Plompton, I recomend me to you, and as I perceive by my son Robart servant, ye say ye will come over and hunt with me; and it please you so to do, ye shal be as hertyly welcome as any man that cam heare of a good space. Ye shall se your arrow fly and your grayhound run, and all thos that comes with you, winter and somer, when it please you to come, as long as I live. As for the other matter, I pas not a little of it; I have yet waide it with my councill; and as ye shall know at our meting, as I am informed, and as I take it, thear ar many dowts by yt. When I speak with you, I will hide nothing from you in this then in no other cause. When ye intend to come, let me know what time, or els ye may hape neither to have me then nor my son at home; but my wife ye shalbe sur to find, and she will send som with you that shall let you se both rid and fallow, if ye will take the paine. I have killed a hind or tow of late, and they ar very fatt this yeare, both in the woods at Tankersley and in my gardin at Thornehill. I thinke ye weare never yet in no grownd of mine, and I never say no man naye. Therfore, the faut is in you and not in me; ye may amend the faut when it please you. The cause of my sending of my servant at this time, is this; he informes me that in your countrie thear is a man that can kill otters very well; wherfor, I have sent him to git him to me for a weke. I asure you, they do me exceding much harme at divers places, and especially at Woodkirk and Thornhill, and lyes in small becks. My folks se them daly, and I can not kill them; my hownds be not used to them. From Sothill,[a] the 8 of November.

By your asured kinsman,

HENRY SAVILL, knt.

After the making herof, or it was sealed, cam my son home from London. Of Wedsday came my Lord of Norfock[b] to the Court. The Spanish Duke is gon; the earle of Hertfort,[c] the Bishop of Winchester,[d] with the French Imbasodor, is gon to the Emporor; the Duke of Sufolk[e] with other remaines at Calisse. The Frenchmen that wear of sea ar gon to Depe haven, and the Inglish men ar of the sea, but the cold weather will sufer no man long to continue of the water. As concerning news of Scotland, give credence to this bearrer. This is my owne hand.

(8 Nov. 1544.)

[a] Sir Henry Savill was owner of Soothill in the parish of Dewsbury, com. Ebor. in right of his wife Elizabeth, daughter and heir of Thomas Soothill of Soothill, esq. who had died 29 Dec. 27 Hen. VIII. 1535.
[b] Thomas Howard, Duke of Norfolk, attainted in 1546.
[c] Edward Seymour, Earl of Hertford, created Duke of Somerset 16 Feb. 1547.
[d] Stephen Gardiner, Bishop of Winchester.
[e] Charles Brandon, Duke of Suffolk, ob. 1545.

LETTER XXIII.

To my right worshipfull Coussin, Mr. William Plompton of Plompton, esquire, this deliver.

Cossin Plompton, I hartely recommend me unto you, thanking you for all your goodnes at all times. I have received your letter by Roger Brindell, and wheare that ye wryte thear is no dowghts if the matter had come to comunication; ye ar the man that I trust, and by you I wold have bene ordered: and if ye had so thought, I wold have confeined myselfe to you. But I perceive the parte is not minded to commone with him; his wife thinks him to light. And I think, consider his qualeties, his living, his posabilete, and confer al togetter, I think, as good chepe as this I shall git a living for him, both as good and as fare. And I am sur ther haith bene comredis won with other far wars then he, excep one faute. And as for that, ther is and haith bene many good men with that faut; it is the thing that he cannot amend. It lets him not to eat, drink, slepe; he can live as well of it I have given him, as though it had desendit to him. And if his brother dy without isew, in all by gift he shall have v hundreth mark land, (and if he wear but inhiretable by the law, he shold be heir to him, but for defaut of heireship, I thinke he will not change his estate in this case;) and for defaute of heires of my body lawfuly begotten, he shall inhirit all that I have. But in the meane onely, his fault so shall not hirt him in no profets. Let this matter pas; I hertyle thank you, as much as if it had come to pase. He is much bownd to you, and, if ever he be able, to do you pleasure. I trust ye shull se him git a living, ere the yeare is past. At York, if ye will come and kill a hind, ye shall be hertyly welcom. Wryten at Sothill, the xxviii of November. Anno 1544, 36 H. 8.

Your asured frind, HENRY SAVILL, knt.[a]

(28 Nov. 1544.)

* The context of this letter has plainly reference to some hoped for settlement in marriage of the writer's illegitimate son, Robart, to which matter an allusion is also made in the preceding letter. The affair, however, seems never to have reached a proposal, because it was perceived the mother of the intended thought a bastard " to light " to wed with her daughter.

LETTER XXIV.

To his right worshipful Coussin, William Plompton, esquire, this deliver.

Cossin Plompton, after my hartie recommendations; your servant sheweth me ye were and have bene very sick, wherof I am very sory. And if your sicknes continue, wheare the commaundment comes forth, send forth your servants and tennants, and send forth your excuse to my Lord Lieutennant, with a letter of the trough of your sicknes, and of the time of the continuance therof; and being advertised of the truth, he will excep of your lawfull and reasonable excuse. And thus hertely far you well. From York, the xxviij of May, Anno 1545, 37 H. 8.

Your asurred kinsman,

(27 May 1545.) HENRY SAVILL.

LETTER XXV.

To my Cossin Plompton this be delivered.

Cossin Plompton, I hartely recommend me urto you. The cause of my wryting to you is, for that Roger Ramy said to me, he thought ye would aboute Low sonday be at Thornhill. Ye shall come to a old howse cleane downe, and as yet litle amended; but ye shall be very welcome, as I can think. I wold be sory that ye shoold take paine, and I not at home when ye come. Tomorrow begging thursday, I must of force ride to Tankerslay, viij miles hence, and mete my Lord of Shrewsburry, who will be thear tomorrow by ij of the clock, and se a showt at a stage, as my keper hath sent me wourd. And of monday, tewsday, and wedsday, theare is apoynted a great number of gentlemen to mette at cocxs at Sheifeild, whear I intend, God willing, to be, and every night will ly at Tankerxlay; soe it will be friday or I come to

Thornhill, which is the xviij (xiiij) of May. Wherfore, I desire you either put of your comming to that day, or take so much paine to come the viij myles to Tankerxlay, whear I have no lodging, but you shall have the best bed the keper haith; and ye shall se a polard or tow, both rid and falow, and se all our good coxs fight, if it plese you, and se the maner of our cocking. Ther will be Lanckeshire of one parte, and Derbeshire of another parte, and Hallomshire of the third parte. I perceive your cocking varieth from ours, for ye lay but the battell; and if our battell be but x^{li} to v^{li}, thear wilbe x^{li} to one laye, or the battell be ended. And whensoever ye come, I require you take time to hunt with me for one weke; bring bowes and gray hounds, and at the time of the year, hownds. A polard is swet now, and I love it best now at this season; and by Whytsonday this year I shall have fatt bucks. And or any red deare be fatt, it will be July, as far as my experience serves. Com when ye will, and such as I have, ye shall se; and bring good stufe, for I warne you they ar wild about Tankerxlay and ill to cach: and if all fale, I have that ar tame enough. I make all these brages to cause you to com, for I never yet did se you in thease parts; and ye shall come no time wrong, fence-time then other. I have tame plenty lyeth out; I can make you game at rid and falow, and stir no rascall. I besich Jesus send us mery meting. Thus hertyly far ye well. This Wendsday at Thornhill, the vth of May, Anno 1546: 38 H. 8.

Your asured frind

(5 *May* 1546.)   HENRY SAVILL, kn^t.

LETTER XXVI.
(No address.)

Right worshipfull, after my most hartiest manner, I recommend me to you. I received your letter of friday; I was buisie a hunting, but as for your suerty, ye shall never be bound to me, for I will not sew you; I had rather louse it. I went immeaddetly to Mr. Gargraves [a] howse, and he was with my father, and so I mist of him. I have drawn an obligation, to be sealed afore you and your servant, Settill, for a knowledge, and my servant shall deliver a hundred marke. And for because I am in no seurty wheare I shall be, when ye or any frind of yours shall call, I shall let another hundred marke with the bearrer herof, of an owre warning to be redy, upon reasonable seurty to be repaid within one yeare And to this bearer I have declared my mind to shew you in all things. And thus I bid you hartely farwell. From Sotthill, the xiiij of September.

Your asured to his power
ROBART SAVILL.[b]

[a] Robert Gargrave, esq. was the fourth husband of Elizabeth Paston, the mother of Sir Henry Savill, kt. The family had afterwards their residence at Nostell-priory, com. Ebor.

[b] Robert Savill, afterwards of Howley, the illegitimate son of Sir Henry Savill before spoken of, ancestor of the Earls of Sussex.

LETTER XXVII.
To the right worshipfull Mr. Plompton, esquire, deliver theis.

After harty commendations premised, this shall be to advertise you, that my Lord Presedent and other of the Kings honnorable comishiners hath delivered to me a precept to cause to com before them at the castle of York, the xvith day of this month of August, a certane number of worshipfull men of Yorkshire, wherof ye be one. Wherfore, I require you to accept this my letter for a suficent warning, for ye to be at the Castle the same xvith day, at x of the clock before nowne, to inquire upon certaine articles and matters which shall be then and thear by the said Comishioners declared upon our sovarayne Lord the Kings behalfe. Wherfore, I pray you, faile not, as ye will answer to the said Comishioners. Thus hartely far ye well. From York this viith day of August.

By yours to comaund
RENOLD BESEY
clerk of the castle of York.

LETTER XXVIII.
To the right worshipfull Mrs. Plompton, at Plompton Hall.

With most harty commendations in Christ Jesus, good Mrs. Plompton, this is to advertis you of the dispatch of such matters as you did commit unto me at my last being with you, wheare that I have traveled as I might of, partly by the ade and help of Mr. Bill,[a] your very frind I think, who hath him most hartily recommended both to you and Mr. Dynes, and hath sent your lozengs for a token. You shall allso receive with this bearrer a letter to Mr. Haymond, feodarry, for your lease, procurred by Mr. Bill, who shewed me that your charges in the Cheker is dispacht, and your Cussin Girlington[b] hath brought your acquitance. And order is taken for you at the Court of the Wards, and all is well stayd, but yet not paid. Your request was moved to Sir Arthur Darcy[c] first, who taketh the matter frindly, as ye shall know. The other gentleman was then by chaunc from the Court, which was the cause of the first talke with Sir Arthur. But in such wise as we may, and shall with honesty take the way which shal be thought the best to you and your frinds. Because you may se the effect of my Lord Treasurrers letter for your lease, I have sent it to you patent and open; and that knowing the effect therof, then you may send it to the feodary yourselfe, which were good that you did with spede convenient. Thus I comit you to the permishion, to him that canne, to will justice, who all your lawful dedes of honesty desires no dought, who I pray long to preserve in health. From my lodge at Howell,[d] this Palme Sunday.

Yours to my litle power
WILLIAM WODRIF.[e]

The cause that I came not now to you is a broken shin, which hath much vexed me.

(*Indorsed*, From my lord at Howell.[f])

(25 *Mar.* 1548.)

[a] Thomas Bill, esq. one of the King's physicians, had granted to him, by indenture dated 16 Nov. l Edw. VI. 1547, the wardship and marriage of William Plumpton, cousin and heir of William Plumpton, esq. deceased, which he by indenture of the 9th Feb. 2 Edw. VI. 1547-8, transferred to Isabel Plumpton, widow, late wife of William Plumpton, esq. deceased. (*Towneley MSS. G.* 24.)

[b] Robert Girlington, see his letter *postea*.

[c] Sir Arthur Darcy, kt. next brother of George, Lord Darcy of Aston.

[d] Howell, or Holywell Grange, was the grange on the lands that had belonged to Nostell Priory, in the parish of Thurnscoe, com. Ebor.

[e] William Woodriff or Woodruffe, the writer of this letter, was apparently a younger brother of the house of Wolley. and uncle of Francis Woodruff, of Wolley, com. Ebor. esq. (*See Pedigree in Hunter's South Yorkshire.*)

[f] Howell Grange was at this date the property of James Lord Montjoy, in right of his wife Catharine, daughter and heir of Sir Thomas Leigh, kt. the original purchaser of the possessions of Nostell Priory in the reign of Henry VIII. Mr. Wodriff may have acted as his agent, and perhaps through him application had been made for the interest of his master at Court by Mrs. Isabell Plumpton, to which this letter was considered a reply; hence the endorsement.

LETTER XXIX.
To the right worshipfull Mrs. Plomton at Plompton hall, widow.

Right worshipfull Mistres, in my harty wise I commend me to you, with thanks given to you for all your gentlenes; certyfying you that as yet my wife hath not laid her belly, but remaineth at her wits end. And since my being with you I have not had iij dayes of health; I thank God albeit. I am better now, which aple, that

I was thinking, by God's helpe, to se you after the holadayes. In the mean time I have sent this knowen bearrer to you for to se you, because I am not all well, praying you to advertis me of your health and wellfare, which I will be glad to hear of, as I wold be any frind I have, as God knoweth, who have you in his keping, and so fare ye well. From Howell grang, this Palme sunday.

    Yours to my litle power
      withowt gile,   WILLIAM WODRIF.

I am sory of the hevines of the death of Mr. Dinis wife.[a]

(Anno 1549-50.)

[a] Ursula, daughter of Richard Aldburgh, and niece of " Ralph Audbrough," the writer of a letter which follows, was married 4th July, 1 Edw. VI. 1547, to Denis or Dyonisius Plumpton, born 9 Oct. 1519, the feast of St. Denis. She left one son, Richard Plumpton, having, it seems, survived her marriage little more than a year.

LETTER XXX.

To his right worshipfull Aunt, Mrs. Isabell Plompton, at Plompton Hall, deliver this.

Right worshipfull and my singuler good Aunt, my deuty to you premised, I have me recommended unto you. This shall be to certyfy you that according to your commaundment haith kept your cort at Sacompte, and there Setle[a], your servant, reseived of tow men that was admited tennements at this your cort iiij [li] save 40[d], and of one power woman xiii[s]. 4[d]; which was admited tennements in rescion he did receive xi[s], which I have written to you, over and above your rents and your estreats. And I desire, good Aunt, to let me know how you will have your corts ordered, whether you will have them kept one or tow times in the yeare, by your next letter;

[a] By charter dated 6th Jan. 5 Edw. VI. 1551-2, Isabella Plumpton granted to Robert Sittills, for term of his life, an annuity of 26l. 2s. 8d. issuing out of lands in Kirkby-upon-Wharfe, or elsewhere within the county of York. *(Towneley MSS. G. 24.)*

and I according to your commaundement therein I shold doe, with the grace of Almighty Jesus, who have you, yours, and all your houshold in his blessed keeping. Written the xth of *Februarii.*
    By yours to comaund
      ROBART GIRLINGTON.[b]

[b] A Nicholas Girlington was one of the many friends and lovers who rode with Sir Robert Plumpton to York, to maintain him in his suit with Suttell and Rocliffe, at the Lammas Assize in the year 1502, and to William Girlington, gent. William Plumpton and Isabel or Elizabeth his wife, by their deed dated 3 Mar. 22 Hen. VII. 1506, conveyed their lands and tenements in Eastofts, in the county of York, for 33l. 15s. *(Chartul. No. 830.)* Burton, in the Pedigree of Babthorpe, printed in his Specimen History of the parish of Hemingborough, marries Robert Babthorpe, the father of Isabel Plumpton, to Joan the daughter of Nicholas Girlington; but this statement is disproved by the evidence that Glover had seen, which renders it more than probable that she was by birth a Hagthorpe. I venture, therefore, to infer from the testimony of this letter a marriage between the father of Robert Girlington, mistaken for Robert Babthorpe, and Joan, half-sister of Isabel Plumpton, of the family of Elson of Selby; for it is only upon this supposition that I can account for her being addressed by him as " my singuler good Aunt." *(See the Note to Letter CLXXIX. p. 118.)*

LETTER XXXI.

To the right worshipfull Mrs. Plompton, of Plompton Hall, be this delivered.

Aunt, this is to certife you that my father-in-law sent one to me ij letters that come from London from Robart Girdlington, one to you which is in hast, as far as my father sent me word to send them as shortly as I could send them to you. Furthermore, I wold have you them sent with Langton; them I give and he wold not carry them. And so I had spoken unto Mr. Egemeton for barneckles, and so I shold have gon over to Lodington to have bought them, and so I let them aloane. And so I desire you have me remembred to my Mistres, and to let hir know that my Lady

servants Hilyeard[a] demaunds halfe a quarter of beanes for their fat swine, and if it weare in condition or no; and if it be not, to alowe the same in the xx quarters that she shold have, and barly in like case. And so to let you know that barly rises of pease, as they say, and I have sold none as yet; and that they ar threshing in the one lath beanes and barley both, for swine makes il work, and so I make them labor as hard as they can for the same. And soe by this bearrer I send you ij letters, and I gave him for his labour xii[d] for coming. No more over to you, but Jesus have you in his kepping. Written this Ladyday at night in hast. And to let you know, wheras ye told me of 6 horses, the which they say the sorrell nag is not of yours, and sayes that ye have but 5; and so I wold answer it. For your hofer, it likes not; I shud a sold it, I truste, for 4[s] or better, if ye will.

    By me   RAFH AUDBROUGH.[b]

[a] Joan, daughter of Ralph Constable of Halsham, com. Ebor. esq. and widow of Sir Christopher Hildyard of Winestead, com. Ebor. kt. who died 29 Hen. VIII. 1538.

[b] Ralph Aldburgh was third son of Sir Richard Aldburgh, of Aldburgh, kt. by Jane, daughter of Sir Thomas Fairfax, of Walton, kt. He had apparently married a sister of Robert Girlington, niece of Mrs. Isabel Plompton, as he speaks of his father-in-law sending on letters to him from the latter. This letter will have been written from Waterton, which is in the parish of Luddington, the place where he meant to have purchased the sea-fowl called barnacles. Waterton had been the residence of Robert Plumpton, and the manor, in the 7th of Eliz. 1565, was yet charged with a rent of 22l. 2s. 8d. to Ann Moreton, then surviving, late wife of Robert Plumpton, for term of her life, by way of dower. At the same date, the manor of Sacombe, com. Herts, was charged with 54s. 4d., descendible, after the death of Dame Isabella Plumpton, to Aldburgh and Garlington, to each of them 26s. 8d. per annum. This letter appears to have been written about the year 1548, after the death of William and Robert Plumpton, during the minority of the son of the latter. Ralph Aldburgh was the steward at Waterton, and his " Mistres," the above-named Mrs. Ann Plumpton, afterward wife of Robert Moreton, of Bawtry, com. Ebor. esq.

LETTER XXXII.

To her worshipful sister Mistres Plompton, at Plompton Hall, deliver these.

Right worshipful sister, after most harty and loving commendations, with like desire of your good health and the long continuance of the same; this shall bee to give you most harty thanks for al your gentlnes unto mee shewid, and in especially for your goodnes shewid unto John Pool my son: he hath you most hartily commended, as your poor kinsman and bedesman, and he desires you, and I both, to take no displeasur with him for his long tarriing here, for as yet he is at no point for his childs part of my husbands goods. Therfore, I desire you, as my trust is, that you will bee so good Aunt unto him. Also I desir to have me commended to my sister Clare and to my son Dennis, sending him Gods blessing and mine, and to al other my kin and frends. Also my son Richard and John commends them unto you and their aunt Clare, and to Master Dennis, and to al other their good frends. And so *Jhesu* preserve you. From Rodburn the 6 of March.

    By your sister to her power
  (6 March 1551-2.)   ANN POOLE.[a]

[a] German Pole, the husband of Ann Pole, the writer of this letter, died 4 Jan. 5 Edw. VI. 1551-2, when German Pole was found to be his cousin and heir, son of Francis, son and heir of the said German, and of the age of seven years. *(Esc. 2 July, 6 Edw. VI. No. 21.)* Mrs. Isabel Plumpton, to whom these letters are addressed, died on the 10th of June in this same year, leaving her second son, Dennis, her only surviving child, to whom Mrs. Ann Pole, his aunt, had stood godmother; on which account she here calls him her son, and sends him God's blessing.

ADDENDA ET CORRIGENDA.

LETTERS WRITTEN TO SIR WILLIAM PLUMPTON.

Letter II. The assumed date of this letter is certainly erroneous. From the phrase, " I may nought be but of Counsell," it is clear that the writer was not in the exercise of judicial functions; moreover, it is well known that the Sheriffs were customarily chosen on the morrow of All Souls, so that it was always in Michaelmas Term that their year of office expired, when they had to be apposed of their greenwax, or in other words to pass their accounts before the Treasurer and Barons of the Exchequer; nor was this process usually delayed beyond the Term. This letter will, therefore, have been written the same year that Sir William Plumpton served the office of Sheriff for Yorkshire, or for the counties of Nottingham and Derby, and prior to the appointment of Brian Rouclíff to be third Baron of the Exchequer, in the reign of Henry VI. The Letters Patent to this effect are teste'd 2 Nov. 38 Hen. VI. 1459, and he was confirmed in his judicial situation 8 May, 1 Edw. IV. 1461.

Letter III. The writer of this letter is erroneously described in the note as of Middleton, com. Derb. Sir Richard Bingham, kt. Justice of the King's Bench, resided at Midleton, com. Warwick; which manor he had in right of his wife Margaret, one of the sisters and coheirs of Baldwin Frevill of Tamworth, to whom he was second husband. He died 22 May, 16 Edw. IV. 1476, and has a monumental inscription to his memory, yet preserved in the church at Midleton. (*Dugdale's Warwickshire, vol. II. p.* 1052.)

Letter IV. This letter should follow Letter V.; the correct date is 19 *May*, 1463.

Letter V. The conjecture in note b is inadmissible; there was a family of Greyndour of considerable eminence in Herefordshire at this period, and the lady of John Earl of Worcester, himself resident on the borders of Wales, was undoubtedly sprung from this stock : on the other hand, the name of Graindorge had merged in Nesfield long before the date of this letter. The near relationship of Thomas Beckwith to the Lord Treasurer may be accounted for in another manner. The mother of Thomas Beckwith is said in the Pedigree of the family entered at the visitation in 1666, to have been a daughter of Sir John Baskervile, the family of which name was seated in Herefordshire. This locality gives a likelihood to their being connected with the Earl of Worcester, and from the designation " Awnte son," here used, we may presume that the lady was half sister to the Earl's father. The date of this letter is determined to the year 1462, inasmuch as John Earl of Worcester, who had been made Lord Treasurer 14 Apr. 2 Edw. IV. 1462, was superseded in his office 24 June, 3 Edw. IV. 1463, by Edmund Lord Grey de Ruthyn. It should be added that no direct proof of Thomas Beckwith having held the office of Escheator of the county of York has been seen by the Editor.

Letter VI. The date of this letter should be 1465; Thomas Goldesburgh became bound with Sir John Norton, kt. to Sir William Plumpton, 1 Oct. 5 Edw. IV. 1465, for performance of covenants before the feast of the Nativity of our Lord next following (*Chartul. n.* 568); " att twentie day of Yoole" will, therefore, have reference to Christmas in that year, i. e. to the *Tres septimanæ Nativitatis*, or interval of time within the third octave of Christmas. In like manner it had been one of the articles of agreement between Robert Rosse, esq. and Sir William Plumpton, 33 Hen. VI. 1454, that the former should find Sir James Pickering, kt. and William Wakefield, esq. or other two men like them, to be bound to the said Sir William by statute merchant in 400li, that he the said Robert shall suffer all the lands to descend upon his son Thomas, who should wed Johan daughter of the said Sir William, that he the said Robert hath by his father or ancestors. By the same covenant, it was agreed that if Johan die within the age of twelve years, then 200li, the money given by Sir William for the marriage, to be repaid, and on the other hand Robert to have the governance of the married couple, and the amount of her jointure, till Thomas, her son, came of age. (*Towneley MS.*) It was, in fact, the usual custom in the feudal age for parents to contract for the preferment of their daughters in marriage, or for an advantageous match for their eldest son, when the parties were yet in infancy; and such marriage was solemnized by the rites of the church, and followed by the removal of the children to live under the same roof, though not yet arrived at the age of puberty. In some instances, there was an express stipulation in the covenant that the parties should not lie together till one or other of them reached a certain age; for it was otherwise the interest of the parents, on whichever side the alliance was most advantageous, to hasten consummation, by reason of the axiom of Canon Law then in force, *Concubitus non consensus facit nuptias*. It also may be collected from the subscriptions to these letters, that the affinity between the parents attached from the time of such solemnization; yet, if the woman at the age of 12 and after, and the man at the age of 14 and after, disagreed either of them to the marriage, they might marry again to others without any divorce, and have the precontract reckoned as if it had never been; on the other hand, if they agreed, then there was need of no new marriage. Thus Margaret Roucliffe, who at the time of her marriage in 1463 had but just completed her fourth year, was residing at Cowthorpe with her father-in-law in 1465, and he in this very letter speaks of her as his daughter, and subscribes himself when addressing her father, " your serviseable brother." These precontracts are hardly reconcileable with the doctrine of the Roman Church, which gives to matrimony the grace and efficacy of a Sacrament, and it may be doubted whether it was so classed by the Canonists before the time of Pope Innocent the Third; if so considered, then the solemnization at so early an age, with the possibility of its being a vain ceremony should the parties disagree, seems to be a suspension of heavenly graces little suited to the nature of so sacred a rite.

Letter VII. " and to Pake also," *lege* Paske, i. e. Easter Term, and *dele* note e.

Letter X. Hugh Pagnam or Pakenham was an officer of Archbishop Kemp in 1441. (*See Historical Notices, p.* lv.) The arms on the tomb of Sir John Pakenham in York minster appear to be *Quarterly*, 1 and 4, Quarterly Gules and Or, in the first quarter a crescent Argent; 2 and 3, Argent, three lilly pots Sable; all within a bordure engrailed Sable; and the same arms were in the head of the P, where his name was woven on some drapery which hung in the choir of the cathedral. (*Harl. MSS.* 1394.) The Suffolk family of the name bear, Quarterly Or and Gules, in the first quarter an eagle Vert.

Letter XVIII. For " with [in] the said manor," *lege* with the said manor, i. e. the thing stolen.

Letter XXVIII. The *Mense Pasche* was the day four weeks from Easter, which Sunday was usually called *Dominica mensis Paschæ*, and always fell in Easter Term; so that an appearance fixed for *Mense Pasche* was, in fact, for Monday in the fourth week after Easter. In 1477, the year in which this letter was written, as may be collected from the allusion to the match in contemplation between Robert Plumpton and Mr. Gascoigne's sister, Easter-day was on the sixth of April, and consequently the morrow of *Mense Pasche* would be the fourth of May.

Letter XXIX. " Untrew peopell of their hands." This was formerly an ordinary English phrase, now entirely lost. Thus Shakspeare, " Thou art a tall fellow of thy hands." *Winter's Tale*, V. 2.

LETTERS WRITTEN TO SIR ROBERT PLUMPTON.

Letter I. note b. For " Wardens," *lege* Warden.

Letter V. n. b. The descent of Edward Plumpton assumed in this note is not capable of proof; and his name is, therefore, omitted in the pedigree among the children of Godfrey Plumpton.

Letter XI. Upon a more careful examination of the Rolls of Parliament, the observation in the note has been found to be unsupported. The Commons prayed the King to resume from the 21st day of August, i. e his accession, all gifts, &c. made by King Henry VI. and the sovereigns of the House of York since the 2nd day of October, 34 Hen. VI. 1455, and they also prayed him to annul all gifts of

Letters Patent made by his majesty before the xx[th] day of January, in the first year of his reign; and the same was enacted. We should, therefore, read in the Letter from the xxi day of August for the ii, and the xx day of January for the iij; substituting also xxxiiij for xxiii yere of King Herre the vi[th]. "I weut" in this letter should be Iwent, *i.e.* weaned, supposed.

Letter XII. In explanation of the gift of a pair of Jeneper beads *pardonet* by my Lady of Syon, these entries among the Privy Purse expences of Henry VII. may be cited. " For offring at Syon at the pardon 13s. 4d. For two botes at pardon tyme at Syon, 1s. 4d." The remark in the note, that the King was at Nottingham when this letter was written, is incorrect, and at variance with the account of the subsequent progress by the Herald in the place cited; for he expressly gives us to understand that the King removed from Nottingham to Doncaster on Saturday, the 15th of April, and that such removal was in the week following his arrival there. This letter bears date on Monday in that preceding week, and was certainly written during the sojourn of the court in Lincoln, where Edward Plumpton, the writer, was in attendance upon his master the Lord Strange.

Letter XV. note [a]. Sir Thomas Bryan, kt. Chief Justice, made his will 7 Feb. 1495-6, which was witnessed by Thomas Betonsar, chaplain, the writer of this letter, and proved 11 Dec. 1500. (*Testamenta Vetusta, vol. II. p.* 450.)

Letter XVIII. There was a long race of Baildons of Baildon in the parish of Otley, continuing to past the middle of the 17th century, when the heiress married Bradwardine Tyndal of Brotherton.

Letter XXI. note [a]. Stephen Eyre, of Hassop, was the eleventh son of Robert Eyre, and Joan de Padley, whose remarkable monument still remains in the church of Hathersedge in Derbyshire, on the borders of the Moors.

Letter XXIII. William Scargill and William Scargill the younger, gentlemen, were among those present on the part of Sir Robert Plumpton at the trial at York, 18 Hen. VII. 1502; it is probable, therefore, that there was a family of this name settled in the vicinity of Plumpton, a junior branch of the Scargills of Thorpe Stapleton. It can hardly be supposed that Sir Richard Tunstall would call the head of the house " one Scaggell."

Letter XXV. note [a]. For " Wednesday, the feast of St. Vitalis," *lege* Tuesday.

Letter XXXI. note [a]. The following is the transcript of the letter of the Earl of Shrewsbury adverted to in this note, contained in Dodsworth's MSS. vol. cxlviii. the date whereof may be referred to the 7 Hen. VII. 1492, as mention is made in it of the field against the King's grace. (*See Letter LXVI. note* a.)

To my right welbeloved frend, Sir Robert Plompton, knight.

Right welbeloved frend, I recommend me unto you, ascertayninge you that it is shewed unto mee by my right welbeloved Dame Joyce Percy, now attendinge upon my wife, how yee, contrary to right and conscience, have interrupted the said Dame Joyce of certain land lyinge within the lordship of Arkinden, and within the county of Yorke, which land was purchased of one Robert Walkingham a by Sir Robert Pearcy, knight, her late husband, deceased, and by him granted unto the said Dame Joyce, as parcell of her joynture, yee now intendinge by meane of a sinistre grant made unto you of the said land by the said Robert continually to keepe the same by extort power contrary to the law, as shee saith. Wherefore, if it bee soe, I greately marvell; willinge and desyreinge you, therefore, that unto such tyme as this matter may be had in good and perfitt examination, yee will in noe wise further intromete or deale with the said land, but suffer the said Dame Joyce and her assignes peaceably to occupy the same, without any manner interruption to the contrary. And if yee, when the said examination shall bee had, shall have any good evidence for your pretence and title in that behalfe that yee of right are

[a] Robert Walkingham and Alice his wife, daughter and coheir of Gallway, sold, 30 Jan. 4 Henry VII. 1488-9, to Dame Joan Plompton, late wife of Sir William Plompton, kt. and to Sir Robert Plompton, kt. her son, in the vill of Plompton, a close called Patrikgarth, and two closes called the Milne closes near Grimball Bridge. Witnesses, William Ingleby, Piers Mydleton, kts. Richard Goldsbrough, Myles Wilsthorpe, Robert Birnand, esquires, Richard Saxton then bailiff of Spofford, Thomas Wood, chaplain, and many others. (*Cartul. No.* 752.)

to have the said land, yee shall thereof have possession and bee recompensed as right requireth. And over this, whereas I am enformed that one Richard Nicoll, late tenant to the said Dame Joyce, was now in the field against the Kings good grace, for the which cause yee have seazed his goods, as it accordeth, I will and desyre you, consideringe the said Dame Joyce was innocent, and nothinge knowinge of his misdemeaninge, yee will see that of his said goods such duties may bee contented as hee oweth unto her by reason of any tenures or holdings, and that yee will tender her in these premisses the rather for my sake, soe as she have not cause to make further suit for her remedy therein, as I trust you. From Ashby,* the 8th day of July.

Your frend,

G. SHREWSBURY.

Letter LXV. note [c]. Sir Henry Wentworth is erroneously called of Woodhouse, com. Ebor. after Fuller, in his List of Sheriffs. He was of Nettlested com. Suff. and ancestor to the lords Wentworth.

Letter LXVI. note [a]. p. 96, and again p. 97. For 1491, *lege* 1492; and before " disposition" add " good." I subjoin a full extract from the inscription on the monument of the Earl of Surrey at Thetford, relating to his government in the North. " And wythin x wekes after his coming out of the towre, ther was an insurrection in the Northe by whom the Erle of Northombrelond was sleyne in the feld, and also the citee of Yorke wonne with a sawte by force.† And for the subduing of those rebells, the Kinge assembled a grete hoste of his subgettis, and toke his iourney towards them from the castell of Hertford; and the said Erle of Surrey made chief captayn of his voward, and apoynted under him in the seid voward the Erle of Shrewesbury, the Lord Hastyngs, Sir Will. Stanley, than being the Kinges Chamberlayn, Sir Rice ap Thomas, Sir Thomas Bowser, Sir John Savage, Sir John Ryseley, and divers other. And whan this jorney was doon, the Capteynes of these Rebelles and many other of them were put to execution. And for the singuler truste that the Kinge had to the seid Erle, and the activite that he saw in him, he lefte him in the North, and made him his Lieuter aunt generall from Trent Northward, and Warden of the Est and Middle Marshes of Englond ageinst Scotland, and Justice of the Forests from Trent Northward, and ther he continued x yeres; and kepte the countrey in peace with policy and many paines taking, withoute whiche it wold nat have been, for that the countrey had ben so lately ponished, and nat withoute desert. And thus he dide the hoole tyme of x yere, saving in the second yere of his being, ther was an insurrexion in the West part of the countrey, with whome the seid Erle, with the helpe of the Kinges true subgettis, fought in the feld, and subdued them at Akworth besides Pomfrett. And besides divers of them that were slaine in the feld, he toke the captaines and put them to execucion, and the residue he sued to the Kinges Highness for ther pardones, whiche he obteined, and wane therby the favour of the countrey. And in the same yere the King went over the see, and laid siege to Bolayn, the seid Erle than remaining ther, notwithstonding that he was appointed to have gone with the King, and had gon, but for the lightnes of the pepule ther, wherefor he was left behind, both for the savegard of the countrey and for defending of the realme, for the singuler truste that he had unto him."

Letter LXXII. *Dele* note [a], and see what is said above, Letter XXIII.

Letter LXXIV. note [a]. There does not appear to have been any Lancashire family of the name of Midleton holding station as gentlemen at this period. In 16 Henry VII. 1501, Jane, widow of David Griffin was wife of Nicholas Talbot, descended of the Lancashire family, and she, it may be presumed, was mother of David, the writer of this letter, and of the wives of .... Midleton and Edward Plumpton. (*Testamenta Vetusta, vol. II. p.* 458.)

* Ashby-de-la-Zouch, the seat of Lord Hastings, brother of the Countess of Shrewsbury.

† The recollection of this assault was fresh in the time of Leland; "Ther was," he writes, " a Fundation of an Hospitale, hard without the very side of Michelgate, of the erecting of Syr Richard of York, Mair of York, whom the Communes of Yorkshir when they enterid into York by brenning of Fisscher-Gate, in the reign of Henry the 7, wold have behedid. But the fundation was never finished." (*Itin. fol.* 61.) And again, " To Waume-Gate 3 Toures, and thens to Fissher-Gate, stoppid up sins the Communes burnid it yn the tyme of King Henry the 7." (*Ibid. f.* 60.)

Letter LXXVII. note b. Richard Cholmley was afterwards a knight. He married Elizabeth daughter of Ralph Nevill of Thornton-Bridge, and died circa 1521, without legitimate issue.

Letter XCIX. note b. For Roxby, *lege* Fenwick. The knight of Roxby was Sir Roger Hastings, mentioned in the Letter of Sir Robert Plumpton in the Historical Notices, p. cxiii, as being near his undoing; and he, it seems, ultimately sold his lands in Pickering-Lythe to Sir Roger Cholmley, kt. (*Lel. Itin. I. p.* 63.)

Letter CIII. note c. This note is a mis-statement; see note a, p. 218.

Letter CX. note e. The prior of St. John's ranked as premier baron in the rolls of Parliament, and was usually styled Lord of St. John's.

Letter CXVI. note b. Thomas Lawrence was of Ashton near Lancaster, son of Sir James Lawrence, kt.

Letter CXIX. note i. Add "George Edgar or Edgore, called Serjeant, 7 Nov. 21 Hen. VII. 1505."

Letter CXXVI. Add this note. "William Wymondeswold of Southwell com. Nott. gent. died in 1520, and lieth buried in the church of St. Nicholas in Nottingham."

Letter CXXXVI. note at foot. The letter from Sir Robert Plumpton to his wife will be found in the Historical Notices of the family.

Letter CXLVI. John Strey of Doncaster, who married Alice, daughter of Sir Roger Hopton of Swillington, com. Ebor. living between 8 and 21 Hen. VIII. was of the family of the writer of this letter. See a description of his monument in the church at Doncaster, in Hunter's South Yorkshire.

Letter CLVIII. note a. l. 3. For letter CLIV. *lege* CLV.

Letter CLIX. For Bramenn Lyvacr, *lege* Bramtun Lynacr. Lands in Brampton were given by Hugh de Lynacre to Adam de Esseburn, and the manor seat of the ancient family of Lynacre was in this parish. At the Conqueror's Survey Ascoit Musard had a manor of ten oxgangs and a half in *Holum, Wadesel* and *Brantune*. The first name subsists in the hamlet of Holy Moor side.

Letter CLXV. n. a. For Lady Darcy, *lege* Lady Nevill. Edith, relict of Ralph Lord Nevill, retained the title of her first husband after her second marriage, as appears from her signature to Letter CLX. and from the order of her interment in the MS. I. 3. in Coll. Arm. In quoting from this manuscript, Dugdale has made an error in the christian name, writing Elizabeth for Edith; the document itself establishes beyond question the pedigree of this noble lady, and I am induced to give it here entire.

" On the xxii day of August, in the yere of our Lorde MVᶜXXIX, the XXI yere of Kyng Henry the Eight, decessed at Stepneth near London, the ladye Edithe Nevyll, and wiff to Thomas Lord Darcy, suster to Will'm Lord Sandis, chamberlain to the King, for whos interrement was ordeyned in maniere folowing :

" Furst, assone as nyght be tyme convenient the body was cerred; oon the Wensday then next folowinge was conveyed from the place havyng the iiii ordres of fryres, the mynystres of the churche, certain gentilmen, garter principall King of armes, Richemont herauld weryng his cote of armes, then the body born by her servants and by certain fryres of the Blacfryres, iiij gret banners at the iiij corners, then folowed the lady Strikeland* and certain other gentilwomen morners to the nombre of vii morners and other gentilwomen. And after my Lord Darcy servants in blacke, xii pore men havyng gownes and hods, went all along the oon syde before the body, bering staff torches, and xii yemen of my said lord bare staff torches abowt the body; and in this ordre keping the high way, went to Radcliff, wher ther was two barges prepared covered with black clothe, garnyshed with her armes. And in the oon barge was the body, the mynestres of the churche, the torche berrers and servants; in the other barge the morners, the gentilmen, and gentilwomen. By cause it was thought that the said lady Nevill died of the gret sykenesse, or ells ther wold have been there a farre gretter compaigne, wiche for dangier of the sykenes my Lord Darcy cawsed them to exchew, for the

* Catharine, daughter and coheir of Ralph Nevill, of Thornton-Bridge, com. Ebor., esq. relict of Sir Walter Strickland of Sizergh, com. Westm. kt.; he died 9 Jan. 18 Hen. VIII. 1526-7, and she became successively the wife of Henry Brough, esq. and William Knivet, esq.

tokens of the gret sykenesse appered on her. And so was conveyed by water to the Kings brigge at Grenewich, were the fryers observants and the paroche met the body, and conveyed it to the fryres; wiche assone as it was entred the myddill part of the churche, the body was set upon two trestills, and the fryres proceeded immediatly to the service of the buryeng. Wiche doon, and the body buried, all the morners with other retorned to the barges ageyn, some to London, and some to Stepneth ageyn; for that nyght ther was certain almes geven bothe in the church-yerde at Stepneth, and alsoo at Grenywich by certain of my Lord Darcy chapeleins.

" On the morne abowt viii of the clocke all the company assembled at Saynt Magnus Churche, and appointed to take their barge, Botolff wharff, and so rowed downe to Radcliff, and there toke in certain gentilmen and gentilwomen, wiche there abode their comyng, and soo rowed downe to Grenewich." (f. 71 b.)

Letter CLXXVII. note b. This statement is incorrect. Sir Christopher Ward died 30 Dec. 13 Hen. VIII. 1521, seized of the manors of Guiseley, Givendale, &c. leaving one daughter and three granddaughters, namely, the daughters of his daughter Anne Nevill deceased, his co-heirs. Of these the daughter then surviving was Joan, wife of Sir Edward Musgrave, of Musgrave and Harcla Castle, com. Westmorland, then aged 34 years; and Catharine, Joan, and Clara were the three daughters of Ralph Nevill, esq. by Anne Ward, deceased, of whom Catharine, then aged 22 years, was wife of Walter Strickland, esq. (afterwards knight), of Sizergh in Westmorland; Joan, aged 21 years, was wife of John Constable, of Burton Constable, in Holderness, esq.; and Clara, aged 14, unmarried. (*Whitaker's Hist. of Leeds, vol. I. p.* 211.) In the dining-room at Sizergh, over the chimney-piece is a shield, quarterly, 1, Strickland; 2, Deincourt; 3, Nevill, with a mullet for difference; 4, Azure, a cross botony Or, Ward; supporters, a stag collared and chained, and a bull with a mullet on his breast: and in another apartment, quarterly Strickland and Deincourt, impaling Nevill and Ward.

Letter CLXXX. note a. l. 5. For Hen. VII. lege Henry VIII.

LETTERS WRITTEN TO MR. WILLIAM PLUMPTON.

Letter I. note a. p. 223, l. 12. For 20 Oct. 3 Eliz. 1561, *lege* 7 Eliz. 1565.

Letter IX. note b. Sir Robert Sheffield the elder, kt. made his will 8 Aug. 1518, and it was proved 28 Feb. 1518-9; the date 10 Aug. 1516, is, therefore, erroneous. (*See Testamenta Vetusta, vol. II.* p. 555.)

ERRATUM IN PEDIGREE.

Issue of Anne Plumpton and Henry Scroop. For Mary *lege* Anne, and for Stephen *lege* Thomas, and *dele* Broughton. The daughter and only child of Henry Scroop of Danby, esq. and Anne Plumpton his wife was Anne, married to Thomas Tempest of Roundhay-Grange near Leeds, esq. second son of Stephen Tempest of Broughton, com. Ebor. esq. and brother and heir of sir Stephen Tempest, kt. who bequeathed Broughton to his nephew Stephen, eldest son of Thomas Tempest and Anne Scroop.

*** The curious incident of the attempted execution of Gilbert de Plumpton for ravishing the daughter of Roger de Guilevast, narrated in the Historical Notices of the family, receives additional illustration from the Abstracts of Charters to Marrick Priory, printed in the fifth volume of that valuable repertory of Ancient Evidences, The *Collectanea Topographica et Genealogica*, page 117, *sub tit.* Hunton, a vill of Richmondshire. From these we learn that Roger de Gulewast was the husband of Helewis, daughter of Roger de Hunton, of whose gift, by the name of Helewis Gulewast, the Priory had land in that vill; and that, with her consent, her husband confirmed the gifts in fee-farm and frankalmoign of one holding of his fief in Hunton. From them the property came into the possession of Gilbert de Plumpton with his wife, and by him five acres and a half of his demesne in the fields of Hunton, were given to the nuns of Marrick. In the course of another descent, (A.D. 1266) Hunton had passed into the hands of Nicholas, son of Robert de Gerdiston, i. e. Garriston, a neighbouring vill.

INDEX OF MATTERS.

Abbot, Anne, Letter from, to Dame Anne Rokeby, to excuse keeping back money by reason of urgent necessity, her household fare described, 229.

Ackworth near Pontefract, field of, xcix, 95[a], 266. The year of its being fought ascertained, xcix [w].

Aldborough (*Burc, Burg*), notices of the early history of, ix [b], xi[a]. Sir Richard, contract of marriage of, with Agnes Plumpton, lxxxiii. Letter from, to sir Robert Plumpton, to bespeak his favourable judgment on behalf of his servant on an award, 84. Challenged together with his servants on the trial of an assize as of kin to the parties, cix. Ralph, Letter from, to Mrs. Isabell Plumpton, concerning the keeping of the Courts of the manor of Sacomb, 256.

Archers, copy of an agreement for service of, in the retinue of a knight, for a year, xlviii.

Ardern, Sir Piers, deputy of William De la Pole, Earl of Suffolk, liii. Henry, Letter from, to Sir Robert Plumpton, his father, soliciting payment of money owing from his deceased lady, 194.

Arms, of Plumpton, when assumed, xix. Ancient emblazonment, *ibid.*[1]. Noticed xxi, liii, lxxxv, lxxxvi, 152 [c]. Of Babthorpe, ci. Of Clifford, lxxxvi. Of Darell, *ib.* Of Foljambe, xxviii [h], liii, lxxxv, lxxxvi, 152[c]. Of Hagthorpe, 218 [a]. Of Hamerton, lxxxvi.

Of Holt, 128 [a]. Of Middelton, 75 [a]. Of Nevill, of Thornton-bridge, 269. Of Pakenham, 226. Of Percy, xix. Of Pilkington, ci. Of Stapleton, lxxxvi. Of Ward, 269. Of Waterton, ci. Of Strickland, 269. Of Wintringham, 152 [e]. Of the Master Forester of Knaresborough Forest, lxxxvi.

A-thington, Willism, Letter from, to Sir Robert Plumpton to assist at the end-making of a dispute referred to arbitration, 81.

Augmentation, Court of, 234, 242.

Award, copy of the terms on, 41. Memorandum of an agreement between parties to submit to, with the judge's hand at foot, 210.

Babthorpe, covenant for the marriage of Isabell, the heir general of, to William Plumpton, xcix. Pedigree of, ci. William, of Osgodby, his suit against Plumpton and ux. 130, *et seq.* Notices of the family of, and their suit with the heirs general, 219, *et seq.* Sir William, the Lawyer, one of the King's Council in the North, cxxv. Final settlement of the controversy, cxxviii.

Banks, Richard, Letter from, to Sir William Plumpton to recommend, 29.

Bans of Marriage, certificate from a rector of the publication of, lxxxi [c].

Barlow, Edwin, [Owen or Ewene,] Attorney of Sir Robert Plumpton, Letter from, to the same, concerning the stopping of a Privy Seal, 114.

Baudkin, 37.

Bedford, John Duke of, copy of the agreement between, and Sir Robert Plumpton, for his services in peace and war, xliii [c].

Bekyns, liii.

Besey, Renold, clerk of the castle of York, Letter from, to Mr. Plumpton, to require his attendance, 252.

Betanson, sir Thomas, chaplain, Letters from, to Sir Robert Plumpton, with news from London, 48, 49. 53. Witness to the will of Sir Thomas Bryan, chief Justice C. P. 263.

Billop, Thomas, Letter from, to Sir William Plumpton concerning the farming of his manor of Kenalton, 20.

Bingham, Sir Richard, Justice of the King's Bench, Letter from, to Sir William Plumpton, to appoint a meeting to settle by treaty a variance between the latter and Henry Pierpoint, 3. Note concerning him, 259.

Birtby, Sir Edward, priest, Letter from, to Sir Robert Plumpton concerning the price of a mail, 110.

Blackwall, Sir Robert, Master in Chancery, clerk of the Parliament, Counsel retained for Sir Robert Plumpton in his suits, 93, 99. His attorney in the Exchequer, 115, 145. Letter from, to the same, concerning the appointment of Sheriffs for the year 1501, and warning him of Master Empson's purpose to proceed by assize, 147.

Bondman, claimed by Sir Robert Plumpton, 54.

Borge-scire, derivation of name, ix [b].

Buckingham, Duke of, alarm created by his rebellion, 44. Sends messengers into the North, 45.

Burgh (Borough), sir Thomas, has the son of Lady Stapleton in ward, 17. Letter from,

to Mr. William Plumpton, for an accommodation of the dispute with Babthorpe, 222.

Byaufiz, sir Henry, Lands of, of the inheritance of his wife Cecilia, daughter of William de Plumpton, settled by fine, xx, xxii [?].

Calverley, William, the older, Letter from, to Sir Robert Plumpton, to recommend, 56.

Canterbury, Hubert Archbishop of, has the Honour of Knaresborough in ward with Robert de Stutevill, xv.

Carlisle, William Sivever Bishop of, correspondence of, noticed, iv. His journey to Colyweston mentioned, 113. Has authority to appoint the Escheator for the county of York, 147. See under York, Abbot of.

Carver, John, Vicar General of Christopher Bainbridge, Archbishop of York, Letter from, and from John Wytaer, his Surveyor and General-reasoner, to Sir Robert Plumpton, concerning the presentation to a chantry, 205.

Castle-Boone, xix.

Catton, Sir William, Canon of Newburgh, Letter from, to Sir Robert Plumpton, soliciting his good offices for his brother in regard to the clerkship of Coxwold, 66.

Chadyrton, Katharine, Letter from, to George Plumpton her brother at Bolton abbey, xxxix. Her visit to the Lord Scrope of Bolton, and his lady described, xl.

Chaloner, Robert, three Letters from, to Sir Robert Plumpton, for money lent, 197, 204.

Chamberlain, Lord, his visit to the North, 15. His saying about labouring on behalf of any of the Earl of Northumberland's men, he being present, 33.

Chancellor, Lord, (George Nevill,) his order in a suit respecting a chantry, 16. At London

with the King, 17. (Thomas Rotherham,) applied to for a letter from the King, 35. (John Alcock,) publishes the King's marriage in Parliament 48.

Chancery, new rule of, 29.

Chantry, Foundation of, in the church of Ripon, xxi. In the church of St. Martin in Mickelgate, York, xxix. In the church of Spofforth, xxxvii. Letter from John Eyre touching the custody of the keys of a, 189.

Claro, derivation of name, x[b].

Cocking at Sheffield, 251.

Collumbell, Henry, Letter from, to Sir Robert Plumpton, concerning Sir Edmund Batmon, 155.

Collyweston, notice of visitors at, 113. Sir William Gascoigne rides thither, 148.

Cologne, confraternity of the Rosary of our Lady of, 50.

Commission, of array, 14 Hen. VI. lii. Of enquiry concerning lands of attainted persons, 38 Hen. VI. lxvi.

Comrades, persons present together at a christening, 63.

Constable, Sir Marmaduke, of Flamborough, one of the arbitrators chosen for the Plaintiffs to treat with Sir Robert Plumpton, cviii. Two Letters from, to Sir William Gascoigne, to appoint a meeting, 207, 209. Purchases the marriage of Jane Sotehill, cxix, 208 [b]. Party to award as her guardian, cxx. Sir John, notice of his marriage and descendants, 208[b]. Sir Robert, Letter from, to Lady Rokesby, offering to assist her to claim arrears, 227. Sir Marmaduke, of Everingham, Letter from, to the same, on family affairs, 228.

Cope, price of material and cost of making, 37.

Cornwall, Richard Earl of, has a grant of the Honour of Knaresborough, xvi. Edmund Earl of, his covenant with Sir Robert Plumpton, respecting forest-easements in Plumpton, xviii.

Coroners, panel on a writ of attaint returned by the, 181.

Coverley, Richard, Letter from, to Sir Robert Plumpton, concerning the dues of the Rector of Spofforth, 105. Mistake of name for Cholmley, 106 [b].

Country, usual term for Jury, 24.

Court, John Rocliff to be placed at, expense of array double, 13.

Court-Baron, called the Three-weeks' court, 32.

Court-rolls, kept in a coffer in the church, 239.

Courtenay, heir to the Earl of Devonshire, arrested, 20.

Cowthorpe, church of, given to the Priory of Helagh by Peter de Plumpton, afterwards released, xviii. Manor of, owed suit and service to Plumpton, 43.

Coxwold, clerkship of, 66.

Cross-days, 152.

Crown, yeomen of the, 20.

D. John, Letter from, to Sir Robert Plumpton, about his suits, and with news, 217.

Dale, abbot and convent of, security for payment of rent, 102.

Dartford, nun professed at, of the order of St. Dominick, 15.

Darcy, Thomas Lord, of Templehirst, note of his being first created a Baron, 187 [a]. Of his matrimonial alliances, 203 [b], 267.

Daysmen, 82.

Dedimus potestatem, writ of, costly and requiring great soliciting, 91. Proceedings upon, 101.

Derby, Freres at, Dame Elizabeth Pole lodged there, 190.

Distress, writ of, proceedings under, described, 167.

Dodington, John, Letter from, to Mr. William Plumpton, upon matters relating to the manor of Sacomb, 237. To Mrs. Isabell Plumpton, for the same, 241. To Mr. William Plumpton, concerning a lease from the Court of Augmentation, 242. To the same, to inform him of the obtaining of a warrant for a doe out of the Parks of Bilton or Hay, 243. To the same, with news of the death of the parson of Sacomb, 243.

Drink-money, xix.

Drury, Sir William, notice of his marriage and descendants, 208 [b].

Durham, (John Shirwood) Bishop of, Richard Cholmley a royal commissioner for levying the duties in arrear, owing to the late, 105. (Richard Fox) Bishop of, has the custody of the lands of Ralph late Earl of Westmorland, during the minority of Ralph Earl of Westmorland, cxv. Lord Privy Seal, 112, 115, 116. (Thomas Ruthall) Bishop of, makes an agreement with William Bedell, concerning the manor of Babthorpe, 218.

Dymes, lands that paid, not assessed, 61.

Edward III. Letter from, to the Mayor and Bailiffs of Rye, to allow Sir Robert de Plumpton, who had landed there from the fleet, to quit his service and return home for the recovery of his health, xxiii [s].

Edward IV. Letter from, with charge not to rob or spoil Sir William Plumpton, lxviii. Of general pardon for same, *ibid.*[t]. Of acquittance from debt by bond for same, *ibid.*[u].

In warrant of the misproof of the charges against, and declaratory of the loyalty of same, and to give protection, lxx. Of pardon for same in the eleventh year of his reign, lxxv. His retinue on coming to London, 17. Said to have given away the property of Sir Thomas Tresham and Sir John Marney, 20.

Eleson, William, of Selby, Letter from, to Sir Robert Plumpton, giving legal counsel, 134. To the same, to appoint a day of meeting, 135. Chosen to peruse the evidence of Sir Robert Plumpton, 151. Arbitrator with Sir William Gascoigne, on behalf of same, cviii. Letter from, to his sister Mrs. Isabell Plumpton, concerning her claim to the manor of Babthorpe, 218. Note explaining his consanguinity to same, *ibid.*[b].

Elton, manor of, claim to the, specified in the award of Richard II. xciii. Note concerning it, xciv [o]. Chantry of, 132.

Emerson, George, confidential friend and attorney of Sir Robert Plumpton, Letters from, to the same, upon matters regarding his suit, and giving advice, 145, 150, 177.

Empson, Richard, has a warrant from Lord Strange for a doe in the park of Hals yearly, 88. His purpose to revive the claim of the heirs-general to the whole succession of Sir William Plumpton made known to Sir William Gascoigne and others, 120. Speaker of the House of Commons, and Serjeant-at-law, 121 [b]. Letter from, to Sir William Gascoigne, to interfere to protect Richard Falbarne against Sir Robert Plumpton and his servants, 122. Spoken of as "the great man Empson," 151. His secret practices, *ibid.* His false craft and utter and malicious enmity, 162. His proceedings against Sir Robert Plumpton detailed, cii. *et seq.* The manor of Kinalton given to him for life, in reward of his maintenance, cvi. His demeanour at the Assize at York, cvii. Petition of Sir Robert Plumpton to the King, setting forth his great maintenance and supportation, cxi. Inquisitions returned by him into the Chancery, cxvi. Executor of Sir Reginald Bray, 177[a]. Chancellor of the Duchy of Lancaster, 208[b]. His execution, cxvii. His daughter, Joan, married first to Henry Sotehill; secondly to Sir William Pierpoint, cxix, cxxi, 208[b].

Emyson, James, Letter from, to Sir Robert Plumpton, on behalf of Lady Ward, desiring his daughter may bear her company at Christmas at Gauthorp, 216.

Error, writ of, put to the making, 165.

Escheator, Thomas Beckwith to be, for Yorkshire, by appointment of the Lord Treasurer, 6. Livery of seizin by Robert Wycard, of the county of Derby, xxvii[b]. Agreement between Edmund Parpoint, of the counties of Nottingham and Derby, and Sir William Gascoigne, to make return of the title of Sir Robert Plumpton to the inheritance of his father, lxxxvii. Office found before William Netilton, of the county of York, *ibid.* Ralph Sacheverell of Hopwell, of Nottinghamshire and Derbyshire, 147. William Crouch, late customer of Hull, of Yorkshire, *ibid.* Livery of seizin by same, 220[e].

Esholt, Dame Alice Chelray, prioress of, her covenant with Sir Robert Plumpton, xlvii[r].

Executors, opinion concerning, 48.

Exigent, 198.

Eyre, Stephen, of Hassopp, Letter from, to Sir Robert Plumpton, concerning a loan of money, 58. Robert, Letter from, to the same, in recommendation of Ralph Haugh, 69. To the same, touching the agreement between him and the said Ralph, *ibid.* To the same, in recommendation of the widow of his farmward, deceased, 140. To the same, touching the marriage contract between their children, 143. To the same, promising to accompany him to the Earl of Shrewsbury at Wingfield, 158. To the same, upon matters concerning the trial by assize against Sir Robert Plumpton at Derby, 160.

Faculty, copy of, by the Vicar General of the Archbishop of York, for George Plumpton to hear reserved cases in confession, xxxv[k]. By the same, for the vicar of Harwood to solemnize marriage in a private chapel in a manor-house, lxxx[r].

Fairfax, Serjeant Guy, saying of, at the Bar, against maintenance, 35.

Fawbergh (Falbarne), Richard, clerk to Bryan Rocliff, one of the feoffees in a settlement, lxxii[b]. Entry by same and his co-feoffees, before statute 1 Ric. III. pleaded, cv. Reentry by same as survivor, and re-feoffment to other persons to the same uses, cvi. Does not dare to apply his business through fear of Sir Robert Plumpton and his servants by reason thereof, 122.

Fees to Counsel, 23, 93, 152[l].

Feodary, 253.

Foder of hay, 21.

Foljambe, notices of the family of, xxvii[b]. Pedigree, xxviii[k].

Fountains, grant to the abbot and convent of, xviii. Letter from John (Darneton), abbot of, to Sir Robert Plumpton in recommendation of a kinsman, 62. Lord of, 82. Farmhold taken of the abbot of, 84.

Frowick, Serjeant, Counsel for Sir Robert Plumpton, 152. Justice of Assize, 153. Chief Justice of the Common Pleas, 165. Note concerning him, *ibid.*[b]

Galtres Forest, named from the wapentake of Girlestre, xi[d]. Its extent, *ibid.* Office of Steward and Master Forester of, belonging to the family of Babthorpe, ci.

Gascoigne, William, brother-in-law of the Earl of Northumberland, in office at Knaresborough, 32. At variance with Sir William Plumpton, *ibid.*[d] Letter to, from the Earl of Northumberland, enjoining him to suffer a prisoner to be at large upon bail, 34. Marriage of his sister to Robert Plumpton, 38. Solemnized in the chapel at Goke-thorpe, lxxix. A fee'd knight of the Earl of Northumberland, xcvi. Notices of his descendants, 34[a]. Sir William, made a Knight of the Bath, xcvii. Summoned by his uncle, the Earl of Northumberland, to Thirsk, on the eve of the insurrection, 61. His influence at Court, 112. His discourse with Mr. Empson, 121. Letter to him from the latter, 122. James Colton and Preston, his servants, 126, 128. Rides to Colyweston, 148. Letter from, to his uncle Plumpton, to excuse his not meeting him through illness, 149. To the same, respecting certain evidence in his custody, *ibid.* One of the arbitrators chosen on behalf of Sir Robert Plumpton to treat with the adversaries at York, cviii. Letter from, to his uncle Sir Robert Plumpton, with various tidings relating to his suit, 175. Offers to send bowmen to aid in the defence of Plumpton-Hall, 176. Counsel for Sir Robert Plumpton, 177. Two letters from Sir Marmaduke Constable to the same, to appoint a time of meeting, 207, 209. Letter from, to his uncle Plumpton, concerning the King's grant to him of the Lordship of Harwood with the wardship of the heir, 214. To the same, to inquire of the date of the birth of his nephew Fairfax, and of the marriage of his cousin Eyre, 215. Treasurer of Cardinal Wolsey, 221[a]. John, esquier, letter from the Earl of Northumberland to, to be ready at an hour's warning, 53. Letter from, to Sir Robert Plumpton his brother-in-law, with a message from his nephew to pay money to Robert Hastings, 148. Ralph, uncle of Sir William Gascoigne, owner of a house in Plumpton, 175. Mary, Letter from the Earl of Northumberland to Sir Robert Plumpton, touching her inheritance, 74.

Girlington, note concerning the alliances of the family of, 256[b].

Gisburn, Ellen, a receipt for legacies bequeathed by, given to the executors of her will, xxix.

Glanvile, Ranulph de, Justiciary under Henry II., historical anecdote of, xvi. Proofs of its authenticity, x*, 270.

Gloucester, Richard Duke of, Constable and Admiral of England, Letter from, to Sir William Plumpton, Steward of the Lordship of Spofford, directing him to restore certain stolen cattle to the owner, 26. Chief Seneschal of the King's Duchy of Lancaster in the North Parts, *ibid.*[a]. Chosen as one of the arbitrators in an award, lxxxix.

Godson, son of Sir Robert Plumpton, of the abbot of Kirkstall, 62.

Gossip, the term used to denote the relationship between a godfather and the parents, 62.

Greenwax, a term of the Exchequer, 2, 92.

Grene, Godfrey, Letter from, to Sir William Plumpton, on legal business, 9. To the same, of his suits, and detailing the particulars of an offer by a mercer of the Cheap for to marry with his sister, 10. To the same, of his suits, and with news of the arrest of divers lords and knights, 18. To the same, on legal business, 29. To the same, respecting an application to the King and the Earl of Northumberland to be continued in his office at Knaresborough, 31. To the same, of his suits, 35. Richard, Letter from, to Sir Robert Plumpton, to excuse his not coming to him, by reason of the commands of the Earl of Northumberland to view his park and game at Topcliff, &c. 79. Elizabeth, Letter from, to the same, with notice of William Tankard's disobeying his orders, 80. Robert, Letter from, to the same, to excuse his not coming to him by reason of his wife's sickness, &c. 83.

Griffith, David, Letters from. See Haverah Park.

Hales, pilgrimage to, 96.

Hall, remarks upon his account of the insurrection of Archbishop Scrope, xxiv.

Hamerton, Sir Stephen, Letter from, to Sir Robert Plumpton, his brother-in-law, to make search for evidence, 63.

Hands, men of their, 38, 89, 262.

Harrington, Hamlett, Letter from, to Sir Robert Plumpton, to inform him of his lands being extended for debt, as his security, 206.

Hastings, Sir John, Dame Isabell, late deceased, late wife to, c. Holds the manor of Sacombe as tenant by the curtesy of England, 129. Action of waste against him, 133, 146. Treats with Sir Robert Plumpton, 136. Sir Roger, at the point of ruin, cxiii. Robert, Letter from, to Sir Robert Plumpton, for loan of money, 144.

Haverah (Hawray, Haw-warray, Awerry, Haywra) Park, in Knaresborough Forest, livery of the game in, by the keepers to Sir William Plumpton, liii[h]. Held by David Griffith, one of the Council of the Earl of Derby, under a patent, and proposed to be leased by him to Sir Robert Plumpton, 94, 96, 97. Letter from the same to Sir Robert Plumpton, informing him of the lease having been drawn up, 99. Letter from Sir Randall Piggott to Sir Robert Plumpton, to certify the price of "palesses" during the time he occupied, 98. Two letters from David Griffith to the same, to solicit payment of the rent, 102, 103. Letter from William Merkenfeild to Sir Robert Plumpton, respecting the purloining of cattle agisted therein, *ibid.*

Hawkesworth, Thomas, Letter from, to Sir Robert Plumpton, to recommend, 109.

Hayboot, xix.

Helperby, details of a serious affray with bloodshed, near, between the men of the forest of Knaresborough and the men of the Archbishop of York, lix.

Henry II. respites the execution of Gilbert de Plumpton, x*. Grants Knaresborough and Burgh to William de Stuteville, xiii.

Henry IV. story of, told by Clement Maidstone, xxv. Grants letters of pardon to Sir Robert Plumpton, after the execution of his son for treason, xxvi.

Henry VI. Letters from, to Sir William Plumpton and others his officers, charging him and the men of the forest of Knaresborough to keep the peace toward the tenantry of the Archbishop of York, of his lordship of Ripon, lvii. To Sir Rich. Tunstall, Sir Thos. Tresham, and Sir William Plumpton, to summon all liege men of the Liberty of Knaresborough to set out to meet the enemy, lxvii. To Sir William Plumpton, to come to him, wheresoever he shall be, with his array, 1.

Henry VII. marriage of, and the Lady Elizabeth, published by the Chancellor in Parliament, 48. Causes the act of attainder to pass against Richard III. and his adherents, 49. Resolves on a journey northward, to do execution on his enemies, 50. At Lincoln, 51. Met by the Earl of Northumberland with the knights his fee'dmen, xcvi. Letter from, to Sir Robert Plumpton, to thank him for his diligence in quelling the insurrection, xcvii. Four servants of the King hanged at the Tower-hill, 87. Letter from, to Sir Robert Plumpton, thanking him for his services in a new commotion, with instructions for his future demeanour, 96[a]. Notice of his expedition into France, 102, 265. Commands the attendance of the Judges and Serjeants at Richmond, 161. Petition of Sir Robert Plumpton to, cxi. Makes him a knight of his body, and grants him letters of protection, cxii. Letters of, for William Plumpton, son of the same, to enjoy the lordships of Plumpton and Idle, cxiii. Continues to favour Sir Robert Plumpton, cxiii.

Hereford, (Thomas Spofford) late Bishop of, to be prayed for by the priest of the chantry founded in the church of Spofford, xxxviii.

Homage, respite of, at the Exchequer, 115.

Housboot, xix.

Hudson, Master Henry, Letter from, to Sir Robert Plumpton concerning the proceedings of the rector of Spofforth, 52. Christopher, Letter from, to Mr. Plumpton, to be allowed to continue to occupy at Beverley, 224.

Hungerford, Mr., son of Lord, arrested, 20.

Hustings, court of, 5.

Idle, complaints to Sir William Plumpton against certain of his servants of, by their fellow servants, 38.

Impereal, a stuff so called, 37.

Indenture, between Sir Robert Plumpton and his mother for her board for a year, xxvii. Of receipt of legacies from executors, xxix. Between the Duke of Bedford and Sir Robert Plumpton, by way of retainer of services as a fee'dman, xlii[g]. Between Sir Robert Plumpton and John de Pancesbery, for same, as a man at arms, xlvi[o]. Between the same and John Fleetham and others, as archers, xlviii. Between the Earl of Westmorland, Sir John Nevill and another, and Sir William Plumpton, to settle terms of an arbitration, 41. Between the same and William Gascoigne, esq. in contemplation of a marriage, lxxix. Between the same and Richard Hamerton, esq. for settlement of property in tail male in contemplation of the same, lxxxiv. Between Sir William Gascoigne and Edmund Pierpoint, Escheator, to find an office and impanel such jury as the former should specify, lxxxvii. Between Sir Robert Plumpton and William Babthorpe, in contemplation of a marriage, and for settlement of property, xcix. Between the same and William Plumpton, his son and heir, for the ordering of their domestic economy, cxxiii. Between the same and Serjeant Yaxley for his fee as Counsel, 152[i].

Indulgence, form of the, granted in aid of an expedition in defence of the Isle of Rhodes at the time of the famous siege, 118[c].

Inquisitio post mortem, instance of the real date of an, being at variance with the regnal year inscribed on the bundle, xvii.[g]

Insurrection, of Archbishop Scrope, xxiii. Translation of the narrative of Polydore Vergil, his partiality, xxiv. Of the commons of Yorkshire in the reign of Henry VII. xcvii, 265. Of the same in the west part of the country in the same reign, xcviii, 95, 265.

Intrusion, suit for, 217.

Joddopkan, Letter from William, to old Lady Plumpton, concerning his duty or debt, 41.

Johnson, John, of York, Letter from, to Sir William Plumpton for venison for a feast to celebrate the saying of his first mass by a priest, 29. Letter from George, clerk, to Mr. Robert Plumpton, on business as his steward at Waterton, 237.

Jointure and dower, may be surrendered by indenture, 47.

Jurors, on an assize, to be solicited privately for their verdict, 131, 132, 160. Or not to appear, *ibid.* 134, 161. To be challenged if sybb, i. e. of kin to the parties, 134. Coroners to be laboured to return an indifferent panel of, 141. Names of, challenged on a trial 18 Hen. VII. cix.

Kinalton, descent of the manor, xxviii[k]. Agreement between Sir Robert Plumpton and his tenant at, for board and lodging for himself and his servants, and provender for their horses twice in the year, 160[d].

Kingsmill, Serjeant, legal opinion of, 132. His character as an advocate, 134. His coming down in a cause costly, 135.

Kirkby Malserd, office of Chief Warden and Master of the chace and warren of, and Nidderdale, granted for life to Sir William Plumpton, lxvi.

Kirkstall, Letter from Thomas (Wymbersley) Abbot of, to Sir Robert Plumpton, his gossip, to recommend, 62. From William Abbot of, to the same, refusing to lend money, 183. Estimated value of, and Arthington nunnery, and of the woods, when in the hands of Archbishop Cranmer, 246.

Knaresborough, formation of forest of, iii. Early history of the Honour of, xi. Granted to William Stuteville, xii. Charter of easements in the forest of, granted by same to Sir William Plumpton, xiv. Honour of, in the custody of Hubert Archbishop of Canterbury, xv. Baron de l'Isle, constable of the castle of, xvi. Honour of, granted by Henry III. to Hubert de Burgh and his wife, xvi. Conferred by same upon the Earl of Cornwall, *ibid.* Agreement between Edmund Earl of Cornwall and Sir Robert de Plumpton, concerning the easements to be enjoyed by the latter in the forest of, xviii. Honour of, given by Edward III. to John of Gaunt, and made parcel of the Duchy of Lancaster, liv. Sir Robert Plumpton, Lieutenant of the Master Forester of, and Constable of the castle of, xxii[y]. Seneschal of the Honour of, xlii, xlix. Steward of the Forest of, xlv. Sir William Plumpton, Seneschal and Master Forester of the Honour and Forest of, Constable for life of the castle of, liii, 24, 31[c]. Tenants of the forest of, make affray with the men of the Archbishop of York of the Lordship of Ripon, lv. With the men of Otley, lvii. Marriage of Sir William Plumpton in the parish church of, lxxvi. Letter from John Felton, groom of the Chamber, and John Ward, groom of the Ewry, to Sir William Plumpton, *Custos* of the castle of, to recommend, 24. Office of Bailiff of the Burgh of, with the farm of certain mills there, leased to Sir William Plumpton by the Duke of Gloucester, 26. The Earl of Northumberland has the chief rule at, 31. Steward, Constable, and Master Forester of, *ib.*[b]. William Gascoigne an officer at, 32, 34. Sir Robert Plumpton an officer at, 55, 79[b], 81, 83, 86. John Fawkes, Steward of the forest of, 78. Sir Henry Wentworth, the King's Lieutenant at Knaresborough, 94. His departure forbidden by the King, 95. Nicholas Leventhorp, receiver of the Honour of, 88[c]. House of St. Robert of, xix. John Craven, Robert Boulton, Robert Teske, Ministers of the same, xxxiii, 22[a], cxxii. Freres of the same indicted and outlawed at the suit of Sir William Plumpton, 9. Bequests of Sir Robert Plumpton to the same, cxxv. Wintringham Hall in, 152[e], cxxxiii. Plumpton's quyer in the church of, 152e. Arms in painted glass in the same, *ibid.*

Kuyes, deles of the, i. e. salted carcasses of Kyloes, *Anglicè* for martisouns en Kuyles, xxx.

Lambton, Percival, Attorney-general of Richard Fox, Bishop of Durham, Lord Privy Seal, Letter from, to Sir Robert Plumpton, concerning the measures taken to avoid his appearance by Privy Seal, 115.

Lancaster, Duchy of, in the North Parts, Knaresborough parcel of, liv. Seneschals, Sir Godfrey Foljambe, xxviii. John de la Pole, xxii[a]. Sir Roger Leche, xlii. William de la Pole, Earl of Suffolk, liii[k]. Richard Harpur receiver-general of the rents of, 70[a].

Lee, Sir Alexander, rector of Spofforth, at variance for his dues with Sir Robert Plumpton, 52, 105. Notice of his warning Edward IV. of an enterprise against his person, *ibid.*[a].

Leventhorpe, Nicholas, Receiver of the Honours of Pontefract and Knaresborough, 88[c]. Robert, Letter from, to Sir Robert Plumpton, advising him of a devotional remedy against the plague. 138.

Lilleshull, Abbot of, Three Letters from the, to Sir Robert Plumpton, respecting the manor of Arkendale, and his conduct as Steward for his House, 63, 64, 65.

Lister, Sir Robert, chaplain to Sir William Plumpton, his evidence, lxxiv. Thomas, Letter from, to Sir Robert Plumpton, to deprecate the suit against his host at York, 133.

London, papers of 3. Skinner of, beheaded, 19. St. Sepulchre church without Newgate, 53. Furnyvalls Inn in Olborn, 124. Clements Inn, 128. Lincolns Inn, 132. The Tyburne, 142. The Angell behind St. Clement Kirk without the Temple barr, 172. Inner Temple, 234. Middle Temple, 13.

Maidstone, Clement, his recital of a miracle, on the authority of George Plumpton, xxv.

Maintenance, charge of, against Sir William Plumpton, with the saying of Guy Fairfax thereupon, 35. Against Sir Richard Empson, on the part of Sir Robert Plumpton, cxi.

Manor, taken with the, phrase explained, 262

Malton, William Eleson keeper of the courts of the Lord Clifford at, 135.

Markenfield, William, Letter from, to Sir Robert Plumpton, to solicit on behalf of a poor neighbour, wronged by his servants, 103.

Marriage, abstracts of covenants of, Robert de Plumpton and Alice Foljambe, xxvii. Stephen de Thorp and Isabella Plumpton, xlii. Sir William Plumpton and Elizabeth Stapleton, xliii. William Slingsby and Joan Plumpton, xlvii. Robert Plumpton and Elizabeth Clifford, lxii. John Rocliffe and Margaret Plumpton, lxx. John Sotehill and Elizabeth Plumpton, lxxi. Thomas Rosse and Joan Plumpton, lxxxiii[u]. 26●. Thomas Middelton and same, lxxxiii. William Beckwith and Elizabeth Plumpton, *ibid.* Sir Richard Aldburgh and Agnes Plumpton, lxxxiii. William Plumpton and Isabell Babthorpe, xcix. Robert Plumpton and Ellen Clifford, cxxix. Griffin Markham and Ellen Plumpton, cxxxi. William Plumpton and Ann Griffin, cxxxii. Sir Edward Plumpton and Frances Arthington, cxxxv. John Plumpton and Anne Towneley, cxxxvi. Evidence of witnesses to the solemnization of, lxiii. Same, when clandestine, lxxvi. *See* Bans, Faculty, Indenture.

Mauleverer, Sir John, at variance with Sir William Plumpton, 23. An officer under John Nevill, Earl of Northumberland, 25. Two Letters from Sir Halnath, Knight of Rhodes, to Sir Robert Plumpton and others, respecting his brother's will and the affairs of his family, 46, 47.

Mense Pasche, the term explained, 262.

Middelton, Thomas, Letter from, to Sir William Plumpton respecting an order of the Lord Chancellor, and with the names of the new Sheriffs, &c. 17. His epitaph in rhyme, 75[a].

Moore, John, Letter from, to Sir Robert Plumpton, in favour of a tenant of Spofford, 77.

Morvill, Hugh de, the murderer of St. Thomas à Becket, *custos* of Knaresborough, xii*.

Nevill, Edith Lady, Letter from, to her daughter Lady Plumpton, condoling with her on her own and her husband's misfortunes, 196. Note of her birth, alliances, and issue, 197[a]. Dorothy Plumpton in her service at Hyrst, 202. Note of the discrepancies of accredited genealogists respecting her, 203[b]. Order of her interment, 268. Sir Robert, Letter from, to William Plumpton, esq. on affairs connected with the death of Sir Robert Sheffield, 230.

Newburgh, Prior of, Letter from the, to Sir Robert Plumpton, to forego his displeasure, 60. Two Letters from the Cellerer of, to the same, concerning lands belonging to the House in his neighbourhood, 67, 68. Two Letters from Canons of, to the same. *See* Catton, Thorp.

Newport, son of Dame Ann Rokeby, 228. Epitaphs of the family of, in Boynton church, *ib.*

Nomen Jesu, feast of, with octave, 130.

CAMD. SOC. 4. 2 O

Norfolk, two gentlemen of the Duke of, beheaded, 10.

Normanvill, William, Under-sheriff to Sir Ralph Ryther, Letter from, to Lady Plumpton, to notify the liberation of a tenant, 185.

Northumberland, Henry Percy, Earl of, guardian of Sir Robert Plumpton, Letter from, to the bailiff of his sister Lady Clifford to distrain, l. Notice of an inroad made by, into Scotland, lxxiv. John Nevill, Earl of, Lord Montague, and Warden of the East Marches, Letter from, to Sir John Mauleverer, to restrain certain partisans from injuring Sir William Plumpton and his servants, 25. Henry Percy, Earl of, influence of, in the North, lxxv. Letters from, to Sir William Plumpton, to solicit the office of bailiff of Sessay for his servant, 26. To the same, to interpose on behalf of a kinswoman, 27. To the same, to forbear a quarrel till he came into the country, 28. To William Gascoigne, esq. his brother-in-law, to deliver a prisoner in the castle of Knaresborough, 34. To Robert Plumpton, esq. for a muster against the Scots, 39. To the same, to command his attendance, 42 *bis*. Meets the King with 38 knights, his fee'd men, xcvi. Letters from, to Sir William Ingleby, Sir Robert Plumpton, and others, to be ready upon an hour's warning, 53. To Sir Robert Plumpton, to cause certain parties at variance to come to him at York, 45. To the same, to commit to ward in the castle of Knaresborough persons within his office who were at the battle of Stoke, or harboured rebels, 54. To the same, to excuse him from riding with him to a day of truce, 36. To the same, to summon him to rendezvous at Thirsk, with such array as he could muster, 61. To the same, requiring him to forbear the pursuit of his quarrel with Sir William Beckwith, 72. To the same, to command his attendance, 73 *bis*. To the same, to aid Mary Gascoigne in her right of inheritance, 74. To the same, giving directions respecting his park at Spofford, 74. To the same, respecting persons hunting therein, 75. To the same, to reconcile differences between two tenants of the same lordship, 76. To the same, concerning William Aldborough and others, for their committal to the castle of Knaresborough, 81. To the same, in reproof for releasing a prisoner under his ward in the castle of Knaresborough, at the request of Sir Thomas Wortley, 86. To the same, to cause a buck of season to be taken in the Forest of Knaresborough, for the use of the Mayor of York and his brethren, *ibid.* To the same, to send him running hounds and a tame hart, 106. To the same, to withdraw his claim to land belonging to the rector of Spofford, 201. To William Plumpton, esq. concerning the right of the Prior of Helagh to a wood in the township of Little Ribston, 226.

Opinion, copy of Counsel's, 195.

Otley, riotous proceedings at the fair there, lvii.

Otters, numerous in Yorkshire, 248.

Oughtred, Jane, labour made to the Earl of Northumberland, for her marriage with a son of Sir John Rocliffe, 175.

Oxford, Earl of, committed to the Tower, 19. Makes confession, and denounces his accomplices, 20. Keeps his Easter at Lavenham, 51. In Essex, 54.

Pakenham (Pagnam, Pakham), Hugh, Letter from, to Sir William Plumpton, to make offer of his services, and to counsel him respecting the excuse to be made to Mrs. F. S. touching the proffer of her hand, 14.

Parliament (1 Hen. VII.), prorogation of, 48. Act of, for resumption of grants, 49. To make it felony to hunt in parks, or to make any manner of prophecies, 50.

Percy, Norman origin of the family of, x. Armorial bearings of, assumed by the family of Plumpton, with difference, xix. Henry Lord, Letter from, to William Plumpton, esq. respecting a claim of customary right in the Lordship of Spofford, 225.

Physician, Letter from Master Anthony, a, to Sir Robert Plumpton, to save him from arrest, 78. Thomas Bill, one of the Physicians of King Edward VI., has the wardship of William Plumpton, cxxviii.

Pigot, Sir Randolph. *See* Haveray Park.

Plague at Plumpton, 138.

Pleadings, care requisite in drawing up, 23. Foreign pleas inadmissible, 30. Copy of replication, 101. Copy of declaration, ciii.

Pledges, in the hands of the abbot of Kirkstall, like to be disposed of, 184.

Plumpton, modern topography, ix. Etymology, *ib.* Early history of, and its lords, ix. *et seq.* Seneschal of, his feoffment, xiii. Manor-place or Hall at, lxxxvi. Fortified as in time of war, cxii. Lower Tower in, cxxxvi. Sold to Daniel Lascelles, esq. and pulled down, cxxxviii.

Plumpton Quire, in Spofforth church, tomb in, xxxii. William Plumpton wills to be buried there, cxxxiii. Monument remaining there, cxxxiv[p]. In Knaresborough church, 152[e]. *See* Knaresborough.

Plumpton, Nigel de, a knight of the Honour of Percy, his seal, xii. His grant to Robert, son of Huckeman, xiii. Compounds for his brother's release and restoration to his wife and lands, xi*. A grant to him of easements and right of chace in the forest of Knaresborough, xvi*. Gilbert de, arrested and condemned to execution by Ranulph de Glanvile, is rescued by the Bishop of Worcester, xvi. *et seq.* Had property in Richmondshire in right of his wife, and was a benefactor to Marrick priory, 270. Peter de, one of the party of the Barons against King John, xvi*. Nigel de, *Inquisitio post mortem* of, xvii. Robert de, his agreement with the Earl of Cornwall for his easements in the forest, xviii. His seal and arms, xix. Cecilia de, heiress of the seneschals of Plumpton, descent of her inheritance, xx, xxi[y]. Sir William de, his seal and arms, xxi. Sir Robert de, a deponent in the Scrope and Grosvenor Controversy, xxii. Obtains leave to return from the King's service by reason of illness, xxiii. Sir William de, notice of the part he had in Archbishop Scrope's insurrection, xxiv. His epitaph, xxv. Robert de, marries the heiress of Foljambe, xxvi. Lodges and boards his mother and her children, xxvii. Alice de, her will, xxxi. Her epitaph, xxxii. Isabella de, her epitaph, xxxii[a]. Richard de, his will, xxxiii. George de, in holy orders, has a faculty to hear reserved cases in confession, xxxv. His will, xxxvii. Retires to Bolton abbey, xxxviii. Sir Robert, a fee'd-man of the Duke of Bedford, xlii. In the expedition to France, xlvi. Tradition that he was slain there, xlix. His epitaph, *ib.* His issue, *ib.* Sir William, his birth and marriage, xliii. Left a minor, l. Sets out for the wars of France, *ib.*

Commissioner of array, lii. Justice and Steward of the Lordship of Knaresborough, lv. Takes part in a bloody affray between the men of the forest and the tenants of the Archbishop of York, *ibid. et seq.* Marries a second wife clandestinely, lxiv. His public career, lxv. At the battle of Towton on the Lancastrian side, lxvii. Obtains the protection of Edward IV. lxviii. A prisoner in the Tower, *ibid.* Tried before the Great Constable of England on a false charge of treason, and acquitted, lxix. Restored to his offices and employments, lxx. Marries his grand-daughters and heirs apparent to Rocliff and Sotehill, *ibid.* Is brought before the official of York for fornication, lxxiii. Makes known his marriage, lxxiv. Adduces legal proof of its solemnization, lxxvii. Settles all his lands on his son by the second venter, lxxviii. His death, lxxxi. His issue, *ibid.* His character, lxxxv. His Correspondence, 1 *et seq.* Robert, eldest son of Sir William Plumpton, settlement on his marriage, lxiii. Evidence of its solemnization, *ibid.* William, married to his brother's widow, lxiv. Slain at the battle of Towton, lxvii. Sir Robert, found heir in tail to his father, Sir William Plumpton, lxxxviii. His disposition in favour of his mother and wife, lxxxix. Submits the matters in dispute with the heirs general to award, *ibid.* His public career, xcvi. Receives the thanks of King Henry VII. for his service in suppressing the insurrection of the Commons of Yorkshire, xcvii. Present at the battle of Ackworth, xcix. Has a second letter of thanks from King Henry for his good service, *ibid.* 96. Is threatened with proceedings in law in the title of the heirs-general by the notorious Empson, cii. 120. Verdict found against him on trial by assize at Nottingham and York, cvi *et seq.* Letter from, to Dame Agnes Plumpton, his wife, to look to the safe keeping and stocking of his place of Plumpton, cx. Petitions the King to have protection for a year, cxi. Is made a knight of the King's body, and exempted from process, cxii. Letter from, to his wife, to send him money, and with news of the disposition of the King and his courtiers towards him, cxiii. Marries a second wife, cxiv. Is reduced to poverty by his suits, cxvii. Confined for debt in the Counter in the Poultry, cxviii. Submits to an award, *ibid.* Is confirmed in the possession of Plumpton, cxxii. Resigns the management of his household to his son, cxxiii. His will, cxxv. His Correspondence, 40, 264. Edward, secretary to Lord Strange, Letters from, to Sir Robert Plumpton, with offers of service, and to inform him of the desire of his adversaries to proceed in the settlement of their claims, 43. To the same, to excuse his not sending before, by reason of the trouble in the country at the time of the Duke of Buckingham's rising against Richard III. 44. To the same, respecting the application of William Plumpton, a bastard son of Sir William Plumpton, for Haveray Park, and with news of the movements of the court, 50. To the same, to inform him of his having communicated with Sir Richard Tunstall, 59. To the same, with news from London, and touching the renewal of leases in the honour of Knaresborough by the Chancellor, 87. To the same, to recommend a servant, 89. To the same, upon

legal matters, 90. To the same, on legal business, and with news of Lord Strange and the Earl of Northumberland, 92. To the same, respecting the lease of Haveray Park, and to defend himself against the accusation of William Plumpton, the bastard, 93. To the same, with the King's commands not to suffer Sir Henry Wentworth to depart from his country, &c. 95. To the same, respecting the grant of Haveray Park, and William Plumpton's feoffment, 97. To the same, touching an office to be found by the Sheriff of Nottinghamshire, 99. To the same, concerning an exchange of land, 100. To the same, with copy of a replication in Chancery, and notice of other legal process, 101. To the same, concerning the letting of a Privy Seal, &c. 112. To the same, that he spoke not with the Bishop of Carlisle, &c. 113. To the same, of the matter of the Privy Seal; counsels him to see and ride a mile or two with "my Lord Privy Seal, when he comes into his country," 116. To the same, to assure him of the report being rife that Mr. Empson intended to attempt matters against him in the title of the heirs-general, 120. To the same, of a widow gentlewoman he purposed to marry, with request to make a settlement for her jointure, 123. To the same, repeating his request, 124. To the same, to make a grant so as to blind the friends of the lady, promising to release after marriage; suggests that Lady Plumpton should send a token by their messenger and give him honourable entertainment for the same purpose, 126. To the same, of the state of the manor of Sacomb, 128. From the same, to Dame Jane Plumpton, concerning the farm of the mill at Knaresborough, 70. Robert Plumpton, senior, bastard son of Sir William Plumpton, Letter from, to his father, on legal business, and with particulars of purchases made for him in London; complains of the delay of the match between his brother Robert and the sister of Mr. Gascoigne, 36. From the same, to Sir Robert Plumpton, respecting rent in arrear, 154. To the same, shewing him the disposition of his tenants in Derbyshire, and urging his presence with twenty horsemen and some sure friends, 156. To the same, with intelligence of the proceedings and designs of his legal adversaries, &c. 172. To Sir Robert Plumpton, Knight of the King's body, to request deliverance of a deed in his custody, 182. Sir Richard, chaplain, Letter from, to Sir Robert Plumpton, with an account of his labours to procure a favourable panel on the assize, 158. Informs Lady Plumpton of the purpose of the adversaries not to press their suit to the King, and meanwhile to impoverish her husband, and all that take his part, cxiv. Dame Agnes, Letter from, to Sir Robert Plumpton, detailing the proceedings against the refractory tenants at Plumpton, 167. To the same, informing him of the interference of the Archbishop of York on behalf of the tenants, 170. To the same, with a remittance of money, letting him know that his son and sixteen of his servants were indicted at the instance of the Archbishop of York, 171. To the same, in answer to an application for money, 184. To the same, of the proceedings against the tenants and servants of Plumpton by the adversaries, 186. To the

same, to ascertain him of acts of ownership on the part of the heirs-general, 188. To Sir Thomas Everingham, to come to her, 172. To Sir Richard Plumpton, chaplain, to write in her name to the Lord Darcy to stop legal process, and on other matters, 187. Dame Isabell, Letter from, to Sir Robert Plumpton, declaring her inability to procure money, and pressing him to make an end; complains of being left destitute, and avows that they are reduced to beggary, 198. William, esq. contracted to marry Isabell Babthorpe, xcix. Has a law suit with William Babthorpe, 141. Letter from, to his father, for instructions, and touching the defence of Plumpton manor, &c. 176. To the same, respecting his suit with Babthorpe, 221. Has a Precept to enjoy the Lordships of Plumpton and Idle, cxiv. Joins in a bond with his father to perform award of the Bishop of Winchester and others, cxix. 210. The manor of Plumpton settled upon him in tail male, cxxiii. His Correspondence, 222. Letter from, to his son Robert, to help the bearer in some legal business, and with other instructions, 234. His will, cxxvii. Robert, Letter from, to his mother, to thank her for sending money, and to beg her to move Lady Gascoigne to write to her brother Lord Latimer to admit him of his household; strongly urges her to read the Scriptures, 231. To the same, with a religious exhortation to read the Scriptures, 233. His Correspondence, 234. Dorothy, Letter from, to her father Sir Robert Plumpton to send for her to come home from Hyrst, 202. Mrs. Isabell, has a grant of the wardship of her grandson, cxxviii. Her Correspondence, 218, 231, 233, 241, 252, *et seq.* William, esq. one of the Catholic refugees in Flanders after the Northern Rebellion, cxxxii. His will, cxxxiii. Sir Edward, transcriber of the family Evidences and Letters, cxxxv. Amount of debts contracted by himself and son in the Civil Wars, cxxxvii. His estate sequestered, cxxxviii. John, captain in the royal army, dies of wounds received at the Battle of Marston-moor, cxxxvii. Robert, the last heir male of the family, conforms to Protestantism, but dies in the profession of the Catholic faith at Cambray, cxxxviii. Pedigree of, in face of page ix.

Pole, German, Letter from, to his father, Sir Robert Plumpton, with an account of his visit to Thornton-bridge; notice of the plague being at Plumpton, 138. To the same, desiring to hear of his speed in his matters, 166. To the same, respecting land not reckoned in the verdict given at the Assizes at Nottingham and Derby lying in Staffordshire; informs him of the unkindness of his grandam, 179. To the same, to congratulate him on obtaining the King's protection royal, &c. 180. To the same, touching the proposals of Ralph Mainwaring to marry Eleanor Plumpton, 192. To the same, concerning same parties, 193. To the same, to make sure means for his peaceable enjoyment of lands bought at Combridge, 211. To the same, respecting same matter, 213. Elizabeth de, Letter from, to Sir Robert Plumpton, with an earnest prayer that he may withstand the enmity of Mr. Empson, and respecting family affairs, 162. To the same, declining to reside with her son at Radburn, &c. 190. Mrs. Ann, Letter from, to Mrs. Isabell Plumpton, to thank her for kindness to her son, 258.

Pont de Burc, *homines de*, xiii.

Prices, sheep, 21. Beans, barley, wheat, 237.

Privy-seals, writs of, easy of procurement, 7. Act concerning them, 112. Bill of all, to be delivered into the Star-chamber, 217.

Privy-Council, Act for, to inspect all the King's grants, 35.

Protection Royal, grant of Letters of, not to be derogatory to justice, 176.

Pullan (Pulleyne), John, Letter from, to Sir Robert Plumpton, on legal business, 132. To the same, on similar matters, and with details of the trials of Perkin Warbeck and the Earl of Warwick, 141. To the same, concerning the underhand dealing of Empson, and with advice how to act, and the names of his counsellors, 150. To the same, to warn him that his adversaries intend surely to attempt the Law against him, &c. 153. To the same, respecting the making of a writ of error, &c. 165. To Sir Richard Plumpton, chaplain, with the office for two feasts, and advising him of legal business, 130.

Pycard (Pichard), Robert, rector of Spofforth, Letter from, to Sir Robert Plumpton, to desist from a claim to land of his glebe, 200.

Ragman, explanation of word, 168 b.

Richard III., copy of an award of, xc *et seq.* Notice of same, 122. Attainted with his adherents in Parliament; their names, 48.

Ripon, kept like a town of war in fair-time, liv.

Risby church, note concerning, 227.

Rocliff, Bryan, third Baron of the Exchequer, of counsel for Sir William Plumpton; Letter from, to the same, touching the passing his account as Sheriff at the Exchequer, 2. To the same, on legal business, 5. To the same, respecting the appointment of Thomas Beckwith to be Escheator, &c. 6. Purchases the marriage of one of the cousins and heirs apparent of Sir William Plumpton, lxx. Letter from, to the same, on legal business, and in reply to a letter mentioning his being freed from restraint; makes allusion to the matches with Ros and Goldsborough, &c. 7. To the same, on money matters; observes on his own practice of not borrowing on papers of London, and on the double cost of having his son at court, 12. His tomb, 8 s. Margaret, Lady, birth of, lxiv. Contracted to marry the son of Bryan Rocliff, lxx. Her feoffment, lxxi. Brought up at Cowthorpe, 8, 261. Sir John, notice of his dispute with the heir-male of the family of Plumpton as claimant in right of his wife, the heir general, lxxx, lxxxix *et seq.* ciii *et seq.* cxix *et seq.* 155 *et seq.* His son designed to be married to Jane Oughtred, 175. Presents to the Chantry of the Holy Trinity at Ripon, cxxvi. Dame Ann, wife of Sir Ingram Clifford, heiress of the family of, cxxix. Projected match between their daughter Ellen and Robert Plumpton prevented by the death of the parties,cxxx.

Rodeburne, blessed Rode of, 179.

Rokeby, Dame Ann, genealogical note respecting, 227 a. Her Correspondence, *ibid.*

Roos, B. Letter from, to Lady Plumpton, the elder, for money lent, 72.

Rose, Maud, Letter from, to Sir Robert Plumpton, for money lent, 171.

Rowkshaw, William, priest at Watton, Letter from, to Sir Robert Plumpton, on behalf of a kinsman owing suit of court, 83.

Ryther, Sir Ralph, Letter from, to Sir Robert Plumpton, to ask for rabbits to stock his ground at Ryther, 106. Sheriff of Yorkshire, 185.

Sacomb, note of the descent of the manor of, 128.

Sailors not able to continue at sea during cold weather, 248.

St. Andrew, John, Letter from, to Sir Robert Plumpton, concerning the offers made for his son's marriage, 137.

St. Elline day, feast of the Invention of the Cross, so called, 71, 160 d.

St. Jago de Compostella, notice of an Indulgence for rebuilding the Hospital of, 151 c.

St. John, Clerkenwell, Sir Robert Multon, sometime Prior of, xcvi. Warden of the East and Middle Marches, xcviii. Letter from Sir John Kendal, prior of, to Sir Robert Plumpton, to thank him for the favour shewn to his nephew, 117. Details respecting him, 118 c. Prior of, sits as one of the Peers upon the arraignment of the Earl of Warwick, 143. Premier Baron of Parliament, 267.

St. Oswald, an annual fast on the eve of, a cure for the plague, 138.

Sanderson, William, bailiff, Letter from, to Sir Robert Plumpton, how Sir John Rocliff and Mr. Anthony Clifford treated him, to force him to pay them rent, 157.

Savill, Sir Henry, Letter from, to William Plumpton, esq. with the valuation of Kirkstall and Arthington, and the rental, from aboard his ship at Tynemouth, 246. To the same, to invite him to hunt with him, and of another matter, viz. the marriage of his bastard son, 247. Postscript of London news, 248. To the same, with his reasons for breaking off the proposed match, 248. To the same, to urge him to send his excuse to the Lord Lieutenant, should his sickness continue, 250. To the same, to come and hunt with him at Tankersley, and of a meeting for cocking at Sheffield. 250. Robert, Letter from, to the same, sending him money, and refusing to take a bone, 251.

Scrope, John, Lord, of Masham, Treasurer of England, Letter from, to Sir William Plumpton on behalf of George Plumpton, touching his annuity, xxxvi. Reception of Mrs. Chadderton at the house of same upon a visit to see his lady, xxxix.

Scrope and Grosvenor Controversy, Sir Robert Plumpton a deponent in the, xxi.

Scriptures. *See* Plumpton.

Scots, Northumberland invaded by the, 39.

Scutage, appointment of, according to the wainage in Plumpton, xiv *et seq.*

Shepe silver, 21.

Sheriffs, notice of the three names for, in the bill sent to the King from the Exchequer in Michaelmas Term, 17, 146.

Sheriff's Tourn, court of, at Knaresborough, 32.

Sherman to dight cloth, 36.

Shrewsbury, Letter from George, Earl of, to Sir Robert Plumpton, to do right to Dame Joyce Percy touching her jointure in Arkenden, 263.

Sotehill, Henry, Attorney-general, of counsel for Sir William Plumpton, purchases the marriage of one of the cousins and heirs apparent of same, lxxi. Notice of, in the Correspondence, 8, 10 c 19 *a, 23. Elizabeth Lady, delivered when an infant, to Henry Sotehill, to be married to his son and heir, lxxi. Sir John, notice of his dispute with the heir-male, lxxxii *et seq.* Note of his death, his monument, 121 c. Dame Elizabeth revives the claim to the estates of the Plumpton family in her widowhood, ciii *et seq.* 121 *et seq.* Marries her son to a daughter of Sir Richard Empson, cvi. Her death, inquisition thereupon, cxvi. Henry, note of his death and place of burial, his issue heirs to their grandmother, cxvii. His widow remarries Sir William Pierpoint, cxix. Joan and Elizabeth, heirs general of Plumpton, agree to submit to an award through their guardians, *ibid.* Note of their marriages and descendants, 208 b.

Soule-mass-day, 80, 164.

Spofford, Steward of the Lordship of, 26.

Stanton, Letter to Sir Robert Plumpton concerning the Lordship of, 111.

Steward, Deed of Sir William Plumpton appointing his brother-in-law John Grene his, lx.

Strange, Lord, prepares to march against the Duke of Buckingham, 44. Keeps the feast of Easter at Lavenham and repairs from thence to the King at Lincoln, 51, 263. Keeps a great Christmas at Latham, 88.

Strey, T., Letter from, to Sir Robert Plumpton, respecting a panel returned by the coroners on a writ of attaint, 181.

Stutevile, his grant, 36, *see* Knaresborough.

Surrey, Earl of, established in the North Parts, xcviii, 95 a. Inscribed memorial of his acts on his tomb at Thetford, extract therefrom, 265. Letter from him, to Sir Robert Plumpton, respecting a gelding lost on the field of Ackworth, 96 a. Instructions from the King to certify to him the number of retainers of assured faith, 97 a.

Swale, John, of Staynley, Letter from, to Sir Robert Plumpton, to recommend, 107.

Taylor, John, Letter from, servant to Sir John Hastings, to Sir Robert Plumpton, to arrange for their meeting at Pontefract, 136.

Testimony of a rector to the publication of bans of marriage, lxxxi c. Of the citizens of York to the worth and honesty of a chapman, xlv. Of certain aged persons to the solemnization of marriage, lxiv. Of Lord Clifford to the contents of a deed of feoffment, lxv.

Thorp, Dame Isabel, her domestic misery, xxxix. Sir Thomas, Canon of Newburgh, Letter from, to Sir Robert Plumpton, to recommend, 67.

Through [thruff], one brought for a tombstone, 229.

Tyson, Norman origin of the family of, x.

Tomlinson, John, servant of Sir Richard Aldborough, Letter from, to Sir Robert Plumpton, to appoint an award, 85.

Tong, Sir John, Commander of Rybston and and Mount St. John's. Letter from, to his father, Sir Robert Plumpton, to thank him for his kind dealing in his absence, 119. Note concerning him, 120.

Towneley, Sir John, Letter from, to Sir Robert Plumpton concerning the death of his kinsman, mischievously made away with, 164.

Treason, heads of charge made against Sir William Plumpton, lxix.

Treasurer, and Barons of the Exchequer, 2. Of York Cathedral, 14.

Tresham, Sir Thomas, committed to the Tower on the confession of the Earl of Oxford, 20.

Tunstall, Sir Richard, established by Henry VII. in the North Parts, xcviii. Steward of the Honour of Pontefract, 52 c. Letter from, to Sir Robert Plumpton, respecting a bondman claimed by the latter, 55. To the same, respecting the non-attendance of William Scargill upon his summons, requiring obedience, 60.

Twisleton, Christopher, Letter from, to Mr. Plumpton, respecting rights in Waterton, 245.

Venison, asked for, to celebrate the saying of his first mass by a priest, 28. Sent by Sir Robert Plumpton to the Cellarer of Newburgh, 67.

Vesci, Ivo de, had the fee of Tison in Plumpton, note concerning him, x c.

Virgil, Polydore, his value as an historian, xxiii. Translation of his narrative of Archbishop Scrope's insurrection, xxiv. Its falsity, xxv.

Visitation of Yorkshire, earliest Plumpton deed copied in the, xii.

Walker, John, Letter from, to Sir Robert Plumpton, to assist his mother in her right, 109.

Warbeck, Perkin, notice of the trial and judgment of, 141. Of the arraignment of his confederates, 142.

Warcop, Robert, of Warcop, Letter from, to Sir Robert Plumpton, in favour of one who had trespassed, 107.

Wards, Court of, 253.

Warwick, Earl of, Letter from the, and Salisbury, Great Chamberlain of England, and Captain of Calais, to Sir William Plumpton, to suffer occupancy of land claimed till time of an award, 16. With the King at London, 17. Earl of, notice of the trial of the, with the names of the Peers who sat in judgment, 142.

Went-brig, Session of Justices at, 113.

Westmorland, Ralph Earl of, has a dispute with Sir William Plumpton concerning land, li. Ralph, Earl of, dies for grief at the loss of his son, in the reign of Henry VII. cxv b.

Winter, severe, 89, 90.

Wittcars, William, Letter from, to Sir Robert Plumpton, or else to Master William his son, on behalf of a poor woman got with child, 109.

Wolf-hunt-land in the forest of Shirwood, suit respecting it, 91, 95, 147.

Woodriff, William, Letter from, to Mr. Plumpton, concerning leases under the Court of Wards during the minority of the heir, 253. To the same, to inform her of his wife being near her time and of his own sickness, &c. 254.

Wool, packed, shipped, and weighed, 20. Weight, stone, and counterpoise, 21.

Worcester, Baldwin Bishop of, instrumental in saving Gilbert de Plumpton from execution, ix. Earl of, Lord Tiptoft and of Powis, Great Constable of England, Sir William Plumpton tried before him at Hounslow and acquitted; his warrant in that behalf, lxix.

Wyvill, Marmaduke Letter from, to Mr. Plumpton, concerning a farmhold in Kirkstainley, 225.

York, St. Martin in Micklegate, xxix. Nether

Ousegate, *ibid.* St. Michael, *ibid.* Cayllom Hall, *ibid.* Skeldergate, xxx. Byshophill, *ibid.* North-street, *ibid.* xxxi. St. Saviour, Adam de Wygan, rector, *ibid.* Chapel of St. Thomas the Martyr in the cathedral church of, lxxiv. Chapel on the bridge at, cviii. The city of, taken by assault, and by burning of Fishergate, xcvii, 265. Siege of, cxxxvii. Meadows of Bishopthorp, near, xxx. Richard (Scrope), Archbishop of, notice of the insurrection of, xxiii. Allusion to him in epitaph of Sir William Plumpton, xxv. Henry (Bowet), Archbishop of, and Legate of the Holy See, xxiii. John (Kemp), Cardinal and Archbishop of, makes a bill of his complaints against Sir William Plumpton and the men of the Forest of Knaresborough, liv *et seq.* William (Booth), Archbishop of, and Legate of the Holy See, xxxviii. George (Nevill), Archbishop of, Lord Chancellor, at London with the King, 17. Thomas (Savage), Archbishop of, Letter from, to William Plumpton, to obey the precept of a replevy, or else to appear before him to show cause to the contrary, 169. Threatens to indict all that aided in ejecting the tenants, 170. Causes a jury to find a true bill, by holding out punishment to such as refused, 171. Letter from, to William Plumpton, not to cut down timber contrary to his agreement, 173. To the same, repeating former command ; the letter of King's protection not to be derogatory to justice, 174. Christopher (Bainbridge), Archbishop of, notice of his letter to the Chapter of Ripon before departure out of England, 205. Thomas (Wolsey), Archbishop of, Cardinal, a Legate to be sent from Rome to him, with full powers, 217. Edward (Lee), Archbishop of, Letter from, to William Plumpton, esq. to arbitrate in a dispute concerning tithe, 235. Abbot of, William (Siveyer), Letter from, to Sir Robert Plumpton to labour the settlement of a controversy, 85. Wishes to arbitrate in a dispute between Sir Robert Plumpton and Kilborne, his servant, 112, *see* Carlisle. Richard, Duke of, attainted, commission to inquire of his lands in Yorkshire, lxvi. Mayor (Robert Hancock) and Aldermen of, Letter from, to Sir Robert Plumpton, to desire that his tenant in York submit his variances with a fellow citizen to their arbitration, 58. Have an order for a buck of season in Knaresborough forest, 86. Sir Richard of, Mayor of, began foundation of a Hospital without Micklegate, design of the Commons of Yorkshire to behead him, 265 *note.* Guild of St. Christopher at, John Skinner, master, lxii. Sub-dean of the Cathedral Church of, Richard Arnall, xxxv. Dean of, Richard Andrews, lxxviii. Official of, Dr. William Poteman, lxxvii. Vicar-general of Lawrence (Booth), Archbishop of, Henry Gillow, lxxx^r. Vicar-general of Christopher (Bainbridge), Archbishop of, *see* Carver.

INDEX OF NAMES OF PLACES AND PERSONS.

Abberford (Habberforth), 71.
Abergavenny (Burgenny), Lord, 142.
Abingdon, John abbot of, 87 ª.
Abney, xciv º.
Acclome, John, cxxxiii, 165 ᵇ.
Aches, William, 122.
Adam, filius Normanni, xiv *.
Addingham, xlvi.
Addle, 82 ᵇ.
Addle-thorpe, cxxxiv.
Adlingfleet, cxxxi.
Agard, Margaret, 48.
Aikton (Aketon), cxv, cxxxi, 68, 197 ˢ.
Ailine, xiii.
Ailmer, 35, 37.
Ainsty (*Annesti*), xii ᵈ.
Alan (Alleyn), 71. John, clerk, 161 ᵇ. Sir John, parson, cxxv.
Albini, Nigel de, xi ᶜ.
Aldborough (*Vetus Burgus*), xvi *. Sir Richard, lxxi, lxxii ᵇ, lxxxiv ᵇ, 27, 255 ª. (Jane Fairfax), 257 ᵇ. Ralph, 255 ª, 257 ᵇ. William, cix, 80, 81. See Index.
Aldclife, 45.
Allestre, Thomas, lxxii ᵇ.
Alneio, Ricardus de, xiv *.
Aluwick, xi.
Alsford, William, 18 ª, 19.
Amcotes, c, cxxix, 223 ᵇ, 245.
Ampleforth, Richard, cxxxvii, 76, 77. John, 200.
Amynton, li ᶜ.

Andrewes, Richard, Dean, lxxviii, lxxxviii.
Angrow (Angrom), William, lxxxviii º. Thomas, clerk, cxxii.
Annias, Rauf, 9.
Anthony, Master, physician, 78. See Index.
Apedale, 90 *.
Ardern, Piers, J. K. B. lxxii ᵇ. Esquire, lxxxi. Henry, 190. See Index.
Arkendale (Arkenden), lxvii ᵍ, cxiv, 64, 65, 197 ª, 264.
Arnall, Richard, subdean, xxxv.
Arthington, Hall, 82. Priory, 246. John, lxxxviii º. Henry, *ibid.* Richard, cxxxvii. William, cxxxv. Henry, cxxxvii. See Index.
Ascyn, John, xli.
Ashby-de-la-Zouch, 265.
Ashford, li.
Ashton, Sir Ralph, of Great Leaver, bart. cxxxvi.
Aske, John, l. Of Aughton, cii.
Askham, Richard, lii, lxxvii. John, lxxii ᵇ.
Aston, John, of Haywood, High Sheriff, 147. (Elizabeth Delves) 137 *.
Astwood, 142 ᵇ.
Atherton, Nicholas, cix.
Atkinson, William, 35.
Aton, Little, lxxxiii.
Attenwyk, xli.
Authorp, William de, parson, xxvi.
Aykrig, Sir Thomas, chaplain, 189.
Aytoun, cxv ᵇ.

Babington, William, lxiii ᵈ, 3 ª. Sir Thomas, of Kinston, 160. George (Anne Constable), 202 ª.
Babthorpe (Babbetorp), 219 *et seq.* Ralph de, 224 *. William, 132, 134, 141. See Index.
Baildon, John, lxxxviii º, 56, 62. Robert (Amice Calverley), 56 *. Walter, cix, 199 ª. Thomas, *ibid.* Family of, 263.
Bakewell, xxviii, *et postea.*
Balderby-en-les-Broome, lxxiv.
Ball, 183.
Banks, Richard, of Newton, lxiii, 46 *. Mr., vi. *see* Index.
Barbor, George, 173.
Barden, Robert, xlviii.
Barker, William, 9 ᵇ. Robert, cix.
Barlow, Edwin,(Owen, Ewene,) 117. William, 128. See Index.
Barnby, 11.
Barnesdale, xcvi.
Barowe, xli.
Barthestortes. See Plumpton.
Barton, John, 66.
Batmon, Sir Edmund, 155.
Bauldiwini, Henricus filius, xv.
Beaston, William, cix. Stephen, *ib.*
Beaumont, John Viscount, 3 *.
Beauvoir, family of, xi.
Becard, Sir Peter, xix.
Becke, Robert, 57, 96 *.
Beckwith, William de, xlviii *. Thomas, liii ᵇ, lvii, lviii, lxxii ᵇ, lxxxii ᵇ. (Elizabeth) 6 ᶜ, 7, 260. Ralph, liii ᵇ. John, of Killinghall, liii ᵇ, lvii. Yeoman, cix. Sir William, of Clint (Elizabeth Plumpton), lxxxii, xcvi, 6 ᶜ, 53, 72. Robert, 93.
Bedford, John Duke of, xlvii. Jasper Duke of, 50. See Index.

Bedale, William, xlv.
Bedell, William, 219, cii.
Bee, Christopher, lx.
Beford, 56, 57.
Beer, John, 245 ª.
Bele, Mr. clerk of the Privy Seal, 112.
Beley, lxviii.
Bekerdike, Thomas, 171, 198.
Bell, Henry, cxxvi. John, 101. Humphrey, 107.
Bencelini, Richardus filius, xiv.
Benigworth, Sarra, wife of Gilbert de, xvi ᶜ.
Bellingham, Richard, xlv. Marmaduke, cxxvii.
Benson, 71. Robert, 114. John, 234.
Bentham, William, 167, 168.
Bentley, 229 ᵇ.
Berkeley, sir William, 48.
Berdall, Richard, 179, 213.
Berners (Barns), Lord, 143.
Berwick, xcvi.
Beske, Richard, cix.
Betfield, lxiii, *et postea.*
Bethom, Sir Edward, priest, 100.
Bevercotes, William (Cecilia Constable), 202 *. Cuthbert, *ibid.*
Beverley, xxxv, lv, 42 *, 221, 224.
Bewott, William, 144.
Bill, Thomas, physician, cxxxviii, 253.
Bilton, xi ᵈ, xiv *, xli, liii ᵇ, 26 *, 149 *. Park, 243.
Bingham, wapentake of, 159. Rector of, xxxv, xxxvii, lii. Sir Richard, li, 3 * (Margaret Frevill), 259. Richard, jun. (Margaret Rempston), 4, 11, 12. See Index.
Bircom. See Plumpton.
Bird, 96. Sir Christopher, parson, 243. John lxxii ᵇ.
Birdforth, xii ᵈ.

Birkine, 234.
Birnand (Brennand), Richard, xlv. Robert, 28, 46, 264 *note.* John, cxxiii.
Bishopthorp, xxx, xliii.
Blackmor Edge, xcvii.
Blackwall, lxxvi ᵇ, 166. Richard, 93 ᶜ. Robert, *ibid.* See Index.
Blithfield, xciii.
Blount, Sir Walter, lxxii ᵇ. Sir James (Delves), 90 *, 100, 102.
Bluet, 142.
Bolesford, xi ᵈ.
Bolton Abbey, xxxviii.
Booth, Sir John, of Barton, 206.
Borough - bridge (Pont-de-Burc), xiv *, xvi *, xlv, lv.
Boteler, Sir Philip, of Woodhall, cxxxiii, 238.
Boulogne, xcix *, 103 *, 266.
Bourchier (Bowischer, Bowser), Sir William, lxviii. Sir Thomas, 265.
Bowett, Henry, archdeacon, xxxv.
Boynton church, 228. John, 228 *. Sir Robert, *ibid.*
Boyvile, John (Alianor), lxxii, 10 ᶜ.
Bozome, Sir Richard, cxxxv.
Brackenholme, cii, 218 * *et seq.*
Bradebelt, Thomas, cix. John, *ibid.*
Bradford, William, lxvi.
Braham (Braem, Braim, Bram), v, xiv, xx, 175 *. Mattheus de, xiii ᶠ, xv. Robert, xliii.
Braistergarth. See Plumpton.
Brakenbury, Sir Robert, 48.
Brakenthwaite, lxxxii. Henricus de, xv. Adam de, *ibid.*
Brampton (Bramtun), 195, 267. William, 49.
Brancepeth, 196 *.

Bray, Sir Reginald, 177.
Brayton, near Selby, 245 *.
Brearton, cxxx, 30, 36. Ricardus, de, xiv *.
Brecknock, 44 *.
Bresteyth (Birstwith), lxviii ᵇ.
Bridy, Ernaldus, xiv *.
Brig, Thomas, liii ᵇ.
Brindell, Roger, 248.
Bristowe, Nichole, 21.
Broke, Lord, 143. Richard, serjeant, 152, J. C. P. 221 *.
Broughton, liii ᵈ, *et postea.*
Broweke, 189.
Brown, Edward, 196 *. John, vicar, lxxvii. Anthonius, J. C. P., cxxix.
Brudnell, Robert, J. C. P. cxx, 210, 222 *.
Brugis in Flanders, 18 *.
Bruis, Rotbertus de, xv.
Bubwith, Robert, clerk, ciii, cvii, cxvii, 122 *, 155 *, 157 *, 159 ᵇ, 165 *, 196 *.
Buck (Boucq), John, knight of Rhodes, 108 *. John, 49.
Buckingham, Duke of, 142. See Index.
Bukton, Dame Isabella de, xxxiv.
Bullock, William, 81, 85.
Bulmer, xii ᵈ. Sir William, 146.
Bunney, Richard, 196 *.
Burgh (Burrow, Brough), xci. Serlo de, xii *. Simon, constable of Rochester Castle, xxiii. Sir Thomas, lxxxi. Richard of the, 26. Clerk, ciii, cvii, cxvii, cxxii, 122 *, 156 *, 157 *, 159 ᵇ, 165 *, 196 *. Henry, 268 *note.*
Burgh-wallis, parson of, cxxv.
Burgundy, Duke of, 19 *.
Burros-asshe (Bargshosham), lxxviii, cxxx.
Burton, Little, 225. Stather, cxxxvi. John, lxi.

Bussenhay, lxii.
Butiller (Butler), Ricardus le, xiii. John, lxi. Family of, of Warrington, xxviii ᵃ.
Button, xciv ᵉ.
Bycroft, Henry, 38.
Bylby, 91.
Byron, Sir Nicholas, of Colwick, 159, 160.

Calton, lxxviii.
Calvados, département du, x.
Calverley, 38 ᵃ. Sir William, cxii, (Agnes Tempest), 56 ᵃ, 181 ᵃ.
Cambray, cxxxviii.
Canterbury, 19 ᵃ. Cranmer, archbishop of, 246.
Cantilupe, William de, lxxxii.
Canwick, Lawrence, 105.
Canworth, lxxxii.
Cape, Edmund, 27.
Capros, Walter, chaplain, xxxv.
Carton, Nicolaus de, xv.
Casson, 42.
Castelton, lxii.
Castley, 81.
Catisby, William, 48.
Cattall, Henry, lxvii.
Cave (North), c, 131 ᶜ, 221.
Cawood, lv, 170, 236. Peres of, lxii. Gervase, 227.
Cecil, Sir William, cxxix.
Chaddesden, xxvii, liii ᵉ.
Chagge, Ricardus de, xiii ᶠ.
Chalner, John, 38.
Chambers (Chambre), Henry de, xlviii. John, lxxxviii, cx. Sir William, chaplain, 125. Christopher, 198.
Chamberlain, William, xlvii.
Chamney, Richard, cxxxvii.

Chapman of Stamford, 10, 11, 12.
Charlston, Sir Richard, 48.
Chasser, John, 125.
Chauncefeild, Joan de, xxx.
Chaworth, Sir Thomas, of Wiverton, xxxvi, xl ᵃ. lxiii ᵈ.
Chelmerton, liii ᵉ, et postea.
Cheney, Sir John, of Shirland, 197 ᵃ.
Chesseman, Edward, 125.
Chesterfield, liii ᵉ, 195.
Chircin, Richard, cxxiii ᵃ.
Chylton, Robert, cix.
Cholmley, Sir Richard, 104. (Elizabeth Nevill), 267. Sir Roger, ibid. Thomas, v. Edward, ib.
Cinghis, Le, x.
Clapeham, Thomas, 22 ᵃ. William, 188. Richarc, ib.
Clarell, Thomas, lii.
Clarence, Duke of, 17.
Clarke, William, 49. Thomas, xlviii.
Clarkson, Stephen, chaplain, cxxvi.
Clare, ix. Bailiff of, cxiii.
Claxton, William, xl ᵃ.
Clerk, Richard, parish clerk of Knaresborough, lxvi.
Clerkenwell, 47, 48.
Clifford, Thomas Lord de, and Westmorland, lxii et seq., ciii. John, Lord de, lxvi, lxxii. Henry, cix, 135. Master Anthony, 155 ᵃ, 157, 171. Sir Ingram (Anne Rocliffe), cxxix.
Clifton, Sir Gervase, lxiii ᵈ, cvii, 208 ᵃ. George, ibid.
Clin, lxxvii.
Clough, Henry, 36.
Coates, Richard, cxiii.
Cock, John, 9 ᵇ.

Cockermouth, Honour of, lxvi.
Cockle, John, 19.
Cocklodge, 62 ᵃ.
Cocus (Cooke) Willelmus, xiii. William, of Ripon, chaplain, cxxvi.
Coke, Hugh, xlviii. Thomas, 58.
Coghill, Thomas, bailiff of Knaresborough, 151.
Colby (Caldby), c, cxxix, 131 ᶜ, 223 ᵃ
Collyweston, cx, 113, 148, 181 ᵃ.
Colow, William, Serjeant, 35.
Colt, 7.
Coltman, William, 43.
Colton, James, 126.
Combes, lxii, et postea.
Combrigge (Combridge), liii ᵉ, 157 ᵃ, 178, 180, 199 ᵃ, 211, 213.
Compton, Thomas, 238.
Connesburgh, 82.
Constable, family of, of Flamborough, xi. Robert, esq. xl. Sir, lxxxi, xcvi, 17. Serjeant, 131, 153. Sir Marmaduke, the elder, 203 ᵃ. Sheriff, 219 ᵈ. John (Joan Sotehill), cxix, cxx, cxxi, 210, 213. Sir Robert, 203 ᵃ, 228 ᵇ. Sir Marmaduke, the younger, (Elizabeth Darcy), 203 ᵃ. Of Everingham (Barbara Suthill), 229 ᵈ. Ralph, of Halsham, 257 ᵃ. John, of Burton Constable, (Joan Nevill), 216 ᵇ, 269. Thomas, fletcher, xlv. See Index.
Conyers, Sir John, of Hornby, lxiii, 17. Sir Richard, xcvi. Sir William, cix. Sheriff, cxii, 181 ᵃ. Lord, 187 ᵃ, 196 ᵃ.
Conyngesby, Humphrey, serjeant, 161 ᵇ. J. C. P. cvii, 222 ᵃ.
Cordall, Sir William (Mary), cxxxvi.
Corneburgh, Willelmus de, xv.

Cornwall, Earl of. See Index. Sir Richard de, xix.
Cotgrave, xxviii ᵇ.
Cotingham, 105.
Coundall, Richard, cix.
Cowper, William, xlviii.
Cowthorpe (Colthorp), xvii, passim.
Coxwold (Cukeswald), 61 ᵃ, 66.
Cragley, Christopher, clerk, xxvii.
Crakemarsh, liii ᵉ, 90 ᵃ, 102, 157 ᵉ, 178, 180, 213.
Cranmer, Thomas, 246 ᵃ.
Crathorn, Sir Ralph, xcvi.
Craven, xi ᵈ. John, xxxiii, lxi. Brother Christopher, 9 ᵇ.
Crempel, aqua de, xiv, xv ᵉ.
Creskeld, lxxxiv.
Creswell, Rogerus de, xiv ᵃ.
Croft, Richard, 19, 25. George, 102. William, 168.
Cropwell, Robert, 66.
Crosse, Robert, xxxiii, xxxiv. Ellen, ib. George, 150.
Croston, xxviii ᵇ. Rector of, xlii.
Croxton Abbey, xix ᵇ.
Crouch, William, Escheator, cxvi. Customer of Hull, 147.
Cukney, cxxii ᵃ.
Cure (Eure ?) James, cx.
Curson, John, lxiii ᶜ, ᵈ.

Dacre, lord, 143.
Dalyson, William, of Laghton in Lindsay, 145 ᵃ.
Danby, Sir Robert, Chief Justice, lxvii, lxviii ᵇ, 19, 22 ᵃ. Richard, 83.
Dance, Master, 221.

Darcy, Sir John, of Hyrst, xl ᶠ. Richard, ib William, ib. Sir, xcvi. Sir Thomas, Lord, cxv, (Dowsabella Tempest), cxvi ᵉ, 187, (Edith Lady Nevill), 196 ᵃ, 203 ᵇ, 219 ᵈ. George, Lord, of Aston, 203 ᵃ, 253 ᶜ. Sir Arthur, 203 ᵃ, 253. Richard, cxxvii.
Darell, Sir George, of Sessay, lxxi, lxxii ᵇ, (Margaret Plumpton), lxxxv, 27 ᵃ. Thomas, See Index.
Dawney, John, lxxxi, lxxxix. Geoffrey, 11 · Sir Thomas, of Cowick, (Edith Darcy), 203 ᵇ.
Darlington, lxxv ᵉ.
Dayvell, George, 66.
Debenham, Sir Gilbert, (Katharine Plumpton), lxxxii.
Dedyser, Sir John, 42.
De la Warr, Lord, 143.
Delves, Sir John, (Lady), 90 ᵃ. John, of Uttoxeter, ib. 102.
Denbigh, 17.
Denny, Edmund, Baron of the Exchequer, 145.
Derby, lii, 161, 190. Thomas Earl of, 44 ᵃ, 51, 54, 94 ᵃ. Margaret Countess of, 113, 114.
Derley (Darley), in the Peke, 69, 70, 155, 157 ᵃ, lxii et postea.
Dertford, 15, 245.
Dewsbury, 10 ᶜ.
Dicthenbi, Robertus de, xv.
Dickenson, William, cix. Thomas, ib. Robert, ib. Roger, ib. Henry, 81. Oliver, cxviii, 194.
Dicton (Kirk-Deighton), lxxvii, 64, 135. Thomas de, xiii ᶠ. Nigellus Pincerna de, xviii ᵇ. Parson of, xxvi. See Butiller.
Dingley, cxxxii, cxxxv.
Dispensator, Simon, xv.
Dobson, John, (Alice), xlix.

Doddington, John, (Eleanor), See Index.
Doncaster, xi ᵃ, 182.
Dodsworth, John, cx.
Doming, John, cix.
Downham (upon-Trent), xxvii ᵇ, xxxv.
Drayate, Robert, (Agnes), 125.
Dremonby, parson, 22.
Drury, Sir William, of Hawstead, (Elizabeth Sotehill), 208 ᵇ.
Dryver, brother Richard, 9 ᵇ.
Ducknanton, 193.
Dudley, cxxvii.
Duske, clerk of the Council of the Court of Augmentations, 242.
Durham, 57. Bishoprick of, 105. Bishop of, Thomas, 129 ᵃ. See Index.
Dyer, Jacobus, J. C. P., cxxix.
Dynoke, sir Robert, of Scrivelsby, cvii.
Dynham, Lord, 143.
Dysney, John, xli.

Eanly, John, Attorney-general, cxx, 210 ᵃ.
Eastburne, cxxx.
Eastoft (Estoft), cii, 220 ᶜ, 223 ᵃ, 256 ᵇ.
Easton, 123.
Eccles, 241 ᵃ.
Eccleston, xxviii.
Edensor, 157 ᵇ, 161 ᵇ, lxii et postea.
Edward I. xviii.
Egmerton, 256.
Eland, William, lxxxi, lxxxix.
Elared, xii.
Elson (Elison, Elson), William, cii, 152, 177, 26, 187, 220. John, 135, 219 ᵃ. See Index.
Elewini, Gamel filius, xii.
Elerker, of Risby, 227 ᵃ.
Elis (Elys), John, clerk, lxii Thomas, cxvii. John, of York, 130, 133.

Elton, lxxviii, xciii, 132.
Elveley (Kirk-Ella), xi ᵉ.
Ely, Bishop of, xxxv.
Emerson, George, 152. See Index.
Emildon, Richard de, xxi.
Empson, sir Richard, See Index.
Epcomp (Thepecampe), 128 ᵃ.
Epworth, lxvi ᶜ.
Esomock, Robert, 37.
Essex, G. filius Petri, comes de, xiii ᵃ. Earl of, 142, 241.
Ethrington, South, lxxxiii.
Even, Thomas, See Rothwell.
Everingham, John, lxxxi. Thomas, of Rockley, 172.
Eure (Evers), William, clerk, lxxviii. Sir William, xcvi.
Exeter, Duke of, 18 ᵃ.
Exilby, Richard, lxxvii. William, lxxxviii ᵃ. Thomas, cix.
Eyre, Robert, of Padley, lxiii ᵃ, 162 ᶜ. Arthur, (Margaret Plumpton), 179, 215. Stephen, (Katharine), 59 ᵃ, 263. Robert, (Joan de Padley), ibid. Thomas, draper of London, (Elizabeth), 11, 13. See Index.

F. Richard, 8.
Fairburne, John, cix.
Fairfax, Richard, 1. Guy, lii, lxiii, lxvi, lxxi, Sergeant, lxxii ᵇ, 23, Sir, 91, 101. J. K. B., xci, Chief Justice, 213 ᵃ. William, 101. J. C. P. 210. Thomas, of Walton, cviii, (Anne Gascoigne), cx, Sir, 215, 257 ᵃ, cxxii. cxxiii ᵃ. Sir Nicholas, of Gilling, 215. William, 215, cxxxiii. Francis, ibid. See Index.
Farnham, xlvii.
Fawkes, John, of Farnley, lvii, lviii, lxiii, 78. Dame Mary, 78 ᵃ.
Feliskirk, 120 ᵃ.

Fellesclif, lxviii ᵃ.
Ferensby, lxvii ᵃ.
Ferman, William, rector, xlii, xlv.
Ferrers, Walter Lord, 48.
Fery, John, lix.
Fewston (Fuston), 23, 25 ᶠ.
Filey, 6 ᵃ, lxxxiii.
Finchley, 165 ᵇ.
Fisher, John, Sergeant, 129 ᵇ, 161 ᵇ.
Fitzwilliams, Hugh, of Sprotborough, xix. Sir Richard, lxxi. Thomas, lxxxi.
Flag-field, liii ᵉ et postea. House, 93 ᶜ.
Flasby, 6 ᵇ, 29. Robertus de, cap. xx ᵇ.
Fleetham, John, xlviii.
Flegge, 238.
Folbaron (Fulburn, Falbarne, Fawberg), 9, 19, 23. Richard, clerk, 122. George, 226. See Index.
Poljambe, Sir Godfrey, xxvi, 195. Sir Edward, of Tideswall, (Cecilia). xciv ᵃ. Thomas, of Walton, xliv ᵃ, li, lxiii ᶜ, xciv ᵃ. See Index.
Follyfoot (Folifait), xx, cxxxi, 67, 175 ᵃ. Poole, 225, 226. Walterus de, xv. Robert, cix.
Fountains, abbey of, xv ᵉ, 86. See Index.
Forest, John, 84.
Formes, James, 188.
Fosse, river, xii ᵈ.
Fox, Henry, lxi, lxii, lxxxix, 41, 92. Mr. 235.
Frank, Edward, 87 ᵃ.
Fray, John, 129 ᵃ.
Frevill, Baldwin, of Tamworth, 259.
Frishmarsh, xli.
Frobisher, John, 182.
Frodes-beri, xiv.
Frost, sir William, (Isabel Gisburn), xxvii, xxix.
Frowick, Thomas, Sergeant, 161. See Index.
Fulham, xxxvii.

INDEX OF PLACES AND PERSONS.

Gainsborough, 237.
Galaway, Robert, 37.
Gamel, filius Elewini, xii.
Gamelbar (Gamel), ix, xi ª.
Garden, Thomas, cix.
Gargrave, William, lxii, lxiii. Robert, (Elizabeth Paston), 252.
Garnet, William, xlv.
Garth, William, li. Thomas, lxii, lxiii. John, lxii, lxiv.
Gascoigne, Sir William, of Gokethorp, xxvi, lii, lxix. (Joan Nevill), 216ª. John, lii. William, esq. lxvi, lxxvi, sir, lxxxi, lxxxvii. Dame, (Margaret Percy), xcviiª. Sir William, cviii, cx, 59, 145, 204, senior, cxxiiiª. Nicholas, cix. Robert, 22ª. John, 34ª, 246, 247. Ralph, 34ª, 74ª. Sir William, (Margaret Nevill), 231, 232ª. *See* Index.
Gaukthorp (Gokethorp), lxxix, 79, 130, 132, 148, 149, 176, 215, 216, 217.
Gefray, John, cix.
Gelsthorpe, Robert, cix.
Gildeford, xiii*¹. Sir Richard, cxiii.
Gillingshire, xvi.
Gillow, Henricus, lxxx.
Gisburn (Gisburgh), John, (Ellen), xxvii, xxx, xxxiii, xxxviii. John, rector, lxxxi. *See* Index.
Girlington, Nicholas, cx, 256ª. William, 256ª, Robert, 253, 257ª.
Glanvile, Ranulph de, vi*. *See* Index.
Glidall, Edward, 238, 241, 242.
Gloucester (Glocestriæ), J. de Gray, Archid. xiii*¹. Duke of, 31. John, 167.
Glusburn in Craven, 160.
Goldsborough (Goldsburgh), lxxxiv ᵇ. Richard de, xiii ᶠ. Sir Richard de, xix, xlviii. Thomas, lxxixᶜ, 8, 260. Edward, Baron of the Exchequer, lxxii ᵇ, lxxxiv ᵈ, 8. Richard, (Alice

Plumpton), lxxxiii, 8 ᵈ, 165ª, 168, 264 note. Mr., 243.
Godard, Sir John, xliv ᵇ.
Gotham, 137.
Gotman, Nicholas, 17.
Goxhill (Gowsell), xl, xli.
Graindorge, Willelmus, xx ᵐ. Family of, 6 ᵇ, 260.
Granger, Sir Thomas, of York, 173.
Grassington (Gersington), *passim.*
Graystock, Dame Joan, 34ª.
Graver, John, cix. The younger, *ib.*
Grene, Sir Richard, xxvii ᵇ. John, de Nuby, xlv, xlvii, 1, 3ª. Godfrey, lxxii ᵇ, 17. Robert, 3ª, 84ª. Isabel, 11. Richard, ci, 3ª, 81, 83, 156. Robert of Newby. (Isabel Tankard), 84ª. *See* Index.
Grenewich, 52, 54, 95.
Gresley, Sir John, lxxi.
Gretham, xvi ª. Of York, 36.
Grey, Lord, of Wilton, 143.
Greyndour, Robert, 6 ᵇ. Family of, 259.
Griffith (Griffin), David, 94, 96, 97, 98ª. (Hervy), 99, (Frances), 103ª, 114, 165 ᵇ. Sir Walter, sheriff, 146, 147. Sir Edward, of Dingley, attorney-general, cxxxii, cxxxiv.
Grimbald-bridge, xviii, 264 note. Staines, xix.
Grimston, Thomas, xli.
Grismere (Grassmere), rector of, xxxv.
Guiseley, 268.
Gyll, Stephen, cix. Myles, *ibid.*

Hackingthorp *(Algrathorp)*, 185.
Hackney (Aknig), 223.
Haget, Geoffrey, 226ª.
Hagthorpe, Thomas, de Brakenholme, 218ª.
Hakfeld, Robertus, xli.
Halaugh, *see* Plumpton.
Haldynby, Robert, ci, cxxxv. Francis, cxxxv.

Hales, 88, 96.
Hall, 142ª, 92. Roger, cxxvii ᶠ. *See* Index.
Halneby (Hawnby), lxxxii, 6 ᵇ.
Hamerton, Lawrence, lxxxiv ᵈ, Richard, lxiii ᵈ, (Elizabeth), lxxiii ᵈ, 63ᶜ. Stephen, lxxii ᵇ, Sir, (Isabel Plumpton), lxxxiv, xcvi. Sir Richard, cx. *See* Index.
Hammond (Haymond), Peter, 246ª. Mr., Feodary, 253.
Hampsthwaite (Hamesthwaite), lxvii ᵠ.
Hanson, 19.
Hanworth, brother William, 9.
Harberch (Arbour) meddow, cxxx.
Hardalsey, William de, xxvii.
Hardistie, John, cix.—Stephen, *ibid.*
Harelaw, xivª.
Harewood (Harwood), lxix, cxv, 134, 197ª, 199ª, 204, 231. Lordship of, 214. Park, 17. Earl of, cxxxviii.
Hargreve, 23.
Harlad, Henry, 161.
Harldre, 9.
Harpur, Richard, 70ª.
Harrigat (Harrowgate), lxvii ᵠ, 168.
Harrington, John, lxii, lxiii. Sir Thomas, lxiii, lxxxix, 17, 48. Sir Robert, 48. Hamlett (Hamnet), of Hyton-hey, 206ª. *See* Index.
Hart, Sir John, rector, 52.
Hassop, xxviii, liii, ci, 59, 70ª, 156, 179, 213, 218ª.
Hastings, William Lord, 15ᶜ, 33ᶠ. Lord, 143, 265 note, 266. John, lxvi. Sir Hugh, lxxxi, lxxxix, xcvi. John, of Fenwick, 53, sir, (Isabel Babthorpe), 145ª, 220ᵈ. Sir Roger, of Roxby, 267. Robert, 148. *See* Index.
Hathersedge, 283.
Haugh, Ralph, 69, 70.
Haveragh Park, 51, 114, 165 ᵇ. *See* Index.

Hawkesworth, Thomas, lxxxviii. *See* Index.
Hawks, Thomas, cxxvii ᶠ. Robert, *ibid.*
Hawkins, John, 14, 15. Ralph, 15.
Hay (Heay) Park, 243.
Haym, Thomas, 159.
Healaugh, 135. Park, priory of, xxii, 226. Henry, prior, xviii. Richard Round, prior, 226ª.
Hegham, 158.
Helme, James, cxi. Ellen, 29.
Helthwait-hill (Elthwate-hill), cxv, 197ª.
Hemingbrough, c, 131ᶜ, 218ª, 221.
Henley, Mr. 242.
Hereford, Thomas Spofforth, Bishop of, xxxvii, xxxviii.
Herryson, John, lxxxviii ᵈ.
Hert, lxv.
Hertford, castle of, 265. Earl of, 248.
Hertlington, Willelmus de, xix. Sir William de, xᵐ.
Heslarton, family of, 6ᶜ.
Hessay (Hessamoor), cxxxvi.
Hesthornmeen, 21.
Heton, John, xxiii.
Hexhamshire, liv.
Heynes, 21.
Hide, Leonard, (Anne Boteler), 240.
Hildyard (Hyliard, Hilliart), Robertus, xl. Sir Robert, xcvi. Lady, 256. Sir Christopher, (Joan Constable), 257ª.
Hilton, Sir Robert de, xl.
Hirst (Templehirst), 203.
Hobert, James, Sergeant, 161 ᵇ.
Holcroft, Thomas, 241ª.
Holden, brother Thomas, 9.
Holebec, xiv.
Holme-upon-Spaldingmore, xi ᶜ, 208, 210, 228.
Holt, Richard, 128ª. Hugh, *ibid.* Mr., 241,

INDEX OF PLACES AND PERSONS.

Holy-moor-side (Holum, Hulme), 195, 267.
Holynagh, James, cix.
Hopton, William de, xlviii. Walter, 48. Sir Roger, of Swillington, 267.
Hopwell, 147.
Horbury, 9, 10, 30.
Hornby in Richmondshire, cxv ᵇ, 197ª.
Horton, Thomas, 100.
Hothom, Elizabeth, xxxiv.
Hotoft, c, cxxix, 223ª. John, 129ª.
Hoton, Jacobus, xli. William, li.
Hoton-field beside Berwick, xcvi, 40.
Howden (Hoveden), 40ᶜ. Roger de, x, xii.
Howell (Holywell) Grange, 254, 255.
Hounslow (Honslough), lxix.
Huby (Heuby), cxv, 197ª, 199ª.
Hucklow, xcivª.
Hudelston, Sir William, xlvii.
Huckman, Robert son of, xiii, xiv, xx.
Hulkil, Robert son of, xiii.
Hull, 228ª, 237.
Humberston, William, lxi.
Hundsley, c, 131ª, 220ª, 223ª, 224ª.
Hungate, William, iii.
Hungerford, Sir Edmund, 19. *See* Index.
Hunsingore, 120ᶜ.
Hunter, Thomas, lx.
Hurdlow, liii *et postea.*
Hussey, Sir William, 12. Chief Justice, xci.
Husworth, brother William, 9 ᵇ, 22ª.
Hybank, *see* Plumpton.
Hykling, lxxviii.
Hyton (Huyton), 207.

Icford, Master Peter de, xxxv.
Idel (Idell), xvi*, *et postea*, 38, 165ª, 175ª, 181ᶜ, 188, 198, 208 ᵇ.
Ilderton, Dame Isabell, 27. Thomas, *ib.*

Illingworth (Elingworth), Richard, 3ª, sir, Chief Baron, 6ª.
Ingaldesthorp, Joan Lady, 10, 15. Sir Edmund, de, 15 ᵇ.
Ingleby (Ingelby, Engelby), William, lii, sir, of Ripley (Joan), liii ᵃ, xcvi, 53ᶠ, 146, 264 note. John, cvii ᵇ, 165ª. Thomas, cxxxiv. William, cxxxv. Sampson, *ib.* Sir William, bart. cxxxv, cxxxvii.
Ingmanthorp, 64ª.
Ireby, William de, xvii.

Ketherton (Catterton), Willelmus de, xviii ᵇ.
Keilway, Robert, Surveyor of the Court of Wards, cxxix.
Kempe, Thomas, (Alice), lxv.
Kendall (Kendell), Richard de, xxvi, xxx. Thomas, cix.
Kenington, lvii.
Kent, Earl of, 142.
Kexby, John, xxxvii.
Kighley, Lawrence, lxxii ᵇ, 22ª. Richard, cix, 161 ᵇ. Thomas, cix. Lawrence, of New Hall near Otley (Anne Lindley), cxvi, 164ª, 203 ᵇ.
Kilborne, Christopher, 112, 113, 116, 130. Thomas, 130.
Killinghall, lvii, lxvii ᵍ, 72.
Kinalton, xxviii *et postea*, 22, 157, 160, 196ª, 208ª. Rector of, 22.
King, Edward, (Mary), cxxxvi.
Kingsmill, John, Sergeant, 132, 134.
Kinston (Cheniston, Kynreston) Place, 156.
Kirby (Kereby), xv.
Kirkby-Malzeard, lxvi.
Kirkby-Overblow (Overblars, Orblaes, Oreblawer, Orblawers), 98ª *bis.* Rector of, xlii, xlv.

Kirkby-Ouseburn, xvª.
Kirkby-super-Wharfe, c, cxxxi, 136, 144, 255ª, Horrington Ings in, c, xxxiii.
Kirk-dighton, 64ª. *See* Dicton.
Kirk-ella. *See* Elveley.
Kirkstall (Cristall), 72. *See* Index.
Knaresborough (Cnardesburgh, Chenardesburgh, Naresburc, Chenaresburg, Knareburg), ix *et postea*, 31, 79, *passim.* John son of Robert de, xxii ᵠ. Thomas, lxxvii, cix. Richard, lxxxi ⁱ. Robert, cix. Blakyfarm in, cxxv. *See* Index.
Knivet, William, 268 note.
Kniveton (Knifton), Nicholas, of Mercaston, xcvii.
Knowle, Ralph, cxxvª.

Lacy, Henry de, xiª.
Lambton (Lampton), cxxiii. Percyval, 114. *See* Index.
Langber (Langburgh), xx, xciii, cxxx.
Landa, prior and convent of, xxxiv.
Langewat, Thomas de, xv.
Langton, 25 ᵇ. Sir John, l. Sir Richard, 99 ᵇ. Sir John, clerk, *ib.*
Lardener, Gilbertus le, xv. Thomas, xivª. Hugo, *ib.*
Lascelles, Daniel, cxxxviii.
Lathom, 45, 89. Anthony, cxxxi. Ralph, 235.
Latimer, Lord, 143. Richard, Lord, 232ª. John, Lord, *ib.*
Lavenham, 51.
Lawe, John of, xlv. Christopher, 140.
Lawrence, Thomas, 149, (Margaret Ward), 216ᵇ, of Ashton, 267, Sir James, *ib.*
Leatham, 234, 235.
Leathley (Lelaia), lxv, cviii ᵠ. Hugo de, xv.
Leckonfield, 27, 28, 34, 42, 73, 87, 175, 227.

Lednam, xli.
Lee, Sir Alexander, rector, 52, 105. Nicholas, 164.
Leeds (Leades), Richard, 81. Mr. 236.
Lees (Leghes), lxxviii, xci.
Leigh, Sir Thomas, 254ᶠ.
Lematon, Ricardus, civis Ebor., xxxvii.
Lenthorp (Leventhorpe), Robert, 60. John, 129ª. *See* Index.
Lincoln, 51, 263. John de Lacy, Earl of, xviiᵍ. Philip, Bishop of, xxxv. Thomas, Bishop of, 35. Thomas, xlv.
Linton, Robert de, xiii ᶠ.
Litton, Sir Robert, Under-Treasurer, 138ª, 148, 166.
Liverpool (Leyrpool), 165 ᵇ.
Liversedge (Liversay), 231.
Lockhaw, liii ᶠ.
Lofthouse, lxvii ᵠ, cv, cxv.
Loftsome, 131ᶜ.
Logge, Thomas of the, 24.
Longsden, acixª.
Lovell, Francis Lord, 48. Sir Thomas, cxi.
Lowh (Low), cxxx.
Loxley, *see* Plumpton.
Luddington, cxxix, 256.
Lumley, William, 41.
Luvet, Robert, xvi ᶜ.
Lynacre, 195. Hugh de, 267.
Lyndley, Percivall, lxxxviii ᶜ, cix. William, lxxxviii ᵈ, cviii, 161 ᵇ. Thomas, of Scutterskelf, cxxiii, 161 ᵇ.

Mainwaring (Manwring, Maywhering), Randolph, of Carincham (Margaret Pole), 192, 193.
Makelay, John de, of Scotton, xxii ᵠ.
Malle, brother John, 22ª.

Mallory (Malary), Sir William, xcvi.
Malton, xi, xii*, 135.
Manche, Département de la, x.
Manfield, Robert, 28.
Mansel, Willelmus, xv.
Mansfield-Woodhouse, lxxviii, 91 ᶜ, 92ª, 99ª. In Shirwood, 147. Chantry at, lxxviii.
March, Edward Earl of, 1.
Markham, Sir John, Chief Justice, 3. Thomas, of Ollerton, cxxx, cxxxi. Griffin, ib. Robert, ib.
Markenfield, xxxv. Sir Thomas de, xlviiiª, 104 ᵇ. Sir Ninian, cx, 104 ᵇ. See Index.
Marley, Richard, 42, 21 ᵇ. John, 42. William, 21. Isabell, 15.
Marney, Sir John, of Layer-Marney, 20.
Marshal (Marescallus), John, x. Master John, lvii. John, 108, 109.
Marston-(moor), cxxxvii, 238.
Martinside, liii ᵉ et postea.
Mason, William, cxxxi.
Mathe (Matge) Lofthouse, cxiv, 197 ᶜ.
Mauleverer (Malyvera), Sir John, xx. Sir Halnath, xlviiiª. Robert, lii, lvii. Sir John, lxxxiv ᵇ, 10, 19. Geoffrey, 19. Sir Halnath, Knight of Rhodes, 46. Halnath, and Robert, ibid. William, 47. Sir Thomas, xcvi, (Elizabeth de la River), 46ª, 53, 85. Richard, cviii, Sir, cxxii, cxxiii ª, Joan Plumpton), 46ª, 85 ᵇ, 131, 179, 197, 199. Sir William, cxxii.
Mauley, Dame Maud de, xxxiii, xxxiv. Peter de, xxxiii.
Mayne, Thomas, lxii. John, 87 ª.
Medley, William, 103.
Mels, Robertus de, xivª.
Melton, 21. Nicholaus de, xx ᵐ. John, de Swyne, xli ᶜ. Sir, lxvi, 3 ᵇ, 4 ᶜ.

Mering, Sir William, 146. Thomas, 171.
Metcalf, Miles, lxxxi, lxxxix. William, of the Inner Temple, cxxxiv.
Metham, Sir Thomas, xcvi.
Meverell, Thomas, 70 ᵇ.
Midleton, xx, 37, upon-the-Wold, c, 131ᶜ, 221, com. Warw. 4, 259. Peter de, xxi. Thomas and Adam, his sons, ib. Sir Nicholas de, xxvi. William, clerk, xxxvii. Of Stokeld, lxxxii, cviii, 74, 175. Thomas, lxxi, (Jane Plumpton), lxxxii, 13, 19, 23, 49, 75, 98 ª. Sir Pers of, xcvi. Nicholas, of Stokeld, 80, 82, 145, 156, 218 ª. Sir William, 235. William, cxxxiv. Sir Peter, cxxxvi. William, cxxxvii. Sir Robert, 48. Family of, 103, 265.
Midlebroke, Edmund, cix.
Milner, Edmund, 159.
Moat in Ightham, 15 ᵇ.
Moginton, 192.
Monyash, liii ᵉ et postea.
Mordaunt, Sir John, of Turvey, 177.
Moreton, John de, xxix. Henry de, ib. Robert, xlviii. Thomas, 64. Robert, of Bawtry, cxxviii, cxxx, cxxxiii, 257ª. Robert, his son, cxxxiii. Family of, cxxxii.
Morvill, Hugh de, xii.
Morwyn, Sir Thomas, Canon of Newburgh, 67. Sir William, Canon, ib.
Moton, Sir Reginald, of Peckleton, 163 ª.
Moubray, Roger de, xi. Robert de, ib. Thomas, Marshal, xxiv.
Mountjoy, Lord, 143. James Lord, (Catharine Leigh), 254 ᵇ.
Moure (Moore), Ralph, cix. George, cxvii.
Moute (Mohaut), John de, xliii.
Moxdale, cxxx.
Musard, Ascoit, 267.

Muston, lxxxiii, 6 ᶜ.
Myming, John, 77.

Nawdon, Thomas, cix.
Neel, Richard, 3 ª.
Nesfield, xvii et postea. William, cx, 29.
Nevill, Ralph Lord, (Edith Sands), cxiv, cxv ᵇ, ª, 267. Sir John, li. Thomas, of Liversedge (Isabel Sheffield), 231 ᵇ. John, of Womersley and Althorp, lxxxv. Sir, 216 ª. Ralph, of Thornton-bridge (Anne Ward), cx, 79, 139, 149, 197, 216, 268 note, 269. John, cx, 139. See Index.
Newbold, xxviii, lxxviii, 195.
Newby, 80, 85. Wiske, 47 ᵇ.
Newcastle-under-line, 103.
Newdigate, John, Sergeant, 146, 210.
Newhall (Newaly), cxvi.
Newsome, xli.
Newton, 175. Near Flaxby, lxxxiv. Near Blithfield, xciii. Cold, or Bank, 29.
Nicholas, the Messenger, 217.
Nicholson, William, xli.
Nicoll, Richard, 265.
Nidd, xivª, xix, lxxxiii, lxxxxvi, 28 ª.
Nidderdale, lxvi.
Norfolk, Katharine duchess of, lxvi, 18 ª. Lord of, 19. John Duke of, 48. Thomas Howard, Duke of, 248.
Normanni, Adam filius, xivª.
Normanvill, Sir William, xxxiii. Sir Thomas, xcvi. See Index.
North, Sir Robert, 183.
Northallerton, lxxv ᶜ.
Northumberland, Earl of, (Robert de Mowbray), xi ᶜ. (John Nevill), 7 ᵇ, 15 ᵇ. (Henry Percy), xxvii ª, l, lxvi, lxxiv ᵉ, lxxxix, xcvi, xcvii, 93, 142, 175, 265. See Index.

Norton, Sir Richard, xlii. Chief Justice, xlvii. Sir John, lxxviii lxxxiv ᵇ, 151, cxv, 197 ª, 210, 260, Esq. cxxviii, 235. Richard, 232ª. Family of, cxxii. William, of Sawley, cxxxvi. William, his son.
Nostell priory, 252 ª, 254 ª.
Nottingham, 451, 95ª, 100, 161, 263.

Ockbrook, lxxviii, ' 54 ª, 183.
Oglethorpe (Oglest op), George, cix. Robert, ib. Edward, 134. Clement, (Cecilia Constable), 208 ᶜ. William, ib.
Oliver, Robert, 234, 245.
Ormond, Lord, 142. John, of Alfreton, 146.
Osberne-stahe-bec Starbeck), xivª.
Osgodby, 223 ª.
Otley, lv, 263. Steward, bailiff, lvii.
Overton, 86.
Oughtred (Owtretᵗ, Ughtred, Utrayte), Sir Robert, of Kexby xcvi, 20, 66. Henry, cviii, 175. Anthony, 175. Robert, 232. See Index.
Ouseflect (Usflet, Uslet, Urslet), cxxxiv. Willough (Wilfes Park in, cxxxv, cxxxvi, cxxxvii.
Owthorp, xxviii ᵇ, lxxviii.
Oxford, Earl of, 18 ª, 142. See Index.

P. Lady, 11.
Padley, 69, 141, 144, 158.
Pakenham (Pakham, Pagnam), Hugh, lv, 261. Sir John, 14, 264. Nicholas, 15. Agnes, ib. See Index.
Palmes, Bryan, of Leathley, Sergeant, cviii 43, 172, 210. Gay, Sergeant, 172 ª.
Pancesbury, William de, xlii.
Pannall, 68.

Parr, Sir William, lxxxix.
Papplewick-moor, 3 ᵇ.
Paston, William, cxiv. Sir John, 19 ª.
Patrington, xli ᵇ.
Paver, William, cix.
Paynell, family of, x.
Peake (Hye Peyke), 21, 161.
Penbroc, (W. Marescallus), comes de, xiii ª ᵗ
Pensax, William, xlviii ª.
Percy, x. Honour of, ib. et postea. William de, x, xii, xvii. Lord, xcviii, 54. Sir Robert, (Joyce), 65, 264. See Index.
Person, John, 57.
Petty, Mr. John, rector, 144.
Petworth, 200, 201.
Picard (Pycard), Robert, lxxxiv. Rector, 269. See Index.
Pierpoint (Pearpointe, Perpoint, Parpoin), Henricus de, senescallus, xviii ¹. Sir Henry, lxiii ᶜ, ᵈ. Henry, of Holme, (Thomas n Melton), 3 ª, 4 ᶜ. John, of Rodmathwaite, 3 ª. Henry, 4. Sir William, cvii, cxx, (Joan Empson), eux, cxxii, 208, 209, 210, 211.
Pigott (Pygott), Ranulph (Randall), xxxiii, lii. Geoffry, lxiii. Richard, Sergeant, lxxii ᵇ, 25. Ranulph, lxxii ᵇ, Sir, cx, 53, 98. Thomas, cviii, 197 ª.
Pikering (Pickering), Sir James, 260. Sir John, xcvi.
Pilkington, Sir John, 31, 35. Sir Thomas, 48.
Pillesley, liii ᵉ et postea, 157 ª, 161 ᵇ.
Playne, William, lxi.
Plumpton (Plompton, Plontone), ix, passim. Lafrinwic in, xii ᶠ. Sabberchdale in, ᵈ. Barthestortes in, xiii. Boundary of, and Roudferlington, xivᵈ. Bircom in, xv ii. Loxley in, ib. Halaugh in, ib. Braisterton,

garth in, xix, Grimbaldstaines in, ib. Hybank in, ib. Rough Farlington in, cxxii. Morhouse in, cxxiii. Patrikgarth and Milne closes in, 264ª. Nigellus de, xi, (Maria, Juliana de Warewick), xvi. Marescallus de, xii. Senescallus de, xiii. Gilbert de, xiii ᶠ. Robert son of Huckman de, ib. xx. Peter de, xvi. Nigel de, xvii. Robert de, (Lucia de Ros), xx. Robert de, (Joan Mauleverer), ib. William de, (Alice Byaufiz), ib. William de, ib. Marmaduke de, xxi. Sir William, (Christiana), ib. Henry de, chap. ib. Sir Robert, (Isabella Scrope), xxiii, (Isabella de Kirkoswald), xxvi. Sir William de, (Alice Gisburn), xxvii, xxx, xxxi. Joan de, xxix. Elizabeth, xxxii. Isabell, xxvii, xxx, xxxi. el. Katharine, xxxi, xxxiv, xl. Richard de, xxvii, xxix, xxx, xxxi, xxxiii. Brian de, xxx, xxxi. Thomas de, ib. George de, xxv, xxx, xxxi, xxxiii, xxxiv et seq. Sir Robert, (Alice Foljambe), xxvi, 195. See Index. Sir William, (Elizabeth Stapleton), xliii, lxi, (Joan Wintringham), 41 ª, 44, 52, 53, 63, 70, 72, 89, 90, 92, 94, 95, 97, 99, 101, 113, 114, 151 ᵉ. See Index. William, bastard, lxxiii, 21, 51, 94, 154 ᵇ. Robert, bastard, lxxiii. See Index. Sir Richard, priest, 80, 130, 152, 173, cxiv, 187, 205, cxiii, 44ª, 262, 263. See Index. Sir Robert, (Agnes Gascoigne), 34 ª, et passim, (Isabell Nevill), cxiv, cxvi, cxviii, cxxiii, cxxv, 194ª, 196, 197 ª, 202, 203 ª, 211, 213, 217, 220. See Index. Thomas, Knight of Rhodes, 112 ª. William, esq. (Isabell Babthorp), 132, 136 ᵇ, 139, 179, 224, 237, 241 et seq. See Index. Eleanor, 139, 167, 192, 193. Dorothy. See Index. Edmund, 204. Clare,

217, 258. Robert, (Ann Norton), 244. See Index. Dennis (Dinis, Dynes), (Ursula Aldborough), 234, 244, 253, 255, 258. Thomas, cxxxvii. See Pedigree of Plumpton.
Plumtree, John, of Nottingham, 5, 7.
Poclington, Robert, 236, 237.
Pole, Ralph, of Radburn (Elizabeth Moton), 138ª, 163ª, 179, 181, 191ª, 214ª. John, (Jane Fitzherbert), 139ᶜ, 191ª. Thomas, ib. Sir Alban, 214. German, (Anne Plumpton), 131, 148, 162, 258 ª. John, 258. Richard, ib. See Index.
Pollard, Hugo, xivª. Sir Lewis, J. C. P. 221 ª, 223 ª. William, clerk, cxvi ᵇ.
Pontefract (Pontfrett, Poymfrett, Pomfrett, Poumfrett), 26, 59, 60, 113, 136. Honour of, xvii, 55, 59. Steward of, 52 ᶜ. Feodary of, xxi. Thomas of, 60.
Porter, 145.
Portington, 228. Master Thomas, 229 ᵇ.
Portsmouth, xlviii.
Potsay, James, 144.
Poule, lxxxiv.
Poynings, Henricus Percy, D'nus de, xxxvii.
Poyntz (Poiner), John, 18ª, 19.
Preston, 103, 128. Sir John, 178. Long, lxxxv ᵇ.
Pudding-stain-cros, xivª.
Pulleyne (Pulane, Pullaine, Polleyn, Pullan, Pullen), John, xliii. Ralph, lviii. William, 36. John, the elder, 55 ᵇ. John, of Knaresborough, (Grace Mauleverer), 45 ª, 46, 47, 55, 81, 153 ᶦ. Bryan, of Gaukthorp, 130, 132. John, cix. See Index.
Pulter, Thomas, of Surrey, 49.
Pynchebek, Thomas, cap. xxix.

Quentin, Thomas, 188.
Queston (Whestoue, Weston), liii ᵉ, xci, xxx.

Radcliffe (Ratcliffe, Ratliff), Sir Richard, 48. William, lxiv. Thomas, cix, 197 ª. Savi e, of Todmerden, cxxxvi.
Rainsford, Sir John, cxv, 197 ª. Edward, ib.
Ralph, William son of, xiii ¹.
Ramy. Roger, 259.
Ratte, John, 49.
Ravenspurn, lxxv.
Reading-burn, 57 ᵇ.
Readshaw, Henry, cix.
Redburn (Rodburne, Rodeburne, Rudburne), 163, 179, 190, 212, 214, 258.
Reding, Hew, cxviii.
Redman (Redmarne, Ridman), Sir Richard, xliii. Richard senior, lii, lviii, cvi, cvi ᵇ. Henry, 214. Edward, 214ª. Joanna, ib.
Reger, John, 159.
Reinerus Dapifer Ranulphi de Glanvilla, xv, xi ª.
Rempston, Sir Thomas, K. G. (Margaret Leeke), xxvii ᵇ xxxvii, xliv, xlv, liii, lxv, civ. Sir Thomas, xl-ii, lii, lxv, 4 ᵈ, 17 ᵇ, 195. William, rector, li . Robert, ib.
Repington, Willelmus, li ᶜ.
Revell, Richard, 49.
Ribstone, Little, Ribstain), xvª, xvi, xx, lxxxii, 196, 200, 201, 227. Frodisbere in, xiv. Godwinnesridding in, ib. Walterus de, xv. Robertus de, xviii ᵇ.
Ribstone, Great, 117, 120, 174.
Ricardus filius Widonis, xivª.
Rice (Rhys), ap Griffin, xvi. Sir, ap Thomas, 266.
Richardson, Robert, cix.

Richmond, 55. Honour of, xvi. Archdeacon of, xxxi, xxxv. Com. Surrey, 161.
Ripley, parson of, xxvi. Robertus de, xv. Henry of, xlviii, lxxxii. Brother John, 9 ᵇ.
Ripon, xxi, xxx, xxxi, xxxiii, xxxv, liv *et seq.* 80, 140, 187, 197 ᵃ, 205, 211 ᵃ, 225. Bondgate in, 189. Bailiff of, lviii, cx ᵃ.
Risby (Resby), 227 ᵃ, 229.
Rishworth, Edmund, cix.
Robinson, William, cix.
Robyn-Hudde-ston, xcvi.
Robyson, Edmund, 188.
Rochester, constable of the castle of, xxiii. Bishop of, 166.
Rodes, Richard, of Knaresborough, cxxxviii.
Roecliff (Rocliffe, Roucliffe), Bryan, of Cowthorpe, lxxi, lxxii ᵇ, lxxx, 8 ᵍ, 122, 259. Thomas, lxxxi. Sir John, (Margaret Plumpton), lxxxviii, 8, 13, 53, 118, 155, 157, 159, 161, 168, 172, 173, 174, 176, 179, 183, 188, 207, 209, 210, 211. *See* Index.
Rokeby, Thomas, of Mortham (Joan Constable), 130, 131 ᵈ. Ralph, 227 ᵃ. Richard, *ib.* Dame Anne. *See* Index.
Roklay, John, 70 ᵃ.
Rollesley, cxxx.
Rookwood (Rokewode), John Gage, 209 ᵃ. Robert Joseph, *ib.*
Rooper, Thomas, lx.
Ros (Roos, Rosse), Willelmus de, xviii¹, xx. Robertus de, xx ᵐ. Petrus de, *ib.* Alexander de, *ib.* Sir Robert, lxiii ᵈ. Robert, of Ingmanthorp, lxxii ᵇ, lxxxi, lxxxii ⁿ, lxxxiv ᵇ, 8, 19, 22 ᵃ, 260. Thomas, lxxxii ⁿ. Thomas, lxxxi, lxxxii ⁿ, 8, 260, 163 ᵃ James, *ib.* Everard de, (Hilaria Trusbut), 64 ᵃ. *See* Index.
Rossell, William, 158. John, of Ratcliff, 159 ᵃ.
Rothwell, Thomas. *See* Even.

Roudferlington (Roth-ferlington), xiv*, xv*. *See* Plumpton.
Routh, Thomas, of Westminster, lxix. David, *ib.*
Rowcester, 178 ᵃ.
Rowley, 224 ᵃ, 227 ᵃ, 229 ᵇ.
Rowland, lxxviii *et postea.*
Rute, brother William, 9 ᵇ.
Rycroft, William, the elder, 38. Younger, *ib.* John, *ib.*
Ryther, 107, 185. Sir William, 34 ᵃ. William, his son, *ib.* Sir Ralph, cix. *See* Index.

S. Mrs. F. 15.
Sacheverell, Sir Richard, cxxii ᵐ, 210. William, steward, 122 ᵃ, 157 ᵇ, 183. Ralph, of Hopwell, 147.
Sacomb (*Seuechamp, Savacum*), 128, 136 ᵇ, 221, 238, 241, 244, 255, 257 ᵇ, c, cxxxi, cxxxiii.
St. Alban's, 238.
St. Amand (Sentmound), Lord, 143.
St. Andrew, of Gotham, John, 137. William, (Margaret Aston), 137 ᵃ.
St. George, Richard, Norroy, xii, lxxxv ᵈ.
St. Leger (Sent Leasur), Alured, 243.
St. Germayn (Seyngermen), Geffrey, 48 ᵇ, 49.
St. Quintin, Sir Thomas, xlvii.
Saltmarsh, Edward, lxxxi.
Sands, Sir William, (Edith Cheney), cxiv, 196 ᵃ. Lord, K. G. cxv, 197 ᵃ, 203 ᵇ, 268.
Sapcott, William, 49.
Savage, Sir John, 266.
Savill, Sir John, cxiv ᵇ. Henry, of Lupset, 246. Robert, of Howley, 246, 247 ᵃ, 249 ᵃ. Sir Henry, of Thornhill and Elland (Elizabeth Soothill), 246 ᵃ, 248 ᵃ. *See* Index.
Saxton, Robert, lxxxviii ᵇ, 75, 100, 264 ᵃ. Thomas, cix, 76, 77.
Scaife, John, cix.

Scarbrough, Thomas, of Glusburne in Craven, 16.
Scargill (Scaggell, Skirgell), William, cix, 59, 60, 101, 168, 263. John, 101. Margaret, *ib.* William, the younger, cix, 263. Sir Robert, of Thorpe-Stapleton, 101 ᵃ. Family of, 263.
Scatergood, 7.
Scotton, xiii, 65 ᵃ. Thorp-Garths in, cxxv. Alexander de, xv.
Scriven, xlvii ᵇ, lxvii ᵇ.
Scrooby, 113.
Scrope, Sir Richard, xxii⁷. Richard, Archbishop, *see* York. Isabella, xxiii, xxxiii ᵇ. William, Lord Treasurer, Earl of Wiltshire, xxiv. Henry Lord, of Masham, xxvi, xxxiii ᵇ. Stephen, Archdeacon, xxxi, xxxiii. John Lord, of Masham, xxxvi, Treasurer of England, xxxvii, xxxix, (Elizabeth Chaworth), xl. John le, xl⁷. Lord, of Bolton. 227 ᵃ. Henry, of Danby, (Anne Plumpton), 270.
Seale (Sole), Sir Anthony, clerk, cxxi, 205.
Sedgwick (Sygskyke), Mr. clerk, 145.
See, of the, (Attsee), Sir Martin, xcvi.
Selay, Henry of, 41.
Selby, 53, 136, 149, 220 ᵃ, 221. Flates in, c, 131 ᵃ.
Sely (Syghly), Sir John, Knight Marshal, 141.
Semar (Seamer), 61, 74, 75, 76.
Serlonis, Willelmus filius, xv.
Sessay, 27.
Settill, Robert, cxxvii, 238, 242, 255.
Sharp, Richard, clerk, 244 ᵃ.
Shaw, Richard, 103.
Sheen, xcviii, 97.
Sheffield, Robert, of Butterwick, lxxxi, lxxx, ix, (Ellen Delves). 90 ᵃ, 100. Sir, 180, 206 ᵃ, 231 ᵇ. The elder, 270. Sir Robert, 230.
Sheriff-Hutton, 96 ᵃ.
Shorthwait, Sir William, chap. lxvii.

Shutley, William, cix.
Shrewsbury, (George) Earl of, 65, 158, 250, 265. *See* Index.
Siclinghall, Robert son of Henry de, xiii ᶠ.
Simpson, Clement, 88.
Skelton, Robert de, chap. 29.
Skinner, John, lxii.
Skipton-upon-Swale, lxxiv.
Skyres (Skiers), Nicholas, cix.
Slepe, 238.
Slingsby, William, of Scriven, xlvii, (Joan Plumpton), xlix. John, the younger, 199 ᵃ, 212.
Smith, John, chap. xxxiv. Francis, of Ashby Folvile, cxxxiv. Francis, his grandson, *ib.* John, 2. Bryan, 21. Robert, 158, 171 ᵃ. William, 180.
Snaith, John, priest, xxxvii.
Sober Hill, 47.
Somerset, Duke of, 18 ᵃ.
Somersham, xxxv.
Soole, Edward, cxviii.
Soothill (Sothill, Sotehill, Suthill, Suttill, Suttell), 248, 249, 252. Gerard, of Redburne, 10 ᶜ. John, of, lxxi. Thomas, 248 ᵃ. Henry, (Anne Boyvile), lxxi, lxxii, lxxix ᵃ, cv, 8, 10 ᶜ. John, (Elizabeth Plumpton), lxxxviii, Sir, of Stokefaston, 155, 159, 161 ᵇ, 169, 208 ᵇ. Henry, (Joan Empson), cvi, 169 ᵃ, 208 ᵃ. *See* Index, *Constable, Drury.*
Southampton, xlvi.
Southwell, xxxv, 100.
Spay, William, xix.
Sparow, Willelmus, cap. xxxi ᵐ.
Spinke, Thomas, bailiff, cxii ᶜ.
Spittle-in-the-street, 106.
Spofforth (Spofford), ix, xiv *et postea*, 26, 75, 76, 78, 168, 197 ᵃ, 225, 226, 227. Rector of, lxxxi ᶻ, 52 ᵇ, 105 ᵃ, 200, 201. Henry de,

---

chap. xxi. Roger de, chap. xxix, xliii. Thomas, *see* Hereford. Johannes Clark de, parcarius, xxxvii ᶠ.
Spounden (Spondon), liii ᶜ, lxv *et postea.*
Squire, Robert, 189.
Stabill, Thomas, 187.
Stafford, Humphrey, 49.
Stainley (Standley), 198, 205. Kirk, 225.
Stainton (Staneton), xiii. Robert son of Jordan de, xiii ᶠ.
Stanhope (Stanop), John, 3 ᵃ. Sir Edward, of Rampton, cvii.
Stanley, Sir William, Lord Chamberlain, 51, 265. Sir Humphrey, of Pipe, 146.
Stansfield, Christopher, 26. Ralph, cix.
Stanton-hall, liii ᵍ *et postea*, 111, 137 ᵃ.
Stapleford, cxxxi.
Stapleton (Stapilton, Stapulton), Sir Bryan, of Carlton, xliii, (Agnes Godard), xliv, lii. Sir Brian, lii, lxiii, lxxii ᵇ, (Isabella Rempston), 17. Bryan, 17 ᵇ, cx, Sir, cxxii ᵃ. Sir William, of Wighill, lxxxiv ᵇ, xcvii, 53.
Stead, William, lxxxviii ᶜ.
Steeton (Steveton), xliii, in Airedale, xlvii, lxxii ᵇ, lxxviii, lxxix ᵍ, xci, 161 ᵇ, 165 ᵃ, 175 ᵃ, 208 ᵃ.
Steris (Staires), Richard, 18 ᵃ, 19.
Stevenson, William, cxxvii ᶠ.
Stockeld (Stockhill), lxxxii, cxxxvi, cxxxvii. Richard de, xiii ᶠ. Baldwin de, *ib.* Nigellus de, xiv*. Sir Richard de, xix.
Stockbridge (Stokke-brigge), xiv*.
Stonden (*Stuo-champa*, Staunton, Standon), cxxxi, 128 ᵃ.
Strange, Lord, (George Stanley,) 44 ᵃ, 88, 89, 93, 113. *See* Index.
Strangways (Strangyshe), Sir James, xcvi. Edward, clerk, cxv ᵇ.
Stratford abbey, 18 ᵃ.

Straungald, Willelmus, xiii.
Strey, John, of Doncaster (Alice Hopton), 267. *See* Index.
Strickland, Sir Walter, of Sizergh (Catharine Nevill), 217, 268, 269.
Studley, Nether or Little, (Studley Roger), xlviii, lxxii ᵇ, cxxi, 44 ᵇ, 124, 163 ᵇ, 175 ᵃ, 199 ᵃ.
Stutevill, William de, xii*, xiii*, xiv*, xv*. Robert de, *ib.* Nicholas de, *ib.* Heirs of, xvi*. *See* Index.
Sudberi, Richard, rector, xlii.
Suffolk, Duke of, (Charles Brandon), 248.
Surrey, Earl of, (Thomas Howard), xcix ᵃ, * 48, 113, 142, 210, 265.
Swale, George, lxxxviii ᵃ. John, cix. *See* Index.
Swaledale, Sir James, rector, xxxvii.
Swan, Christopher, 87 ᵃ.
Swillington, 60 ᵃ. Sir Robert, xlvii ᵍ. Ralph, Attorney-gen. 221 ᵃ.
Sykerwham, Robert, lxxxix ᵇ.

Tadcaster, 150.
Talbot, Sir Gilbert, cxiv ᵃ. Nicholas, 266.
Talboys (Tailbose), George, (Elizabeth Gascoigne), 34 ᵃ, 113. Sir Richard, *ibid.*
Tanghe, Ricardus de, xiv*.
Tancred (Tancred), George, 45. William, 45 ᵃ, 80, 85 ᵃ.
Taylor (Toyller, Talloyr), Thomas, chap. 105 ᵃ. John, 144, 189. Robert, 167. *See* Index.
Tempest, Sir John, lxiii, lxvi, ciii, 56 ᵃ. John, cx. Sir Richard, of Giggleswick in Ribblesdale, cxvi ᵇ, 203 ᵇ. Thomas, of Roundhay-grange, 270. Stephen, of Broughton, *ib.*
Tewkesbury, lxxv, 20 ᵈ.
Thetford, xcix ᵐ, 265.
Thirleby, lxxxii ᵃ.

Thirsk, xcvii, 61.
Thomas, Sir Rice ap, 266.
Thoresby, John, bailiff, lvii.
Thorn, John, lxiv.
Thornby, Nicholas. chap. xxix, xxxi.
Thornton, Sir Richard, priest, 92. John, 104.
Thornton-bridge, lvi, lix, la, 139. Wood, lviii. Beck, lxxxiii.
Thorp, xli ᵇ, ᶜ, cxxx. Sir Stephen, x ᶠ, of Gowsell, (Isabella Plumpton), xxxix, xl, xli. Stephen de, xl. Robertus de, jun. xli ᶜ. John, xlvii ᵈ. Thomas de, liii ᵇ. William, 103. *See* Index.
Thorold, Sir Anthony, of Marston, 208 ᵇ.
Thurland, Edmund, of Gamston on Idle, cxxxi. Family of, cxxxi.
Thurnscoe, 254 ᵈ.
Thury-Harcourt, x.
Thwaites, John, Jii, lxvi. Thomas, lxiii.
Tideswell (Tidswall), liii ᵍ *et postea.*
Timble (Tymble), Great, 25 ᵇ. Robert of, 25.
Tindale, liv.
Tirwhit, Robert, 129 ᵃ.
Tison, Gislebert, x, xi. Adam, xc.
Tockwith, 149.
Tomlinson, John, 81, 82, 84. *See* Index.
Tong, Sir John, 117. William, 120 ᵃ. Margaret, *ib.* Isabel, *ib.*
Topcliffe (Toplif), 1, lxxv ᵉ, 16, 27, 39, 79.
Topclyff, 43.
Tor, John of, 21.
Towneley, 164. (Geoffrey), 103 ᵃ, 111, 115, 164, 165 ᵇ. Richard, of Towneley, cxxxvi. Christopher, of the Carr, cxxxvii. *See* Index.
Towyll, Robert, 159.
Trent, piscary of Maredyke-garth in, cxix.
Tresham, Sir Thomas, of Rushton, lxvii, 20.
Trey, Mr. 229.
Trongton, John, 118, 119.

Troway (Truberui), 195.
Trumyll, Richard, 160.
Trusbut, Hilaria, 64 ᵃ.
Tuly, parson, 30, 31.
Tunstall, Sir Richard, lxvii, xcviii, 52, 95 ᵃ, 264. *See* Index.
Turberville (Trobilfeild), Sir John, 141.
Turndike, liii ᵍ *et postea.*
Turnham, Robertus de, xiii*¹.
Turvile (Tufell), William, of West Leke, 160.
Tutbury, 17.
Twisleton, John, (Alice Latham), alderman of London, 235 ᵇ. Christopher, of Barlow or Barley, (Anne Beer), 245 ᵃ. *See* Index.
Twyford, liii ᵍ *et postea.*
Tyndal, Bradwardine, of Brotherton, 263.
Tynderley, Sir John, 140.

Vavasor, Robertus le, xiii ᶠ, xv, xiv*. Willelmus le, xiv*. Malgerus le, xiv*. Johannes le, xviii ᵇ. John, of Newton, lxiii, 175, 175 ᵃ. John, Sergeant, lxxxix. J. C. P. cvii, 159 ᵇ, 161 ᵇ. Henry, lxvi. Sir, of Hazelwood, 14, 17. Henry, cviii. Sir William, cxxix.
Vaughan, Dr. Edward, (Bishop of St. David's,) 166.
Veesy, Master John, Dean of the King's chapel, cxiii, 206 ᵃ.
Vernon, Sir Richard, li, lxiii ᶜ, ᵈ. Sir William, 3 ᵃ.
Vesci (Vassy), x. Ivo de, *ib.* xi. William de, xvii. Henry (Bromflet) Lord, 135 ᵇ.
Vignolles, Bernard de, 120 ᵃ.
Vilers, family of, xxviii ᵃ.

Ulvesby, Patricius de, xx ᵐ.
Unthank, John, xlv.
Ure (Yure), xiii*, lvi.

Wade (Wayde, Wadd), Thomas, 25. Robert, cix. John, 145.
Wadesel (Wadshelf), 267.
Wadsmill, cxxxi.
Waferer, William, cxxxi.
Wake, Roger, 49.
Wakefield, 204. William, xlvii q, lvii, 260. Henry, cx.
Walensis, Stephanus, xviii b.
Walker (Waukar), John, cxiii, 184. See Index.
Walkingham, Thomas de, xv. Robert, 64, (Alice Gallway), 264.
Walshe (Walste), John, 49. John, J. C. P cxxix, 223 a.
Walworth, John, lviii.
Waman, Christopher, 129. William, ib.
Warbeck, Perkin, 120 a. See Index.
Ward, Rogerus, miles, xxxvii f. Armiger, ib. Sir, xlviii a, lxiii d. Nicholas, xlvii q, 46. Sir Christopher, of Givendale (Margaret Gascoigne), lxxxix l, xcvi, cviii, cx,cxii, 34 a, 46 b, 53, 56, 139 g, 149, 181 a, 216 b, 269. Robert, clerk, 83. Thomas, 103. Edmund, 185, 186. Of Breeton, 30.
Wardlow (Werdlow, Worderplow), liii g et postea.
Ware, 128.
Warkworth, 26, 73, 76, 81.
Warrington (Warynton), 99.
Warter, Richard, 9 b.
Warwick, Earl of, (Richard Nevill), lxxv, xciv o, 7 b, 18 a, (Edward Plantagenet), 54, 87 a. Richard de, xvi a a. See Index.
Water (Awater), John, Mayor of Cork, 142 a.
Waterton, c, cxxviii, cxxix, cxxxi, cxxxiii, cxxxvii, 136, 220 c, 223 a, 232 a, 235, 237 a, 245, 257 a. Sir Robert, lii.
Watkinson, of Pontefract, 60.
Watkyn, Walter, Herald, 49.
Watling-street, xiii a.
Watson, 101.
Watton, cxxxi. (Quatton) 83, 221. At stone, 239 b.
Weeton (Withetun, Wetton), 199 a. Willelmus de, xv. Alexander de, ib.
Wellensis, S. archidiaconus, xiii a t.
Welwick-thorp, xli c.
Wentbridge, 113.
Wentworth, Sir Henry, of Nettlested, xcviii, 94, 95, 265.
Westhall, cxxvi.
Westminster, Whitehall at, 141.
Westmorland, Ralph Earl of, xxxiii, cxiv, cxvi, 197 a, 199 a, 203 b. See Index.
Weston, lxxxiii. Sir Richard, cxiii. Richard, J. C. P. cxxix, 223 a. See Index, St. John's.
Westwick, Patricius de, xx m.
Wetherby (Wederby), lxxxviii.
Whalley, William abbot of, 103 a.
Whele, 9, 35.
White, William, mayor of York, 57.
Whitehill, William, l.
Whitfield, Nicholas, lxiv.
Whitgift, cxxxiv, cxxxvi.
Whitteny (Witney), xlii.
Whixley (Quixley), Sir John, chap. lxxxvi, lxxxix l, 41, 79.
Whytehead, Percival, cix.
Wiclif, xlvii q.
Widonis, Ricardus filius, xiv a.
Wigmore, 5.
Willelmus filius Serlonis, xv.
William son of Ralph, xiii f.
William, Morgan, 206 a.
Willingham, 238 a.
Willough (Wilfe) Park, cxxxv, cxxxvi.
Willoughby, Lord, 143. Sir Henry, of Wollaton, 160.
Willymot (Willemett), John, 160.
Wilson, John, 68. Richard, Recorder, cxxxviii. Thomas, ib.
Wilsthorpe (Wivelstrop), Robertus de, xv. Miles, 23, 46, 85 a, 264 a. Guy, cxxii. Sir Oswald, 235.
Wiltshire, Earl of. See Scrope.
Winchester, 54. Bishop of, (Henry Beaufort), xlii. Bishop of, (Richard Fox), cxi. 210. Bishop of, (Stephen Gardiner), 248.
Windsor, 24. Sir Andrew, 210.
Wingfield, 158.
Wintringham, Thomas, (Alice Dobson), xlix, lxxvi, lxxvii, 41 a. Joan, lxiv, lxxiii, lxxiv, lxxvi, lxxvii. John, chap. lxxxix a.
Wistow, c, 131 r, 221.
Wodfeld, 217.
Woller, 27 b.
Wood, William, chap. lii. Walter, cix. Richard, ib. Lancelot, ib. James, ib. Myles, ib. Thomas, ib. chap. 264 note. Robert, 167.
Woodal (Woodhall), 218 a.
Woodhouse, cxxii w.
Woodkirk, 248.
Woodruffe, Francis, of Wolley, 254 c. See Index.
Woolden (Wouden), 241.
Worcester, viii, ix, x. Thomas Earl of, 40. John, Earl of, (Elizabeth Greyndour), 15 b, 17. See Index.

Wormhill, liii g et post ea.
Worsley (Wortesley), Sir Walter, lxxi.
Wortley, Sir Thomas cx w, 86.
Woyd, Mr. 221.
Wray, cxxx.
Wressle, 40, 46, 73, 226.
Wright, 192.
Wroes, William, 55.
Wryghame, of Knaresborough, 202.
Wulwich, 15.
Wycard, Robert, xxvii b.
Wydmerpole, William, cxxx.
Wygan, Adam de, rector, xxxi.
Wymeswold (Wymondeswold), William, 160, 267.
Wynpenne, John, 82.
Wythers, John, 205.
Wythornwyke, xli c.

Yaxley, John, Sergeant, 152, 153.
Yeo, Nicholas, (Elizabeth), 13 b.
York (Everwyke), x iv, xxvii, xxxix, xlv, lii, lv, lxvii, lxviii, lxxx t, xcvi, cvii, cx, 1, 37, 42, 45, 57, 58, 119, 133, 154, 164, 165 a, 173, 181, 183, 206 250, 253, 265. Sir Richard, 265 note. Richard, cxxvii. See Index.

Zouche (Such), Ivo le, xxxi. William le, Lord, of Haryngworth and Lord St. Maur (Katharine Plumpton), lxxxiii. John Lord, ib. 48, 146. William, of Morley, 146.

FINIS.

J. B. NICHOLS AND SON, 25, PARLIAMENT STREET.